"Philip Deloria and Neal Salisbury have brought together some of the best scholars writing about American Indian peoples and given them topics that both reflect and expand the new scholarship on Indian history and culture. The volume is a virtual compass for readers and scholars interested in American Indians."

Richard White, Stanford University

"If you need to know where the practice of American Indian history has been; better yet, if you need and want to catch up with where it's going, you will need *A Companion to American Indian History*. Each essay, in its own right, gives an important stylistic and substantive shove to the new writing of American Indian history while it offers the latest, best word in dutiful exegetical historiography. The *Companion* is the bridge-building, critical, enlightened, reflexive work the editors hoped for, and more, since its bridge-dynamiting challenges to Indian history are graceful and graciously delivered."

Rayna Green, National Museum of American History

"Historians are exceedingly well served by this *Companion* on Native peoples of the USA, north-western Mexico, Canada, and Western Greenland."

Antiquity

"This volume testifies to the strength and comprehensiveness of the *Blackwell Companions to American History* series… The selection of writers and topics is excellent, and the quality of the historiographical essays matches or supersedes the spate of recently published books that have attempted similar tasks… The essays go beyond a mere listing of sources to intelligently integrate shifts in interpretation over time and to indicate weaknesses in the existing canon of knowledge. Academic researchers, general readers, and members of Native American communities can all profit from these sophisticated essays … this reference work deserves a place in all libraries, and it should be widely used to spark further debate."

Choice

BLACKWELL COMPANIONS TO AMERICAN HISTORY

This series provides essential and authoritative overviews of the scholarship that has shaped our present understanding of the American past. Edited by eminent historians, each volume tackles one of the major periods or themes of American history, with individual topics authored by key scholars who have spent considerable time in research on the questions and controversies that have sparked debate in their field of interest. The volumes are accessible for the non-specialist, while also engaging scholars seeking a reference to the historiography or future concerns.

Published

A Companion to the American Revolution
Edited by Jack P. Greene and J. R. Pole

A Companion to 19th-Century America
Edited by William L. Barney

A Companion to the American South
Edited by John B. Boles

A Companion to American Indian History
Edited by Philip J. Deloria and Neal Salisbury

A Companion to American Women's History
Edited by Nancy A. Hewitt

A Companion to Post-1945 America
Edited by Jean-Christophe Agnew and Roy Rosenzweig

A Companion to the Vietnam War
Edited by Marilyn B. Young and Robert Buzzanco

A Companion to Colonial America
Edited by Daniel Vickers

A Companion to American Foreign Relations
Edited by Robert D. Schulzinger

A Companion to 20th-Century America
Edited by Stephen J. Whitfield

A Companion to the American West
Edited by William Deverell

In preparation

A Companion to the Civil War and Reconstruction
Edited by Lacy K. Ford

A Companion to American Technology
Edited by Carroll Pursell

A Companion to African-American History
Edited by Alton Hornsby

A Companion to American Immigration
Edited by Reed Ueda

A Companion to American Cultural History
Edited by Karen Haltunnen

BLACKWELL COMPANIONS TO HISTORY

Published

A Companion to Western Historical Thought
Edited by Lloyd Kramer and Sarah Maza

A Companion to Gender History
Edited by Teresa A. Meade and Merry E. Wiesner-Hanks

BLACKWELL COMPANIONS TO BRITISH HISTORY

Published

A Companion to Roman Britain
Edited by Malcolm Todd

A Companion to Britain in the Later Middle Ages
Edited by S. H. Rigby

A Companion to Tudor Britain
Edited by Robert Tittler and Norman Jones

A Companion to Stuart Britain
Edited by Barry Coward

A Companion to Eighteenth-Century Britain
Edited by H. T. Dickinson

A Companion to Nineteenth-Century Britain
Edited by Chris Williams

A Companion to Early Twentieth-Century Britain
Edited by Chris Wrigley

In preparation

A Companion to Britain in the Early Middle Ages
Edited by Pauline Stafford

A Companion to Contemporary Britain
Edited by Paul Addison and Harriet Jones

BLACKWELL COMPANIONS TO EUROPEAN HISTORY

Published

A Companion to the Worlds of the Renaissance
Edited by Guido Ruggiero

A Companion to the Reformation World
Edited by R. Po-chia Hsia

In preparation

A Companion to Europe Since 1945
Edited by Klaus Larres

A Companion to Europe 1900–1945
Edited by Gordon Martel

BLACKWELL COMPANIONS TO WORLD HISTORY

In preparation

A Companion to the History of the Middle East
Edited by Youssef M. Choueiri

A COMPANION TO AMERICAN INDIAN HISTORY

Edited by

Philip J. Deloria and Neal Salisbury

Blackwell
Publishing

© 2002, 2004 by Blackwell Publishing Ltd
except for editorial material and organization © 2002, 2004 by Philip J. Deloria and Neal Salisbury

BLACKWELL PUBLISHING
350 Main Street, Malden, MA 02148-5020, USA
9600 Garsington Road, Oxford OX4 2DQ, UK
550 Swanston Street, Carlton, Victoria 3053, Australia

First published 2002
First published in paperback 2004 by Blackwell Publishing Ltd

2   2005

Library of Congress Cataloging-in-Publication Data

A companion to American Indian history/edited by Philip J. Deloria and Neal Salisbury.
         p. cm. – (Blackwell companions to American history; #4)
     Includes bibliographical references and index.
     ISBN 0-631-20975-1 (alk. paper) – ISBN 1-4051-2131-9 (alk. paper : pbk)
     1. Indians of North America – History. I. Deloria, Philip Joseph. II. Salisbury, Neal
   III. Series.
   E77.C74 2001
   970′.00497–dc21   2001018461

ISBN-13: 978-0-631-20975-1 (alk. paper) – ISBN-13: 978-1-4051-2131-6 (alk. paper : pbk)

A catalogue record for this title is available from the British Library.

Set in 10/12.5 Galliard
by Newgen Imaging Systems, Chennai, India
Printed and bound in the United Kingdom
by TJ International, Padstow, Cornwall

The publisher's policy is to use permanent paper from mills that operate a sustainable forestry policy, and which has been manufactured from pulp processed using acid-free and elementary chlorine-free practices. Furthermore, the publisher ensures that the text paper and cover board used have met acceptable environmental accreditation standards.

For further information on
Blackwell Publishing, visit our website:
www.blackwellpublishing.com

Contents

Contributors

Patricia Albers
Professor of American Indian Studies, University of Minnesota

Taiaiake Alfred
Associate Professor in the Faculty of Human and Social Development and Director, Indigenous Governance Program, University of Victoria

Betty Bell
Associate Professor of English, Women's Studies and American Culture, University of Michigan

Jennifer Brown
Professor of History, University of Winnipeg

Regna Darnell
Professor of Anthropology, University of Western Ontario

Philip J. Deloria
Associate Professor of History and American Culture, University of Michigan

Gregory Evans Dowd
Associate Professor of History, University of Notre Dame

R. David Edmunds
Watson Professor of American History, University of Texas at Dallas

Donald Fixico
Professor of History; Director, Indigenous Nations Studies Program, University of Kansas

P. Jane Hafen
Associate Professor of English, University of Nevada, Las Vegas

Alexandra Harmon
Associate Professor of American Indian Studies, University of Washington

Sidney L. Harring
Professor of Law, City University of New York School of Law, Queens College

Eric Hinderaker
Associate Professor of History, University of Utah

Tom Holm
Professor of American Indian Studies, University of Arizona

Lee Irwin
Associate Professor of Religious Studies, College of Charleston

John E. Kicza
Professor of History, Washington State University

Clara Sue Kidwell
Professor and Director of Native American Studies, University of Oklahoma

Tsianina Lomawaima
Professor of American Indian Studies, University of Arizona

Jay Miller
First Nations Culture and Language Education, Prince Rupert Program, Simon Fraser University

L. G. Moses
Professor of History, Oklahoma State University

Nancy Parezo
Professor of American Indian Studies, University of Arizona

Willard Hughes Rollings
Associate Professor of History, University of Nevada, Las Vegas

Theresa Schenck
Assistant Professor of Comparative American Cultures, Washington State University

Pauline Turner Strong
Associate Professor of Anthropology, University of Texas at Austin

Russell Thornton
Professor of Anthropology, University of California, Los Angeles

Louis S. Warren
Associate Professor of History, University of California, Davis

Approximate locations of selected Native American Peoples at the time of contact (source: James Wilson, The Earth Shall Weep: A History of Native America. New York: Grove Press, 1998, p. vii).

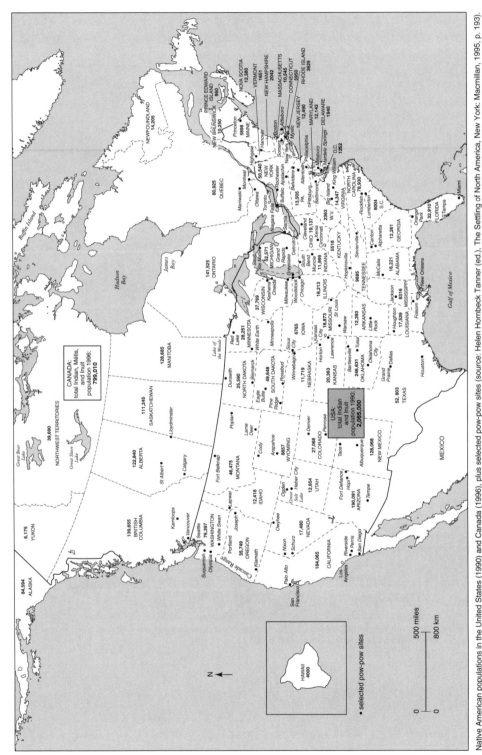

Native American populations in the United States (1990) and Canada (1996), plus selected pow-pow sites (source: Helen Hornbeck Tanner (ed.), The Settling of North America, New York: Macmillan, 1995, p. 193).

* Canadian territory of Nunavut established within Northwest Territories (1999). Population, 27,039.

Introduction

What is American Indian, Native American, or First Nations history? What are its boundaries? Its methods? Its struggles and debates? What is its relation to the broader, interdisciplinary field of American Indian Studies? No single book could hope for a definitive answer to these questions, for they imply a coherence that is – and probably should be – lacking. A single volume may, however, aspire to discuss basic ideas, survey useful writings, trace developing intellectual patterns, and propose questions that may structure Native American history in the years to come. That, indeed, is our goal for this book. It is meant to serve as a useful reference guide to concepts and literatures while at the same time moving readers to think deeply about the issues at stake.

Indian history – as it is and has been preserved, narrated, and owned by native people – is absolutely central to any thinking about American Indian pasts. First Nations history-telling exists in oral traditions and written texts, in autobiographies and "as-told-to" narratives, in geographies and memories throughout Indian country. Over the last several decades, however, its place has shifted: rather than existing as the *subject* of inquiry, Indian history has become a critical *agent* of history-telling itself – both in local native communities and in the world of global intellectual discourse. A fundamental premise of this book is that, in addition to changes driven by the transformations of North American scholarship during the last generation, First Nations history has been utterly remade by the challenges and engagements of Native American people within and without the academy.

Since the 1960s, American Indian history has also emerged as a distinct and significant field of academic study in predominantly Euro-American institutions. During those decades, a significant number of historically minded anthropologists have joined with historians interested in thinking about culture and about narrating the stories of people who had fallen out of history-telling in the past. Often based in colonial or Western American history, they began to read each other's work and to gather at conferences such as the annual meetings of the American Society for

Ethnohistory. The resulting interdisciplinary approaches have been reinforced by a shift in interest by some archaeologists toward Indian–European relations, as opposed to "prehistory." Changes in social and political climates during the 1960s and 1970s generated additional interest in Indian histories, and created a context in which Indian people began to question dominant historical narratives and to insist that their own stories be heard in both popular and academic venues. As scholarship and pedagogy in both the social sciences and the humanities have increasingly emphasized multicultural approaches to their various subjects, American Indian history has grown in stature, analytical power, and diversity of approach.

Graduate students in early American history now routinely read works of Indian history as they prepare for their comprehensive examinations and many choose Native American topics for their dissertations. For later periods, Indian history has become *de rigueur* for historians of the American West, and growing numbers of specialists in other areas are likewise finding it central to their understanding of the role of race and ethnicity in American life and in the formation of American identities. In short, the field is becoming mainstreamed. Meanwhile, historians of Native America continue to expand their reach. Their histories long ago ceased to end at Wounded Knee or some other moment thought to mark the final "disappearance" of Indian people. As many of the essays here make clear, historians and ethnohistorians have explored innumerable dimensions of Native American history in the twentieth century. They have also contributed to the rich interdisciplinarity that characterizes so much of recent scholarship. Their forays into cultural studies, identity issues, global history, gender studies, and other developing areas of inquiry make clear that the field will continue to change and to command the attention of a wide range of historians and other scholars for some time to come.

In this *Companion*, we have tried to capture the thematic breadth of the First Nations history that has developed during the last generation. In many cases, the themes we have selected represent established scholarly traditions that have been energized by new intellectual paradigms introduced by both native and non-native thinkers, by both historians and non-historians. The study of native languages, for example, has a long history in North American scholarship. So too do the issues surrounding European empire, Indian religious expression, and native kinship, family, and community. Other themes reflect traditional historical questions less frequently applied to native people. What has labor and work meant to Indians, particularly as they entered the wage labor markets of the nineteenth and twentieth centuries? Can we think about Indians and warfare in ways that escape the stereotypes engendered by the conquests of New England and the Great Plains? How have native people responded to the opportunities and pressures of the fine art market?

American Indian history has not failed to be influenced by other emerging fields of scholarship as well. These include new approaches drawn from environmental history, comparative history, and gender history. And Indian history has taken up an array of compelling questions surrounding performance, identity, cultural brokerage, race and blood, captivity, adoption, and slavery. In many other cases, First Nations history has proven essential to the interests and goals of contemporary Native American people. Legal studies, federal and state political relationships, issues of health and education and sovereignty – these fields represent scholarly interests that have, in large part, been driven by Indian initiatives. Finally, certain themes in this book focus more deliberately on Indian people's own expressions of Indian pasts, presents, and futures. Native literature has been one of the most important venues for such expressions, but the reader will also find essays on historiography and traditional systems of knowledge.

There are twenty-five essays in this book, each of which occupies a place both within the study of history and within other fields as well. In writing about spiritual traditions, for example, author Lee Irwin speaks both to Indian history and to the study of comparative religion. He speaks as well – as do many of the authors in this *Companion* – to those occupied with the relatively new, interdisciplinary, native-centered field of American Indians Studies. Since the late 1960s and early 1970s, native scholars have worked hard to unify their studies in academic departments and programs such as those now operating at the University of California at Los Angeles and at Davis, the University of Minnesota, and the University of Arizona. Native American Studies has been a truly cross-disciplinary enterprise, incorporating creative writers, educators, political scientists, lawyers, linguists, sociologists, historians, and others. Indeed, several of the contributors to this volume occupy positions in Native Studies departments or programs.

Indian Studies casts a wide net, and, looking at themes or subjects, one might easily imagine this volume as a *Companion to American Indian Studies* rather than Indian *history*. We've not chosen that route, largely because of the way we've asked writers to conceptualize their essays. Indian Studies quite rightly focuses on issues and problems, using the insights of history and other disciplines as analytical cutting tools. From an American Indian Studies perspective, a field such as "education," for example, would be examined not only through the lenses of the past, but also through those of the present. Such an examination might include a treatment of the politics of federal, state, and tribal funding, educational theory and research, longitudinal and comparative studies of native and other "minority" educational institutions, and so on. Instead, we've asked our contributors to think historically. Their charge has been to present the state of American Indian history in their particular fields, tracing its historical development, the changes that have occurred in the last few decades, and the contemporary issues that have sparked the most interesting and productive debates. We've asked them to consider the contributions of both Indians and non-Indians, and to indicate the directions the field appears most likely to follow during the next decade.

American Indian history has developed in relation to a set of problems, opportunities, and unique situations. As told by Europeans and white Americans, First Nations history has traditionally, and perhaps inevitably, narrated the story of Euro-American conquest. The earliest histories offered stories and interpretations that quivered with mythic power and groaned under the weight of the ideologies of white cultural superiority and Indian backwardness. Most of us are familiar with these ideologies to the point that an obligatory catalog of images of either Indian savagery or nobility is unnecessary. But subsequent historians have in general had to take conquest and the myths that accompanied it as their point of departure. Such departures have not been easy, for all of us – both Indian and non-Indian – have had a harder time escaping those myths than we might allow. What has been increasingly clear, however, is the ways in which those myths have been tied to the workings of power, and the ways in which our contemporary tellings of Indian pasts continue to be tied up in the same way.

Since so much Indian history has been created at a remove from Indian people, historians have often become – and are sometimes trained to become – accustomed to separating their own narratives from those either of Indian people or of the government and corporate officials who continue to impact Indian lives. But because many Indian people have forced the issue, historians of native America have learned anew the ways in which the telling of an Indian past can have political consequences for the present. Politics, power, and the ongoing legacies of conquest will always make the writing of Indian history a problematic endeavor.

In large part, this reality stems from the unique relations that most Native American people have with federal governments, a relationship that is still misunderstood by most citizens of the United States and Canada. Treaty relationships and subsequent legal decisions and legislation have embedded Indian people in power struggles with state, provincial, and federal governments in ways unlike any other ethnic or racial group. History, for Indian people and for historians of Indian North America, does not simply revolve around abstract questions of identity, "what happened when" issues, or "objective" assessments of the past. Rather, every historical narrative has the potential to change lives and policies in the contemporary world. All Indian scholarship, whether the author chooses to recognize it or not, exists in relation to this complicated, difficult, and often painful reality. In that sense, then, it is strictly impossible to separate Indian history from the concern with contemporary issues that has often characterized American Indian Studies. Even as they strive to represent historical analyses and the historical development of intellectual fields, many of the essays in this book also reflect and engage contemporary concerns.

As American Indian history becomes ever more a part of a new global indigenous history, these issues will only grow more difficult. We think they will also grow more compelling and more interesting. It is our deepest hope that the realities of power and politics will not lead Indian scholars to exclude non-Indians from Indian histories. It is also our hope that non-Indian scholars will not shrug off Indian history as something too difficult or too remote for them to pursue. Rather, we hope that enlightened, critical, and reflexive writing in Indian history can be a place where bridges can continue to be built – between Indians and non-Indians, between history and ethnography, between intellectual investigation and social action.

For that reason, we've sought out authors – Native American and non-native – who are engaged in this kind of bridge-building. We've also encouraged approaches that call rigid dualisms – Indian and white, myth and truth, history and ethnography – into question. Like many of the authors, we believe that language conveys power, and we have chosen to use an assortment of words to describe native people. These include tribal designations in both English and native languages, and the words "Indian," "native," "Native American," "First Nations," and "indigenous." We recognize the problems and limitations of these words. We also recognize the ways that Indian/native/indigenous people have made them their own. The tension that sometimes surrounds these words illustrates in six-letter bits the complexities that dog the maintenance, retention, and reshaping of culture in the colonial/post-colonial settings that have led, over the long term, to this book.

We would like to thank Susan Rabinowitz and Ken Provencher, our editors at Blackwell, for their patient support of this project. We also thank Patricia Murphy at the University of Colorado and Stephanie Ziegler at Smith College for their help with word-crunching and disk maintenance, and Timothy Willig at the University of Massachusetts, Amherst, for compiling the bibliography at the end of the volume. Phil Deloria would like to thank his wife, Peggy Burns, for her unrelenting calm, as well as Roger Echo-Hawk and Angela Cavender Wilson, two Indian intellectuals who could hardly be more different, yet who have helped form some of the under-standings that underpin this book.

1

Historiography

PHILIP J. DELORIA

In 1997, Native historian Donald Fixico observed that more than 30,000 books had been written about American Indians. The number may have been conservative then, and it has certainly been surpassed since. Visit the call numbers between E51 and E99 in even the smallest library and marvel at the prodigious outpouring of writing on Native people. As you browse those impressive stacks, however, don't forget that books and libraries are not the only ways of recording and communicating a past. It's worth bearing in mind one of Fixico's other calculations: roughly 90 percent of those books were written by non-Indians (Fixico, 1997: 3). Fixico's observations suggest at least three central historiographical problems. First of all, how do we make sense of this vast library of texts, this Western canon of Indian history? Second, even if we could order this canon, how would we then situate it in relation to the multiplicity of Native histories, each of which poses political and epistemological challenges to the Western tradition of history-telling itself? And third, can we imagine histories that problematize or perhaps even transcend dualisms like Indian/non-Indian, linear/cyclical, or oral/literate?

These problems defy easy solution, particularly in the course of a short essay. Indeed, the very notion of historiography – a history of history-writing – immediately raises an even deeper horizon of critical questions. How do people use their pasts to perceive, imagine, and perpetuate ideas about cultural and social difference? How have historical narratives reflected the relations of power between various groups of Native people and various groups of Europeans? Can we even begin to perceive the complex connections between social, political, economic, and environmental transformations and the psychic and cultural changes that are refracted through the historical consciousness of the writer or the storyteller?

Historiography – and particularly in a cross- or multicultural context – requires us to think about epistemology – how we know what we know – in complex ways. First, one has always to confront the epistemology of *difference*: how have non-Indian writers understood Indians to be different? And, by extension, how have Indians conceptualized non-Indian difference? Second, one has to think about the ways that epistemologies have changed across *time*. How was the historical consciousness available to Francis Parkman in the mid-nineteenth century different from that available to John Neihardt in the early twentieth? And how were they both different from subjects like Black Hawk and Black Elk, both of whom narrated their own histories? In this essay, I plan to think first about grappling with the Western tradition of historical writing. The essay will then raise the question of Native historiography, before finally trying to come to terms with the hybrid understandings of the past that inevitably characterize our contemporary acts of history-telling.

Let us return first to the library. Traditional historical categories offer one useful way of ordering the material. We could parse those 30,000-plus books using words like military, political, diplomatic, social, cultural, women's, race, class, gender, sexuality, environmental, family, and so on. "Indian" would mark a kind of commonality, but "Indian histories" would fit into other categories as well. One can see the opportunities and the problems with books such as Walter Williams's *The Spirit and the Flesh*, Will Roscoe's *The Zuni Man-Woman*, and *Two Spirit People*, edited by Sue-Ellen Jacobs, Wesley Thomas, and Sabine Lang. All are "Indian histories" that, one might argue, fit more easily into the broader categories of gender and sexuality. Alternatively, we might use an ordering scheme that relies more directly on discipline or method. The categories would be different: archaeology, ethnology, ethnography, ethnohistory, myth and symbol, folklore, sociology, policy studies, and so on. But both kinds of categorizations, while useful, don't generally meet the requirement laid down by the "history" in the word "historiography" – the explanation of change over time.

Historical periodization creates different kinds of categories, divisions that are temporal rather than methodological or topical. Like all categories, these necessarily do harm to their subjects – in this case, the continuity and flux of change over time. Historiographical periodization implies, for example, that one can distill complex historical consciousnesses down to recognizable definitions and examples. We know this to be untrue. Yet periodization can also be an exercise in ordering that makes change visible in productive ways. In that spirit, I want to suggest four broad historical periods in Indian history-writing, each of which has overlaid, rather than supplanted, those that have come before. Each suggests changes in social, political, and epistemological positions within non-Indian societies that have helped to produce new kinds of history-writing. Obviously such crude paradigms will obscure shifts and subtleties, but it is also true that additional historiographical inquiry will derive its analytical power by breaking down these and other categories. With that caveat and invitation, let us proceed:

1 Frontier History: In which spatial metaphors explain Indian–non-Indian difference in simple terms of geography, conflict, and eventual (and often predestined) conquest (from contact to the present).
2 Racial/Developmental Hierarchy: In which more complex structures result from scientific efforts to explain difference within a larger human landscape (from the late eighteenth century to the present).

3 Modernist History: A post-frontier paradigm in which people imagine social
   boundaries to be fixed, while simultaneously retaining the possibility of their tran-
   scendence (from the late nineteenth century to the present).
4 Postmodern/Postcolonial: Contemporary writing in which texts and histories seek
   to deal with the tension between the liberating dissolution of boundaries and the
   constant reshaping of them as political memories of the colonial past (roughly,
   post-World War II to the present).

Frontier

Frederick Jackson Turner's 1893 formulation of "the frontier" serves as a useful starting place, for if it marks the beginning of a series of academic "frontier" histories, it
also represents the supposed *end* of the conditions that powered a long tradition of
popular history-writing (Turner, 1920). Turner saw American history in spatial terms,
a moving boundary between European civilization and Indian savagery. He didn't
talk much about Native people, but he did codify the very old notion of a line that
separated Indian and non-Indian. That line defined the terrain of physical, political,
economic, and social struggle and it carried with it the expectation that white America
would inevitably triumph. Turner's address – and his subsequent scholarship – insisted
that Americans had arrived at the endgame of a national teleology. In that sense, it
also serves as a useful marker of the modernist tradition of Indian historiography.

As Francis Jennings has pointed out, this spatial reading of Indian history as a contest between the savage and the civilized has origins as old as European colonization
itself (Jennings, 1975: 6–12). Frontier paradigms suggest a relation between the ways
in which Europeans understood cultural and racial difference and the ways in which
they understood empire and colony. Imagined around race, faith, economy, gender,
and geographical expansion, frontier oppositions mapped space and human difference together in ways that used the past to naturalize European dominance. The
distinct colonial experiences of different European powers produced, within this paradigm, different kinds of histories. In New France, historians such as Gabriel Sagard
(*Histoire du Canada*, 1636), Pierre Boucher (*Histoire Véritable et Naturall*, 1633),
and François DuCreux (*Historia Canadensis*, 1664) began recording frontier pasts
characterized by economic and religious encounters. Spanish colonial historians had
to confront pasts marked by greater violence and more frequent conflict. Their uses
of history are perhaps best illustrated by the famous 1550–1 debate between
Bartolomé de Las Casas, who criticized the excesses of Spanish conquest, and Juan
Ginés de Sepúlveda, who argued that one could easily conceive of a "just war" against
Indians who were "slaves by nature." Likewise, Gonzalo Fernández de Oviedo y
Valdés (*Historia general y natural de las Indias*, 1537, 1557) and Francisco López de
Gómara (*Historia de las Indias*, 1552) offered prominent historical readings of the
Spanish colonial past that naturalized both conquest and Indian difference.

European writers, be they French, English, Spanish, Dutch, Russian or other,
assumed that Indians and Europeans confronted each other across a vast social
chasm, and their histories link Indian difference together with European expansion.

In New England, Increase Mather's *Brief History* (1676), John Underhill's *Newes from America* (1638), William Bradford's *Of Plymouth Plantation* (1620–47, published in 1856), and John Winthrop's *History of New England* (2 vols., 1825–6) all represent early American histories that rely on the notions of an Indian–white boundary and physical conquest for their analytical and narrative force. Further south, Samuel Purchas, William Byrd, John Smith, and others offered regionally inflected histories using the same model.

Perhaps the most powerful American genre in this tradition was the captivity narrative, a form that produced writings as diverse as Mary Rowlandson's 1682 captivity and Sarah Wakefield's 1864 book, *Six Weeks in the Sioux Teepees.* The early captivity narrative prefigured later modernist writing in its use of the metaphor of culture-crossing, but it ultimately insisted upon a cultural difference understood through a geography of conflict. Captivity, as Richard Slotkin has observed, offered one of the few legitimate excuses for being on the far side of the frontier boundary. To know Indian society and history, one had to learn it under duress. Even a sympathetic figure like Daniel Gookin, who crossed the boundary as a missionary, proved unable to escape the dualist visions of the frontier. Along with Slotkin, Christopher Castiglia and June Namias, among others, have offered significant analyses of this literature. Wilcomb Washburn and Alden Vaughan have both edited collections of captivity narratives.

Nineteenth-century historians made only subtle alterations to the formula that placed opposed societies fighting across a frontier boundary. And indeed, their writing reflected the prerogatives of American manifest destiny itself, as much a colonial and imperial project as those of England, France, and Spain. Timothy Flint (*Indian Wars of the West*, 1833), James Hall (*Letters from the West*, 1828, among others), and Francis Parkman were among the multitude of nineteenth-century historians captured by a clear and simple sense of boundary. Parkman's *Conspiracy of Pontiac* (1851), for example, used an Indian-war past to help explain a nineteenth-century present, Indian wars both recent and impending. Seeing white America as "metal," combining flexibility and strength, Parkman viewed Indians as metaphorical rock, their inflexibility explaining their eventual doom. "You can rarely change the form without destruction of the substance," he argued. "Races of inferior energy have possessed a power of expansion and assimilation to which [the Indian] is a stranger; and it is this fixed and rigid quality which has proven his ruin. He will not learn the arts of civilization, and he and his forest must perish together" (p. 63). Parkman later went on to write the monumental seven-volume study *France and England in North America* (1865–92) which, along with the works of George Bancroft and William Prescott, make up the dominant nineteenth-century histories of American frontier colonialism.

The story of Indian frontier conflict became a staple of popular history, with frequent retellings in a variety of forms. These included drama, the penny press, Indian-fighter autobiographies, memoirs of overland trail migration, Wild West show performances, historical paintings, such as those of Frederic Remington, and "serious" popular histories, like Theodore Roosevelt's *Winning of the West* (1889–96), which portrayed American development as one long Indian war.

Turner was Roosevelt's contemporary, and his famous thesis essentially founded the twentieth-century field of Western American history, which has been the subsequent resting place for this particular historical paradigm and a frequent location for the study of Indian history. Although the Turnerian frontier has been attacked by numerous historians and transformed by neo-Turnerians and cultural pluralists, the notion of a line or zone that demarks Indian–white conflict has continued to resound as a key trope in Indian–European history. Popular history continues to use frontier models. And one can continue to find scholarly studies that focus on unambiguous conflict between Indians, settlers, and the federal government. Several publishers have established core constituencies of both historians and readers who continue to find in this particular category a meaningful history. Among many others, Kerwin Lee Klein (*Frontiers of Historical Imagination*, 1997) has written an excellent survey of the transformations of the frontier idea in relation to Indians.

An equally interesting part of this tradition is the body of scholarship that has looked critically at the ways the relation between a spatialized sense of racial and cultural difference and the act of conquest have been expressed in history, literature, and art. Roy Harvey Pearce's classic *Savagism and Civilization* (1953) was one of the first modern works to examine this discourse of difference in American history, and Pearce has been ably followed by Richard Slotkin (particularly *Regeneration through Violence*, 1973 and *The Fatal Environment*, 1985), Robert F. Berkhofer, Jr. (*The White Man's Indian*, 1978), Brian Dippie (*The Vanishing American*, 1982), and others. Each of these writers seeks to show how the frontier metaphor was both product and precursor of the various kinds of social dislocations Indian people have suffered throughout American history. Gordon Sayre (*Les Sauvages Américains*, 1997) and Olive Dickason (*The Myth of the Savage*, 1984) expand this treatment to cover the French. Benjamin Keen (*The Aztec Image in Western Thought*, 1971) and, from a moralist literary-critical position, Tzvetan Todorov (*The Conquest of America*, 1984) have examined the discourses in Spanish examples. Among others, Anthony Pagden (*European Encounters with the New World*, 1993; *Lords of All the World*, 1995) has discussed European ideologies broadly and comparatively.

Finally, as probably the most familiar tradition in American history-writing, the notion of frontier conflict between spatially defined civil and savage societies has been a significant target for Native historians as well. In addition to the classic Native writers of the nineteenth and early twentieth centuries (see Hafen, this volume) more recent Indian critiques have invariably had to confront various elements of the frontier paradigm. Vine Deloria's *Custer Died for Your Sins* (1969) offered a model for the historically inflected polemic. The works of Elizabeth Cook-Lynn, Jack Forbes, Ward Churchill, Donald Grinde, Scott Momaday and others have utilized the idea of coherent cultural boundaries, while at the same time criticizing the way those boundaries have been called into being.

Racial Science and Hierarchies

Implicit – and often explicit – in the frontier tradition has been the question of race, which has been inextricably linked to notions of savagery and civilization. If frontier writing has its roots in the colonial encounter, then more complex, hierarchical considerations of race might be seen as having a slightly later starting point. In this second tradition, one sees a change in structure from dualism and a single firm boundary between two societies to social evolution, with its concomitant rankings of the racial endowments of multiple peoples. If the first tradition has been aptly suited to explain continuing colonial conflict, the second has been just as useful for thinking about the scattering of people *within* the boundaries of the United States and the world at large. Indians, Africans, whites, the black Irish, Latinos, and Asians – where did each of these groups of people fit in relation to each other? And how did one come to the knowledge that would allow one to make the necessary distinctions?

The practices and procedures that characterized the scientific study of race inevitably influenced Indian history-writing. These represent a diverse range of ideas, from early speculation concerning Indian origins to amateur ethnology to the classic Social Darwinism of the late nineteenth and early twentieth centuries to today's tortured debates over racial difference. Particularly in the early cases, ethnologists and historians assumed that different peoples could be ranked on a scale (rather than an absolute boundary) that ran from varying levels of primitivism and savagery to varying levels of civilization. And while this tradition has its own popular historical representations, it more significantly signals the beginning of the ongoing relation between science and history in the creation of knowledge about Indian people (Bieder, 1986; Hinsley, 1981; Pagden, 1993).

One mode of scientific racialism revolved around the question of origins (see Darnell, this volume, for a discussion of mono- and polygenesis). James Adair's *History of the American Indians* (1775) might be seen as an early example in this particular historiographical tradition. Adair, who traded with several Southeastern tribes and married among the Chickasaw, hypothesized that Indian people occupied a unique racial position as the remnants of the lost tribes of Israel. Similarly, in the early nineteenth century, artist George Catlin suggested that the Mandans were "white," the survivors of a Welsh expedition. Later historians would look for origins among the Norse, Greeks, Egyptians, and others. *The Book of Mormon* (1829–30), for example, constructed a thorough American prehistory for Indian people, placing them squarely within the "lost tribes" tradition. Like these other treatments, *The Book of Mormon* had then to account for racially "superior" Indian people (that is to say, "white") who occupied positions near the savage bottom of the developmental scale. The *Book* explains this inconsistency historically, offering a North American past of devastating war and cultural declension.

Some scholars – and more particularly, the popular media – continue today to speculate about Indian origins and development in racial terms. The flurry over Kennewick Man, a supposedly "caucasoid type" found amidst material 9,300 years old, suggests the ongoing nature of this racialist tradition. The semantic slippages between the technical term "caucasoid," the racialist term "caucasian," and the popular media gloss "white" raise loaded questions about Indians, Europeans, and North American history. The tension in such instances results from complementary instincts – either the sympathetic naming of Indians as "white" or the less-benign claiming of North America for Anglos. In the first instance, non-Indian accounts might elevate "noble" Indians above other races by granting them whiteness. In the second, they might relegate Indians to the bottom of the hierarchy by positing a North American prehistory crudely colored "white." In either case, the linkages between science, racial hierarchy, and history can be surprisingly consistent across time. David Hurst Thomas's *Skull Wars: Kennewick Man, Archaeology, and the Battle for Native American Identity* offers a brilliant reading, placing Kennewick in larger historical context (2000).

Early ethnology often narrated Indian pasts in similar ways. As they sought to understand Indians, writers like John Heckewelder, Henry Rowe Schoolcraft, Peter Duponceau, and Samuel Morton wrestled with the tension between the absolute difference of the frontier model and the hierarchical difference suggested by natural science. Lewis Henry Morgan, for example, made what would become a classic anthropological move, from the detailed descriptive study of difference found in *League of the Ho-de-no-sau-nee, or Iroquois* to the comparative racial and linguistic studies of *Ancient Society* (see Darnell, Miller, this volume). In *League*, Morgan (like proto-ethnographer Heckewelder before him) investigated and described the customs, beliefs, rituals, structures, and histories of a single group of native people. According to Morgan, the Iroquois were "advanced" in relation to other Indians, but they lacked the progressive spirit to ascend the racial hierarchy. "The hunter state," Morgan insisted (despite abundant evidence of Iroquois agriculture), "is the zero of human society and while the red man was bound by its spell, there was no hope of his elevation" (p. 141). In passages such as this, Morgan saw a hierarchy that connected the "zero" of Indianness with the agricultural civilization of Euro-Americans. Samuel Morton's *Crania America* (1839) sought to reveal the nature of American racial hierarchies through a combination of physical anthropology (measuring the cranial capacity of different racial groups) and phrenology (finding markers of racial character in skull formations).

The writings of a third ethnologist, Henry Rowe Schoolcraft, offer a complex sense of the mingled development of three strands in the intellectual history of race and Indians. In *Western Scenes and Reminiscences* (1853), Schoolcraft's early impressions of Indians followed the oppositional logic of the frontier. "The word 'Indian,'" he recalled, "was synonymous then, as perhaps now, with half the opprobrious epithets in the dictionary" (p. 65). But Schoolcraft found himself working among Indian people, and saw an opportunity for scientific investigation. After a cross-racial marriage, and years as an Indian agent, natural historian, and collector of Indian stories and histories, Schoolcraft claimed he had learned to reject much of the frontier model. Indians, he said, should be studied as a distinct branch of the human race. Focusing on language, government, and religion, Schoolcraft undertook, in several different projects, an ethnological and literary catalogue of the culture and history of the native people of the Great Lakes and prairies. His output included *Algic Researches* (1839), *Oneota* (1844–5), *Notes on the Iroquois* (1846), and *Historical and Statistical Information* (1851–7). When thinking comparatively, he was able to place racially defined Indians in relation to a white society parsed along hierarchical class lines. "As a class of men," he observed, "native speakers, without letters or education, possess a higher scope of thought and illustration, than the *corresponding class* in civilized life" (p. 67). And this insight nudged Schoolcraft toward a third notion, that of evolutionary change. "The old idea that the Indian mind is not susceptible of a high or advantageous development," he argued, "rests on questionable data" (p. 67). Schoolcraft, one should note, concluded his remarks with a return to frontier dualism, insisting that native religion kept Indians "beyond the pale of civilization" (p. 68). Elsewhere, he argued that it was not simply that Indian societies could not advance – they had actually declined.

And yet, with the notion of evolutionary change, Schoolcraft pointed to future permutations of racialist thinking. With the publication of Darwin's *Origin of Species* in 1859, intellectuals began wondering not just about racial difference, but about its historical development. Anthropological writers such as Edward Tylor (1871) formally posited a single "culture," with people moving along a prescribed evolutionary path that led from the savage to the civilized. Indians represented a stalled branch. "They," anthropologists argued, are what "we" once were – a living representation of an earlier history (Stocking, 1968). The potted histories offered by late nineteenth- and early twentieth-century government policy makers, missionaries, and anthropologists, for example, placed Indians on such a social evolutionary trajectory.

Much of the writing on Indians from the latter part of the nineteenth century is oriented toward policy. The Indian Rights Association, for example, was only one of many groups who naturalized the idea of a developmental hierarchy. Taking a social evolutionary past for granted, they looked toward a future characterized by rapid Indian development, and they made this narrative concrete through the so-called "Assimilation" policies. With white assistance, Indians could, in effect, escape the frontier model and move up the hierarchy to become civilized, Christian, and economically rational (Hoxie, 1984). Although tempered by the rise of cultural relativism after World War II, such developmental assumptions continue to live on today, underpinning federal and state policy, church missionary activity, and educational dogma.

Modernist History

Turner's 1890 ending of the frontier marked another, equally significant moment of change in white historical consciousness concerning Indians. The Wounded Knee massacre, also in that year, seemed to many to be the final battle of the imperial struggle for North America. Indians immediately looked different when seen through the lens of what Renato Rosaldo has called "imperialist nostalgia" (Rosaldo, 1989). With a modern sensibility tuned toward regret, much Indian history-writing continued to see the past through the metaphor of boundaries – only now those boundaries were not so much spatial and impenetrable as they were temporal and permeable (P. Deloria, 1998).

Nostalgia permeates this tradition and it led writers to invert and to dissolve older, "frontier" boundaries while at the same time retaining the racial privilege that came with the developmental hierarchy. Helen Hunt Jackson's 1881 *A Century of Dishonor*, for example, did not engage the scientific concern with race that continued to mark much historical writing. And while it accepted the dualistic division that characterized the frontier school, it flip-flopped the values assigned to civilization and savagery. Jackson offered a history of white American barbarism, an empathetic inversion that would frequently mark modernist writing.

But if inversion was one component of this historiographical tradition, so too was the anthropological notion that one might participate in an Indian world, at least on a small scale. Columbia anthropologist Franz Boas and his students led the way in replacing the rigid racial divisions of the nineteenth century with the more permeable cultural boundaries of the twentieth. Salvage anthropology – the logical descendant of a Social Darwinian linking of history and science – proved most amenable to the notion that one could cross time and culture to gather up an Indian past (Stocking, 1968). Yet most ethnographers were not thinking historically, for salvage anthropology insisted upon Indians frozen in an "ethnographic present." Rather, amateur historians such as Stanley Vestal, E. A. Brininstool, George Hyde, and Walter McClintock went among Indian people and gathered information for biography and history.

Perhaps the quintessential expressions of this modernist boundary-crossing revolve around the Lakota holy man/Catholic catechist Black Elk. In 1931, poet John Neihardt visited Black Elk in search of the historical material that eventually became *Black Elk Speaks* (1932), and later, *When the Tree Flowered* (1951). Neihardt's writing (or is it Black Elk's speech? – the relations of literary production are confused, to say the least) overflows with modernist regret, nostalgia, and the inversion of civil and "savage" sympathies. In 1947, Joseph Epes Brown, deeply moved by Neihardt's book, made a similar visit to Black Elk's home, where he stayed for several months. The result was *The Sacred Pipe* (1953), which, like *Black Elk*, blurs the boundaries between subject and recorder. Neihardt's author tag, for example, reads "as told through," while Brown simply writes "recorded and edited by ..." In such writing, culture-crossing tended to be an individual issue, and so many similar works are biographical in nature. William Wildschut and Two Leggings, Frank Linderman and Pretty Shield and Plenty Coups, Brininstool and Luther Standing Bear, Vestal and White Bull, Walter Dyk and Left Handed, Leo Simmons and Don Talayesva, among many others – these biographies and "as-told-to" histories all bear the mark of the relationship between writer and anthropological informant. And this form has continued to have resonance and power, particularly when adapted by historically minded anthropologists such as Paul Radin (Crashing Thunder), Nancy Oestreich Lurie (Mountain Wolf Woman), and Margot Liberty (John Stands In Timber). Recent popular writings include, among others, the various collaborations with Richard Erdoes (*Lame Deer, Seeker of Visions*, 1972; *Lakota Woman*, 1990; *Ohitika Woman*, 1993; *Crow Dog*, 1995; among others), Vada Carlson (*No Turning Back*, 1964), and Mark St. Pierre (*Madonna Swan*, 1991).

Perhaps the most significant moment in the modernist tradition, however, was the formal linking of history and ethnography, two disciplines that had been dancing together for over one hundred years. Founded in 1954, the American Society for Ethnohistory focused on bringing the methods of ethnographic fieldwork and the documentary evidentiary bases of American Indian history into explicit interdisciplinary dialogue (Axtell, 1981). Ethnohistory has thrived in the years since, and many of the classic recent works of Indian history have come from its adherents. Indeed, many of the chapters in this volume reflect the productive historical investigations undertaken by ethnohistorians in fields such as demography, commerce, religion, law, land tenure, and politics, among many others. Ethnohistorians have, in addition, brought an increasing historiographical self-consciousness about their field, its direction, and its basis of knowledge and authority. Among the many noteworthy texts are edited collections like Nancy O. Lurie and Eleanor Leacock's *North American Indians in Historical Perspective* (1971), William R. Swagerty's *Scholars and the Indian Experience* (1984), Calvin Martin's *The American Indian and the Problem of History* (1987), Colin Calloway's *New Directions in American Indian History* (1988), Jennifer S. H. Brown and Elizabeth Vibert's *Reading Beyond Words* (1996), Donald Fixico's *Rethinking American Indian History* (1997), Devon Mihesuah's *Natives and Academics* (1998), and Russell Thornton's *Studying Native America: Problems and Prospects* (1998).

In many ways, however, ethnohistory is simply the logical development of modernist boundary-crossing traditions. As Kerwin Klein has argued, the blurring of genres that finds historians doing fieldwork and anthropologists writing "library dissertations" has "emptied ethnohistory of its methodological content" (Klein, 1997: 212). Ethnohistory now confronts issues that problematize its familiar practices and call out for new approaches to the telling of an Indian past. Those changes have come, in part, from epistemological shifts that have altered recent understandings of history. And they have come, in part, out of the critical presence of native people in the familiar practices surrounding the production of knowledge.

Native Narrative

Before we can grapple with these issues, however, it is vital that we return to the question, bracketed so many pages ago, of native narration of native pasts. As white Americans have created a library of Indian history, native people have themselves been engaged in the ongoing production of Indian histories. And if we insisted on thinking about this first body of historiography in terms of accreting layers, each driven by historical shifts in the conditions under which history was produced, we should do no less for native histories. The historiography that emerges is every bit as complex, if perhaps less easily captured, for native historical traditions are as diverse as tribes themselves. Indian people have persistently maintained oral records. Some of those records have changed; others have remained relatively unchanged. Native people have meticulously preserved the past in spiritual understandings and collective memories of place. They have recorded the past in various written forms, including mnemonics, images, and books. And they have reshaped it in order to meet social, cultural, and political challenges. Indian history – as possessed and produced by native people – has been as complicated and time-bound a process as it has been for non-Indians. In this, they have been no different from any group of people in the world.

Native historians have insisted that, simply because the practice of oral tradition and oral history has been so often invisible to the library, does not mean that it lacks legitimacy. While academic debates concerning the nature of orality and literacy continue, scholars such as Jan Vansina have demonstrated that oral tradition can preserve information across broad spans of time (Vansina, 1985). And native oral histories have their own social and cultural legitimacy outside of academic judgements, which have often been less concerned with meaning and context and more focused on verifiable facticity. This is an ironic focus, given the problematizing of fact and the emphasis on context that has characterized the post-structuralist awareness so much a part of recent Euro-American history-telling. Nonetheless, as Angela Cavender Wilson points out, oral history – when seen in a Native context – has certain affinities with Euro-American history, operating, for example, under similar constraints (Wilson, 1997). Stories are repeated under certain conditions, at certain times of the year, in connection with certain landscapes, and, in many cases, are subject to the "peer review" of knowing audiences. The Navajo Blessingway, for example, is a history that, one might argue, has remained largely unchanged across significant spans of time and hundreds of retellings through exactly this kind of oversight.

And yet, it is clear that there are distinctions to be made between, for example, oral *traditions* that are held and renewed collectively and oral *histories* that may be personal and biographical. In a wide-ranging treatment of Indian history-telling, Peter Nabokov suggests complicating three familiar categories of native historical narrative: myth, legend, and folktale. "Myths" are sacred stories that take place in an earlier world and are held as absolute truths (Nabokov, 1996). As Keith Basso has shown, such stories continue to exist as vital collective narratives about the past – histories – that give explanatory meaning to the world of the present. Apache place stories, in this case, link contemporary landscape and culture to origins that have become essentially timeless (Basso, 1996). "Legends" maintain their link to what might be called "Western" historical time – they contain human characters and factual content. "Folktales" exist as fictional literature, educational and entertaining. They include "just so" stories, trickster tales, ghost stories, jokes, and other informal expressions. Nabokov includes within this category "trickster" histories that are explicitly constructed as tools for political struggle. Obviously the categorical lines are just as blurry in this accounting as they are in the Euro-American historical traditions already discussed. Apaches, to return to Basso's example, do not simply live in a static, mythic world. They create new histories about newly created places, revealing the gaps and fissures in any scheme that would sift out temporal distinctions among native histories.

But Indian histories are not simply defined by forms, contents, and acts of narration. Oral traditions and histories (like written texts) have constantly had to confront the question of reading – a confrontation that origin stories always face: should they be heard as literal depictions of historical events, as some proponents advise? Or do they really function as metaphorical "pseudo-histories" containing renditions of cultural circumstances rather than history, as most academic scholars suggest? Roger Echo-Hawk (2000) has inquired into the historical content of origin stories, and he proposes to employ academic tools to excavate arguably historical settings from narratives that feature an accumulated overburden of culturally specific interpretive detail.

This endorsement of academic analysis as the basis for deciding historicity could easily be viewed as an affirmation of intellectual imperialism, a forced fitting of Western historical consciousness on histories that are not meant to be considered so, and yet another attack on origin stories and oral history – the heart of Indian historiographical traditions. A counter to such critique might be to suggest that the major precepts of academic analysis, such as checks for veracity and questions of authorship, readership, and context, ought to be recognized as a vital part of the tradition of Indian history-telling and not as the sole domain of imperialistic non-Indian history. In the end, the search for common ground between distinctive historiographic traditions may yield insight into shared principles of history, bringing greater complexity into the creation of the stories we tell about the past. But encounters between deeply entrenched, coexisting worldviews are never easily negotiated. Where one observer sees common ground, another might see contested territory, a place of collision between imperialistic winners and victimized losers.

Native people have also recorded the past in ways that are not exclusively oral. Plains winter counts, for example, function as mnemonic devices, with each picture representing a memorable (oftentimes an idiosyncratic) event that allows the recollection of a given year (Mallery, 1883/1972). And though the counts are arranged in the form of a circle, they do in fact allow a "linear" conception of the relationship of one or more past events. In addition to recording personal and collective narratives, the Cherokee syllabary was sometimes used to record calendar information in a similar way. And of course, native people have recorded their own personal and collective histories, both in native language orthographies and in written English.

Nineteenth-century Indian historians tended to be exceptional figures such as William Apess, George Copway, Samson Occam, and a very few others. But by the twentieth century, many native people had worked their way inside mission Christianity and academic disciplines such as anthropology. Their cross-cultural writings, often inflected by the traditions of modernist history, frequently tried to use the past to make a case for contemporary Indians. Anthropologists Arthur C. Parker, Edward Dozier, J. N. B. Hewitt, and D'Arcy McNickle, writers Zitkala Sä, Pauline Johnson, Charles Eastman, and John Joseph Mathews – these were only a few of the native people who offered Indian histories as part of their literary output (Hoxie, 1992).

The diversity of tribal experience makes it difficult to attempt any general periodization of native history-telling. Nonetheless, one might suggest, as a starting point, three broad periods: (1) an "oral/traditional" period in which people used and recalled significant events as temporal markers embued with historical and cultural significance, characterized, on the plains, for example, by the invention of winter counts; (2) a period shaped by Christianization, in which mergings of the ideologies and tropes of the Bible with those of oral traditions became relatively common, shaping the nature of historical discourse among Indian people; (3) a period shaped by academic and non-academic scholarship, in which detailed ethnographic and historical inquiry into Indian history helped reshape native conceptions and narrations of the past. Such a periodization is not meant to suggest wholesale rewritings of Indian pasts, but rather to cast into relief the subtle transformations in epistemology and narrative which inevitably accompany the passage of time and cultural transmission.

Since the 1960s, then, we have seen Indian people playing increasingly important roles in transforming the library of non-native histories. The political upheavals of the

1960s not only made non-Indian historians more sensitive to issues, they also created the social and political contexts for the development of an Indian academic history. In 1972, for example, D'Arcy McNickle was named the first director of the Newberry Library's Center for the History of the American Indian, which has offered a home to many native scholars ever since. The first American Indian Studies programs came of age in the early 1970s, and, like the McNickle Center, helped create native intellectual centers for new approaches to Indian history. The list is significant, for many of these scholars have been at the forefront of Indian history: Jack Forbes at the University of California, Davis; Duane Champagne at UCLA; Gerald Vizenor, Terry Wilson, and Clara Sue Kidwell at UC Berkeley; Vine Deloria, Scott Momaday, Tom Holm, Ophelia Zepeda, and others at the University of Arizona; Elizabeth Cook-Lynn at Washington State; Oren Lyons and John Mohawk at SUNY; Michael Dorris at Dartmouth; Rupert Costo and Jeanette Henry at UC-Riverside.

Yet it is also the case that one cannot track a clean trajectory for recent Indian history beginning in the late 1960s. In Chicano history, for example, one can point to a generation of Chicano Ph.D. recipients, the so-called "class of 75." Mario T. Garcia, Albert Camarillo, Oscar Martinez, Juan Gomez-Quinones, Ricardo Romo, Richard Griswold del Castillo, among others, have moved through their careers together, producing an initial burst of dissertation-based scholarship, sustained training of multiple generations of students, and the development of a Chicano historical canon. The products of a different political milieu, Indian intellectuals more frequently turned to law or literature than to history or anthropology. And so in many ways, it was not entirely the voices of Indian intellectuals that pushed history and ethnohistory to open up to native perspectives. It was also the presence of Indian subjects – informants, readers, and students – who insisted upon making themselves heard.

Postmodern and Postcolonial

With that, we can now turn to consider the present moment in Indian history-telling which, it strikes me, is one of achievement, activism, and uncertainty. Earlier, I used the words "postmodern" and "postcolonial" as descriptive terms, and, despite the shared trendiness of the "post" prefix, I suggested that one might see them as being in tension with one another. I've argued that "frontier," "hierarchical," and "modern" schools of history-writing can be visualized in terms of the boundaries between Indians and others that have been imagined, inverted, and problematized. A rigid and largely impermeable frontier boundary mirrored the ideologies of colonial and imperial contest. A set of ranked distinctions put the problems of racial and ethnic distinctiveness in a reassuring order. And if modernists have clearly marked the boundaries between Indian and other, they have done so in order to transgress those same markers of difference. However one defines "postmodernism," it seems apparent that sometime over the last few decades we've entered a moment in which such boundaries have essentially disintegrated (Jameson, 1991).

One can see this disintegration in a social sense, for example, as cross-racial marriage and mixed-blood identity have become important issues in both history and

sociology. One can see it in the most recent census data, in which the Indian population skyrocketed beyond any rational demographic explanation and which suggests
that non-Indians, having rejected certain ethnic borders, are simply choosing an identity that suits them. One sees it in aesthetics, as "Indian" themes in art and literature
have become accessible to the entire world. In politics and the media, we've watched
the dissolution of distinctions between public and private and between news and
entertainment. And among all the other places one might point, one also sees it in
the telling of history.

In addition to traditional treatments of politics and law, recent scholarship has
often focused more on the fluidities of culture and identity, particularly in socially
ambiguous situations. Gerald Vizenor, Richard White, Tsianina Lomawaima, Alan
Taylor, Craig Womack, James Merrell, Delphine Red Shirt, Alexandra Harmon, Greg
Sarris, Margaret Connell Szasz, James Clifton, among many others, have looked at
confused moments that have cast up individuals characterized by multiple identities
(see Hinderaker, this volume). What to make of figures like Simon Girty or Hendrik
Aupaumut or boarding school children or Wild West show performers? The answers
have often revolved around the ways in which cultural and social borders have been
confused or demolished. White's *Middle Ground* (1991) and Merrell's *Indians' New
World* (1989), for example, use structuring metaphors that suggest worlds characterized by shattered social structure and consequent rebuilding. *Contact Points* (Cayton
and Teute, 1998), an important recent collection of essays, insists on a redefined
frontier, one conceived around "contested spaces" where "kinetic interactions" create "new cultural matrices, American in their eclecticism, fluidity, individual determination and differentiation" (p. 2). Rather than considering the dynamics of visible
boundaries, such studies gain their coherence by examining subjects or groups in a
broad and multiplicitous "cultural field" in which clarity is lacking and identities are
cobbled out of confusion and conflict.

Pomo writer Greg Sarris's outstanding *Mabel McKay: Weaving the Dream* (1994)
stands as an icon of this postmodern ambiguity. In the book, Sarris weaves coherence
out of the blurred threads of his own identity, that of Mabel McKay, his personal and
scholarly encounters with her, the space of the reservation and the city. By the time
he is through, there is little left of the lines formerly used to distinguish Indian from
non-Indian, historian from subject, literature from history, nature from supernature.
Many non-Indian writers have celebrated the general sense of liberation that comes
with such an embrace of ambiguity. Others have rejected it, preferring a more conservative approach to questions of truth and difference. But except as they have
included questions of "multiculturalism" and educational representation, the so-
called "culture wars" being fought among non-Indian intellectual elites have often
been irrelevant to many native writers. What has mattered has been the other
context, that of postcolonialism (although one should note that many Indian writers
hesitate over the term itself).

A full postmodern embrace of the individual subject can easily result in an attenu-
ation of the importance of history. What comes to matter is not so much the cause-
and-effect of the past as it is the ways individuals and groups have figured themselves
out in the midst of trying circumstances. Postcolonial approaches also focus on the

individual, often the colonized person who finds a place and an identity through the institutions of those who have done the colonizing. But the postcolonial focus on the individual is different, for it requires a confrontation with the history that created those trying circumstances (Ashcroft, Griffiths, and Tiffin, 1995; Bhabha, 1994). The youngest generation of Indian historians, it seems to me, is concerned to insure, in Kwame Anthony Appiah's apt phrase, that the "post" in postcolonial is not the same as the "post" in postmodern (Appiah, 1992). That is, in the midst of an incredibly productive historical focus on boundary dissolution and ambiguity, native historians are also insisting on recognizing and reshaping boundaries both in the past and in the present.

Any reinstallation of boundaries will, perhaps necessarily, include issues of identity politics in the production of history. Perhaps never more than now, the question is being raised: who should do Indian history? For what audience and for what reason? Young Indian historians such as Angela Cavender Wilson and Anton Treuer, who insist on the primacy of native language history and oral tradition, are passionate advocates for the preservation of cultural difference in a postmodern world. To argue otherwise would be to allow tribal people, histories, and traditions to dissolve into a global melting pot far more effective and pernicious than the failed program of assimilation of a century ago. But while these writers seek a certain purity – Indian histories largely devoid of the colonialist documents of the conquerors, researched in native languages among native elders – they also have to account for the impurities of histories written in a postmodern moment. The "pure products" as James Clifford has said, reworking William Carlos Williams, have "gone crazy" and there's no going back (Clifford, 1988). The desire for purity is, of course, a political desire. In that sense, native-originated history ought to be considered on the same terrain as the equally political non-native histories we've discussed. But if we choose to mark Indian history as political, let us make doubly sure that we mark the politics that underlie non-Indian histories as well, rejecting the claims to objectivity and truth that have empowered those histories.

This multivalent reality suggests to me that future Indian histories may well be produced in a self-conscious collision, the politics and epistemology of purity and difference clashing with the politics and epistemology of ambiguity and fluidity. Thus, one can see in Angela Wilson's work an assertion that Indian oral history functions in ways similar to European history, with specific checks and balances for something called "accuracy." At the same time, however, Wilson also insists that the epistemology of oral tradition is radically different and that, in its difference, it challenges Western ways of knowing. A paradox, then: histories overlap in method and practice. But histories are also written and told to reject such overlaps, for practice is always marked by power, and history has always been crucial to thinking about – and contesting – power.

The best evidence for the continued working of power in history lies in the fact that the frontier school of Indian historiography is alive and well, as are the proponents of modernist desire and the voices of scientific racialism. This essay has, in effect, been working through an ongoing set of authorial positions. Power relations continue to make it possible for Euro-Americans to choose to write history through

Euro-American lenses such as frontier, hierarchy, crossing. In challenging those power relations – both directly and through the maintenance of Indian distinctiveness – it's equally possible for native people to write history through a strictly native lens. Intellectually, however, neither position seems tenable, for neither does justice to what is, at least in terms of the last 500 years, a thoroughly cross-cultural history. The best contemporary scholarship treats Indians and non-Indians in a changing world, with historical consciousnesses that are the products of that world and of those changes. Such scholarship recognizes the need to both dissolve and reassert boundaries at the same time.

Writing contemporary Indian history requires a creative weaving together of contradictions. First, the political demands made by those concerned with colonial/postcolonial issues require any historian – Indian or non-Indian – to engage in a self-reflexive consideration of *difference* in the epistemology of history. How *are* Indian people and Indian histories different, both in terms of the past and in terms of the project at hand? Second, the realities of the postmodern moment require historians to engage in a self-reflexive consideration of *change* in the epistemology of history. How are the Indian histories of today *not* the Indian histories of the past? Somehow, historians – Indian and non-Indian alike – need to escape the tendency to force each other to choose loyalties from a dichotomous vision that splits history into two untenable camps.

In the end, the most interesting new Indian histories will come from Native people who have been able to look the Euro-American library full in the face, learning its politics, its lessons, and its secrets. They will also come from non-Native people who have been able to transcend the library and look Native people full in the face, understanding their politics and their pasts. And they will come from individuals who are naturally positioned in between and who work to develop their narratives with a full awareness of difference and ambiguity, and change and timelessness.

BIBLIOGRAPHY

Appiah, Kwame Anthony 1992: *In My Father's House: Africa in the Philosophy of Culture* (New York: Oxford University Press).

Ashcroft, Bill, Gareth Griffiths, and Helen Tiffin (eds.) 1995: *The Post-Colonial Studies Reader* (New York: Routledge).

Axtell, James 1981: "Ethnohistory: An Historian's Viewpoint," in *The European and the Indian: Essays in the Ethnohistory of Colonial North America* (New York: Oxford University Press).

Basso, Keith 1996: *Wisdom Sits in Places: Landscape and Language Among the Western Apache* (Albuquerque: University of New Mexico Press).

Berkhofer, Robert F. 1978: *The White Man's Indian: Images of the American Indian from Columbus to the Present* (New York: Knopf).

Bhabha, Homi 1994: *The Location of Culture* (New York: Routledge).

Bieder, Robert 1986: *Science Encounters the Indian, 1820–1880: The Early Years of American Ethnology* (Norman: University of Oklahoma Press).

Brown, Jennifer S. H. and Elizabeth Vibert (eds.) 1996: *Reading Beyond Words: Contexts for Native History* (Orchard Park, NJ: Broadview).

Calloway, Colin 1988: *New Directions in American Indian History* (Norman: University of Oklahoma Press).

Castiglia, Christopher 1996: *Bound and Determined: Captivity, Culture-Crossing, and White Womanhood from Mary Rowlandson to Patty Hearst* (Chicago: University of Chicago Press).

Cayton, Andrew R. L. and Fredrika Teute 1998: *Contact Points: American Frontiers from the Mohawk Valley to the Mississippi, 1750–1830* (Chapel Hill: University of North Carolina Press for the Institute of Early American History and Culture).

Clifford, James 1988: *The Predicament of Culture: Twentieth-Century Ethnography, Literature, and Art* (Cambridge, MA: Harvard University Press).

Deloria, Philip 1998: *Playing Indian* (New Haven: Yale University Press).

Deloria, Vine 1969: *Custer Died for Your Sins* (New York: Macmillan).

DeMallie, Raymond J. 1984: *The Sixth Grandfather: Black Elk's Teachings Given to John G. Neihardt* (Lincoln: University of Nebraska Press).

Dickason, Olive 1984: *The Myth of the Savage and the Beginnings of French Colonialism in the Americas* (Edmonton: University of Alberta Press).

Dippie, Brian 1982: *The Vanishing American: White Attitudes and U.S. Indian Policy* (Middletown: Wesleyan University Press).

Echo-Hawk, Roger 2000: "Ancient History in the New World: Integrating Oral Traditions and Archeology in Deep Time," *American Antiquity* 65(2) (April): 267–90.

Fixico, Donald (ed.) 1997: *Rethinking American Indian History* (Albuquerque: University of New Mexico Press).

Hinsley, Curtis 1981: *Savages and Scientists: The Smithsonian Institution and the Development of American Anthropology, 1846–1910* (Washington, D.C.: Smithsonian Institution Press).

Hoxie, Frederick 1984: *A Final Promise: The Campaign to Assimilate the Indians, 1880–1920* (Lincoln: University of Nebraska Press).

Hoxie, Frederick 1992: "Exploring a Cultural Borderland: Native American Journeys of Discovery in the Early Twentieth Century," *Journal of American History* 79 (December): 969–95.

Jackson, Helen Hunt 1881: *A Century of Dishonor: A Sketch of the United States Government's Dealings with Some of the Indian Tribes* (New York: Harper Brothers).

Jacobs, Sue-Ellen, Wesley Thomas, and Sabine Lang (eds.) 1997: *Two-Spirit People: Native American Gender Identity, Sexuality, and Spirituality* (Urbana: University of Illinois Press).

Jameson, Fredric 1991: *Postmodernism, or the Cultural Logic of Late Capitalism* (Durham: Duke University Press).

Jennings, Francis 1975: *The Invasion of America: Indians, Colonialism, and the Cant of Conquest* (Chapel Hill: University of North Carolina Press for the Institute of Early American History and Culture).

Keen, Benjamin 1971: *The Aztec Image in Western Thought* (New Brunswick: Rutgers University Press).

Klein, Kerwin Lee 1997: *Frontiers of Historical Imagination: Narrating the European Conquest of Native America, 1890–1990* (Berkeley: University of California Press).

Leacock, Eleanor and Nancy Oestreich Lurie 1971: *North American Indians in Historical Perspective* (New York: Random House).

Mallery, Garrick 1972: *Picture Writing of the American Indians* (Washington, 1883; New York: Dover).

Martin, Calvin 1987: *The American Indian and the Problem of History* (New York: Oxford University Press).

Merrell, James 1989: *The Indians' New World: Catawbas and Their Neighbors from European Contact through the Era of Removal* (Chapel Hill: University of North Carolina Press for the Institute of Early American History and Culture).

Mihesuah, Devon 1998: *Natives and Academics: Researching and Writing about American Indians* (Lincoln: University of Nebraska Press).

Morgan, Lewis Henry 1851: *League of the Ho-de-no-sau-nee, or Iroquois* (Rochester: Sage and Brothers).

Namias, June 1993: *White Captives: Gender and Ethnicity on the American Frontier* (Chapel Hill: University of North Carolina Press).

Nabokov, Peter 1996: "Native Views of History," in *The Cambridge History of the Native Peoples of the Americas*, eds. Bruce Trigger and Wilcomb Washburn, 2 vols. (Cambridge: Cambridge University Press).

Pagden, Anthony 1993: *European Encounters with the New World: From Renaissance to Romanticism* (New Haven: Yale University Press).

Pagden, Anthony 1995: *Lords of All the World: Ideologies of Empire in Spain, Britain and France c.1500–c.1800* (New Haven: Yale University Press).

Parkman, Francis 1962: *The Conspiracy of Pontiac* (Boston, 1851; New York: Collier).

Pearce, Roy Harvey 1953: *Savagism and Civilization: A Study of the Indian and the American Mind* (Baltimore, 1953; Berkeley: University of California Press).

Rosaldo, Renato 1989: *Culture and Truth: The Remaking of Social Analysis* (Boston: Beacon Press).

Roscoe, Will 1991: *The Zuni Man-Woman* (Albuquerque: University of New Mexico Press).

Sarris, Greg 1994: *Mabel McKay: Weaving the Dream* (Berkeley: University of California Press).

Sayre, Gordon 1997: *Les Sauvages Américains: Representations of Native Americans in French and English Colonial Literature* (Chapel Hill: University of North Carolina Press).

Schoolcraft, Henry Rowe 1853: *Western Scenes and Reminiscences: Together with Thrilling Legends and Traditions of the Red Men of the Forest* (Buffalo: Derby, Orton, and Mulligan).

Slotkin, Richard 1973: *Regeneration through Violence: The Mythology of the American Frontier, 1600–1860* (Middletown: Wesleyan University Press).

Slotkin, Richard 1985: *The Fatal Environment: The Myth of the Frontier in the Age of Industrialization, 1800–1890* (New York: Atheneum).

Stocking, George 1968: *Race, Culture, and Evolution: Essays in the History of Anthropology* (New York: Free Press).

Swagerty, William R. 1984: *Scholars and the Indian Experience: Critical Reviews of Recent Writing in the Social Sciences* (Bloomington: Indiana University Press for the D'Arcy McNickle Center for the History of the American Indian, Newberry Library).

Thomas, David Hurst 2000: *Skull Wars: Kennewick Man, Archaeology, and the Battle for Native American Identity* (New York: Basic).

Thornton, Russell 1998: *Studying Native America: Problems and Prospects* (Madison: University of Wisconsin Press).

Todorov, Tzvetan 1984: *The Conquest of America: The Question of the Other*, trans. Richard Howard (New York: Harper & Row).

Turner, Frederick Jackson 1920: *The Frontier in American History* (New York: Henry Holt).

Vansina, Jan 1985: *Oral Tradition as History* (Madison: University of Wisconsin Press).

Vaughan, Alden and Edward Clark (eds.) 1981: *Puritans Among the Indians: Accounts of Captivity and Redemption, 1676–1724* (Cambridge, MA: Belknap Press).

Washburn, Wilcomb (ed.) 1975: *The Garland Library of Narratives of North American Indian Captivities* (New York: Garland).

White, Richard 1991: *The Middle Ground: Indians, Empires, and Republics in the Great Lakes Region, 1650–1815* (New York: Cambridge University Press).

Williams, Walter L. 1986: *The Spirit and the Flesh: Sexual Diversity in American Indian Culture* (Boston: Beacon Press).

Wilson, Angela Cavender 1997: "The Power of the Spoken Word: Native Oral Traditions in American Indian History," in D. Fixico, ed., *Rethinking American Indian History* (Albuquerque: University of New Mexico Press).

Part One

Contacts

2

First Contacts

JOHN E. KICZA

On October 12, 1492, natives of a Bahama island met the captain of a Spanish expedition as he landed. Such encounters would be repeated numerous times in North America over the next couple of centuries. Oftentimes, however, the local people knew of the Europeans even before meeting them. Furthermore, with increasing frequency the material goods and diseases – and more rarely, the animals – that they had brought to the Americas preceded their arrival. Though undoubtedly impressed by certain of their attributes, the natives did not cower before the Europeans, nor were they mystified by them. Instead they endeavored to make sense of them within the context of their long-established cultures.

This chapter considers the nature and impact of early contact between the peoples of North America and the Europeans who entered their territories. It devotes its early sections to Spanish interaction with the indigenous societies of the Caribbean and Mexico before turning to the Southwest and Southeast of the present United States, important regions which the Spanish explored and colonized before other European nations. We will then turn to the Northeast coast, where Indian peoples had dealt with fishermen and traders from different European countries for over a century before the English settled in New England and the French in Canada.

Overall, this chapter concentrates on the initial perceptions and interactions between the natives and the Europeans in these major zones of North America, and presents the dynamic responses of the indigenous peoples to changes brought by the newcomers. Coverage stops with the establishment of stable colonies and extends beyond 1650 only when some significant process is being traced. The chapter develops comparisons between the individual cases and highlights numerous commonalities. It notes salient scholarly perspectives and debates regarding these early encounters and comments on recent and emerging research trends.

The Impact of the Spanish on the Caribbean Peoples

The indigenous peoples of the major Caribbean islands, generally termed Tainos, numbered in the low millions, practiced swidden (slash-and-burn) agriculture based on manioc cultivation, lived in substantial communities organized around kinship groups, and organized themselves into chiefdoms. Hence, despite the tropical environment, their material culture and social and political organization substantially resembled those of the Eastern Woodlands Indians of the North American mainland.

Spanish expansion typically emphasized active colonization of a new region rather than trade alone. On his first voyage, Columbus seized seven natives – several of whom soon escaped – to display in Spain and to train as translators for subsequent expeditions. (Such kidnappings became common among European explorers.) He commanded some 1,200 men (no women) to settle Hispaniola on his second voyage. Despite some conflicts between Taino chiefdoms and intrusive Spaniards, native leaders did not initially try to drive off the Spaniards. They sought alliances with them against local rivals, but staunchly resisted political subordination. The Spanish searched for precious metals instead of planting crops, and they remained dependent on the natives for food. The two sides traded considerably with each other, commonly combining these exchanges with ritual feasting and gift-giving. The Spanish did not undertake systematic religious conversion in the first decades, nor did they dispute native land ownership.

Many colonists mated with native women. A 1514 census indicates that perhaps 40 percent of the Spaniards lived with Indian women. But these men soon suffered from official discrimination, the governor denying them additional lands. Also, perhaps a hundred early settlers chose to live in native communities, a pattern repeated among early colonists throughout the Americas.

In the Caribbean the Spanish continued their longstanding practice of ruling newly occupied regions through local headmen. Taino leaders who refused to provide laborers for mining enterprises were put in chains or even executed. The Spanish also requisitioned foodstuffs as tribute. This unrelenting demand for workers and supplies disrupted indigenous crop production. Famine resulted as early as 1495–6, and many chiefs thereupon began armed resistance. Some communities fled into the hinterland. One group withdrew into the rugged backcountry in 1519 and withstood all onslaughts until 1533, when it was pardoned by the governor.

A protracted period of warfare and devastation ensued, much of it involving Spanish attacks against independent communities. The indigenous style of warfare, which stressed close combat over ambush and flight, proved generally ineffective. The incessant warfare did inspire unprecedented cooperation among Taino provinces, including a coalition of fourteen *caciques* (chiefs) in one campaign.

The indigenous population plummeted as a consequence of warfare, the harsh treatment of workers, and especially disease. Epidemic diseases brought from the Old World caused the near elimination of the Tainos by 1550. Influenza may have afflicted Hispaniola as early as 1494, causing the death of many natives – and some Spaniards. In 1518, the island was racked by smallpox. By 1520, the Tainos numbered no more than 25,000, a population decrease of around 98 percent in a single generation. The colonists responded by searching the other major islands for replacements, accelerating Spanish exploration that led to the discovery of Florida and Mexico.

The ethnohistorical study of the early Caribbean has been severely restricted by the sparse extant documentation. Centuries of warfare and the tropical climate have destroyed most local records. Official reports and several second-hand chronicles provide the bulk of the surviving evidence. The virtual elimination of the indigenous Caribbean population has prevented anthropologists from examining cultural practices in much depth. Few modern authors have written about the native peoples in the initial decades of contact. Samuel M. Wilson (1990) has composed easily the best book on the peoples of Hispaniola, focusing on the chiefs. As few additional documents are likely to emerge, a deeper understanding of the early Caribbean may well depend on archaeological discoveries. Kathleen Deagan (1988, 1995) has adeptly synthesized the findings to date. The Spanish conquest of the Aztec empire, on the other hand, has generated an abundant historiography, one that includes early Spanish and indigenous writing, nineteenth-century American writing by historians such as William Prescott, and a range of contemporary interpretations.

The Spanish Conquest of the Aztec Empire

Spain's Caribbean colonies were near stagnation, yielding little wealth, and attracting few immigrants – or even significant governmental attention – when Cortés' expedition conquered the massive and wealthy Aztec empire in 1519–21. While the issue of the population of central Mexico remains hotly debated, most scholars agree that the island-capital of Tenochtitlan contained over 200,000 people, and the empire embraced some millions of subjects. The Aztecs could readily sustain armies of some tens of thousands in the field for prolonged periods. Though it consisted of 371 city-states organized into 38 provinces, the empire was less than a century old when the Spanish arrived, and many of these societies had been subordinated for only a few decades. All retained their individual ethnic identities, local rulers, and religious and historical traditions. Uprisings against Aztec rule were common. Some provinces dispatched envoys to Cortés and even proposed military alliances.

In a highly original book, literary critic Tzvetan Todorov argued that the Aztec conquest occurred largely because the Spanish did a superior job of manipulating signs and understanding the character and intentions of their opponents (1984). The primary reason they could do so, he posited, was their ability to communicate through writing. The Aztecs remained preliterate, doomed by omens and an inability to improvise, thoroughly bound to tradition and ritual. Todorov's provocative piece has influenced cultural studies scholarship with its theoretical intricacies and historical grounding, but it also inspired a strong and compelling response from ethnohistorians of Mesoamerica.

Inga Clendinnen (1991) and James Lockhart (1993) address Todorov's thesis most directly. They point out that both the set of omens that supposedly foreshadowed the Aztec defeat and the depiction of Montezuma as a hapless emperor were invented by indigenous writers at least several decades after the conquest in an effort to understand the defeat within the native historical tradition. Incidents and statements chosen by Todorov to exemplify Aztec dependence on ritual seem in fact to be misunderstandings of Mesoamerican rhetorical conventions and diplomatic protocol.

To the contrary, the peoples of Mexico did not display overwhelming awe toward the Spaniards. They viewed them as a previously unknown, foreign ethnic group whose aims and values largely paralleled theirs. In his magisterial study *The Nahuas after the Conquest*, James Lockhart (1992) points out that so many central Mexican and Spanish cultural practices resembled each other that for a long time both societies thought that they were virtually identical. He has termed this "double mistaken identity." This perspective enabled the natives to retain many traditional practices, as the colonial authorities incorrectly viewed them as local adoptions of Spanish norms.

Colonial indigenous chronicles, which typically reflect the viewpoint of the authors' ethnic provinces, commonly portray the Spanish as similar in nature and behavior to their native rivals. Only descendants of the former imperial center treat the Aztec defeat as a cataclysm. Many native annals and chronicles ignore or barely mention the Spanish conquest: they are more likely to note the arrival of Christianity and the construction of the first church in their province.

The Aztecs did not regard the Spanish as gods, but as outsiders whose powers remained still undetermined. Cortés even told the first imperial official he met that he represented a foreign monarch; the official responded that his emperor was fully as powerful. Throughout North America, native societies typically regarded Europeans initially with respect. They treated captive Europeans as slaves, however, and fought or conducted diplomacy with European expeditions. Whatever awe some natives may have initially held toward the newcomers rapidly dissipated with experience.

The conquest period is replete with instances of natives taking the initiative and manipulating the Spaniards to their own ends. The ruler of Cempoala, the first province to side with the Spanish, advised Cortés to organize several nearby provinces against the Aztecs. When the Tlaxcalans, the Aztecs' longstanding enemies, sided with the Spanish, they insisted that they attack an Aztec fortress. They may later have deceived the Spanish into massacring the population of Cholula, a rival province.

Scholars of the conquest of Mexico generally point to the same set of contributing factors – superior Spanish military technology (including horses); the European tradition of total war; the Mesoamerican emphasis on capturing rather than slaying one's enemies, coupled with an inflexible command structure; the numerous native provinces that sided with the invaders; and the impact of epidemic disease on the Aztecs – but they disagree profoundly on the significance that should be given to each. Ross Hassig (1988, 1992, 1994) has systematically studied the Mesoamerican tradition of warfare and the Spanish conquest. He emphasizes the fragmentation of the Aztec empire, the contribution of native allies of the Spanish, and the famine inflicted on the defenders of Tenochtitlan – an island city – by cutting off supplies from the mainland. Alfred W. Crosby, Jr. (1972) argues that the smallpox epidemic that erupted in Mexico as the Spanish began their siege was decisive, for it afflicted the city's population to an unprecedented extent, disrupted the civil and military hierarchies, and caused the Aztecs to doubt their cause (for the foreign invaders were immune to the disease).

Inga Clendinnen (1991) and Hugh Thomas (1993) are less monocausal in their explanations, but note the tremendous devastation that the Spanish (and their allies, to some extent) inflicted on the Aztecs. They point out that the attackers did not merely impose a passive siege around Tenochtitlan, but had to invade and level the city to force it to capitulate. (It is significant that the Spanish force suffered few casualties during the several months of their aggressive siege, while the defenders endured horrible losses.) A lack of warriors and foodstuffs may be the ultimate reason for the Aztec defeat, but such might never have been attained without daily onslaughts – generally successful – by the Spanish forces.

The scholarship on the native societies in the colonial period has a distinguished heritage. The voluminous documentation produced about and by these complex cultures has long attracted top researchers. In recent decades historians have analyzed previously unutilized records composed by indigenous peoples in their own languages. Scholars practicing "The New Philology" have examined what individuals and groups in native communities actually did and, often, how they explained themselves in their own words, with minimal external intervention in the account. Notable books by Louise M. Burkhart (1989), S. L. Cline (1986, 1993), Robert Haskett (1991), James Lockhart (1992), and Rebecca Horn (1998), complemented by numerous articles by them and others, have illuminated the resilience and dynamic character of these indigenous societies.

The Spanish in the American Southwest

The desert north of Mexico contained mostly nomadic peoples, with several semi-sedentary societies thriving along river basins. The Spanish settled this vast, largely desolate area only because of its substantial silver deposits. For several decades the colonists had little military success against the nomadic tribes, which fought with bows and arrows and used ambushes. Ultimately, these tribes accepted treaties that required them to settle in villages under Spanish missionaries in return for a stipulated amount of European goods each year. European diseases and manufactured goods (the latter by 1533) flowed into northern Mexico and the American Southwest along trade routes that had connected these regions with the civilizations of central Mexico for some two thousand years.

The Coronado expedition of over 300 Spaniards (including at least three women), 1,000 central Mexican Indians, and 1,500 horses and pack animals explored much of the region in 1540–2. The participants expected to find a land like central Mexico: they discovered instead a demanding landscape, where water and foliage were rare. But the well-watered upper Rio Grande River basin supported substantial communities of semi-sedentary agricultural peoples, the Pueblos. Conflict soon ensued over Coronado's demands for supplies and authority. But with the expedition's return to central Mexico, the Spanish largely left the Pueblo Indians alone for over half a century.

The Spanish did not undertake to colonize the Southwest until 1598. Then, Juan de Oñate, a Zacatecas mining heir, led some 500 people into Pueblo territory. He required that native leaders swear fealty to the crown, but within a year the community of Acoma killed eleven Spaniards. In retaliation, the colonists killed over 800 inhabitants, many of them women and children, as they retook the community. A number of captives were forced into servitude.

As late as 1639, fewer than 300 colonists resided in New Mexico. The Spanish population remained small until after the Revolt of 1680, and Santa Fe remained the sole settlement of any size. The total number of Spaniards who fled the province in 1680 did not exceed 800; at most a few hundred had been killed. Few Pueblos lived among the colonists, remaining instead in their traditional communities. The Spaniards' dependent labor force largely consisted of Navajos, Apaches, and members of other tribes whom the colonists had "redeemed" from captivity by other tribes.

The number of Pueblo Indians plummeted during the century. Around 1500, their population may have reached nearly 250,000 distributed among some 130 settlements. But a 1678 survey found only 17,000 Pueblos residing in 46 communities. Epidemic disease and drought-induced famine caused most of the decrease. The colonists' demands for maize as tribute exacerbated the periodic food shortages.

The Pueblos had long occupied a central position in trading systems throughout the Southwest. The Spanish occupation greatly disrupted these patterns, which were so crucial in a region of scarce resources. The Navajos and Apaches became alienated from the Pueblos and raided them for the goods no longer available through trade.

Ramón Gutiérrez (1991) provides a systematic and stimulating consideration of Pueblo culture and its modification under the Spanish. In a prize-winning book, he cast the pre-contact Pueblo way of life as pacifist in orientation, with female sexuality as the primary shaping force, sustaining peace and integrating foreign elements into the culture. Women enjoyed sexual discretion, and their vital economic functions gave them political and familial authority as well. Gutiérrez enumerates how the Pueblos used their traditional values to make sense of the Spanish presence and how their beliefs and practices were affected by it. However, Gutiérrez often substantiates general assertions with only one or two examples and depicts a cultural homogeneity throughout the region that seems problematic. American Indian scholars raised numerous questions about the book that have led to serious re-evaluations of its argument and use of evidence.

A small number of Franciscans arrived in the early 1600s to convert the Pueblos, and they resided in Pueblo communities. Their ability to transform native culture was severely limited and only some modifications occurred. Many Pueblos viewed baptism as a death ritual, for it often occurred just before a person's demise. They understood the cross to be a prayer-stick, while the friars understood just the opposite. The friars drew a parallel between the kachina cult and the cult of the saints. Traditional dances for good crops continued, but combined with devotions toward appropriate saints.

Fifteen years of drought and famine, exacerbated by Navajo and Apache raids, led to the Revolt of 1680, which took on the characteristics of a revitalization movement. Some Pueblos once again performed forbidden dances and harkened to their religious leaders. Already in 1672, one community had burned its church and killed the friar. In the late 1670s, Popé, a religious leader from San Juan, traveled among communities promoting rebellion. He called for renewed respect for kachinas, saying that they had already bestowed special powers on him.

Perhaps 8,000 warriors took part in the highly successful 1680 revolt. Only a few communities refused to participate. Some Spaniards were killed, but most fled to Santa Fe, where they were besieged for nine days. In desperation the defenders fled to the nearest Spanish fort, El Paso. But despite the despoiling of churches and destruction of livestock and other European introductions, only partial cultural purification took place. The Pueblos retained most of their adopted European material culture and also some aspects of Christian doctrine.

Don Diego de Vargas, commanding 60 soldiers, led the reconquest of New Mexico in 1692. Most community leaders met him peacefully and submitted to Spanish authority. But resistance emerged over the next year. Pueblo warriors occupied Santa Fe in 1693, and Vargas routed them only after a siege. By the early 1700s, however, the colonists felt secure enough to move away from the garrison at Santa Fe to found two additional towns.

Spain's Impact on the American Southeast

The Southeast contained some of the most populated and complex societies north of central Mexico, enjoying the benefits of a productive agricultural system that regularly rendered surpluses. Trading networks connected these sophisticated cultures to each other and to less complex societies on their periphery. Settlements had grown progressively larger and many contained large temples and platforms. In the half millennium before the arrival of Europeans, distinct political capitals emerged, with chiefdoms as the dominant political structures.

The Spanish had a profound early impact on these societies, although they would withdraw from most of the region rather quickly and establish few settlements there. Juan Ponce de León visited the Florida peninsula as early as 1513; he was killed on his return in 1521. In 1526, Lucas Vázquez de Ayllón, a colonial official, led some 600 colonists to settle the "land of Chicora" in what became South Carolina. He was inspired by the glowing description given by a native kidnapped from that area some years earlier, whom the Spanish named Francisco de Chicora. Upon arrival, Francisco and several other captives escaped into the interior. The colonists found the area to be lacking in resources and lightly populated. A harsh winter killed three-quarters of them (including Ayllón), and the survivors returned to the Caribbean.

In 1527, Pánfilo de Narváez led 300 men into western Florida. (Even at this early date, the Spaniards found the Indians in possession of woven cloth, shoes, canvas, and ironware washed up on the shore.) Narváez tried to rule the Apalachees through a captive headman, but they responded with surprise attacks, their longbows inflicting significant casualties. Disease also debilitated the Spaniards. Many of the survivors built barges to return to Mexico. After some years Alvar Nuñez Cabeza de Vaca and three companions returned overland via the American Southwest; his account is a classic primary source for Spanish–Indian contact. These brief Spanish inroads into Florida were sufficient to transmit epidemics to the natives. When the de Soto expedition landed a decade later, its chroniclers noted widespread devastation from disease. Some settlements were entirely deserted.

Though scholars have highlighted those few European captives who became shamans or traders, most suffered worse fates. The Florida Indians seized a number of shipwreck survivors. Many were slain; those kept alive were sometimes relegated to slavery. Juan Ortiz, a captive from the Narváez expedition, had been cruelly tortured and was slated for execution when a family decided to keep him as a slave. De Soto ultimately rescued him more than a decade later.

With higher death rates from Spanish aggression but particularly from the new diseases, the populations of many Southeastern societies declined steadily over decades. Some peoples responded by increasing the adoption of outsiders into their communities. Now, however, those adopted might occasionally be Spanish or African rather than Native American. Incorporating such people into their societies required revolutionary redefinitions of community and ethnicity. But this enhanced adoption of outsiders slowed demographic decline only slightly. It could not provide sufficient substitutes to replace the substantial human losses.

Hernando de Soto's large and destructive expedition throughout the Southeast (1539–43) did not usually cause the indigenous societies great distress, despite his policy of pillage and intimidation. Notice of de Soto's approach often reached communities in time for them to flee into the hinterland or to organize a resistance. On a few occasions several tribes joined forces against the invaders. But while they inflicted some casualties on the Europeans, de Soto's men always prevailed, killing numerous opponents with their swords, horses, and vicious dogs.

New epidemics accompanying the expedition caused heightened loss of life over the following several decades, emptying even more settlements. This demographic collapse severely damaged indigenous culture in the Southeast, reducing the construction of ceremonial mounds and the frequency and scale of warfare. Craft specialization diminished. Local societies could no longer produce abundant agricultural surpluses, and settlement patterns became more dispersed, while the authority of paramount chiefs decreased.

When the expedition returned to Mexico in 1543 after de Soto's death, it left behind hundreds of pigs brought along as a food supply. These proliferated and became an important source of animal protein for the natives. Earlier explorers had apparently introduced peach trees and watermelon, and the local peoples cultivated them avidly. Finally, the glass beads and small metalware items brought by de Soto spread along trading routes. Initially, chiefs hoarded them as status items; but in the seventeenth century so many manufactured goods entered the region that they became much more widely distributed.

Most Spanish activity in the Southeast after 1570 revolved around Franciscan missions in central and western Florida and along coastal Georgia, which were vital to demarking the empire's northern border. The few priests had to base themselves in existing Indian settlements, for they could not coerce the natives into freestanding missions. More than thirty missions were situated among the Guales, Timucuas, Apalachees, and Apalachicolas. In 1655, some 26,000 natives lived in these districts. Many of them labored periodically for the residents of San Agustín. The Franciscans declined to send envoys to the heavily populated societies farther west because they would lack the military protection this substantial fortress provided.

As most missions were staffed by only a single priest, their religious impact was limited. The Franciscans had to acknowledge the prevailing native hierarchies. Customary housing patterns also endured. But the conversion of some residents disrupted religious traditions, bringing tension and sometimes conflict to community and kinship groups. The greatest impact of the missions was the dramatic decrease of the native population from unhealthy conditions and outbreaks of epidemic disease. Some Timucuan communities totally disappeared. Uprisings were common among mission Indians: a series of devastating assaults in 1702–4 from English-sponsored tribes in Carolina to the north largely ended the Florida missions (see Dowd, this volume).

Although some chiefdoms had thrived for several centuries without major disruptions, none of them survived unscathed the impact of the Spanish expeditions and colonizing efforts of the sixteenth century. Aggressive armies passed through the region almost every generation, inflicting highly destructive attacks and seizing supplies and laborers. They spread epidemic diseases that decreased the native population for years after their departure. Famines sometimes resulted. Political structures and settlements became smaller and simpler, as people dispersed in response to disease outbreaks. Others fled from their homelands. Remnant societies combined with each other to form new ethnicities. Such were the fruits of contact.

In the 1910s, 1920s, and 1930s, Herbert Bolton essentially founded a school of Spanish borderlands scholarship. Examining Spanish colonial institutions – the mission, the entrada, the presidio, the trade fair – he limned a Spanish line stretching from Florida through Texas to central California. In a series of books, articles, and edited primary sources, Bolton and his students examined the dynamics of contact and colonization surrounding this "rim of Christendom" (Magnaghi, 1998). Recent scholars, such as David Weber, have drawn on this tradition. Yet it has also become apparent that within the possibilities set by Spanish imperial structure, contact situations unfolded in many different ways depending on the specific interests and practices of different native groups. As we have seen, even Spanish practices varied across time and region, making Mexico, Florida, and the Southwest very different pieces in a "rim" of Spanish Christendom. And, of course, the Spanish represent only one of the European societies making contact with native people.

The English in the American Southeast

By the time the English came to the Southeast in the 1580s, the preceding Spanish ventures had already transformed native life. The initial English settlement at Roanoke Island, composed entirely of men and intended as a privateering base, quickly failed. A second attempt recruited families, each promised over 500 acres of land. The local natives may have been initially impressed by the colonists' technology, particularly their weaponry, and their seeming ability to spread disease while remaining immune themselves. But this high regard soon dissipated, and the settlers became caught up in traditional tribal rivalries, with different groups seeking to recruit them against their enemies. Some native communities split internally over whether to welcome the Europeans or not.

Feeling militarily weak and outnumbered, the colonists attempted to intimidate the neighboring peoples and seized their provisions to remedy their shortages. In 1590, after an absence of three years, relief vessels arrived to find the colony abandoned. Some evidence indicates that its survivors had moved north for protection under the Powhatan confederacy.

The Jamestown colony of 1607 shared some characteristics with the Roanoke enterprise. The initial colonists were all men. Though inadequately supplied, they showed little interest in cultivating their own food and died in great numbers in the hot lowlands. The leaders aspired to make fortunes from mining precious metals and exploiting native laborers, but had no success. They only shifted to cultivating tobacco when these initial plans proved unfeasible. Like other coastal societies, the Powhatans had interacted with members of various European countries over the preceding decades, and the chiefs appreciated that differences existed among the Europeans.

While the Spanish recognized native rights to the land and to their own leaders, the English did not. Instead they seized property they coveted, and tried to have indigenous leaders recognize the English monarch's sovereignty. Such strategies rarely succeeded until a tribe had been decimated and stripped of its resources. The English never entertained the massive absorption of Indians into their colonial societies, as did the Spanish. As early as 1610, Jamestown was placed under new laws intended to minimize the integration of natives into the settlement. They further stipulated that nearby tribes should be subjugated and required to pay tribute, with recalcitrant chiefs to be incarcerated. Also unlike the Spanish, the English brought no missionaries with them, showing, in fact, little interest in converting the natives. Finally, finding no immediately exploitable resources in the region comparable to the abundant wealth in central Mexico, the Spanish treated the Southeast as the northern periphery of their empire, maintaining only a modest presence in one corner of it. For the English, however, the same region represented the most promising economic zone to which they could aspire on the mainland. Hence from the earliest years of settlement they continued to invest men, money, and goods, transforming the indigenous way of life in the process.

Jamestown remained dependent on the Powhatan confederacy for foodstuffs for several years. Further, recognizing their military disadvantage, the English maintained a continual military alert. But the abundant vacant land eliminated conflicts over resources until tobacco emerged as a commercial crop. The Powhatans showed no awe of the English. The settlers died in great numbers in an environment in which the Powhatans had long thrived. Epidemic disease did not afflict them for a couple of decades. Some settlers abandoned the colony to live in native communities. In the early years, Powhatan played a waiting game to see if the English would eventually thrive, and also possibly provide assistance against rival tribes as he expanded his small empire. But as early as 1610, the settlers showed their military might by attacking the Paspaheghs, a people friendly to Powhatan, and their ruthless style of warfare by killing the children and keeping the women. A haughty female chief was put to the sword.

The emergence of tobacco as a cash crop guaranteed the colony's survival. Many more English flocked to Jamestown, heightening the demand for land. The colony had little regard for the indigenous population, for trade with them had declined, particularly as food became more abundant, and the natives showed they would never become a dependent labor force – though some young men did work on settlers' estates to earn money to purchase European goods. Natives moved freely around Jamestown and routinely borrowed English tools, boats, and the like. Numerous Indians were falling into debt, probably from their deepening reliance on manufactured items. The first epidemics hit the Powhatans in 1617 and 1619.

By 1622, the Powhatans, now led by Opechancanough, feared losing their lands and their population and being overrun by the English. They therefore tried to destroy the colony in a concerted military attack. They killed a fourth of the colonists and then withdrew in traditional native style, figuring that the survivors would see that they had been defeated and would withdraw from the region. But instead the English counterattacked and burned down Powhatan settlements and storehouses, killing indiscriminately. The Powhatans continued to behave in traditional manner, killing male captives but retaining the women as workers until they were ransomed a year later. They could not curtail the influx of people and material from England, despite all their efforts, and became ever a smaller minority on their own lands and more dependent on European goods. The colonists no longer maintained any idea of living alongside the natives. Instead they claimed more and more land, refusing to recognize native ownership. They also frequently raided native communities, forcing the various peoples farther into the interior, where they were often absorbed by more powerful tribes.

In 1644, the aged Opechancanough led his people in one more assault against the colonists, killing some 400 and taking many prisoners. Yet again, the Powhatans did not follow up on their successful initial attack, enabling the English to regroup. The colonists now took the offensive, killing some natives, forcing many others to flee, and selling prisoners as slaves. By 1646, the Powhatan empire was no more, and Opechancanough was killed while an English prisoner. His successor agreed to a treaty stating that he held his lands as a subject of the king of England, to whom he even paid a modest annual tribute. No Indians were allowed into English-controlled territory without permission.

The natives of the Carolinas had been far more directly affected by the early Spanish expeditions into the Southeast than were those of Virginia. Their populations had been reduced by epidemics and they had somewhat greater exposure to European goods. Then left largely alone for several generations until English traders arrived around 1670, their numbers recovered somewhat, and their leadership, ceremonies, and customs stabilized. The Carolina tribes sought to profit as middlemen, providing European goods to peoples in the interior, while colonial traders strove to prevent this by traveling into the interior themselves.

By the middle of the seventeenth century, some Carolina peoples – especially the Westoes – were armed and financed by Virginia traders to raid native settlements deep into the hinterland to capture slaves. Expeditions even penetrated deep into Spanish Florida, most notably destroying the Apalachees in 1702–4. These were exchanged for imported items and sold into slavery on Virginia tobacco plantations. These vulnerable tribes were finally able to acquire firearms from Carolina merchants for protection, once this rival colony to Virginia was founded a couple of decades later. Over subsequent decades, the balance of military power shifted repeatedly among the Southeastern peoples, so the predators in one period sometimes became the hunted in the next.

Describing the encounters of peoples of Eastern North America – and especially those of the Southeast – with Europeans and their influences, James Merrell has remarked that they faced three waves: disease, traders, and settlers. But the early contacts are much more varied and complex than this single sequence. For example, sometimes they had to deal with Spanish expeditions before disease made any impact. In other cases the primary initial threat was other tribes raiding for slaves to trade. With the exception of Jamestown and other English settlements, contact situations in the Southeast until recently received relatively less scholarly attention. Recent treatments by Merrell (1989), Helen Rountree (1990, 1993), Peter Wood, and others (1989) have shed new light on the South and Southeast.

The English in the American Northeast

The coastal peoples of the Northeast had numerous dealings with Europeans over more than a century before the first English colony was established there in 1620. In just the first decade of the sixteenth century, on at least four occasions explorers kidnapped a total of perhaps a dozen Mi'kmaqs. In the 1520s Verrazzano traded with Indians who had done so previously with other Europeans and were very selective in their choices. Peoples along the entire east coast obtained diverse European items during the sixteenth century. Such goods quickly entered longstanding trading networks and reached societies located far in the interior, sometimes decades before Europeans arrived in their territory.

The Europeans especially coveted the furs the Indians obtained from trapping and hunting. As some coastal tribes became more dependent on European goods, they resorted to hunting full time, neglecting other subsistence pursuits and relying on outsiders for their food supplies. Tribal chiefs found their power enhanced, as custom dictated that they receive a share of each hunt and as Europeans made known their preference for dealing with single leaders. This translated into more goods that leaders could redistribute to their people in return for greater authority and prestige. Neighboring societies competed more frequently over hunting zones and access to European traders. Warfare increased, and seemingly became more deadly, as the traditional practice of blood feuds was replaced – or at least combined – with elimination of one's opponent from a certain territory. Traders could substantially determine the outcome of indigenous warfare through the provision of firearms.

But by the perverse logic of contact with Europeans, the native groups most successful – and hence most intimate with these outsiders – were thereby most likely to be exposed to the epidemic diseases they carried. Archaeological findings have reinforced documentary evidence of widespread deaths from epidemics decades before the founding of colonial settlements. This rapid depopulation weakened native cultures, and perhaps caused them to question their religions and traditional healers who could offer no remedy for these horrible afflictions.

Initially, Indians desired only certain items, such as colored glass beads, which they could readily incorporate into their religious systems and their established material culture. Axe blades and copper implements, for example, might be worn as adornments rather than used as tools. In some early exchanges, the Indians rejected cloth goods, even silk, in favor of items that Europeans – and subsequent observers – valued only as trinkets. Use of these foreign items was initially restricted to native leaders, who found in them enhanced prestige. Such objects were incorporated into traditional religious practices, often being buried with the dead. But within two generations, European cloth, metal tools, and firearms were distributed more widely throughout the native population as their practical utility became generally recognized. Scholars have long puzzled over the meanings associated with markets, trade, and commodities themselves in these early contact situations. How did Indians value "trinkets" and utilitarian goods? How did trade change native societies? To what extent did Indian people adopt profit motives and other market understandings? How slowly or rapidly did such changes occur? The debate between Hammell and Trigger over how Indians perceived and used European goods and how widely such items were distributed, for example, seems to reflect the different time period examined by each author (Miller and Hammell, 1986; Hammell, 1987; Trigger, 1991).

As the Eastern Woodlands Indians periodically shifted their village locations, they acquired only such goods as could be conveniently carried. Their level of consumption was thus inherently limited. Nor did they seem to recognize the existence of market forces. Once an exchange value had been established, they expected it always to prevail and were unreceptive to pleas from European traders that supply and demand had changed. The Indians were discerning consumers, insisting on specific types and quality of goods, sometimes even demanding particular designs. They likewise insisted that trade be conducted within the framework of indigenous customs, with much discussion, eating and drinking, and the giving of gifts before the commencement of business negotiations.

Once the English in New England, the Dutch in New Netherlands, and the French in Canada had established colonies and begun a lively competition for beaver pelts, the interior societies greatly increased their harvest of hides and soon depleted these animals over a broad area. Certain native peoples responded by competing to become crucial middlemen between the coastal colonies and the suppliers far in the interior. Indigenous warfare seems to have increased and become more deadly as a consequence.

Calvin Martin has argued that when epidemic diseases began to decimate native societies and traditional sacred invocations failed to cure the victims, the natives blamed the animals, whom they stripped of their spiritual aura (Martin, 1978). They then trapped them into extinction. But this view has received various criticisms. Native peoples historically switched quite pragmatically from one religious leader to another and from one sacred belief to another – within cultural parameters – in their insistence on spiritual effectiveness in bringing about cures and military victories. Further, animal overkill may have preceded the onset of epidemics. The natives placed a high value on leisure, often prizing it over the extra effort required to bring in more pelts. Also, they seem to have responded more to the tangible benefits they obtained from European traders than to any loss of belief in the beneficial sacredness of the animal world. Turning away rather quickly from trade for purely decorative items, the native peoples sought instead cloth and metal goods that improved their lives in tangible fashion (Krech, 1981).

When the first settlers of Massachusetts arrived in 1620, they found a land recently devastated by disease. Epidemics had swept through the native communities of the Northeast in 1616–18, reducing the population by 75–90 percent, and leaving many villages and agricultural fields vacant. Threatened by peoples of the interior who were intact and powerful, the coastal peoples initially welcomed the settlers as potential allies. But they resisted the colonists' persistent efforts to subordinate them. They insisted on being treated as sovereign peoples and demanded the political ritual and gift-giving that characteristically accompanied native diplomatic affairs. Soon, however, the colonists began to pressure the natives over land ownership and legal jurisdiction in disputes, refusing to recognize their sovereignty. Factionalism increased within tribes and villages, engendered by disputes over how to respond to pressures from the colonists and also by certain limited efforts at religious conversion.

A wave of smallpox in 1633 reduced the remaining native societies even further, decimated their leadership, and opened up yet more land to the Puritans. While the indigenous population plummeted, English immigrants continued to arrive in substantial numbers, ever worsening the ratio between the two groups. In the second half of the 1630s, the settlers undertook a major military campaign against the resolutely independent Pequots. The tribe was nearly eliminated, with those not killed being sold into slavery and a remnant group fleeing from the region. Long dominated by the ideological heirs of the New England Puritans, the historiography of early Indian–European encounters in New England broke open in the last quarter of the twentieth century. Works by Jennings (1975), Salisbury (1982), and others have stressed the perspectives and experiences of natives, as well as the English, in order to highlight the intercultural dimensions of contact and colonization.

The French in Canada

French interaction with the peoples of eastern Canada dates from the mid-1530s, when Jacques Cartier made two voyages up the St. Laurence River. The people he encountered showed an immediate eagerness to barter: they may already have traded with passing ships. As early as Cartier's second voyage, the headman of Stadacona tried to prevent the French from proceeding upriver in order to control trade with those tribes. Relations between the French and Stadacona's chiefs became so frayed that Cartier decided to construct a fort protected by a moat. But when many of the French became ill from scurvy – with some dying – during the winter of 1535–6, the natives provided them with a remedy made from tree bark. Like Columbus, Cartier returned to France with kidnapped Indians after each voyage.

Hostilities arising from a third Cartier voyage (1541–2) poisoned Franco-Indian relations on the St. Laurence for several decades. Only in the 1580s did French fur traders begin frequenting the region, and only in 1608 did they establish a permanent settlement, when Samuel de Champlain constructed a trading house that eventually became Quebec City. Unlike the Spanish and the English the French never colonized in great numbers and they avoided land disputes with the natives. Few French women immigrated to early New France, and many colonists mated with Indian women, further cementing ties between the two peoples. The French did not assert sovereignty over indigenous societies. Disputes between the two sides were commonly resolved by negotiations. The French well appreciated that their small population in Canada depended on native allies for its economic viability and for military support against hostile tribes and European rivals.

The fur trade persisted as the colony's economic base until the British takeover in the late eighteenth century. French traders remained heavily dependent on Indian trappers for pelts. The natives always saw trade as a component of a larger political and military alliance rather than as an independent activity. When Champlain set up his trading house, the local Indians insisted that he join them against their foes, the Iroquois. Champlain's few muskets had the desired impact and the Iroquois were routed, with many taken captive.

The fur-trading tribes did not obtain European goods only for consumption. The Hurons, the first native group to become indispensable middlemen in the fur trade, bartered imported wares with tribes farther west, thereby enhancing their status. Huron chiefs, with more gifts to distribute, enhanced their authority with their fellow tribesmen and in diplomatic negotiations.

The Indians of eastern Canada suffered greatly from epidemic diseases. The Hurons were among the most afflicted, rendering them vulnerable to military onslaughts from the Iroquois. But in time the Iroquois themselves were hard hit by disease. Both societies had their populations cut by more than half in the twenty years following the onset of the epidemics in the mid-1630s.

The early and continuing role of Jesuit missionaries had a major impact on the native cultures, strengthening their ties to the French, but also causing factionalism within communities. Initially, the Indians accepted missionaries for fear of exclusion from the fur trade if they refused. By displaying their technological abilities, forecasting eclipses and other natural events, and their greater effectiveness at healing, the Jesuits encouraged the natives to believe they had supernatural powers. They proselytized natives in their own communities and recognized their chiefs. Unlike the Spanish, they did not erect independent missions. Nor did they show open disdain for indigenous culture and attempt to Europeanize their followers. Yet tension and animosity developed within communities when some members converted while others did not. Converts no longer participated in public festivals and rituals, undercutting the reciprocity that was so central to native culture. Some converts refused to fight alongside traditionalists.

Economic relations and demographic ratios dictated a quite distinct experience for the peoples of eastern Canada compared to those societies to the south, that were beleaguered in turn by the Spanish and English. The French did not subject them to concerted warfare or to attacks on their sovereignty or ownership of land. The few French settlers well appreciated that they remained at the forbearance of the local societies and that the Indians were indispensable to the profitable functioning of the fur trade. Certainly, the Jesuit missionaries had some modifying effect on native culture, but even here they sought reconciliation of belief systems and rituals more than the elimination of indigenous traditions. Epidemics, though, devastated the native peoples in a manner quite comparable to their counterparts to the south.

Concluding Remarks

The early contacts between North American native societies and European explorers, traders, and settlers discussed in this essay argue the centrality of epidemic disease and control over human and natural resources in shaping these interactions. In most cases, both the native and European groups continued confident in the superiority of their own cultures. They were not intimidated by the new people they encountered, and rather readily incorporated new goods and techniques into their cultural practices and fundamental beliefs. In the evolving situation of the early contact period, for example, with deaths from disease and sometimes heightened warfare, native people often turned to indigenous traditions, adopting captives and remnant societies.

Both natives and newcomers remained sure of their own interpretations of one another. Yet moments of contact also opened the door to the creative cross-cultural misunderstandings discussed by James Lockhart and Richard White (*The Middle Ground*). Some of the most interesting scholarship in this area focuses on the meetings of Europeans and Pacific Islanders (Dening, 1980; Sahlins, 1995; Obeyesekere, 1992), and its insights have made their way into Americanist studies. It is no coincidence that Greg Dening, an Australian historian of Pacific contact, introduces a recent edited volume on identity in early America, *Through a Glass Darkly* (Hoffman et al., 1997). Such innovations in cultural analysis, however, remain necessarily undergirded by considerations of military, social, economic, and biological power.

When Europeans coveted the lands, precious metals, or labor resources of the indigenous societies, they sought to subordinate Indians. When, however, the local peoples maintained a central role in trade, as with furs, or were crucial as military allies, they generally retained their autonomy. Settlers and natives typically negotiated their relationships and terms of exchange informally and on site. The sponsoring countries did not develop overarching policies toward indigenous peoples, certainly not in this still inchoate formative period.

Even peoples far removed from the European presence felt its impact. Coastal tribes traded imported goods to those of the interior; epidemic disease spread across the countryside, often along trade routes; and European animals such as swine and horses were adopted by distant peoples.

The native cultures responded resourcefully and selectively to the unprecedented challenge represented by the increasing European presence. Few natives chose to live among the colonists. Indigenous societies endeavored to retain their ethnic identities, autonomy, and cultural traditions before the duress and great changes that surrounded them.

BIBLIOGRAPHY

Axtell, James 1985: *The Invasion Within: The Contest of Cultures in Colonial North America* (New York: Oxford University Press).

Axtell, James 1997: *The Indians' New South: Cultural Change in the Colonial Southeast* (Baton Rouge: Louisiana State University Press).

Burkhart, Louise M. 1989: *The Slippery Earth: Nahua–Christian Dialogue in Sixteenth-Century Mexico* (Tucson: University of Arizona Press).

Calloway, Colin G. 1997: *New Worlds for All: Indians, Europeans, and the Remaking of Early America* (Baltimore: Johns Hopkins University Press).

Clendinnen, Inga 1991: "'Fierce and Unnatural Cruelty': Cortés and the Conquest of Mexico," *Representations* 33: 65–100.

Cline, S. L. 1986: *Colonial Culhuacan, 1580–1600: A Social History of an Aztec Town* (Albuquerque: University of New Mexico Press).

Cline, S. L. (ed.) 1993: *The Book of Tributes: Early Sixteenth-Century Nahuatl Censuses from Morelos* (Los Angeles: UCLA Latin American Center Publications).

Cook, Noble David 1998: *Born to Die: Disease and New World Conquest, 1492–1650* (Cambridge: Cambridge University Press).

Crosby, Alfred W., Jr., 1972: *The Columbian Exchange: Biological and Cultural Consequences of 1492* (Westport, CT: Greenwood Press).

Deagan, Kathleen 1988: "The Archaeology of the Spanish Contact Period in the Caribbean," *Journal of World Prehistory* 2(2): 187–233.

Deagan, Kathleen (ed.) 1995: *Puerto Real: The Archaeology of a Sixteenth-Century Spanish Town in Hispaniola* (Gainesville: University Press of Florida).

Dening, Greg 1980: *Islands and Beaches: Discourse on a Silent Land, Marquesas, 1774–1880* (Honolulu: University Press of Hawaii).

Díaz del Castillo, Bernal 1986: *Historia de la conquista de Nueva España* (Mexico City: Editorial Porrúa).

Duncan, David Ewing 1995: *Hernando de Soto: A Savage Quest in the Americas* (New York: Crown Publishers, Inc.).

Fitzhugh, William M. (ed.) 1985: *Cultures in Contact: The Impact of European Contacts on Native American Cultural Institutions, A.D. 1000–1800* (Washington: Smithsonian Institution Press).

Gutiérrez, Ramón A. 1991: *When Jesus Came, the Corn Mothers Went Away: Marriage, Sexuality, and Power in New Mexico, 1500–1846* (Stanford: Stanford University Press).

Hammell, George R. 1987: "Strawberries, Floating Islands, and Rabbit Captains: Mythical Realities and European Contact in the Northeast During the Sixteenth and Seventeenth Centuries," *Journal of Canadian Studies* 21(4): 72–94.

Haskett, Robert S. 1991: *Indigenous Rulers: An Ethnohistory of Town Government in Colonial Cuernavaca* (Albuquerque: University of New Mexico Press).

Hassig, Ross 1988: *Aztec Warfare: Imperial Expansion and Political Control* (Norman: University of Oklahoma Press).

Hassing, Ross 1992: *War and Society in Ancient Mesoamerica* (Berkeley: University of California Press).

Hassig, Ross 1994: *Mexico and the Spanish Conquest* (London: Longman).

Hoffman, Ron, Mechal Sobel, and Fredrika J. Teute (eds.) 1997: *Through a Glass Darkly: Reflections on Personal Identity in Early America* (Chapel Hill: published for the Omohundro Institute of Early American History and Culture by the University of North Carolina Press).

Horn, Rebecca 1998: *Postconquest Coyoacan: Nahua–Spanish Relations in Central Mexico, 1519–1650* (Stanford: Stanford University Press).

Hudson, Charles and Carmen Chaves Tesser (eds.) 1994: *The Forgotten Centuries: Indians and Europeans in the American South, 1521–1704* (Athens: University of Georgia Press).

Jaenen, Cornelius J. 1976: *Friend and Foe: Aspects of French–Amerindian Cultural Contact in the Sixteenth and Seventeenth Centuries* (New York: Columbia University Press).

Jennings, Francis 1975: *The Invasion of America: Indians, Colonialism, and the Cant of Conquest* (Chapel Hill: University of North Carolina Press).

Kicza, John E. 1994: "Dealing with Foreigners: A Comparative Essay Regarding Initial Expectations and Interactions between Native Societies and the English in North America and the Spanish in Mexico," *Colonial Latin American Historical Review* 3(4): 381–97.

Knaut, Andrew L. 1995: *The Pueblo Revolt of 1680: Conquest and Resistance in Seventeenth-Century New Mexico* (Norman: University of Oklahoma Press).

Krech III, Shepard (ed.) 1981: *Indians, Animals, and the Fur Trade: A Critique of "Keepers of the Game"* (Athens: University of Georgia Press).

Kupperman, Karen Ordahl 1984: *Roanoke: The Abandoned Colony* (Totowa, NJ: Rowman & Littlefield).

Lockhart, James 1992: *The Nahuas after the Conquest: A Social and Cultural History of the Indians of Central Mexico, Sixteenth through Eighteenth Centuries* (Stanford: Stanford University Press).

Lockhart, James (ed.) 1993: *We People Here: Nahuatl Accounts of the Conquest of Mexico*, intro. and trans. by James Lockhart (Berkeley: University of California Press).

Magnaghi, Russell 1998: *Herbert E. Bolton and the Historiography of the Americas* (Westport, CT: Greenwood Press).

Malone, Patrick M. 1993: *The Skulking Way of War: Technology and Tactics Among the New England Indians* (Baltimore: Johns Hopkins University Press).

Martin, Calvin 1978: *Keepers of the Game: Indian–Animal Relationships and the Fur Trade* (Berkeley: University of California Press).

Merrell, James H. 1989: *The Indians' New World: Catawbas and Their Neighbors from European Contact through the Era of Removal* (Chapel Hill: University of North Carolina Press).

Milanich, Jerald T. 1995: *Florida Indians and the Invasion from Europe* (Gainesville: University Press of Florida).

Miller, Christopher L. and George R. Hammell 1986: "A New Perspective on Indian–White Contact: Cultural Symbols and Colonial Trade," *Journal of American History* 73(2): 311–28.

Morgan, Edmund S. 1975: *American Slavery, American Freedom: The Ordeal of Colonial Virginia* (New York: W. W. Norton & Co.).

Obeyesekere, Gananath 1992: *The Apotheosis of Captain Cook: European Mythmaking in the Pacific* (Princeton: Princeton University Press).

Ramenofsky, Ann F. 1987: *Vectors of Death: The Archaeology of European Contact* (Albuquerque: University of New Mexico Press).

Richter, Daniel K. 1992: *The Ordeal of the Longhouse: The Peoples of the Iroquois League in the Era of European Colonization* (Chapel Hill: University of North Carolina Press).

Rountree, Helen C. 1990: *Pocahontas's People: The Powhatan Indians of Virginia through Four Centuries* (Norman: University of Oklahoma Press).

Rountree, Helen C. (ed.) 1993: *Powhatan Foreign Relations, 1500–1722* (Charlottesville: University Press of Virginia).

Rouse, Irving 1992: *The Tainos: Rise and Decline of the People Who Greeted Columbus* (New Haven: Yale University Press).

Sahlins, Marshall 1995: *How "Natives" Think: About Captain Cook, for Example* (Chicago: University of Chicago Press).

Salisbury, Neal 1982: *Manitou and Providence: Indians, Europeans, and the Making of New England, 1500–1643* (New York: Oxford University Press).

Salisbury, Neal 1996: "Native People and European Settlers in Eastern North America, 1600–1783," in *The Cambridge History of the Native Peoples of the Americas*, Volume I: *North America, Part 1*, eds. Bruce G. Trigger and Wilcomb E. Washburn (Cambridge: Cambridge University Press), pp. 399–460.

Sauer, Carl Ortwin 1969: *The Early Spanish Main* (Berkeley: University of California Press).

Sauer, Carl Ortwin 1971: *Sixteenth Century North America: The Land and the Peoples as Seen by the Europeans* (Berkeley: University of California Press).

Thomas, David Hurst (ed.) 1989–91: *Columbian Consequences*, 3 vols. (Washington, D.C.: Smithsonian Institution Press).

Thomas, Hugh 1993: *Conquest: Montezuma, Cortés, and the Fall of Old Mexico* (New York: Simon & Schuster).

Todorov, Tzvetan 1984: *The Conquest of America: The Question of the Other*, trans. by Richard Howard (New York: Harper & Row).

Trigger, Bruce G. 1985: *Natives and Newcomers: Canada's "Heroic Age" Reconsidered* (Kingston and Montreal: McGill-Queen's University Press).

Trigger, Bruce G. 1991: "Early Native North American Responses to European Contact: Romantic versus Rationalistic Interpretations," *Journal of American History*, 77(4): 1195–215.

Trigger, Bruce G. and William R. Swagerty 1996: "Entertaining Strangers: North America in the Sixteenth Century," in *The Cambridge History of the Native Peoples of the Americas*, Volume I: *North America, Part 1*, eds. Bruce G. Trigger and Wilcomb E. Washburn (Cambridge: Cambridge University Press), pp. 325–98.

Wallace, Anthony F. C. 1970: *The Death and Rebirth of the Seneca* (New York: Alfred A. Knopf, Inc.).

Weber, David J. 1992: *The Spanish Frontier in North America* (New Haven: Yale University Press).

White, Richard 1991: *The Middle Ground: Indians, Empires, and Republics in the Great Lakes Region, 1650–1815* (Cambridge: Cambridge University Press).

Wilson, Samuel M. 1990: *Hispaniola: Caribbean Chiefdoms in the Age of Columbus* (Tuscaloosa: University of Alabama Press).

Wood, Peter H., Gregory A. Waselkov, and M. Thomas Hatley (eds.) 1989: *Powhatan's Mantle: Indians in the Colonial Southeast* (Lincoln: University of Nebraska Press).

3

Wag the Imperial Dog: Indians and Overseas Empires in North America, 1650–1776

GREGORY EVANS DOWD

Historiography

When Indian history took root in the early American field in the 1970s and 1980s, it did so largely – but not entirely – as an exotic, anthropological species called ethnohistory. Until then, Indians had played little role in the dominant contest between the scholarly progressive and whiggish traditions. At the same time, a more conservative imperial tradition took notice of Indians as difficult, colorful obstacles. While these three schools focused on the eastern seaboard, from out of the West came a "Spanish Borderlands" school, and from out of Canada came a cluster of important works attending to New France (see Weber, 1992; Frégault, 1955). Both challenged the narrow Anglocentrism of the imperial school, but only as its hostile cousins, for they shared its disposition toward Indians. Neither they nor the imperial school affected the increasingly fiery debates between progressives and Whigs, which left Indians in the shadows as demography, class, Christianity, and republicanism contended for the attention of early Americanist scholars. Indians – hard to count, generally non-Christian, and outside the social structure and the *polis* – did not seem much to belong.

During the 1970s, some early American scholars caught up with the civil rights, "red power," and environmental movements. Scholars of a neo-progressive bent, such as Francis Jennings (1975) and Gary Nash (1974), and a few scholars of a neo-Whig inclination, most notably James Axtell (1972), joined such Canadian scholars as W. J. Eccles (1969) and ethnohistorian Bruce Trigger (1976) to include Indians as critical figures in their histories. Already Wilbur Jacobs (1950), with borderlands training, had been moving with his students in the same direction. By the middle of the 1980s Indian studies became one of the most dynamic areas of colonial North American history. Ethnohistorians, such as Anthony F. C. Wallace (1969), diligently at work for a generation, attracted the interest of a newer coterie of professional historians, and the word "empire" again appeared in the titles of early American histories. Anti-imperial world-systems theory attracted several scholars (Jennings, 1984, 1988; White, 1983; Delâge, 1985), all of whom owed an ironic debt to the imperial school, which had at least acknowledged Indians.

This essay will explore the history and recent historiography of Native Americans' relations with the rising overseas empires of Spain, Russia, France, and the Netherlands in the region now comprising the United States and Canada. It moves in rough clockwise fashion, from encounters in the Southeast, westward across the Southwest to California, northward to the Pacific Northwest, eastward through Canada and the Great Lakes, and finally shifting southward to the Atlantic Northeast. There it remains for a time, examining the intricate historiography of French and British imperial relations with the Iroquois League, before turning to the role of Indians in the imperial wars of the mid-eighteenth century. The goal is to illuminate the history of Indian relations with the European empires by raising comparisons and by viewing those relations in a larger continental context. The essay pays less attention to some topics that are discussed in other chapters of this volume (see Rollings; Albers; Brown and Schenck).

As European nation-states built empires in the Americas, they claimed possession of vast regions by right of papal grant, discovery, conquest, occupancy, or improvement. Rarely did they concede that Indians possessed *dominium* or, to use the modern term, sovereignty (see Alfred, this volume). Sixteenth-century Spanish jurists came the closest to such a concession. They recognized prior Indian dominion but at the same time declared such dominion as subject to easy forfeiture when Indian violations of Spanish rights, according to sixteenth-century Christendom's norms, gave Spain a just cause for conquest (Williams, 1990). Seventeenth- and eighteenth-century English and French colonizers did not much bother with the possibility of Indian dominion. Anthony Pagden (1995) has suggested that, unlike the Spanish, the English and French avoided justifying their sovereignty with arguments from just conquest and instead denied Indian sovereignty in the first place on the putative grounds that the natives failed to improve the land (*terra nullius*). Patricia Seed (1995) has ethnographically interpreted the different rites through which each European nation claimed possession of America. Whatever the accuracy of these subtle readings, the differences among the justifications of the various European nations could not have meant much to Indians. At root, European powers agreed more than they disagreed on the issue of Indian sovereignty. So firmly did Europeans share such convictions by the eighteenth century that all colonial powers made treaties with one another in which they exchanged Indian land with abandon, much to the implicated Indians' horror and disgust.

Even in direct dealings with Indians, Europeans did not concede sovereignty. The "treaties" they made with Indians did nothing to admit the fundamental integrity of Indian independence, however the word "treaty" might, to modern ears, ring of a true deal between independent powers. The Dutch and the English employed the treaty mechanism much less frequently than historians assume; indeed the word "treaty" itself was used loosely in the seventeenth century, and not very commonly (Dickason, 1989). To be sure, negotiations for land often represented a genuine European accommodation to native demands, protocols, and goals. Occasionally,

Europeans recognized – however mistakenly – the sovereign leadership of Indian "kings," but such recognition usually suited the deeper purpose of buttressing one European crown's claim to fundamental sovereignty against that of a European rival (Hinderaker, 1996). While Europeans often conceded measures of what today would be called aboriginal "title" or self-government, there is little evidence that European powers ever allowed a serious consideration of Indian sovereignty or dominion to make a difference in their actions. That the idea of Indian sovereignty went for the most part unacknowledged speaks volumes about imperial attitudes toward Indians (Williams, 1990; Jones, 1982; Dickason, 1989).

The postcolonial, subaltern studies movement, so important to recent debates in the history of India, has had little direct impact on American Indian historical scholarship. Yet many investigations of the practices of Native American subalterns and mediators in overseas colonialism reveal how those roles effectively complicated the Europeans' assumptions of sovereignty. From La Florida to California, the Spanish depended upon some Indians to exercise a degree of leadership. In La Florida Franciscans captured and intensified an aboriginal tributary system (Bushnell, 1989; Hann and McEwan, 1998; Milanich, 1999). Spanish authorities incorporated Pueblo *caciques* into New Mexico's administrative structure, particularly to secure Indian labor and tribute (Gutiérrez, 1991). Similarly, in California, according to Steven Hackel (1994), Indian subalterns employed their status as native leaders to negotiate with the Spanish in the interest of their people.

With great variations, this effort to recruit a subaltern native leadership would be made by every other empire in the colonies, but Spain, intruding among some of the more hierarchically organized societies in North America, had more success. Russians, French, Dutch, and Britons, to be sure, cultivated Indian leaders, but rarely did they integrate Indians into a hierarchical, European-dominated society. Once again, the nature of pre-existing Indian societies profoundly influenced the imperial system in North America. Nonetheless, Indian individuals everywhere emerged alongside Europeans as "culture brokers" or mediators between empires and indigenous nations (Richter, 1988; White, 1991; Merrell, 1999).

By 1776 Indian peoples – organized in hundreds, perhaps thousands, of small-scale societies – had encountered the overseas empires of Spain, England, France, the Netherlands, and Russia, and the continent had everywhere witnessed dramatically accelerated cultural change, powerful imperial conflict, massive demographic and ecological transition, and profound political transformation. So thorough were these changes that until recently, most scholars assumed that they were inevitable.

The denial of inevitability is the hallmark, perhaps even the project, of much of the scholarship on empires and Indians in the 1980s and 1990s. European powers did not always look like promising candidates for imperial expansion as the colonial era opened, and their own national compositions were liquid and changing, rent with expansion, amalgamation, fusion, warfare, and sometimes rebellion. The European turbulence, swirling outward, encountered autonomous American winds and swept them into an unpredictable vortex. Some Indian peoples were able to respond to the invasion of overseas empires with new, still-independent political arrangements that sometimes built upon processes under way *before* the peoples had regular, sustained contact with Europeans (Salisbury, 1996). Notable examples include the rise and augmentation of the Iroquois League, the formation of the multi-ethnic Creek confederacy, the expansion of the Lakotas, and the creation or ethnogenesis of the Catawba, Choctaw, Crow, Comanche, and Seminole peoples (Galloway, 1997; Merrell, 1989; Sturtevant, 1971; Trigger, 1985; Jennings, 1984; Anderson, 1984, 1999). Indians often welcomed and sustained newcomers, usually with the hope – not always misplaced – that they could bend the newcomers to their own purposes and even incorporate them into their own peoples (Salisbury, 1982; Kupperman, 1980). Other peoples capitalized on the presence of Europeans to form powerful alliances, such as the Great Lakes Indians' alliances with France and the Iroquois League's flexible "Covenant Chain" with Great Britain (White, 1991; Richter, 1992). Indians also played a variety of economic roles in the colonies. In short, so much was up for grabs in the national or political identities of so many peoples – European and American – that the inevitability of an Anglo-American triumph north of the Rio Grande is no longer taken for granted. Once a sturdy feature of the old imperial school, it now seems a topic worthy of conversation in pipe-smoke under gaslight.

Francis Parkman once declared that where Spain conquered and Britain dispossessed the Indians, France "embraced and cherished" them (Jaenen, 1976: 7). The reality was more complex. North American Indians had widely differing cultures, societies, and politics. The fact that Spain, operating in the southern reaches, tended to encounter more hierarchically organized societies shaped its relations with Indians, as did the fact that France dealt more frequently with relatively egalitarian societies. Though all European powers strove to make vassals of Indians and to fix certain Indian leaders as key players in the imperial project, the Spanish had the most success, a fact that almost certainly reflects Indian, not European, realities. The nature of Indian alliances influenced all imperial histories, as did even the various established Indian diplomatic protocols – whether in Alaska or Louisiana.

Spain

Spain first penetrated and established colonies in what is now the United States. (See Kicza, this volume.) In 1565, Pedro Menéndez de Aviléz placed the first enduring Spanish colony in St. Augustine, in the neighborhood of the Timucuas. Though he scattered small, short-lived posts and missions from Charlotte's Bay (Florida) to the York River (Virginia), only St. Augustine survived into the early seventeenth century. When the Spanish arrived, the Timucuan-speaking peoples may have numbered around 200,000. Whatever the initial size of the population, it diminished to as low as 1,000 by the end of the seventeenth century. This represented a far greater decline than that among the Apalachees, whose numbers fell from perhaps 50,000 at contact to 10,000 by 1675. Disease was likely the primary culprit. But especially after 1633, when Timucuas, Guales, and Apalachees came under the sway of the Spanish, a Franciscan mission system and the labor regime it imposed to feed its missionaries and garrisons also took their toll. Many Indians found Franciscan rule oppressive. Individual Indian flight was a common response, and the people sometimes rose in rebellion: Guales of coastal Georgia rebelled in 1597, Apalachees in 1647, and Timucuas in 1656. The Apalachee revolt saw seven of eight missions torched, three missionaries killed, and enormous battles between Apalachee rebels on the one side and victorious intertribal-Spanish forces on the other. The Timucuan revolt remains distinctive in that missionaries were deliberately spared; many of the Timucuans had become Catholic, indeed some of their leaders had become literate and coordinated their activities in handwriting. With Apalachee assistance, mounted Spanish troops put the rebellion down (Milanich, 1999; Hann, 1988, 1996; Hann and McEwan, 1998; Bushnell, 1989).

English-sponsored invasion, not Indian rebellion, ended the mission system, anni-hilating, enslaving, and dispersing its thousands of neophytes. From the 1670s, Indian allies of South Carolina began raiding the thatched, wattle-and-daub missions for slaves and altar goods to sell in the English market. Between 1702 and 1710, raids by hundreds of armed Creeks, Yamasees, and other Indians, along with English troops, wiped the mission villages off the map. The most devastating of these raids came in 1703–4 when South Carolinian James Moore and thousands of Indian allies carried off over 4,000 people. No body of Catholics and few bodies of Indians would suffer more in the history of what is now the United States. One Spanish official estimated in 1710 that 12,000 Indians had been enslaved. The missions, of which the Franciscans had established more than 150 over several generations, lay in shambles as those who escaped the onslaughts fled for their lives. St. Augustine and its satellites remained, attracting and inviting Indians as well as slave fugitives from the English. Many other Indians joined the enlarging Creek "confederacy," whose emerging multi-cultural entities actually gained population in the disease-ridden eighteenth century. The Creeks and their later offshoots, the Seminoles, not the Spanish, would dominate the culture of much of the Southeast until displaced by Anglo-Americans in the late eighteenth and early nineteenth centuries (Hann, 1988, 1996; Milanich, 1999).

Spain would leave more durable marks in the Rio Grande region, but here too the empire faced serious setbacks. (See Kicza, this volume.) Culturally, the region was highly complex, with varied Indian societies speaking many different languages. Of the perhaps 60,000 to 80,000 Pueblo people, there were eight separate groups in clusters of small town organizations on the Rio Grande – the Piro, Tompiro, Kere (or Keresan), Northern Tiwa, Southern Tiwa, Tano, Towa, and Tewa – and two further west: the Zuni and the Hopi. Sharing considerably in material culture and somewhat in religion, these peoples spoke a half dozen distinct languages, and traded and fought both among one another and with the more scattered and mobile Utes and Apachean (including Navajo) peoples. Already these many Indian peoples had formed a shifting quilt of enclaves, establishing a unique pattern of cultural geogra-phy that, with great changes in the particulars, would endure throughout the colo-nial period and into the present. Almost every imaginable form of acculturation would appear in the valley and its surroundings, and here the Indian societies – expe-rienced from the outset in dealing with others – would prove to be among the most obviously resilient and enduring in the history of North America (Spicer, 1962).

By 1680 there were almost 2,500 colonists in New Mexico, but the Indians' num-bers had fallen dramatically in the pueblos of the Piro, Kere, Southern Tiwa,

Northern Tiwa, Tano, Towa, and Tewa. Disease undoubtedly took the major toll, but so did drought, periodic rebellion, and exploitative labor. The seventeenth century also saw increasing attacks by Utes, Apaches, and Navajos. Inspired by Spanish slave-raiding expeditions against them, by the Spaniards' disruption of their traditional trade with various Pueblos, and by the stories of Pueblo refugees from Spanish exploitation living among them, these non-farming neighbors of the Pueblos gradually gained horses and proved formidable opponents. As the new Christian sacred world did not appear to be favoring them, Pueblo Indians began turning back to older beliefs and practices. Franciscans responded to such revivals of traditional religion with charges of witchcraft and idolatry, and they punished some forty-seven religious leaders before the Pueblos rose in rebellion against what one scholar considers a Spanish "theocracy" (Knaut, 1995; Gutiérrez, 1991; Anderson, 1999). The religious character of the Pueblo revolt of 1680 is clear. Of the three main leaders, two, Popé and Catiti, led Pueblo ceremonies. Overcoming tremendous language barriers, the Pueblos of the valley forced the Spanish out of the upper Rio Grande. Fleeing Spaniards and Pueblo supporters took refuge in El Paso del Norte (founded 1659), leaving behind 396 dead, twenty-one of them priests (Bowden, 1981; John, 1975).

The remarkable unity that Pueblos had forged as a weapon against Spain proved fragile; conflict among and within the towns erupted, and after twelve years, Spain capitalized on the divisions to reconquer the Rio Grande. Again, resistance met severe reprisals; at Santa Fe in 1693, seventy captured Pueblo Indians were publicly executed and some 400 people of all ages and both sexes were sentenced to ten years of servitude. A subsequent revolt in 1696 killed twenty-six Spaniards (five of them priests), but it was suppressed with Pueblo assistance (Espinosa, 1988). For all this, Spain's reconquest was not recapitulation. French influence on the Great Plains, and the growing power of the emergent Comanches, had by now created new dangers to New Mexico. The threat of violence from displaced Southern Plains peoples, some armed with French trade guns, encouraged the reconciliation of Pueblos and Spaniards; even Hopis, far to the west and persistently independent, extended olive branches to the Spanish as the eighteenth century drew to a close (John, 1975).

Within this new, more violent context, the colony's religious mission declined, as it did also in La Florida in the wake of the disastrous slave raids. Franciscans failed to recover their theocratic rule, and presidios became more central to the colonizing project. These were not simply military garrisons with flying companies of mounted men, but centers for patronage and negotiation. Franciscans among the Pueblos adapted to the changes, learning for the most part to ignore "idolatrous" practices celebrated out of their sight. Nonetheless, the Pueblo population continued to drop in the Rio Grande Valley; it amounted to some 10,000 people by the end of the Spanish period, a mere sixth of what it had been in Oñate's day (Knaut, 1995; John, 1975).

Spanish explorers had skirted and penetrated the coasts of Texas since 1519 and California since 1542. Spanish expansion into northern Mexico and into the upper Rio Grande had vast cultural repercussions in the central and lower valley, and beyond, as Indians displaced by settlers or by epidemics forged new relationships and as horses and firepower expanded trade networks and Indian alliances on the Plains (Anderson, 1999). But not until the late seventeenth century in eastern Texas and the eighteenth century in California did Spain establish a presence. Much as French activity in La Florida had drawn a defensive Spanish response, so did French activity in Louisiana and Russian and British activity in the Pacific Northwest draw New Spain to secure its flanks in Texas and California. As in La Florida and New Mexico, soldiers and missionaries undertook the political task of checking European competition, with missionaries initially dominating the enterprise.

Short-lived Spanish missions were placed among the Caddos of east Texas in 1690 and again in 1716. Consisting of at least three separate and far-flung alliances in Louisiana, Arkansas, and Texas, the agricultural Caddos emerged as key players in the diplomacy of the region, gaining arms from the French and trading them with the Comanches, Wichitas, and Tonkawas. All of these groups were, along with others in Texas, called the "Norteños." By 1793, Spain had founded as many as eight presidios and forty missions in Texas. But at no one time was Spain able to garrison more than five presidios, and none of the missions, save those around San Antonio and at Goliad, successfully converted Indians. Even in those two places missionaries faced frequent, sometimes collective, desertion. Death rates within the missions were depressingly high, outpacing birth rates in most years (Smith, 1995; Anderson, 1999).

In California, the Franciscan Junípero Serra placed the first mission at San Diego in 1769, and by 1776 he had extended his reach to San Francisco. Because the Catholic Church has advanced Serra to the brink of canonization, his treatment of Indians has become the subject of heated debate. Severe corporal punishment, ordered by missionaries, including Serra, is well documented. Some of the best demographic work on Indians has established – though the precise figures are likely to remain a mystery – a vast population decline, attributable not only to disease but also to dietary deficiencies and a severe labor regimen (Jackson and Castillo, 1995; Cooke, 1976).

In New Mexico after 1696 and in La Florida after 1710, the centrality of the missions faded in the face of increased militarization. The process intensified toward the end of the eighteenth century, and swept California as New Spain "secularized" missions in its northern borderlands. Throughout the century, Indian enemies of Spanish Texas and New Mexico gained firepower, expanded their political and military organization, and strained the poor resources of the presidio system (Weber, 1992; Hurtado, 1988; Anderson, 1999).

San Antonio de Béjar, with its presidio (1718) and five missions, would form the center of Spanish Texas by the 1760s. Its social fabric included African, Spanish, and mestizo settlers from New Spain, recent immigrants from the Canary Islands (1731), as well as Texas mission Indians, though the last were largely segregated from town life until late in the century. Remnant bands of coastal Karankawas and Coahuiltecans made up the neophytes. Colonists faced chronic labor shortages, and they converted retaliatory strikes against Apaches into slave-raiding expeditions – often protested against by missionaries. Apaches also found themselves dislodged by the expansion of the Comanches onto the southern Great Plains in the early eighteenth century. San Antonio was thus frequently at war with various Apache peoples: intense warfare occurred in 1720–5 and 1731–9, and a massive Apache attack on the city in 1745 was repelled only with the assistance of armed mission Indians. As Spanish colonists became convinced that they had not the power to dominate the still-independent and increasingly well-armed Norteños, they made peace with such peoples as the Lipan and Natagé Apaches after 1749, and the Comanches, Tonkawas, and Wichitas after the 1770s. But they remained at odds with eastern Apaches (including the Jicarilla Apache, Mescalero Apache, and Kiowa Apache peoples) throughout the colonial period (Chipman, 1992; Teja, 1995; Hinojosa, 1991; Smith, 1995).

The Spanish by no means took full possession of the Southwest. The Yumas of California and Arizona provide but one example of a people who expelled the colonizers and then kept them at bay. Initially cooperative with Spanish colonizers, Yumas successfully rebelled in 1781 and would remain largely independent until the American period (Weber, 1992).

Throughout the sixteenth century, Spain's colonial enterprise had developed in North America without serious European interference. And even into the seventeenth and eighteenth centuries, the only colony in New Spain's northern frontiers to face the genuine threat of European conquest was La Florida. There the threats were manifested with extreme force. The Spanish empire asserted its sovereignty over large tracts of North America, rejecting that of "conquered" Indian peoples. The reality on the ground, however, proved to be immeasurably more complicated.

Russia

Russians had provoked Spain's advance into Alta California. Vitus Bering and Alexi Chirkov first sailed eastward in 1741 from Kamchatka, beginning a lucrative sea-otter pelt trade. Despite their resistance, the Unangan and Sugpiat peoples – known to the Russians as "Aleuts" – fell subject to this highly exploitative Russian thrust. During the first fifty years, Russians held entire villages hostage for the good behavior of Aleut men serving as hunter-slaves. By century's end, Russians had imposed a regular form of serfdom on many of the remaining Aleuts, forcing labor from all adult males. Disease, as always, took a heavy toll (Gibson, 1978).

Toward the end of the century the Russians conquered Kodiak Island, which became the base of operations for the Golikov-Shelikhov Company that spearheaded the Russian colonization of the Sitka and Yakutak Bay area in Tlingit territory. Here the Russians met the more hierarchically and broadly organized Tlingits and Haidas. Russians attempted to influence Tlingit and Haida clan and village political structures through such means as elevating "medal chiefs" and offering privileges to cooperative leaders. But they never made vassals of the Tlingits; constant negotiation and periodic warfare characterized relations (Gibson, 1978; Dean, 1995). Here, as elsewhere, empire was highly contested, appearing differently to the colonizers than it did to their ostensibly subject Indians.

France

Nowhere more than in New France did Indian action and protocols shape both imperial policy and rivalries with other European powers. France launched the first sustained effort in North America with its colony at Quebec (1608), which remained the heart of a French North American enterprise that eventually touched Indians across most of the continent. Yet as early as 1630, the English and the Dutch out-numbered the French in eastern North America by a ratio of twenty-seven to one (Trudel, 1966: 438–9). This uneven ratio of *Canadiens* to their southern colonial enemies goes far toward explaining the close ties of Canada to its Indian neighbors.

By the 1660s, the French had established a far-flung network of alliances with many of the peoples of the Great Lakes region. Initially, the Hurons of the Ontario peninsula provided the outlet for an intertribal alliance, but by 1649 they had been decimated by diseases and defeated by the Five Nations Iroquois League. Survivors fled, alongside their Ottawa, Potawatomi, and Ojibwa allies, temporarily to settle the region south of Lake Superior. By the time many of these peoples returned eastward to the Michigan peninsula in the 1660s, the French proved at last able to supply them adequately with traders and firearms (Trigger, 1976; White, 1991; Delâge, 1985). The resulting Upper Great Lakes alliance lasted a century, decisively shaping the history of eastern North America.

Sustained by exchanges of arms for military services, the alliance also featured some striking ideological props, for example a flexible rhetorical device so convenient that French officials were later able to employ it in Louisiana. Indians agreed to call the French governor and his representatives "Father" – indeed they may have come up with the designation on their own. But delighted as French officers were with the term, they were unable to convince Indians that it implied a subordinate's obedience to a French patriarch. Instead, the French "fathers" found they had to act as did Indian fathers, somewhat distant and above all generous, especially with gifts of European manufacture. Furthermore, "fathers" had to mediate disputes among their "children" if they wished to sustain the alliance against the Iroquois, the Dutch, and later the English (Galloway, 1989; White, 1991).

France would find the role of "father" enormously taxing, for it meant often being sucked into Indian wars fought for Indian, not imperial, purposes. Most notable were the Fox (or Mesquakie) Wars, though even the wars against the British-allied Indians of the Southeast were of dubious value to France. The cost of supplying Indian allies embarrassed colonial officials, not so much fiscally as politically: crown officials resented having to pay warriors they could not control (Edmunds and Peyser, 1993; White, 1991; Merrell, 1989; Desbarats, 1995).

Whereas scholars once assumed that Indian–European trade ties led rapidly to Indians' economic dependence on Europeans, some have rejected that argument, at least for the French. Richard White (1991) and W. J. Eccles (1983) have suggested that French garrisons and French imperial policy depended upon Indians. France, rather than expanding its empire in the interest of commerce, subsidized its Indian commerce, and thereby its Indian allies, to expand its imperial claims. White challenges the idea of Indian dependency itself, arguing that European products had not so completely replaced those of native design and were not so readily available to Indians as to generate abject dependence on the trade. While most scholars applaud the recognition that imperial governments and settlers had to rely upon Indians to accomplish their goals, White's narrower argument that Indian peoples in the Great

Lakes region remained economically independent of France and Europe until the 1760s has met opposition. Daniel Richter (1992), Bruce Trigger (1991), Denys Delâge (1985), and others see signs of Indian dependence on the market – a significant disadvantage vis-à-vis Europe – at very early dates.

Daniel H. Usner's (1992) study of the lower Mississippi Valley provides a different approach. Examining the trading practices of various peoples, he finds that Indians, free Africans and African-Americans, and even slaves exhibited surprising levels of independence in their engagement with Euro-Americans and Europeans in the regional market. He never doubts the importance of European-made goods to all the region's peoples, but he does stress that Europeans and their governments were unable to achieve direct control over the regional economy until the full expansion of the plantation economy after 1783.

The idea that France was more open than other Europeans to Indians was not new in Francis Parkman's day; it grew out of an Anglo-American recognition that New France, more successfully than British North America, had won and fielded Indian allies. The notion would indeed become a French conceit, what Cornelius Jaenen (1976, 1982) has debunked as the mythical notion of the *génie colonial*. Recent scholars attribute French "success" in Indian diplomatic and military relations less to a peculiar, natural, cultural, or intellectual Gallic affinity for "natives," and more to the material dimensions of demography and economy. Their studies cast French colonists and a variety of Indian peoples together in forms of mutual dependence, not mutual admiration. Low French populations combined with a relatively high French level of material wealth to provide unique conditions for successful alliances (White, 1991; Galloway, 1989; Dickason, 1984).

If demographic weakness is central to any explanation of French diplomatic success with Indians, the picture of success is itself accurate only at a high degree of abstraction. At the local level, one finds striking French failure everywhere. Some of France's successful alliances were realized only by alienating other Indians. Far from experiencing a warm and enduring French embrace, Five Nations Iroquois, Mesquakies, Chickasaws, and others faced Gallic invasions. Louisiana's record is particularly mixed. As in New France, officials were able to convince allied Choctaw and Tunica Indians to address them as "fathers" because of the term's ambiguity among cultures with drastically different conceptions of fatherhood. French officials aggressively seized upon the opportunity presented by widespread Indian hostility to the English during the Yamasee War and built Fort Toulouse (1717) among the Alabaman confederates of the Creeks. The next year, with vast Indian support, the French took Pensacola from the Spanish. But for all this success, Louisiana faced many failures. In 1715 Antoine Lamothe Cadillac blundered into a needless war with the Natchez when he failed to conform to native diplomatic protocols. In the series of Natchez wars that followed, hundreds of colonists and many more Indians were killed. Wars between the French and the Chickasaw did little to impress France's Choctaw allies with French military prowess. Nor were French officials able to resolve disputes over cross-cultural murders as factions of alienated Choctaws courted the English. The result was a severe Choctaw Civil War (1747–50) that devastated Louisiana's principal Indian ally on the eve of the Seven Years War. One may find much talent in French colonial Louisiana, but one must look elsewhere for a peculiar colonial genius (Usner, 1992; Galloway, 1989; White, 1983).

Despite the limited success of the French in Louisiana, their grand alliance with the Great Lakes Indians was the avant-garde of their empire until the Seven Years War (1756–63). Even after the fall of New France in 1760, Ottawas, Ojibwas, Potawatomis, and other former allies at times sought a resurrection of the fallen French North America, a call for imperial restoration that was without parallel. While Indians elsewhere courted Spain, Russia, Great Britain, or the Netherlands as allies, nowhere else did Indians forge alliances across wide tribal boundaries and organize to seek the restoration of a fallen overseas empire in America. The anomaly is a mark of France's failure to have its way, to be truly sovereign, over much of its claimed territory.

The Netherlands

New Netherland was a famously polyglot colony, heavily colored by Algonquian cultural forms, even as the Dutch West Indian Company (WIC) infiltrated the coastal Algonquian and interior Iroquoian worlds. Together, Indian and Dutch traders developed a trade jargon based on Algonquian languages, and the Dutch adopted, exchanged, and briefly became economically dependent upon wampum. Between 1625 and 1654 the WIC planted colonies from the Mohawk to the Delaware River. It competed successfully until the late 1630s with the English for control of the Connecticut Valley fur trade, and in the 1650s it absorbed tiny Swedish and Finnish colonies on the Delaware River. Trade dominated life, and the low population limited its threat to Indians until the eve of the English conquest in 1664, when Dutch numbers rose dramatically to some 10,000 (Trelease, 1960; Dennis, 1993; Delâge, 1985).

The Dutch initially established good relations with the various Algonquian-speaking peoples of the Hudson Valley, especially the Mohicans in the neighborhood of Fort Orange (later, Albany), some 120 miles north of Manhattan, and the Munsees, Wappingers, and related peoples around the mouth of the Hudson. These peoples fared quickly for the worse. The Dutch found trade relations with the Mohawks more advantageous than with the Mohicans, and shifted their alliances accordingly. Fort Orange had long been a rival to New England and New France for the regional fur trade, and by 1663 it had long been trumping its enemies. So successful was one colonist, Arent van Curler, in mediating relations with the Mohawks that variations of "Curler" became terms of respect used by Six Nations Indians for any good Dutch or, later, English mediator. Van Curler was not alone, and in outposts like Schenectady several Dutch traders married Mohawks (Richter, 1992).

Along the lower Hudson River, however, Munsees lost crops to Dutch livestock and grew highly indebted to Dutch merchants. At the same time, they faced the dramatic blundering of Governor Willem Kieft, who demanded tribute and provoked a war (1639–45). New Netherland's forces, which included English who had settled on Long Island, spared neither women nor children as they destroyed several villages, most notably Pavonia (1643) and Poundridge (1644). Well-armed Indians, meanwhile, pinned the colonists down, inhibited farming, and reduced the colony to desperation. Peace, when it came, was negotiated. Kieft was recalled and replaced as governor by Peter Stuyvesant. Indian casualties were high, perhaps exceeding a thousand persons killed (Trelease, 1960).

One of Stuyvesant's major accomplishments was to take the Delaware Valley from Sweden. The Swedes had established Fort Christina (1638), which became the heart of New Sweden, a small, poor colony with little access to the European goods and supplies necessary for the Indian trade. In the early 1650s, Sweden's Johan Rising arrived with settlers and supplies, and the little colony was soon at war with the Dutch. Stuyvesant invaded and absorbed the colony. When he returned to New Amsterdam, his own colony was again at war with local Munsee Indians, increasingly alienated by Dutch merchants who traded more actively with the Mohawks. The Dutch may have been correct in their estimation of the Mohawks as more valuable trading partners than the increasingly hostile Algonquian-speaking peoples of the Hudson Valley, but they paid a dear price for ignoring their near neighbors. When English forces came by land and sea to take the colony in 1664, Stuyvesant could not even think of calling up local Indian allies (Trelease, 1960).

Overseas Empires and the Iroquois League

The Mohawks, the eastern "door" of the Five Nations Iroquois, inhabited their "Longhouse," or League, with the Oneidas, Onondagas, Cayugas, and Senecas. The League originated a century before contact, and it has in the past been viewed as an aggressive, expansionist empire in its own right. Scholars today doubt that the term "empire" suits an entity that was less political than ceremonial, that existed less to make conquest abroad than to maintain peace at home, that had no metropolitan center, no bureaucracy, no taxes, and no army. Even the Iroquois conquests – a subject of evocative, romantic, and for some colonies, self-interested history – have been debunked (Jennings, 1984). But if the Iroquois are no longer seen to have possessed an empire, their history continues to fascinate scholars. Much of the best anthropological and historical scholarship, and indeed much of the history of French, Dutch, and English colonies, visits the Longhouse (Fenton, 1998; Tooker, 1978; Webb, 1984). The League dealt extensively with other Indian peoples and with three of the empires; by the 1740s, its "Covenant Chain" with Great Britain, along with the rival Upper Great Lakes' Indians alliance with France, formed two great networks that bound strategic relations throughout much of eastern North America. Both were by then fraying dangerously, however, producing local crises that precipitated the Seven Years War.

Scholars have long recognized that great violence convulsed the entire Great Lakes region in the mid- to late seventeenth century, and they have long known, too, that despite its colonial aspect the violence was not under imperial European direction. By the late 1640s, the Mohawks and their League brethren devastated the Ontario peninsula and the region south of Lake Erie. George T. Hunt (1940) argued that the violence was about trade and plunder; Indians fought one another for goods and the control of trade routes. Francis Jennings (1984) and W. J. Eccles (1983) modified

Hunt's thesis, viewing the Iroquois less as piratical raiders or conquerors of Indian enemies than as warriors and statesmen aggressively seeking to control the diplomacy of the interior, and willing to negotiate with Europeans in the process.

Daniel K. Richter (1992) further modified the "Beaver Wars" interpretation, insisting that the League, was, first of all, less a political than a ceremonial union. The so-called Beaver Wars did have economic causes but were *also* the result of sacred readings of a worldly disaster: epidemic disease, which had halved the population to 10,000 in the space of a generation. According to tradition, captives and scalps could calm the anguished souls of the deceased and their still-living relatives, and captives could help repopulate the League. War provided desperate solutions to problems of depopulation, at least until the mid-1660s, when the first round of the Beaver Wars ended in a series of negotiations. However, the second round of intensified wars, from the 1680s to 1701, misfired badly. The League's former enemies, by this time well-armed and often in concert with French troops, struck back, devastating much of Iroquoia and ultimately causing the Iroquois to make peace with their neighbors in 1701. If the Iroquois had gained a western empire in the first round of Beaver Wars, it was erased in the second. But J. A. Brandão and William A. Starna (1996; see also Brandão, 1997) have argued strongly that, however badly the League suffered, its enemies were also exhausted and anxious for an end to bloodshed. The League secured a favorable peace in 1701, allowing it shared access not only to good hunting territories in what is now Ontario and Michigan, but also to the important diplomatic and trading venues of Montreal and Detroit.

Matthew Dennis (1993) focused even more directly on the sacred dimension of League policy. In his view, warfare itself has been drastically over-emphasized. The League was, he insists, less about war than about peace, and most of its seventeenth-century history can be interpreted as a quest for the incorporation and adoption of strangers. Thus the wars themselves were in part the offspring of a noble dream, to amalgamate the Dutch, French, Algonquian, and Huron peoples under the Great Tree of Peace. Only in the face of widespread disease and in the wake of the Jesuit intrusion into Iroquoia in the 1650s and 1660s – leading to a departure *en masse* of Catholic converts to Canada – did the dream dissolve. In its sad wake, the Iroquois turned from the Great Tree of Peace and toward the idea of military alliance with their new English neighbors, an alliance termed the Covenant Chain.

The workings of the League, and the nature of its "Covenant Chain" with Great Britain, are related subjects with large literatures. William Fenton (1998) and Bruce Trigger (1976) suggest that, although the League was not a full-blown state, it served political ends: it inhibited violence among its members and it institutionalized the resolution of members' disputes. Indeed, League members generally refused to go to war against one another until the American Revolution. But it did not promise unity in war or diplomacy, and certainly did not realize such unity for any extended period during the colonial period. Richter (1992) argues that imperialism shaped League politics, as factions divided along lines he calls francophilic, anglophilic, and neutral. And he hints that divisive League politics may have been responsible for the unintentional emergence of the much vaunted policy of Iroquois neutrality after 1701, referred to by Anthony F. C. Wallace (1969) as the Iroquois "play-off system."

The Covenant Chain, sometimes confused with the Iroquois League, was another matter altogether. Variations of the metaphor "chain" were common in the language of colonial–Indian relations in the seventeenth and eighteenth centuries. After the Third Anglo-Dutch War left New York firmly in English hands in 1674, the English had the good fortune to inherit, along with several key Dutch mediators, the Dutch relationship with the Iroquois League. As early as 1677, the phrase "Covenant Chain" entered the official record of Anglo-Iroquois negotiations. For the League and for the English, the relationship provided – or promised to provide – a measure of security against French-allied attacks, the reconciliation of trade imbalances, and a way to negotiate mutual disputes over trade, boundaries, and isolated killings. Additionally, for the British, it promised a way of controlling nearby Indian neighbors. Mohawk intervention at English urging, for example, contributed to the isolation of New England's enemies in King Philip's War (1675–6). For the League, it augmented Iroquois prestige, while for the English, who early on viewed the League as subject to the Crown, it enlarged the British empire (Jennings, 1984).

When the British failed to support the League militarily against French-allied invasions of the late 1680s, however, the League made its famous treaties in 1701. Teganissorens, also known as Dedanisora, accompanied by thirty-seven others, treated with the French and French-allied tribes at Montreal, gaining access to the interior trade. Meanwhile at Albany, Iroquois leaders allowed Western Indians access to Albany merchants, and they yielded to New York lands they did not possess, while avoiding firm military commitments. It was a remarkable success (Brandão and Starna, 1996). For twenty years, war had failed the League, except to the immediate south, where the League capitalized on the collapse of the Susquehannocks to gain authority over the upper Susquehanna River. Indians from throughout the East took refuge there under League auspices (Jennings, 1975). When the Tuscaroras of North Carolina, defeated by the English, moved to the northern stretches of the valley, they were welcomed as junior partners and became the sixth nation of the League.

In the early eighteenth century, the British continued to view the League as closely bound by the Covenant Chain. Such reasoning enabled colonists to declare authority, not only over the League, but over all its supposed dependents on the Susquehanna and, more importantly, over all its claimed lands, which stretched preposterously beyond the Alleghenies into Kentucky and Illinois. Delaware Indians proved to be particularly vulnerable to this arrangement. The collective strength of the League and the British colonies persuaded Delawares to surrender lands in the Delaware Valley. In exchange they would receive homes on the Susquehanna where they would live under League protection, but without title to their adopted homelands. The League gained a southern buffer in the Susquehanna Valley against the setters' expansion while the British obtained a vast new territory in the upper Delaware Valley for settlement.

Yet even during this period, divisions originating at the village level plagued the League. Deeply disappointed by New York's neglect during the French–Indian invasions of 1687, Senecas especially grew wary of the English. They allowed the establishment of a French trading post at Niagara in 1720 and a French garrison there in 1723. Mohawks, conversely, tilted enough toward the British to permit Fort

Oswego on Lake Ontario in 1727. The famed Iroquois play-off system existed less as a policy of the central council-fire than as that center's struggle to hold as independent villages took matters into their own hands. Some villagers sought even more independence, and emigrated after 1720 from their Seneca "castles" to repopulate the Ohio Valley. These "Mingos," as they came to be called, while still occasionally involved with the League, effectively pursued their own goals. Migrating with others to the Ohio Valley, they joined the larger defection from the Covenant Chain by the League's purportedly dependent Indian nations: Delawares, Shawnees, and other Algonquian inhabitants of the Susquehanna Valley. Seeking land and game, they carried memories of dispossession at the hands of British and League authorities to a region where the French beckoned (McConnell, 1992).

Northeastern Indians and the Anglo-French Wars, 1744–1763

While the Covenant Chain wore thin through internal division and external migration, the grand French alliance with the upper Great Lakes Indians faced similar troubles. Some former allies of the French migrated southeastward along the southern shore of Lake Erie. A leader among them stands as an example: the Wyandot, Angouriot. Disgruntled with French policies urging constant war on Chickasaws, Cherokees, and other Southeastern Indians, Angouriot established Sandusky in 1740. Wyandots under Orontony followed him to the place, and they invited British traders, whose trading posts appeared in the Upper Ohio in 1741. Prior to and during King George's War (1744–8), the flow of French trade goods was interrupted on the high seas, and French officials and their close Indian allies came very close to facing open revolt in the Great Lakes. Sandusky folk and other dissident migrants killed five French traders, and Orontony sent one of the scalps to Pennsylvania in a clear bid for a British alliance. Many of the peoples on whom the French thought they could depend considered secret proposals to drive the French from the Lakes, but despite a flare-up of anti-French violence in 1747 from Green Bay to Michilimackinac to Fort Miami to Detroit, no general conflict erupted (White, 1991; Edmunds, 1978). Still, leading alliance chiefs – French, Métis, and Indian – were alarmed. When King George's War ended, these leaders prepared to regain control. Thus two great alliance systems, the Covenant Chain and the Great Lakes alliance, looked to the Ohio region and saw defection. It was as if two tall trees with shallow roots leaned toward one another as high imperial winds rose. Indian folk migrations were shaping imperial decisions.

The Seven Years War would alter the imperial maps of North America as much as any conflict to come, and it profoundly influenced affairs around the world. The war had many causes in Europe and elsewhere, but it began with Indian defectors in the Ohio country as much as it did with empires; its initial skirmishes involved Indian as well as colonial gunmen in the Allegheny's tributary valleys and forests. For two years before any empire officially declared war, Indians and colonials both rallied and shot at one another; the turbulence sucked in imperial armies.

In the last decade or so of the twentieth century, scholars took seriously the idea that Indians were not only allies or mercenaries, but that Indian action helped bring on the war (Jennings, 1988). Daniel Richter (1988) had already suggested that village politics could shape imperial power. Richard White (1991) then outlined the process by which French officials struggled to gain control over their deteriorating alliance in the Great Lakes. Important Ottawas and Chippewas supported, even led, the effort to assert greater control over the region. Forces composed of Upper Great Lakes Indians dominated the early actions that drew British attention to the region. Most notable was the attack at Pickawillany in 1752, when a primarily Indian–Méti force violently shut down British trade. Similarly constituted forces, accompanied by French officers and troops, helped establish French forts on the Upper Ohio at Presque Isle, Venango, Le Beouf, and Duquesne. These actions attracted the visit of George Washington in 1753, his botched invasion of 1754, and the disastrous effort by General Edward Braddock and his British regulars and colonial militiamen to seize Fort Duquesne in 1755. The men who defeated Braddock were for the most part Great Lakes Indians. They saw the maintenance of the Great Lakes alliance as very much their fight – and they were determined to win the struggle for human loyalties that, far more than land, had brought on their war. They were able, through early military successes against the British, to rally to their cause such erstwhile members of the Covenant Chain as Delawares, Shawnees, and Mingos. The result was a massive Indian–French alliance against the British colonies. The British lost most remaining northern Indian support later in 1755, after hundreds of Iroquois, mostly Mohawks, collided with a French and Canadian force south of Crown Point, New York. The battle was a stand-off and the Six Nations remained divided, so the Mohawks quietly disengaged until they could more confidently expect British victory in 1759 (Jennings, 1988).

If Indian action and interest contributed to the explosion of this great American war, Indian allies could not prevent France's defeat. The British proved to be better supplied with everything from people to foodstuffs to manpower to gunpowder – indeed gunpowder was manufactured nowhere in Canada. Indian dependence on unavailable French ammunition hampered Indian warriors late in the war. Like England, France sent to America fine generals who misunderstood Indians; unlike England, France could not afford to ignore Indian realities. The Marquis de Montcalm, according to Ian Steele (1994) in an expansion of earlier interpretations by W. J. Eccles (1969) and Guy Frégault (1955), deeply misunderstood these realities, fought according to European forms, and alienated his best allies. France itself became increasingly mindful of the enormous cost and small benefit North America had provided to the home country. And as the war ended, France surrendered its North American colonies and its claims to vast lands it had never peopled. Louisiana went to Spain by a secret treaty in 1762, and Canada to Britain by the formal Treaty of Paris (1763). Indians were not parties to either agreement.

The empires of France, Spain, and Great Britain had followed every precedent in disregarding Indian sovereignty as they divided the continent in the closing years of the Seven Years War. At the capitulation of Montreal (1760), Britons gained the French claim to Canada and the French posts in the west. But the treaties of 1762 and 1763 meant a massive reshuffling of land. As their terms became known in the spring of 1763, the sheer audacity outraged many Indians, who organized to nullify those terms in what has come to be known as Pontiac's War (1763–5).

Like the Seven Years War, Pontiac's War was an imperial crisis in which Indians, Britons, and French officers (the last still awaiting official evacuation orders) argued or fought about the place of Indians in the British North American empire. Historians from Francis Parkman to Richard White (1991) are in agreement that British officers helped to precipitate the war by terminating key French practices at the French posts they now controlled in the American interior, most notably the giving of gifts, including guns, to firm up relations and mediate disputes. These British decisions signaled British intentions to master Indians, and many former allies of France turned once more against their former enemies. Indeed throughout Pontiac's War, Indians sought French assistance and predicted the revival of New France and the rising of the defeated French king. Britons, convinced by such seeming loyalty that French North Americans encouraged the crisis, blamed Jesuits, traders, and the remaining French officers in Louisiana and Illinois of a vast conspiracy. In fact, Indians had decided to make war; they received very little clear French encouragement or assistance. The war also had a millennial dimension, as Indians seeking to restore the French counterweight to British North America appealed to sacred powers in a nativistic movement. Against them, for the most part, were Indian Christians. Throughout the east, whether among Protestant Oneidas or Catholic reserve Indians of the St. Lawrence, Christian Indians either opposed the anti-British war or were its most reluctant supporters (Dowd, 1990, 1992).

Although British officers carried orders to march through Indian villages spreading fire and death, soldiers killed few Indians directly, and they burned no villages west of the Appalachians. A smallpox epidemic, to be sure, was deliberately initiated at British Fort Pitt, although it is possible that the contagion – already present in the Upper Ohio – had arrived through other vectors. The war ended in a series of treaties, and Britons learned in its course that it was cheaper and easier to adapt to native protocols than to insist on a mastery the empire lacked the power to enforce. Indians too, short of ammunition, convinced of the demise of New France, and cognizant of their material dependence upon trade with Europeans, conceded to the British the possession of several key posts. They thus acknowledged a new, highly ambiguous, relationship with Great Britain (White, 1991; Jennings, 1988). The issue of sovereignty was left unsettled.

The conflagrations of the 1750s and 1760s – born of political struggles among Indian villagers and of Indians' determination to defend their independence and their established ways of dealing with Europeans – demonstrate the limits of both French–Indian cooperation and British colonial mastery. They also bring home to scholars the critical influence of Indians on North American history. The Seven Years War, very much an Indian crisis in its American origins, brought about great colonial changes in government – the elimination of New France, of French Louisiana, and of Spanish La Florida. Viewed in combination with Pontiac's War, the Seven Years War convinced the British imperial government that American colonials could not defend themselves and should pay taxes to defray the army's expenses. The two wars thus contributed to the series of imperial crises that brought on the American Revolution.

Indians, Colonial History, and Revolution

Any modern colonial historian would have to account for Indians as shapers of colonial politics, which may explain why the old imperial school, with its mastery of administrative detail, noticed Indians all over the record. From the very earliest establishment of European colonies, Indians shaped political affairs. (See Kicza, this volume.) Subsequent Indian rebellions, moreover, forced dramatic changes in imperial organization from Florida, where the Timucua rebellion (1656) led to the recall of governor Diego de Rebolledo, to California, in the Yuma case, over a century later. The Pueblo Revolt not only shut down New Mexico's government for twelve years, but reoriented it thereafter. Indian affairs forced administrative change almost everywhere. Iroquois defeats of New France led to the royal takeover of the previously corporate colony in 1663. France's Louisiana Company (Compagnie des Indies) likewise collapsed in the wake of the Natchez uprising of 1729. To be sure, the Dutch West India Company survived long enough to be dislodged by English arms, but Indians had already shaken up New Netherland's government. Governor Kieft's recall following his disastrous war against the Indians is but one example. In the English colonies the pattern is also clear. Massachusetts, Plymouth, and the Carolinas all had their charters revoked as a result, at least partially, of royal investigations following disastrous Indian wars: King Philip's or Metacom's War (1675–6), and the Yamasee War (1715–16). Virginia lost its longest-serving seventeenth-century governor as a result of Bacon's Rebellion (1676), in which Indian policy played a critical role. Rumors of Catholic–Indian conspiracies dislodged Maryland's proprietary government during the Glorious Revolution.

In the late eighteenth century, the British imperial administration found itself, like France before it, increasingly devoting royal troops and resources either to fight or to manage Indians – even after the conquest of French Canada. The most significant result of this intensifying imperial attention to the colonies was the greatest of all changes in colonial governance, that brought on by the American Revolution, the event that marks the beginning of the end of overseas empires in America (Jennings, 1988). So could the native tail powerfully wag the imperial dog in the unpredictable colonial world.

BIBLIOGRAPHY

Anderson, Gary Clayton 1984: *Kinsmen of Another Kind: Dakota–White Relations in the Upper Mississippi Valley, 1650–1862* (Lincoln: University of Nebraska Press).

Anderson, Gary Clayton 1999: *The Indian Southwest, 1580–1830* (Norman: University of Oklahoma Press).

Axtell, James 1972: "The Scholastic Philosophy of the Wilderness," *William and Mary Quarterly* 3rd series, 29: 335–66.

Bowden, Henry Warner 1981: *American Indians and Christian Missionaries: Studies in Cultural Conflict* (Chicago: University of Chicago Press).

Brandão, José António 1997: *Your Fyre Shall Burn no More: Iroquois Policy toward New France and its Native Allies to 1701* (Lincoln: University of Nebraska Press).

Brandão, J. A. and William A. Starna 1996: "The Treaties of 1701: A Triumph of Iroquois Diplomacy," *Ethnohistory* 43: 209–44.

Bushnell, Amy Turner 1989: "Ruling the 'Republic of Indians' in Seventeenth-Century Florida," in Peter H. Wood et al. (eds.), *Powhatan's Mantle: Indians in the Colonial Southeast* (Lincoln: University of Nebraska Press), pp. 134–50.

Chipman, Donald E. 1992: *Spanish Texas, 1519–1821* (Austin: University of Texas Press).

Cooke, Sherburne F. 1976: *The Population of the California Indians, 1769–1970* (Berkeley: University of California Press).

Dean, Jonathan R. 1995: "'Uses of the Past' on the Northwest Coast: The Russian American Company and Tlingit Nobility, 1825–1867," *Ethnohistory* 42: 265–302.

Delâge, Denys 1985: *Le Pays Renversé: Amérindiens et européens en emérique du nord-est, 1600–1664* (Quebec: Boréal). Trans. Jane Brierley as *Bitter Feast: Amerindians and Europeans in Northeastern North America, 1600–1664* (Vancouver: University of British Columbia Press, 1992).

Dennis, Matthew 1993: *Cultivating a Landscape of Peace: Iroquois–European Encounters in Seventeenth-Century America* (Ithaca: Cornell University Press).

Desbarats, Catherine M. 1995: "The Cost of Early Canada's Native Alliances: Reality and Scarcity's Rhetoric," *William and Mary Quarterly* 3rd series, 52: 607–39.

Dickason, Olive Patricia 1984: *The Myth of the Savage and the Beginnings of French Colonialism in the Americas* (Edmonton: University of Alberta Press).

Dickason, Olive Patricia 1989: "Concepts of Sovereignty at the Time of First Contacts," in L. C. Green and Olive P. Dickason (eds.), *The Law of Nations and the New World* (Edmonton: University of Alberta Press), pp. 143–295.

Dowd, Gregory Evans 1990: "The French King Wakes up in Detroit: 'Pontiac's War' in Rumor and History," *Ethnohistory* 30: 254–78.

Dowd, Gregory Evans 1992: *A Spirited Resistance: The North American Indian Struggle for Unity, 1745–1815* (Baltimore: Johns Hopkins University Press).

Eccles, W. J. 1969: *The Canadian Frontier: 1534–1760* (New York: Holt, Rinehart and Winston).

Eccles, W. J. 1983: "The Fur Trade and Eighteenth-Century Imperialism," *William and Mary Quarterly* 3rd series, 40: 341–62.

Edmunds, R. David 1978: *Potawatomis: Keepers of the Fire* (Norman: University of Oklahoma Press).

Edmunds, R. David and Joseph L. Peyser 1993: *The Fox Wars: The Mesquakie Challenge to New France* (Norman: University of Oklahoma Press).

Espinosa, J. Manuel (trans. and ed.) 1988: *The Pueblo Indian Revolt of 1696 and the Franciscan Missions in New Mexico: Letters of the Missionaries and Related Documents* (Norman: University of Oklahoma Press).

Fenton, William N. 1998: *The Great Law and the Longhouse: A Political History of the Iroquois Confederacy* (Norman: University of Oklahoma Press).

Frégault, Guy 1955: *La Guerre de la Conquête* (Montreal: Fides). Trans. Margaret M. Cameron as *Canada: The War of the Conquest* (Toronto: Oxford University Press, 1969).

Galloway, Patricia 1989: "'The Chief Who is Your Father': Choctaw and French Views of the Diplomatic Relation," in Peter H. Wood et al. (eds.), *Powhatan's Mantle: Indians in the Colonial Southeast* (Lincoln: University of Nebraska Press), pp. 254–76.

Galloway, Patricia 1997: *Choctaw Genesis, 1500–1700* (Lincoln: University of Nebraska Press).

Gibson, James R. 1978: "European Dependence upon American Natives: The Case of Russian America," *Ethnohistory* 25: 359–85.

Gutiérrez, Ramón A. 1991: *When Jesus Came, the Corn Mothers Went Away: Marriage, Sexuality, and Power in New Mexico, 1500–1846* (Stanford: Stanford University Press).

Hackel, Steven W. 1994: "The Staff of Leadership: Indian Authority in the Missions of Alta California," *William and Mary Quarterly* 3rd series, 51: 347–76.

Hann, John H. 1988: *Apalachee: The Land Between the Rivers* (Gainesville: University Press of Florida).

Hann, John H. 1996: *History of the Timucua Indians and Missions* (Gainesville: University Press of Florida).

Hann, John H. and Bonnie G. McEwan 1998: *The Apalachee Indians and Mission San Luis* (Gainesville: University Press of Florida).

Hinderaker, Eric 1996: "The 'Four Indian Kings' and the Imaginative Construction of the First British Empire," *William and Mary Quarterly* 3rd series, 53: 487–526.

Hinderaker, Eric 1997: *Elusive Empires: Constructing Colonialism in the Ohio Valley, 1673–1800* (New York: Cambridge University Press).

Hinojosa, Gilberto M. 1991: "The Religious Indian Communities: The Goals of the Friars," in Gerald E. Poyo and Gilberto M. Hinojosa (eds.), *Tejano Origins in Eighteenth-Century San Antonio* (Austin: University of Texas Press), pp. 61–83.

Hunt, George T. 1940: *The Wars of the Iroquois: A Study in Intertribal Trade Relations* (Madison: University of Wisconsin Press).

Hurtado, Albert 1988: *Indian Survival on the California Frontier* (New Haven: Yale University Press).

Jackson, Robert H. and Edward Castillo 1995: *Indians, Franciscans, and Spanish Colonization* (Albuquerque: University of New Mexico Press).

Jacobs, Wilbur R. 1950: *Diplomacy and Indian Gifts: Anglo-French Rivalry along the Ohio and Northwest Frontiers, 1748–1763* (Lincoln: University of Nebraska Press).

Jaenen, Cornelius J. 1976: *Friend and Foe: Aspects of French–Amerindian Cultural Contact in the Sixteenth and Seventeenth Centuries* (New York: Columbia University Press).

Jaenen, Cornelius J. 1982: "Les Sauvages Amériquains: Persistence into the Eighteenth Century of Traditional French Concepts and Constructs for Comprehending Amerindians," *Ethnohistory* 29: 43–56.

Jennings, Francis 1975: *The Invasion of America: Indians, Colonialism, and the Cant of Conquest* (Chapel Hill: University of North Carolina Press).

Jennings, Francis 1984: *The Ambiguous Iroquois Empire: The Covenant Chain Confederation of Indian Tribes with the English Colonies* (New York: Norton).

Jennings, Francis 1988: *Empire of Fortune: Crowns, Colonies and Tribes in the Seven Years' War in America* (New York: Norton).

John, Elizabeth A. H. 1975: *Storms Brewed in Other Men's Worlds: The Confrontation of Indians, Spanish and French in the Southwest, 1540–1795* (College Station: Texas A & M University Press).

Jones, Dorothy 1982: *License for Empire: Colonialism by Treaty in Early America* (Chicago: University of Chicago Press).

Knaut, Andrew L. 1995: *The Pueblo Revolt of 1680: Conquest and Resistance in Seventeenth-Century New Mexico* (Norman: University of Oklahoma Press).

Kupperman, Karen Ordahl 1980: *Settling with the Indians: The Meeting of English and Indian Cultures in America, 1580–1640* (London: J. M. Dent & Sons).

McConnell, Michael N. 1992: *A Country Between: The Upper Ohio Valley and Its Peoples, 1724–1774* (Norman: University of Oklahoma Press).

Merrell, James 1989: *The Indians' New World: Catawbas and Their Neighbors from European Contact through the Era of Removal* (Chapel Hill: University of North Carolina Press).

Merrell, James 1999: *Into the American Woods: Negotiators on the Pennsylvania Frontier* (New York: Norton).

Milanich, Jerald T. 1999: *Laboring in the Fields of the Lord: Spanish Missions and Southeastern Indians* (Washington and London: Smithsonian Institution Press).

Nash, Gary 1974: *Red, White, and Black: The Peoples of Early America* (Englewood Cliffs, NJ: Prentice-Hall).

Pagden, Anthony 1995: *Lords of All the World: Ideologies of Empire in Spain, Britain and France, c.1500–c.1800* (New Haven and London: Yale University Press).

Richter, Daniel K. 1988: "Cultural Brokers and Intercultural Politics: New York–Iroquois Relations, 1664–1701," *Journal of American History* 75: 40–67.

Richter, Daniel K. 1992: *The Ordeal of the Longhouse: the Peoples of the Iroquois League in the Era of European Colonization* (Chapel Hill: University of North Carolina Press).

Salisbury, Neal 1982: *Manitou and Providence: Indians, Europeans, and the Making of New England, 1500–1643* (New York: Oxford University Press).

Salisbury, Neal 1996: "The Indians' Old World: Native Americans and the Coming of Europeans," *William and Mary Quarterly* 3rd series, 53: 435–58.

Seed, Patricia 1995: *Ceremonies of Possession in Europe's Conquest of the New World, 1492–1640* (New York: Cambridge University Press).

Smith, F. Todd 1995: *The Caddo Indians: Tribes at the Convergence of Empires, 1542–1854* (College Station: Texas A & M University Press).

Spicer, Edward 1962: *Cycles of Conquest: The Impact of Spain, Mexico, and the United States on the Indians of the Southwest, 1533–1960* (Tuscon: University of Arizona Press).

Steele, Ian K. 1990: *Betrayals: Fort William Henry and the "Massacre"* (New York: Oxford University Press).

Steele, Ian K. 1994: *Warpaths: Invasions of North America* (New York: Oxford University Press).

Sturtevant, William 1971: "Creek into Seminole," in Eleanor Burke Leacock and Nancy Oestreich Lurie (eds.), *North American Indians in Historical Perspective* (New York: Random House), pp. 92–128.

Teja, Jesús F. de la 1995: *San Antonio de Béxar: A Community on New Spain's Northern Frontier* (Albuquerque: University of New Mexico Press).

Tooker, Elizabeth 1978: "The League of the Iroquois: Its History, Politics, and Ritual," in Bruce G. Trigger (ed.), *Handbook of North American Indians*, vol. 15: *Northeast* (Washington, D.C.: Smithsonian Institution Press).

Trelease, Allen W. 1960: *Indian Affairs in Colonial New York* (Ithaca: Cornell University Press).

Trigger, Bruce G. 1976: *Children of Aataentsic: A History of the Huron People to 1660* (Montreal: McGill University Press).

Trigger, Bruce G. 1985: *Natives and Newcomers: Canada's "Heroic Age" Reconsidered* (Kingston and Montreal: McGill-Queens University Press).

Trigger, Bruce G. 1991: "Early Native North American Responses to European Contact: Romantic versus Rationalistic Interpretations," *Journal of American History* 77(4): 1195–215.

Trudel, Marcel 1966: *Histoire de la Nouvelle France: Le Comptoir, 1604–1627* (Montreal: Fides).

Usner, Daniel H. 1992: *Indians, Settlers, and Slaves in a Frontier Exchange Economy: The Lower Mississippi Valley before 1783* (Chapel Hill: University of North Carolina Press).

Wallace, Anthony F. C. 1969: *The Death and Rebirth of the Seneca* (New York: Alfred A. Knopf).

Webb, Stephen Saunders 1984: *1676: The End of American Independence* (New York: Alfred A. Knopf).

Weber, David 1992: *The Spanish Frontier in North America* (New Haven: Yale University Press).

White, Richard 1983: *The Roots of Dependency: Subsistence, Environment, and Social Change among the Choctaws, Pawnees, and Navajos* (Lincoln: University of Nebraska Press).

White, Richard 1991: *The Middle Ground: Indians, Empires, and Republics in the Great Lakes Region, 1650–1815* (New York: Cambridge University Press).

Williams, Robert A. 1990: *The American Indian in Western Legal Thought: The Discourses of Conquest* (New York: Oxford University Press).

4

Health, Disease, and Demography

RUSSELL THORNTON

The Native American population of the total Western Hemisphere underwent drastic decline following European contact and its associated colonialism. Some population recovery occurred. The extent of any recovery is open to debate, however, since estimates of aboriginal population size for the hemisphere vary widely. These estimates range from the mere 8.4 million suggested by Alfred L. Kroeber (1939), to 53.9 million arrived at by William Denevan (1992) to more than 100 million asserted by Henry Dobyns (1966, 1983); some 75 million seems a reasonable estimate, as I have argued elsewhere (Thornton, 1987: 25). Population recovery for the Western Hemisphere is also a function of how historic and contemporary indigenous populations are defined. Such definitions are equally open to debate, and vary considerably from country to country in the hemisphere. The censuses of different countries, for example, enumerate Native Americans differently and the way in which a country enumerates Native Americans may vary from census to census. As a result, good figures do not exist as to the size of the current total Native American population of the Western Hemisphere and we do not know how current definitions of the populations relate to aboriginal populations. Certainly, the total population is smaller than the estimated 75 million circa 1492. (Some people have suggested informally a current size of 50 million.) It can only be said with certainty that specific Western Hemispheric populations were destroyed, more or less "permanently" reduced, or declined sharply but experienced some subsequent population growth. (And some populations are even far larger today than in 1492, depending on how the populations are currently defined.) It may be pointed out, however, that the overwhelming majority of the more than 5.8 billion people alive in the world today are descendants of the 500 million occupants of the Eastern Hemisphere in 1492. The past 500 years have witnessed unparalleled population growth for those of the Eastern Hemisphere, while the Native Americans of the Western Hemisphere have struggled to survive as distinct populations.

Native North America

As the size of the aboriginal population of America north of present-day Mexico is debated by scholars, so too do they debate the magnitude of population decline. The classic estimate of aboriginal population size for this area is by James Mooney. Early in the twentieth century, he estimated individual Native American tribal populations, summed them by regions, and then totaled the regions to arrive at an estimate of 1,152,000 for North America north of the Rio Grande River at first (extensive) European contact (see Mooney, 1928; see also Mooney, 1910). Generations of subsequent scholars generally accepted Mooney's estimate, although Alfred Kroeber (1939: 131–66, esp. 131–4) considered it excessive for the California area and lowered it to barely over 1 million. Kroeber then suggested that "Mooney's total of about 1,150,000, reduced to 1,025,000 by the California substitution, will ultimately shrink to around 900,000, possibly somewhat farther" (1939: 134).

These early estimates were challenged in 1966, when Henry Dobyns (1966) used depopulation ratios to assert an aboriginal population size for North America north of Mexico of between 9.8 and 12.25 million. He did so by calculating the average rate of decline for American Indian groups that had fairly well-known population histories and then multiplying nadir populations by the average rate to achieve aboriginal population size estimates. In 1983, Dobyns (1983) again used depopulation ratios (from epidemics) but this time included possible carrying-capacities of Native American environments and technologies to estimate some 18 million aboriginal Native Americans north of Mesoamerica (an area including northern Mexico as well as present-day United States, Canada, and Greenland).

The vast majority of scholars now agree that Mooney significantly underestimated aboriginal population size for the area north of the Rio Grande and thus also the baseline from which aboriginal population decline may be fully assessed. The problem is that he did not consider the possibility of significant population decline prior to his dates of first extensive European contact, which ranged from AD 1600 to 1845, depending on the region in question (see Ubelaker, 1992: 287–8; Thornton, 1987: 25–8). On the other hand, most scholars also consider Dobyns's estimates to be excessive. There is little consensus for a higher population figure: estimates have varied from around 2 million by Douglas Ubelaker (1988) to almost 4 million (reduced from an earlier estimate of almost 4.5 million) by William M. Denevan (1992 [1976]: xvii–xxix) to the slightly more than 7 million estimate I arrived at and continue to use (see Thornton and Marsh Thornton, 1981: 47–53; Thornton, 1987: 25–32). (For a recent, thorough consideration of North American estimates see Daniels, 1992.) My estimate includes somewhat more than 5 million people for the conterminous United States area and somewhat more than 2 million for present-day Canada, Alaska, and Greenland combined.

Such dissension notwithstanding, substantial depopulation did occur after European arrival and colonization; there is no argument about this point. The Native American population of the United States, Canada, and Greenland combined reached a nadir population of perhaps only 375,000 at around 1900 (Thornton, 1987: 42–3), although it may have been somewhat higher (see Ubelaker, 1988 for a higher nadir figure).

Through the 1990s, "holocaust" emerged as the metaphor to view the population collapse of Native Americans accompanying European expansion into this hemisphere. Likewise, this "holocaust" has emerged as crucial to understanding the full impact of colonialism upon Native Americans and their subsequent social, cultural, biological, and perhaps psychological changes. Native American societies and cultures and Native Americans as biological and psychological entities were all impacted by demographic collapse following 1492. The social and cultural collapse accompanying demographic change are well known. Not so well known are biological changes through selective mortality in epidemics and "population bottlenecks" whereby populations contract and then expand, producing biological differences between the two points.

Population Decline and the Epidemic Disease "Myth"

The effects of "Old World" diseases on Native American populations of the Western Hemisphere have been important in the debate on aboriginal population size and decline, and their role has been extensively discussed. There were considerably fewer infectious diseases here than in the Eastern Hemisphere. New diseases which impacted native populations include smallpox, measles, the bubonic plague, cholera, typhoid, diphtheria, scarlet fever, whooping cough, malaria, and yellow fever, as well as some venereal diseases. America was not a "disease-free" paradise before the Europeans arrived, however; serious diseases were present, particularly tuberculosis and diseases caused by treponemas, e.g. syphilis, yaws, pinta. Nevertheless, one scholar concludes that "it is quite clear that the two worlds of disease were different enough so that the post-Columbian effect of Old World diseases on the Native Americans was devastating" (Merbs, 1992: 36).

Scholars have also shown that the life expectancies of Native Americans did not differ that much from those of their European counterparts, with their complement of infectious diseases. Life expectancies for Native Americans – generally in the twenties to early thirties – were kept relatively low by famine, nutritional deficiency diseases (e.g. pellagra), warfare, parasites, dysentery, influenza, fevers, and other ailments in addition to tuberculosis and treponemal infections (Thornton, 1987: 37–41; Newman, 1976; Reinhard, 1990).

Reasons for the relatively few infectious diseases in this hemisphere are not fully understood. They surely include, however, the existence of fewer domesticated animals, from which many human diseases arise. Perhaps they include the presence of fewer large centers of population concentration, which foster many diseases. They probably include a low overall population density in this hemisphere, a condition hindering the survival of many diseases.

It is generally thought that humans came first to America from Asia, and the Native American descendants of these first humans here have common ancestors at some point in history with contemporary Asian peoples. Most argue that the *Homo sapiens sapiens* who would become Native Americans migrated across cold and barren Beringa (the land connecting both hemispheres at certain times) and moved into the interior of North America across present-day Alaska and Canada, probably along the eastern edge of the Canadian Rocky Mountains. Some argue, however, that humans came here first by boat, along the northwest coast of North America. There were perhaps three migrations: one, the Paleo-Indians, as early as 40,000 years ago; a second, the Na-Dine, as recent as 12,000 years ago; and a third, the Eskimo [Inuit] and Aleutian Islanders, about 9,000 to 10,000 years ago. These migrations across Beringa (or over water) may have served as a filter restricting pathogens from entering the Western Hemisphere, as such organisms cannot survive in extremely cold temperatures.

In any event, Native Americans lacked immunity to new diseases from Europe and Africa. Native Americans lacked prior exposure to specific diseases such as smallpox and measles, whereby recovery typically provides lifelong immunity. Thus new diseases produced "virgin soil epidemics" in which a new disease spreads to virtually all members of a population (and may be particularly virulent) (see Crosby, 1976). Native Americans in 1492 also seemingly were remarkably genetically homogeneous. Because of this viral infections were pre-adapted to successive hosts and never encountered a wide variety of new immune response (see Black, 1992). Technically, they had "a lack of genetic polymorphism in the MHC (major histocompatibility complex) alleles," as a young Passamaquoddy immunologist expressed it to me. This characteristic reflects a lack of historic contact with many diseases to which their immune systems could "adapt," meaning that Native Americans were unusually susceptible to diseases from the other hemisphere. These diseases and the apparent relative homogeneity of the Native American population in dealing with the new diseases caused widespread population reduction. There is no question about this.

The timing and magnitude of "Old World" disease episodes and subsequent depopulation, however, is still being debated. Soon after European arrival in the Western Hemisphere, diseases devastated American Indian populations in areas of present-day Mexico, the Caribbean, and Central and South America. Some scholars have also argued that diseases moved northward early in the sixteenth century from European settlements in the Caribbean and Mesoamerica and spread to North America through early European explorations, colonies, slave raids, shipwrecks, and other native contacts (see, for example, Dobyns, 1983; Upham, 1986).

The diseases, according to these scholars, infected native populations in both the Southeast and the Southwest of present-day United States during the initial decades of the sixteenth century. They frequently culminated in epidemics and pandemics that devastated Native American populations of not only these regions but other regions as well. Consequently, they assert, the aboriginal population of North America was exceedingly large, but was reduced greatly by epidemic disease prior to significant historical documentation.

Scholarly research has generally refuted arguments regarding continent-wide pandemics of smallpox and other diseases during the sixteenth century. As Larsen (1994: 109) concludes with respect to smallpox, "archaeological, historical, and bioarchaeological studies provide compelling evidence that the arrival of Europeans did not occasion a sudden pandemic of smallpox in the early sixteenth century."

Significant population decline in the Southeast, and perhaps in the Southwest, did begin *sometime* during the sixteenth century. Some research (e.g., Ramenofsky, 1987; Smith, 1987) supports the notion that it was caused by epidemic disease in the Southeast (and Mississippi Valley region); similarly, it is possible that smallpox was present early in the Southwest (see Upham, 1986, 1987; Reff, 1987). Still debated is whether sixteenth-century diseases in the Southeast – and by implication, the Southwest – occurred as region-wide pandemics, as more isolated epidemics, or even as mere episodes (see, for example, Smith, 1987; Blakely and Detweiler-Blakely, 1989; Thornton, Warren, and Miller, 1992; Zubrow, 1990). More likely, the pattern of disease "was a patchwork affair, striking some populations and not others at various times" (Larsen, 1994: 109). Neither the epidemic disease pattern in North America nor the depopulation of Native American peoples by epidemic disease are fully understood by scholars, however.

Human populations constantly change in composition as members are born, die, or move into or out of the population. As discussed elsewhere (Thornton, Miller, and Warren, 1991), the underlying population patterns may be termed a "demographic regime," that is, determinants of fertility, mortality, and migration which, interacting together, produce population growth, decline, or stability over a particular time. Such patterns are typically relatively stable, and influence the population's ability to respond to disturbances such as those caused by disease episodes.

It was likely not the *direct* effects of any single epidemic or even any single disease which produced the long-term population reduction of most Native American groups. Disturbances such as epidemics may result in only short-term population decline as populations may return to pre-disease levels of population growth, decline, or stability. For example, I (Thornton, Miller, and Warren, 1991) have simulated this for smallpox epidemics. Herring (1994) has illustrated that recovery of a Native American population occurred following the influenza epidemic of 1918–19, and Boyd (1992) has shown the temporary effects of a smallpox epidemic as well as the longer effects of a measles epidemic. Similarly, the historian William H. McNeill (1976: 150) concluded: "the period required for medieval European populations to absorb the shock of renewed exposure to plague seems to have been between 100 and 133 years, that is, about five to six human generations." Population recovery may even occur following repeated cycles of different diseases. The "Black Death" plague in Europe from 1347 to 1352 caused huge population losses, as there was population reduction because of the cyclic recurrence of the plague and the occurrence of other diseases such as typhus, influenza, and measles. European populations did recover, although not until late in the fifteenth century; however, they did recover (Gottfried, 1983: xv–xvi, 129–35, 156–9).

The indirect effects of disease episodes appear more important in population decline. Such effects include the social disruption accompanying epidemics, as described, for example, by Neel and others (Neel et al., 1970; Neel and Weiss, 1975; Neel, 1978) among the Yanomama Indians of South America and discussed by McGrath (1991). They also include decreased fertility accompanying reduced fecundity due to the disease or resulting from marital disruption, such as the loss of a spouse. The nature of Native American societies, including pre-existing patterns of social organization, also influenced population reduction and/or recovery, as I have shown regarding the Tolowa of northern California (Thornton, 1984b, 1986; see also Zubrow, 1990; Decker, 1991; Boyd, 1992; Larsen, 1994).

Native American population decline resulted not only from European and African diseases but also from the many effects of colonialism, subtle or otherwise. As Larsen (1994: 110) summarizes, the emphasis on disease "has overshadowed a host of other important consequences of contact such as population relocation, forced labor, dietary change, and other areas." Colonialism also interacted with disease to produce population decline: Meister (1976: 165) notes that "later population decline resulting from disease was made possible because Indians had been driven from their land and robbed of their other resources."

Native American societies were removed and relocated, warred upon and massacred, and undermined ecologically and economically. All of these products of colonialism caused population decline due to fertility decreases as well as mortality increases, as I (Thornton, 1988) have pointed out and as Stannard (1990) has analyzed regarding Native Hawaiians. The Cherokee "Trail of Tears" from the Southeast to Indian Territory, for example, produced substantial population losses, partly from the mortality of diseases such as cholera but also from decreased fertility and increased mortality due to malnutrition and starvation (Thornton, 1984a). Southern California Indians were missionized, which confined them in new disease environments that took a demographic toll via both fertility and mortality (see, for example, Walker and Johnson, 1994). Their eventual displacement resulted in selective outmigration and lower fertility as well as assimilation (see Harvey, 1967). Northern California Indians were subjected to pseudo war and outright genocide as well as the destruction of their traditional patterns of subsistence (see Thornton, 1984a, 1986; Thornton and Walker, 1998). And while it is hard to address direct effects on mortality and fertility, Plains Indians lost much of their social and cultural life and most of their economic base when the great herds of buffalo were destroyed (Thornton, 1987: 51–3).

Population Recovery

After some 400 years of population decline beginning soon after the arrival of Columbus in the Western Hemisphere, the Native American population north of Mexico began to increase around the turn of the twentieth century. The U.S. Census Bureau's decennial enumerations indicate a Native American population growth for the United States that has been nearly continuous since 1900 (except for an influenza epidemic in 1918 that caused serious losses and some changes in enumeration procedures) to more than 1.4 million by 1980 and to more than 1.9 million by 1990. (Changing definitions and procedures for enumerating Native Americans used by the U.S. Bureau of the Census also had an effect on the enumerated population size from census to census during the twentieth century.) To this may be added some 740,000 Native Americans in Canada in 1986 (575,000 American Indians, 35,000 Inuit [Eskimos], and 130,000 Métis) plus some increase to today and perhaps 30,000

Native Americans in Greenland. The total then becomes some 2.75 million in North America north of Mexico. This is obviously a significant increase from the perhaps fewer than 400,000 around the turn of the century, about 250,000 of which were in the United States; however, 2.75 million remains far less than the estimated 7 million circa 1492. It is also but a fraction of the total current populations of the United States (250 million in 1990) and Canada (more than 25 million in 1990) (Thornton, 1994a).

U.S. Census enumerations also provide self-reported tribal affiliations and ancestries. The 1990 Census reported the ten largest tribal affiliations in the United States as Cherokee, 308,000; Navajo, 219,000; Chippewa (Ojibwa), 104,000; Sioux, 103,000; Choctaw, 82,000; Pueblo, 53,000; Apache, 50,000; Iroquois, 49,000; Lumbee, 48,000; and Creek, 44,000 (U.S. Bureau of the Census, 1993: figure 2). About 11 percent of those identifying as Native American in the 1990 Census did not report a tribal affiliation.

This population recovery was in part a result of lower mortality rates and increases in life expectancy as the effects of "Old World" disease and associated colonialism lessened (see Thornton, 1987: 159–85; Snipp, 1989: 66–9). For example, some data indicate that life expectancy at birth increased from 51.6 years in 1940 to 71.1 years in 1980, compared with a change from 64.2 years to 74.4 years in the life expectancy of whites during the four decades (Snipp, 1989: 67–9). Nonetheless, the health status of American Indians remains very poor. Their rate of diabetes, for example, is twice that of whites, and they are three times more likely to die of diabetes than are whites; their alcohol-related death rate is over five times that of the general population; and their suicide rate is over half again that of the U.S. population. Similarly, Indian people continue to suffer from cirrhosis, influenza, and pneumonia, and perinatal and early infancy diseases at greater rates than the general population (see, for example, Thornton, 1987: 169–72).

The population recovery also resulted from changing fertility patterns and adaptation through intermarriage with non-native peoples during the twentieth century, whereby American Indian birth rates have remained higher than those of the average North American population (Thornton, Sandefur, and Snipp, 1991). Early in the twentieth century, at around the point of the Native American population nadir in the United States, the fecundity and fertility of Native Americans – particularly "full bloods" – was of considerable concern to government officials (see U.S. Bureau of the Census, 1915: 157–9). Soon, however, fertility increased; indeed, the twentieth-century recovery of the Native American population of the United States has been driven by Native American fertility increases and Native American fertility levels higher than those of the total United States population (Thornton, Sandefur, and Snipp, 1991), while mortality decreases have also occurred. In 1980, for example, married American Indian women 35 to 44 years of age had a mean number of children ever born of 3.61 in comparison to 2.77 for the total U.S. population and only 2.67 for the white segment of the population (Thornton, Sandefur, and Snipp, 1991: 360). Intermarried American Indian women generally had lower fertility rates in 1980 than American Indian women married to American Indian men; however, intermarried, American Indian women still had higher fertility than the total U.S. population (Thornton, Sandefur, and Snipp, 1991: 362, 364–5).

The very nature of this population history and recovery has had and continues to have profound effects upon the Native American population, particularly on questions of who Native Americans are and how they define themselves, at both the group and individual levels. Many remnant American Indian groups in the eastern United States, for example, joined with the Iroquois and were adopted by them, as were the Tuscarora who fled northward from the Carolinas to escape the slave trade. Similarly, the migration of various tribes into the Mississippi River valley and their amalgamation there has been illustrated: Brain (1971) noted that the Natchez changed marriage rules to adopt other Indians as relatives. My earlier study of the Tolowa and Yuki Indians of northern California indicates that depopulation in and of itself was not the only factor determining tribal survival. Included along with magnitude of depopulation was a difference in reservation experiences. The Yuki were placed on a reservation with other tribes, intermarried with them, and thereby became merged with other tribes of the Covelo Indian Community of Confederated Tribes of the Round Valley Indian Reservation. Also included were pre-existing patterns of social organization – Tolowa kinship patterns allowed the easy incorporation of female outsiders into the tribe through marriage but offspring were defined as Tolowa since Tolowa society is both patrilocal and patrilineal (Thornton, 1984b).

Various new "Native American" groups were created in response to the demographic events of Euro-American contact. The Métis of Canada and the United States–Canadian border are the most well-known: this Indian–white "racially mixed" group was created, they say, "nine months after the first white man set foot in Canada." New peoples also include the Lumbee, and historically prominent tribes such as the Catawba. New peoples also encompass many and varied triracial groups throughout the Atlantic, southeastern, and southern states. James Mooney (1907) of the Smithsonian surveyed many of these peoples in the early 1900s and found a strong sense of Indian identity along with a fear of being absorbed into the African-American population. William Harlen Gilbert, Jr. (1946: 438), of the Library of Congress, surveyed such communities in the mid-1940s, and found "little evidence for the supposition that they are being absorbed to any great extent into either the white or the Negro groups." In fact, he found they were increasing in size. (The total population for these groups in 1960 was estimated at 100,000 by Berry [1963: 57].)

"Old" and "New" Native Americans

The twentieth-century increase in the Native American population reflected in successive censuses of the United States was due in part to changes in the identification of individuals as "Native American." The U.S. Census enumerates individuals as of only one race. Since 1960 the U.S. Census has relied on self-identification to ascertain an individual's race. Much of the increase in the *American Indian* population – excluding Eskimos (Inuit) and Aleuts – from 523,591 in 1960, to 792,730 in 1970, to 1.37 million in 1980, to more than 1.8 million in 1990, resulted from individuals not identifying as American Indian in an earlier census but identifying as such in a later census. (Some 7 million Americans had some degree of Native American ancestry.)

It may be estimated, for example, that about 25 percent of the population "growth" of American Indians from 1960 to 1970, about 60 percent of the "growth" from 1970 to 1980, and about 35 percent of the "growth" from 1980 to 1990 may be accounted for by these changing identifications (Passel, 1976; Passel and Berman, 1986; Thornton, 1987: 220–1; Harris, 1994: 583; Eschbach, 1995: 89). In other words, the "error of closure" – the difference between a natural increase and the enumerated population from one time to another (assuming no migration) – was 8.5 percent in the 1970 census count, 25.2 in the 1980 count, and 9.2 in the 1990 count (see Passel, 1976; Passel and Berman, 1986: 164; Harris, 1994: 583).

Why did this occur? The political mobilization of Native Americans in the 1960s and 1970s along with other ethnic pride movements may have lifted part of the stigma attached to a Native American racial identity. This would be especially true for persons of mixed ancestry who formerly may have declined to disclose their Native American background for this reason. Conversely, however, individuals with only minimal Native American background may have identified as Native American out of a desire to affirm a marginal ethnic identity and their "romanticized" notion of being Native American.

Tribal Membership Requirements

Many different criteria may be used to delimit a population. Language, residence, cultural affiliation, recognition by a community, degree of "blood," genealogical lines of descent, and self-identification have all been used at some point in the past to define both the total Native American population and specific tribal populations. Of course, each measure produces a different population, and which variables are ultimately employed to define a population is an arbitrary decision. The implications for Native Americans, however, can be enormous.

Native Americans are unique among ethnic and racial groups in their formal tribal affiliations and in their relationships with the United States government. Today, 317 American Indian tribes in the United States are legally recognized by the federal government and receive services from the U.S. Bureau of Indian Affairs (U.S. Bureau of Indian Affairs, 1993: 54364–9). There are some tribes recognized by states but not by the federal government. There are also some 217 Alaska Native Village Areas identified in the 1990 Census, containing a total of 9,807 American Indians, 32,502 Inuit (Eskimo), and 4,935 Aleuts (U.S. Bureau of the Census, 1992: table 2). In addition, there are about 125 to 150 tribes seeking federal recognition and dozens of others who may do so in the future. Contemporary American Indians typically must be enrolled members of one of the 317 federally recognized tribes to receive benefits from either the tribe or the federal government. To do so, they must meet various criteria for tribal membership, which vary from tribe to tribe and are typically set forth in tribal constitutions approved by the U.S. Bureau of Indian Affairs. Upon membership, individuals are typically issued tribal enrollment (or registration) numbers and cards that identify their special status as members of a particular American Indian tribe.

The process of enrollment in a Native American tribe has historical roots that extend back to the early nineteenth century. As the U.S. government dispossessed native peoples, treaties established specific rights, privileges, goods, and money to which those party to a treaty – both tribes as entities and individual tribal members – were entitled. The practices of creating formal censuses and keeping lists of names of tribal members evolved to insure an accurate and equitable distribution of benefits. Over time, Native Americans themselves established more formal tribal governments, including constitutions, and began to regulate their membership more carefully, especially in regard to land allotments, royalties from the sale of resources, distributions of tribal funds, and voting. In the twentieth century, the U.S. government established additional criteria to determine eligibility for benefits such as educational aid and health care.

The federal government also implemented the Wheeler-Howard Act (or Indian Reorganization Act) of 1934, under which most current tribes are organized. The Act was "the culmination of the reform movement of the 1920s led by John Collier," and "reversed the policy of allotment and encouraged tribal organization" (Prucha, 1975: 222). The Act encouraged tribes to have written constitutions, containing a membership provision. Generally, these constitutions were either first established or, if already existent, modified after the Act of 1934. (A few groups, however, have no written constitution; the Pueblo of Taos does not, for example: they say they have "a traditional form of Government.")

A variety of court cases have tested tribal membership requirements. From the disputes, American Indian tribal governments won the right to determine their own membership: "The courts have consistently recognized that in the absence of express legislation by Congress to the contrary, an Indian tribe has complete authority to determine all questions of its own membership" (Cohen, 1942: 136).

Individuals enrolled in federally recognized tribes also receive a Certificate of Degree of Indian Blood (referred to as a CDIB) from the Bureau of Indian Affairs specifying a certain degree of Indian blood, that is, a blood quantum. The Bureau of Indian Affairs uses a blood quantum definition – generally a one-fourth degree of Native American blood – and/or tribal membership to recognize an individual as Native American. Each tribe, however, has a particular set of requirements – generally including a blood quantum – for membership (enrollment) of individuals in the tribe. Typically, a blood quantum is established by tracing ancestry back through time to a relative or relatives on earlier tribal rolls or censuses where the relative's proportion of Native American blood was recorded. In such historic instances, more often than not it was simply self-indicated.

Enrollment criteria have sometimes changed over time; often, the change has been to establish minimum blood quantum requirements. For instance, in 1931, the Eastern Band of Cherokee Indian established a one-sixteenth blood quantum requirement for those born thereafter (Cohen, 1942: 5). Sometimes the change has been to establish higher requirements: the Confederated Salish and Kootenai Tribes have tightened their membership requirements since 1935, and in 1960 established that only those born with a one-quarter or more blood quantum could be tribal members (Trosper, 1976: 256). Conversely, tribes may reduce their blood quantum requirements, sometimes even eliminating a specified minimum requirement. Cohen

Table 4.1 Blood quantum requirement of American Indian tribes by reservation basis and size

	Blood quantum requirement		
	More than ¼	*¼ or less*	*No minimum requirement*
Number of tribes	21	183	98
Reservation-based	85.7%	83.1%	63.9%
Median size	1,022	1,096	1,185

Note: Information not available on 15 tribes.

Source: U.S. Bureau of Indian Affairs (unpublished tribal constitutions and tribal enrollment data obtained by the author).

(1942: 136) writes: "The general trend of the tribal enactments on membership is away from the older notion that rights of tribal membership run with Indian blood, no matter how diluted the stream. Instead it is recognized that membership in a tribe is a political relation rather than a racial attribute." Blood quantum requirements for membership in contemporary tribes vary widely from tribe to tribe. Some tribes, such as the Walker River Paiute, require at least a one-half Indian (or tribal) blood quantum; many tribes, such as the Navajo, require a one-fourth blood quantum; some tribes, generally in California and Oklahoma, require a one-eighth or one-sixteenth or one-thirty-second blood quantum; and many tribes have no minimum blood quantum requirement but only require a documented tribal lineage. A summary of the blood quantum requirements for federally recognized tribes is presented in table 4.1.

In 1990, about one-fourth of the Native American population, some 437,079 American Indians (and 182 Inuit [Eskimo] and 97 Aleuts), lived on 314 reservations and trust lands; about half of these, some 218,290 American Indians (and 25 Inuit [Eskimo] and 5 Aleuts), lived on the 10 largest reservations and trust lands: Navajo Reservation and trust lands, 143,405; Pine Ridge Reservation and trust lands, 11,182; Fort Apache Reservation, 9,825; Gila River Reservation, 9,116; Papago Reservation, 8,480; Rosebud Reservation and trust lands, 8,043; San Carlos Reservation, 7,110; Zuni Pueblo, 7,073; Hopi Pueblo and trust lands, 7,061; and Blackfeet Reservation, 7,025 (U.S. Bureau of the Census, 1993: 1). Alaskan Eskimos (Inuit) and Aleuts present a somewhat different picture from American Indians. Most are tied to small, local communities, representing ancestral grounds rather than government reservations.

American Indian tribes located on reservations tend to have higher blood quantum requirements for membership than those not located on reservations. As indicated in table 4.1, more than 85 percent of tribes requiring more than one-quarter blood quantum for membership are reservation-based, whereas less than 64 percent of the tribes having no minimum requirement are reservation-based. Those tribes on reservations have seemingly been able to maintain *exclusive* membership by setting higher blood quanta since reservation location has generally served to isolate the tribe from non-Indians and intermarriage with them. Tribes without a reservation base have maintained an *inclusive* membership by setting lower blood quanta for membership since their populations interacted more with non-Indian populations and intermarried with them. As additionally indicated in table 4.1, tribes with more restrictive blood quantum requirements tend to be somewhat smaller than those with a less restrictive blood quantum requirement, although the differences are not particularly striking.

In the early 1980s the total membership of federally recognized tribes was about 900,000. Therefore, many of the 1.37 million individuals identifying themselves as American Indian in the 1980 Census were not actually enrolled members of federally recognized tribes. In fact, only about two-thirds were. In the late 1980s the total membership of these tribes was somewhat more than 1 million (U.S. Bureau of Indian Affairs, unpublished data); hence, only about 60 percent of the more than 1.8 million people identifying themselves as American Indian in the 1990 Census were actually enrolled in a federally recognized tribe.

Differences between self-identification and tribal enrollment varied considerably from tribe to tribe. Most of the 158,633 Navajos enumerated in the 1980 Census and the 219,198 enumerated in the 1990 Census were enrolled in the Navajo Nation; however, only about one-third of the 232,344 Cherokees enumerated in the 1980 Census and the 308,132 Cherokees enumerated in the 1990 Census were actually enrolled in one of the three Cherokee tribes (the Cherokee Nation of Oklahoma, the Eastern Band of Cherokee Indians [of North Carolina], or the United Keetoowah Band of Cherokee Indians of Oklahoma) (Thornton, 1990: 170–2; 1994a). Thus the Navajo Nation is the American Indian tribe with the largest number of enrolled members, but more individuals identifying as Native American identified as "Cherokee" in the 1980 and 1990 Censuses than as any other tribe.

The nature of the population recovery of Native Americans has produced different distinctive Native American populations along both "racial" and tribal lines. "Racial" heterogeneity has been produced whereby many individuals with few "Native American genes" are within the Native American population, defined either tribally or by the U.S. Census (or by most other methods). It has also produced tribal variations, not only in terms of membership requirements but more importantly in terms of whether or not an individual is a tribal member. A dichotomy has emerged between Native Americans and tribal Native Americans.

Urbanization and Intermarriage

By the beginning of the twentieth century, surviving Native American groups in the United States had been redistributed. Much of this occurred during the nineteenth century with Native American removals, the establishment of the reservation system, and the subsequent elimination and allotment of some reservations. According to the 1990 Census, the ten states with the largest Native American populations were: Oklahoma, 252,000; California, 242,000; Arizona, 204,000; New Mexico, 134,000; Alaska, 86,000; Washington, 81,000; North Carolina, 80,000; Texas, 66,000; New York, 63,000; and Michigan, 56,000 (U.S. Bureau of the Census, 1993: figure 3).

A redistribution of Native Americans has also occurred through urbanization in the United States. Only .4 percent of the American Indians in the United States lived in urban areas in 1900. By 1950, this had increased to 13.4 percent; however, by 1990, 56.2 percent of American Indians lived in urban areas (Thornton, 1994b). Important in this urbanization was the migration to urban areas, some of which occurred under the Bureau of Indian Affairs relocation program which began in 1950 to assist American Indians in moving from reservation (and rural) areas to selected urban areas (Thornton, 1994b). U.S. cities with the largest Native American populations are New York City, Oklahoma City, Phoenix, Tulsa, Los Angeles, Minneapolis-St. Paul, Anchorage, and Albuquerque (Thornton, 1994b).

The above-described pattern of requiring low percentages of Indian blood for tribal membership and dealing with the federal government to certify it may be seen in part as a result of "a demographic legacy of 1492." As the numbers of Native Americans declined and Native Americans came into greater contact with whites, blacks, and others, Native American peoples increasingly married with non-Indians. As a result, they have had to rely more and more on formal certification as proof of their "Indianness." This pattern has accelerated with urbanization as it has increased the numbers of non-natives that Native Americans have encountered and thus raised intermarriage rates of Native Americans with non-natives: today, almost 60 percent of all American Indians are married to non-Indians. Moreover, it has been argued that the "new Native Americans" who changed their census definitions of themselves, as discussed above, are more likely to be intermarried.

Urbanization has also seemingly brought about some decreased emphasis on Native American tribal identity. About 20 percent of American Indians enumerated in the 1970 Census reported no tribe, but only about 10 percent of those on reservations reported no tribe while about 30 percent of those in urban areas reported no tribe. Comparable data from the 1980 and 1990 Censuses are not available: the 1980 Census indicated about 25 percent reported no tribal affiliation (Thornton, 1987: 238); the 1990 Census indicated about 15 percent reported no tribal affiliation. As indicated in the 1990 Census, only some one-fourth of all American Indians speak an Indian language at home; however, census enumerations also indicate that urban residents are far less likely than reservation residents to speak an Indian language, or even participate in tribal cultural activities.

If these trends continue, both the genetic and the tribal distinctiveness of the total Native American population will be greatly lessened. A Native American population comprising primarily "old" Native Americans strongly attached to their tribes will change to a population with a predominance of "new" Native American individuals who may or may not have tribal attachments or even tribal identities. It may even make sense at some point in the future to speak mainly of Native Americans as people of Native American ancestry or ethnicity.

BIBLIOGRAPHY

Berry, Brewton 1963: *Almost White: A Study of Certain Racial Hybrids in the Eastern United States* (New York: Macmillan Company).

Black, Francis L. 1992: "Why Did They Die?" *Science* 258 (December 11): 1739–40.

Blakely, Robert L. and Betinna Detweiler-Blakely 1989: "The Impact of European Diseases in the Sixteenth-Century Southeast: A Case Study," *Midcontinental Journal of Archaeology* 14: 62–9.

Boyd, Robert T. 1992: "Population Decline from Two Epidemics on the Northwest Coast," in *Disease and Demography in the Americas*, eds. John W. Verano and Douglas H. Ubelaker (Washington, D.C.: Smithsonian Institution Press), pp. 249–55.

Brain, Jeffrey P. 1971: "The Natchez 'Paradox'," *Ethnology* 10: 215–22.

Cohen, Felix S. 1942: *Handbook of Federal Indian Law* (Albuquerque: University of New Mexico Press).

Crosby, Alfred W., Jr. 1976: "Virgin Soil Epidemics as a Factor in the Aboriginal Depopulation in America," *William and Mary Quarterly* 33: 289–99.

Daniels, John D. 1992: "The Indian Population of North America in 1492," *William and Mary Quarterly* 49: 298–320.

Decker, Jody F. 1991: "Depopulation of the Northern Plains Natives," *Social Science Medicine* 33: 381–93.

Denevan, William M., ed. 1992: *The Native Population of the Americas in 1492*, 2nd edn. (Madison: University of Wisconsin Press; 1st edn. 1976).

Dobyns, Henry F. 1966: "Estimating Aboriginal American Population: An Appraisal of Techniques with a New Hemispheric Estimate," *Current Anthropology* 7: 395–416.

Dobyns, Henry F. 1983: *Their Number Become Thinned: Native American Population Dynamics in Eastern North America* (Knoxville: University of Tennessee Press).

Eschbach, Karl 1995: "The Enduring and Vanishing American Indian: American Indian Population Growth and Intermarriage in 1990," *Ethnic and Racial Studies* 18: 89–108.

Gilbert, William H., Jr. 1946: "Memorandum Concerning the Characteristics of the Larger Mixed-Blood Racial Islands of the Eastern United States," *Social Forces* 25: 438–47.

Gottfried, Robert S. 1983: *The Black Death* (New York: Free Press).

Harris, David 1994: "The 1990 Census Count of American Indians: What Do the Numbers Really Mean?" *Social Science Quarterly* 75: 580–93.

Harvey, M. R. 1967: "Population of the Cahuilla Indians: Decline and Its Causes," *Eugenics Quarterly* 14: 185–98.

Herring, D. Ann 1994: "There Were Young People and Old People and Babies Dying Every Week: The 1918–1919 Influenza Pandemic at Norway House," *Ethnohistory* 41: 73–105.

Kroeber, Alfred L. 1939: "Cultural and Natural Areas of Native North America," *University of California Publications in American Archaeology and Ethnology* 38: 1–242.

Larsen, Clark Spencer 1994: "In the Wake of Columbus: Native Population Biology in the Postcontact Americas," *Yearbook of Physical Anthropology* 37: 109–54.

McGrath, Janet W. 1991: "Biological Impact of Social Disruption Resulting from Epidemic Disease," *American Journal of Physical Anthropology* 84: 407–19.

McNeill, William H. 1976: *Plagues and Peoples* (Garden City, NY: Anchor Doubleday).

Meister, Cary W. 1976: "Demographic Consequences of Euro-American Contact on Selected American Indian Populations and Their Relationship to the Demographic Transition," *Ethnohistory* 23: 161–72.

Merbs, Charles F. 1992: "A New World of Infectious Disease," *Yearbook of Physical Anthropology* 35: 3–42.

Mooney, James 1907: "The Powhatan Confederacy, Past and Present," *American Anthropologist* 9: 129–52.

Mooney, James 1910: "Population," in *Handbook of American Indians North of Mexico*, vol. 2, ed. Frederick W. Hodge, *Smithsonian Institution, Bureau of American Ethnology Bulletin* no. 30 (Washington, D.C.: U.S. Government Printing Office), pp. 286–7.

Mooney, James 1928: "The Aboriginal Population of America North of Mexico," in *Smithsonian Miscellaneous Collections*, vol. 80, ed. John R. Swanson, pp. 1–40.

Neel, James V. 1978: "Population Structure of an Amerindian Tribe, the Yanomama," *Annual Review of Genetics* 12: 365–413.

Neel, James V., W. R. Centerwell, Napoleon A. Chagnon, and H. L. Casey 1970: "Notes on the Effect of Measles and Measles Vaccine in a Virgin-Soil Population of South American Indians," *American Journal of Epidemiology* 91: 418–29.

Neel, James V. and Kenneth M. Weiss 1975: "The Genetic Structure of a Tribal Population, the Yanomama Indians. XII. Biodemographic Studies," *American Journal of Physical Anthropology* 42: 25–51.

Newman, Marshall T. 1976: "Aboriginal New World Epidemiology and Medical Care, and the Impact of Old World Disease Imports," *American Journal of Physical Anthropology* 45: 667–72.

Passel, Jeffrey S. 1976: "Provisional Evaluation of the 1970 Census Count of American Indians," *Demography* 13: 397–409.

Passel, Jeffrey S. and Patricia A. Berman 1986: "Quality of 1980 Census Data for American Indians," *Social Biology* 33: 163–82.

Prucha, Francis Paul, ed. 1975: *Documents of United States Indian Policy* (Lincoln: University of Nebraska Press).

Ramenofsky, Ann F. 1987: *Vectors of Death: The Archaeology of European Contact* (Albuquerque: University of New Mexico Press).

Reff, Daniel T. 1987: "The Introduction of Smallpox in the Greater Southwest," *American Anthropologist* 89: 704–8.

Reinhard, Karl J. 1990: "Archaeoparasitology in North America," *American Journal of Physical Anthropology* 82: 145–63.

Smith, Marvin T. 1987: *Archaeology of Aboriginal Cultural Change in the Interior Southeast* (Gainesville: University of Florida Press).

Snipp, C. Matthew 1989: *American Indians: The First of This Land* (New York: Russell Sage).

Snow, Dean and Kim M. Lanphear 1988: "European Contact and Indian Depopulation in the Northeast: The Timing of the First Epidemics," *Ethnohistory* 35: 15–33.

Stannard, David E. 1990: "Disease and Infertility: A New Look at the Demographic Collapse of Native Populations in the Wake of Western Contact," *Journal of American Studies* 24: 325–50.

Thornton, Russell 1984a: "Cherokee Population Losses during the Trail of Tears: A New Perspective and a New Estimate," *Ethnohistory* 31: 289–300.

Thornton, Russell 1984b: "Social Organization and the Demographic Survival of the Tolowa," *Ethnohistory* 31: 187–96.

Thornton, Russell 1986: "History, Structure and Survival: A Comparison of the Yuki (Unkomno'n) and Tolowa (Hush) Indians of Northern California," *Ethnology* 25: 119–30.

Thornton, Russell 1987: *American Indian Holocaust and Survival: A Population History since 1492* (Norman: University of Oklahoma Press).

Thornton, Russell 1988: Discussion of the session "A Return to Old Killing Grounds: Recent Epidemiological Studies of North American Indians," 1988 Annual Meeting of the American Society for Ethnohistory, Williamsburg, Virginia.

Thornton, Russell 1990: *The Cherokees: A Population History* (Lincoln: University of Nebraska Press).

Thornton, Russell 1994a: "Population," in *Native Americans in the 20th Century: An Encyclopedia*, ed. Mary B. Davis (New York: Garland Publishing Company), pp. 461–4.

Thornton, Russell 1994b: "Urbanization," in *Native Americans in the 20th Century: An Encyclopedia*, ed. Mary B. Davis (New York: Garland Publishing Company), pp. 670–2.

Thornton, Russell, ed. 1998: *Studying Native America: Problems and Prospects* (Madison: University of Wisconsin Press).

Thornton, Russell and Joan Marsh Thornton 1981: "Estimating Prehistoric American Indian Population Size for United States Area: Implications of the Nineteenth Century Population Decline and Nadir," *American Journal of Physical Anthropology* 55: 47–53.

Thornton, Russell, Tim Miller, and Jonathan Warren 1991: "American Indian Population Recovery following Smallpox Epidemics," *American Anthropologist* 93: 20–38.

Thornton, Russell, Gary D. Sandefur, and C. Matthew Snipp 1991: "American Indian Fertility History," *American Indian Quarterly* 15: 359–67.

Thornton, Russell and Philip L. Walker 1998: "Health, Nutrition, and Demographic Change in Native California." Paper presented at the Annual Meeting of the American Association of Physical Anthropology, Salt Lake City, Utah.

Thornton, Russell, Jonathan Warren, and Tim Miller 1992: "Depopulation in the Southeast after 1492," in *Disease and Demography in the Americas*, eds. John W. Verano and Douglas H. Ubelaker (Washington, D.C.: Smithsonian Institution Press), pp. 187–95.

Trosper, Ronald L. 1976: "Native American Boundary Maintenance: The Flathead Indian Reservation, Montana, 1860–1970," *Ethnicity* 3: 256–74.

Ubelaker, Donald S. 1992: "The Sources and Methodology for Mooney's Estimates of North American Indian Populations," in *The Native Population of the Americas in 1492*, 2nd edn., ed. William M. Denevan (Madison: University of Wisconsin Press), pp. 243–88 (1st edn. 1976).

Ubelaker, Douglas H. 1988: "North American Indian Population Size, A.D. 1500 to 1985," *American Journal of Physical Anthropology* 77: 289–94.

U.S. Bureau of the Census 1915: *Indian Population of the United States and Alaska, 1910* (Washington, D.C.: U.S. Government Printing Office).

U.S. Bureau of the Census 1992: *1990 Census of Population. General Population Characteristics. American Indian and Alaska Native Areas* (Washington, D.C.: U.S. Government Printing Office, September).

U.S. Bureau of the Census 1993: *We the ... First Americans* (Washington, D.C.: U.S. Government Printing Office, September).

U.S. Bureau of Indian Affairs 1993: "Indian Entities Recognized and Eligible to Receive Services from the United States Bureau of Indian Affairs," *Federal Register* 58: 54364–9.

Upham, Steadman 1986: "Smallpox and Climate in the American Southwest," *American Anthropologist* 88: 115–28.

Upham, Steadman 1987: "Understanding the Disease History of the Southwest: A Reply to Reff," *American Anthropologist* 89: 708–10.

Walker, Philip L. and John R. Johnson 1994: "The Decline of the Chumash Indian Population," in *In the Wake of Contact: Biological Responses to Conquest*, eds. C. S. Larsen and G. R. Milner (New York: Wiley-Liss), pp. 109–20.

Walker, Philip L. and Russell Thornton 1996: "Health, Nutrition, and Demographic Change in Native California." Paper presented at the Second Conference on a History of Health and Nutrition in the Western Hemisphere, Columbus, Ohio.

Zubrow, Ezra 1990: "The Depopulation of Native America," *Antiquity* 64: 754–65.

Part Two

Native Practice and Belief

Native American Systems of Knowledge

CLARA SUE KIDWELL

In American historical consciousness, Indians are often imagined as children of nature, hunters roaming over vast areas from which they took only what they needed to survive and no more. The popular image belies the remarkably sophisticated techniques that native peoples used to control their environments. New work in archaeology and ethnohistory has revealed much about the intellectual sophistication of American Indians in North America and the ways in which they observed, understood, and sought to control their environments. Recent scholarship suggests that native agricultural practices, for instance, were much more diverse and subtle than the image allows. Native systems of knowledge are difficult to describe, for while they often reflect familiar Western processes – observation, deduction, hypothesis, experimentation – they also rest upon fundamentally different understandings of a world that can be alive with intent and will. Recent scholarship has sought to describe native knowledges as they existed prior to contact and as they changed in relation to European introductions. In terms of contact, that scholarship has focused on processes of adaptation rather than acculturation. The result is a richer understanding of the ways in which the worldviews of different cultures converge and diverge over time. This essay will reflect briefly on the relation between native and non-native systems of knowledge, examine some of the most important areas of Indian knowledge, and consider the nature of native adaptation.

Native American and European Systems of Knowledge

The image of Peter Minuet purchasing the island of Manhattan from the Indians for $24 worth of beads and trinkets is part of the mythology of American culture. The commonly held belief that wampum – easily seen as just another bead – was the Indians' form of money is part of that mythology. Both ideas reflect a peculiarly Western notion that objects can be assigned a specific value and used as money.

Minuet's exchange reinforces the idea that the Indians had no concept of the value of land and were merely intrigued by gaudy baubles. The use of wampum strings and belts woven of wampum beads is understood in the Western terms of buying and selling, rather than what it actually was – a signifier of a contractual relationship.

The idealized bead, then, becomes a way of viewing different cultural understandings of the world and of human relationships. It can also be used to explore a historical assumption – that a technologically superior Western civilization, with its metal tools, weapons, and modes of mass production, overwhelmed native peoples and native systems of knowledge. It gives us a way of understanding that exchange of objects can introduce new knowledge and information that cause historical change in culturally specific ways. And if we find a bead "good to think with," so too can we apply its insights to kettles, guns, horses, and the myriad other objects that lie at the nexus of intercultural trade and imagination.

Native American systems of knowledge are often characterized as religious or magical. Native people explained their environments in terms of immanent power manifest in physical reality, a power that aroused feelings of awe. *Manido* in Algonquian languages, *Orenda* in Iroquoian languages, and *Wakan* in Siouan languages – these are all terms for this immanent power (Williams, 1973: 190–1; DeMallie, 1987: 28–35; Hewitt, 1902: 33–46). These terms designate things that are out of the ordinary, that have unusual characteristics, or that behave differently. The capacity to act or to express difference is seen as evidence that the forces of nature have will and volition. The natural world is thus an intentional one, filled with beings, human and other, who exercise will and choice.

At one point in his fieldwork among the Ojibwa, A. Irving Hallowell asked an old man: "Are *all* the stones we see about us here alive?" The man reflected a while and answered, "No! But *some* are." The question and the answer epitomize a crucial distinction between native and Western systems of knowledge. Hallowell was trying to establish a linguistic category, a place for a word in a descriptive and analytical hierarchy. For the old man, *some* stones were important, for they had the potential to *act* (Hallowell, 1976: 362–3).

Western science presupposes a nature composed of physical forces acting according to laws. Those forces have no personal aspect. They can be understood rationally because their behavior is lawful, rather than willful. Laws are based on systematic observation of the natural environment and the ability to predict the outcome of events based on perceived natural patterns. As we know, however, Europeans also had traditions of knowledge that admitted the possibility of an active will in nature. Enlightenment rationality was not Europe's only mode of thought.

At the time of initial contacts between native peoples and European colonizers, for example, the European world was still alive with Aristotelean doctrines of natural place, which decreed that objects fell because they sought to reach the center of the earth. More important, the Christian idea of God's will and natural order was lodged equally firmly in place. God might intervene in human and non-human affairs, but always on the side of his Christian believers. Colonizers attributed the diseases that struck Indian populations after contact, for example, to God's divine intervention on their behalf. John Winthrop in 1634 wrote that the natives around Boston "... are neere all dead of the small Poxe, so as the Lord hathe cleared our title to what we possess…" (Pearce, 1965: 19). Colonization and enlightenment, however, went hand in hand, and scientific rationalism gained in epistemological power as the colonial drama unfolded.

European science was based in concepts of lawful behavior of natural forces. Native American beliefs were based on the willful behavior of those forces. The one presupposed fixed and rational ways of understanding those laws. The other looked toward intimate interaction with the forces of nature through dreams, visions, ceremonies, and through intuitive and personal ways of comprehending and controlling those forces. Europeans observed in the world the work of God and marveled at its order. Native people in the Americas saw themselves as active agents in bringing events about because of their ability to establish relationships with the beings who populated the world.

The "beads and trinkets" that so fascinated Indians may not have been exotic so much as they were similar to objects that had spiritual powers in Indian cultures. Crystals, for example, were used in divining because they projected light and shifted the perspective of things viewed through them. Glass beads were similar to crystals (Miller and Hammell, 1986: 315–18). Wampum beads, laboriously cut and shaped from the coahoag shells found on beaches along the New England coast, had sacred significance. Wampum belts carried in a physical sense the sacred words that were spoken into them, and they thus became records of understandings and agreements (Salisbury, 1982: 149).

Confronted with the unfamiliar, Indians found ways to put European technology into their own systems of thought. They often reasoned by analogy, adopting new goods when they recognized similarities to things that they already used. The Tsimshian on the Pacific Coast in the nineteenth century replaced deer hooves with brass thimbles on the fringes of dance aprons. The analogy of hooves and thimbles lay in the rhythmic sound that accompanied the dance. The basic Tsimshian understanding of the dance remained the same (Barnett, 1942: 23–6).

Within their own systems of thought, Indians also reasoned by metaphor, organizing categories of beings by their relationships to the physical world around them and seeing physical phenomena as manifestations of spiritual power. Where analogies are based on similarities of form or function, metaphors establish a sense of identity between two objects. Analogies make the unknown familiar because of its resemblance to something that is known. A metaphor, however, is deeply embedded in culture because it depends on existing, shared assumptions about the nature of relationships between objects. In contact situations, one might link the two. A European bead is like a wampum bead; the wampum bead is both physical object and metaphorical embodiment of human thought, speech, and action. .

Copper kettles have similar significance as analogy and metaphor. Many native peoples used clay cooking pots, but the French in Canada introduced literally thousands of copper and brass kettles into the trade. The Mi'kmaq in Nova Scotia began to use them not only for cooking (analogy) but also in their burial practices (metaphor). In some cases kettles were flattened to line the floor of a grave, and in some graves they were used to hold offerings. In some, kettles were found broken or slashed with an axe to ceremonially kill them so they could accompany the spirit of the deceased. The idea that kettles had souls vastly amused early French traders, but their use as grave goods indicates their cultural significance to the Mi'kmaq (Martin, 1975: 114–15; Turgeon, 1997: 11–15). A copper kettle may replace a clay pot as a container for a soul. It may be "killed," i.e., broken, so it can accompany the soul of the deceased to another world. The killing assures that it will not be put to further use in the land of the living. The kettle thus takes its place in a cultural system of knowledge.

Subsistence

Corn is often synonymous with American Indian cultures in grade school textbooks, and indeed corn, beans, and squash were, and in some areas still are, the agricultural staples of historic Indian villages. But agriculture in North America began not with corn but with the domestication of sunflowers in the Midwest and Northeast by about 4000–1000 BC. Jerusalem artichokes, another widely used food source, are actually tuberous roots of a species of sunflower. The appearance of domesticated squash in central Missouri as early as 2300–2000 BC indicates the development of an independent agricultural hearth in the Eastern Woodlands. Native people cultivated marsh elder, knotweed, maygrass, and goosefoot, plants that would be considered weeds in modern society, for their oil and protein-rich seeds (Cowan, 1985: 207–17).

Although corn was domesticated in northern Mexico about 4000 BC, and introduced into the American Southwest in about 1300 BC, it did not appear in the Northeast until about 200 BC, and it remained a relatively minor crop in the agricultural complex until about the beginning of the Mississippian period around AD 750 (Yarnell, 1993: 17, 22–3). Bottle gourds and Devil's Claw were also part of the agricultural complex in the Southwest, the former used for containers and the latter for fibers used to make baskets (Heiser, 1985: 63–7).

Domestication of plants entails systematic observation and use of the natural environment. It is thus the most basic form of science in human activity. It implies an understanding of the outcome of events, for example, that seeds will reproduce their own kind. It also involves systematic modification of the environment. Plants that flourished in the wild in flood-disturbed river bed environments moved easily into human-disturbed environments around villages. Wild plants produced large numbers of small seeds and fruits that dropped easily from the plant so they could propagate themselves. Women, the primary gatherers in Indian societies, favored plants with larger and tighter seed and fruit clusters that did not scatter easily. Because of selection, plants lost the ability to spread their own seeds, and humans had to take responsibility for propagation by deliberately harvesting and planting seeds. Morphologically, domesticated plants have larger and thinner-coated seeds than wild plants.

If the domestication of corn is a result of systematic human activity, native stories about the origin of corn demonstrate the metaphorical nature of Indian understandings of their relationship with the natural world. In the Cherokee story, Selu, the mother, and her husband, the hunter Kintuah, have two sons. Selu provides a delicious food (corn) but will not reveal its source. Her sons follow her one day and find her rubbing skin from her body into a basket, where it becomes grains of corn. They then fear her as a witch, and when she discovers that they know her secret, she tells them that they must clear the ground in front of the cabin, kill her, and drag her body seven times around the ground. The brothers kill her, but they clear only seven small spaces, and they drag her body around them only twice. Thus, corn grows only in some places, and Cherokees work their fields only twice (Mooney, 1982: 242–5).

The story identifies Selu as mother, as source of food, as earth, and her death is necessary to bring forth the life of corn, identifying her with the seasonal cycles of planting and harvesting and the alternation of seasons. The fact that her blood must touch the earth associates the female menstrual cycle and power to give birth with the growth of the corn, and women's work as farmers is further association of female fertility with the fertility of the earth. The knowledge associated with corn and other domesticated plants rested on observation and experimentation *and* upon a metaphorical, spiritual understanding of the world. The fact that corn was widely used throughout North America attests to a ready acceptance by native people of a food source analogous to others that had already been independently domesticated.

Time and History

The cycles of the natural environment oriented native people to the repetition of events rather than to the linear progression that preoccupied Europeans. The Christian world-view pointed toward the ultimate end of salvation. Native worldviews were more often concerned with events that repeated themselves on a regular basis – the growth and harvest of crops, the mating and migration of animals, the movements of stars and planets. Yet, if astronomy rests upon cycles, it is nonetheless a quintessentially histori-cal discipline. Recognition of patterns in celestial events depends on accumulation of data over extended periods of time, usually greater than those of the lifetime of a single observer, and it requires some form of record-keeping.

Although the best known evidence for sophisticated astronomical knowledge in the Americas is from Mayan, Aztec, and Incan sources, Indian people in North America also left permanent records of their knowledge in medicine wheels and building align-ments. Fajada Butte, near the Pueblo ruins in Chaco Canyon, New Mexico, is one such site. There, a spiral carved into a rock face is exactly bisected by a dagger of light on the day of the summer solstice. At the winter solstice, two daggers touch the edges of the spiral, enclosing it in a frame (Sofaer, Zinser, and Sinclair, 1979: 283–91). Medicine wheels in Saskatchewan indicate that the Blackfeet may have oriented their tipis on a north–south axis that allowed observation of eastern sunrise solstice sites; oral traditions tell of calendar men who observed the sun to predict certain cere-monies (Kehoe and Kehoe, 1977: 85–95). In the Big Horn Mountains of Wyoming, a circle of stones with spokes and cairns forms a medicine wheel. Sight lines across the cairns point to the rising of the sun at the summer solstice and possibly to the helical rising of Sirius, Rigel, and Aldebaran. It was constructed about AD 1500 (Eddy, 1974: 1035–43).

The sun, however, is not simply an inanimate body subject to observation. It is often the metaphor that embodies relations between humans and the world. Its passage from winter solstice point to summer solstice point is accomplished because people give it energy through their ceremonies. The Soyal, a nine-day Hopi ceremony conducted around the winter solstice, assures that the sun will be able to rise from his southern "house" and begin his journey back across the sky. Niman Kachina marks the summer solstice (McCluskey, 1982: 42; Fewkes, 1920: 496). The timing is determined by systematic observation of the sun's rising and setting points along the horizon for several days before the solstice (McCluskey, 1982: 39–40). The Hopi system is based on both empirical observation and cultural belief. The points along the horizon that sun watchers observe have been identified based on long periods of earlier observation. The basic assumption is that the sun is a spirit, but that he follows a regular path through the sky. Likewise a group of Lakota elders has explained how the path of the sun through the constellations corresponds with the geography of the Black Hills (*Paha Sapa*). And those correspondences exist in relation to certain Lakota rituals performed at specific times and places (Haile, 1947; Goodman, 1992).

The Pleiades are another important celestial marker of planting seasons. In the Northern Hemisphere they are a winter constellation. The dates of their first and last appearance in the night sky depend upon the latitude of the observer, and they generally correspond to the times of the first and last killing frosts. These dates for the Seneca communities in present-day New York state (approximately 42° north latitude) are generally between October 10–15 and May 15–19. Seneca corn requires approximately 120 days of frost-free weather to mature, a period well within the period of 153 to 163 days of the Pleiades' absence from the sky. The zenith passage of the Pleiades marks the mid-point of the frost season and traditionally has been the signal for the beginning of the traditional Seneca Midwinter Ceremony. The Seneca believed that the stars were spirits who danced above the longhouse (Ceci, 1978: 306–8).

Although major ceremonies may be timed by annual celestial events such as the appearance of the Pleiades directly overhead or by solstices, the more important calendric event for American Indian tribes was the waxing and waning of the moon. The combination of the appearance of the moon and the occurrence of events in nature served to give months names like "Moon of Ripe Choke Cherries" (Mandan – July). Astronomical knowledge continues to be used in the timing of elements of the Girls' Puberty Ceremony in the contemporary Mescalero Apache tribe. The main singer in the ceremony times the final song of the ceremony to end exactly at sunrise by watching the rotation of the stars of the Big Dipper through the smokehole of the tipi in which the ceremony is held. The song is responsible for "pulling the sun over the horizon" but its timing depends upon precise knowledge of celestial movements (Farrer, 1991: 38–59).

The importance of systematic observation of celestial bodies can be inferred from the appearance of a standardized unit of measure in the alignment of mounds. At the Toltec Mounds site in central Arkansas, this standard (called the Toltec module) is 47.5 meters, and the 18 mounds in the complex and their surrounding embankment are spaced at various extensions of this basic unit. Two mounds are the primary reference points for the module and are aligned to summer and winter solstices. Similar spacing and solstice alignments have been found for 28 mound sites in the lower Mississippi River valley. At Cahokia, the great mound complex across the Mississippi River from St. Louis, the module was "extended in magnitude out to 22 times and even 44 times."

Fully 75 percent of the Mississippian mound sites analyzed by scholars also feature one or more solar alignments, and some showed equinoctial and stellar sightings (most often of Vega and Sirius). Complex alignments of massive mounds with solar phenomena indicate that the builders were capable of mobilizing both long-term record-keeping of some form and the resources of a wide-spread population. From the mound tops they could announce times for planting and harvesting floodplain gardens (Rolingson, 1990: 27–50).

In Mesoamerica, the Mayans and Aztecs viewed a sky much different from that of their European conquerors. In the temperate latitudes of Europe, the movement of the sun along the horizon is much more dramatic than in the tropics, where the sun moves more directly overhead through a much narrower range of the horizon (Aveni, 1980: 40). The next brightest object in the sky after the sun and the moon and most dramatic in its complex movements across the sky, the planet Venus was both deity and focus of observation and record-keeping (Thompson, 1966: 262–3). The Dresden codex, a Mayan hieroglyphic text, described in mathematical notations the path of Venus in relation to the sun, its periods of appearance in the sky as the morning star and then the evening star, and gave a table of lunar eclipse predictions, another indication of the sophistication with which the Maya realized the relationship between the sun and moon in their passage through the night sky. The numerical values in the table are mathematically consistent in recording the pattern of the 584-day solar cycle of Venus, but the dates of actual appearance and disappearance of the planet did not coincide with the math, and corrections (roughly equivalent to the leap year in the Gregorian calendar) were inserted in the tables (Aveni, 1980: 189–90). Building alignments also served as permanent records of astronomical observations. At Caracol Tower at Chichen Itza, a Mayan site dating to about AD 800, windows aligned with the further northernmost and southernmost helical rising of Venus and the point of disappearance of the Pleiades from the sky on the date of the vernal equinox (Aveni, 1980: 261–2, 264–6).

The Mayan sense of history is connected to a calendar system that evolved over a long period of time, beginning probably with the Olmec culture that flourished from *ca.* 1500–600 BC, and that was capable of recording cycles of long duration (Lounsbury, 1970–80: vol. 15, p. 813). The calendar was a combination of two systems – a sacred calendar of 260 days (the *Tzolkin*), and a 365-day solar calendar referred to as the Vague Year – both of which allowed observation and metaphorical interpretation. The Sacred Year and the Vague Year created a 52-year cycle called the calendar round. The combination of day names in the *Tzolkin* and the Vague Year gave a unique identity to each day in the calendar round, which made it possible to record unique historical events. It took 18,980 days (or 52 years) to return to the same combination of named and numbered days that began this cycle (Lounsbury, p. 765).

The Aztecs who arrived in the valley of Mexico in the thirteenth century AD inherited the Mayan calendar system and marked the end of the 52-year cycle with a ceremony called the "Binding of the Years," which involved the sacrifice of a captive to feed the sun with blood to sustain its strength for the next cycle. The timing of the ceremony was determined by the zenith passage of the Pleiades (Krupp, 1982: 9–13). The Mayans also had a day count, by which they reckoned the absolute number of days in their history. Although the day count might imply a linear sense of history, the cycle of the calendar round seems to have been the more important concept. Calendar notation included glyphs designated as day carriers, and crucial calendric conjunctions were occasions for changes in political leadership. The deaths of rulers and the accession of new rulers were memorialized in dates on stelae, and because these transitions had occurred and would occur, the Mayans and Aztecs essentially remembered the future based on what had happened in the past (Farriss, 1987: 577). Although the Mayan and Aztec cultures differed dramatically from Hopi culture, there is an underlying similarity in the concerns of their calendar systems. Human efforts maintained the cycles of the sun for both the Aztecs and the Hopi. The primary concern for all three cultures was the repetition of events in understandable ways – what had happened before must surely happen again.

Indian people were also generally aware that the lunar year did not correspond to the solar year. A Ho-Chunk (Winnebago) calendar stick dating from the nineteenth century recorded not only two precise, non-arithmetic records of observable lunar years of twelve months, but also notations that incorporated a thirteenth intercalary month every three years in order to bring the lunar calendar into phase with the solar tropical year (Marshack, 1985: 27–51).

Acculturation and Accommodation

Beads and trinkets (brass bells, mirrors, buttons) were only a small part of the complex of European trade goods introduced to native people. Indians replaced their own goods with metal utensils, trade cloth, and guns. They did not, however, automatically accept all the trade goods they were offered. Salisbury points out (1982: 52–3) that in the early sixteenth century, the Narragansetts accepted a wide variety of goods because trade was a way of establishing alliances, whereas the Abenaki, who had no interest in alliances with European explorers and fishermen, demanded only metal utilitarian goods that could be substituted for stone tools.

The anthropological paradigm of acculturation presupposes that cultures are characterized by discrete sets of traits and values, and in the historical experience of contact between cultures, those of the dominant society are accepted by and replace those of the subordinate society (Redfield, Linton, and Herskovits, 1936: 149–52). From the cultural presumption that European technology was superior to native technology, scholars have argued that trade goods led to the decline or transformation of Indian cultures. Stone Age culture must necessarily give way to European Iron Age culture (Quimby, 1966: 3).

The vast literature on the Indian trade generally stresses Indians' growing dependence on both European goods and alcohol as factors in the degradation of Indian cultures. Initially amazed at the uses of axes, knives, and guns, Indians very quickly recognized the superiority of these items to their own tools and put aside their traditional implements in favor of these trade goods. They soon became dependent upon them in ways that led to change in native economies. Jennings (1975: 86) summarizes the situation: "New commodities replaced old. Iron and steel implements made copper and stone obsolete. Instead of exchanging surpluses of their own products, the tribes abandoned their crafts in order to concentrate on obtaining surpluses of the goods desired by Europeans."

Indians were not, however, uncritical consumers or unwary buyers. Malone (1993: 37) concludes that Indians were selective in their adoption of foreign products. "Favored goods usually satisfied functional or symbolic needs already existing in the aboriginal culture." Although Indians were generally terrified by guns in their first encounters, they soon learned their usefulness in hunting and warfare. Indians in New England also learned quickly to mold bullets and sharpen the flints of their weapons. They could replace broken stocks and salvage parts from damaged weapons, but repairing mechanisms and metal parts of guns was generally beyond their skill, and for those purposes they relied on blacksmiths (Malone, 1993: 45, 95).

Guns also took their place in some native systems of thought. The report of the gun was analogous to the sound of thunder, which was in turn associated with rain, fertility, crops, and renewal. The Cherokee integrated guns into their Green Corn Ceremony. Frank Speck reported that in the 1930s, men carried guns during the ceremony and fired them at periodic intervals. Gunshot became the source of the spiritual power of thunder and rain (Speck and Broom, 1983: 47).

In contemporary Yuchi culture in Oklahoma, guns are still used in the Lizard Dance. They continue to represent thunder, but their firing replaces lost elements of songs whose words formerly summoned thunder (White Deer, 1995: 11). The Cheyenne, on the other hand, believed that thunder and lightning were malevolent beings and fired guns to drive them off. Mandan ceremonial leaders consecrated guns in a ritual closely resembling other purification rites. The Blackfeet attempted to cure illnesses in horses by loading a gun with powder and firing it at the horse's side. The shock might cure the horse (Ewers, 1997: 49–50). For the Heiltsuk on the Northwest Coast, Harkin (1997: 86) maintains that "The rifle is iconic of the Heiltsuk notion of corporeal causality." Its bullets penetrate the human body in the same way that objects can be injected into a person's body by witchcraft. This action at a distance appears as a form of power; guns might easily be seen as part of witchcraft. In sum, the gun entered native systems of knowledge as metaphor, analogy, substitute, and wholly new practice.

Guns also allowed Indians to alter their environments through more efficient hunting. Guns and metal traps could more easily kill animals, and they led to the depletion of animal populations, especially the deer and beaver whose skins were important in the trade. Calvin Martin (1978) has argued, however, that even the rapid disappearance of beavers in northeastern hunting territories can be explained by looking at native worldviews. Indians, according to Martin, believed that the beavers were angered by their adoption of elements of the white man's culture and were withdrawing deliberately from contact with Indian hunters. Disappearance of animals from traditional hunting grounds and large-scale animal deaths from disease were seen as animals "making war" on humans, and Indian hunters felt justified in retaliating by making war on the animals. Martin's provocative thesis presented a classic "systems of knowledge" problem – how did Indian people understand ecology, technology, and the fur trade? His work was challenged almost immediately by Indian people and anthropologists alike (Krech, 1981). The thesis was based on flimsy evidence and, despite Martin's attempt to construct a native perspective, his argument adopted non-Indian assumptions about war and spiritual belief.

Yet Martin was right in thinking that the complex interplay of human beings and spiritual powers operating in the natural environment could help explain the adoption of European technology by Indian tribes. The Chippewa integrated the term "Manitou," their word for transcendent spiritual power, into their name for glass beads, *manitôminens*, *min* (berries), *ens* (a diminutive), roughly translated as "small sacred berries." Steel was *manitobiwâbik*, sacred iron. The Dakota word for power is *Wakan*, which can be translated as something that is difficult to understand, and *maza wakan* (sacred iron, a gun) demonstrated its power to act in mysterious ways (White, 1994: 369). Bradley (1987: 110) argues that the Iroquois acquired trade goods which, because of their mysteriousness, represented power. As evidence he cites the sudden appearance of grave offerings after European contact, a custom rarely practiced before, and the vast quantity of trade items among those offerings, along with shells, crystal, and copper, indigenous materials denoting power. European goods were fully adopted into the potlatch ceremony on the Northwest Coast. Daniel Cramner, who hosted a great Kwakiutl potlatch in 1921, gave cash, gas boats, and pool tables to two chiefs, commenting "It hurt them." The sentiment is totally in keeping with the intent to shame or humiliate high-ranking guests in order to establish one's own social privileges (Codere, 1966: 117). As products of European systems of knowledge, the trade goods that made their way into native knowledge systems offer difficult but suggestive opportunities for thinking about cultural interaction and exchange.

Science and Ethnoscience

The seventeenth and eighteenth centuries in Europe saw the rise of the scientific revolution. Nicholas Copernicus proposed a sun-centered mathematical model of the universe. Galileo Galilei established laws describing the acceleration of falling bodies and asserted the physical reality of planetary motion. Using observational data from the Danish astronomer Tycho Brahe, Johann Kepler determined the elliptical shape of planetary orbits. Isaac Newton promulgated the law of gravity, and Carl van Linne established his great classification system for plants and animals. The intellectual achievements of the scientific revolution codified and classified the cycles and patterns of nature into immutable laws.

Native people, as we have seen, recognized cycles and patterns too, but they saw them in terms of relationships between humans and the environment. The Linnean system proposed that sexual organs were the main factors in the classification of plants. The Navajo classified plants as male and female, based on qualities associated with gender rather than sex. Woody plants are male, while slender, flexible plants are female. External form determines. Ethnoscience, then, involves understandings of Native systems of classification which, like European systems, operate within their own cultural logics. Plants may be classified together because they grow in proximity with each other. Appearance, history, spiritual position – these and other factors helped define classificatory position. Many plants may be broadly classified as medicinal because of the effects they have upon the human body.

Such effects constituted the basis for healing in Native societies, and they also mark the point at which European and Native practices converged. The European medical doctrine of simples was based on similarities between physical characteristics of plants and aspects of the human body. Indian uses of plants were based on the belief that plants as living beings had powers that affected the well-being of human beings. Physical similarity between plants and the human body was an indication of a special relationship. The juice of milkweed (*Asclepius sp.*), for example, was used among the Ojibwa for female complaints. Bloodroot (*Sanguinaria canadensis*) was widely used in a variety of ways, from a dye to a strong emetic. When a Chippewa woman in Minnesota today digs roots, leaves a pinch of tobacco in the hole, and ends her prayer to the plant with *Megwich* ("Thanks"), she still expresses this belief in the spiritual nature of the plant.

Many white settlers in America adopted Indian herbal medicines. White trillium, for example, was called "squaw flower" by whites who put it to the same use as Indians, an aid in childbirth. A number of plants used by American Indians have been listed in the United States *Pharmacopeia* (Vogel, 1970: 267, 336–7, 354–6, 384–5). Although ethnographers scoffed at Indian curing ceremonies as mere superstition, patent medicines based on supposed Indian formulas became popular during the nineteenth century, and books on Indian herbal medicines were widely used (Gibson, 1967: 34–9, 74–9; Hallowell, 1965: 239–41). Ironically, the failure of native healers to deal with European-introduced epidemic diseases such as smallpox, measles, and cholera often served to discredit them and promoted acceptance of Christian missionaries (Axtell, 1985: 97–8).

Orality and Literacy

Writing was one of the most amazing skills that Europeans brought to North America. Indeed, Axtell (1985: 102–3) maintains that the Hurons were awed by the ability of French Jesuits to read and write, activities that they took as a sign of mysterious power. For people who believed that human thought was a causal element in the processes of the natural world and influenced things at a distance, the ability of Europeans to know about distant events by reading messages was a sign of spiritual power. Europeans, of course, had their own belief in the power of the word of God to transform Indians into Christians. Christian hymns could counter native songs, which missionaries sometimes considered incantations to the devil (Calloway, 1991: 48). Priests and ministers labored to reduce Indian languages to written form so that native people could read the word of God and be transformed by it.

The introduction of literacy to Indian people was done with the main intent of converting them to Christianity, which was as important as technology in changing native knowledges. Christianity, for example, introduced a linear concept of time to people whose oral traditions were based in cyclical memories of past events (Todorov, 1992: 80–1). The repetition of the past was less important than a striving toward the future, and the printed page itself forced linearity upon meaning (Ong, 1982: 121).

The association of writing and Christianity discouraged many adult Indians from adopting literacy, although mission schools made an impact on their Indian students. It was not until 1821 that Sequoyah, a Cherokee who knew no English, devised a syllabic form of writing for the Cherokee language. The *Cherokee Phoenix*, the tribal newspaper, published articles in English and Cherokee beginning in 1828. It became a major vehicle for expressions of sentiments in favor of and opposed to the proposed government policy of Indian removal (McLoughlin, 1984: 183–5, 233). The publication of constitutions and laws in the Cherokee and Choctaw languages during the late 1820s is striking evidence of the changing circumstances wrought by technology and literacy. Indian nations sought to prove that they had become civilized and capable of living with their white neighbors while inexorable forces of American expansion pushed them to the west.

Continuity and Change

The major divergence between American Indian and European systems of knowledge lies in the perception of the role of human beings in the processes of nature. In European science, humans manipulate circumstances to test the validity of laws through experiments. In Indian cultures, human action in reciprocal relationship with spiritual action brings about the cycles of the environment. The Hopi, for example, would not think of not performing their ceremonies to see if the sun would remain at rest. To do so would risk the continuation of their world. Human beings are an integral part of the processes of the natural world, not observers who stand outside those processes.

Columbus's world in 1492 was still alive with mysterious forces. Alchemists sought the Philosopher's Stone, which had the power to transmute base metals into gold. Magnetism was understood as an invisible fluid that acted between objects. In many respects, will in natural objects was part of the European world as well as the American Indian world. Columbus charted his voyage to the New World with crude instruments – an hourglass to tell time, the mariner's compass for direction, and a simple quadrant to shoot the angles of stars above the horizon. Dead reckoning and a good deal of luck got him to the Americas. His religion convinced him in his later years that he had actually discovered Eden on earth (Morrison, 1942: 183–96). But the urge that drove Europeans to explore and to seek material wealth in unknown regions was also part of the intellectual renaissance that led to the development of modern science. Greek philosophers knew theoretically that the world was round, but Columbus's and Magellan's voyages gave physical proof of the fact.

Europeans brought to the native people of these newly discovered lands new systems of knowledge – a belief in the absolute power of the Christian God and a technology based on metal, mechanical energy, and domesticated animals. Where Indian goods were handmade, unique objects, European-manufactured trade goods could be produced uniformly in large quantities. The sheer abundance of strings of beads may have amazed Indians who laboriously drilled each shell bead of a wampum belt by hand. Even as it connects different peoples, then, a bead also reflects different systems of cultural knowledge.

Indian people became increasingly dependent on European goods as their traditional subsistence patterns changed under the impact of European settlement, the effects of European diseases, and the introduction of domesticated livestock. The intellectual change in worldview was less dramatic, however, as Indian people found ways to integrate new ideas into their own systems of knowledge. Though they might adopt metal hoes to work their fields, Cherokee women could still understand that the story of Selu, the corn mother, encompassed many layers of meaning and association between corn and human life. The story showed the essential importance of natural cycles in human life.

Guns made hunting more efficient, and they exacerbated intertribal warfare, both conditions that led to cultural change. They were also, however, a new form of thunder that fit into older ceremonies that renewed human relationships with the spiritual world. Anthropologist Marshall Sahlins argues that new influences change a culture even when they are adopted into seemingly traditional forms (Sahlins, 1985: 138–9). But perhaps the truest sign of cultural change was not dependence on guns in hunting, war, and ritual, but the more dramatic moments when Indian leaders agreed to support schools to expose their citizens to "the benefits of instruction in the mechanic and ordinary arts of life" (Treaty with the Choctaw, 1825, cited in Kappler, 1904–41: vol. 1, p. 212). Missionaries measured the progress of civilization among the Choctaws in the number of cards, spinning wheels, and looms used by women in the Nation (Schermerhorn, 1814/1846: 20–1). When Indians expressed an interest in learning new skills to replace the old, the process of cultural adaptation and change was well underway.

Yet, in varying degrees, Indian people have continued to pursue traditional ceremonies that keep them grounded in the cycles of nature. The Yuchi Lizard Dance and variations of the traditional southeastern Green Corn Ceremony are still performed in parts of Oklahoma. The Hopi ceremonial cycle is maintained on the mesas in central Arizona. The Makah tribe of Neah Bay, Washington has regained the right to hunt whales for subsistence, now using gasoline-powered boats and explosive powered harpoons, rather than the traditional cedar canoes and yew wood harpoons. Although Sahlins maintains that the more things remain the same, the more they change, in many cases systems of knowledge based on seasonal and religious cycles coexist with modern and changing technology.

BIBLIOGRAPHY

Aveni, Anthony 1980: *Skywatchers of Ancient Mexico* (Austin: University of Texas Press).
Axtell, James 1985: *The Invasion Within: The Contest of Cultures in Colonial North America* (New York and Oxford: Oxford University Press).

Barnett, H. G. 1942: "Invention and Cultural Change," *American Anthropologist* XLIV (January–March): 17–32.

Bradley, James W. 1987: *Evolution of the Onondaga Iroquois: Accommodating Change, 1500–1655* (Syracuse: Syracuse University Press).

Calloway, Colin G. (ed.) 1991: *Dawnland Encounters: Indians and Europeans in Northern New England* (Hanover and London: University Press of New England).

Ceci, Lynn 1978: "Watchers of the Pleiades: Ethnoastronomy among Native Cultivators in Northeastern North America," *Ethnohistory* 25(4) (Fall): 301–17.

Codere, Helen 1966: "Daniel Cranmer's Potlatch," in *Indians of the North Pacific Coast*, ed. Tom McFeat (Seattle: University of Washington Press).

Cowan, Wesley C. 1985: "Understanding the Evolution of Plant Husbandry in Eastern North America: Lessons from Botany, Ethnography and Archaeology," in *Prehistoric Food Production in North America*, ed. Richard I. Ford. Anthropological Papers, Museum of Anthropology, University of Michigan, No. 75 (Ann Arbor: University of Michigan), pp. 205–44.

DeMallie, Raymond J. 1987: "Lakota Belief and Ritual in the Nineteenth Century," in *Sioux Indian Religion: Tradition and Innovation*, ed. Raymond J. DeMallie and Douglas R. Parks (Norman: University of Oklahoma Press), pp. 28–35.

Densmore, Frances 1928: "Uses of Plants by the Chippewa Indians," in *Forty-fourth Annual Report of the Bureau of American Ethnology to the Secretary of the Smithsonian Institution 1926–1927* (Washington, D.C.: Government Printing Office), pp. 279–397.

Eddy, John A. 1974: "Astronomical Alignment of the Big Horn Medicine Wheel," *Science* 184: 1035–43.

Ewers, John C. 1997: *Plains Indian History and Culture: Essays on Continuity and Change* (Norman: University of Oklahoma Press).

Farrer, Claire R. 1991: *Living Life's Circle: Mescalero Apache Cosmovision* (Albuquerque: University of New Mexico Press).

Farriss, Nancy M. 1987: "Remembering the Future, Anticipating the Past: History, Time, and Cosmology among the Maya of Yucatan," *Comparative Studies in Society and History* 29 (3) (July): 566–93.

Fewkes, Walter J. 1920: "Sun Worship of the Hopi Indians," *Smithsonian Institution, Annual Report for 1918* (Washington, D.C.: Government Printing Office).

Gibson, Arrell M. 1967: "Medicine Show," *American West* 4(1): 34, 74–7.

Goodman, Ronald 1992: *Lakota Star Knowledge: Studies in Lakota Stellar Theology* (Rosebud, SD: Sinte Gleska University).

Haile, Berard 1947: *Starlore among the Navaho* (Santa Fe, NM: Museum of Navajo Ceremonial Art).

Hallowell, A. Irving 1965: "The Backwash of the Frontier: The Impact of the Indian on American Culture," in *The Frontier in Perspective*, ed. Walker D. Wyman and Clifton B. Kroeber (Madison: University of Wisconsin Press), pp. 229–58.

Hallowell, A. Irving 1976: "Ojibwa Ontology, Behavior, and World View," in *Contributions to Anthropology: Selected Papers of A. Irving Hallowell* (Chicago: University of Chicago Press), pp. 357–90.

Harkin, Michael E. 1997: *The Heiltsuks: Dialogues of Culture and History on the Northwest Coast* (Lincoln and London: University of Nebraska Press).

Heiser, Charles B., Jr. 1985: "Some Botanical Considerations of the Early Domesticated Plants North of Mexico," in *Prehistoric Food Production in North America*, ed. Richard I. Ford. Anthropological Papers, Museum of Anthropology, University of Michigan, No. 75 (Ann Arbor: University of Michigan), pp. 57–72.

Hewitt, J. N. B. 1902: "Orenda and a Definition of Religion," *American Anthropologist* n.s., IV: 33–46.

Jennings, Francis 1975: *The Invasion of America* (Chapel Hill, University of North Carolina Press).

Kappler, Charles J. 1904–41: *Indian Affairs: Laws and Treaties*. 5 vols. (Washington, D.C.: Government Printing Office).

Kehoe, Thomas F. and Alice B. Kehoe 1977: "Stones, Solstices, and Sun Dance Structures," *Plains Anthropologist* 22 (76), part 1: 85–95.

Krech, Shepard, ed. 1981: *Indians, Animals, and the Fur Trade: A Critique of "Keepers of the Game"* (Athens: University of Georgia Press).

Krupp, E. C. 1982: "The 'Binding of the Years,' the Pleiades and the Nadir Sun," *Archaeoastronomy: The Bulletin of the Center for Archaeoastronomy* 5: 9–13.

Lounsbury, Floyd G. 1970–80: "Maya Numeration, Computation and Calendrical Astronomy," in *Dictionary of Scientific Biography*, ed. Charles C. Gillispie, 16 vols. (New York: Scribners), vol. 15, pp. 759–818.

Malone, Patrick M. 1993: *The Skulking Way of War: Technology and Tactics among the New England Indians* (Baltimore: Johns Hopkins University Press).

Marshack, Alexander 1985: "A Lunar-Solar Calendar Stick from North America," *American Antiquity* 50(1): 27–51.

Martin, Calvin 1975: "The Four Lives of a Micmac Copper Pot," *Ethnohistory* 22(2) (Spring): 111–33.

Martin, Calvin 1978: *Keepers of the Game: Indian–Animal Relationships and the Fur Trade* (Berkeley: University of California Press).

McCluskey, Stephen C. 1982: "Historical Archaeoastronomy: The Hopi Example," in *Archaeoastronomy in the New World*, ed. A. F. Aveni (Cambridge: Cambridge University Press), pp. 31–59.

McLoughlin, William G. 1984: *Cherokees and Missionaries, 1789–1839* (New Haven: Yale University Press).

Miller, Christopher J. and George R. Hamell 1986: "A New Perspective on Indian–White Contact: Cultural Symbols and Colonial Trade," *Journal of American History* 73 (2) (Sept.): 311–28.

Mooney, James 1982: *Myths of the Cherokee and Sacred Formulas of the Cherokees, from the 19th and 17th Annual Reports B.A.E.* (Nashville: Charles and Randy Elder).

Morrison, Samuel Eliot 1942: *Admiral of the Ocean Sea: A Life of Christopher Columbus* (Boston: Little, Brown and Company).

Ong, Walter J. 1982: *Orality and Literacy: The Technologizing of the Word* (London and New York: Methuen).

Pearce, Roy Harvey 1965: *Savagism and Civilization: A Study of the Indian and the American Mind* (Baltimore: Johns Hopkins University Press).

Perdue, Theda 1998: *Cherokee Women, Gender and Culture Change, 1700–1835* (Lincoln and London: University of Nebraska Press).

Quimby, George Irving 1966: *Indian Culture and European Trade Goods* (Madison: University of Wisconsin Press).

Redfield, Robert, Ralph Linton, and Melville J. Herskovits 1936: "A Memorandum for the Study of Acculturation" *American Anthropologist* XXXVIII: 149–52.

Rolingson, Martha Ann 1990: "The Toltec Mounds Site: A Ceremonial Center in the Arkansas River Lowland," in *The Mississippian Emergence*, ed. Bruce D. Smith (Washington D.C.: Smithsonian Institution Press), pp. 27–50.

Sahlins, Marshall David 1985: *Islands of History* (Chicago: University of Chicago Press).

Salisbury, Neal 1982: *Manitou and Providence: Indians, Europeans, and the Making of New England, 1500–1643* (New York: Oxford University Press).

Schermerhorn, John F. 1814: "Report Respecting the Indians Inhabiting the Western Parts of the United States," *Collections of the Massachusetts Historical Society*, II, second series (Boston, 1814; reprinted Charles C. Little and James Brown, 1846).

Smith, Bruce D. 1992: *Rivers of Change: Essays on Early Agriculture in Eastern North America* (Washington, D.C. and London: Smithsonian Institution Press).

Sofaer, Anna, Volker Zinser, and Rolf M. Sinclair 1979: "A Unique Solar Marking Construct," *Science* 206: 283–91.

Speck, Frank G. and Leonard Broom 1983: *Cherokee Dance and Drama* (Norman: University of Oklahoma Press).

Thompson, J. Eric S. 1966: *The Rise and Fall of Maya Civilization*, 2nd edn. (Norman: University of Oklahoma Press).

Todorov, Tzvetan 1992: *The Conquest of America*, trans. Richard Howard (New York: HarperPerennial).

Turgeon, Laurier 1997: "The Tale of the Kettle: Odyssey of an Intercultural Object," *Ethnohistory* 44(1) (Winter): 1–29.

Vogel, Virgil J. 1970: *American Indian Medicine* (Norman: University of Oklahoma Press).

White, Bruce M. 1994: "Encounters with Spirits: Ojibwa and Dakota Theories about the French and Their Merchandise," *Ethnohistory* 41(3) (Summer): 369–405.

White Deer, Gary 1995: "Pretty Shellshaker," in *Remaining Ourselves: Music and Tribal Memory*, ed. Dayna Bowker Lee (Oklahoma City: State Arts Council of Oklahoma), pp. 11–14.

Williams, Roger 1973: *A Key into the Language of America* (1643), ed. John J. Teunissen and Evelyn J. Hinz. Detroit.

Yarnell, Richard A. 1993: "The Importance of Native Crops during the Late Archaic and Woodland Periods," in *Foraging and Farming in the Eastern Woodlands*, ed. C. Margaret Scarry (Gainesville: University Press of Florida), pp. 17–23.

6

Native American Spirituality: History, Theory, and Reformulation

LEE IRWIN

Throughout the twentieth century, the study of Native American religions was dominated by three primary ethnographic vectors: studies of individual religious leaders or visible practitioners; intensive "cultural" studies of the role of rites, ceremonies, and beliefs in a specific native community; and comparative theorizing that cuts across religious practices in search of common unifying themes. These studies have been based primarily in the perceptions, observations, and theories of non-native observers. Often these non-native, written observations have then been used as primary sources for the subsequent study of native religions. Further, the context of Christian missionization, anthropological categorical reductions, and a surplus of historical narratives written by non-native observers has resulted in the dominance of an "outsider" understanding of native religions. Indian beliefs and practices have frequently been recorded in limited selections in the form of monographs and field reports by those often unfamiliar with the language and thought worlds of native practitioners. Subsequently, there can exist significant tensions between the actual spiritual beliefs and practices within a given native community and the external literature on the religion of that community authored by non-native scholars.

In order to gain a sense of the complexity of indigenous native spiritual traditions and their transformations in the twentieth century, it is necessary to consider the dialogical interfaces between native practitioners and the non-native observers whose written productions have dominated the field. The heart of religious practice within native communities is not a written text, nor is it an explicitly rationalized creed, nor is it usually based in a dogmatic set of required beliefs. In general, native religions are flexible, have nuanced interpretations based in personal experience, and revolve around the sanctioned leadership of those regarded as knowledgeable through many years of training and specialized experience. Each community has its own unique patterns, language, and social structures that intimately unite religious beliefs and social practices in a holistic worldview. Further, communally distinctive rites are tied to native systems of knowledge based in many generations of close observation, precise symbolic coding, and complex behavioral and linguistic forms of intergenerational communication (Kidwell, this volume). These systems of knowledge are locally developed and tied to specific environments. While this knowledge was shared between groups, significant differences can also be found between communities sharing mutual or adjoining territories.

In most cases, the specific language of each group is crucial for the correct performance of religious actions; it is equally important in the act of interpretation. Native people classify religious knowledge through linguistic categories associated with diverse types of practitioners, ritual leaders, experienced elders, and a number of special societies, all empowered to moderate and supervise the practice of specific rites and communal religious events. Such events are embedded in social codes of respect, proper behavior, and ethical attitudes. They often help sanction leadership roles ranging from kin relations and society membership to varying degrees of social and political influence through elected or inherited leadership. The whole is embedded in a sacred landscape whose contours and places are rich in stories, remembered events, cosmological structures, and which resonate the power of sanctified places through a symbolic understanding of the interdependent relationships between place, plants, animals, and human beings.

In the overall sense, context is more crucial than text for native religions. A text isolated from its performative, social, and religious context is apt to be seen as a radical diminishment (and distortion) of the religious event. The emotional, symbolic, and spiritual content communicated through spoken, sung, and enacted words often registers a communal understanding that is not reducible to a representational text (Gill, 1981). This problem is made even more complex by the significance attributed by native religionists to the sacred qualities of the languages used in prayer and ceremony (Powers, 1986). Descriptive works, particularly those written by non-native observers, often fail to adequately represent the complexity of native religious life. The gap between the performative context, its symbolic processes, gestures, objects, prayers, invocations, and communal narratives, and the written descriptive account is immense. Written descriptions of actual religious practices simply cannot contain the full nuances that pervade and legitimize the means through which a ceremony empowers and enriches the practitioners. Further, all native religions have undergone often radical historical transformations that are frequently absent in descriptions that present native religions as "timeless" creations of a mythicized, archaic past. The written history of Native American religions, then, is often burdened by misunderstanding, romanticization, and biased misconception. In part, these problems stem from the irreducibility of religious experience to scholarly text. In part, they also originate in the problems of cross-cultural translation. It is also the case, however, that such problems must also be seen in the context of political oppression and the denial of the legitimacy of native peoples to practice native religions (Irwin, 1996/7).

In reviewing the history of scholarly productions on native religions, there are four (heuristic) areas of study that reflect the various predispositions taken by scholars. These four may be summarized historically as: early descriptive ethnography by literate non-native observers; folklore collections and anthropological monographs concerning specific native religions; thematic and comparative religious studies; and contemporary native (and co-authored) productions of the late twentieth century. Writers and scholars in each of these areas have tended to produce characteristic works reflecting historically shared cultural biases toward the subject of native religion. Each area still has its active scholars, though anthropological studies in native religion have declined whereas comparative religious studies have increased, although slowly and as a minor discipline within the larger field of comparative world religions. For those who are unfamiliar with the study of native religions, a good overview is given in Champagne (1994: 441–523) and a useful history of native religious studies with extensive bibliography is found in Hultkrantz (1983).

Early Descriptive Ethnography

With over 500 native communities, each practicing its own spiritual traditions in a context tied to local landscapes, seasonal rites, major life changes, a unique language, and a multitude of special ceremonies and practices generally closed to outsiders, it is no surprise that there is only a fragmentary, piecemeal historical record of native religions. While the earliest religious ethnography (Taino) dates back to 1496, everything recorded is fragmentary and isolated by the writers' lack of familiarity with the wider contexts of native religion. I use the term "descriptive ethnography" loosely to mean usually brief, sporadic descriptions of native beliefs, practices, or "customs" acquired from only a few native individuals. Often there is little understanding of religious practice as a whole, and inevitably native "religions" in such descriptions are subsumed into an overarching rhetoric that diminishes native practices while celebrating Euro-American Christian values (Tinker, 1993). No early ethnography escapes this early paradigm of comparison; native religions are "pagan" or "savage" or (later) "primitive" in contrast to Christian beliefs. By implication, therefore, they were seen as hardly worth studying or recording, and such records are often "curiosities" of exotic "savage customs" whose significance for native practitioners is dismissed or largely misunderstood. While genuine curiosity and interest may have motivated observers, the same observers commonly recorded native religious activities as "childlike" and "superstitious."

Such attitudes are seen clearly in the writings on native religions by early Spanish Franciscan and French Jesuit authors. While these volumes contain a multitude of early observations on native religious practices or beliefs, they are subsumed into a Christian rhetoric that thoroughly "demonizes" all native religions and their practitioners. Native religious images were all regarded as "idols" and native religious leaders as "servants of the devil," "necromancers," or "conjurers" – terms that persisted into the early twentieth century. Arriving in Mexico, the invaders burned and destroyed all "idols," dismantled temples, and persecuted native priests. The working assumption, among Catholic missionaries, was that while native peoples had "religion," it was a worship of "demons and idols" and must therefore be overthrown. Thus the Christian mythic world was projected onto native peoples and their religious world was reduced to an alien construct – native religions were strictly engaged in demonic practices. Sahagún (*ca.* 1560), the Franciscan priest who learned the Nahua language and collected detailed ethnography on Aztec religion, was motivated by a desire to combat the demonic aspects of Nahua religion. The demonization of native religions in Mexico is discussed by Cervantes (1994) but has not yet been thoroughly studied in the rest of North America, where it was a common strategy among missionaries.

Even more restrictive were Europeans who represented native people as having no religion whatsoever. Many Jesuit authors saw nothing but "very tenacious customs" that could not be described as religion in terms familiar to Euro-Christian missionaries. Such observers overlooked thoroughly complex native ceremonies, religious beliefs, and social relations that gave meaning and coherence to native life. This wholesale denial of native religions lasted well into the nineteenth century. Some writers were more receptive to the intrinsic value of native languages and beliefs and yet Gabriel Sagard (*ca.* 1632) could blithely write, "their language is defective in words for many things ... like Trinity, Glory, Paradise, Hell, Church, etc." Such statements are less concerned with understanding difference than they are with using linguistic distinctions to assert superiority. A similar denial or incorporation into Christian mythos can be seen clearly in English colonial sources as well. For example, William Strachey in 1612 writes of the Powhatan, "their chief god is no other than the Devil." Robert Beverley (*ca.* 1705) and John Lawson (*ca.* 1712) write extensively on Virginia Indian religions but always with an eye to denouncing their "pagan" or "superstitious" character. And yet, many native peoples did become members of Christian communities, thus creating an alternative "native religion" in the form of native Christianity (Rollings, this volume).

Over time authors emerged who did not seek to deny the value of native religion and were collectors of exotic aspects of native cultures. Artists, explorers, and early ethnographers attributed some value to native religions but often as "survivals" of a more primitive age. People like Maximilian, Prince of Wied, who was an astounding collector of everything "Indian," along with artist Carl Bodmer, recorded many details (and objects) of native religions along the Missouri in the 1830s. Artist George Catlin recorded two volumes of notes along with many hundreds of drawings and paintings depicting native ceremonies he claimed to have witnessed. Henry Schoolcraft, whose wife was Chippewa, in 1859 produced a two-volume work containing many details of native religion. Schoolcraft, like many before and after him, constantly fails to make any clear distinctions between native groups. This problem plagues many early ethnographic sources; generalizations are made for "Indian religion" which simply blur the differences between the real beliefs and practices of specific peoples, creating instead an abstract "mental picture" of Indian religion related to no group at all. If missionaries "demonized," then secular ethnographers transformed native religious experiences into abstract, dehistoricized portraits.

Some observers wrote on religion more specifically; for example, Johann Georg Kohl (*ca.* 1860) among the Ojibwa; Stephen Powers (*ca.* 1877) among the California Indians; Gideon Pond (*ca.* 1867), Stephen Riggs (*ca.* 1880), and James Owen Dorsey (*ca.* 1894) among the Dakota. Yet their narrowly constrained writing tends toward abstraction, generalizing observations of specific actors into "essential" representations of whole peoples. This part-for-whole analogy satisfied a general popular interest in Indian culture when it no longer was seen as a direct threat but rather as a fading image of the past. But it also tended toward abstractions based on fragmentary information neither contextualized nor actually understood. In these cases, and many like them, the native religious worldview was shrunk to often arbitrary examples isolated from a full account of the specific communal practices and beliefs. Writers like George Bird Grinnell (*ca.* 1910) among the Cheyenne and Pawnee and Walter McClintock (*ca.* 1910) among the Blackfeet represent examples of somewhat more comprehensive writing. These men lived with native peoples and collected much that is valuable in understanding the specifics of Cheyenne or Blackfeet religions in the nineteenth century. But both distanced themselves by proclaiming the superiority of "Western civilization" and both tended to see native peoples from a romanticized perspective as "noble savages" whose days were bound to pass. Both engaged in salvage ethnology that fixed native religions in an archaic past and refused to admit the actual historical transformations saturating every aspect of native life.

Anthropology and Native Religions

In 1851 Lewis Henry Morgan, with the help of Seneca ethnologist Ely Parker, published his work on Iroquois culture and the religion of Handsome Lake. This publication marks the beginning of anthropological studies of native religions. In 1879, Major John Wesley Powell became the first director of the Bureau of American Ethnology (BAE). As a dedicated evolutionist interested in native languages, Powell promoted the study of native culture, religion, and mythology as remnants of a more "barbaric" age whose survival was threatened by the Indian Removal Act (1830) and the so-called "decline" of native life in the face of the aggressive settlement of the west. Powell, influenced by Morgan's evolutionary scheme – savagery–barbarism–civilization – wrote concerning Indian mythology of North America that "all these tribes are found in the higher stages of barbarism" (Hultkrantz, 1983: 9). While not all those who published in the BAE Annual Reports and Bulletins shared this perspective, many did, and most saw traditional native culture (and religion) as "survivals" from an age now past or fading. This attitude continued well into the mid-twentieth century. Yet much of the BAE's published work represents the most detailed and specific information now available for nineteenth- and early twentieth-century native religions. Many of these volumes contain a wealth of details on native religious practice and ceremonies, though with a frequent lack of attention to the native epistemologies that underpinned ceremonial actions. More problematically, these volumes often recorded native religions as "in decline" and refused to view processes of historical adaptation as viable expressions of positive change in native religions.

James Mooney's work (1900) on the Ghost Dance, recently rereleased, deserves special mention as it includes within it the first attempt to describe Native American religions in historical terms (1991: 662–792). Mooney traces the history of Native American religious movements, most motivated by attempts to sustain or reclaim traditional native religious values and practices. Mooney no longer restricted native religions to static, local "traditional" paradigms disconnected from historical processes of interaction and development. He wrote on Neolin (*ca.* 1764) and the Delaware

Prophet movement, Tenskwatawa the Kispoko-Shawnee prophet (*ca.* 1820), Kenekuk (*ca.* 1840) the Kickapoo religious leader, Tavibo and the 1870 dreamer dance movement of the Northwest, and the associated movements of the Wanapam religious leader Smohalla (*ca.* 1880), and the Shaker religious movement led by John and Mary Slocum (Squaxin, *ca.* 1880s). These foreground an extensive treatment of Wovoka (Jack Wilson, d. 1932), the Paiute Ghost Dance leader, and of the beliefs, practices, songs, and history of the Ghost Dance movement, including the tragic killing of over 300 Lakota at Wounded Knee (1890). Most of these leaders have been subjects of more recent scholarship (Edmunds, 1983; Herring, 1988; Ruby, 1989; Ruby and Brown, 1996), but there are few overviews of the entire history of the movements they led (Irwin, 1996/7).

Unfortunately, many early anthropologists and folklorists ignored Mooney's attempt to give historical depth to native religious cultures. Many BAE ethnographies isolated native cultures in a past that was seen as no longer viable in a Christian-scientific present. While native peoples might interact and modestly influence each other, core cultural practices were bracketed by an idea of "tradition" thoroughly isolated from contemporary adaptations of inherited beliefs or practices. Ethnographers valued "old ways" while ignoring adaptation, survival, and the reconstitution of native thought and action in a world destroyed by settlement, genocide, and restriction to reservations. In this context, "religion" was "traditional religion" – that is, religion unaffected by modern (or even Christian) influences. This bracketing out of more recent influences gives these works a static quality that contributes to a continuing tendency among many non-native scholars to over-value the past and to devalue the present as less meaningful in terms of religious beliefs or practices.

Similarly, anthropologists and folklorists rarely showed native religions as playing a central or critical role in determining social action or in motivating cultural behavior. They had little or no training in comparative religions, knew nothing about the study and history of other world religions and, in compensation, tended to develop religious theories in complete isolation from the larger discourses within the academic study of religion. In many ways, the latter was a reaction to a fervent missionary presence that continued to attack native religions as pagan and barbarous. Some BAE publications managed to avoid the extremes of either denouncing native religions as pagan superstitions or of ignoring and minimalizing them. Alice Fletcher, for example, working with both James Murie (Pawnee, d. 1921) and Francis La Flesche (Omaha, d. 1932), produced very credible works on both Pawnee (22nd Annual Report, 1904) and Omaha religion (27th Annual Report, 1906). Native author Francis La Flesche wrote many articles on Omaha, Osage, and other native religions. John Hewitt (Tuscarora, d. 1937), working with linguist Erminnie Smith, wrote on Iroquois language and cosmology (21st, 1903, and 43rd Annual Report, 1908). Edward Goodbird (Hidatsa, d. 1938) published with G. L. Wilson his life story (1914) with many details on Hidatsa religion, and Arthur Parker (Seneca ethnologist, d. 1955) published the "Code of Handsome Lake" (1912).

Under the influence of Franz Boas, anthropologists wrote many monographs and articles on native culture and religion. While the theoretical impact of Boas on anthropology was significant, his contribution was slight in the area of religion. Boas typically saw religion as a minor area of concern and as more or less a by-product of other social processes (Hultkrantz, 1983: 18). His interest, and those of his many students, was on the overall "culture pattern" and on a "historical method" of determining the influence of adjoining native cultures. While he collected useful linguistic texts, his concern lay in dissemination and amalgamation of culture traits, not in the integrative, explanatory, or classificatory functions of religious beliefs. Subsequently, many of Boas's students, while stressing the importance of fieldwork and text collection, tended to minimize the importance of native religions. For example, Boas's 1930 treatment of Kwakiutl religion, written with the help of George Hunt (Kwakiutl) whom Boas does not credit, is strictly linguistic and shows little sensitivity toward the more cohesive functions of religion. Nevertheless, many of the native texts gathered by Boas and his students represent primary linguistic sources for the study of nineteenth- and early twentieth-century native religion.

Emerging anthropological theory contributed strongly to a disjunction between non-native and native perceptions of religion. First, anthropologists applied evolutionary theories which placed native religion and culture on the lower stratum of development. Secondly, they marginalized the role of native religions in indigenous social life. In general, throughout this period, native religions were seen as peripheral to Euro-American interests, which turned on the theoretical construction of cultural categories and various analytic schemes. Commonly anthropologists, folklorists, and religionists treated native religion as "superstition" and as wholly secondary to analytic theories that gave precedence to social-cultural influences based largely in non-native behavioral models. This was a direct inheritance of earlier views of European and later American "social scientists" who simply assumed the superiority of their own culture and intellectual worldview. Scientific rationalism continued this displacement of religion from the center of native life, focusing primarily on structural and functional ideas often alien to native religious values.

While anthropologists described many rituals and ceremonies during this period, they displayed an obvious lack of attention to or understanding of the underlying native epistemologies that sustained the ceremonies. Robert Lowie, for example, collected detailed information on Absalooke (Crow) religion but saw such religion as reducible to a "religious thrill" that motivated ritual behavior – an idea utterly at odds with Crow explanations (Fitzgerald, 1994). Paul Radin collected many texts in Winnebago, including a biography of Winnebago peyotist Sam Blowsnake (*ca.* 1926), but thought of the trickster figure as reflecting a "non-descript person obsessed by hunger and … sexuality" (Radin, 1956: 165). Clark Wissler, working with Blackfeet native D. C. Duvall, recorded religious beliefs, dreams, and stories but few explanations, being primarily interested in material culture. On the other hand, Wissler also supported Pawnee ethnologist James Murie in his recording of Pawnee ceremonies and their many complex bundle rites. Working with Lakota religionist George Sword, Thomas Tyon, and other Lakota, James R. Walker (b. 1849) recorded valuable beliefs but also constructed his own version of Lakota myth using ideas borrowed from Greek classical mythology. Frank Linderman (*ca.* 1930s) published on the life of Crow leader Plenty Coups and Crow medicine woman Pretty Shield but recorded religious beliefs in a fragmentary and disjointed fashion. Some co-produced work stands out, for example Frank Speck's 1931 work with Delaware Big House leader Witapanoxwe and his 1949 work with Cayuga-Oneida ethnologist Alexander General on the mid-winter rites of the Cayuga.

During this same period many native authors published works relevant to the study of native religions, independent of anthropology. Many of these works have been overlooked and ignored by mainstream non-native academics. Delaware author Richard Adams (*ca.* 1910) published several works on Delaware religion reflecting contemporary attitudes toward religion. Wahpeton-Mdewakanton Dakota author Charles Eastman (*ca.* 1910) wrote many books, several relevant to religious studies. Eastman criticized non-native writers for denouncing native religions or reducing them to parodies of actual native religious life. He also supported the idea of assimilation into mainstream American life and sentimentalized the past (Warrior, 1995). Eastman represents the inner tensions between being both Native and Christian, and he sought to epitomize native religions insofar as they contributed a positive view of native peoples (Treat, 1996). Anishinaabe author Gerald Vizenor (1994) calls Eastman a "warrior of survivance" who sought to overcome the tragedy of Wounded Knee (where he helped treat the wounded) by remembering native traditions in a more positive light. Brulé writer and religionist Luther Standing Bear (d. 1939) also wrote several works related to Lakota religion, as did Yankton ethnologist Ella Deloria (d. 1971) who published a collection of Dakota texts (*ca.* 1933) and a fictive biography of a traditional female Lakota life. Osage writer and ethnologist John Joseph Mathews (d. 1979) also contributed to this growing literature on the boundaries between native and non-native values and perspectives in the struggle for authentic self-representation (Warrior, 1995).

Comparative History of Native Religions

The next phase of the study of native religions, beginning in the mid-1920s, built on ethnology already collected and moved toward works that attempted to compare local traditions and to identify shared religious practices. Edward Curtis's (1907–30) twenty-volume ethnographic and photographic survey, for example, contains sections on native religion for every community he visited. Such writings also integrated an increasingly ethnohistorical perspective into the study of specific communities. During this period, some authors began to incorporate historical perspectives into descriptive ethnographies by identifying specific, historically identifiable "religious movements." Leslie Spier (*ca.* 1930), building on Mooney, wrote on Klamath Ghost Dance and on the historical development of the "prophet dance" in the Northwest. John R. Swanton wrote on Creek Indian religion by collecting a multitude of historical writings to produce a synthetic overview of Indians of the southeast United States. Charles Hudson (*ca.* 1976), building on Swanton, later produced a more analytic work on "southeast" Indians. These works show a new methodological drive to assemble a wide variety of written texts from the earliest period to the present. These texts then served as resources for a categorical analysis of native religions in geographic areas said to share "cultural traits."

These works are significantly limited, however, by the tendency to conflate (or "essentialize") various ethnic groups and to draw sweeping generalizations which, once again, turn local historical practices into abstract intellectual idealizations. A more significant synthesis is found in James Howard's (1968) publications on pre-contact religion and the "southeast ceremonial complex" – a construct based in the marriage of archaeology and historical ethnography. Contemporary works in this direction are found in Galloway (1989). Ruth Benedict's (1923) writing on the "guardian spirit complex" throughout North America is a classic example of comparative trait analysis, with sweeping conclusions that turn the non-native construct of "guardian spirit" into a highly dislocated abstract idea. In her work on "patterns of culture" she further attempted a comparative analysis by distinguishing between the individualistic "Dionysian" Plains religions and the communal "Apollonian" Pueblo religions, further conflating the individual groups by a delimiting construct based in "culture areas." Benedict's work shows the influence of mid-twentieth-century "personality and culture" behavioralism. It also sought to explain native cultural differences by applying comparative models from an ancient "classical" past (Greece). Such "differences" reduce native behavior to remote and archaic norms and thereby reinforce an understanding of native peoples as idealized types in contrast to the complexity, diversity, and differences found in contemporary native communities.

A more useful early comparative study on the topic of "shamanism" is Willard Park's research with the Paviotso. Park gives simple but useful definitions of a "shaman" as one who has "direct relationships with spirits ... and acquires supernatural power through direct personal experience." Shamans stand in contrast to priests who are ritual experts, even though Park notes an overlap between the two (Park, 1975: 10). Frank Speck, A. Irving Hallowell, and Edgar Siskin all contributed to discussions on types of native healers and "conjurers" – a dismissive term used well into the twentieth century that masks many native linguistic distinctions and terms. The construct of "shaman" is itself problematic, stemming as it does from the Evenki-Tungus peoples of central Siberia. Mircea Eliade's (1964) comparative work on shamanism further obscures the role of religious specialists in native communities while making seriously mistaken observations for North America. Every native community had its own systems of classification based in native lexicons that have continued into the present, often undergoing revision and reclassification. More contemporary treatments of the subject are found in John Grim (1983) and Åke Hultkrantz (1992).

By mid-century, many scholars combined fieldwork and archival research. William H. Gilbert's history of Cherokee society and religion was based on archival research using the Payne-Butrick manuscripts in the Newberry Library. Alfred W. Bowers's (*ca.* 1950s) many publications on Mandan and on Hidatsa social and ceremonial organization are excellent compilations of existing historical resources, fieldwork, and appreciation for the central role of religion in native life, as are Father John Cooper's (*ca.* 1950s) writings on A'ani/Gros Ventres religion. While based on native narratives and long-term relationships with native practitioners, all these works tend to ignore contemporary problems of adaptation and change, particularly the impact of Christianity. Native religions are given a fuller explication in these works but they tend to divorce narratives of the "old ways" from current struggles, often by the same practitioners, to adapt to cultural changes that had profound impact on religious identity.

Consider, on the other hand, San Juan anthropologist Alfonso Ortiz, who has written an excellent native-oriented work on Tewa religion, *The Tewa World* (1969), that shows how important it is to explicate the full epistemology that underlies the practice and worldview of Pueblo religion and how the impact of Spanish culture and Christian missionization changed (and did not change) Pueblo culture. Ortiz's work stands out as a unique native view that thoroughly confirms the sophistication and complexity of Pueblo religious beliefs. The writing on the Plains Sun Dance is equally revealing. The Sun Dance tradition was early recorded among the Arapaho (G. A. Dorsey), the Crow (Lowie), the Blackfeet (McClintock and Wissler), and the Oglala (Walker). This early research was synthesized by Spier (*ca.* 1921) in terms of diffusion and trait distribution. But these works record little of what motivates or gives meaning or explanation to the ceremony as a religious activity (Hultkrantz, 1983: 55). Even though the Sun Dance was suppressed by the Bureau of Indian Affairs, practices continued and resurfaced in the 1970s, giving birth to more Sun Dance literature among the Ute (Jorgensen), the Cheyenne (Powell), the Shoshone-Crow (Voget, 1984), and the Lakota (Holler, 1995). Native Lakota Sun Dance and religious leaders like Black Elk (d. 1950), John Fire Lame Deer (d. 1976), Frank Fools Crow (d. 1989), and Leonard Crow Dog, as well as Crow Sun Dance leader John Trehero (d. 1985) and Tom Yellowtail, all have co-produced biographies critical to the study of northern Plains Sun Dance traditions. The Sun Dance tradition has increasingly become the source of a resurgent pan-Indian expression of native religious identity that has been adopted by some native groups for whom it was formerly marginal or non-existent. Many native practitioners from northern Plains communities in which the Sun Dance is central regard this popularization with great skepticism. The underlying tensions revolve around issues of religious solidarity, strategies of spiritual affirmation, and historical changes, all frequently in conflict with "traditionalized" views of local native religious practice.

Another thematic area is the study of the peyote movement and its development in the Native American Church (NAC) after 1918. Unfortunately most of this literature takes a view of peyote as a "hallucinogen" and thereby diminishes the native religious explanations for its use as a spiritually empowering sacrament. Rationalist descriptions of the practice as producing "hallucinations" is part of the ongoing denial of native religious beliefs and values. Associating peyote with "drugs" is a falsification of the religious motives and native epistemologies that regard peyote as a sacred substance that gives visionary power and guiding insight to sincere practitioners. Many peyotists have been persecuted for following their religion and NAC has waged a long battle to gain recognition and protection for the sacramental use of peyote. Some peyote rites are non-Christian, others are extensively Christian, and some combine varying degrees of both. The literature is fairly extensive and begins with Weston La Barre's original study of the "peyote cult." Other primary studies include works by J. S. Slotkin, David Aberle, Omer Stuart, Paul Steinmetz, and peyote roadmen (leaders) Sylvester Brito and Leonard Crow Dog; there is also an excellent collection of articles edited by Huston Smith and Reuben Snake (Snake and Smith, 1996). This last is particularly valuable as it is the only work to give extensive materials from actual peyote practitioners as well as clear descriptions of the rites recorded by lifelong peyote roadmen. In 1994, Public Law 103-344 made the transportation and use of peyote "for traditional ceremonial purposes" legal – a law as yet untested in the courts (Weaver, 1998: 227).

In 1953 Åke Hultkrantz published his comparative study of the concept of the "soul" among native peoples of North America, and Joseph Epes Brown published his account of the "seven rites" of Oglala holyman Black Elk. These two publications mark the entry of comparative religious scholars into the field of native religious studies. Brown (1964) also published a short monograph which attempts to summarize a universally shared epistemology for native religions, based primarily on his research among the Lakota. This work applies ideas drawn from other world religions and seeks to integrate native traditions into a global perspective. In 1979, Hultkrantz published a one-volume survey of native religions based on thematic topics that cut across many diverse communities. Hultkrantz maintains that the category of the "supernatural" is intrinsic to native thought, an idea now repudiated by many contemporary authors who contend that native religionists never saw a distinction between the natural and the supernatural, a distinction imported from Christian metaphysics. Western metaphysical ideas and intellectual categories too easily obscure the cultural differences that mark the unique and special features of a native religion so valued by its practitioners.

Native religionists have rarely displayed interest in articulating abstract theories of religion that would show the commonality of practices and beliefs with other native communities. Instead, the emphasis has fallen on the unique, linguistically centered, specific cultural practices and oral traditions that best characterize the primary spiritual values of a particular community. For example, George Horse Capture (A'ani/Gros Ventre) published *The Seven Visions of Bull Lodge* (1980) as a remarkable first-hand native account of A'ani vision quest rites and the inner life and values of a renowned A'ani healer and pipe-keeper. Such a narrative highlights the unique features of A'ani spiritual life as invested in specific rites or objects owned by clan or family line and shows how the vision experience is part of the development of an A'ani religious worldview. Another example is Percy Bullchild's (1985) account of Blackfeet oral traditions on creation and religious beliefs. Bullchild's book has been largely ignored by non-native scholars because it clearly shows syncretic influences; yet it is exactly these influences that are shaping much of contemporary native religious development.

Many scholarly works have tended to ignore contemporary changes and the complex intersection of native identities within a variety of social and religious contexts, each of which acts to shape religious attitudes. Authors have continued to bracket out problems of native Christianity, pan-Indian influences, and political actions that address problems of religious oppression. Issues of historical transformation or the importance of new social contexts (urban life, non-native education, popular American culture, etc.) on native religions are often ignored and thus perpetuate a tendency to think of native religions as most authentic in the past. While some studies show a genuine respect for native religions in an ideal sense, they often fail to ground observations in the complexity of changing religious traditions and the dislocation of native religious practices in a largely hostile or manipulative non-native cultural climate.

In contrast to the comparative perspective, in 1972 Yankton author Vine Deloria Jr. published his famous work, *God Is Red: A Native View of Religion* (reissued, 1994). This work marks a transition to contemporary scholarship on native religions. Its two central concerns are the failure of the U.S. government to protect native religions from secular encroachments and the misinterpretation of native religions by non-native scholars. Deloria is concerned with the many false stereotypes of "Indians" that continue to undermine the authentic concerns of native religionists. He is particularly critical of the absence of native voices in the representation of native religion. Popular press and movie images create a fictive version of native peoples completely alienated from the reality of contemporary reservation and urban life. Reservation religion is not locked into a static past but is undergoing constant change and transformation, as it always has; native religions are not static, but dynamic and constantly engaged in processes of renewal. Deloria also heavily critiques Christianity and Christian missionaries for their aggressive rejection of native religious perspectives.

Deloria sees native traditions as locally grounded in geographic, spatial narratives that fully empower local ritual and religious behaviors. These traditions cannot be easily transported to other localities, much less stripped of their local narrative and symbolic orientations. Rather than chronological history, the geographic locale is primary in establishing the basic patterns of religious action. The focal point of the geographic orientation is found in the local symbolizations of nature in aesthetic religious forms: in a Sun Dance lodge, in sandpaintings, in pipe bowls, medicine bundles, or ceremonial dress. Further, these forms are tied to dreams, visions, and a variety of cognitive states unique to advanced practitioners of the religions. Native religious epistemology is grounded in a synthesis mediated between ritual practices in local, highly revered settings and a receptivity to natural forms imbued with power that exceeds normal human awareness. Such mediation by religious leaders is regarded as entirely natural and a function of proper relations between human beings and all species that inhabit a local area. The disbelief of outsiders is basically irrelevant; what is crucial is kinship, communal relationships, and responsibilities within the religious group. Communal membership is an irreducible fact; religious knowledge is particular, local, and culturally distinctive to the community. These issues set the stage for contemporary writings on native religions (Irwin, 1998).

Contemporary Native Spirituality

In 1982, David Carrasco published *Quetzalcoatl and the Irony of Empire*, which is strongly influenced by Mircea Eliade and the comparative study of world religions. Despite its comparative focus, *Quetzalcoatl* is a ground-breaking book, for it takes a central figure from Aztec life and surveys its historical development under the impact of colonization. Carrasco shows clearly how Aztec religious thinking and ceremony is embedded in its own unique epistemology, symbolism, and iconography, and how the Aztec and Nahua sought to reinterpret Aztec religion in the post-conquest period. The following year, Christopher Vecsey published his work on Ojibwa religion, showing how the impact of Christian missionization resulted in the formation of new religious identity among present-day Ojibwas. William McLoughlin (1984) likewise published a compendium on the Cherokee Ghost Dance as an extensive historical overview of the multiple interfaces between "traditional" and native Christianity. In 1985, Clifford Trazfer edited a special volume of essays on Native American prophets (*American Indian Quarterly*, vol. 9(3)) that is a pointedly historical survey of outstanding native religious leaders placed directly in the dynamics of cultural conflict, each struggling to redefine religious traditions in the light of missionization and the impact of new religious ideas.

These volumes clearly illustrate a new concern for more historically grounded approaches to the study of native religions, approaches that emphasize the dynamics of historical confrontation between native and Euro-American cultures. In that process, the struggle to redefine native religions is clearly linked to strategies of survival initiated by native religious leaders. Within their respective communities, these leaders sought to institute changes that would preserve core native values while also accommodating, in various degrees, government policies aimed at suppressing native religion. Raymond DeMallie and Douglas Parks's (1987) edited volume is another landmark, representing a synthesis of native and non-native authors writing on past and present Lakota religious traditions, as well as contemporary issues such as peyote, Christianity, and women's role in native religion. This volume elucidates the value of a dialogical approach to the study of native religions, gathering together a variety of voices and refusing to privilege non-native scholars over native practitioners. Other works that show an increased sensitivity to the historical transformations of native religions are Frisbie (1987) on Navajo sacred bundle traditions, Gruzinski (1989) on the "god-man" of the Mexican highlands, Ruby (1989) on the northwest coast religious leaders Smohalla and Skolaskin, Joel Martin (1991) writing on southeastern native religions as motivating the 1814 Muskogee revolt, Armin Geertz's (1994) work on Hopi prophecy, and Howard Harrod's (1995) excellent work on Mandan-Hidatsa religion. All of these emphasize the historical conditions of colonialism and they see strategies of cultural innovation and resistance as an intrinsic feature of native religious adaptation in the face of religious bias and the politics of oppression.

If such works reflect a new scholarly sensitivity toward issues of history and power, the last decades have not been without other problems. We have seen, for example, the publication of popular works by native authors who claim to represent the spiritual traditions of their community but who are viewed by many other natives as "plastic Indians" – a term applied to natives and non-natives who claim falsely to represent native religions. Mohawk scholar Christopher Jocks (in Irwin, 1997) has discussed this "spirituality for sale" that continues to disempower the sacred character of native religions. The late twentieth-century popularization and imitation of native religions after centuries of oppression and denial is another stage in the unequal power relations between native communities and dominant cultural production. Can spirituality be transformed into saleable products disconnected from communal approval and the sanction of community religious leaders? In fact, many works claiming to "represent" native religious culture have been repudiated by the natal communities of the authors. Many non-native persons have also made doubtful claims to native identity in order to capitalize on the current popularity of native religions.

In the 1990s there also appeared a significant number of co-authored works related to individuals who are either practitioners or leaders in native religions. These are usually written by a non-native and issued under both names. Many have been autobiographical. Richard Erdoes's life of peyote road woman Mary Crow Dog, for example, tells the story of the second standoff at Wounded Knee (1973) and its connection to Lakota spirituality. Erdoes also co-authored two other works: one with Lakota pipe-carrier Archie Fire Lame Deer and another with peyote roadman and healer Leonard Crow Dog. These books have been criticized for their failure to clarify the role of the non-native author. Such books tend as well to locate their subjects at the heart of native spirituality, when the authors may be marginal within their native communities.

An example of a co-authored work which gives a lucid portrait of one woman's struggle to maintain her native religious identity in a radically changing world is Miwok-Pomo author Greg Sarris's (1994) excellent book on dreamer, healer, and renowned basket-maker Mabel McKay. This is a fine example of new directions in co-authored ethnography. Sarris writes in a dialogical, narrative mode that captures the relationship between himself and Mabel McKay in a poignant way. There is no attempt to summarize or essentialize either her personhood or her life, nor to make any claims about her role within the Pomo community other than the respect she received from many of her contemporaries. It is a story of a remarkable woman whose spiritual influence on those around her was a lasting testimony to her Pomo spiritual heritage (Irwin, 1998). Michael Fitzgerald (1994) also published a sincere, readable, co-authored work on the life of Crow Sun Dance leader Tom Yellowtail. Mark St. Pierre and his Oglala wife, Tilda Long Soldier, published an excellent, semi-biographical account (1994) of female religious traditions among the Lakota, gathered with the help of many women who contributed to the volume. Arlene Hirschfelder and Paulette Molin (1992), Duane Champagne (1994), and Fred Hoxie (1996) have all produced encyclopedic works that contribute to the study of native religions.

The increasing presence of Indian people in the field has created more opportunities for dialog, while bringing native issues to the fore. In 1995, for example, Robert Allen Warrior published his important *Tribal Secrets: Recovering American Indian Intellectual Traditions*. This book deals not only with native religions and literature, but also with the question of Native American "intellectual sovereignty" – a theme that is primary in the reconstitution of the study of native religious traditions. Warrior traces the intellectual history of native thought through three periods: first, the post-Wounded Knee (1890) massacre and the formation of goals of assimilation and partnership with friends-of-Indians groups by isolated native intellectuals; second, the struggle between reservation religionists who resisted assimilation and the romanticizing of the native past; and third, the rebirth of native identity led by Vine Deloria Jr. and the emergence of confrontational ideologies and an aggressive local nationalism no longer willing to accept mainstream definitions of native religion or identity. What do native people say about native identity, religion, and culture? This question cannot be answered in the abstract but must engage complexity, diversity, difference, tension, ambiguity, and multivocal perspectives irreducible to simple "universals." Warrior discusses Deloria's writings on religion in depth, emphasizing that "traditions" are guidelines to an experiential, process-oriented way of living. He raises important methodological questions for the future study of native religions by recognizing the intellectual rights of native scholars to define and articulate unique perspectives on the role and significance of religion in shaping native intellectual history.

Contemporary works on Native American religions have continued to emphasize the priority of native voices in determining authentic representation. Native authors George Tinker (1993) and James Treat (1996) have written critical works on native Christian identity and the problematic history of missionization. Assimilation of native peoples within Christianity is by no means an annulment of native identity; in fact, ideas within these volumes suggest that native people continue to value being native in ways that enhance and give new meaning to the Christian experience (Weaver, 1998). Another concern is the ongoing issue of religious freedom that has become paramount in determining local development of native religions; many court cases have marked the history of religious oppression, including issues of burial rights and the control of native dead (Vecsey, 1993; Wunder, 1996).

Changes in the study of native religions through the 1990s have contributed to the emergence of a more dialogical approach, one that views native peoples as engaged in creative processes of spiritual transformation that value the past while also seeking indigenous self-definition in the present (Thorpe, 1996). Further, studies in native religions are no longer isolated from the contemporary dynamics of political action and the search for a more just and equitable recognition at the state and federal level of government (Wunder, 1996). Native religions cannot be bracketed in the historical past nor regarded as illegitimate simply because they do not conform to non-native romanticized stereotypes of artificially constructed bygone eras. Contemporary native concerns challenge scholars to disassemble the essentialized views of past native cultures in order to see them as highly complex, living traditions fully engaged with problems of religious identity that intersect many diverse areas of social life. Native religions cannot be reduced to "traditional" reservation ceremonies, but must include the urban, Western educational politics of identity negotiation, gender diversity, and cultural boundaries that are constantly shifting and realigning. Future research will necessarily address gender concerns, religious political rights, control of burial remains, emergent theologies of native Christianity, and a thorough revisioning of native religious history. Clearly, the study of native religion is undergoing a major transformation, and it is equally clear that future work will require an increasing emphasis on the dynamics of historical transformation, as well as a recognition of native intellectual rights in the ongoing interpretation of native religions (Irwin, 1997, 1998).

BIBLIOGRAPHY

Benedict, Ruth F. 1923: *The Concept of the Guardian Spirit in North America* (Menasha, WI: American Anthropological Association).

Brown, J. E. 1964/1982: *The Spiritual Legacy of the American Indian* (Pendel Hill, 1964; New York: Crossroads Press, 1982).

Bullchild, P. 1985: *The Sun Came Down: The History of the World as My Blackfeet Elders Told It* (San Francisco: Harper & Row).

Carrasco, D. 1982: *Quetzalcoatl and the Irony of Empire: Myths and Prophecies in the Aztec Tradition* (Chicago: University of Chicago Press).

Cervantes, F. 1994: *The Devil in the New World: The Impact of Diabolism in New Spain* (New Haven: Yale University Press).

Champagne, D. (ed.) 1994: *Native America: Portrait of the Peoples* (Detroit: Visible Ink Press).

Deloria, V., Jr. 1972/1994: *God Is Red: A Native View of Religion* (New York, 1972; Golden, CO: North American Press, 1994).

DeMallie, R. (ed.) 1984: *The Sixth Grandfather: Black Elk's Teachings Given to John G. Neihardt* (Lincoln: University of Nebraska Press).

DeMallie, R. and D. Parks (eds.) 1987: *Sioux Indian Religion: Tradition and Innovation* (Norman: University of Oklahoma Press).

Edmunds, R. D. 1983: *The Shawnee Prophet* (Lincoln: University of Nebraska Press).

Eliade, Mircea 1964: *Shamanism: Archaic Techniques of Ecstasy* (Princeton, NJ: Princeton University Press).

Farella, J. R. 1984: *The Main Stalk: A Synthesis of Navajo Philosophy* (Tucson: University of Arizona Press).

Fitzgerald, M. O. 1994: *Yellowtail, Crow Medicine Man and Sun Dance Chief: An Autobiography* (Norman: University of Oklahoma Press).

Frisbie, Charlotte J. 1987: *Navajo Medicine Bundles or Jish: Acquisition, Transmission, and Disposition in the Past and Present* (Albuquerque: University of New Mexico Press).

Galloway, P. (ed.) 1989: *The Southeast Ceremonial Complex: Artifacts and Analysis* (Lincoln: University of Nebraska Press).

Geertz, A. 1994: *The Invention of Prophecy: Continuity and Meaning in Hopi Indian Religion* (Berkeley: University of California Press).

Gill, S. 1981: "Sacred Words: A Study of Navajo Religion and Prayer," *Contributions to Intercultural & Comparative Studies*, 4 (New York: Greenwood Press).

Grim, J. 1983: *The Shaman: Patterns of Religious Healing among the Ojibway Indians* (Norman: University of Oklahoma Press).

Gruzinski, S. 1989: *Man-Gods in the Mexican Highlands: Indian Power and Colonial Society, 1520–1800* (Stanford: Stanford University Press).

Harrod, H. L. 1995: *Becoming and Remaining a People: Native American Religions on the Northern Plains* (Tucson: University of Arizona Press).

Herring, J. B. 1988: *Kenekuk, the Kickapoo Prophet* (Lawrence: University of Kansas Press).

Hirschfelder, A. and P. Molin (eds.) 1992: *The Encyclopedia of Native American Religions: An Introduction* (New York: Facts on File).

Holler, C. 1995: *Black Elk's Religion: The Sun Dance and Lakota Catholicism* (Syracuse: Syracuse University Press).

Howard, James A. 1968: "The Southeast Ceremonial Complex and Its Interpretation," *Memoirs of the Missouri Archaeological Society*, no. 6, pp. 1–164.

Hoxie, F. E. 1996: *Encyclopedia of North American Indians* (Boston: Houghton Mifflin Company).

Hultkrantz, Å. 1979: *The Religions of the American Indian* (Berkeley: University of California Press).

Hultkrantz, Å. 1983: *The Study of American Indian Religions* (New York: Crossroad Publishing Company).

Hultkrantz, Åke 1992: *Shamanic Healing and Ritual Drama: Health and Medicine in Native North American Religious Traditions* (New York: Crossroad Press).

Irwin, L. (ed.) 1996/7: *To Hear the Eagles Cry: Contemporary Themes in Native American Spirituality, American Indian Quarterly* (Special Issue), vols. 20(3 & 4) (1996), 21(1) (1997).

Irwin, L. 1997: "Freedom, Law and Prophecy: A Brief History of Native American Religious Resistance," *American Indian Quarterly* 21(1): 35–56.

Irwin, L. 1998: "Native Voices in the Teaching of Native Religions," *Critical Review of Books in Religion* 11: 97–147.

Lewis, T. 1990: *The Medicine Men: Oglala Sioux Ceremony and Healing* (Lincoln: University of Nebraska Press).

Martin, Joel W. 1991: *Sacred Revolt: The Muskogees' Struggle for a New World* (Boston: Beacon Press).

McLoughlin, W. G. 1984: *The Cherokee Ghost Dance: Essays on the Southeastern Indians, 1789–1818* (Macon, GA: Mercer University Press).

Mooney, J. 1991: *The Ghost-Dance Religion and the Sioux Outbreak of 1890* (BAE 14th Annual Report, 1893) (Lincoln: University of Nebraska Press).

Noel, D. 1997: *The Soul of Shamanism: Western Fantasies, Imaginal Realities* (New York: Continuum Press).

Ortiz, A. 1969: *The Tewa World: Space, Time, Being and Becoming in a Pueblo Society* (Chicago: University of Chicago Press).

Park, W. 1938/1975: *Shamanism in Western North America: A Study of Cultural Relations* (1938) (New York: Cooper Square Publishers, 1975).

Powers, W. 1986: *Sacred Language: The Nature of Supernatural Discourse in Lakota* (Norman: University of Oklahoma Press).

Radin, P. 1956: *The Trickster: A Study in American Indian Mythology* (New York: Bell Publishers).

Rice, J. 1991: *Black Elk's Story: Distinguishing its Lakota Purpose* (Albuquerque: University of New Mexico Press).

Ruby, R. H. 1989: *Dreamer-Prophets of the Columbia Plateau: Smohalla and Skolaskin* (Norman: University of Oklahoma Press).

Ruby, R. and J. A. Brown 1996: *John Slocum and the Indian Shaker Church* (Norman: University of Oklahoma Press).

Sarris, G. 1994: *Mabel McKay: Weaving the Dream* (Berkeley: University of California Press).

Schlesier, K. H. 1987: *The Wolves of Heaven: Cheyenne Shamanism, Ceremonies, and Prehistoric Origins* (Norman: University of Oklahoma Press).

Snake, Reuben and Huston Smith 1996: *One Nation under God: The Triumph of the Native American Church* (Santa Fe, NM: Clear Light Publishers).

St. Pierre, M. and T. Long Soldier 1994: *Walking in the Sacred Manner: Healers, Dreamers, and Pipe Carriers – Medicine Women of the Plains* (New York: Simon & Schuster).

Thorpe, D. (ed.) 1996: *People of the Seventh Fire: Returning to the Lifeways of Native America* (Ithaca: The Akwe:Kon Press, Cornell University American Indian Program).

Tinker, G. E. 1993: *Missionary Conquest: The Gospel and Native American Cultural Genocide* (Minneapolis: Fortress Press).

Treat, J. (ed.) 1996: *Native and Christian: Indigenous Voices on Religious Identity in the United States and Canada* (New York: Routledge).

Vecsey, C. 1983: *Traditional Ojibwa Religion and its Historical Changes* (Philadelphia: American Philosophical Society).

Vecsey, C. 1993: *Handbook of American Indian Religious Freedom* (New York: Crossroads Press).

Vizenor, G. 1994: *Manifest Manners: Postindian Warriors of Survivance* (Hanover, NH: University Press of New England).

Voget, F. W. 1984: *The Shoshoni-Crow Sundance* (Norman: University of Oklahoma Press).

Warrior, R. A. 1995: *Tribal Secrets: Recovering American Indian Intellectual Traditions* (Minneapolis: University of Minnesota Press).

Weaver, Jace (ed.) 1998: *Native American Religious Identity: Unforgotten Gods* (Maryknoll, NY: Orbis Books).

Wunder, J. R. (ed.) 1996: *Native American Cultural and Religious Freedom* (New York: Garland Publishing).

7

Indians and Christianity

WILLARD HUGHES ROLLINGS

In this matter of change, people are like the grass. They toss and sway and even seem to flow before the forces that make for change, as grass bows to the wind. But the rude force moves on, people are found still rooted in the soil of the past. Again, like grass, people produce seed; and the seed will fly with the wind and finding a friendly soil and climate, start a new generation. To change, yet to remain steadfast – that would seem to be the need of all living things. (McNickle and Fey, 1970: 3)

Continuity and change characterizes the history of all peoples, but the European invasion of North America was so rapid and devastating that compromise and continuity take on a richer and more complex meaning in the history of North American Indians. The words of Salish Métis author and activist D'Arcy McNickle and Harold Fey provide an appropriate metaphor for Indian–European relations. Native Americans were the grass while Europeans constituted the "rude force" moving across North America, bringing enormous, incomprehensible changes for the native inhabitants. Europeans introduced new technologies, weapons, plants, animals, and pathogens to the Indians' North American world. They also carried their culture, their ways of looking at and making sense of the world, and their way of assessing the value and spiritual position of people, places, and things. A fundamental component of their culture was, of course, their religion – Christianity.

The principal colonizers of North America – Spanish, French, and English – were all Christians. Although they adhered to a variety of faiths, ranging from the Roman Catholicism of the Spanish to the Puritan Protestantism of England, they shared a European-centered, Christian worldview. Their religious practices varied in detail and emphasis, but all worshiped a single, patriarchal God who had created the universe and all animate and inanimate substances within it. The Europeans' confidence in the exclusive truthfulness of Christianity played varying roles in their efforts at conquest and colonization. For some, spreading Christianity among the heathen was integral to those efforts, while for others conversion of the Indians was secondary to goals of dispossession, domination, or exploitation.

Despite enormous variations in beliefs and practices, all Native American religions recognize humans as but one of many spiritual creatures inhabiting the universe. Humans maintained their place within the universe through acts of reciprocity toward one another. Religious ritual was the means by which they expressed reciprocity, thereby helping maintain the required balance in the universe. In contrast, Christian colonizers sought to fulfill the biblical injunction to "be fruitful and multiply, and fill the earth, and subdue it; and rule over the fish of the sea and over the birds of the sky and over the cattle and over all the earth, and over every creeping thing that creeps on the earth" (Genesis 1:28).

This belief in the supremacy of humankind over nature, so firmly embedded in Judeo-Christian culture, was entirely alien to the native peoples of North America. They could not conceive of a world solely dominated by humans. Native American theology/mythology is replete with animals playing critical interactive roles with humans. This was in striking contrast to Judeo-Christian traditions in which animals play minor roles at best. In the entire Bible there are only two instances of animals speaking to humans. In Genesis 3:1–4, the serpent, an agent of evil, persuades Eve to violate Yahweh's instructions, and in Numbers 22:28–30, Balaam's ass protests his beating on Balaam's journey to Moab.

Europeans believed that, among the earth's myriad life forms, only humans possessed spiritual value, and they arranged their cosmos according to a hierarchical construct in which their God reigned supreme over the world he had created. Humankind existed somewhere below God and the angels but definitely above the natural world. In Genesis 2:19, God gives Adam (mankind) the power to name all of the animals. Also in Genesis (chapters 7–8), Noah chooses the animals to save from the great flood. Christians were culturally conditioned to seize, control, and consume nature. With an ethos centered on social, natural, and supernatural worlds shaped by reciprocity, Indians never understood European ideologies of human domination and nature's submission.

Through critical assessment of historical documents, scholars can often determine the chief goals of the Europeans and the ways in which Christian beliefs and practices, including missionary efforts, reinforced those goals. Such inquiries are possible not simply because Europeans were literate and left written records of their thoughts and deeds. They are also facilitated by the fact that most scholars are themselves products of a European Judeo-Christian heritage that helps them to grasp the actions and motives of past Christian figures, even at a cultural and historical distance.

This intellectual and cultural affinity simply does not exist for Euro-American scholars looking at Native American spirituality. Indians practiced a wide variety of religions. In North America at the beginning of the European invasion there were more than twenty million Native Americans, speaking in over four hundred languages and dialects, worshipping countless deities in immeasurable ways, all generally incomprehensible to the Europeans. Those diverse beliefs and practices would be recorded in writing largely by outsiders – literate Europeans and Euro-Americans who understood little if anything about native spirituality. More often than not, they produced their accounts long after their Indian subjects had been attacked by catastrophic epidemics that had killed up to 90 percent of native populations. In oral cultures where religious traditions and beliefs were preserved in the minds of practitioners, pandemic diseases destroyed indigenous libraries and seminaries. Under such conditions, only the fragments of religions survived.

Despite the variety and diversity of experiences they depict, most studies of Indians and Christianity have been until recently simple historical narratives couched in Christian theology. Early studies of Christian missionaries, for example, depicted them in heartrending narratives as individuals who made great sacrifices to go among the uncivilized heathen to bring them the word and way of life of the one true, Christian, God. Individuals such as fathers Eusebio Kino and Junipero Serra were frontier saints who wanted only to save the heathen of Sonora and Alta California. French Jesuits like Claude Allouez and Jacques Marquette endured the harsh Canadian winters to save Indian souls for Christ. John Eliot and Thomas Mayhew were tireless saints who sought to bring the good word to the Natives of New England. Narcissa and Marcus Whitman were self-sacrificing martyrs murdered by the bloodthirsty savages they were trying to save. Such early studies were framed by Euro-Americans as contests and conflicts between the well-intentioned Christian believers and the non-believing Indians.

These sympathetic interpretations of missionaries were followed by reactive studies, often focused on the cultural destruction conducted by the Christians. In these counter-narratives, Serra and Kino were genocidal emissaries of the Spanish Empire, while Allouez and Marquette were intent on paving the way for French domination. By a similar logic, Eliot and Mayhew appeared as handmaidens of Puritan hegemony, and the Whitmans as agents of the aggressive and racist United States.

The more sophisticated studies that emerged during the late twentieth century reveal a history of Indians and Christianity that is more complex than stories of either cultural survival or destruction. This more recent scholarship has uncovered a diverse and complex set of processes that varied according to time, people, and circumstances. The older and simpler interpretations of attack and resistance have been replaced by a richer set of questions about Native Americans and their myriad responses to Christianity. Such responses run a long gamut, from utter rejection to complete acceptance of Christianity. In between lies a complex terrain of religious and cultural exchange: traditionalist–Christian factionalism, the simultaneous practice of Christianity and traditional religions, be it overt or covert, conversion with aggressive proselytizing, partial conversion, pretended conversion, the creation of Native–Christian hybrid faiths. And while these analytical categories are at best very rough, each needs to be considered when undertaking a case study. (In addition to works cited elsewhere in this chapter, see Taylor, 1996; Radding, 1998; Weber, 1989; Bowden, 1981.)

One of the most destructive effects of proselytization was factionalism. Seventeenth-century French Jesuits went among the Natives of southeastern Canada and recorded vivid, detailed accounts of Native American life in their *Jesuit Relations* (Morrison, 1986). These accounts grudgingly conceded that the Indians had religion, but labeled it primitive and savage. While rejecting the very premises of native theology, the Jesuits used indigenous religions as foundations upon which to teach the Indians Christianity. In this respect they were diametrically opposed to both Protestant and Franciscan Catholic practices. Nevertheless, Jesuits initially insisted that indigenous practices were sinful and had to be repudiated by Indian Christians. The combination of different Christian belief systems and still vital native spiritualities often led to factional disputes. Among the Huron (Wendat) in the 1640s, for example, Christian–traditionalist factionalism resulted in a bitter internal division that left them vulnerable to defeat and dispersal by the Iroquois in 1648–9 (Trigger, 1976; Salisbury, 1992).

Recent scholars on French colonialism in North America tend to dismiss earlier generalizations that characterized the process in terms of either conflict or Indian acculturation to French culture and values. Instead they analyze the complex and changing interaction between the French and the Indians. They reveal the outright rejection of the missionary message by some and the willingness of others to incorporate Christian symbols and rituals into their traditional practices. These scholars examine the impact of disease on the conversion process and the role of the expanding French trade in creating physical and spiritual change among the Natives (Trigger, 1976; Jaenen, 1976; Delâge, 1993; Tanner, 1987; Bonvillain, 1986; Dickason, 1984; White, 1991).

Following the demise of the Huron Confederacy, for example, the Jesuits modified their tactics, enabling some Indians to accept some elements of the new faith and incorporate them into their spiritual lives. In 1667 Jesuit Father Claude Allouez visited the Mesquakie Indians. Recently defeated by the Seneca, the Mesquakie were willing to listen to the new shaman and add his manitou (spiritual power) to their pantheon. They allowed Allouez to erect a large cross in a village, and in 1671 when village warriors prepared to attack the Sioux they painted their bodies, shields, and weapons with crosses. The attack was successful but when Mesquakie warriors, again adorned with Christian symbols, launched another attack a year later, they were defeated. Upon returning home, they tore down the cross and refused to permit Allouez to return to the village (Miller, 1955: 251; White, 1991: 7–10).

Other Indians likewise first read aspects of European culture in terms of their own cosmologies. When English Puritans arrived in New England, they wanted to convert the natives there to Christianity. But Puritanism, with its emphasis on the role of the individual outside the context of the group, and its beliefs in heaven and hell, sin, guilt, and domination, was so alien to the Massachusett, Pawtucket, and Wampanoag peoples that they simply ignored it at first (Salisbury, 1982: 38, 56). At the same time, however, these and other New England Native Americans were interested in English material goods. Believing that the metal tools, cooking pots, axes, cloth, and guns possessed spiritual qualities, the natives read European technology as a manifestation of manitou. The new goods were evidence of the newcomers' manitou, and the New England Natives believed that they could secure that power within their own spiritual frameworks. In order to acquire the new items, they exchanged gifts with the Europeans in a manner consistent with their spiritual system of reciprocity. (Salisbury, 1982: 37–9; Salisbury, 1999: 114–15). The physical act of exchanging material goods was familiar to both peoples, but its meaning was very different for each. Europeans thought they were engaged in a simple economic activity, while the Natives believed they were engaged in a religious ritual, exchanging gifts to acquire spiritual power and cement friendships. Ironically, they were both correct.

Working in eastern Massachusetts Bay, Puritan missionary John Eliot met with limited success among Massachusett and Pawtucket Indians – those most devastated by epidemics and in closest proximity to English settlements. In 1644 Massachusetts Bay created a "praying town," Natick, for its first "praying Indians." There Eliot set about to complete the process of converting the residents to Christianity, whereby they could transcend their "savage" state and become "civilized" humans. Colony law forbid the praying Indians to practice their own religion, and compelled them to observe the Christian Sabbath and attend Puritan church services. Eliot, other Englishmen, and, eventually, native preachers and teachers provided religious instruction. By 1674, Eliot had created 14 praying towns, forerunners of modern reservations, whose inhabitants would be kept separate from both hostile settlers and non-Christian Indians. He attempted to persuade praying Indians to change their appearance, dress, food, polity, and economics to become civilized Christian Indians (Salisbury, 1974; Axtell, 1985).

Meanwhile, other Puritan missionaries enjoyed some success among those Indians most isolated from contact with both colonists and other Native peoples. In particular, the Wampanoag of Martha's Vineyard incorporated Christian missions into their spiritual and social lives. Living on an island and outnumbering the Puritans, they escaped the pressing Puritan demands for land that their fellow Wampanoag and other Indians confronted on the mainland. When a new round of epidemics struck in the mid-1640s, and their shamans were unable to stop the death and suffering, several island leaders professed the new faith. But the Wampanoag did not simply "convert." They created their own Wampanoag Christianity which served their needs and yet was consistent with their cultural values and practices. Native ministers assumed traditional shamanistic functions and redesigned the ritual calendar to include both Christian holidays and Wampanoag ceremonial occasions that entailed feasting, singing, and dancing (Ronda, 1980).

Immediately prior to King Philip's War (1675–6), missionaries sought to expand their activities as the English moved into previously uncolonized Indian homelands. Missionaries were one of the sources of Native resentment that fueled the war. After the bloodshed of the war and the defeat of the Natives, Puritan conversion efforts declined (Salisbury, 1974; Axtell, 1985: 179–217, 243–7; Lepore, 1998). The hatred engendered by the violence of the war convinced most colonists that the Indians were mere savages incapable or unworthy of conversion. Missionaries and some others continued to work with natives, but made little headway. One reason for this was that while a minority of former praying Indians continued to identify as Christians, few new converts were forthcoming until the advent of the Great Awakening revivals of the 1740s.

Whereas missionaries were never the direct targets of violence in New England, Pueblo Indians in the Upper Rio Grande Valley directed their ire particularly at Franciscan missionaries living among them during the Pueblo Revolt (1680). When Don Juan Oñate arrived with Franciscan missionaries to found the colony of New Mexico in 1598, the Pueblo people were uninterested in Catholic Christianity. Over the next several decades, however, some Pueblos began to welcome the Christian God into their cosmology. There were enough superficial similarities between the beliefs and practices of Roman Catholics and Pueblos that many natives could reconcile the two. Each had a distinct priesthood whose members employed ritual chanting in their religious ceremonies. Each had elaborate altars at the sites of their rituals, and had complex religious calendars. Roman Catholic saints whose past acts had raised them to sainthood were comparable to the Pueblo mythic figures who had accomplished great deeds and were remembered and revered by the Pueblo. Both were remembered and honored by the performance of dance, drama, and ritual (Bowden, 1975).

But the two worldviews directly conflicted in more fundamental ways. The Franciscans preached that the followers of Christ decided as individuals to become Christians, thus separating themselves markedly from non-Christians. Pueblos, on the other hand, believed that humans were inextricably connected to their communities and that everyone was certain to reach the other world after death, regardless of his or her earthly behavior. As one Pueblo Indian described it, "to die in a pueblo is not to become dead but to return to the only real life there is; one changes houses and rejoins the ancestors" (Bowden, 1975: 224). Whereas the Spanish spoke of a world controlled by a single heavenly creator who directed his people to exploit the resources of the earth, the Pueblo believed that all patterns of life had been created when they emerged from beneath the earth. They believed that the patterns were eternal and needed to remain synchronized with natural rhythms. The earth was sacred, and the Pueblo people were only one of the many types of beings who inhabited it. The eternal rhythms of this holy place were maintained by orderly and sacred behavior, unlike for the Spanish who insisted only on the conquest and domination of nature and humanity (Bowden, 1975).

The Franciscan priests, however, vigorously repudiated the Pueblos' religion as pagan and attacked their sacred sites and objects. Raiding the sacred chambers (kivas) in the pueblos, they destroyed Kachina masks, altars, prayer sticks, and sacred rattles – all material manifestations of the Pueblo religion. These attacks forced the Pueblo to make terrible choices. They could either abandon their way of life and become Spanish peasants, adopt some of the superficial and visible features of Catholicism while continuing to practice their old religion in secret, or drive the Spanish away.

The Pueblo peoples of New Mexico did all three. Some avoided the missions altogether, but many more continued to practice their faith secretly while attending church, seemingly converted to Catholicism. But as Franciscan attacks on the kivas and religious leaders intensified during the 1670s, the compromises became too great for the Pueblos. A combination of drought and disease (evidence that Catholicism was having destructive rather than beneficial effects), along with brutal suppression of their traditional religion, led the Pueblo to stage the singlemost successful rebellion against Europeans anywhere in colonial North America. Led by a San Juan Tewa shaman, Popé, the Pueblos destroyed the missions, burning the statues of saints and other Catholic icons, and washed themselves with yucca suds to cleanse themselves of Christianity (Bowden, 1975; Weber, 1992; Knaut, 1995).

By 1696, the Spanish had regained control of most of the region. Their control was now tempered, however, by the Pueblo successes of 1680. The Spanish compromised on matters of religion. In the words of Borderlands scholar John Kessell

(1989), the Spanish of New Mexico became religious pragmatists and accepted a synthesis of Roman Catholicism and Pueblo religions. The Franciscans returned to Indian communities, but they accepted a limited participation in Pueblo life. Franciscan priests performed baptisms, officiated at marriages, and supervised burials, but they no longer interfered – at least overtly – with traditional religious practice.

The Pueblos of the Rio Grande Valley also compromised. They allowed the Catholics to build churches in their Pueblos, they allowed priests to celebrate mass in the churches, and they accepted baptism. They modified Catholicism to fit within the existing systems of their religion. They observed Christmas and Easter, but with little emphasis on the birth, death, and resurrection of Jesus. Instead Pueblo people used the Christian holidays as opportunities to hold traditional dances and make offerings to elders. Pueblo people attended mass but refused to go to confession; perhaps to avoid giving up spiritual secrets; or simply because of an inability to reconcile Catholic notions of sin and priestly absolution with their Pueblo worldview (Spicer, 1972: 506–8).

Like the Pueblos, other Indians violently rejected the imposition of Christianity and its accompanying cultural demands. Living in an isolated and remote region to the west of the Rio Grande Valley, the Hopi also rose up and attacked the Franciscan missions in 1680. Thereafter they practiced their traditional faith undisturbed until the late nineteenth century when Christian missionaries, aided by the federal government, moved onto their lands. The Ipai and Tipai people of southern California violently rejected Franciscan attempts to convert them and repeatedly attacked the mission of San Diego de Alcala to drive the Spanish from their lands. In 1847 the Cayuse Indians, ravaged by epidemic disease and angered by the brutal behavior of Protestant missionaries Marcus and Narcissa Whitman, killed them and destroyed their mission (Hackett, 1942; Knaut, 1995; Castillo, 1989: 385–91; Jeffrey, 1991: 205–19).

When traditional ways became irrelevant to new realities, some Indians created new faiths that incorporated familiar symbols and ritual with new ideologies. Sometimes these were combined in a syncretic faith; in other cases natives followed two religions simultaneously. Jesuit missionaries working in Baja California and Northern Sonora during the seventeenth and eighteenth centuries experienced such syncretism when they combined small native communities into larger villages, and tried to change the Indians' lives and to convert them to Catholicism. The most energetic and "successful" of these Jesuits was Father Eusebio Kino. In 1696 he established a series of mission churches among the Tohono O'Odham rancherias in the Santa Cruz Valley in present-day southern Arizona and Sonora. The Jesuits learned the languages of the people, and allowed the Indians to retain the form and substance of their traditional religions. Sonoran Indians incorporated their traditional ceremonies within Roman Catholic ritual. The Opatas, Mayo, and Yaqui created their own unique Christianity (Spicer, 1972: 505).

After Spain expelled the Jesuits from its American colonies in 1767, the native people took over and operated the mission churches by themselves. The Yaqui continue to celebrate Christian holidays filled with indigenous symbolism and ritual. Holy Week, the last week of Lent, is still celebrated with a combination of Jesuit Catholicism and indigenous Yaqui symbol and ceremony. During the week, they re-enact the arrest, trial and execution of Jesus. Within the Christian pageant, *chapeyeka*, coyote dancers of the Yaqui military society, capture Jesus for the evil Pharisees (*fariseos*) and guard him until Holy Saturday (The Gloria), the day before Easter Sunday. In a long series of rituals throughout that holy day, evil is defeated by small boys dressed as angels, along with *pascolas,* Yaqui fiesta dancers, and deer dancers performing to insure and sanction the defeat of evil and the resurrection of Jesus (Painter, 1986: 241, 471–93).

In Alta (Upper) California, where Spanish missionary activity began in 1769, the encounters between Franciscans and Native Americans have produced debates and controversies among non-academics and scholars alike. The early twentieth-century scholarship of Herbert Bolton and his later follower, John Francis Bannon, insisted that the Franciscans, led by Father Junipero Serra, tried to save the Indians and improve their lives (Bolton, 1917; Bannon, 1964). The missionaries immediately set about to transform them into Spanish peasants tied to the life and land of the Franciscan missions. The "mission myth," in which selfless padres taught lazy, naked Indians discipline, religion, and the virtues of hard work, survives even today in California tourist literature (Pohlmann, 1974: 1).

Later scholarship challenged the vision of devoted priests working among docile mission Indians. Cahuilla scholar Rupert Costo and Jeanette Henry Costo (1987) depicted the Franciscans as ruthless agents of genocide, intent on destroying the California Indians' culture while exploiting their land and labor. According to this "genocidal myth," the Franciscans put the mission Indians to work as slave labor at the missions and oppressed them solely for the profit of the Roman Catholic Church.

The reality of the California missions system and the nature of Christian conversion lies somewhere in between these two myths. The more recent work of Steven Hackel (1997) provides a clearer understanding of California mission realities. Hackel argues that mission Indians maintained their communities and successfully resisted many of the Franciscans' demands and pressures to abandon traditional culture despite the multiple upheavals and abuses arising from Spanish colonization.

Although the mission Indians were forced to convert, there is little evidence that the conversions were genuine spiritual conversions. The history of Alta California reveals that once the missions were secularized the Indians dispersed. When the missions were transferred to private hands after Mexican independence, few Indians remained at the churches. While some remained on the ranchos created from the former missions, the rancheros were more interested in cattle than the spiritual welfare of their workers. Those who left the missions often moved to the coastal communities where they found work created by the opening of the Mexican trade frontiers.

Following the annexation of California and the gold rush of the late 1840s, California Indians confronted Anglo-American violence as well as the end of the economies that had supported them. Large numbers moved to Euro-American communities and, in the face of massive mortality and exploitation, they created hybrid traditional–Catholic cultures and communities (Hurtado, 1988: 126, 201, 210; Phillips, 1993: 100; Haas, 1995: 91–3, 105).

With the gradual defeat of a region's tribes by the combination of warfare, disease, and alcohol, white Americans evicted Indians and seized their lands, or confined them on small reservations where missionaries and teachers forced an alien culture upon them. Following colonial precedents, and despite constitutional injunctions to separate church and state, Christian missionaries served as agents of the federal government. In 1819 the United States Congress passed the Indian Civilization Act to provide funding for "the civilization of the Indian tribes" (Prucha, 1984, vol. 1: 181). The agents for this civilization program were Christian missionaries who eagerly accepted federal funding and established missions through Indian country. Throughout the nineteenth century both Protestant and Roman Catholic missionaries worked with the federal government's support to facilitate the assimilation of Native Americans into American society. An integral part of this assimilation process was the elimination of native culture and the conversion of Indians to Christianity. Indian children were placed in reservation schools and educated in white cultural ways, and some were taken forcibly from their families and educated in distant boarding schools where Christianity was an integral part of the curriculum (see Lomawaima, this volume).

Thousands of Native Americans converted to Christianity during the eighteenth and nineteenth centuries. While the nature of their conversions remains unclear, ample evidence exists to show that many Indians exchanged their traditional spiritual beliefs for Christian ones. Individuals like Samson Occam (Mohegan), William Apess (Pequot), George Copway (Anishinabe), Kanchi (Choctaw), Electra Quinney (Housatannuck), Daniel Adams (Mohawk), Willie Folsom (Choctaw), and Duane Porter (Anishinabe) became preachers who spread a message of Indian Christianity among their people and to sympathetic white audiences.

As early as the Great Awakening of the mid-eighteenth century, some Native Americans were separating the message of Christianity from the behavior of its European and Euro-American messengers. Samson Occam, a Mohegan who converted to Christianity at the age of sixteen, became a teacher and minister in Native communities in New York and southern New England. He became an ardent spokesman for Native Americans and preached Christian sermons against the corrupting influences that had arrived with the whites, alcohol in particular. After raising money for the creation of an Indian school (Dartmouth College), Occam discovered that the school was intended primarily for white students. Convinced that Native Americans would never find justice in white society, he gathered together a group of southern New England Indians from several tribes to move west, away from whites. At the invitation of the Oneida, they created the Brotherton community on that tribe's land in upstate New York. The Brotherton community later accompanied the Oneida in a move further west to Wisconsin, again attempting to practice Indian Christianity away from the corrupting influence of whites (Strong, 1996; Blodget, 1935).

A later New England Indian convert was even more blatant in his condemnation of white Christians. William Apess, a Pequot born in Massachusetts, worked to convert Native Americans to Christianity to improve the quality of their lives. He believed that Jesus was the means to recapture harmony, and preached a religion that promised hope within a familiar framework (Noley, 1998). Apess accepted the Christian notion of sin, but differed with Euro-American Christians on its true nature. He believed that sin was the disruption of a harmonious life and creators of the disharmony were the true sinners. Attracted to the egalitarian nature of the Methodist faith he became a minister in 1829, and used the pulpit to advocate Indian rights. As an itinerant Methodist minister he became the leading Native American advocate of the era, writing several books denouncing mistreatment of New England Indians in both the past and the present and leading a revolt of Mashpee Wampanoag against the authority of whites who controlled their community and church (O'Connell, 1992).

George Copway (Kahgegagahbowh), a Rice Lake Ojibwa, grew up amid the chaos generated by tens of thousands of whites bringing disease and alcohol to western Ontario during the 1820s. In his autobiography, *Life, History and Travels* (1847), Copway reveals that dreams and visions, important elements of traditional Ojibwa religion, convinced him to accept Christianity (Brown and Brightman, 1988). He was specifically attracted to Methodism because of its egalitarian ideology and its strong stand against alcohol. Copway's conversion seemed complete, for throughout his book *Running Sketches of Men and Places* (1851), he rejects the Native spiritual ethos in favor of a white Christian one, as revealed in passages such as, "Man is the one for whom this world is made." Copway pursued an active and successful life as a Methodist missionary and author (Smith, 1996: 134–5).

In other instances, however, Indians actively and simultaneously practiced two cross-cultural religions. The renowned Oglala Black Elk was a Lakota *wicasa wakan* (Holy Man) who was simultaneously a Roman Catholic catechist working to establish Catholicism among his people. Although converting to Catholicism in 1917, Black Elk continued to play an active role in traditional Lakota Sun Dances. Both Clyde Holler (1995) and Michael Steltenkamp (1993) have carefully examined Black Elk's theological bi-culturalism. While neither of these scholars has solved the mystery of such spiritual duality, they provide insights into the act of simultaneous worship in multiple cultures.

For many Indian peoples, the impact of colonization was so severe that neither traditional religion nor Christianity sufficed to explain in meaningful terms the new realities of their lives. Virgin soil epidemics killed as many as 80 percent of the Native Americans of North America (Crosby, 1976; see also Thornton, this volume). The impact of such losses is incomprehensible today. The European presence dramatically changed Native American economies. European traders used metal goods, guns, and liquor to lure Indians into the larger capitalist market economy then emerging around the Atlantic. As a result, many Native American communities became dependent on their trade with Europeans. Quite frequently, after exhausting local game resources they needed to obtain European trade goods, Indians began invading their neighbors' territories. The result was frequent and deadly warfare that brought further losses of population and devastation of communities. Whenever traders added alcohol to their inventories, Native American societies were torn still further apart. In many instances when neither traditional religion nor Christianity were able to stop the strife, strain, death, and overall sense of spiritual crisis caused by European invasions, Indian people created new religions to revitalize their lives and cultures. While striking departures from both traditional beliefs and Christianity, the new movements usually reflected the influences of both.

A common feature of most of the revitalization movements was the presence of a messianic figure who, divinely inspired, directed the transformation of Native peoples' lives and cultures. In the eighteenth century, Neolin, also known as the Delaware Prophet, advocated a new way of life and a rejection of European culture for his people and others in the Ohio Valley–Great Lakes region. In the early nineteenth century Handsome Lake created a new religious foundation for the Seneca. At about the same time Tenskwatawa, also known as "the Shawnee Prophet," sought to unite the tribes of the Old Northwest under his pan-Indian revitalization faith. In the late nineteenth century, the Paiute prophet Wovoka shared his Ghost Dance movement with Indians from throughout the West. Both Handsome Lake and Wovoka revered Jesus as a major prophet, and Tenskwatawa conducted ceremonies that were influenced by the Catholic communion service (Dowd, 1992b; Wallace, 1969; Moses, 1985; Mooney, 1896; Hittman, 1997).

Religious revitalization movements were frequently associated with political movements that sought to maintain native control of Indian cultures and lands. When Neolin preached spiritual renewal and pan-Indianism, he was joined in 1763 by the Ottawa political leader, Pontiac, in resisting British takeover of the Ohio–Great Lakes forts recently abandoned by the French. Tenskwatawa, the Shawnee Prophet, preached nativism and worked alongside his brother Tecumseh to unite tribes to defend their lands against the United States' efforts to dominate the Old Northwest. While the political dimension of revitalization movements was critical, scholars have frequently placed an undue emphasis on it. Recent work by Dowd (1992b) and Martin (1991) has redirected attention to the spiritual foundations of such movements.

Whereas early revitalization movements usually became pan-Indian because their prophets crossed tribal boundaries, the Ghost Dance of the late 1880s saw a reversal of this pattern. Indian people from all directions traveled, usually by train, to visit Wovoka at his home at Walker Lake in Nevada. There they heard him describe his prophecy of a return of all the dead ancestors and animals, a stark contrast to the death and destruction that nearly all western Indians had experienced during the preceding generation or two. Visitors from Indian Territory took the message of Wovoka's prophecy home and practiced it according to his dictums, but without disrupting familiar cultural patterns. Others adapted it to their own circumstances and cultural contexts. After visiting Wovoka, for example, Teton Lakota leaders Short Bull and Kicking Bear took the Ghost Dance back to Pine Ridge where tensions festered between the people and nearby army troops.

The results of the revitalization movements varied according to time and circumstance. That of Neolin and Pontiac largely failed in the face of British determination to establish firm control of the Ohio–Great Lakes region. Its legacy remained, however, to inspire Tenskwatawa's movement. The latter was crushed by the violence of the War of 1812. Wovoka's Ghost Dance ended for the Lakota on a cold morning in December 1890 when army troops massacred Big Foot's dancers at Wounded Knee. Although the Ghost Dance continued peacefully in Indian Territory for several years, it eventually faded away when life there failed to improve (Stewart, 1987: 222). On the other hand, Handsome Lake's prescription for a new way of life revived the

Iroquois, and his code is still followed by many Seneca, Cayuga, Oneida, Tuscarora, Onondoga, and Mohawk people in New York and Ontario (Wallace, 1969).

The peoples in Indian Territory who abandoned the Ghost Dance turned soon thereafter to another new hybrid faith that centered around collective use of the hallucinogenic drug, peyote. The chaos and crowding of native peoples and cultures in Indian Territory, combined with continued invasions by whites, perpetuated a sense of spiritual crisis. The ritual use of peyote as a means of undertaking a spiritual passage came to Indian Territory in the late nineteenth century from Mexico and South Texas. Many Indians who took peyote in Indian Territory and elsewhere did so to fulfill the quest for visions that was central to the spiritual traditions of many Indian cultures. At the same time, however, Jesus often figured in their visions.

Peyote was, and remains to this day, a controversial substance. Some whites and Indians believed it was a harmful drug and should be outlawed, while others claimed that it was, like the wine used in Christian communion ceremonies, a sacred sacrament. In an attempt to protect their religion and legitimize the use of peyote, followers organized the Native American Church in 1918 (Stewart, 1987: 222). The federal government did not halt the Native American Church in Indian Territory because its faith was sufficiently couched in Christian terms, was sufficiently discrete in its practice, and because its followers included the more politically cooperative Indians of the region. Nevertheless, Native American Church members fought almost continuously through the twentieth century to practice their religion. The most recent blow was *Employment Division, Department of Human Resources of Oregon, et al., v. Alfred L. Smith, et al.* (1990), in which the Supreme Court ruled that states can deny employment to Native American Church members on the grounds that peyote is an illicit drug, not a holy sacrament.

While some Indians turned to the Native American Church at the turn of the twentieth century, others, educated at Christian boarding schools, converted to Christianity as a means of bridging the gap between white and Native cultures. In the tradition of Occam, Apess, and Copway some became outspoken advocates of Indian rights. The most notable among these converts was Charles Eastman (Ohiyesa), a Wahpeton and Mdewakanton Dakota who had survived the Santee Conflict of 1862. Educated at Dartmouth, he received a medical degree from Boston College. He was the first doctor to tend to the survivors of the carnage of the Wounded Knee Massacre, and its horrors shaped his life.

Like Apess and others, Eastman accepted Christ's truths, but was repelled by the divergence of American society from Christ's teaching. He attempted to serve as a cultural translator to explain Indian spirituality to Euro-Americans. He explained his purpose at the beginning of his *Soul of the Indian* (1911): "I have attempted to paint the religious life of the typical American Indian as it was before he knew the white man. I have long wished to do this, because I cannot find that it has ever been seriously, adequately, and sincerely done. The religion of the Indian is the last thing about him that the man of another race will ever understand" (Eastman, 1971: ix–x).

Eastman's mission has continued beyond his time, as Native American spiritual leaders and politically minded writers have confronted Indian realities and Christian theology. During the New Deal, Commissioner of Indian Affairs John Collier strengthened the status of native religions while ending the use of missionaries in boarding and day schools. The democratic rhetoric of World War II and, later, the Civil Rights movement of the 1960s sparked a cultural resurgence that inspired many Natives to seize greater control of their lives and property. Some Native Americans now direct Christian churches while others have abandoned Christianity and revived older religious practices with traditional songs, rites, practices, and beliefs (Deloria, 1994: 4–24; Nagel, 1996).

Native Americans have recently begun to talk and write openly about their religions in public. While there is now a great deal of discussion about all facets of Native religion and the place of traditional spirituality in today's world, the significant feature of the recent flowering is the fact that Native Americans have seized control of the dialogue. They are directing the discourse (Irwin, this volume).

Some Native Americans insist that Native American religions and Christianity are inherently incompatible and that no compromise between them is possible. Vine Deloria Jr., the son of an Episcopal priest and a graduate of a Christian seminary, wrote a powerful challenge to Native Christians with his *God Is Red* (1972). Deloria argues that because of fundamental differences between their worldviews, Native Americans and Europeans can never reconcile their religious beliefs. He asserts that Native Americans base their religions on place and largely ignore time, while those of European heritage focus on time and discount place. Western Christians focus on history to prove the validity of Jesus' message. They attempt to place Jesus in historical time and claim that his legitimacy rests on the historical proof of his existence. Indians, on the other hand, pay attention to the message and do not try to prove the historical existence of the messenger. Lakota people are not concerned with White Buffalo Woman's exact place in history but rather with her message and its application to their present lives (Schultz and Tinker, 1996: 63). Native Americans' religious focus is on their communities in the present, and if their prayers and rituals work, that success in itself is sufficient evidence of their religion's validity. Deloria (1994: 103; 1999) claims that this focus represents something more than spiritual pragmatism, explaining that tribal ritual and ceremony are so integral to a community's very being that the facts about its origins in time are immaterial.

Deloria's arguments have triggered serious debate among Native Americans. While some agree completely with him, others insist that Native Americans can and continue to create meaningful religious compromises consistent with tradition and Christianity. Indian Christians maintain that they can remove Jesus and Christianity from the colonizers' hands altogether, accepting Christ's teachings and making Christianity theirs by placing Christ within a spatial context without reference to a historical one. They insist that it makes no difference whether Christ was in Galilee or Gallup, that his message is consistent with their traditional religions. While the debate is significant, the real value of the issues raised is the simple fact that they are being argued about by Native Americans.

James Treat, for example, has edited a collection of twenty-one essays by Indian Christian writers entitled *Native and Christian: Indigenous Voices on Religious Identity in the United States and Canada* (1996). His fine introduction focuses on contemporary Native Christian narrative discourse. The collection offers a wide range of essays on Native Christianity. George Tinker and Paul Schultz urge Indian Christians to begin the process of shifting the individualistic nature of Christianity to one of community. Robert Allen Warrior challenges Christian liberation theology, arguing that tribal peoples must carefully examine Christian theology before embracing it as a pattern for liberation. He reminds readers that the biblical story of Israel and Canaan legitimizes Israel's conquest of Canaan, whereas tribal peoples must identify with the indigenous people of Canaan. He points out that Yahweh commanded Israel to invade Canaan and smite the indigenous people and suggests that tribal peoples look elsewhere for justice and peace. Other contributions range from Sister Marie Therese Archambault's essay about the need to "de-evangelize" native people to Sister Juanita Little's discussion of the nature of her Indian Catholicism.

While these and other Native authors contribute to the development of a Native Christian discourse, others have rejected Christianity altogether or worked to develop an even broader view. Cherokee scholar Jace Weaver (1998) has edited a collection on contemporary Native American religious concerns, *Native American Religious Identity: Unforgotten Gods*. The readings reveal the diversity of religious experience and expression of Native peoples after 500 years of colonialism. It includes essays about traditional Native religions, Indian Christianity, and syncretic religions by Native writers such as Homer Noley Jr., Donald Grinde Jr., Tweedy Sombrero, Craig Womack, and Freda McDonald. Taken together, the seventeen essays demonstrate the diversity of experience and expression in Native American Christianity.

Since the mid-twentieth century, Native scholars have turned the discussion of Native Americans and Christianity on its head. Once controlled by non-Indian Christian theologians and the historians who followed them, the leading scholarship now comes from Native People, both Christian and non-Christian themselves. As historians, theologians, and autobiographers, Native authors are producing sharp, sophisticated scholarship on the nature of the interaction of Indians and Christianity. While scholars continue to struggle to make sense of the fragments of Indian visions and voices from the past, they need not struggle to understand the present. For Native Americans are writing and speaking, and all scholars have to do is pay attention.

BIBLIOGRAPHY

Axtell, James 1985: *The Invasion Within: The Contest of Cultures in Colonial North America* (New York: Oxford University Press).

Bannon, John Francis 1964: *Bolton and the Spanish Pioneers* (Norman: University of Oklahoma Press).

Blodget, Harold 1935: *Samson Occom* (Hanover: Dartmouth College Publications).

Bolton, Herbert E. 1917: "The Mission as a Frontier Institution in the Spanish-American Colonies," *American Historical Review* 23: 42–61.

Bolton, Herbert E. 1936: *Rim of Christendom: A Biography of Eusebio Francisco Kino, Pacific Coast Pioneer* (New York: Macmillan).

Bonvillain, Nancy 1986: "The Iroquois and the Jesuits: Strategies of Influence and Resistance," *American Indian Culture and Research Journal* 10: 29–42.

Bowden, Henry W. 1975: "Spanish Missions, Cultural Conflict, and the Pueblo Revolt of 1680," *Church History* 44: 217–28.

Bowden, Henry W. 1981: *American Indians and Christian Missions: Studies in Cultural Conflict*. Chicago History of American Religion Series (Chicago: University of Chicago Press).

Brown, Jennifer S. H. and Robert Brightman 1988: *"The Orders of the Dreamed": George Nelson of Cree and Northern Ojibwa Religion and Myth, 1823*. Manitoba Studies in Native History III (St. Paul: Minnesota Historical Society Press).

Castillo, Ed D. 1989: "The Native Response to the Colonization of Alta California," in David Hurst Thomas (ed.), *Columbian Consequences,* vol. 1: *Archaeological and Historical Perspectives on the Spanish Borderlands West* (Washington, D.C.: Smithsonian Institution Press), pp. 377–94.

Comaroff, Jean and John Comaroff 1991: *Of Revelation and Revolution: Christianity, Colonialism and Consciousness in South Africa* (Chicago: University of Chicago Press).

Costo, Rupert and Jeanette Henry Costo (eds.) 1987: *The Missions of California: A Legacy of Genocide* (San Francisco: Indian Historical Press).

Crais, Clifton C. 1992: *White Supremacy and Black Resistance in Pre-Industrial South Africa: The Making of the Colonial Order in the Eastern Cape, 1770–1865* (Cambridge: Cambridge University Press).

Crosby, Alfred 1976: "Virgin Soil Epidemics as a Factor in the Aboriginal Depopulation in America," *William and Mary Quarterly* 33: 289–99.

Delâge, Denys 1993: *Bitter Feast: Amerindians and Europeans in Northeastern North America, 1600–1664*, trans. Jane Brierley (Vancouver: University of British Columbia Press).

Deloria, Vine, Jr. 1994: *God Is Red: A Native View of Religion* (Golden: Fulcrum Publishing).

Deloria, Vine, Jr. 1999: *For This Land: Writings on Religion in America* (New York: Routledge).

Dickason, Olive Patricia 1984: *The Myth of the Savage and the Beginnings of French Colonialism in the Americas* (Edmonton: University of Alberta Press).

Dowd, Gregory E. 1992a: *A Spirited Resistance: The North American Indian Struggle for Unity, 1745–1815*. The Johns Hopkins University Studies in Historical and Political Series (Baltimore: Johns Hopkins University Press).

Dowd, Gregory E. 1992b: "Thinking and Believing: Nativism and Unity in the Ages of Pontiac and Tecumseh," *American Indian Quarterly* 16: 309–35.

Eastman, Charles 1971: *The Soul of the Indian* (Boston: Houghton Mifflin Co., 1911; New York: Johnson Reprint Corporation, 1971).

Haas, Lisbeth 1995: *Conquest and Historical Identities in California, 1769–1936* (Berkeley: University of California Press).

Hackel, Steven W. 1997: "The Staff of Leadership: Indian Authority in the Missions of Alta California," *William and Mary Quarterly* 54: 347–76.

Hackett, Charles W. (ed.) 1942: *Revolt of the Pueblo Indians of New Mexico and Otermín's Attempted Reconquest, 1680–1682*, 2 vols. Coronado Cuarto Centennial Publications, 1540–1940, vols. 8–9, George P. Hammond (gen. ed.) (Albuquerque: University of New Mexico Press).

Harrod, Howard L. 1971: *Mission among the Blackfeet* (Norman: University of Oklahoma Press).

Hittman, Michael 1997: *Wovoka and the Ghost Dance*, ed. Don Lynch (Lincoln: University of Nebraska Press).

Holler, Clyde 1984: "Black Elk's Relation to Christianity," *American Indian Quarterly* 8: 37–49.

Holler, Clyde 1995: *Black Elk's Religion: The Sun Dance and Lakota Catholicism* (Syracuse: Syracuse University Press).

Hurtado, Albert L. 1988: *Indian Survival on the California Frontier* (New Haven: Yale University Press).

Jaenen, Cornelius J. 1976: *Friend and Foe: Aspects of French–Amerindian Cultural Contact in the Sixteenth and Seventeenth Centuries* (New York: Columbia University Press).

Jeffrey, Julie Roy 1991: *Converting the West: A Biography of Narcissa Whitman* (Norman: University of Oklahoma Press).

Keller, Robert H. 1983: *American Protestantism and United States Indian Policy, 1869–82* (Lincoln: University of Nebraska Press).

Kessell, John L. 1989: "Spanish and Pueblos: From Crusading Intolerance to Pragmatic Accommodation," in David Hurst Thomas (ed.), *Columbian Consequences*, vol. 1: *Archaeological and Historical Perspectives on the Spanish Borderlands West* (Washington, D.C.: Smithsonian Institution Press), pp. 127–38.

Knaut, Andrew L. 1995: *The Pueblo Revolt of 1680: Conquest and Resistance in Seventeenth-Century New Mexico* (Norman: University of Oklahoma Press).

Lepore, Jill 1998: *The Name of War: King Philip's War and the Origins of American Identity* (New York: Knopf).

LiPuma, Edward 1998: "The Genesis of Maring Christianity: The First Quarter Century, 1955–1980," *Ethnohistory* 45: 621–55.

Martin, Joel W. 1991: *Sacred Revolt: The Muskogees' Struggle for a New World* (Boston: Beacon Press).

McNickle, D'Arcy and Harold E. Fey 1970: *Indians and Other Americans: Two Ways of Life Meet* (New York: Perennial Library).

Miller, Walter B. 1955: "Two Concepts of Authority," *American Anthropologist* 57: 271–89.

Mooney, James 1896: "The Ghost-Dance Religion and the Sioux Outbreak of 1890," in *Fourteenth Annual Report (Part 2) of the Bureau of Ethnology to the Smithsonian Institution, 1892–1893* (Washington, D.C.: Government Printing Office).

Morrison, Kenneth M. 1986: "Montagnais Missionization in Early New France: The Syncretic Imperative," *American Indian Culture and Research Journal* 10: 1–23.

Moses, L. G. 1985: "The Father Tells Me So! Wovoka: The Ghost Dance Prophet," *American Indian Quarterly* 9: 335–51.

Nagel, Joane 1996: *American Indian Ethnic Renewal: Red Power and the Resurgence of Identity and Culture* (Oxford: Oxford University Press).

Noley, Homer 1998: "The Interpreters," in Jace Weaver (ed.), *Native American Religious Identity: Unforgotten Gods* (New York: Orbis Books), pp. 57–8.

O'Connell, Barry (ed.) 1992: *On Our Ground: The Complete Writings of William Apess a Pequot* (Amherst: University of Massachusetts Press).

Ortiz, Alfonso 1969: *The Tewa World: Space, Time, Being and Becoming in a Pueblo Society* (Chicago: University of Chicago Press).

Painter, Muriel Thayer 1986: *With Good Heart: Yaqui Beliefs and Ceremonies in Pascua Village*, Edward Spicer and Wilma Kaemlin (eds.) (Tucson: University of Arizona Press).

Parsons, Elsie Clews 1996: *Pueblo Indian Religion*, 2 vols. (Lincoln: University of Nebraska Press).

Phillips, George Harwood 1993: *Indians and Intruders in Central California, 1769–1849* (Norman: University of Oklahoma Press).

Pohlmann, John Ogden 1974: "California's Mission Myth." Ph.D. dissertation, University of California, Los Angeles.

Prucha, Francis Paul 1962: *American Indian Policy in the Formative Years* (Cambridge, MA: Harvard University Press).

Prucha, Francis Paul 1976: *American Indian Policy in Crisis: Christian Reformers and the Indian, 1865–1900* (Norman: University of Oklahoma Press).

Prucha, Francis Paul 1984: *The Great Father: The United States Government and the American Indians,* 2 vols. (Lincoln: University of Nebraska Press).

Radding, Cynthia 1998: *Wandering Peoples: Colonialism, Ethnic Spaces, and Ecological Frontiers in Northwestern Mexico, 1700–1850* (Durham, NC: Duke University Press).

Ronda, James P. 1980: "Generations of Faith: The Christian Missions of Martha's Vineyard," *William and Mary Quarterly* 38: 369–94.

Salisbury, Neal 1974: "Red Puritans: The 'Praying Indians' of Massachusetts Bay and John Eliot," *William and Mary Quarterly* 38: 27–54.

Salisbury, Neal 1982: *Manitou and Providence: Indians, Europeans, and the Making of New England, 1500–1643* (Oxford: Oxford University Press).

Salisbury, Neal 1992: "Religious Encounters in a Colonial Context: New England and New France in the Seventeenth Century," *American Indian Quarterly* 16: 501–9.

Salisbury, Neal 1999: " 'I Loved the Place of My Dwelling': Puritan Missionaries and Native Americans in Seventeenth-Century New England," in Carla Gardina Pestana and Sharon V. Salinger (eds.), *Inequality in Early America* (Hanover, NH: University Press of New England), pp. 111–33.

Schultz, Paul and George Tinker 1996: "Rivers of Life: Native Spirituality for Native Churches," in James Treat (ed.), *Native and Christian: Indigenous Voices on Religious Identity in the United States and Canada* (New York: Routledge).

Smith, Donald 1996: "George Copway," in Frederick E. Hoxie (ed.), *Encyclopedia of North American Indians* (Boston: Houghton Mifflin Co.).

Spicer, Edward H. 1972: *Cycles of Conquest: The Impact of Spain, Mexico, and the United States on the Indians of the Southwest, 1533–1960* (Tucson: University of Arizona Press).

Steltenkamp, Michael F. 1993: *Black Elk: Holy Man of the Oglala* (Norman: University of Oklahoma Press).

Stewart, Omer 1987: *Peyote Religion: A History* (Norman: University of Oklahoma Press).

Strong, John A. 1996: "Samson Occom," in Frederick E. Hoxie (ed.), *Encyclopedia of North American Indians* (New York: Houghton Mifflin Co.), pp. 434–6.

Tanner, Helen Hornbeck 1987: *Atlas of Great Lakes Indian History* (Norman: University of Oklahoma Press, for the Newberry Library).

Taylor, William B. 1996: *Magistrates of the Sacred: Priests and Parishioners in Eighteenth-Century Mexico* (Stanford: Stanford University Press).

Treat, James (ed.) 1996: *Native and Christian: Indigenous Voices on Religious Identity in the United States and Canada* (New York: Routledge).

Trigger, Bruce G. 1976: *Children of Aataentsic: A History of the Huron People to 1660* (Montreal: McGill-Queen's University Press).

Wallace, Anthony F. C. 1956: "Revitalization Movements," *American Anthropologist* 58: 264–81.

Wallace, Anthony F. C. 1969: *The Death and Rebirth of the Seneca* (New York: Knopf).

Weaver, Jace (ed.) 1998: *Native American Religious Identity: Unforgotten Gods* (New York: Orbis Books).

Weber, David J. 1989: "Blood of Martyrs, Blood of Indians: Toward a More Balanced View of Spanish Missions in Seventeenth Century North America," in David Hurst Thomas (ed.), *Columbian Consequences*, vol. 2: *Archaeological and Historical Perspectives on the Spanish Borderlands East* (Washington, D.C.: Smithsonian Institution Press), pp. 429–48.

Weber, David 1992: *The Spanish Frontier in North America* (New Haven: Yale University Press).

White, Richard 1991: *The Middle Ground: Indians, Empires, and Republics in the Great Lakes Region, 1650–1815* (Cambridge: Cambridge University Press).

Wunder, John 1994: *"Retained by the People": A History of American Indians and the Bill of Rights* (Oxford: Oxford University Press).

8

Kinship, Family Kindreds, and Community

Jay Miller

Native peoples have always lived in mutually supportive communities whose members included diverse ranks and species. Communal ties exist at many different levels – immediate and extended families, "fictive" kin relations that make community members into family members, "made" kin relations with strangers, and a broad understanding of the relatedness of animals, plants, and landscapes (see Irwin, Kidwell, this volume). The nature of these relations has changed during the last 500 years, but kinship itself, with its ties, obligations, and sanctions, has continued to structure most – if not all – native societies. Likewise, as a critical part of social analysis, kinship has long been the focus of ethnographic study. Indeed, in many ways kinship studies have defined scholarship just as surely as kinship itself helps define Indian worlds.

Based on a cultural interpretation of biology rather than straight genetics, any kinship system is largely taken for granted by its members, who regard it as somehow innate. Europeans, for example, often imposed a naturalized Protestant notion of the "feeble family" – a married pair with children – on the native "full family." A grouping of all who ate, slept, worked, and lived together, whether by birth, adoption, marriage, or proximity, the "full family" seemed to many Indian people equally innate and natural. Scholars have sought to put analytical order, not only on "full" and "feeble" families, but on an even greater diversity of kin relations. Families (as an abstracted analytical unit) mesh into larger kinship networks that scholars have defined using three well-known types – unilateral, bilateral, and ambilateral.

Unilateral (one-sided) kinship occurred in more complicated and populous societies where it was traced only through the father, only through the mother, or through each parent for different purposes. In these cases, family households were submerged within *lineages*, transgenerational linkages through fathers and sons or through mothers and daughters within larger institutions. But patrilineages and matrilineages were not mirror images of each other because men always took the public community positions of leadership in both. In other words, while men were both leaders and kinsmen because of who their fathers were in a patrilineage, for a matrilineage-based community, kinship depended on mothers but leadership passed from brothers to nephews through the common link of a woman who was sister to the office holder and mother to the inheritor, as described for the Iroquois and Hopi since the 1600s.

Lineages are, in turn, components of larger groupings such as *clans*, *phratries*, and, sometimes, *moieties*. While lineages rarely have a name apart from the oldest living grandparent, all of these larger clanship units are named formally. Whether a patriclan or a matriclan, real or metaphorical kinship was traced among all clan members, so they could not marry each other. And when, for example, a member of the Turtle clan traveled, he or she would receive a warm welcome and open hospitality in any Turtle clan household, even of another tribe. The virtues of this mystical bond of clanship, therefore, are readily apparent because of the wide range of kin, mutual caring, and supportive protection which are automatically assumed among clans-people. If a member is hurt, injured, or killed, men of the same clan as the victim are obligated to take revenge or otherwise seek justice.

Clans, in turn, gather into *phratries*, often on the basis of some logical parallel that forbids intermarriage. Thus, clans called Crane, Frog, Sand, and Willow might belong to a Water phratry. Among the Hopi, phratries protect rituals owned by clans from extinction. A ritual's last official will teach its rite to a man in another clan within that same phratry so it can then take over hosting that rite.

Moieties, whether composed of phratries or only of basic households, divide a community into two halves, bisecting the universe into sky or earth, land or water, right or left, and any other likely opposition. In the south, moieties called Red and White, symbolic of War and Peace, characterized the sophisticated Mississippian farmers, the ancestors of tribes who later emerged in the Southeast such as Creeks, Cherokees, Choctaws, and Catawbas. Along the upper Mississippi and Missouri River, various Siouan peoples had Earth or Sky moieties, each composed of a number of clans aligned into land, water, and air phratries. Among the Pueblos of the Southwest, Summer and Winter, also known as Squash and Turquoise, defined the characteristic halves.

Bilateral (both-sided) systems included only about three generations. They focus around a set of individuals who form a *kindred*, a unit also found in modern American society. Members of a kindred can be traced through both the mother and the father as far as acceptable memory allows. Among tribes, therefore, kindreds were huge. In practice, however, kindreds functioned in terms of significant individuals who guided and directed the membership. Most commonly, a *nodal* kindred formed around the node of a married couple, and, after their deaths, around a cluster of their children, siblings (brothers and sisters) with their spouses and children. A typical example is the *tiospaye* of the Lakota, larger than a married couple for protection but smaller than a tribe to be easily fed. In cases where an office or fetish was inherited, successors formed the descent line of a *stem* kindred, as with the transmission of certain sacred bundles among towns of the Skidi Pawnee confederacy.

Ambilateral (chosen sides) descent can be traced through both parents, with the resulting discrete units called *septs*, though actual residence determines which of the possible septs someone belongs to at that moment. Where primogeniture or primacy is vital, high ranks trace membership in a *ramage* composed only of privileged links such as that from first-born son to first-born son, who in turn marry only first-born daughters, important in the proper inheritance of high or chiefly rank, as among Wakashans of central British Columbia.

Thus, kinship was and is not everywhere the same. Settling among the farming towns of the Northeast, Frenchmen came face to face with elaborate "mother right" matrilineal systems. Again and again, across North America, curious observers would discover yet another tribe or nation with what came to be technically called matrilineal descent, because it challenged or contrasted so strongly to their own naturalized "father right" of kinship traced through men.

Inland in central New York, the Hodenosaunee, renamed Iroquois, gave a strong political cast to their matrilineality by assigning each of the fifty name-titles of the *royaner* (federal chiefs) of their league to a particular matriline of mothers–daughters within a matriclan named for an animal, plant, or other species-like natural entity. These clans formed phratries and moieties, all traced through women composing the original league of Five Nations (Mohawk, Oneida, Onondaga, Cayuga, and Seneca).

This array of descriptive kinship terms has its own history. While features of Iroquois and related Huron matrilineality were mentioned in *Jesuit Relations*, perhaps the earliest analytical treatment of native kinship came from Joseph-François Lafitau (1685–1740) in his two-volume comparison of the Iroquois with ancient Hebrews, Egyptians, Greeks, and Romans (1724). Indeed, for over a century training in the classics proved vital in establishing frameworks for the interpretation of Indian kinship diversity. Unfortunately, this framework – set in a racist, colonial, Eurocentric context – was avowedly evolutionary, with England or France set unabashedly at its apex.

The most influential of these interpretations was articulated in the massive research and publications of Lewis Henry Morgan (1818–81), the "inventor [or father!] of kinship studies." Life experiences in central New York did much to precondition Morgan's interest in kinship. He came from a large wealthy family of half-siblings, married his own cousin, and suffered the loss of his children while away conducting kinship research among tribes in the West.

Trained as a lawyer, Morgan became involved in a men's literary club that modeled itself loosely on the Iroquois Confederacy. He became interested in land frauds that threatened to dispossess remaining Iroquois, and he befriended Ely S. Parker (Hasanoanda), a sixteen-year-old Seneca interpreter and lobbyist who went on to become a civil engineer, Civil War aide to Ulysses Grant, and first native Commissioner of Indian Affairs.

In return for his help in the struggle for their homeland, the Parker family assisted Morgan in his research on Iroquois society, thus pointing the way toward his scholarly career. Relying on his knowledge of Latin and law, Morgan adopted classical terms in order to generalize his findings, though not all have remained in use. Nor was his terminology consistent, using, for example, both tribe and gens for what is now called clan, as in his *League of the Ho-de-no-sau-nee, or Iroquois* (1851). Still, Morgan's treatment is remarkably sophisticated, covering recent history, geography, leadership, councils, beliefs, rituals, reforms by the prophet Handsome Lake, dances, games, settlements, clothing, grammar, trails, place-names, and failures of United States Indian policy.

Having worked out Seneca kinship terminology with the Parkers in 1846, Morgan was delighted to discover a similar pattern in 1858 among the Ojibwa near Marquette, Michigan, where he was pursuing the legal work for railroads that, in time, made him wealthy. Financial security allowed him to pursue his consuming, detailed, intellectual interest in kinship terminology and systematics. Following established procedure, Morgan made a list of 286 possible terms for degrees of kin relationship by descent or marriage. During the early summers of 1859–62, he visited many tribes in the West, filling out these schedules carefully and consistently. Supported by William Cass, Secretary of State and himself a scholar of Great Lakes Indians, Morgan sent copies of this schedule to Indian agents and, seeking global comparisons, to foreign diplomats.

With meticulous care, Morgan assembled and analyzed these lists in his monumental *Systems of Consanguinity and Affinity of the Human Family*, finished in 1866, accepted by the Smithsonian as Contributions to Knowledge 17 in 1868, but not published until 1870. Using known linguistic classifications, he arranged the schedules into so-called families (Darnell, this volume). Seeing the "families" in terms of social evolution, he named each after a useful invention thought to characterize a particular stage. Adopting Aryan from "plowing" and Turanian from "horsemanship," he coined for native North Americans the Ganowanian family (from Seneca *gano* "arrow" + *wa-a-no* "bow") and gave lists for 80 tribal examples, divided by language stock into branches according to topographical region, geographical subregions, male or female line, and "rovers" or villagers.

In contrast to American political divisions – town, county, and state – he regarded Ganowanians as organized by tribe, nation, and confederacy, "founded respectively upon consanguinity, dialect, and stock-language" (Morgan, 1870: 141). For all of humanity, he argued, kin-term systems were either descriptive or classificatory, depending on whether primary terms were modified to apply to each relative separately and distinctly (e.g. mother's brother) or to generalized clusterings (e.g. uncle) of like relationship (Morgan, 1870: 12).

Pursuing larger implications of these data in terms of social evolutionary tenets, Morgan outlined a model of "human progress" in his *Ancient Society, Researches in the Lines of Human Progress from Savagery through Barbarism to Civilization* (1877). In the book, he distinguished the social development of the community (Societas) from the political development of the state (Civitas). Though now embarrassing and discredited, what makes *Ancient Society* constantly useful is the raw data it marshals and its unhesitating willingness to compare societies cross-culturally. Rome and Greece are treated the same way as Australians, Iroquois, and other American nations. Morgan's terminology here is modern and consistent, using gens for clan, phratry for clan clusters, along with tribe, nation, and confederacy for land-based polities. Still missing, however, were terms for lineage and moiety.

Despite its Anglocentrism, Morgan's work truly laid the foundation for much subsequent Americanist research. Later American and British scholarship did not invent a whole new focus (Reining, 1972; Fortes, 1972), but instead returned to data in *Systems of Consanguinity and Affinity of the Human Family*. In Morgan's own lifetime, Scottish writers used his forms to refute some of his own arguments. His spellings have been updated and his lists filled out, but Morgan's data remain fundamental to all subsequent work in kinship. He forever changed the way in which all human societies were studied.

The American West and Northwest presented the next great challenges for this developing model of ancient American (and world) kinship. John Wesley Powell of the Bureau of American Ethnology gathered substantive data on the Numic speakers of the Great Basin, noting polyandry (a woman with several husbands at the same time) and resource territories. Powell proved unable to grasp nodal kindreds as the bases of these small and scattered communities, and he too let himself be misguided by a social evolutionary schema.

Columbia University's Franz Boas, a founder of academic anthropology, researched extensively in the Pacific Northwest and trained several native people to record tribal ethnographies in their native languages. His closest collaborator was George Hunt, son of a Tlingit mother and Scottish trader father raised at Fort Rupert where the dominant tribe was the Kwakiutl (now included among Kwakwaka'wakw, "those who speak Kwakwala").

The entire Northwest Coast is filled with exceptions to many cherished rules, and it particularly calls into question crude linkages between language, subsistence, and social organization. Though fishers and gatherers, Northwest Coast nations organized themselves as confederacies or chiefdoms similar to the most intensive farmers. Along the modern Alaska–Canada border, matrilineal peoples symbolically based themselves in "houses," variously expressed as cedar plank longhouses, inherited crests and treasures, and corporate holders of fisheries, lands, names, and ranks assumed to be immortal.

Along the mid-coast, among Wakashans like the Kwakwaka'wakw, people talked about their membership in *numaym*, a stem kindred that baffled Boas. Understanding of these non-unilineal groupings came in the 1960s among scholars who had worked in the Pacific among islanders with similar systems (Davenport, 1959). To existing understandings of unilineality and bilaterality was now added ambilaterality, with "ambi-" indicating that members had a choice in tracing their affiliations. Thus, almost a century after Boas first grappled with the *numaym*, further comparative work in the Pacific (Firth, 1957) revealed the importance of choice and claims to prestige for many patterns of descent.

Final clarification of the issue came from a Toquaht chief on the west coast of Vancouver Island, who reminded a Welsh anthropologist (Kenyon, 1980: 86), confused about local kinship, that the Nootkan system was much like her own with nobles concerned about both existing kinship and pedigreed descent traced through genealogies of first-borns, while commoners had only kinship to trace relationships to people living in the here and now.

Of Boas's students, Robert Lowie had the greatest concern with kinship (Graburn, 1971), but it was Alfred Kroeber (1909), seeking to avoid Morgan's classificatory/descriptive dichotomy, who first codified eight basic kinship principles. These are: differences between persons of the same or of separate generations, between lineal and collateral relationship, of relative age within one generation, of sex of relative, of sex of speaker, of sex of person through whom relationship exists, of "blood" relatives or by marriage, and of life condition of the linking persons through whom relationship exists.

Forty years later, George Peter Murdock (1949: 101) condensed these as the criteria of generation, sex, affinity, collaterality, bifurcation, polarity, relative age, speaker's sex, and decedence. Though not common, decedence, a change in kin terms after the death of a linking relative, occurs along the Pacific coast (Miller, 1999: 122–9). In all societies, of course, death calls for circumlocutions and polite forms, rather than the use of separate kin terms. Often, these consisted of adding tags, lexicals phrased as "the late," or actual necronyms (death names) for defining classes of people who are mourning specific types of relatives (cf. Buchler and Selby, 1968: 170).

Among Coast Salish, decedence was such a prominent and wide-ranging feature that it was applied to both affinals (in-laws) and collaterals ("blood" kin on the sides). While expected remarriages explain the affinal shifts, new kin terms for collaterals appear problematic because they involved surviving siblings (aunts and uncles) and their niblings (nieces and nephews), the children of the deceased, who then came under their care for the sake of "family" honor and prestige (Miller, 1999).

In all societies, marriage is an alliance between larger families, expanding a network of kin to care for children, both natural and adopted. Rank has always been a factor in these arrangements, because every society has a range of proper and disorderly members. Stable, supportive marriages, with betrothal before birth, often marked high status, while casual liaisons did not. Members of leading families had stable unions so that their homes could provide havens for those orphaned and displaced within the community.

In many native societies, a wedding began as a series of visits and exchanges that lasted as long as the alliance. The mother of the groom or her representative brought meat and "male foods" to the bride's family, returning with small gifts. Then the bride's mother came to the groom's family with plant and other "female foods" to show that her daughter knew how to take care of a family. Extreme respect shown after marriage to in-laws, as among Apaches and others, forbid any speech with a mother-in-law, though they shared the same home. In contrast, same-age in-laws, intended for remarriage at the death of a spouse, engaged in ribald joking to prepare them emotionally and socially.

All kindred or clan institutions influenced marriage choices in Native America, and are reflected in six standard kinship types, based on how "cousins" (using the American English term) are classified. Each type, named for the culture in which it was first identified, is found throughout the Americas (Edmonson, 1958), and suggests a scale of increasing complexity. The Hawaiian (Generational) type does not recognize any distinctions except that of siblings, "brother" and "sister," so everyone in your generation is either one or the other. Similarly, everyone in the older generations is "father" or "mother," and "grandfather" or "grandmother." Eskimoan, shared with modern America, has separate terms for siblings and for cousins, as well as for parents and for uncles and aunts. Iroquoian makes the fine distinction between siblings and cross cousins, the children of your parents' opposite-gender siblings (father's sisters and mother's brothers). Children of your parents' same-gender siblings were parallel cousins (children of father's brothers and mother's sisters). Since your male parent and his brothers are all called "father" and your female parent and her sisters are all called "mother," Iroquoians called parallel cousins "brothers" and "sisters," reserving their "cousin" term for cross cousins. The Sudanese type carefully distinguishes siblings, from cross, from parallel cousins.

Most complex are the Crow and Omaha types, which involve clans, matrilineal for Crow and patrilineal for Omaha. Sometimes, to allow for affiliation with the father's clan among Crow or mother's clan among Omaha, a child will be described as born *of* the proper clan and *for* the clan of the other parent. In addition to sibling and cousin terms, a special transgenerational term sorts out the linkage and clan of the other or "for" parent. Among Crow, this term applies to father's sisters and all the women who transmit his clan and matrilineage. For Omaha, the term is "mother's brothers," who do the same for her clan and patrilineage. Often, among leading families, marriages occur at least once between the same two clans in each generation to perpetuate a position of power and influence to children.

During Boas's last decade (he retired in 1939 and died in 1941), University of Chicago anthropologist A. R. Radcliffe-Brown helped shift Americanist research toward a functional mode. Among his lasting contributions was to insist, after a century, that scholars return to Morgan's argument that kin terms and social institutions were mutually interdependent. Scottish writers had long argued that such terms were only "salutations" of little theoretical or institutional import.

In particular, Radcliffe-Brown directed Fred Eggan (1906–91), the premier authority on Americanist kinship for fifty years, to probe Morgan's 1870 schedules yet again. Eggan's long career provides numerous milestones in the technical study of Americanist kinship systems, from the publication of a classic collection in honor of Radcliffe-Brown (Eggan, 1937, 1955) to a recent tribute by his students (DeMallie and Ortiz, 1994). Eggan and students such as Alexander Spoehr studied the way in which native kinship systems – as terms, relationships, categories, and behaviors – underwent changes due to pressures toward American bilateral, patricentric, kindreds based on "feeble families." Indeed, the major change in native societies has been the growing importance of the so-called nuclear family, a couple and their children, insisted upon by missionaries, government agents, and law courts. Yet these studies show that the "nuclear family" but was not only imposed upon Indian people, but was also used by them as one strategy for living in a hostile world.

"The individual family," observed Alexander Goldenweiser in 1915, "does not often appear as a specific social, ceremonial, economic, or political unit," since the sole contribution by a married couple is "education" in etiquette, life skills, and lore (Goldenweiser, 1915: 365). Since a native "full family" could include several wives, and rarely several husbands, it was more of a kindred. Chief Moses of the Colvilles, when repeatedly told to give up all of his many wives but one, responded that he would never "break up his family." White male scholars early concluded that since the father-headed household and family was the culmination of human development, matrilineality was lower in scale (although above chaotic promiscuity). The shift from mother- to father-right, therefore, was regarded as an important step in human social evolution.

A century later, it is clear that societies can and do shift from matrilineal to patrilineal patterns and vice versa, depending on the needs of either gender to cooperate in life skills and tasks. While a shift to patrilineality seems to be unencumbered, the reverse requires an intermediate stage of double descent, where fathers or mothers confer different inheritances on their children, as among the Keresan Pueblos of New Mexico. Classic examples include farming tribes who enthusiastically adopted horses in the 1700s and moved out onto the Plains as bison hunters, abandoning matrilineality for either weak patri- or bi-lineality.

At mid-century, several significant volumes dealing with kinship appeared, including Robert Lowie's masterly summary *Social Organization* (1948), George Peter Murdock's sociological and statistical *Social Structure* (1949), Claude Lévi-Strauss's innovative *Elementary Structures of Kinship* (1949, English translation 1969), which presented exchange and alliance theory on a global scale, and Eggan's own *Social Organization of the Western Pueblos* (1950).

Looking at the Hopi, Eggan (1950) developed an all-purpose Pueblo model based in the "abstract" matrilineage and expanding into clans, phratries, moieties, and towns. He then argued that differing structures among Zuni, Keresan, and Tanoan Pueblos were variations produced by ecology and by history – increased proximity to Spanish and then American authority and towns. As an intellectual ideal, Eggan's model has been much discussed. Additional fieldwork among these Pueblos, including efforts by Edward Dozier and Alfonso Ortiz, both Tewas with Ph.D.s in anthropology, suggest that modern Pueblos, speaking languages of four very different families with very different origins, are similar in name only.

In particular, Keresan Pueblos, whose language is an isolate, share a culture distinctively their own, though Eggan tried to divide them into western and eastern segments in order to bridge the matri-Hopi and the bilateral Tewa. Instead, based on fieldwork at Cochiti in the Rio Grande, far to the east of Hopi, Robin Fox (1967a, 1967b) found a double descent system based in matriclans and patri-kivas (religious chambers). Jay Miller (1972) further explored a model based on gender, with woman a subset of man and left having priority over right, to explain variations among seven modern Keresan towns as logical permutations and to predict a missing eighth town destroyed about 1700. The regional significance of esoteric Keresan priesthoods among other Pueblos, moreover, added a prehistoric dimension that implicates the Keresans as builders of Chaco Canyon.

Ortiz's (1969) research in his home Pueblo of San Juan explicated the importance of Summer/Winter moieties, patrilines, and priesthoods of "made people" for understanding Tewa society. A similar breakthrough in understanding moieties came when fieldworkers visited Tsimshian towns that had not moved to trading posts or missions in the period 1830–60. Boas and his student Viola Garfield had consistently reported four phratries called Orca, Raven, Eagle, and Wolf (Halpin and Seguin, 1990). Yet these in-place towns had moieties, like neighboring Haida and Tlingit (Miller, 1981, 1997). It then became apparent that moieties had long been the north coast pattern, though relocation of the downriver Tsimshian towns gave an impression of phratries. John Dunn (1984), by analogy with Australian kinship, called these four groupings semi-moieties and found mythological and social evidence linking Orca with Wolf and Raven with Eagle. Moreover, comparing regional kinship terms, he traced a macro-Crow system across three very different languages, whose high-ranking families frequently intermarried now as in the past.

New theoretical strategies were introduced in 1964 when, after years of toil, Floyd Lounsbury, a brilliant Iroquoian linguist, published a mathematically formal description of kinship semantics (1964a), using Morgan's terms from Seneca though his own work centered on the Oneida. He also presented a formal account of Crow-Omaha systems (1964b), with stated rules to derive major variants that had been virtually ignored.

During the 1970s, attention shifted from such formalism to the pragmatic uses of kin terms. Scholars began studying how terms are applied in real-world situations according to personal intentions among actual or would-be kinspeople. Indeed, in small communities where everyone can be related in multiple ways, someone can be addressed as an "aunt" in the morning when everyone is visiting happily, a "cousin" in the afternoon when money is being asked, and "damn you" at night during a fight. Sometimes relationships are briefly if playfully denied so that teams can be formed for a gambling game, since a firm rule usually prevents kin from betting against each other. Rather than give up gambling, it is easier to give up the relationship for a short time.

This observation, of course, was not new but merely became a focus for systematic inquiry. In his *Omaha Sociology* (1884), James Owen Dorsey inserted a frequent disclaimer about some fixed rule of kinship: "Two Crows denies it." In 1911, *The Omaha Tribe* by Alice Fletcher and Francis La Flesche presented a magisterial overview of this Siouan community, gifted with the insights of La Flesche, himself the fluent Omaha son of Joseph La Flesche (Iron Eye), one of the moiety tribal chiefs. Seeking to reconcile differences with the Fletcher/La Flesche monograph, Dorsey made further inquiries among Omaha leaders, sometimes resulting in vague answers. Much later, R. H. Barnes (1984) suggested that the many overburdening Omaha rules for and against marriages with various members of other clans were expediently bypassed by maintaining short genealogical memories, deliberate amnesia in the service of alliances. Of greater note, Barnes (1990: 222) discovered a touch point in the "potential for embarrassment between Two Crows and Joseph La Flesche" caused by the marriage of Sioux Solomon, Two Crows' brother, to New Moon Returning, Alice Cline La Flesche Solomon, the second wife of the widowed Francis La Flesche, who married her in 1879, had a child, but became estranged by 1881 and divorced her for adultery in 1883.

Francis La Flesche spent his adult life as an anthropologist dedicated to revealing the complexities of native philosophies. Among his more controversial acts was the purchase and removal to Harvard's Peabody Museum of Omaha sacred objects. In 1989, Omahas of Nebraska repatriated the Sacred Pole known as *Umon'hon'ti* "Real Omaha" that was the axis and beacon of their universe (Ridington and Hastings, 1997). In 1991, its female twin, the White Buffalo Hide known as *Tethon'ha*, came back to stay, after being stolen for a century. With the return of these male and female sacra, Omaha people anticipate a renewal of their community, both materially and spiritually, on their own terms. The importance of such objects points to the larger dimensions of kinship organization – that of the community as a whole.

While kinship has long been at the defining core of anthropology, community studies have been interdisciplinary across the humanities and social sciences. Though most intense in the 1930s, interest in community studies dates back to the nineteenth-century efforts of Swiss-born Albert Gallatin – diplomat, Jefferson's Secretary of the Treasury, and comparative linguist. Indeed, in the Americas, interest in local community scholarship was long stimulated by Swiss and Scottish thinkers, countries known for their intense regionalism.

At the same time that Morgan was collating kinship schedules, the United States was moving into the Southwest. Early military reconnaissance reports drew scholarly attention to the Pueblos as communal, farming, ritually complex, apartment builders. Indeed, the richness, diversity, and complexity, along with intense suspicion and insularity, of all Southwestern native peoples – including Pueblos, Pimans, Utes, Navajos, Apaches, and Quechans – encouraged research that proceeded from community to community. Swiss-born Adolph Bandelier was perhaps the first to study communities. Under Boas and Leslie White, however, such separatism became a formal research strategy.

Similarly inspired, Frank Speck studied East Coast Indian people on a community by community basis, as have his students. A. Irving Hallowell (1992), for example, expanded the concept of community and culture for all of anthropology when Ojibwa people called his attention to the many "persons" of their universe who were other-than-human. These immortal beings of awesome meaning and purpose help define any native sense of community, though they have largely been ignored or avoided by academics (Galloway, 1995; White, 1991).

Kinship terms, learned within the household, might be applied throughout the universe. Terms such as "mother" and "father" applied to a broad range of individuals, only some of them human, who were equally persons in native belief. Thus, the Earth and other sustaining forces might be addressed as "mother" in prayers, while "father" indicated the Sun and various supernatural beings who instructed, protected, and sometimes threatened a child.

To be viable, communities existed within a system of checks and balances whose tensions crossed species and extended beyond the eco-system to the eco-spiritual. From a native perspective, local communities were defined on the basis of sound. All those living within hearing of the distinctive village call, drumbeat, waterfall, and distinguishing dialect could be regarded as belonging to that community. At least once a year this membership was given public expression at one or more major unifying rituals.

Positioned between place and planet, any community and its constituents required the sponsorship of immortals that were the real "owners" of that territory. The most powerful of all served as patrons, virtual totems, of the community through generations of linkages with its hereditary leaders. This array of place, people, patron, and purpose can be seen, for example, in the mystical totemic (from Ojibwa "emblem, friend, mate") expressions among the Maritime Abenaki. Vital links between kindreds and lands took the form of an animal crest, explained in an epic concerning a Giant Frog who swallowed all the water. As thirst became unbearable, "people" moaned they were as dry as a particular animal – a turtle, beaver, wolf, trout, haddock.

Frog was killed, then crushed under a birch tree to force out the water, which ran down the trunk and branches, to form rivers and lakes. During this flood, people became their various animal species, emblems for unifying humans, animals, and their ancestral lands and waterway (Speck, 1915a, 1915b, 1917, 1935; Strong, 1929).

Along the Klamath River of northern California, after the beginning of the Karuk world, various immortals sank into the earth in special places. They are visited each year during a world renewal ceremony called the Fixing. During the course of ten days, a priest goes to each spot to light fires, pray, make offerings, sweep away refuse, and set aright stones and other landmarks. Keeping his right hand empty, and his legs crooked, he seeks to attract "luck," the coveted ability to bring wealth and well-being (Kroeber and Gifford, 1949). His entourage includes men and boys who shoot arrows to fix the earth in place, and two women who reshape a sand mound and provide firewood so that the priest can stand through the final night looking up at the Karuk sacred mountain. The next day, the White Deerskin or another Dance is performed to display heirloom treasures. The Fixing prevents famine, disease, and cataclysm. By recognizing local immortals, by showing respect for the landscape, and by setting landmarks on firm footings like the focal mountain, the Karuk world is remade, steady and reliable as a community of relationships.

In the frozen north, Yup'ik of southwest Alaska believe in a primordial, undifferentiated universe whose shifting and permeable boundaries depend on human attention to rules, especially for sharing food, providing gifts, and making up for what others lack. Kinship and community define the nature of human and non-human behavior. A proper person was ever concerned to restrict his or her breath, sight, thought, speech, and body movement; carefully wearing a belt and hood to limit their actions, deter unclean influences, and hold in their life force. Weapons, tools, and containers were carefully made and decorated both to please that artifact itself and to attract game animals.

Before going after seals, hunters prepared beautiful weapons, kayaks, and gear that would appeal to the animals. Women sewed new clothing for the men, who also fumigated their bodies and tools (sitting mat, pack basket, food supplies, and kayak) so as to smell like the land, which attracted seals. Immediately after a seal was killed, it was anointed with fresh water on its mouth and four flippers. Similar regard was shown to land animals, except the five-point anointing used seal oil, because these "persons" yearned for the sea. Yup'ik people demonstrated their active awareness of human duties toward the greater moral universe, where they connected as community members (not as isolated or alienated individuals) by supplying what other "persons" lacked – fresh water to seals, light and heat to belukha whales, and dry land to fish.

A good hunter focused on making a passage, a clear way, between himself and the animals he hunted, constantly thinking about and working hard to attract their attention. Clearing snow away from any openings provided a clear view of a man's face so animals could decide to offer him their own flesh. After proper treatment of their outer remains, the spirits of these animals were reborn. Indeed, for Yup'ik, existence was an endless cycle of birth and rebirth, with the same "persons" (both human and non-human) interacting over eons within self-perpetuating communities. Today, as in the past, Yup'ik out on the tundra "feed the land" by burying food and offerings to show their regard for this larger mindfulness. Everything has to be done with slow, careful deliberation to avoid offense. Berries are picked with individual regard, and a good person always turns driftwood to give it a new outlook.

Communities and kinship relations have been transformed repeatedly by various kinds of historical change. According to the careful work of Francis La Flesche with Osage native priests, after uniting on the earth as Sky and Earth moieties, they reorganized their community three times, each phrased as a "move to a new country." First came an internal reordering begun by Water people of the Earth division, with the Isolated Earth priests responsible for a symbolic "house" where all Osage children were named, the Land (particularly Bear and Puma) priests given charge of the "house" where war ceremonies were held, and war or hunt leadership assigned to the Bear, Water, Sky, and Isolated Earth.

Prompt action, however, was impossible because of this excessive ceremonial, so a second reordering improved military tactics, though each expedition was still led by a priest. This "move" allowed various clans, as needed, to organize three types of war parties – composed of men from all the clans, a few clans within one moiety, or a single clan. The third move, by two chiefs from the Ponka clan of the Earth and the Sky clan of the Sky, instituted the civil government. Such leaders held vigil until a spirit patron revealed to each the contents of a great bundle, either medicines (symbolized by cormorant and a root shaped like man and woman) or long life (symbolized by pelican and tattooing).

The goal of this complex religion was a community composed of kin, unbroken lines of descendants stretching far into the future. Today, having deliberately "unloaded" older religious strictures, many Osage people have reordered once again through the Big Moon peyote rituals of the Native American Church, an institution that provides a larger sense of community across the tribes, languages, and races who share its songs, rituals, and tipi churches.

Because natural disasters, from flooding and volcanic eruption to enemy attacks, were ongoing, native communities constantly broke up and reformed, always around the special relationship between local totem and leading lineage, either by inheritance or by revelation. Intermarriage outside of kinship degrees also added to the mix of communities, though the extent of remixing after European devastation was particularly intense. Still, the consistent use of language and kinship reckoning from those former spiritually based communities set the standard for all newcomers.

Today, after at least 500 years, native kinship has proved remarkably resilient. Matrilineality, which has been particularly attacked, survives in the Northeast and Northwest because chiefships and rituals are still derived from mothers. Matrilines can now live far apart, in separate homes instead of a shared longhouse, because phone, van, fax, and e-mail keep everyone in touch. No full family is too poor that someone will not have access to this equipment, perhaps at work or the tribal headquarters. Young people lured away from reserves and reservations to earn a decent living and raise a family nonetheless return for the annual powwow or ceremonial, and they too phone home. Later, when they retire on a pension, they return home to live and, often, to help with the costs of ceremonies if they do not take up religious duties themselves.

Even now, members of the First Nations of the Americas uphold the axiom that everything comes down not to a matter of money but to a matter of kinship. Who is connected to whom, from mortals to immortals, defines these tribal universes as much today as it has always done in the past.

BIBLIOGRAPHY

Bailey, Garrick (ed.) 1995: *The Osage and the Invisible World, From the Works of Francis La Flesche* (Norman: University of Oklahoma Press).

Barnes, R. H. 1984: *Two Crows Denies It: A History of Controversy of Omaha Sociology* (Lincoln: University of Nebraska Press).

Barnes, R. H. 1990: "A Legacy of Misperception and Invention: The Omaha Indians in Anthropology," in James Clifton (ed.), *The Invented Indian: Cultural Fictions and Government Policies* (New Brunswick: Transaction Publishers), pp. 211–36.

Buchler, Ira and Henry Selby 1968: *Kinship and Social Organization: An Introduction to Theory and Method* (New York: The Macmillan Company).

Davenport, William 1959: "Nonunilinear Descent and Descent Groups," *American Anthropologist* 61: 557–69.

DeMallie, Raymond and Alfonso Ortiz (eds.) 1994: *North American Indian Anthropology: Essays in Society and Culture* (Norman: University of Oklahoma Press).

Dorsey, James Owen 1884: "Omaha Sociology," *Bureau of American Ethnology Annual Report* 3.

Dunn, John 1984: "International Matri-moieties: The North Maritime Province of the North Pacific Coast," in Margaret Seguin (ed.), *The Tsimshian: Images of the Past, Views for the Present* (Vancouver: University of British Columbia Press).

Edmonson, Munro 1958: "Status Terminology and the Social Structure of North American Indians," *American Ethnological Society Monograph* 30.

Eggan, Fred (ed.) 1937: *Social Anthropology of North American Tribes* (Chicago: University of Chicago Press).

Eggan, Fred 1950: *Social Organization of the Western Pueblos* (Chicago: University of Chicago Press).

Eggan, Fred (ed.) 1955: *Social Anthropology of North American Tribes*, enlarged edn. (Chicago: University of Chicago Press).

Eggan, Fred 1966: *The American Indian: Perspectives for the Study of Social Change* (Cambridge: Cambridge University Press).

Fienup-Riordan, Ann 1990: *Eskimo Essays. Yup'ik Lives and How We See Them* (New Brunswick: Rutgers University Press).

Fienup-Riordan, Ann 1994: *Boundaries and Passages: Rule and Ritual in Yup'ik Eskimo Oral Tradition* (Norman: University of Oklahoma Press).

Firth, Raymond 1957: "A Note on Descent Groups in Polynesia," *Man* 57: 4–7.

Fletcher, Alice and Francis La Flesche 1911: "The Omaha Tribe," *Bureau of American Ethnology Annual Report* 27: 17–660.

Fortes, Meyer 1972: "Kinship and the Social Order: The Legacy of L. H. Morgan," *Current Anthropology* 13(2) (April): 285–96.

Fox, Robin 1967a: *The Keresan Bridge: A Problem in Pueblo Ethnology* (London: Athlone Press, London School of Economics, Anthropological Monograph 35).

Fox, Robin 1967b: *Kinship and Marriage: An Anthropological Perspective* (Middlesex: Penguin).

Galloway, Patricia 1995: *Choctaw Genesis, 1500–1700* (Lincoln: University of Nebraska Press).

Goldenweiser, Alexander 1915: "The Social Organization of the Indians of North America," in Franz Boas et al. (eds.), *Anthropology of North America* (New York: GE Stechert and Co.), pp. 350–78.

Graburn, Nelson 1971: *Readings in Kinship and Social Structure* (New York: Harper & Row).

Hallowell, A. Irving 1992: *The Ojibwa of Berens River, Manitoba. Ethnography into History*. Case Studies in Cultural Anthropology, Jennifer S. H. Brown (ed.) (Fort Worth: Harcourt Brace Jovanovich College Publishers).

Halpin, Marjorie and Margaret Seguin 1990: "Tsimshian Peoples: Southern Tsimshian, Coast Tsimshian, Nishga, and Gitksan," in Wayne Suttles (ed.), *Handbook of North American Indians* vol. 7, *Northwest Coast* (Washington, D.C.: Smithsonian Institution Press), pp. 267–84.

Kenyon, Susan 1980: *The Kyuquot Way: A Study of a West Coast (Nootkan) Community* (National Museum of Man, Mercury Series, Canadian Ethnology Service 61).

Kroeber, Alfred 1909: "Classificatory Systems of Relationship," *Journal of the Royal Anthropological Institute* 39: 77–84.

Kroeber, Alfred and Edward Gifford 1949: *World Renewal: A Cult System of Native Northwest California* (Berkeley: University of California, Anthropological Records 13 (1)), pp. 1–156.

Lafitau, Joseph-François 1724: *Moeurs des sauvages ameriquains, comparées aux moeurs premiers temps* (Paris: Saugrain l'aine).

Lévi-Strauss, Claude 1969: *The Elementary Structures of Kinship*, trans. James Harle Bell, John Richard Von Sturmer, and Rodney Needham (Boston: Beacon Press) (original French publication, 1949).

Lounsbury, Floyd 1964a: "The Structural Analysis of Kinship Semantics," in Horace G. Lunt (ed.), *Proceedings of the Ninth International Congress of Linguists* (The Hague: Mouton), pp. 1073–93.

Lounsbury, Floyd 1964b: "A Formal Account of Crow- and Omaha-Type Kinship Terminologies," in Ward Goodenough (ed.), *Explorations in Cultural Anthropology* (New York: McGraw-Hill Book Company), pp. 351–94.

Lowie, Robert 1936: "Lewis Henry Morgan in Historical Perspective," in *Essays in Anthropology, Presented to A. L. Kroeber* (Berkeley: University of California Press).

Lowie, Robert 1948: *Social Organization* (New York: Holt, Rinehart & Winston).

Miller, Jay 1972: "The Anthropology of Keres Identity." Ph.D. dissertation, Rutgers University.

Miller, Jay 1981: "Tsimshian Moieties and Other Clarifications," *Northwest Anthropological Research Notes* 16(2): 148–64.

Miller, Jay 1997: *Tsimshian Culture: A Light through the Ages* (Lincoln: University of Nebraska Press).

Miller, Jay 1999: *Lushootseed Culture and the Shamanic Odyssey: An Anchored Radiance* (Lincoln: University of Nebraska Press).

Morgan, Lewis Henry 1851: *League of the Ho–de–no–sau–nee, or Iroquois* (Rochester: Sage and Brothers).

Morgan, Lewis Henry 1870: *Systems of Consanguinity and Affinity of the Human Family* (Smithsonian Contributions to Knowledge XVII).

Morgan, Lewis Henry 1877: *Ancient Society, Researches in the Lines of Human Progress from Savagery through Barbarism to Civilization* (New York: Henry Holt and Company).

Murdock, George Peter 1949: *Social Structure* (New York: The Free Press).

Murdock, George Peter (ed.) 1960: "Social Structure in Southeast Asia," *Viking Fund Publications in Anthropology* 29.

Ortiz, Alfonso 1969: *The Tewa World: Space, Time, Being, and Becoming in a Pueblo Society* (Chicago: University of Chicago Press).

Reining, Pricilla (ed.) 1972: *Kinship Studies in the Morgan Centennial Year* (The Anthropological Society of Washington).

Ridington, Robin and Dennis Hastings 1997: *Blessing for a Long Time: The Sacred Pole of the Omaha Tribe* (Lincoln: University of Nebraska Press).

Speck, Frank 1915a: "The Family Hunting Band as the Basis of Algonkian Social Organization," *American Anthropologist* 17(2): 289–305.

Speck, Frank 1915b: "The Eastern Algonkian Wabanaki Confederacy," *American Anthropologist* 17(3): 492–508.

Speck, Frank 1917: "Game Totems among the Northern Algonkians," *American Anthropologist* 19(1): 9–18.

Speck, Frank 1935: "'Abenaki' Clans – Never, 1935," *American Anthropologist* 37(3): 528–30.

Spier, Leslie 1925: "The Distribution of Kinship Systems in North America," *University of Washington Publications in Anthropology* 1(2): 69–88.

Strong, William Duncan 1929: "Cross Cousin Marriage and the Culture of the Northeast Algonkian," *American Anthropologist* 31: 277–88.

Tax, Sol 1955: "From Lafitau to Radcliffe-Brown: A Short History of the Study of Social Organization," in Fred Eggan (ed.), *Social Anthropology of North American Tribes* (Chicago: University of Chicago Press), pp. 443–81.

White, Leslie 1959: *The Indian Journals, 1859–62 of Lewis Henry Morgan* (Ann Arbor: University of Michigan Press).

White, Leslie (ed.) 1964: "Introduction," in *Ancient Society* by Lewis Henry Morgan (Cambridge, MA: The Belknap Press of Harvard University), pp. xii–xlii.

White, Richard 1991: *The Middle Ground: Indians, Empires, and Republics in the Great Lakes Region, 1650–1815* (Cambridge: Cambridge University Press).

9

American Indian Warfare: The Cycles of Conflict and the Militarization of Native North America

TOM HOLM

Most historians view warfare as a bloody progression of weapons development, state-building, the rise of "civilized" nations with geopolitical aspirations, and the concomitant escalation of conflict on a grand, even global, scale. Since Carl von Clausewitz penned his famous treatise on warfare (published in 1832, after his death, as *Vom Krieg* or *On War*), scholars have defined war as a political act in which winning a decisive battle over a given enemy was the ultimate goal. Total warfare thus became "decisive," "true," "modern," or even "civilized" warfare, at least in terms of defining a particular human behavior or institution.

Limited wars could be fought, but even they were assumed to be instituted for political reasons and to have concrete results. They could be decisive, but only if a state could compel its citizens to accept conquest as the outcome of a relatively small war. A limited war might fail to achieve the desired results simply because an entire society might not accept defeat on the basis of one or two lost battles, especially if its military arm remained intact.

In a geopolitical sense, therefore, the total destruction of a society's will to oppose conquest as a result of the destruction of its armed forces was and is an overriding consideration in war. And, according to most scholars, only hierarchical, centrally controlled states can conduct "true" or "decisive" war because only these kinds of states can compel their populations to go to war in the first place and to accept its outcome at the end of a conflict. In short, only "true" states can make "true" war (Keegan, 1993: 16–22; Turney-High, 1973: 227–53).

From this line of reasoning, scholars have concluded that "pre-states" or "tribes" could not make true war because they lacked the organizational structures or coercive institutions able to compel citizens to accept whatever decision was made on the battlefield or in negotiations ending a war. Thus, "pre-states" – by definition – fought "primitive" warfare, which was neither made for geopolitical concerns nor fought to destroy decisively an opponent's will to fight. "Primitive" war came to be defined as "tribal" conflict – quite deadly but without real goals as defined by a central state organization.

These narrow definitions placed Native American peoples, prior to contact with Europeans, in the category of pre-states. And as pre-states, tribes could not have made true war. Rather, they were continuously engaged with traditional enemies in long-term duels that had no geopolitical consequences. Native Americans, according to this line of thought, were locked in a stasis of "primitive" conflict that was illogical, inconclusive, and chaotic. Moreover, "primitive" warfare seemed to Europeans to have been bereft of formality – the "rules of engagement" or "codes of conduct" in military parlance – and was therefore "uncivilized" at best and "savage" at worst. European colonists and their academic descendants have implied that were it not for European imperialism, North America would have continued in a state of perpetual and violent anarchy. "Primitive" Native American warfare was a Hobbesian nightmare in which unorganized groups apparently fought for the simple pleasure of spilling blood (Keeley, 1996: 3–24).

This is an ideological view. By insisting on Indian savagery, such interpretations painted European military conquest as a civilizing action. Yet all too often, non-indigenous scholars have passively accepted this view of Native American warfare, depicting it as functional only in terms of revenge, gaining access to new hunting grounds, obtaining booty and women, or providing warriors with the opportunity to demonstrate their individual prowess and courage in combat. Never, according to anthropologist Harry Holbert Turney-High, did Indian people rise above the "military horizon," becoming actual states with real political aspirations (Turney-High, 1973: 23–8).

Other interpreters arrive at similar conclusions. Some linear-minded scholars, for example, have described war as "progressive," suggesting a "punctuated equilibrium mechanism" of weapons development (O'Connell, 1989: 3–12; Brodie and Brodie, 1973: 7–13; Dupuy, 1980: 337–43). As the punctuated equilibrium hypothesis of war has been articulated, a new weapon or weapons system will gain ascendancy for a short time. Then, an opposing force will adopt for itself the new technology. This adoption leads to weapons symmetry and a long period of stasis in warfare until a new system of "war-winning" technology is adopted and used to conquer a less technologically developed foe. Thus, chariotry, compound bows, the Roman "Spanish" sword, the long lance, crossbows, cannon, rifles, battleships, aircraft, submarines, and tanks move from strategic to tactical weapons as opponents develop symmetrical technologies. In this historical scenario too, Native Americans are seen as primitives. At best, scholars describe the tribes as Neolithic societies, technologically static, and thus unable to evolve above "pre-state" status. Consequently, Native American warfare is often described as being locked on the lowest step of an "evolutionary ladder" of war.

Other scholars have recognized, however, that multiple factors have often caused organized human conflict – including that of states – to run in cycles of limited-indecisive and total-decisive warfare. Western European history is replete with examples of this historical trend. The Roman Empire, for instance, possessed a professional standing army that waged total wars for the sake of territorial conquest and to subordinate other groups to the Roman will (Keegan, 1993: 265–6). After horse peoples from the eastern steppes finally defeated Rome, Europe settled during the Middle Ages into a geopolitical stasis of smallish kingdoms and principalities, in which only select groups of noble warriors had the right to bear arms. The knights and nobles basically made limited war among themselves, leaving civilian populations, on which they based their wealth and status, more or less alone. Warfare during the age of chivalry was limited to clashes between nobles, their retainers, and, sometimes when needed, groups of peasants wielding little more than farm implements. Medieval battle focused on the capture, for ransom, of opposing knights, lords, and sundry other wealthy combatants. A fief or two might be acquired during a war; but by and large, European warfare during the Middle Ages was brief, colorful, and far less deadly to large numbers of people than when Roman armies traversed the continent seeking to subjugate or destroy entire societies (Dyer, 1985: 48). Total war raised its head again during the Crusades, but settled back into a chivalric stasis soon after.

There is a growing body of evidence that supports the idea that Native North America has gone through similar kinds of limited-indecisive and total-decisive warfare that occurred in Europe and, indeed, all over the globe. When Europeans first made their appearance in North America, many Native American groups had become what military historian John Keegan called "complicit partners" in particular forms of warfare with traditional foes (Keegan, 1993: 108). This meant that American Indians had certain, generally understood reasons for going to war and possessed what western Europeans could think of as rules of engagement and codes of conduct in combat. One might argue that, at the moment of contact with Europeans, Native peoples were practicing limited-indecisive forms of war on their own terms and that they had attained a kind of equilibrium of combat. It was this equilibrium that scholars would eventually define as static, "pre-state," and "primitive" warfare.

The North American equilibrium of limited-indecisive warfare generally consisted of raiding – and defending against raids – and highly formalized, pitched battles. Raiding, for the most part, served an economic function. Goods were taken from traditional enemies, carried back to the home community, and distributed among tribal members and relatives. The tribes of the Northwest Coast formalized these kinds of give-aways into their potlatches, which aggressively validated a family's status and continually renewed mutually beneficial intra-group relations (Driver, 1975: 209–10). Some tribes in the Southwest and on the Plains raided farming groups for foodstuffs and other material goods. Among the more sedentary groups of the Eastern Woodlands, war parties raided to obtain material goods such as cured skins and even sacred objects. As in other cultural areas in North America, the raiders redistributed the goods seized to their fellow villagers.

Native North Americans also conducted raids in order to seize people. On the Northwest Coast captives might become slaves and, like material goods, could be given away in potlatches (Driver, 1975: 315). But the taking of captives held much deeper meaning for many other tribes. In what has been termed the "mourning war," Iroquois raiders undertook to replace deceased relatives. The foundations of mourning warfare lay in the basic understanding of kinship in tightly knit Iroquois communities. Death in a family caused great grief and the assumption that when a kinsperson died or was killed, the group's collective power was "diminished in proportion to his or her individual spiritual strength" (Richter, 1983: 530–7). Grief was therefore considered to be as destructive to a society as a plague, famine, or, indeed, as a total-decisive war.

The Iroquois, as well as many other tribes, formally adopted captives, in particular women and children. Race or ethnicity apparently meant little in these adoptions; once adopted, the captive became just another kinsperson to be instructed in the particular tribe's sacred history and traditions. Total assimilation was the ultimate goal of adoption. From a purely functional point of view, adoption, especially of female captives, served to broaden a tribe's gene pool. Given the strict injunctions in native North America against incest, bringing in "new blood" was entirely beneficial.

On the other hand, killing or the ritualized execution of some captives also served a purpose in war. In many cases, scalps were taken to prove that a raiding party had indeed avenged the death of a tribal member and the bereaved would literally "dry their tears" with the trophy. The widespread ritual of the "scalp dance" allowed non-combatants the chance to vilify the enemy, reaffirm tribal superiority, and assuage their grief for a recently deceased tribal member.

The ritual execution of mostly male captives served exactly the same function. A captured warrior might be tortured, by various means, to death. The manner of the captive's death was extremely important. If he endured the torture courageously – singing songs, deprecating his torturers' exertions, and stoically ignoring his pain – he would be praised as a worthy sacrifice for a dead relative. He would be addressed in kinship terms and revived with food and water and even allowed to rest periodically during his ordeal (Abler, 1988). In turn the courageous captive would know that even in death he had bested his enemy's attempts to break him. His status as a warrior remained intact and he actually died triumphantly. A captive's shared understanding of the meaning of ritual execution perhaps best illustrates the idea of a "complicit partnership" in organized violence (Keegan, 1993: 21–46). Culture, in this case, is every bit as important as politics in the waging of war.

James Adair, a long-time trader among the Southeastern tribes during the eighteenth century, summed up warfare in his *History of the American Indians*. According to Adair, some Cherokee headmen:

> told me that they never waged war, but in revenge of blood; and that in such cases, they always devoted the guilty to be burnt alive when they were purifying themselves at home, to obtain victory over their enemies. But otherwise they treat the vanquished with the greatest clemency, and adopted them in the room of their relations, who had either died a natural death, or had before been sufficiently revenged, though killed by the enemy. (1930: 161)

Adair also asserted that raiding parties were "usually satisfied with two or three scalps and a prisoner" (p. 416). In short, such warfare, while made to end grief through revenge or replacing a lost kinsperson by way of adoption and assimilation, was nevertheless waged on a limited scale.

Ritual execution served a very different purpose in Aztec warfare. The Aztec waged "flower wars" in order to capture individuals for sacrifice to the Aztec deities. In one form of ritual sacrifice, a warrior, adopted as a son by his captor, was tethered to a raised platform and forced to fight representatives from the various Aztec warrior sodalities. The adopted captive was armed with a feathered war club while his opponents in the ritual carried their usual obsidian-bladed swords. He was never killed outright but wounded over and over again with cuts from the extremely sharp obsidian blades until finally he dropped from exhaustion and loss of blood (Keegan, 1993: 111–12).

Although the primary purpose of Aztec warfare might have been cultural – the taking of captives for ritual sacrifice – the Aztecs also fought for political reasons, primarily the maintenance and expansion of their empire. The Aztec empire, however, was hegemonic rather than territorial or colonial (Hassig, 1992: 83). Aztec armies did not become occupation forces or serve as protection for Aztec colonizers. Aztec warriors, in reality, were only semi-professional. In addition to their training for combat and serving in actual warfare, Aztec warriors were artisans, agriculturists, and nobles with political responsibilities. Aztec armies were raised for specific purposes, such as quelling rebellions, subduing a particular city, or a "flower war." They fought pitched battles that were rigidly linear in their tactics and highly ritualized in their procedures. The Aztec considered the taking of prisoners exceptionally important; in fact, the number of opposing warriors an Aztec captured determined his status in Aztec military culture (Hassig, 1995: 37–40). Often the simple threat of having an Aztec army in the field was enough to force a given enemy's submission. Even Aztec war, waged by a powerful state, was limited rather than total, a fact made abundantly clear by the Spanish conquistador Hernan Cortés, who recruited allies among people not fully dominated by the Aztecs.

While the Aztecs' pitched battles could become quite bloody and merciless, other Native American groups engaged in combat that more closely resembled an athletic contest. Groups native to what is now California, for example, fought perhaps the most benign and balanced form of war ever to have existed. According to Malcolm Margolin, who carefully researched the tribes of Monterey Bay in northern California before preparing his frankly non-academic book *The Ohlone Way*, tribal warfare in the area was heavily ritualized to the point of being almost bloodless. An aggrieved group would send a messenger to the tribe suspected of causing an injury in order to challenge its warriors to a formal battle. The date and the site of the battle were arranged and both sides began making ceremonial preparations for the coming conflict. On the date set for the battle the warriors of the two groups formed lines facing one another. After exchanging insults and singing their battle songs, the warriors shot special war arrows at their opposing lines. At the death or even the severe wounding of a warrior, the battle would cease. The two sides retired to heal their wounds and take part in ceremonies that expiated the trauma of battle. Following the cleansing ceremonies and a celebration, the victors went to the enemy village to make amends. A celebration then occurred in the losing side's village and arrangements were made whereby the victors paid what amounted to blood money to those who lost a relative in the battle. The Ohlones thought that this kind of reciprocity was the only way that peace could be re-established (Margolin, 1981: 108–14).

Of course, other pitched battles fought in native North America were not so bloodless. None of the tribes, however, sought the utter destruction of an enemy's society or the colonization of an enemy's territory. Native American warfare in the fifteenth century was rarely total, in the sense that it completely dispossessed an enemy of land, identity, and culture. Even "empires" like that of the Aztecs or that of the Powhatan Confederacy in Virginia were not inclined to colonize, fortify, or otherwise occupy the territories of subjugated groups. They may have exacted tribute, but they did not deny one another's right to exist. Even bitter, traditional enemies were complicit partners in the forms and rituals of Native American warfare. Win or lose, battles with traditional enemies reinforced tribal identities and renewed intra-tribal relationships. Warfare was not only limited and restrained but the product of the tribal sense of balance and natural order (Holm, 1996: 42–5).

It had not always been that way. Native North American organized violence, like European conflicts, may have moved in cycles of limited-indecisive and total-decisive war. Many tribal oral traditions indicate that unrestrained, highly organized violence had in fact occurred in the past. That this form of political warfare did not seem to exist when Europeans landed in North America suggests that Native Americans were in the limited-indecisive phase of a historical cycle (Jennings, 1976: 146–66). More important, perhaps, is that tribal sacred histories, as well as some scholarly works, indicate that the tribes deliberately chose this form of warfare as an alternative to total-decisive conflict.

One of the best-known origin stories is the *Wallum Olum* of the Delawares or Lenni Lenape. The *Wallum Olum* has long been a controversial text. The most recent version, edited, translated, and annotated by David McCutchen (1993), is often conjectural rather than substantive, as for example in his maps of Delaware migration over the Bering Strait. Still, Linda Poolaw, the Grand Chief of the Delaware Nation, gave the book her authoritative, eloquent, and enthusiastic endorsement. Jay Miller suggests that some parts of the *Wallum Olum* ring true, while others perhaps do not (Miller, 1994).

As a sacred history, the *Wallum Olum* is not unlike other Native American migration stories, which tell of great journeys, epic battles, and wholesale displacements of other groups. And whoever drew its pictographs knew both defeat and victory in prolonged decisive warfare. Basically, the *Wallum Olum* is the record of a long eastward march across the North American continent. The Delawares crossed ice floes, mountains, and frozen lakes in their journey, but they also fought numerous great wars with the various groups of people they encountered along the way. By their own lights they were on a trek to find a land wherein they would establish a free, bountiful, and peaceful society. From the perspective of those whose lands were being traversed, however, the Delawares were interlopers. In one part of the *Wallum Olum* the Delawares found themselves living on the Great Plains during one of the many lengthy pauses during their migration. There they collided with the land's prior inhabitants. According to McCutchen, "Lenape [Delaware] victories became mixed with costly defeats. The future seemed to offer only more war and bloodshed as the Lenape faced an ever-increasing price for their territory beside the Rockies. The Lenape determined to leave, and they set off eastward on the long journey across the Great Plains" (1993: 104).

The wars did not end when they left the high plains. As the Delawares came to the banks of what may have been the Mississippi River, they encountered the Talega, possibly a group associated with the Mississippian Temple Moundbuilder culture. Frightened by the number of Delawares, the Talega decided to attack them. The resulting war lasted through the regimes of at least seven Delaware sachems. It eventually ended in a decisive Delaware victory and the Talega were driven southward (McCutchen, 1993: 107–11).

The Creeks also have a migration story centered on a long journey to the east. As told by Creek chief Chekilli at a conference with the English held in Savannah in 1735, the Creeks emerged from the earth's "mouth, and settled nearby." The earth unfortunately was angered by the Creeks and "ate up" a large portion of their population. Some escaped this disaster and "journeyed toward the sunrise." At one point in their journey, the Creeks attacked a town so that each tribal member could "have a house when it was captured." In what looks like decisive war, they attacked and killed all but two of the people living in the town. These they pursued until they came across another group of people – the Apalachicolas – who gave them black drink as token of friendship and persuaded the Creeks to "lay down the bloody tomahawk" (Lankford, 1987: 113–16).

While the Delawares and the Creeks essentially admitted that they had intruded upon other people's territories during their migrations and displaced, rightfully or wrongfully, those who stood in their way, other tribes tell of being oppressed by interlopers. The Sioux story of how the Badlands of South Dakota were formed, for example, tells of their subjugation by fierce groups of people who had entered the Great Plains from the west. As the story was told to Ella E. Clark, this new, bellicose group:

> Want[ed] the high tableland for themselves only, [and] they drove off the other people. They claimed all the grass for their own horses, killed the best of the game, and refused to allow other tribes to set up camp as in the old days....Again and again the Sioux and their friends from the north and the east fought for their ancient hunting ground, but the mountain tribe from the west defeated them. Many of their warriors died in battle. (1989: 309)

In the end, the Sioux sacrificed and appealed to the Great Mysteries for help. The spirits then sent a great storm and earthquake that obliterated the camps of the fierce tribe from the west. The Badlands were formed as a result of this great catastrophe.

The Iroquois migration story recounts a tale of oppression equal to that of the Sioux. A nation known as the Adirondacks, or "porcupines" or, literally, "Barkeaters" defeated the Iroquois in a great war that cost many lives. Thereafter, the Iroquois or, more properly, the Hotinonsonni, were forced into a state of servitude and had to pay tribute to the Barkeaters in the form of animal skins and meat. During the time of their oppression the Hotinonsonni prayed for help from the spirit world, stored provisions for a journey, and planned their escape from the Barkeaters. One night under the cover of darkness, they took flight. They packed up their stores and set out in canoes up the St. Lawrence River. The Barkeaters soon found out that the Hotinonsonni had made a bid for freedom and sent out a large war party to overtake them on the river. Near the mouth of the Oswego River the Barkeater war party and the Hotinonsonni fought another great battle. This time, the Thunder People intervened and helped the Hotinonsonni, sending a great storm that selectively overturned the Barkeater canoes. On land picked out near the site of the great battle, the Hotinonsonni established their Longhouse (Akweks, 1972: 11–20).

Other origin narratives and a few published ethnographic studies mention migration and subsequent territorial conquests in ways that suggest total-decisive wars. The Athabascan migration from the Subarctic to the Southwest certainly resulted in territorial acquisition and conflict (Driver, 1975: 49). The Aztecs moved into the central valley of Mexico and began a series of costly wars to reclaim the Toltec empire (Hassig, 1995: 125–8). The Cherokees were an offshoot of the Iroquoian language family who apparently migrated from the region of the Great Lakes to the southern Appalachian mountains. Once established in the mountains, the Cherokees held their position there against numerous attacks until forced to remove in the 1830s (Mooney, 1897–8: 15–21).

A few pre-Columbian archaeological sites also provide evidence of high casualty rates resulting from great and violent battles. Consider, for example, the Crow Creek site, located some eleven miles north of Chamberlain, South Dakota. It contained the skeletal remains of 486 individuals and is dated from around 1325. The remains were found in a fortification ditch – the more outward of two and presumably the more recent – surrounding a village of some fifty earth lodges. The ditch had not been completed at the time of the massacre. According to Patrick Willey, in his *Prehistoric Warfare on the Great Plains: Skeletal Analysis of the Crow Creek Massacre Victims*, the bodies had been left above ground for approximately a month, then interred in two distinct burials with a sixteen-inch layer of sterile soil between them. There were many fewer young adult females present in the mass burials "than expected," leading the excavators to think that whoever raided the village took a large number of female captives. Moreover, because there was a lack of fly larvae found among the bones, the massacre itself very likely took place during the winter. The remains showed marks of scalping, traumatic skull fractures, and the telltale signs of decapitation on the neck vertebrae.

Willey estimated the size of the village based on historic Arikara villages along the upper Missouri River and guessed the population to have been somewhat over 800 (831 or 810 depending on the arithmetic) individuals. Given the 486 skeletons, Willey tentatively concluded that approximately 60 percent of the entire village had been killed in the battle (Willey, 1990: xv–xxx). Perhaps the attackers enjoyed a technological advantage. But if their arms were technologically symmetrical, as seems likely, the attacking force must have greatly outnumbered the defenders – perhaps by as much as three-to-one.

Does Crow Creek offer evidence for Indian "states" waging total war? Although not necessarily "states" as we would recognize them today, both attackers and defenders clearly possessed a sophisticated social structure. The large attacking force had to be equipped, motivated, and maneuvered in the midst of a South Dakota winter. The defenders were in the middle of a public works project, building a second and much larger defensive redoubt. Quite clearly both groups possessed a political system capable of maintaining order and mobilizing for war. Seen in this context, Crow Creek was no more an example of "primitive warfare" than were the battles of Waterloo, Cold Harbor, the Argonne Forest, or Iwo Jima. Both the attackers and the defenders at Crow Creek were members of well-organized polities, visible in the Euro-American context using the term "state."

But such questions of perception and definition extend beyond words like "state." For much of American history, war defined relations between native people and Europeans, if not in fact then in the white imagination. The ideological apparatus surrounding Indian "savagery" makes it difficult to discuss war without reinforcing older stereotypes. Some scholars, for example, have suggested that sites like Crow Creek "prove" that Native Americans were far more bellicose and murderous than "civilized" people (Keeley, 1996: 68, 71–98; Bamforth, 1994: 95–113). The archaeological record, however, suggests that they are actually anomalous among Native American sites and indicate that massacres were at best sporadic occurrences (Willey, 1990: xv).

Native American tribal states existed before the Europeans and they had indeed experienced total-decisive warfare. But the tribal origin and migration stories also emphasize that peace and order was the preferred and, by tribal lights, natural state of human existence. All of the war narratives conclude with the establishment of peace and harmony as the desired state. How then, after surviving the chaos of destructive, total wars, did native groups become complicit partners in what was often limited, indecisive ritual warfare?

Very likely most tribes, after surviving these catastrophic episodes of violence, rejected total-decisive war as a means to a political end. Most tribes continue to demonstrate a strong antipathy toward aggression, organized or otherwise. At the same time, however, groups must maintain harmonious relationships within their communities, and this requires mechanisms for dealing with aggression and conflict. Many Native American societies relied on an extensive system of social rewards to maintain in-group harmony. Children might be praised for learning life skills; young women for bearing children; adult females for nurturing and artisanship; adult males for leadership; elders of both sexes for preserving culture and conducting necessary ceremonies.

Few societies, however, offered social rewards to young males beyond those given for their participation in combat. Historian Gwynne Dyer has argued that, in a purely biological sense, young males are the most expendable members of any given society and therefore bear the brunt of fighting (Dyer, 1985: 9). In doing so, they are accorded a degree of status within the group and are praised for their valor or self-sacrifice as well as for their participation in time-honored ceremonies. War-linked ceremonies in Native American societies usually have to do with cleansing an individual warrior of the "taint" of aggression caused by the trauma and chaos of war (Holm, 1996: 39).

The ceremonies of war have to be maintained to insure group identity. The warrior is praised, not necessarily for going to war, but for participating in a tribe's unique ceremonies and thus preserving its power and relationship with the spirit world. The society, in turn, shows support for the individual combatant and, at the same time, recommits itself to more peaceful pursuits and a return to normality.

It has also been argued that young males may be intrinsically aggressive and need some kind of outlet, such as ritual war, for these tendencies. By directing male aggression outwardly, so the argument goes, the tribes are better able to maintain harmony within. Whatever the case, re-directing male aggression or having them participate in ceremonies, warfare may indirectly be seen as a way for young males to interact positively with the rest of a given society.

There is some evidence to demonstrate that Native American groups essentially waged ritual warfare in order to assure young males of their positive roles in society and to provide an outlet for youthful aggression, while at the same time insuring that not too many of them would be killed in the process. A few scholars have argued that ritual warfare reflected the distinct separation in Native American societies between female and male physical spiritual powers (Dowd, 1993: 4–9). Females are born with the power to reproduce; males, on the other hand, are born without power and have to seek and obtain it from the spirit world. Menses is, in itself, a force that can block or negate other powers. Similarly, Clifton B. Kroeber and Bernard L. Fontana have argued persuasively that female power is often associated with the ability to reproduce and nurture. Women not only gave birth and nurtured children but became, in many tribal cultures, the primary sowers and reapers of the soil. In effect, women "could perform most or even all essential community chores: tend the hearth, bear and raise children, and plant, cultivate and harvest the calories needed to stay alive." As a result, the "worth of males, their dignity as human beings, was challenged to the utmost." This "imbalance in the sex division of valued status" led to the development in most Native American societies of distinct male and female roles and relationships: female power was associated with the activities of life (childbearing, cultivation), male power with death (war, hunting) (Kroeber and Fontana, 1992: 169).

In 1802, Creek elder Efau Harjo succinctly outlined the roles and expectations for young males in his own society: "There is among us … old customs, one of which is war. If the young men … wish to practice the ways of the old people, let them try themselves at war, and when they have tried let the chiefs interpose and stop it" (Brown, 1971: 26). Efau Harjo no doubt captured the essence of Native American warfare immediately prior to the coming of the whites.

What the Creek elder did not mention, however, was the fact that the arrival of Europeans had caused widespread changes in Native American warfare long before 1802. Anthropologists Neil L. Whitehead and R. Brian Ferguson have argued that "both the transformation and intensification of war, as well as the formation of tribes, result from complex interactions" in what they call the "tribal zone." This zone "begins … where centralized authority makes contact with peoples it does not rule." Traditional indigenous groups experienced the introduction of new technologies, animals, diseases, plants, and philosophies, often even before colonizers appeared in their midst. These changes disrupted existing systems and social relationships, thus "fostering new alliances and creating new kinds of conflicts" (Whitehead and Ferguson, 1996: 191).

Whitehead's and Ferguson's ideas certainly apply to the total-decisive wars recounted in the various tribal migration narratives. Delawares and Creeks may well have disrupted native groups on whose lands they intruded. Sites like Crow Creek suggest equally intensified social conflict. But their ideas apply equally well to the transformation of Native American warfare from its limited-indecisive state in the fifteenth century to what it became as a result of the European invasion. In short, the arrival of the whites in the New World touched off a new round of total-decisive warfare and widespread territorial displacement among native North Americans. And it is this particular cycle of warfare that defined the ways Europeans understood Indian combat.

The return of this kind of war was perhaps inevitable, for at the same time as Europeans embarked on a new round of imperialism they were themselves in the middle of a revolution in warfare. During the fourteenth and fifteenth centuries, Europe was ravished by frequent dynastic duels, seriously threatened by the expansion of Islam, and shaken by the introduction of gunpowder. A product of feudalism, mounted knights had spent a lifetime training for combat and owed their existence to a limited form of warfare waged primarily against others of similar training and temperament. Now, they were suddenly knocked from their saddles with weapons wielded by social inferiors. Guns and cannon brought Europe back to total-decisive war. By the fifteenth century, Europe had emerged as a conglomeration of competing and warring states. As Columbus made his voyages to the New World, the Old World was ablaze. The Ottoman Empire had conquered Constantinople with siege guns; Spain had expelled the Moors with the aid of gunpowder; and the French were rampaging through Italy armed with light, mobile cannon (Dupuy, 1980: 106–7). Colonialism raised the stakes of total war in Europe. Colonies meant economic gain. With new-found wealth, rulers could buy weapons and mercenaries, fortify their borders, and raise armies to do their political bidding. Warfare in Europe soon spiraled out of control (O'Connell, 1989: 124–37). Such was the context that European states brought to the Americas.

It has been tempting to apply a technological determinist argument to the conquest of the Americas. The four-century-long struggle for North America, however, cannot so easily be typified as a relentless duel between superior European firepower and Native American tenacity. Cortés did not simply blast his way into Tenochtitlan and destroy the Aztec Empire; neither did the Dutch, English, French, or Americans easily overrun Native American lands. The "Indian Wars" were far more complex. Perhaps most significant, these wars involved whole societies versus whole societies rather than armies against armies. In that sense, the Indian Wars were total-decisive, and they resulted in the militarization of entire communities. They also brought about new alliances and the appearance of completely new militarized groups among both the indigenous and the colonizing peoples.

On the surface, it appears that Native Americans were, from the outset, more thoroughly militarized than their European opponents. It has been assumed that among all "primitive" or tribal peoples every able-bodied male is considered a warrior. This assumption gives Native American groups 100 percent military participation ratios. So-called "civilized" societies are presumably more complex and have a greater degree of role specialization. Hence, not everyone is, or needs to be, a warrior. "Civilized" groups, then, are presumed to have much lower military participation ratios.

On the other hand, neither were Native American tribes as heavily militarized as this assumption suggests. Warfare among the tribes was always voluntary. Moreover, able-bodied males in Native American societies participated in their tribe's economic life: they were hunters, priests, shamans, cultivators, artisans, and fishermen as well as warriors. That they were given more social rewards as warriors does not diminish their other contributions to their communities. Like most European and American troops, they were not professional soldiers. In addition, the belief systems of most tribes held that bad omens could and should deter warriors from taking part in combat. If a vision told a warrior that he or possibly the entire war party would be unsuccessful, it was likely that a raid or an entire war would be canceled. Given these beliefs and the other expectations of males in Native American societies, the tribes would have been hard-pressed to have full military participation at any time.

In any case, however, military participation ratios meant little or nothing in the wars for the possession of North America. Spain, for example, first sent the *Conquistadors*, a group of thoroughly militarized individuals who were veterans, or the sons of veterans, of the wars to rid Iberia of the Moors and Jews. English colonists, who for the most part had few combat experiences and little military training, were more than willing to be organized as militia to protect their territorial claims. The French at first were the least militarized of the major colonial powers to come to the Americas; but after they became involved in a series of wars with the British, France sent a large number of regular soldiers to American shores. It is likely the case that the colonizers were as militarized as any Native American group; perhaps even more so, simply because they had both professional soldiers and a highly motivated, well-armed, and predominantly male civilian population.

The first wars between Native Americans and Europeans set the tone for those that followed. Cortés' conquest of Mexico, for example, was not the result of overwhelming firepower or superior tactics. By and large, it was the outcome of the Spanish ability to exploit the enmities between the Aztecs and other groups, in particular the Tlaxcaltecs, disrupt the traditional patterns of Aztec warfare, and take advantage of the debilitation and demoralization of the Aztec population caused by disease and other hardships. For the Spanish who followed Cortés the war against the Aztec empire was ruthlessly total and decisive. It was Clausewitzian political war with a vengeance (Hassig, 1995: 236–50; Shurkin, 1979: 101–4; McNeill, 1989: 183; Crosby, 1973: 49).

The English colonists followed much the same pattern of conquest in wars against the Powhatan Confederacy, the Pequots in 1637, and the Wampanoags, Narragansetts, Nipmucs, and Pocumtucks during what has been dubbed "King Philip's War." From the very founding of the Plymouth, Massachusetts Bay, and Jamestown colonies, the entire adult male populations of each were mobilized into local militia companies and prepared to eradicate any and all Native American resistance. The Virginians used total war – the firing of villages and crops, taking hostages, and the wholesale massacres of those who lent support to Native American warriors – to debilitate and finally defeat the Powhatan Confederacy as early as the 1620s (Steele, 1994: 37–58).

In New England, the colonists utilized nearly the same tactics to defeat the Pequots. It might also be added that the entire New England Native American population had been devastated by disease several years beforehand. The attack on a large

Pequot stronghold in 1637 was especially horrific. The English set fire to the village and simply slaughtered everyone who tried to escape the conflagration. Even the colonists' Narragansett and Mohegan allies protested against the terrible massacre; not only did it run counter to their own particular form of warfare but it was unspeakably brutal (Malone, 1991: 100–4).

In 1675, the Wampanoags and Narragansetts under the leadership of Metacom, or King Philip, rebelled against the English colonists in a total war. Armed now with trade weapons and utilizing fire to spread panic and ruin fortifications, they fell upon the outlying white settlements. Using their old tactics of ambush and raiding and combining these with different armaments, the warriors outfought the English at nearly every turn. The tribes, highly militarized now and taking every advantage of terrain and cover, used surprise, maneuver, sound planning, and excellent intelligence, and nearly defeated the English at their own newly revived system of total-decisive war. In the end, however, the English exploited the knowledge of their Native American Christian converts, adopted Native American tactics, and eventually defeated King Philip in 1676 (Malone, 1991: 105–25; Utley and Washburn, 1977: 47–52).

Several years before King Philip's War, Europe had undergone a devastating series of conflicts known as the Thirty Years War, which, curiously enough, resulted in Europe's return to the practice of limited, formalized battle. The wars primarily pitted the Catholic against the Protestant nation-states and, almost from the beginning, set a standard for brutality not seen in Europe since the Roman Legions ransacked Germany and the Balkans. Literally exhausted by the long and costly war, the European belligerents signed the Treaty of Westphalia in 1648. They reached an unwritten consensus that limitations would be placed on war. European armies reverted to formalized, linear tactics, fought battles in frontier areas, and, most importantly, avoided civilian populations. The battles they fought during this period of limited warfare were no less bloody – soldiers stood shoulder to shoulder and exchanged volleys of musketry from ranges of less than 40 yards, causing appalling casualties – but they were far less costly in terms of the devastation that might have been wrought upon cities and villages. A ruler might lose a province or two as a result of a particular battle, but by and large thereafter Europe maintained a "balance of power" until the Napoleonic wars (Dyer, 1985: 60–6).

Yet despite the changes in European warfare, conflict in the colonies remained total-decisive. Colonial militia, along with those who taught them – primarily other Native Americans – were still the deadliest foes with whom Native Americans had to contend. During the late seventeenth century a series of wars erupted between competing imperial powers (Dowd, this volume). Native American client states became heavily involved in these colonial wars, fought between Great Britain and France, as auxiliaries and allies. For the European, Native American, and Euro-American combatants, the wars were a mixture of European tactics, guerrilla warfare, and vestiges of tribal ritual combat. European linear tactics were notably unsuccessful except when European professionals met on the battlefield, and Europeans increasingly mixed total war with Indian tactics.

The culminating conflict was the French and Indian War, and its first battle, a resounding British defeat at the hands of Native American warriors, pushed Britain to adopt Indian strategies (Keegan, 1995: 110, 126–33). In 1755, two regular infantry regiments under the command of Major General Edward Braddock marched to destroy the French-built Fort Duquesne at the junction of the Allegheny and Monongahela rivers. Braddock enlisted several American militia groups from Virginia and North Carolina and instructed them in close-order formations and volley musketry. A small blocking force met Braddock's advance guard and forced it back onto the main column. Meanwhile, Native American warriors had infiltrated the heavily wooded high ground on both of Braddock's flanks. Well-aimed fire from the Native American positions took its toll – several officers, including Braddock himself, were killed or wounded in the initial exchange of gunfire. Finally, its officers dead or incapacitated, caught in a pocket of white smoke discharged by hundreds of muskets, with the air seemingly filled with lead projectiles, and unable to see its enemy, Braddock's command simply lost its cohesion, turned into a mob and fled the field (Utley and Washburn, 1977: 77–88).

The British learned from Braddock's defeat. James Smith, an Anglo-American captive who would later urge Americans to adopt "the Indian mode of warfare," flatly asserted that Native American tactics had defeated Braddock (Smith in Loudon, 1971: 125–7, 242–3). As a result, the British simply allowed the colonial militia to run amok in wars against Native Americans. American militiamen, spurred on by a British bounty placed on Indian scalps, burned, pillaged, and massacred Native Americans with a ferocity equaling that of the Thirty Years War (Steele, 1994: 228).

Unlike the Thirty Years War, however, these appalling depredations did not result in a reversion to limited warfare in North America. Instead, they continued without let-up or remorse, setting a pattern for later American warfare. The wars also created a domino effect, forcing Native American groups far from the center of the struggle in the east to militarize and adopt new outlooks regarding war. This westward extension of total warfare also created new alliances, new wars, and completely new militarized tribal states – not an uncommon occurrence among indigenous groups on the frontiers of colonial empires (Ferguson and Whitehead, 1992: 2–30; Whitehead, 1992: 127–50).

A short history of the Cherokees in the latter half of the eighteenth century illustrates the pattern well. During the French and Indian War the Cherokees at first remained loyal to British interests. Some 400 Cherokees had in fact taken part in General John Forbes' expedition against Fort Duquesne three years after Braddock's ill-fated attempt to capture the French bastion. As this group was returning to Cherokee country they ran afoul of some Virginia militiamen and during some ensuing skirmishes lost seventeen of their number. They also killed some militiamen, for whom the Virginians demanded vengeance. But the Virginians also responded to the colonial government's fifty-pound bounty on Indian scalps. Total war erupted, lasting from 1759 to 1761. During this period, the Virginia and Carolina militia burned towns and crops, enslaved a large number of Cherokees, and generally wreaked havoc throughout Cherokee country. In turn, the Cherokees laid siege to two British outposts, forts Prince George and Loudon, massacring the garrison of the latter in 1760. But it proved difficult for the Cherokees to live as a militarized state. The following year, out of utter exhaustion, the Cherokees signed a peace treaty with the British

Crown (Steele, 1994: 228–33; Mooney, 1897–8: 40–5). Like the Pequots and the Aztecs, they too had been debilitated by outbreaks of smallpox, the loss of crops, and relentless combat.

But European advance created other militarized tribes. When the American Revolution broke out, for example, the Cherokees were placed in a political quandary. A bifurcated system, the Cherokee state government consisted of a "white" council of "Beloved Men" who handled domestic disputes, seasonal ceremonies, and any and all civil problems, and a "red" council headed by a Principal War Captain, a Red Priest, and a "Red Woman" who had jurisdiction over the nation during a war (Gearing, 1962: 47–54). The Red Woman sanctioned war and had jurisdiction over the fate of captives; the Red Priest conducted the ceremonies that began and ended wars; and the War Captain made strategic decisions and led the warriors in battle.

In 1775, the American uprising caused this system serious harm. Knowing that the Cherokees were locked into a treaty with Great Britain and coveting Cherokee lands for themselves, a large number of Virginians began to mass for an attack on the Cherokee Nation. Dragging Canoe, a head warrior from the town of Malaquo, and by then Principal War Captain of the nation, began military operations in cooperation with the British agent, John Stuart. By early 1776, though, Stuart had been forced to leave his headquarters in Charlestown and relocate in British-held Florida, cutting off the Cherokees from British gunpowder and shot. Dragging Canoe, intent on protecting the nation and carrying on the war against the Americans, was betrayed by the Red Woman, Nancy Ward, who was then married to a white settler. The Virginians invaded Cherokee country and began a campaign of burning, looting, and slaughter. The Beloved Men of the council – the civil or white half of the Cherokee government – were genuinely frightened into making peace overtures to the Americans. The British had abandoned them and the Americans were making all-out war.

In the end, the Cherokee council betrayed Dragging Canoe, who, in turn, established new towns along the Hiwasse River in Tennessee and vowed to continue the war. Dragging Canoe's followers, who became known as the Chickamaugas, carried the war on until 1794, when Dragging Canoe's successor, John Watts, finally signed a treaty with the Americans at Tellico Blockhouse (Evans, 1977: 179–87). Other Chickamaugas, however, had already migrated west, presumably to distance themselves from the encroaching Americans. One band of Chickamaugas emigrated to Arkansas, where they became involved in a deadly war with the Osages. The Osage War lasted until 1818, when a treaty was signed establishing the Cherokee Nation West on new lands in what is now Oklahoma (Brown, 1971: 471–6).

The Chickamaugas essentially became a new, militarized Native American polity. The towns Dragging Canoe founded would eventually be reincorporated in the old Cherokee Nation, as were those Chickamaugas who did not migrate west. In fact, some of those who in later years would become leaders of the Cherokee Nation – John Ross, Major Ridge, John Walker – were from the Chickamauga towns (Evans, 1977: 187). But the Chickamauga polity – and the portion of it that would become the Cherokee Nation West – maintained a separate government and made independent decisions regarding policy. The Chickamaugas, for example, sent a contingent of warriors to aid the northern confederacy of tribes under the Miami chief Little

Turtle in its defeats of two U.S. armies in 1790 and 1791. They also allied themselves with the Shawnees and Creeks (both former enemies) to carry on a war against the white settlers in Tennessee (Dowd, 1993: 106–9). After the Cherokee Nation West became involved in the war with the Osages, its leaders formed military alliances with some Delawares, Creeks, Choctaws, and Comanches in order to deal the Osages a crushing blow at Claremore Mound in 1818 (Brown, 1971: 471). Dragging Canoe had sponsored a successful secessionist movement that led to the formation of a relatively short-lived but thoroughly militarized tribal state in the west.

This abbreviated history of Cherokee militarization and political change was repeated dozens of times by a number of Native American groups between 1790 and 1890, particularly in the trans-Mississippi west. New tribal states and alliances came together to stop the onslaught of Euro-American expansion. Some tribes, or tribal factions, allied themselves with the whites against traditional enemies. Others – like the Osages – found themselves caught up in struggles resulting from the displacement of already militarized groups.

The Teton Sioux or Lakota, for example, rose to military power on the Plains in the wake of such displacement. For a long time, the Lakotas had practiced a highly ritualized form of warfare. A system of graded war honors known as "coup" and practiced by all of the Plains groups emphasized touching an enemy, capturing a weapon, or stealing a horse over any actual killing. During the early nineteenth century, however, displaced, militarized groups like the Cree (former French allies), armed with trade guns, entered Lakota territory and initiated another round of total-decisive warfare (Secoy, 1992: 65–77). Young Lakota men, who could have gained standing as hunters, athletes, orators, craftsmen, shamans, dancers, and singers as well as warriors, found themselves focused on war as a means of obtaining valued status. This kind of social compulsion, in addition to the "fortress" mentality that results from being surrounded by enemies, produced changes in the way the Lakota fought. By the 1850s they were thoroughly militarized and had transformed their government. Leadership began to fall upon skilled tacticians like Red Cloud, persons with extraordinary powers associated with warfare like Crazy Horse and Sitting Bull, and to men known to have exhibited extreme courage in battle like Gall.

Such transformations have continued to resonate among Native people. Many Indians served as scouts and soldiers in the nineteenth-century United States military, and some tribes continue to speak of having maintained a "warrior ethos." In the two World Wars, Indian people enlisted in the armed forces in large numbers, highly disproportionate to their population (Bernstein, 1991; Britten, 1997). The same trend held true in Korea and Vietnam and it continues to hold true today. Veterans – whether the famous Navajo Code Talkers or peacekeepers in Kosovo – are highly honored by their home communities, and warfare continues to be an important way of interacting with the world and defining the boundaries of one's own society.

With the European incursion, Native Americans entered a renewed cycle of conflict and militarization. Many groups in fact rose above what Turney-High called the "military horizon" – the ability to wage total-decisive war – which was, by his lights, the precursor to statehood. Migration stories and sacred histories suggest that they had already done so in the past. The cycle had begun with intruders but when territorial boundaries had been established the tribes reverted to formalized, ritual war. The European invasion set a similar cycle into motion once again.

Euro-Americans went through the same cycle. The image of the peaceful white settler trying to eke out an existence from the land and only taking up arms in the defense of meager property rights is sheer fantasy. In actuality, Native Americans had more to fear from civilians than from the several professional armies they fought. For one thing, American pioneers were better armed than most professional soldiers. In the colonial period, American settlers carried accurate flintlock rifles that were exceptionally effective in forest warfare, while the French, British, and, later, American forces were armed with inaccurate, smoothbore muskets effective only in close-quarter, European-style battles. After the Civil War, the U.S. Army would not adopt new and deadly repeating rifles because it was feared that the troops would waste ammunition (Hallahan, 1994: 191–210). American civilians, however, had no such qualms, and firms such as Winchester and Colt sold thousands of their new repeating rifles and pistols to homesteaders, ranchers, businessmen, miners, and even outlaws. America became perhaps the most heavily armed nation ever to exist.

More importantly, the American civilian population became one of the most thoroughly militarized *societies* in existence. The early colonies at Jamestown, Plymouth, and Massachusetts Bay required every male to enter the local militia. From those points onward through time, Americans thought of military service, even on a local level, as an expression of loyalty to the state, which, in turn, was ultimately responsible for securing their property rights. And from Greek times, Europeans had equated property rights with the right, as well as the responsibility, to bear arms (Keegan, 1993).

Warfare has everything to do with social cohesion, and killing Indians was a powerful expression of American identity. As a result, most of the infamous massacres of Native Americans came at the hands of local American volunteers, militia, and even vigilantes. New England militiamen burned villages and slaughtered the Pequots; Virginia volunteers burned towns and crops in Cherokee country; in California the Indian Island massacre was carried out by a local group of vigilantes; the horrors of the Sand Creek massacre were perpetrated by the Denver barflies who signed up with the 3rd Colorado Volunteers under Methodist minister John M. Chivington; and the wanton slaughter of the Arivaipa Apaches at Camp Grant in 1871 was organized and carried out by a Tucson citizens' group.

The four hundred years of total-decisive war for the continent of North America was a Thirty Years War on a grand scale. Whole societies were militarized to the point that the more normal activities of hunting, raising crops, conducting ceremonies, and rearing children became secondary to the waging of war. As in Europe during the period 1618 to 1648 whole areas of Native North America were depopulated and entire societies displaced. Disease, of course, played its part. And armies carry disease more easily than they do their weaponry. Total, political war, as reintroduced in North America during the sixteenth century, ultimately devastated the indigenous populations that had, in the past, chosen to limit and restrain warfare. Out of that devastation, though, Indian people have re-emerged, oftentimes through the same military institutions that once threatened them. Whether American society has ceased waging decisive war on Indian culture and society, however, remains an open question.

BIBLIOGRAPHY

Abler, T. and M. H. Logan 1988: "The Florescence and Demise of Iroquoian Cannibalism: Human Sacrifice and Malinowski's Hypothesis," *Man in the Northeast* 35: 1–26.

Adair, J. 1930: *Adair's History of the American Indians* (1775), ed. S. C. Williams (New York: Promontory Press).

Akweks, A. 1972: *Migration of the Iroquois* (Mohawk Nation at Akwesasne, NY: White Roots of Peace).

Bamforth, D. B. 1994: "Indigenous People, Indigenous Violence: Precontact Warfare on the North American Great Plains," *Man* 29(1): 95–115.

Bernstein, A. 1991: *American Indians and World War II* (Norman: University of Oklahoma Press).

Britten, T. 1997: *American Indians in World War I: At War and at Home* (Albuquerque: University of New Mexico Press).

Brodie, B. and F. M. Brodie 1973: *From Crossbow to H-Bomb* (Bloomington: Indiana University Press).

Brown, J. P. 1971: *Old Frontiers* (Kingsport, TN, 1938; reprint, New York: Arno Press, 1971).

Clark, E. E. 1989: *Indian Legends from the Northern Rockies* (Norman: University of Oklahoma Press).

Clendinnen, I. 1991: *Aztecs* (New York: Cambridge University Press).

Crosby, A. W., Jr. 1973: *The Columbian Exchange: Biological and Cultural Consequences of 1492* (Westport, CT: Greenwood Press).

Dowd, G. E. 1993: *A Spirited Resistance* (Baltimore: Johns Hopkins University Press).

Driver, H. 1975: *Indians of North America* (Chicago: University of Chicago Press).

Dupuy, T. N. 1980: *The Evolution of Weapons and Warfare* (New York: Bobbs-Merrill).

Dyer, G. 1985: *War* (Homewood, IL: Dorsey Press).

Evans, E. R. 1977: "Notable Persons in Cherokee History: Dragging Canoe," *Journal of Cherokee Studies* 2: 176–89.

Ferguson, R. B. and N. L. Whitehead 1992: "The Violent Edge of Empire," in R. B. Ferguson and N. L. Whitehead (eds.), *War in the Tribal Zone* (Santa Fe, NM: School of American Research Press).

Gearing, F. 1962: "Priests and Warriors," *American Anthropological Association Memoir* 93, no. 64.

Hallahan, W. H. 1994: *Misfire: The History of how America's Small Arms Have Failed Our Military* (New York: Scribner's).

Hassig, R. 1992: "Aztec and Spanish Conquest in Mesoamerica," in R. B. Ferguson and N. L. Whitehead (eds.), *War in the Tribal Zone* (Santa Fe, NM: School of American Research Press).

Hassig, R. 1995: *Aztec Warfare* (Norman: University of Oklahoma Press).

Holm, T. 1996: *Strong Hearts, Wounded Souls* (Austin: University of Texas Press).

Jennings, F. 1976: *The Invasion of America: Indians, Colonialism, and the Cant of Conquest* (New York: W. W. Norton and Company).

Keegan, J. 1993: *A History of Warfare* (New York: Vintage Books).

Keegan, J. 1995: *Fields of Battle* (New York: Alfred A. Knopf).

Keeley, L. H. 1996: *War Before Civilization* (New York: Oxford University Press).

Kroeber, C. B. and B. L. Fontana 1992: *Massacre on the Gila* (Tucson: University of Arizona Press).

Lankford, G. E. (ed.) 1987: *Native American Legends, Southeastern Legends* (Little Rock, AR: August House Publishers).

Loudon, A. 1971: *A Selection of Some of the Most Interesting Narratives of Outrages Committed by the Indians in Their Wars with the White People;* vol. I, 1808; vol. II, 1811; reprint Harrisburg Publishing Company, 1888 (most recent reprint, New York: Arno Press 1971).

Malone, P. M. 1991: *The Skulking Way of War* (Baltimore: Johns Hopkins University Press).

Margolin, M. 1981: *The Ohlone Way: Indian Life in the San Francisco-Monterey Bay Area* (San Francisco: Heyday Books).

McCutchen, D. (ed. and annot.) 1993: *The Red Record: The Wallum Olum, the Oldest Native North American History* (Garden City, NY: Avery Publishing Group).

McNeill, W. H. 1989: *Plagues and Peoples* (New York: Anchor Books).

Miller, J. 1994: Review of McCutchen (1993). *American Indian Culture and Research Journal* 18(1): 187–90.

Mooney, J. 1897–8: *Myths of the Cherokee*. Bureau of American Ethnology Report, 19th Annual Report (Washington, D.C.; reprinted Nashville, TN: Charles and Randy Elder, Booksellers, n.d.).

O'Connell, R. L. 1989: *Of Arms and Men* (New York: Oxford University Press).

Richter, D. K. 1983: "War and Culture: The Iroquois Experience," *William and Mary Quarterly* 40: 529–37.

Secoy, F. R. 1992: *Changing Military Patterns of the Great Plains Indians* (Lincoln: University of Nebraska Press).

Shurkin, J. N. 1979: *The Invisible Fire* (New York: G. P. Putnam's Sons).

Steele, I. K. 1994: *Warpaths* (New York: Oxford University Press).

Turney-High, H. H. 1973: *Primitive War, Its Practice and Concepts* (Columbia: University of South Carolina Press).

Utley, R. M. and W. E. Washburn 1977: *Indian Wars* (New York: American Heritage).

Whitehead, N. L. 1992: "Tribes Make States and States Make Tribes: Warfare and the Creation of Colonial Tribes and States in Northeastern South America," in R. B. Ferguson and N. L. Whitehead (eds.), *War in the Tribal Zone* (Santa Fe, NM: School of American Research Press).

Whitehead, N. L. and R. B. Ferguson 1996: "Deceptive Stereotypes about 'Tribal Warfare'," in W. A. Haviland and R. J. Gordan (eds.), *Talking About People* (Mountain View, CA: Mayfield Publishing Company).

Willey, P. S. 1990: *Prehistoric Warfare on the Great Plains* (New York: Garland).

Part Three

Language, Identity, and Expression

10

Languages: Linguistic Change and the Study of Indian Languages from Colonial Times to the Present

Regna Darnell

North American anthropology developed a broader scope than its European counterpart, including not only linguistics but also ethnology, prehistorical archaeology, and physical anthropology. Linguistics has offered useful organizational principles that have helped tie together these diverse approaches. Ethnological interpretation of the cultural and linguistic diversity of American Indian people, for example, has been inseparable from questions of language typology, genetic classification of languages, the relation between language and worldview, and the future of often endangered languages in contemporary Indian communities. And if language has been central to intellectual understandings of Native people, it has been equally implicated in policy questions. Language and linguistic classification, for example, have sometimes been used in place of written Indian histories to trace Indian pasts and to group related tribes together for settlement on reservations. Linguistic change is the conceptual glue that holds together this package of issues, each to be taken up here in turn.

Language Typology

Early recorded observations by fledgling Americanists tended to underestimate the linguistic diversity of the continent, which was masked particularly because many of the languages described were members of the far-flung Algonquian linguistic stock. Scholars thus hypothesized that all American languages shared fundamental properties distinguishing them from the languages of Europe. These so-called polysynthetic languages incorporated many basic grammatical relations within the verb to form what in familiar Indo-European languages would be a complete sentence. For example, Sapir and Swadesh (1946: 106) broke down the internal structure of the single word which translated the English sentence "He will give it to you," in Wishram

("will-he-him-thee-to-GIVE-will"), Takelma ("WILL'GIVE-to-thee-he.or.they.
in.future"), Southern Paiute ("Give-will.visible.thing-visible.creature-thee"), Yana
("ROUND'THING-away-to-does.or.will-done.unto-thou-in.future"), Nootka
("THAT-give-will-done.unto-thou.art"), and Navajo ("thee-to-transitive-will-
ROUND'THING.IN.FUTURE"). Polysynthesis in turn was correlated with the
evolutionary development of the American Indians, in a peculiar form of racism ema-
nating from Charles Darwin (1809–82) by way of Herbert Spencer (1820–1903).

The impulse to typological classification united a first generation of linguistic
scholars in the early days of American independence. These amateur linguists were in
close touch with European colleagues who sought descriptive and interpretive data
to map the world's languages and rank them in degree of progress toward European-
style Enlightenment. Many of these early Americanists were statesmen as well as
scholars. Most were armchair students of the American Indian, utilizing data collected
by practical men on the frontier in their capacities as agents of civilization through
army, commerce, or missionary enterprise.

These new ethnologists of the late eighteenth and early nineteenth centuries
included: Albert Gallatin (1761–1849), Peter Stephen Duponceau (1760–1844),
John Pickering (1777–1846), Thomas Jefferson (1743–1826), James Madison
(1751–1836), and Benjamin Smith Barton (1776–1815). They met to share their
findings at the American Philosophical Society founded in 1743 in Philadelphia by
Benjamin Franklin (1706–90). More pragmatically inclined contributors were Henry
Rowe Schoolcraft (1793–1864) and Lewis Cass (1782–1866), whose actual contacts
with various Indian tribes provided grist for interpretations of Indian history and
culture (Andresen, 1990; Bieder, 1986).

Enlightenment rationalists, in Europe as well as in America, sought universal principles of grammar to shed light on the origins of language. In the absence of direct
evidence (i.e., written documents) for American Indian history, they assumed that
"primitive" languages were both simpler and older than the "civilized" languages of
Europe. Within this framework, actual encounters with Indians proved ambivalent.
At the same time scholars categorized Indian customs as "primitive," they also recognized what Duponceau called the "wonderful organization which distinguishes the
languages of the aborigines of this country from all other idioms of the known
world" (quoted in Andresen, 1990: 101). Duponceau, in 1819, first used the term
"polysynthetic" to characterize the indigenous languages of the Western
Hemisphere. The elegance of those languages, he thought, betrayed a more sophisticated past that had been lost through cultural degeneration (Bieder, 1986: 27–8).
The next year, Pickering designed a uniform orthography for all known Indian languages (Andresen, 1990: 105).

Albert Gallatin, Secretary of the Treasury under presidents Jefferson and Madison,
had studied Indo-European philology in his native Switzerland before emigrating to
the United States in 1780. Relying on questionnaires circulated to Indian agents and
missionaries at his request by the Secretary of War, Gallatin attempted the first classification of American linguistic diversity on philological principles. The 1836 synopsis
of his work, however, already shifted from genetic or historical classification to
language typology, taking for granted the polysynthetic character of all the languages
and the inevitable progress of the Indians from savagery to barbarism and ultimately

to civilization. Languages provided the new American nation with a way to measure the present state of the Indians and their progress in European terms.

Gallatin grouped 81 vocabularies into 28 irreducible linguistic families postulated to share a common origin. He rejected Duponceau's degeneration argument, citing emerging archaeological evidence for cultural (and presumably linguistic) continuity from the Mound Builders of the Mississippi Valley to contemporary Indian tribes. Agriculture, for Gallatin, was the key to further progress. Linguistic structure and cultural achievement continued to be linked.

An increasingly racist climate developed during the following decade, invoking polygenesis (multiple origin of human races) as well as degeneration to explain the savagery of the Indians. Gallatin's impassioned defenses of Enlightenment rationalism in 1845 and 1848 focused on the achievements of the indigenous civilizations of Central and South America as evidence that further progress was possible, indeed likely. Asian origin of the Indians seemed to confirm the monogenetic origin of the entire human species. Gallatin sought a democracy which incorporated the American Indian. His arguments against scientific racism led Gallatin to focus less on genetic classification of languages and more on broad typological features shared by all Indian languages.

Daniel Garrison Brinton (1837–99), a prominent Philadelphia Quaker physician and amateur ethnologist, dominated the American Philosophical Society's Indian researches in the succeeding generation. He held the first professorship of anthropology in North America, at the University of Pennsylvania beginning in 1886, although he had neither students nor salary (Darnell, 1988). Like Gallatin, he emphasized the "psychic unity of mankind" and the monogenetic origin of the human species. What he called "the American Race" (Brinton, 1891) shared a cultural level of evolution, with the characteristic polysynthetic linguistic structure. Brinton emphasized the expressive richness of aboriginal languages (Hallowell, 1960: 43) and introduced the typological framework of Wilhelm von Humboldt (1767–1835) to a North American audience (Brinton, 1885). Again like Gallatin, he emphasized the high cultures of the central continent. Brinton argued that all known human languages were fully rational, thus producing an early version of cultural relativism (the view that all cultures are equally valuable in their own terms).

Brinton adopted the comparative method of Indo-European philology to interpret the descriptive data of ethnology (Brinton, 1891). Philology, like mythology, offered a guide to the underlying thought patterns of "primitive" mankind. Humboldt's concept of "inner form" allowed Brinton to model language as a universal symbolic resource. Like Humboldt, he placed more emphasis on grammar and typology than on vocabulary and the historical relationships of languages. The "structural plan" of the American languages, Duponceau's polysynthesis, was crucial in classifying languages of the world into a small number of types according to their characteristic processes of word formation (Brinton, 1885). On a global scale, therefore, Brinton's cultural relativism vied with an underlying evolutionary racism (the view that cultures are ranked in achievement and value, thereby justifying social inequality).

Brinton's reputation was considerably eclipsed by the increasing professionalization of Americanist anthropology and by the concomitant critique of cultural evolution by Franz Boas in the late nineteenth century (Darnell, 1988, 1998). Boas ignored the subtleties of Brinton's non-unilinear evolution, in which cultures were not locked into a single sequence of development but linguistic change was progressive and creative. Individual aboriginal people would adopt Indo-European inflectional structures in the course of their inevitable assimilation to mainstream American customs. By the end of Brinton's life, language typology based on an evolutionary model was rapidly giving way to genetic classification of languages as the preferred means of organizing their diversity and reconstructing their unwritten histories.

Genetic Classification

Despite the pioneering efforts of Gallatin and Brinton to impose order on the cultural and linguistic diversity of the continent, absence of a systematic overview proved an increasing impediment to western settlement and development. John Wesley Powell (1834–1902) realized that the only way to organize this diversity for practical administration of Indian affairs and for scholarly interpretation was linguistic classification. He adopted Gallatin's questionnaire method to supplement the vocabularies already in the possession of the Smithsonian Institution, under whose umbrella the Bureau of American Ethnology was established by Congress in 1879. Although the entire Bureau staff worked on the linguistic classification, particularly on first-hand fieldwork to fill gaps in knowledge of the various tribes, only Albert Gatschet (1832–1907) was trained in Indo-European philology. The classification, in any case, appeared in 1891 under the sole authorship of Powell as Director of the Bureau. The dominant imagery was of mapping, of filling blank spaces, of locating and categorizing the various Indians.

Unlike his typologically inclined predecessors, Powell emphasized vocabulary rather than grammar as the basis of genetic or historical classification of languages. Grammar, in his view, reflected an evolutionary stage of development rather than the particular historical circumstances of related groups. Detailed histories were urgently needed for extending administrative control and settling Indians on reservations. Powell adopted the social evolutionary framework of Lewis Henry Morgan's *Ancient Society* (1877). Morgan (1818–81) postulated a universal sequence from savagery to barbarism to civilization, each with three sub-stages marked by progress in technology. Powell, in his previous career as a geologist, had modelled land use in the arid lands of the American Southwest as a relationship between environment, technology, and culture, and carried out first-hand fieldwork among the Utes and Shoshones, often dismissed by cultural evolutionists as mere "root-digging savages." He emphasized non-material culture and creative adaptation, adding a fourth stage – Enlightenment, the civilization to which American democracy was heir and which at least some (individual) Indians might aspire to share. Surprisingly, however, Powell did not accept the genetic relationship between Ute, Shoshone, and Nahuatl, the language of the Aztec empire, although the connection had been made earlier in the century. Powell did not attempt seriously to reconcile his typological and evolutionary views with his classificatory and historical ones when he turned to what he considered the primarily pragmatic questions of linguistic classification.

Untrained in linguistics, Powell relied on inspection of word lists for cognates (related words reflecting common origin of the two languages). His assistant for the linguistic classification was Henry Henshaw (1850–1930), a taxonomic biologist. For Powell, therefore, the difficulty was obtaining vocabularies. Anyone could then identify historically related languages. He was uninterested in relative positions within the larger linguistic families; data were rarely adequate, and in any case Powell wanted a practical overview. Thus, Powell's list of linguistic families did not distinguish between the far-flung Algonquian or Athabascan language families and the many apparent isolates, not connected to any larger unit.

Powell recognized 55 stocks without presenting evidence of the cognates on which his genetic conclusions were based. He discussed connections he rejected, noting that further research might resolve their validity. Interestingly, Powell rejected two consolidations of linguistic stocks suggested by Franz Boas as a result of his fieldwork on the Northwest Coast, sponsored in part by the Bureau.

Powell did not expect his classification to be taken as a rigidly codified entity. But his contemporaries, both in Indian administration and in the emerging professional discipline of anthropology, needed an interpretive framework to sort out the diversity of languages and cultures of the continent. The Powell classification provided the only such framework. Moreover, once it was in place, Powell himself turned to other questions. After his death in 1902, possibilities for dramatic revision receded as the Bureau battled for its continued existence (Darnell, 1998).

A second linguistic classification also appeared in 1891, although Daniel Brinton's *The American Race* subordinated linguistic classification to more general ethnological interpretations. His thirteen genetic units were in principle based on grammar as well as on vocabulary. In practice, however, grammatical data were unavailable for many languages. Moreover, Brinton included South American languages which were even less well known than those of the United States and Canada. An appendix of comparative word lists allowed readers to assess Brinton's consolidations of languages and language families. Many, however, appear to be based more on geographical contiguity than on linguistic evidence *per se*. Brinton's most prescient proposal was his acceptance, contra Powell, of the Uto-Aztecan stock.

The relationship between the classifications of Powell and Brinton remains ambiguous (Darnell, 1998). Brinton implied that he was denied access to the Bureau database, but Bureau archives confirm that the decision was his, in order to claim originality for his conclusions. The imminence of the Brinton classification lent urgency to the release of the Bureau version, though it was considered by Powell and his staff as still in progress.

Despite a hiatus in classificatory activity after 1891, fieldwork continued on particular languages, gradually amassing a database for reassessment of linguistic relationships. In the first two decades of the twentieth century, Franz Boas (1858–1942) came to dominate American anthropology, moving its institutional base from Bureau and museum to universities. Boas trained a generation of students with professional credentials along the German graduate model, setting new professional standards for the emerging discipline of anthropology.

Linguistics was crucial to the Boasian program. Early students, accepting Boas's injunction to salvage ethnology and linguistics, wrote dissertations consisting of grammar, texts, and dictionary of an American Indian language. Boas himself was a self-taught linguist who assumed that anyone was capable of producing such work. Among the classic early generation of Boas's students, only Edward Sapir (1884–1939) specialized in linguistics. Sapir came to Boas already trained in Indo-European philology and transposed it to the study of unwritten American Indian languages. He, rather than Boas, would bring a new level of sophistication to the classification of North American linguistic families.

Sapir eagerly placed his linguistic talents and methods at the service of fellow Boasian ethnologists. Like Powell, the early Boasians needed a classificatory framework for cultural and linguistic diversity. Boas (1911) had already argued cogently that race, language, and culture were independent classificatory variables whose results could not be assumed to coincide. Sapir took for granted this rejection of the facile assumptions of evolutionary anthropology and went on to specify methods for ethnological reconstruction of the culture histories of particular American Indian groups, using language to replace the written records of European histories. A single culture history for the continent, as expected by earlier typological evolutionary linguists, was impossible. Rather, Sapir sought evidence of which groups had shared a common history at some point in the past.

Archaeology was virtually non-existent when Sapir wrote his classic *Time Perspective in Aboriginal American Culture: A Study in Method* in 1916. Following Boas's exemplary Northwest Coast format, Sapir dutifully noted diffusion or borrowing of various cultural traits whose present distributions could be interpreted in historical terms, using the culture area as an organizing frame. But the core of Sapir's essay contended that language was unique among cultural forms in its ability to distinguish between "archaic residue" and "diffusional cumulation" (Swadesh, 1951). Sound changes in language were not consciously understood and therefore not subject to manipulation by individuals within culture; thus, they preserved systematically their divergence from a common prototype. Borrowing could not produce such regular change.

Encouraged by the enthusiastic response to his codification of the implicit Boasian historical method, Sapir returned to the question of an overall linguistic classification. His own fieldwork and analysis, particularly in collaboration with Alfred Kroeber (1876–1960) and Roland Dixon (1875–1934) in California, had already begun to consolidate many of the Powell stocks. Kroeber and Dixon initially assumed that observed lexical similarities across the state of California were due to diffusion. Between 1903 and 1919 (Darnell, 1990a, 1998) they moved gradually to interpreting the same lexical data in genetic or historical terms, proposing two new super-stocks in California: Hokan and Penutian.

Sapir, meanwhile, had provided incontrovertible evidence of linguistic relationship through a series of detailed sound changes in the Uto-Aztecan and Athabascan stocks. He connected Wiyot and Yurok, two small languages of California, renamed Ritwan, to the far-flung Algonquian linguistic family. Ritwan was received with considerable skepticism because of the geographical discontinuity between the parts of the super-stock, but the connection has been upheld by further work (Campbell, 1997; Campbell and Mithun, 1979; Goddard, 1997). The diffusional logic of Boasian historical particularism perhaps encouraged his colleagues to read Sapir's evidence in spatial rather than temporal terms. Lacking his linguistic training, many were unable to judge the particular evidence. Kroeber probably represented the majority when he accepted Sapir's new connections on the basis of his authority and "genius" rather than the evidence for particular cases.

Sapir extended Kroeber and Dixon's California Hokan and Penutian stocks to much of southern North America in the former case and to Oregon, the Plateau, and even Mexico in the latter. With these connections in place, Sapir was ready to rewrite the Powell classification, although he worried that colleagues would think he had lost his mind. In December 1920, after a flurry of letters to trusted assessors about his increasing enthusiasm for consolidation of stocks, Sapir presented his six-unit classification, accompanied by a hand-drawn map, at the annual meeting of the American Association for the Advancement of Science. It was published in a brief note in *Science*, the journal of the AAAS, early in 1921, without evidence (which Sapir undoubtedly believed was already available in the reports he and various colleagues had published over the past two decades).

Boasian reaction was divided between exhilaration at the new level of generalization and rejection of the very possibility of reliably distinguishing the effects of genetic relationship from those of diffusion at the time depths implicit in Sapir's superstocks. The most articulate opponent of the new dispensation was Boas, who was sufficiently distressed by what he considered Sapir's abandonment of established methodological principles to explicitly reject in principle the historical work of Sapir, Kroeber, Paul Radin (1883–1939), and others. Boas (1920) reiterated that he had once made some rather radical proposals himself – the very ones that Powell had rejected in 1891 – and recanted in favour of attributing the similarities to diffusion. His preferred methodology had shifted considerably as his Northwest Coast fieldwork moved from linguistic survey to folklore elements and text collection, from language to culture history and folklore.

Despite Boas's strictures, Sapir's classification was convenient and his contemporaries, especially those who were not trained for or interested in the linguistic details, adopted it wholesale as a framework for Americanist ethnology.

A better-known version of the six-unit classification, albeit without the map, appeared in the *Encyclopaedia Britannica* in 1929. Sapir stated his case cautiously, emphasizing an intermediate level of classification between his own six units and the 55 of the Powell classification (see table 10.1). Changes from the 1921 version were minimal and not based on further fieldwork; he merely filled gaps in the continental map. The intermediate units were not, or should not be, controversial. Some were based on his own work, others on that of Kroeber and Dixon, or of other Boasians. The consolidation into larger units appealed to Sapir precisely because of its potential use for ethnological reconstruction. Despite increasing interest in cultural integration and personality and culture after about 1910, the Boasian paradigm remained fundamentally historical. Mapping the diversity of tribes as small independent units made no historical sense to Sapir. The six units, in contrast, could provide insight into the distant past. This classification was the culmination of the "method" promised in *Time Perspective* in 1916. It was also Sapir's final foray into linguistic classification. In the last decade of his life, he worked on particular Athabascan languages and returned to Indo-European, as well as pioneering in interdisciplinary social science studies of the impact of culture on personality (Darnell, 1990a). What could be known about

Table 10.1 North American linguistic classifications

	Sapir 1929	Sapir (Implicit)	Powell 1891
I	Eskimo-Aleut	Eskimo	Eskimo
II	Algonquian-Ritwan	*Algonquian-Ritwan	Algonquian, Beothukan, Wiyot, Yurok
		*Mosan	Waskashan, Chemakuan, Salish
		Kootenay	Kootenay
III	Na-dene	*Tlingit-Athabascan	Haida, Tlingit, Athabascan
		Haida	
IV	Penutian	*California Penutian	Miwok, Costanoan, Yokuts, Maidu, Wintun
		*Oregon Penutian	Takelma, Coos (-Siuslaw), Yakonan, Kalapuya
		*Plateau Penutian	Waiilatpuan, Putuamian, Sahaptian
	Chinook	Chinook	Chinook
		Tsimshian	Tsimshian
		(Mexican Penutian)	—
V	Hokan-Siouan	*Hokan	Karok, Chimariko, Salinan, Yana, Pomo, Washo
		*Coahuiltecan	Tonkawa, Karankawa, Coahuiltecan
		*Tunican	Tunica, Atakapa, Chitimacha
		*Iroquois-Caddoan	Iroquois, Caddoan
		Yuki	Yuki
		Keres	Keres
		Timucua	Timucua
		Muskhogean	Muskhogean
		Siouan	Siouan, Yuchi
VI	Aztec-Tanoan	*Uto-Aztecan	Nahuatl, Pima, Shoshonean
		*Tanoan-Kiowan	Tanoan, Kiowa
		?Zuni	Zuni

* Twelve units Sapir considered accepted by most of his colleagues. The reduction of Powell's 55 stocks to 23 reflected the work of Sapir's generation. The further reduction to six units, he considered to be his own work.

the history of the American Indians on the basis of linguistic classification had reached closure.

The six-unit classification remained the unreflexive standard in American Indian linguistics and anthropology for several decades, confirmed by the so-called consensus classification of 1964 under the aegis of Carl Voegelin and Indiana University. The accompanying map, essentially following Sapir, was widely circulated and headed off broadscale revision of the linguistic classification or rethinking of its evidence and method.

More recent classificatory work, however, has been consistently conservative, taking many of Sapir's proposals as undemonstrated if not undemonstrable. Campbell and Mithun (1979) revisited the question of classification in an edited volume with specialist assessments of major language families. They proposed 62 stocks, a few more than suggested by Powell. This is not, however, merely a rerun of his classification. Campbell and Mithun proposed rigorous standards for comparative linguistic work, relying particularly on detailed sound correspondences. The classification recognized such large units as Algonquian-Ritwan, Nadene, and Eskimo-Aleut, but split Sapir's Hokan and Penutian into a series of linguistic isolates.

Campbell and Mithun display a residual, perhaps habitual, loyalty to the six-unit Sapirian synthesis: isolates are presented in the order they appear in Sapir's groupings (see table 10.2). Further work may demonstrate some of these connections.

Over twenty years later, the conservatism initiated by Campbell and Mithun (1979) has attained considerable momentum, reflected in the rhetoric of two crucial recent assessments (Campbell, 1997; Goddard, 1997). Table 10.2 compares Campbell's current version to the previous one, rearranging his stocks to follow the 1979 listing. The changes are minor: Algonquian-Ritwan is now called Algic; intervening work has demonstrated the genetic connection of Miwok and Costanoan, Sahaptian-Klamath-Molala, and Takelman and Kalapuyan. Progress comes through specific incremental investigations.

Both Campbell and Goddard review the history of the classification of American Indian languages, emphasizing the detailed proposals of Powell and his predecessors, especially Gallatin, with considerably less attention to Sapir's proposals or the ethnological logic that motivated them (cf. Darnell, 1990a).

Campbell and Goddard are responding in part to a resurgence of dramatic consolidation by Joseph Greenberg, whose controversial proposal (1987) involves only three linguistic stocks for all of North and South America: Eskimo-Aleut, Na-dene (in Sapir's broad sense), and Amerind (everything else). Given the methodological standards of proof of the current consensus classification, Greenberg's evidence is simply not talking about linguistic classification in the same sense. Even those (few) linguists who are sympathetic in principle have been hard pressed to defend the particular cognates proposed by what Greenberg calls "multilateral comparison." The classification has been received with enthusiasm, however, by archaeologists, biological anthropologists, and some ethnologists, who seek distant time perspective (in some cases, a reintegration of the traditional subdisciplines of anthropology).

The logic of Greenberg's argument is reminiscent of Sapir's *Time Perspective* and of the six-unit classification that followed. Sapir, however, would have argued that he

Table 10.2   Present conservative consensus classifications

	Campbell and Mithun 1979	*Campbell 1997*
1	Eskimo-Aleut	Eskimo-Aleut
2	Nadene	Tlingit-Athabaskan/ Tlingit Eyak-Athabaskan
—	Haida isolate	Haida
3	Algonquian-Ritwan	Algic Algonquian Wiyot-Yurok
4	Muskogean family	Muskogean
5	Natchez isolate	Natchez
6	Atakapa isolate	Atakapa
7	Chitimacha isolate	Chitimacha
8	Tunica isolate	Tunica
9	Tonkawa isolate	Tonkawa
10	Siouan family	Siouan
11	Iroquoian family	Iroquoian
12	Caddoan family	Caddoan
13	Yuchi isolate	Yuchi
14	Yuman family	Yuman
15	Seri isolate	Seri
16	Pomoan family	Pomoan
17	Palaihnihan family	Palaihnihan
18	Shastan family	Shasta
19	Yanan family	Yana
20	Chimariko isolate	Chimariko
21	Washo isolate	Washo
22	Salinan family	Salinan
23	Karok isolate	Karuk
24	Chumashan family	Chumashan
25	Cotoname isolate	Cotoname
26	Comecrudo isolate	Comecrudo
27	Coahuilteco isolate	Coahuilteco
28	Aranama-Tamique isolate	—
29	Solano isolate	—
30	Esselen isolate	Esselen
31	Jicaque family	—
32	Subtiaba-Tlapanec family	Subtiaba-Tlapanec

Table 10.2 Contd.

	Campbell and Mithun 1979	Campbell 1997
33	Tequistlatecan family	Tequistlatecan
34	Yokuts family	Yokutsan
35	Maiduan family	Maiduan
36	Wintuan family	Wintuan
37	Miwok family	Miwok-Costanoan Miwok
38	Costanoan family	Costanoan
39	Klamath-Modoc isolate	Sahaptian-Klamath Molala
40	Sahaptian family	Sahaptian-Klamath- Molala
41	Cayuse isolate	Cayuse
42	Molala isolate	Sahaptian-Klamath- Molala
43	Coos family	Coosan
44	Alsea isolate	Alsea
45	Siuslaw-Lower Umpqua isolate	Siuslawan
46	Takelma isolate	Takelman Takelma
47	Kalapuya family	Kalapuyan
48	Chinookan family	Chinookan
49	Tsimshian isolate	Tsimshian
50	Zuni isolate	Zuni
51	Kiowa-Tanoan family	Kiowa-Tanoan
52	Uto-Aztecan family	Uto-Aztecan
53	Keresan family	Keresan
54	Yukian family	Yukian
55	Beothuk isolate	Beothuk
56	Kutenai isolate	Kutenai
57	Karankawa isolate	Karankawa
58	Chimakuan family	Chimakuan
59	Salish family	Salishan
60	Wakashan family	Wakashan
61	Timucua isolate	Timucuan
62	Adai	Adai
	(Campbell and Mithun 1979: 39–46; Goddard 1997: 320)	(Campbell 1997: 86–8)

used the same method as the conservatives, only adding the intuition or historical imagination that many of them seemed to lack. From Sapir's point of view, the proper comparison would doubtless have been his fellow Boasian Paul Radin's attempt in 1919 to reduce the linguistic stocks of native North America to a single unit. This proposal was received universally as ludicrous; it was probably the final straw in Boas's repudiation of his students' linguistic consolidations.

At the millennium, classification has again retreated from the foreground of American Indian linguistics. Work continues on subclassification and relative dating of successive splits within particular linguistic stocks. Earlier enthusiasm for absolute dating by what Morris Swadesh called glottochronology has also fallen out of favour in linguistics, although archaeologists and some cultural anthropologists continue to employ it. Areal linguistics clarifies diffusional processes and their internal dynamics. But work at distant time depth on the basis of limited evidence remains largely in abeyance and will continue to do so for the foreseeable future.

Grammatical Categories and Psychological Reality

Not all early twentieth-century Americanist linguistics focused on genetic classification. The Bureau of American Ethnology, after its 1891 synthesis, turned to the grammars of particular languages, selected to represent the diversity of structural or grammatical patterns across Native North America. Franz Boas, whose linguistic and ethnological surveys on the Northwest Coast had set new standards for fieldwork and scientific reporting, was appointed Honorary Philologist to oversee the new collaborative project (Darnell, 1998; Stocking, 1974).

Boas was in a unique position to organize what became the *Handbook of American Indian Languages*. His graduate students at Columbia University had absorbed sufficient linguistics to produce grammatical sketches alongside their ethnological work. The twin poles of Boasian anthropology were history, paradigmatically represented by Boas's ethnological studies of folklore element diffusion on the Northwest Coast, and psychology, which Boas understood to mean the spirit of a people encapsulated in the grammatical categories of their particular language. It was a typological framework without the earlier evolutionary overlay.

Boas's "Introduction" to the first volume of the *Handbook* in 1911 rejected the evolutionary expectation that race, language, and culture would coincide necessarily. Rather, each of the three variables had its unique trajectory in the histories of particular groups. His interest in the psychological character of individual languages was consistent with the particularity of his historical approach and with his systematic critique of evolution. He examined each language on its own terms, just as he sought the unique history of each culture.

The categories of Indo-European grammar, inherited from Greek and Latin, could not be applied to unrelated languages without distorting the unique native point of view encoded in each language. Boas drew on a German Romantic tradition associated with Wilhelm von Humboldt: the spirit of a people inhered in the inner form of their language (Bunzl, 1996). This essential tie between language and thought – the core of personal and community identity – looks backward to the evolutionary typology of Gallatin, Brinton, and Powell, and forward to the linguistic relativity hypotheses elaborated by Boas's foremost linguistic student, Edward Sapir, and his student, Benjamin Lee Whorf (1897–1941).

The interests of Boas and the Bureau overlapped substantially (Darnell, 1998, 1999). The *Handbook* project, as Boas conceived it, revitalized the earlier typological study of American Indian grammatical or morphological processes but without its overtones of evolutionary racism. Since little interpretation was provided in the grammars, one consequence of Boas's inductive method of presentation was that the Bureau's evolutionary commitments were not directly challenged. What Carl Voegelin and George Stocking (1974) called the "Boas plan for the study of American Indian languages" in particular grammars remained largely implicit.

Boas insisted on a standard format of order and organization for synchronic description, accompanied by a brief illustrative text. He intended the grammars to provide a model for further standardization and professionalization of American Indian linguistics. To this end, he exercised surprisingly dictatorial control over the work of his students, former students, and selected collaborators from the older anthropological establishment. Missionaries and Bureau staff were pointedly left out. One student was excluded (from the profession as well as from the project) for failure to report back to Boas at regular intervals from the field. Sapir's sketch of Takelma, his Columbia dissertation, appeared only in the second volume of the *Handbook* in 1922 because it was too long, it included diachronic (historical) analysis, and Sapir did not follow the standard format. The quality of Sapir's grammar was never in question, but that, for Boas, was not the point.

As North American linguistics developed professional autonomy from anthropology, the psychological fit between the spirit of a people and the categories of their language became less relevant to linguistic description. Sapir continued to be interested in language typology; his emphasis on American Indian examples of structural difference in word formation processes in his book, *Language* (Sapir, 1921b), distinguishes it from Leonard Bloomfield's book of the same title a few years later (Hymes and Fought, 1975). Sapir remained firmly within the Boasian alternation of history (genetic classification) and psychology (of grammatical categories) as foundations for the study of language.

Sapir considered the standpoint of the native speaker both in his grammars of particular languages and in his formulation of the concept of the phoneme, the meaningful patterning of sound, in 1925 (Darnell, 1990a). In 1933, he made explicit the "psychological reality" of the phoneme. Meaningful sounds are not objective phenomena. Sapir emphasized sound patterning within the larger structure of a particular language; sounds are not understood in isolation from other sounds. Sapir followed the established Boasian principle that the psychological (i.e., typological) character of a language is located in its grammatical categories. For Sapir more than for Boas, however, the typological argument was also a structural one, emphasizing patterns of contrast more than the forms themselves.

The so-called Sapir–Whorf hypothesis, foreshadowed in Boas and articulated in some of Sapir's work, was developed by Benjamin Lee Whorf during Sapir's final illness and after his death. Whorf argued that the categories of a particular language shaped the way its speakers thought (usually without their conscious awareness) and mediated between them and the outside world. Whorf's collected essays (1956) appeared posthumously under the rubic "language, thought, and reality." Best known to his contemporaries as one among the cohort of American Indian linguists trained by Sapir, he wrote grammars of Milpa Aztec and Hopi.

Whorf's successors have read his claims about linguistic relativity more dramatically and literally than they were undoubtedly intended (Darnell, 1990a). "The Whorf theory complex" (Lee, 1996) was a sophisticated amalgam of reflections on the consequences of a world characterized by linguistic diversity. Whorf in fact talked about "habitual thought" rather than about linguistic determinism. His contrast between the grammatical categories of Hopi and what he called Standard Average European was not intended to essentialize cognitive capacities of speakers of either language, but rather to enjoin "multilingual consciousness" as the key to cross-cultural tolerance in a liberal democracy.

American structuralism (Hymes and Fought, 1975) aspired toward scientific description of languages during the 1940s and 1950s, primarily by removing questions of meaning from the model of grammatical description. In this context, Whorf was read as claiming one-to-one correspondence between language and culture. Linguists and anthropologists attempted to test this correlation empirically, with limited success.

Contemporary explorations of the relation between language, thought, and reality (e.g., Gumperz and Levinson, 1996; Lucy, 1992) are thoroughly revisionist. Whorf receives cursory citation as a predecessor, but the new cognitive science emphasizes universals over cultural and linguistic diversities, rationalism over realism (what Whorf meant by "reality"), and empiricism over idealism (his wish to apply the insights of Americanist linguistics to building a better world). Whorf's interest in grammatical categories and their psychological importance for individual speakers of a language appears naive in a framework focusing on the (neurologically hard-wired) capacities of all human beings, regardless of the language(s) they speak. Mind is taken to be modular, thought to proceed according to schemas and plans having more to do with biology than with culture, embodied in ways including non-verbal as well as verbal patternings. Different belief systems, encoded in language, are understood as variations on a common pattern of universal conceptual assumptions.

At the same time, Americanist linguistics since Sapir and Whorf has turned more seriously to the pragmatic study of language use and of the emergence of meaning through contextualized interaction. There is renewed emphasis on agency, the ability of individuals to shape the world around them. Ethnographic work along these lines has returned to some of the humanistic questions of Boas, Whorf, and Sapir, particularly in the context of rapidly changing contemporary Native American societies in which language is a key to cultural and personal identity.

Contemporary Language Preservation Efforts

The study of American Indian languages within anthropology has foregrounded accessing the Native point of view. But the focus gradually has shifted from the psychological reality of grammatical categories to the organization of cultural knowledge in narrative form. Boasian grammars were expected to include illustrative texts. Elicitation of isolated paradigms was deemed a less valid source of data than consecutive speech, preferably spontaneous. Much of Boas's legendary five-foot shelf of Kwakiutl ethnography consists of texts, presented with minimal commentary, illustrating both language and culture in the words of native speakers. Many of these texts were collected and recorded by Boas's primary consultant and translator George Hunt, although they were published under Boas's name as primary author. Sapir and other Boasians also taught consultants to write their languages and continue the work of text collection after the anthropologist/linguist left the field. Despite ambivalent co-authorships, the resulting documents provide invaluable evidence today of Native points of view at the time they were collected.

The textuality of the Americanist tradition at the intersection of anthropology and linguistics is undeniable (Darnell, 1990b, 1992, 1999). Sapir was particularly active in moving from the point of view of the particular Native consultant ("informant" in the language of his day) to individual personality as both creating and created by cultural forms. He came to argue that a culture had as many versions as it had individual members.

The American Indian linguistic texts collected by the Boasians and their successors serve today as fundamental documents, especially in light of encroaching language loss. Many aboriginal American languages are extinct; others continue to function with varying degrees of endangerment. Only a few are unproblematically viable for the foreseeable future.

Contemporary Native American communities across the continent are engaged in programs of language maintenance and revitalization. These draw on existing anthropological and linguistic literature to jog the memories of elders who have not used their first languages for a long time. They also seek to reintegrate information about traditional culture that has ceased to function in everyday practices. Existing texts frequently document both linguistic and cultural change. Collaborations between linguists and Native communities have become commonplace, while community members are trained in linguistics and language pedagogy.

Authorship of texts is now attributed to their producers. Sapir collected texts on Kutchin, an Athabascan language of the Northwest Territories, in 1923 at a summer camp in Pennsylvania; he never visited a Kutchin community and never published John Fredson's texts. In 1982, these texts were published by the Alaska Native Languages Center in Fairbanks under the name of John Fredson (with a modest notation that Edward Sapir recorded them). The orthography and translation resulted from consultation with the contemporary Kutchin community. The linguistic value of these texts is immeasurably enhanced by the powerful political message of the transfer of ownership of the words back to the community of the original speaker. Taking intellectual property from an oral tradition is as significant an appropriation as taking material objects and skeletal remains. The ethical ground has shifted considerably, making the anthropologist facilitator and translator rather than author.

One consequence of the trend toward community control of cultural materials and language programs has been increasing inseparability of linguistic and cultural issues in American Indian scholarship. Silver and Miller (1997), for example, subtitle their textbook "Cultural and Social Contexts." Languages can no longer be isolated from their use in particular communities at particular points in time. Language change has a social dimension. Concern with use as well as structure of language has developed as an area of Americanist linguistics and anthropology primarily since the 1960s under the rubric of ethnography of speaking (Murray, 1994).

In some communities, English is now the only language shared by elders and young people. Traditional forms of storytelling, however, demonstrate considerable continuity from aboriginal languages into English. The textual emphasis continues in new media. Traditional knowledge once transmitted exclusively through oral tradition may now be recorded on sound tapes, videotape, or published in written form so that future generations will have the benefit of the knowledge accumulated by this generation of elders.

Linguists and anthropologists have been active in collecting, editing, and publishing such texts, both in traditional languages and in English. The most extensive philological enterprise results from the felicitous long-term collaboration of linguist H. C. Wolfart and Plains Cree elder and linguist Freda Ahenakew at the University of Manitoba in Winnipeg. Their text editions (Ahenakew and Wolfart, eds., 1992, 1997; Wolfart and Ahenakew, eds., 1993) are presented in Cree and English, often with Cree syllabic script, with grammatical apparatus enabling linguists or non-speakers from the Native community to read the texts. The narrators are elders, mostly women, who record their own experiences in a natural pedagogical context targeted to a Native audience. This long-term project provides a model for other communities with a critical mass of traditional language speakers of all ages.

Elders from other First Nations (the Canadian term for Native American) communities are forced to speak in English if they want to be understood by their grandchildren. Julie Cruikshank (1990) at the University of British Columbia has worked in intensive collaboration with three traditional women elders of the Southern Yukon, to present their autobiographies in English. These texts interweave traditional cultural knowledge and personal experience. They are invaluable documents reflecting the rapid culture change of the past century and the efforts of aboriginal communities to preserve their identity through language and traditional transmission of knowledge.

In Southwestern Ontario, few young Anishnabek (Ojibwa) speak their traditional language fluently. But efforts to preserve the experiences of the elders (and revive the language) continue unabated. Native artist and writer Barry Milliken (1997) returned to his home community to record the stories of Annie Rachel Shawkence, medicine woman and elder of Stony Point Reserve. The narrative authority of these stories enhances the community's highly contested claims to land and self-determination.

These representative examples indicate the vitality of contemporary efforts to preserve traditional languages and forms of transmitting traditional knowledge across the United States and Canada today. American Indian languages have changed and are still changing, as all languages do. Increasingly, this change is in the hands of Native American communities, though past and present scholars have provided critical resources for language maintenance and revitalization.

BIBLIOGRAPHY

Ahenakew, Freda and H. C. Wolfart (eds.) 1992: *Kohkominawak Otacimowiniwawa: Our Grandmothers' Lives as Told in Their Own Words* (Saskatoon: Fifth House Publishers).

Ahenakew, Freda and H. C. Wolfart (eds.) 1997: *Eki-pe-kiskinowapahtihicik. Their Example Showed Me the Way: A Cree Woman's Life Shaped by Two Cultures* (told by Emma Minde) (Edmonton: University of Alberta Press).

Andresen, Julie T. 1990: *Linguistics in America 1769–1924* (New York: Routledge).

Bieder, Robert E. 1986: *Science Encounters the Indian, 1820–1880: The Early Years of American Ethnology* (Norman: University of Oklahoma Press).

Boas, Franz 1911: "Introduction," *Handbook of American Indian Languages. Bureau of American Ethnology Bulletin* 40: 1–83.

Boas, Franz 1920: "The Classification of American Languages," *American Anthropologist* 22: 367–76.

Brinton, Daniel Garrison 1885: "The Philosophic Grammar of American Languages as Set Forth by Wilhelm von Humboldt, with a Translation of an Unpublished Memoir by Him on the American Verb," *Proceedings of the American Philosophical Society* 22: 306–54.

Brinton, Daniel Garrison 1891: *The American Race: A Linguistic Classification and Ethnographic Description of the Native Tribes of North and South America* (New York: N.D.C. Hodges)

Bunzl, Matti 1996: "Franz Boas and the Humboldtian Tradition," in *Volksgeist as Method and Ethic* (ed.) George W. Stocking, Jr. (Madison: University of Wisconsin Press), pp. 17–78.

Campbell, Lyle 1997: *American Indian Languages: The Historical Linguistics of Native America* (Oxford: Oxford University Press).

Campbell, Lyle and Marianne Mithun (eds.) 1979: *The Languages of Native America: Historical and Comparative Assessment* (Austin: University of Texas Press).

Cruikshank, Julie 1990: *Life Lived Like a Story* (Lincoln: University of Nebraska Press).

Darnell, Regna 1988: *Daniel Garrison Brinton: The "Fearless Critic" of Philadelphia* (Philadelphia: University of Pennsylvania Department of Anthropology).

Darnell, Regna 1990a: *Edward Sapir: Linguist, Anthropologist, Humanist* (Berkeley and Los Angeles: University of California Press).

Darnell, Regna 1990b: "Franz Boas, Edward Sapir and the Americanist Text Tradition," *Historiographia Linguistica* 17: 129–44.

Darnell, Regna 1992: "The Boasian Text Tradition and the History of Canadian Anthropology," *Culture* 17: 39–48.

Darnell, Regna 1998: *And along Came Boas: Continuity and Revolution in Americanist Anthropology* (Amsterdam and Philadelphia: John Benjamins).

Darnell, Regna 1999: "Theorizing the Americanist Tradition: Continuities from the Bureau of American Ethnology to Franz Boas," in *Theorizing the Americanist Tradition*, (eds.) Lisa Valentine and Regna Darnell (Toronto: University of Toronto Press).

Fredson, John 1982: *John Fredson Edward Sapir Haa Googwandak* (Fairbanks: Alaska Native Languages Center).

Gallatin, Albert 1836: *A Synopsis of the Indian Tribes of North America. Transactions and Collections of the American Antiquarian Society* 2: 1–422.

Gallatin, Albert 1845: *Notes on the Semi-Civilized Nations of Mexico, Yucatan and Central America. Transactions of the American Ethnological Society* 1: 1–352.

Gallatin, Albert 1848: "Introduction," *Hale's Indians of North-west America and Vocabularies of North America. Transactions of the American Ethnological Society* 2: xxiii–clxxx, 1–130.

Goddard, Ives (ed.) 1997: *Handbook of North American Indians,* vol. 17: *Languages* (Washington, D.C.: Smithsonian Institution).

Greenberg, Joseph 1987: *Language in the Americas* (Stanford: Stanford University Press).

Gumperz, John and Stephen Levinson (eds.) 1996: *Rethinking Linguistic Relativity* (Cambridge: Cambridge University Press).

Hallowell, A. Irving 1960: "The Beginnings of Anthropology in America," in *Selected Papers from the American Anthropologist, 1888–1920* (ed.) Frederica de Laguna (Washington D.C.: American Anthropological Association), pp. 1–90.

Hymes, Dell and John Fought 1975: *American Structuralism. Current Trends in Linguistics 13: Linguistic Historiography* (ed.) Thomas Sebeok (The Hague: Mouton), pp. 903–1176.

Lee, Penny 1996: *The Whorf Theory Complex: A Critical Reconstruction* (Amsterdam and Philadelphia: John Benjamins).

Lucy, John 1992: *Language Diversity and Thought: A Reformulation of the Linguistic Relativity Hypothesis* (Cambridge: Cambridge University Press).

Milliken, Barry (ed.) 1997: *Annie Rachel Mshkikiikwe: Stories from an Elder of the Kettle and Stony Point First Nation* (London, Ontario: Centre for Research and Teaching of Canadian Native Languages).

Morgan, Lewis Henry 1877: *Ancient Society* (New York: Henry Holt).

Murray, Stephen O. 1994: *Theory Groups and the Study of Language in North America: A Social History* (Amsterdam and Philadelphia: John Benjamins).

Powell, John Wesley 1891: *Indian Linguistic Families of America North of Mexico. Seventh Annual Report of the Bureau of American Ethnology* (Washington, D.C.: Government Printing Office).

Sapir, Edward 1916: *Time Perspective in Aboriginal American Culture: A Study in Method* (Ottawa: Department of Mines, Geological Survey of Canada, Memoir 90, Anthropological Series 13).

Sapir, Edward 1921a: "A Bird's Eye View of American Languages North of Mexico," *Science* 54: 408.

Sapir, Edward 1921b: *Language: An Introduction to the Study of Speech* (New York: Harcourt, Brace and World).

Sapir, Edward 1929: "Central and North American Languages," *Encyclopaedia Britannica,* 14th edition, vol. 5, pp. 138–41.

Sapir, Edward and Morris Swadesh 1946: "American Indian Grammatical Categories," *Word* 2: 103–12.

Silver, Shirley and Wick R. Miller 1997: *American Indian Languages: Cultural and Social Contexts* (Tucson: University of Arizona Press).

Stocking, George W., Jr. 1974: "The Boas Plan for the Study of American Indian Languages," in *Traditions and Paradigms in the History of Linguistics* (ed.) Dell Hymes (Bloomington: Indiana University Press), pp. 454–84.

Swadesh, Morris 1951: "Diffusional Cumulation and Archaic Residue as Historical Explanations," *Southwestern Journal of Anthropology* 7: 1–21.

Whorf, Benjamin Lee 1956: *Language, Thought, and Reality: Selected Writings of Benjamin Lee Whorf* (ed.) John B. Carroll (Cambridge, MA: MIT Press).

Wolfart, H. C. and Freda Ahenakew (eds.) 1993: *Kinehiyawiwininaw Nehiyawewin. The Cree Language is Our Identity: The La Ronge Lectures of Sarah Whitecalf* (Winnipeg: University of Manitoba Press).

11

Performative Traditions in American Indian History

L. G. MOSES

From southwest of the plaza, the drums begin; rhythmic, cadenced, faint. The men of Isleta parade from the kiva on this day of celebration and giving, dressed in their ribbon shirts of red and white: first the drummers, then the caciques, next the mayor-domos, followed by the war captains, and finally the dancers. In the plaza, bordered by cottonwood arbors, the male dancers, joined by women wearing ornate mantles, take their places.

It is September 4, the festival of San Agostinito. Twice already this forenoon, the dancers have come from the church. In 1604, the Spaniards named it to honor St. Anthony, to whom Catholics pray when they have lost something, sometimes themselves. St. Anthony's antedated any Christian relic in tidewater Virginia or anti-nomian New England. Destroyed in the 1680 Pueblo Revolt, the charred ruins of the first great church served as the foundation for the new basilica. The church today, washed alabaster by attentive hands, cools the penitent seeking succor from the dusty plaza at noon.

When the Spaniards retreated from Santa Fe in 1680 within days of the revolt, they took south with them as hostages those citizens of Isleta who would plight, when threatened by the crucifix and the sword, their affection for Holy Mother Church, the Holy Office, and the wholly ruthless sons of Castile. Some of the Christian Tiwas remain today at a place they named Isleta del Sur. But three hundred souls, hungry for the vistas of home, and having affirmed their devotion to the gods of Aragon and Castile, returned to Isleta, and became, according to legend, the most Catholic of the Pueblos. They dug a grand kiva, however, far from the plaza and the church. For all the *Pater Nosters* and *Ave Marias*, this sacred dance, the giveaway, originates from the kiva, the holiest of places, where no outsider ever ventures.

The dancers, men and women in alternating columns, enter the plaza. The slow, shuffling half-steps mark the beat of the drum and stress alternate syllables of the singers. Three times they circle the enclosure. At the end of the last circuit, the mothers of the village surround the dancers. They carry baskets filled with goods – not the bread that has made Isleta famous, or pottery or blankets; but instead plastic laundry baskets from Wal-Mart, stuffed with the goods that inspire the spectators to close the distance between themselves and the revelers. The children of Isleta, swept toward the dancers by their aunts and sisters, take up their posts. The mothers toss the gifts to the crowd. The children, who had been pelting the tourists with "Bomb Bags" (aluminum foil wrapped bicarbonate tablets from China that, when pinched, are mixed with water and become explosive), are able to recover some of the generosity of their relations, and symbolically the economy of the Pueblo survives for another year.

Performance, as the False Face ceremony among the Iroquois would suggest, wears many visages. Sacred or secular, secret or public, for Native or non-Native audiences – performance in American Indian history is as old and varied as human habitation on the continent; as new and vibrant as the latest "non-traditional" color scheme adopted by a fancy dancer.

From Irving Goffman to Judith Butler, scholars have agreed that performance is essential to thinking about identity, both individual and collective. In the multicultural interactions between Indians and non-Indians, performance illumines questions about cultural identity, about processes of cultural change, syncretism, hybridity, blending, mixture, and parallelism. At the same time, performance can also reveal the workings of power in the relation between Indians and Europeans. These are two different categories of questions, fused together in dance, song, act, and exhibition.

Before attending to these issues, however, it is worth considering briefly the sources available for the historical study of performative traditions. The performative tradition is as much a story about the observer as the observed. Generations of spectators, the vast majority of them non-Indian, have pondered the meaning of dancing and singing tribes, studying performance in "the wild," upon the stage, within the arena, recorded digitally on a plastic disk, or projected upon a screen. Indians in the flesh (and often in pantomime) have danced, sung, ridden, acted, joked, or re-enacted their way into the consciousness of such observers, often altering their performances for specific kinds of spectators.

Perhaps the most prominent spectators have been anthropologists. As noted elsewhere in this volume, the nineteenth-century idea of the "vanishing American" gave a sense of urgency to the founders of the modern discipline of anthropology in the United States. The "science of mankind," as it came to be called, depended on salvaging what remained of Indian cultures in presumably pristine form.

Developmentalism dominated the thinking of the first generation of professional anthropologists in the United States. Expanding upon Lewis Henry Morgan's ideas about the stages of civilization, many ethnologists believed that they could recover some of the lost history of modern civilizations by study of the "primitive" survivals. Driven by this possibility, the collection of data sometimes became an end in itself. Such data, according to the ideal, would provide future generations of scholars (and ironically, as it turns out, many Indians themselves) with resources with which to write studies of social and cultural development.

In their race to collect artifacts and data, these anthropologists nevertheless established, albeit obliquely, areas of research rich in performative traditions. The series of

Bulletins and *Annual Reports* of the Bureau of American Ethnology, as well as the Smithsonian Institution's *Miscellaneous Collections*, helped organize anthropological thought in the United States (Hinsley, 1981: 147–52; Bieder, 1986: 243–6). When it came to questions of performance, the central organizing principle was often not performance itself, but rather the study of religion.

Religious ritual invariably offers a performance particularly attuned to issues of identity and cultural cohesiveness. Indeed, religion, like other kinds of cultural performance, preserves social continuity while at the same time promoting social change. Howard L. Harrod examines these dynamics in *Becoming and Remaining a People: Native American Religions on the Northern Plains* (1995). Much like salvage anthropologists, but in a different context, Harrod has claimed a larger purpose, viewing religion as an effort to bring the richness, depth, and cultural complexity of past societies into coincidence with contemporary cultural heirs. Some of the descriptive and theoretical material from religious studies, then, easily finds its way into questions surrounding Indian performance.

The history and ethnography of performative traditions depend on a variety of source materials ranging from the observations of early travelers, explorers, and fur traders writing in the languages of Europe to the large body of work produced in the nineteenth and twentieth centuries by cultural anthropologists and archaeologists. Despite their obvious biases, such observations were nevertheless first-hand. They remain important sources for retrieving historical data on Native American traditions and rituals, and can be productively used to understand the issues surrounding performance. In the hands of skilled ethnohistorians, such texts can animate studies of Native American cultures (Harrod, 1995).

Unlike these earlier observers, anthropologists and archaeologists have frequently made their observations about performative traditions from particular theoretical perspectives that undoubtedly shaped the process and results. Even so, anthropological records in the area of religious traditions and performance practices have been descriptively rich. And theoretical frameworks have themselves proved extremely useful. Loretta Fowler's *Shared Symbols, Contested Meanings* (1987), for example, has influenced the way scholars approach cultural identity (and by extension, the performative tradition) and the ways that identity has been and continues to be symbolized among, in this case, the people of the Northern Plains.

Like Native oral traditions, performances are shared knowledge expressed aurally and visually in contained temporal moments. They have been equally subject to the continued reluctance of some historians outside Native American studies to accept the viability of oral "texts." In fact, however, there have often been convergences between American Indian memories recorded in the early twentieth century and observations reported in the eighteenth and nineteenth centuries. This, more than anything else, can be used to demonstrate convincingly that oral traditions and practices, or memories of them, are not as suspect as they might seem to less experienced researchers. As Harrod's evocative phrase "communities of memory" suggests, native societies conserve tradition while possessing the creative capacity to reinterpret traditions and practices (Harrod, 1995: xviii). Oral/aural cultures may as easily conserve as they innovate, and vice versa.

Memories are mediated within Indian communities. Morris Foster's Comanche informants, for example, had much to say about how and why they remembered what they did (Foster, 1991). Likewise, Julie Cruikshank's *The Social Life of Stories* is brilliant in its comments on the power of memory and the ways in which knowledge and memory get shared, negotiated, and by extension, performed. Luke E. Lassiter argues that stories told by and for the community, and those told by and for academics, are very different (Lassiter, 1997). American Indian societies have organized knowledge and experience into shared structures of meaning. Upon this the creative imagination of the people worked, producing both the continuities and discontinuities observed and recorded by cultural anthropologists. Native American groups have incorporated new religious and performative elements from Europeans and from other Indian groups for generations. But they did not do so without actively reinterpreting traditions and rituals, reshaping them to fit their own needs. Performance, then, has served as the concrete expression of creative cultural imagination, of borrowing and mixing, of the retaining of some traditions and rituals and the reshaping of others (Harrod, 1995; Irwin, 1994; Holler, 1995; Crummett, 1993). And perhaps nowhere have the questions surrounding cultural change and persistence in a world of interaction been so compelling as in Indian dance.

Embodying both a religious and a secular component, dance lives at the heart of American Indian performative tradition. Some authors have seen dance as encompassing first principles, the deep core of culture. Richard Drinnon, for example, suggests that human survival may depend on relearning dance, in Martha Graham's sumptuous phrase "the secret language of the body" (Drinnon, 1987: 113). For that bodily "language" speaks directly to a culture's relation to the natural world, and the path that leads to spiritual interconnectedness must be trod metaphorically on dancing feet. The Hopi are frequently offered as people wise in the ways of nature's syndicalism. In every season they venerated the "Mighty" or "Magnificent" Something. "And at the spiritual center of their great affirmation," Drinnon writes, "was the dance, the moving means of interweaving life, culture, land" (p. 109).

In sacred homelands and upon reservations, the tradition of performance marked the changes of the season if not the passage of time (Whorf, 1956: 58–60). And performance can express not only relations with nature, but social relations as well. For each of the Hopi mesas, the integration of politics, religion, and the environment occurs through the performance of public acts of faith and supplication. What Albert Yava and Edmund Nequatewa do for First and Second Mesas respectively, Peter Whiteley does for Bacavi (Yava, 1978; Nequatewa, 1993; Whiteley, 1988).

Howard Meredith suggests that in Euro-American cultures, the stuff of politics – propositions, arguments, and metaphorical systems – are competitive and adversarial. Argumentation exists as a sort of warfare, and winning at all costs achieves high marks of social approval. The Southern Plains tribes by comparison (and in common with many other Indian people) express their visions of the world and of their societies in propositions set forth in forms of dance (Meredith, 1995: 3).

Yet if dance materialized first principles and social expression, it too was subject to the change that accompanies cultural contact. The aesthetics of Indian dance, for example, demonstrate particularly well the separation between white observer and

Native observed. On an 1829 tour of the Old Northwest, Caleb Atwater compared Indian dancing to classical theater (Atwater, 1975 [1830]: 130). Atwater, unlike so many other observers, seems not to have let his "civilized prejudices" get in the way. In contact with Indians he could not help using a particular cultural lens to view distinct – and therefore unique – Native cultures.

Reginald and Gladys Laubin, historians, dancers, and Indian hobbyists, write that, though art and dance occurred innately in Indian cultures, "almost like breathing," Indians themselves never regarded dancing as art. Having imposed the category "art" onto dance (and found Indians wanting), the Laubins carried out their own logic, assuming a culture in decline. The only way Indian dancing could be preserved was through public interest. Dance, they thought, had already lost its significance and importance for Indians (Laubin and Laubin, 1989: 84). An extraordinary statement. Even within the category "art," it is vitiated by the careers of such ballerinas as Rosella Hightower, Yvonne Choputeau, and Maria and Marjorie Tallchief, to say nothing of an entertainer like Molly Spotted Elk, dancer, actor, and cabaret singer, or the innumerable dances occurring in urban and reservation dance grounds (Livingston, 1997; Tallchief and Kaplan, 1997; McBride, 1995).

Euro-Americans have tended to perceive tribal dances as entertainment rather than argument, as "art" rather than life, as cultural vestige rather than ongoing creation. No less difficult have been questions about cultural change, adaptation, and acculturation. Can one imagine at the same time a "traditional" culture, fixed in time and character, and a culture that changes regularly in reaction to new kinds of contacts? Coincident with the growth in popularity of Wild West shows, for example, came the modern Indian rodeo and powwow, where displays of *Western* skills and artistry offered status and financial rewards. In the case of the powwow, it also became a means by which people could retain, restore, or, in certain instances, create through adaptation a modern American Indian identity. Building upon older cultural content, they create an adaptive "pan-Indian" culture for those persons long separated from their landed heritage.

Most of the current writing about powwows proceeds from the assumption that dance represents an important set of accommodations to the cultural and social change that has occurred in Indian communities, particularly in the twentieth century. Historian Clyde Ellis, for example, suggests that dance is best understood as a way to discern important strategies of adaptation that have deep cultural meaning. The contemporary Southern Plains powwow, then, represents a carefully articulated expression of identity and cultural maintenance (Ellis, 1999). Many other works also share an interest in how dance reflects not only an adaptation to outside forces, but also a set of negotiations based on internal pressures as well (Lassiter, 1998; Foster, 1991; Powers, 1990).

The same holds true for music, so closely joined to dance as to be synonymous. Severt Young Bear of the Porcupine Singers at Pine Ridge has written that "song and dance can't really be separated. ... We never dance without singing and we rarely sing without dancing" (Young Bear and Theisz, 1994: 38). American Indian music and dance have become, according to William K. Powers, socially heritable signs of American Indian cultural vitality and identity. Whereas Powers' interpretation, which turns on cultural retention and creativity, differs from older notions of Indian culture in decline, his interest in musical performance shares a long history.

Ethnomusicological research in North America has built upon a tradition that began in the nineteenth century with the work of Alice C. Fletcher among the Omahas. It may have found its greatest expression in the work of Frances Densmore in the twentieth century. The focus of that tradition, however, has been on collection, often at the expense of synthesis and analysis. With the technological achievements in recording dating from the 1950s, however, the number of published articles and monographs, including pure descriptions of expressive culture, have steadily declined. In some respects, the sheer volume of recordings represents another source for ethnographers of music.

One might place music and dance in a classificatory system distinguished on two levels: as either "traditional" or "popular"; and as either "tribal" or "intertribal." By their very nature, traditional forms are always predominantly tribal. Popular forms are distinguished by their diffusion even into the non-Indian community. Tribal music and dance are always traditional in structure and function – they are usually associated with individual tribes. Intertribal music and dance may also be traditional in structure; but they are not always so in function. "Tribalism," again borrowing from William K. Powers, deals with a classification of things; whereas "intertribalism" deals with a classification of processes. Tribalism and intertribalism are therefore dialectical, two systems operating coterminously. Persons participate in both systems, performing both specific "tribal" and broadly based "Indian" identities (Powers, 1980: 212–16).

Tribal music and dance represent historical continuity. There is, of course, historical change within each tribe; but the rate of change is slower than the diffusion of traits in intertribal music and dance. Tribal music and dance may persist for decades or even centuries. Intertribal music and dance may change from one season to the next. The relationship between the two is dynamic. Intertribal changes reflect and synthesize tribal changes. Tribalism reinforces ethnic identity and relates music and dance to other social and cultural categories that are meaningful within individual tribes. Intertribal music and dance reinforce American Indian identity at a level where this identity is more directly threatened by non-Indian influences. The two systems, as in regional powwows, often operate in the same arena (Powers, 1980: 216; Nettl, 1967).

Powers has also offered three reasons why professional singing has emerged in the last half century. First, the proliferation of recording companies in the 1950s had consequences for the growing professionalism of Indian singers. The recording, editing, and titling of songs, and the writing of liner notes created a system of classification where none had existed previously (except perhaps in the language of the ethnomusicologist). Second, songs themselves became identified by genre, region, and tribe. Finally, Western musical technology became widely available to Indian singers and song groups. Among their baggage, traveling song groups carried public address systems, commercially manufactured drums, and tape recorders (Powers, 1990: 162). Even the way various song groups dressed became part of the performance itself, as well as a means for differentiating one group from another (Young Bear and Theisz, 1994: 44).

Contemporary American Indian music is performed under a big tent. It ranges from the innovative flute music of Carlos Nakai and John Rainer, Jr.; to the bluesy work of John Trudell and Indigenous; to other genres, from Folk/Country, to Urban, to Reservation Rap. There are small local radio stations, syndicated shows, and internet players. The field has grown so large and disparate that by 1999, the second annual Native American Music Awards were being presented in sixteen categories, including "Best Radio Station" (reservation radio has some of the most innovative programming in North America) and "Best Rap/Hip Hop Artist." Aside from listening in the audience or to the radio, awareness of this musical scene is best achieved through reading in the ephemeral press in such journals as *Rolling Stone, Cowboys & Indians, Native Peoples*, and *Native Artist* (in some respects replacing the defunct *Indian Artist*).

Back in the heyday of salvage anthropology, it had been the fashion in social science research to view Indians as part of a pure but dying culture. Left unexamined was the capacity for change. Thus, it was always the oldest member of the tribe to be consulted in matters of art – painting, singing, dancing. This quest for purity blinded researchers to the fact that Indians had creatively *changed* their music and dance. Innovation, ironically, was the very attribute associated with the Western world's definition of art (Heth, 1992: 14). Repetition of songs and dances secure the survival of ancient social, religious, and curing ceremonies; but the creation and performance of new songs and dances are equally necessary to ensure sustained interest and continuity (Lassiter, 1998; Little Coyote and Giglio, 1997).

Music and dance, originally integrated into virtually all tribal institutions, have become institutions in themselves, not only within Native societies, but also in American society itself. Singers and dancers are now symbolic of the continuation of American Indian cultures that do not threaten, but rather enrich the dominant culture. Whereas once Indian ceremonials were dismissed as heathenish or suppressed as being dangerous, the relatively benign acceptance of Indian pageantry allowed adaptive Indian cultures again to flourish.

Most of the major powwows celebrated today had their origin at the turn of the twentieth century, when Indian fairs received a blessing from the federal government. Ironically, at that same moment, that same government moved to restrict traditional religious dances. The freedom to be – or remain – Indian began to be increasingly manifested in secular and public spheres. Dance and song occurred within a calendar of events and at places outside usual settings, whether a rodeo arena, a coliseum, an auditorium, or a theatrical stage (Powers, 1990: 161). This particular transformation suggests that we look at performance not only for its window into cultural change and persistence, but also for the ways it reveals the workings of power, domination, and resistance in Indian–American relations.

Performance as ritualized "Native" behavior – dance, religious ceremonial, oration and the like – could, salvage anthropologists believed, serve the ends of science. Re-created performance for mass, and largely white, audiences, by contrast, celebrated a much larger story of American civilization. Wild West shows and films looked nostalgically to the recent past, leaving science and anthropology behind and turning instead to popular history and myth. The shows took public performance by Indians to the level of mass entertainment. In this way, the Native performative tradition also came to encompass "Indian" imagery, and thus reinforced the Native place in the American imagination.

Richard Slotkin observes that Wild West shows have proved easy targets for historians. They recreated the national legend of the "Winning of the West," which included near-annihilation of the buffalo and the military victory over the Indians. Buffalo Bill and the legion of imitators that followed became metaphorical agents of a ravaged wilderness, exploiters cast as heroes. Their faithful Indian adversaries became symbols of debauched humanity (Slotkin, 1973: 564–5).

Wild West shows were not reality, but they were *something*. They created "mythic" spaces that combined reality with legend, past with present. They ritualized history by acting out the myths that had been made of history (Slotkin, 1981: 34). Not always appreciated was the fact that for over half a century, Indian people participated in the creation and performance of that myth-history.

There are two schools of thought about Indian participation in Wild West shows. One, echoing an earlier generation of Indian policy reformers, generally excoriates the whole notion of Indians in aspic. Indian performers were dominated, degraded, and pathetic. The other, building upon an ethnohistorical tradition of observation from the perspective of the participants, finds Indian agency. Native performances, according to this view, offered a means both to preserve and to celebrate American Indian cultures and their histories. This analytical dichotomy may be a false one, for in exercising agency, Indian performers also reinforced stereotypes, ideas that would later be used to rationalize policies that *were* dominating and degrading.

Raymond Stedman sees a progression of Indian stereotypes, as if they moved after the fashion of westward expansion. The frontier of Indian tales changed from the pedestrian natives of the Eastern Woodlands to the distant West of Indians on horseback. The world of performance likewise changed from stage to arena to silver screen. Romantic poets abandoned the Noble Savage as the last of his race. Publications shifted from the "gentlemanly publishing house" to the mass-market penny press (Stedman, 1982: 79–80).

In the 1970s and 1980s, revisionism took the path of least resistance, particularly in film imagery, which tended simply to trade savage stereotypes for noble. With *Soldier Blue* and *Little Big Man*, Indians became peaceful villagers trying to avoid the search-and-destroy missions of the U.S. Cavalry. More to the point, film studies scholarship also criticized earlier images, many of which descended through the Wild West shows of Buffalo Bill Cody. Gretchen Bataille and Charles Silet seemed to hold Buffalo Bill personally responsible for negative images, noting that his Wild West firmly established Indians as figures of entertainment along with the "stage Irishman and the comic Jew" (Bataille and Silet, 1980: xxii). Donald Kaufmann saw Indian entertainers as the first victims of "media bias." Once Hollywood absorbed stereotypes from the Wild West shows, he argued, history discarded Indians as a shaping force (Kaufmann, 1980: 22). The continued marketing of Wild West show imagery in film, long after Buffalo Bill had quit the planet, represented for some people the "filmic cultural genocide" for American Indians (Friar and Friar, 1972: 70).

Because Wild West shows created stereotypes about Indians that have persisted for much of the twentieth century, the performers themselves have often been treated as victims, dismissed as irrelevant, or simply ignored. Recent writing by cultural historians and ethnohistorians, however, has abandoned the victimology of an earlier generation. As vital participants rather than simple victims, they have in fact achieved a kind of agency missing from earlier critiques of the Wild West show imagery (Slotkin, 1992: 75; White, 1994: 9). For Richard White, the imaginative creation of a diverse and performative West – with its roots in Buffalo Bill – prepared the way for a new history that re-examined lived nineteenth-century experience in a region much more diverse than the one imagined by Frederick Jackson Turner (p. 54).

In my own writing, I've tried to amend the view that entrepreneurs such as Buffalo Bill relentlessly exploited the "Show Indians," as they were called by people in the Indian Office. I took my lead from an earlier observation made by Vine Deloria that Buffalo Bill and the first generation of Show Indians spent their declining years playacting the exploits of their youth. They seemed to realize in the deepest sense that even a caricature of their youth may have been preferable to the homogeneity demanded by mainstream American culture (Deloria, 1981: 56). *Wild West Shows and the Images of American Indians* examines the lives and experiences of Show Indians largely from their own point of view. Their performances – the dances, re-enactments of battles, and living in village encampments – may actually have helped to preserve cultural heritage through decades of forced assimilation (Moses, 1996).

The government itself contributed to a modern cross-cultural performative tradition by creating alternate imagery in direct competition with the Wild West shows. It encouraged Indians to take part in local historical plays and pageants to portray history and ethnography "correctly." Indian Commissioner William A. Jones (1897–1905), for example, championed performances that portrayed Indians as competent farmers and workers. In a fashion, Indians displayed themselves effectively by presenting the products of their fields and workshops. Such exhibits had first been tried at world's fairs and at international expositions in New Orleans, Nashville, Atlanta, Jamestown, Portland, and Seattle. The work of Indian schoolchildren also became a focus of exhibition. Model Indian schools, with performing students in attendance, appeared at the Columbian Exposition (1893) and the Louisiana Purchase Exposition (1904) (Rydell, 1984, 1993; Moses, 1996).

Perhaps the most dramatic example of governmental support of the performative tradition in direct opposition to Wild West show imagery occurred in the decision to allow Carlisle Indian School to compete on the football field. For a number of years after its founding in 1879, Carlisle provided its students with up to the equivalent of an eighth-grade education. By the early twentieth century, it had advanced to about the twelfth grade. Yet its young adult male students would compete on the field against the students of Harvard, Pennsylvania, Brown, Bucknell, and the like. Then as now, big-time college athletics has been vexed by corruption. Scandals in the football program also engulfed Carlisle and contributed to its closure in 1918. But for a number of years, Carlisle's Redmen competed against the nation's most privileged youth.

The performance of football at Carlisle had multiple meanings, at once a means of cultural transformation and a mode of cross-cultural mediation. Here too, it is worth noting the disjuncture between performer and audience – and indeed between Carlisle's Indian hometown fans and the primarily white spectators the team encountered on the road. Whereas press accounts were filled with allusions of frontier conflict, the founder and superintendent of Carlisle, Richard Henry Pratt, used victories to remind the students that they had defeated white men at their own game precisely because they were becoming white men (Adams, 1995; Steckbeck, 1951; and for multiple meanings of football at Haskell, see Bloom, 1996). As in the Wild West shows, Indian cultural agency and empowerment existed alongside a relative lack of economic, social, and political power.

Long before the government allowed Indian students to perform in public, or Indian farmers to compete in tribal-agricultural fairs during the first decade of the twentieth century, there developed a similar tradition, that of the "educated" Indian appearing at the annual conference of the Friends of the Indian at Lake Mohonk, New York. At these conclaves the Indians performed, in a sense, as "aspirational images" for reservation Indians, and they usually endorsed the reformers' version of acculturation. Persons such as Charles Eastman, Carlos Montezuma, Marie Baldwin, Gertrude Bonnin, and Susan LaFlesche Picotte testified to rapt audiences on the efficacy of mainstream education (if not always its administration) at those schools run by the Bureau of Indian Affairs (Hertzberg, 1971; Wilson, 1983; Iverson, 1982; Mathes, 1993). They organized themselves as the Society of American Indians and, worried about popular imagery, debated early on whether they would admit non-acculturated members. The society collapsed after World War I, and in the 1920s reform efforts were able to relax the combat to preserve Indian cultures under attack. More positive images of Indians emerged, influenced in part by the struggles of the Pueblo people, who adopted a particularly performative kind of politics.

Similar to an earlier tour organized around the Ponca leader Standing Bear, holy men and tribal chairmen from the Rio Grande pueblos traveled throughout the eastern seaboard and in cities along the West coast to publicize the plight of the Indians. As in the Wild West shows, Indians had only to "be themselves." Unlike the Lake Mohonk Indians, these delegates from the "ancient present" asked only to be left alone. One could make a case that these performances helped to shift public attitudes, which in turn helped to change federal policies in the 1930s (Dilworth, 1996: 14).

At the beginning of the twentieth century, the imagery of the United States' thirty-year war, the staple of Wild West shows, found new life in film. As in the performative tradition of the shows themselves, Indians got to play the parts – that is until filmmaking closed many of its branch offices and settled in southern California, and turned to white actors (Moses, 1996; Everson, 1992: 12). By the 1970s, however, reacting perhaps to the racialism of the Vietnam War, Hollywood rediscovered Indians playing Indians, and a small group of actors, among them Will Sampson and Chief Dan George, found a measure of success (Rollins and O'Connor, 1998). In the 1980s and 1990s a range of popular film and television – *Dances with Wolves, Last of the Mohicans*, the made-for-TV movies created by Ted Turner, *Northern Exposure, Twin Peaks*, and many others – brought a new generation of talented Indian actors to the American public. These included Graham Greene, Gary Farmer, Rodney Grant, Tantoo Cardinal, Irene Bedard, Wes Studi, among others.

At present, Native Americans not only continue to act in films and television, but also with such movies as *Powwow Highway* (1988), *Medicine River* (1993), and

Smoke Signals (1998), they also occasionally write screenplays and sometimes direct. In addition, there are many fine – if struggling – young Indian documentary film-makers. The number of Indian actors, screenwriters, and directors is not so large, nor their filmography so varied and rich, as to suggest a substantial "performative tradition" (Schneider, 1999). Nevertheless, they have developed a small but significant presence in contemporary film.

Indians perform culture and identity in complex political ways as well, evoking what Gerald Vizenor describes as "post-Indian warriors of simulation." In someone such as Russell Means one encounters an activist, a radical, a prisoner in the dock, an unsuccessful vice-presidential candidate, an actor simulating the actual "last of his race," and a trickster creating new stories about tribal rights, philosophies, and traditions (Vizenor, 1994: 16–21). With his hired gun Marvin J. Wolf assuming the role of "Arizona John" Burke, he became his own Buffalo Bill Cody, selling his story large (Means, 1995).

Likewise, there seems room for growth in the tradition of "plastic Medicine Men," leaders, in Rayna Green's words, of "a tribe called Wannabe" (Kehoe, 1990; Green, 1988). But in addition to the outright poseurs (Jamake Highwater, for example) that frequently find themselves outed in the pages of *Indian Country Today*, there are those persons with familial and ethnic ties to Native American communities who have built upon the celebrated career of Nick Black Elk, to become first visionaries and then performing philosophers. Many have found a congenial audience in the New Age movement, combining elements of "the shaman" with that of the "public Indian," updating and mystifying figures such as Charles Eastman at Lake Mohonk or the leaders of the All Pueblo Council who shared a New York stage with John Collier in the 1920s.

There is a thriving business in generic Native American spirituality, from seminars to spiritual exercises, complete with books and audio cassettes. The place of actual Indians in this branch of the "personal growth" phenomenon of the 1980s and 1990s is complex. Some, for example Sun Bear and Rolling Thunder, are self-identi-fied, whereas others such as Wallace Black Elk or John Redtail Freesoul have legitimate, or at least identifiable, claims on Indianness. Such "simulations" speak of the multiple ways some Indian people create themselves – while being created – in relation to the power represented in images and materialized in social, political, and economic relations.

One sees the dilemmas surrounding power, culture, and performance with particular clarity in Indian rodeo. The pageantry and formulaic portions of rodeo owe much to the Wild West shows. Still, the skills demonstrated in that portion of the program described as "cowboy fun" – riding, roping, and wrestling various critters to the ground – came out of the work in stock-raising and droving that went West and grew up with the country. And before the turn of the nineteenth century, Indian people were actively participating in ranching on and off the reservations. Particularly for the bison tribes, ranching was about cultural transformations that were simultaneous *retentions* of older practices.

And when Indians became cowboys, they also celebrated their prowess in the arena as well. Yet despite their professed desire for Indian assimilation, many white Americans did not want to see Indians as cowboys, particularly in rodeo performances, and they segregated the sport. As a result, Indians created their own rodeo circuit, an act of agency, resistance, and cultural creativity. Peter Iverson asserts that Indian rodeo reinforces the importance of place, of competition, of achievement, and of the family (Iverson, 1994; Iverson and MacCannell, 1999). It is all about cultural change and continuity, power and performance.

The lines waver – at one moment the clarity of white racial discrimination, at another the cultural blur encapsulated in Iverson's assertion that cowboys are Indians (and vice versa). What effect this cultural mix will have on the performative traditions of the coming century remains unclear. In the increasingly urban West, special enclaves such as reservations and ranches, both of which support complex cultures of performance, remain on a kind of cultural endangered species list (Iverson, 1994; Iverson and MacCannell, 1999). And in North America as a whole, where performance and identity seem so tightly linked, the dynamics of performance – Indian and non-Indian, public and private, individual and collective – will demand the attention of scholars, indeed, of us all.

At the giveaway during the closing public ceremonies of the feast day of St. Augustine at Isleta Pueblo in the fall of 1997, instead of the round loaf of bread I had been lusting after, I caught a box of animal crackers tossed into the crowd. I shared them with two young boys who had only recently been pelting me and other outsiders with "Bomb Bags." When our throats became dangerously thick, I bought three orangeades from a plaza merchant at a price that would have made a New York street vendor blush. It was enough to inspire a Koshare to point his finger and laugh.

Ethnohistorians of the Pueblo Indians tend to stress continuity rather than innovation; but it is in that border region between coherence and invention that so much of the performative tradition thrives today in Indian Country. As Joe Sando informs us, though the Pueblos are an ancient people whose history goes back into the farthest reaches of time, traditional history survives in the many additions that have been made, as events have shaped and altered lives. In reverent narration, through the art of ritual dance and mime, the Pueblo people relate their history, passing it down the generations. And thus, for example, sixteenth- and seventeenth-century Spaniards appear in the ritual narratives of the present (Sando, 1992: 21).

As a reminder, perhaps it is well to end this essay on performance by looking at the Matachines Dance of the upper Rio Grande valley. It is a ritual drama performed on certain saints' days in Pueblo Indian, Nuevo Mexicano, and Hispano communities in the upper Rio Grande valley and elsewhere in the American Southwest. Two rows of masked male dancers wearing mitre-like hats with elongated ribbons down the back dance the Matachines. In the Rio Arriba area of New Mexico, a dozen or so masked figures accompany a young girl in white and her partner, an adult male dancer wearing a floral corona headdress. Another man or boy dressed as a bull will join them. Two clowns complete the ensemble. The floral-crowned man is known as Montezuma, or El Monarca, whereas the female child partner is called La Malinche. Several sets of movements to the accompaniment of violin and guitar make up the dance. The presentation of the dancers, exclusive of the procession and recession, takes roughly forty-five minutes to an hour (Rodriguez, 1996: 2).

The Matachines dance probably derives from medieval European folk dramas signifying conflict between Christians and Moors. Spaniards brought it to North America and used it as a ritualized story to convert the Indians to Christianity. In that other Old World of the sixteenth century, Iberian elements merged with aboriginal forms in central Mexico. It came up the trail with Don Juan de Oñate in 1598. As performed today in the greater Southwest, the Matachines dance symbolically blends centuries of Iberian–American ethnic relations and provides a syncretic foundation upon which individual Indian and Hispanic communities have built their own particular thematic complex (Rodriguez, 1996: 147–9; Gutiérrez, 1991).

The Matachines dance presents a distinctive pattern in the upper Rio Grande valley and is generally considered to be identical among Indians and Hispanos. Nevertheless, the ways in which these two major ethnic communities perform and view the dance differ significantly. Both are elementally Christian; but most Pueblos claim that Montezuma, portrayed by the figure of El Monarca, brought them the dance from Mexico. Hispanic villagers, in comparison, attribute its introduction to either the colonizer Oñate, the re-*conquistador* Don Diego de Vargas, or Cortés himself. The drama depicts the arrival of Christianity among the Indians and is paradigmatically associated with the expulsion or conversion of the Moors in Spain. The dance thus has equally historical – but different – meanings for each ethnic group. For those who brought it and for those who "accepted" it, Christianity's arrival in the region obviously had different consequences (Rodriguez, 1996: 1–2).

Although conquest dramas originally re-enacted the subjugation and humiliation of Indians at the hands of their oppressors, with time Pueblo performers appropriated, altered, and subtly subverted that meaning, changing the dynamics of performed power. Performances came to include broad, comic gestures, contradictory sayings, and farce. Over the generations the Pueblos made the Matachines their own, taking over its organization and filling the majority of roles. Thus, even though they enlisted outsiders, for the most part Indians ended up portraying the intruders rather than the other way around. Indeed, part of the power of Matachines symbolism lay in the fact that the masked dancers portrayed themselves and others – and their own ideas about themselves – regardless of outside perception. Merging the dance with their own ceremonial calendar gave the Pueblos a measure of control over how the story of their extorted conversion would be remembered and told within their own communities (Rodriguez, 1996: 144–5).

As Montezuma's gift to the Pueblos, the dance synchronically proclaims alien rule yet offers a hidden means to subvert it under the mask of submission. In such places as Taos, San Juan, Jemez, and Picuris, each pueblo negotiates the consequences of Spanish domination according to the particulars of its history, environment, and modern character. The details of this negotiation and what the pueblo makes of them are metaphorically illustrated in the performance (Rodriguez, 1996: 146–7).

Perhaps in their own time, the Pueblos will ritualize the effects of other Americans upon their cultures (Sando, 1992: 21). Just as they have done with the Matachines dance, they will doubtlessly incorporate those varied influences into *objets d'art*, dance, song, or ritual. Pueblo people, and by extension all American Indian communities, continue persistently to retain their culture and their arts. The performative tradition persists; and, as always, it builds as it goes, sustaining the people for yet another year.

BIBLIOGRAPHY

Adams, David Wallace 1995: *Education for Extinction: American Indians and the Boarding School Experience, 1875–1928* (Lawrence: University Press of Kansas).

Atwater, Caleb 1975: *Remarks Made on a Tour to Prairie du Chien, Thence to Washington City, in 1829* (New York: Arno Press).

Bataille, Gretchen M. and Charles L. P. Silet (eds.) 1980: *The Pretend Indians: Images of Native Americans in the Movies* (Ames: Iowa State University Press).

Bieder, Robert E. 1986: *Science Encounters the Indian, 1820–1880: The Early Years of American Ethnology* (Norman: University of Oklahoma Press).

Bloom, John 1996: "'There Is Madness in the Air': The 1926 Haskell Homecoming and Popular Representations of Sports in Federal Indian Boarding Schools," in *Dressing in Feathers: The Construction of the Indian in American Popular Culture*, ed. S. Elizabeth Bird (Boulder: Westview Press), pp. 97–110.

Cruikshank, Julie 1998: *The Social Life of Stories: Narrative and Knowledge in the Yukon Territory* (Lincoln: University of Nebraska Press).

Crummett, Michael 1993: *Sun Dance* (Helena, MT: Falcon Press).

Deloria, Vine, Jr. 1981: "The Indians," in *Buffalo Bill and the Wild West*, eds. David H. Katzive et al. (New York: The Brooklyn Museum), pp. 56–8.

Dilworth, Leah 1996: *Imagining Indians in the Southwest: Persistent Visions of a Primitive Past* (Washington, D.C.: Smithsonian Institution Press).

Drinnon, Richard 1987: "The Metaphysics of Dancing Tribes," in *The American Indian and the Problem of History*, ed. Calvin Martin (New York: Oxford University Press), pp. 106–13.

Ellis, Clyde 1999: "'We Don't Want Your Rations, We Want This Dance': Song, Dance, and the Evolution of the Contemporary Southern Plains Powwow," *Western Historical Quarterly* 30 (Summer): 133–54.

Everson, William K. 1992: *The Hollywood Western* (New York: Citadel Press).

Foster, Morris W. 1991: *Being Comanche: A Social History of an American Indian Community* (Tucson: University of Arizona Press).

Fowler, Loretta 1987: *Shared Symbols, Contested Meanings: Gros Ventre Culture and History, 1778–1984* (Ithaca: Cornell University Press).

Friar, Ralph E. and Natasha A. Friar 1972: *The Only Good Indian ... The Hollywood Gospel* (New York: Drama Book Specialists Publishers).

Green, Rayna 1988: "The Tribe Called Wannabee: Playing Indian in America and Europe," *Folklore* 99: 30–55.

Gutiérrez, Ramón 1991: *When Jesus Came, the Corn Mothers Went Away* (Stanford: Stanford University Press).

Harrod, Howard L. 1995: *Becoming and Remaining a People: Native American Religions on the Northern Plains* (Tucson: University of Arizona Press).

Hertzberg, Hazel W. 1971: *The Search for an American Indian Identity: Modern Pan-Indian Movements* (Syracuse: Syracuse University Press).

Heth, Charlotte 1992: "Introduction – American Indian Dance: A Celebration of Survival and Adaptation," in *Native American Dance: Ceremonies and Social Traditions*, ed. Charlotte Heth (Washington, D.C.: Smithsonian Institution Press), pp. 1–17.

Hinsley, Curtis M., Jr. 1981: *Savages and Scientists: The Smithsonian Institution and the Development of American Anthropology, 1846–1910* (Washington, D.C.: Smithsonian Institution Press).

Holler, Clyde 1995: *Black Elk's Religion: The Sun Dance and Lakota Catholicism* (Syracuse: Syracuse University Press).

Irwin, Lee 1994: *The Dream Seekers: Native American Visionary Traditions of the Great Plains* (Norman: University of Oklahoma Press).

Iverson, Peter 1982: *Carlos Montezuma and the Changing World of American Indians* (Albuquerque: University of New Mexico Press).

Iverson, Peter 1994: *When Indians Became Cowboys: Native Peoples and Cattle Ranching in the American West* (Norman: University of Oklahoma Press).

Iverson, Peter and Linda MacCannell (Photographer) 1999: *Riders of the West: Portraits from Indian Rodeo* (Seattle: University of Washington Press).

Kaufmann, Donald L. 1980: "The Indian as Media Hand-me-down," in *The Pretend Indians: Images of Native Americans in the Movies*, eds. Gretchen M. Bataille and Charles L. P. Silet (Ames: Iowa State University Press), pp. 20–7.

Kehoe, Alice B. 1990: "Primal Gaia: Primitivists and Plastic Medicine Men," in *The Invented Indian: Cultural Fictions and Government Policies*, ed. James A. Clifton (New Brunswick, NJ: Transaction Publishers), pp. 193–209.

Lassiter, Luke E. 1997: "'Charlie Brown': Not Just Another Essay on the Gourd Dance," *American Indian Culture and Research Journal* 21: 75–104.

Lassiter, Luke E. 1998: *The Power of Kiowa Song* (Tucson: University of Arizona Press).

Laubin, Reginald and Gladys Laubin 1989: *Indian Dances of North America: Their Importance to Indian Life* (Norman: University of Oklahoma Press).

Little Coyote, Bertha and Virginia Giglio 1997: *Leaving Everything Behind: The Songs and Memories of a Cheyenne Woman* (Norman: University of Oklahoma Press).

Livingston, Lili Cockerille 1997: *American Indian Ballerinas* (Norman: University of Oklahoma Press).

McBride, Molly, with forewords by Eunice Nelson-Bauman and Jean Archambaud Moore 1995: *Molly Spotted Elk* (Norman: University of Oklahoma Press).

Mathes, Valerie Sherer 1993: "Dr. Susan LaFlesche Picotte: The Reformed and the Reformer," in *Indian Lives: Essays on Nineteenth- and Twentieth-Century Native American Leaders*, eds. L. G. Moses and Raymond Wilson (Albuquerque: University of New Mexico Press), pp. 61–90.

Means, Russell 1995: *Where White Men Fear to Tread: The Autobiography of Russell Means*, with Marvin J. Wolf (New York: St. Martin's Press).

Meredith, Howard 1995: *Dancing on Common Ground: Tribal Cultures and Alliances on the Southern Plains* (Lawrence: University Press of Kansas).

Moses, L. G. 1996: *Wild West Shows and the Images of American Indians, 1883–1933* (Albuquerque: University of New Mexico Press).

Nequatewa, Edmund 1993: *Truth of a Hopi: Stories Relating to the Origin, Myths and Clan Histories of the Hopi* (Flagstaff, AZ: Northland Press).

Nettl, Bruno 1967: "Studies in Blackfoot Indian Musical Culture, Part I," *Ethnomusicology* 11: 141–60.

Powers, William K. 1980: "Plains Indian Music and Dance," in *Anthropology on the Great Plains*, eds. W. Raymond Wood and Margot Liberty (Lincoln: University of Nebraska Press), pp. 212–29.

Powers, William K. 1990: *War Dance: Plains Indian Musical Performance* (Tucson: University of Arizona Press).

Rodriguez, Sylvia 1996: *The Matachines Dance: Ritual Symbolism and Interethnic Relations in the Upper Rio Grande Valley* (Albuquerque: University of New Mexico Press).

Rollins, Peter C. and John E. O'Connor 1998: *Hollywood's Indian: The Portrayal of the Native American in Film* (Lexington: University Press of Kentucky).

Rydell, Robert W. 1984: *All the World's a Fair: Visions of Empire at American International Expositions, 1876–1916* (Chicago: University of Chicago Press).

Rydell, Robert W. 1993: *World of Fairs: The Century-of-Progress Expositions* (Chicago: University of Chicago Press).

Sando, Joe S. 1992: *Pueblo Nations: Eight Centuries of Pueblo Indian History* (Santa Fe: Clear Light Publishers).

Schneider, Wolf 1999: "Irene Bedard: Native America's Most Successful Actress Shares the Secrets of Her Success," *Cowboys & Indians* 7 (October/November): 158–63.

Slotkin, Richard 1973: *Regeneration through Violence: The Mythology of the American Frontier, 1600–1860* (Middletown, CT: Wesleyan University Press).

Slotkin, Richard 1981: "The Wild West," in *Buffalo Bill and the Wild West*, eds. David H. Katzive et al. (New York: The Brooklyn Museum), pp. 27–44.

Slotkin, Richard 1992: *Gunfighter Nation: The Myth of the Frontier in Twentieth-Century America* (New York: Harper Perennial).

Steckbeck, John S. 1951: *Fabulous Redmen: The Carlisle Indians and Their Famous Football Teams* (Harrisburg: J. Horace McFarland Co.).

Stedman, Raymond William 1982: *Shadows of the Indians: Stereotypes in American Culture* (Norman: University of Oklahoma Press).

Tallchief, Maria and Larry Kaplan (Contributor) 1997: *Maria Tallchief: America's Prima Ballerina* (New York: Henry Holt & Company).

Vizenor, Gerald 1994: *Manifest Manners: Postindian Warriors of Survivance* (Hanover: Wesleyan University Press).

White, Richard 1994: "Frederick Jackson Turner and Buffalo Bill," in *The Frontier in American Culture: An Exhibition at the Newberry Library, August 26, 1994–January 7, 1995/Essays by Richard White and Patricia Nelson Limerick*, ed. James R. Grossman (Berkeley: University of California Press), pp. 7–65.

Whiteley, Peter 1988: *Bacavi: Journey to Reed Springs* (Flagstaff, AZ: Northland Press).

Whorf, Benjamin Lee 1956: *Language, Thought, and Reality: Selected Writings of Benjamin Lee Whorf*, ed. John B. Carroll (Cambridge, MA: MIT Press).

Wilson, Raymond 1983: *Ohiyesa: Charles Eastman, Santee Sioux* (Urbana: University of Illinois Press).

Yava, Albert 1978: *Big Falling Snow: A Tewa-Hopi Indian's Life and Times and the History and Traditions of His People*, ed. and annot. Harold Courlander (New York: Crown Publishers).

Young Bear, Severt and R. D. Theisz 1994: *Standing in the Light: A Lakota Way of Seeing* (Lincoln: University of Nebraska Press).

12

Indigenous Art: Creating Value and Sharing Beauty

NANCY PAREZO

Like others around the world, the indigenous peoples of North America have a rich history of artistic production and a contemporary output that is extensive and varied. Historically, each Native American/First Nation society has produced a wide variety of aesthetically pleasing items. These distinctive art forms have been, and currently are, used for a number of cultural purposes: as personal expressions of self, spiritual gifts to supernaturals, symbols and metaphors, reflections of the landscape, symbols of social relationships and ethnic identity, historic documents, objects to be admired for their beauty and usefulness, trade items, and marketable commodities. As a result of this multiplicity, Native American art has been dynamic in its meanings, forms, and intent, while remaining part of coherent artistic traditions that have been admired, and sought after by peoples around the world. Native American art has taken on new meanings – and new values – as it has been exchanged and embedded in a range of new cultural settings.

Due to its multivocal nature, art has been used to study almost all aspects of Native peoples' cultures and societies. Art has been employed, for example, to classify cultures. Scholars have long been fascinated, for instance, with the ways Native artists have visualized the land. In some cases art forms reflect a region's raw materials: pottery in the Southwest, wood carvings in the Northwest Coast, sealskin parkas in the Arctic, porcupine quill decorated moccasins in the Northeast. For the last hundred years, scholars have used such correlations to define culture areas and cultural groupings. Similarly, continuities and changes in art styles and material culture media have been used by archaeologists to identify and distinguish particular cultures and social groups.

Scholars have also used Native arts to study the impact of culture contact, for post-contact arts reflect the nature of European and Euro-American colonialism, capitalism, technological change, ethnic tourism, trade, ghettoization, marginalization, and cultural borrowing and appropriation. Such impacts generate their own list of further issues: intellectual property rights, national, individual, and group identity, patterns of assimilation and acculturation, cultural preservation, and ethnogenesis, to name a few. Scholars have been equally concerned with how art is embedded in contemporary art worlds – how it has been collected, borrowed, appropriated, and displayed by non-Native communities. Art, in short, has offered a window opening on all aspects of Native culture. At the same time, it has proven the occasion for debates about aesthetics, creativity, and art itself.

Native arts also resonate with the enduring vigor of indigenous peoples' cultures and the centrality of Native voices in narrating native stories. But art has pushed such arguments beyond the strictly visual. As Mohawk historian Deborah Doxtator (1996: 11) has noted, "Visual metaphors impart meanings that sometimes do not have words to describe them." Indeed, the appropriate use of symbols in aesthetic production and display has been a battleground in which Native artists and scholars have questioned the established ways of studying Native peoples and their arts.

While the record of scholarship on the art of each society is uneven, its total corpus is impressive. An entire paper could be written on recent works in textiles, pottery, baskets, paintings, sculpture, or photography. Likewise, the literature on Native art tends to be regional. Focusing exclusively on the Plains rather than the Arctic, for example, produces different conclusions about gender and art, the development of painting, stylistic developments in clothing, or the nature of contemporary art markets. Scholars working in different media and in different regions have recognizable preferences for topics thought to be appropriate for specific art types. Plains weapons and tools, for example, often go with analyses of raw materials and technology; Pueblo pottery with how artists interact with Mother Earth. Limiting one's scope to a certain region, like limiting it to certain media, affects what is known about Native art and can easily bias a general survey of scholarship on indigenous art.

This essay will not discuss most of the contemporary and historic literature on indigenous arts, which amounts to thousands of articles and books. It will, however, present some overall issues and concerns evident in post-1980 scholarship on Native American art, especially in terms of art production, aesthetics, display, and repatriation. How do we define Native art? How do we locate it in time and space? In terms of identity and authenticity? How do we situate it in terms of market economies and manufactured goods, institutional influences on media and styles, and the larger worlds of contemporary art? Can art – as an analytical category – help make sense of repatriation and other issues facing contemporary artists? These issues will have an important theoretical impact on future work in American Indian Studies.

Anthropology and Art History: Disciplinary Bases for the Study of Native Art

In general, scholarship dealing with Native American art has been based in anthropology with more recent interest evidenced by art historians. Rarely has history, sociology, or economics been concerned with art or aesthetics. This disciplinary exclusivity has meant that Native art historically and discursively reflects anthropology's categories and intellectual concerns. To understand contemporary scholarship and the critiques of Native artists and scholars, then, one must understand the goals, strengths, and weaknesses of past work. It should be remembered, of course, that any academic endeavor reflects American and Canadian cultural norms, social stereotypes, and preconceptions about indigenous peoples. While Native American art is factual, knowledge about it is provisional, because any interpretation of "native," "ethnic," or "primitive" art is part of the past and present discourses of colonialism and capitalism.

Since the inception of anthropology, its practitioners have focused on art because physical objects last longer than the spoken word. They have a physical existence of their own, apart from the people who made and used them. Art can be contextualized, decontextualized, and recontextualized in ways that intangible information cannot; objects can be seen, touched, collected, and appreciated by people in other societies, including researchers. Artifacts can take on new meanings in new situations never envisioned by makers, including a scholarly study or a museum exhibit. Artifacts, as indigenous art used as scholarly data is called, have been employed to provide researchers with insights on how culture operates, to interpret human behavior, and to document how societies have changed over time. Art has been adopted as inferential data to understand a culture's meanings, symbolism, and worldviews, and as direct evidence of culturally specific aesthetic preferences. The range of anthropological studies in this genre is extensive and reflects the theoretical thrusts of the field at various times: universal stylistic evolution (1890s), technology and morphology (1910s–1930s), technology and social organization (1910s–1950s), craft revivals (1920s–1930s), functionalism (1940s), culture element distributions in time and space (1930s–1940s), psychology, cognition, ethnoscience, and aesthetics (1940s–1950s), "primitive art" and fine art (1940s–1980s), folklore (1970s–1980s), ethnoarchaeology (1970s–1990s), structuralism (1960s–1970s), semiotics (1970s–1980s), cultural criticism (1990s) (see Thompson and Parezo, 1989).

Some theoretical foci, such as the study of art as evidence of culture change or the description of stylistic canons, have continued undiminished, although scholars have used more refined (or at least new) terminology over time. Anthropological surveys of object types, for example, have remained prevalent. These studies tend to focus on development in regions, focusing on technology or stylistic change (Tanner, 1983; Whiteford, 1988). Such surveys are most prevalent in archaeology, although there are several good examples in cultural anthropology (Nabokov and Easton [1989] or Krinsky [1996] on architecture, Archuleta and Strickland [1991] on painting, or Batkin [1987] on Puebloan pottery). The archaeological literature is replete with descriptions of pottery, rock art, stone and bone tools, architecture, and perishable materials from specific sites or regions. This range of evidence (preserved whole objects and fragments) is used to understand culture and human behavior through time. Art in these surveys is still employed to identify cultures, define cultural development, establish chronologies, reconstruct pre-contact societies, and document environmental adaptations.

This anthropological basis of scholarship has had a profound influence on what is known and not known about Native American art. There is a great deal of information about: (1) social "functional" needs expressed through art, that is, how societies use art for religious, political, economic, and social ends. This includes statements made by artists about themselves as a people or nation; (2) the specific art inventory of each Native society at specific points in time; (3) production techniques for each medium; and (4) the development of styles and their correlation with social complexity. Also, since the historic life of a group is partly written in their art, much is known about how culture change is echoed in artistic change. Anthropologists, for example, have penned thousands of words documenting how the introduction of agriculture influenced pottery design in the Southeast and how the diffusion of art style and religious ideas from Mesoamerica affected mortuary art in Woodland areas. Ethnohistorians have learned how confinement on reservations affected men's tipi designs, and how the Canadian government's outlawing of the potlatch curtailed the making and use of carved rattles along the Northwest Coast.

A great deal of study has also led to insightful understandings about ideological symbols in specific cultures' artistic traditions, especially as these relate to design identification, gift-giving, economics, and worldview (Whitten and Whitten, 1993). But it is in this latter area, as well as in the realm of aesthetics, that more work needs to be undertaken. I do not know of a single anthropologist who does not feel that his/her translations of artistic value are incomplete. As a corpus of knowledge, anthropology is weak in understanding cultural play in art, art's multiple intra-cultural meanings and how these are valued. Advances also need to be made in elucidating ethnographically relevant classificatory schemes, in obtaining information on artistic manipulation of language symbols and the visual senses, and in figuring the ways groups evaluate craftsmanship and assign value. In short, much work needs to be done on what constitutes beauty.

Art history, the discipline that specifically studies aesthetic development, has devoted little attention to Native American art until recently. This is because scholars had to overcome the philosophical barriers inherent in the assumption that "real" art requires a self-composed, contemplative or aesthetic attitude on the part of artist, viewer, and critic. Since Native art is always useful art, art historians dismissed it as craft. In addition, art historians excluded Native art, with the exception of Aztec, Mayan, and Incan pieces, as methodologically unknowable because scholars lacked critical information on individual artists and provenance as well as the written documents that are the basis for their interpretative studies. A third barrier has been the assumption that indigenous cultures lacked the values or understandings that gave significance to post-Renaissance European art. These included the hierarchical valuation of painting over "decorative arts," representational depictions over geometric or abstract design, and innovation and individual insight over continuity and community tradition. Art history was simply not sure that Native American creations met their definition of "real" art as individual non-reproducible creations that convey unique visions and evoke emotional responses.

Some art historians have undertaken work that has value for contemporary understanding of Native art (Berlo, 1992; Mathews and Jonaitis, 1982). They have analyzed style, the manner in which a work is articulated through color, shape, perspective, symmetry, and pattern, as both cultural convention and individualistic creation. While acknowledging that styles are unique to specific places and time periods, most artistic studies have been formalistic. The concepts used to describe styles have relied on Euro-American criteria developed for painting and naturalistic sculpture: thus rock art becomes playful abstract designs or naturalistic depictions rather than symbols through which artists communicate with the supernatural. While art historians saw this as a unified, universalistic approach to diverse cultural forms, Native American critics today contend that it is evidence of inherent ethnocentric bias: "When Native American art is studied as part of art history or explored in the studio, the past is usually emphasized. Romantic misconceptions of Native Americans as non-technological Stone Age artisans dominate the literature, thereby reinforcing the tendency to dismiss the evolving contemporary Native American culture" (Farris-Dufrene, 1997: 15). As a quick review of scholarly and popular art journals shows, art appreciation, like the study of art by anthropologists or art historians, involves an ideological framework within which people evaluate, using their own established cultural criteria, the success by which raw materials have been aesthetically manipulated. For art history, the criterion has been indigenous art's fit with the stereotype of the anonymous Noble Savage who produces primitive art. This in turn has been based on the assumption that historic and contemporary Indians are less authentic than their pre-contact ancestors, due to corruption by the industrial West.

The Contemporary Literature

Recent scholars have attempted to break away from these assumptions by being intentionally interdisciplinary. Their work blends art history with empirically based theoretical and descriptive ethnography (Duncan, 1988; Phillips, 1994b; Szabo, 1994; Vastokas, 1986–7; West, 1993). Interpretative in intent and grounded in postmodern critiques of traditional disciplinary paradigms, the most notable studies are those that use concepts developed in literary criticism, cultural and critical studies, Marxism, phenomenology, and French structuralism. Coming from these perspectives, authors have been interested in historically situating issues of gender, power, patronage, representation, image production, and the influence of Euro-American culture on Native aesthetics. Researchers have also been compelled to address the concerns of the international art community and consumers who want to be assured that they are purchasing "authentic" Indian art. Most vitally for American Indian Studies, important recent scholarship has been generated by the concerns of artists who want their voices and interpretations heard.

Each of these constituencies – producers, consumers, and scholars – has a stake in the production and dissemination of knowledge about art, creating unique characteristics that distinguish the literature on Native art from other literatures addressing American Indian topics. Most important, perhaps, is that contemporary art literature is dichotomized by a popular/scholarly split. The popular literature is more extensive than scholarly writings and tends to focus on consumer/collector issues: the identification of cultural, historical, and individual styles and their development over time, concern for detailed attribution and provenance of a piece, and, of course, authenticity. Books are large-format and lavishly illustrated, for the color photographs are as important as, if not more important than, the text. This helps potential collectors identify what art they should purchase (Jackna and Jackna, 1998). The particular value of Native art is stressed through words such as "treasures," "sacred art," "spiritual," and "ancient." Photographs of "museum quality" pieces demarcate "worth," defining what is the best of the established traditions and what will be new styles. In the late 1980s and 1990s, publications incorporated extensive quotes and interviews with Native artists as a way of substantiating authenticity. Artists are now highlighted as individuals rather than anonymous "primitive" artists, which was the rhetorical strategy in the past. Value, however, is still defined primarily by authoritative individuals, generally Euro-American writers who have served as judges in the numerous Native American art shows held throughout North America since the 1920s. What they include and do not include in popular books helps the buying public decide which art forms are economic and aesthetic investments.

The popular literature affects the ability of Native artists to compete in the national and international art market. Five journals – *American Indian Art Magazine, Native Peoples, Native Artist, Southwest Art*, and *Indian Artist* – concentrate on Native American historic and contemporary art. *American Indian Art Magazine* contains articles by professional and dedicated avocational scholars. It focuses on museum collections and collectors, object types, conservation issues, technology and design, identification of cultural styles, symbols and motifs through time, and the exploration of the corpus of individual historic artists. Authors rarely address theoretical issues, for the journal's editorial policies discourage both theory and jargon. They also discourage articles on contemporary art forms (especially those that have not been established through success in the marketplace or legitimized by appearance in museum collections), non-traditional media, or Native artistic experimentation with anything that smacks of the tourist market. Thematically, *American Indian Art Magazine* has devoted issues to specific object types: baskets, pottery, beadwork. These are important contributions for they provide extremely detailed information on construction techniques and stylistic comparisons that help readers learn about cultural and temporal variety. Journals such as *Southwest Art, Indian Artist*, or *Native Peoples* focus on the contemporary art scene and have interviews and short biographical sketches penned by professional journal writers, many of whom are an emerging group of Native American journalists and freelance writers. All four journals are marketing tools as well as informative dissemination vehicles and contain information on museum and gallery exhibits, shows, and places where consumers can purchase art for themselves.

These journals also reflect another feature of Native American art worlds – Native art's marked nature as exotic, ethnic art as opposed to fine art. By and large, journals devoted to fine art and the general art market have not focused on Native American art, except for an occasional theme issue (approximately once every ten years) or when a controversy surfaces at some major East Coast or Los Angeles exhibit. (Exhibits in Indian Country or other parts of the United States are never considered worthy of notice by any mainstream art journals. This effectively eliminates from notice and discussion all rural markets and the major locales of urban Indian artistic strength: Tulsa, Oklahoma City, San Francisco, Santa Fe, Seattle, Phoenix-Scottsdale.) Less than 1 percent of Native American artists are considered "established" or "noteworthy" enough to warrant interviews or mention of their retrospective exhibits; this low number is actually a percentage roughly equivalent to the mainstream art market, where only about 5 percent of artists are discussed in major art journals. These silences in taste-setting art journals (*Art in America*, for example, or *Contemporary Visual Arts*) and their editorial exclusions (that is, where dissemination occurs and in what form) make up an important part of the economic structure of contemporary art worlds.

Another important feature of the current (and historic) literature on Native American art is that it is institutionally based: the majority of scholarly and popular work is undertaken and disseminated through museums and galleries as ephemeral exhibit labels, brochures, and exhibition catalogues. This means that the nature and purpose of museums in American society, and the issues that affect their current undertakings, influence the choice of topics that scholars are researching. Such topics include collecting activity by colonial nation-states, representation and authenticity issues, debates over the appropriate venues for the display of Native art (art museums versus natural history museums), and repatriation. It is evident that the nature of modern American, Canadian, and European institutions affects both Native artists and all researchers (Ames, 1992; Phillips, 1998).

The result of this museum base for art research – and a feature that distinguishes the study of art from other areas focusing on Native American culture – is that a significant amount of scholarship is disseminated through exhibition catalogues, often of limited distribution. These catalogues are quite varied, although all tend to be well illustrated in order to recapture the visitor's viewing experience and to encourage visitors to learn more about the media they have seen. Some catalogues document specific exhibits and deal either directly with art forms (Hardin, 1983), the artistic development of an artist's or group of artists' work (Dobkins, 1997), art forms that are part of a social institution, such as the potlatch (Jonaitis, 1991), or the permanent collections of an institution (Jonaitis, 1988).

Other catalogues deal with more encompassing theoretical topics, such as authenticity, tourism, adaptation, religion, or humor. While art is pervasive in such books and exhibits, the emphasis is more often on its contextualization within the framework of cultural continuity and change within Native societies. Consider, for example, the exhibit "Indian Humor," developed by Cherokee artist Sara Bates, which traveled under the auspices of San Francisco's American Indian Contemporary Arts (1995–9). This exhibit focused on Native artists' collaborative efforts to counter popular notions that Indians are stoic and serious by problematizing and satirizing stereotypes of the Noble Savage and by demonstrating how different forms of humor play vital roles in self-awareness and identity (Bates, 1995). Other examples include the many excellent catalogues produced by Atlatl, a Native-run arts organization in Phoenix. One of the best of these is *Women of Sweetgrass, Cedar, and Sage* (1986) which explores issues of gender in Native art production and the frustration women artists have in breaking into a male-controlled art establishment.

The titles of recent exhibitions reveal some of the key themes being explored by artists and curators. These can be divided into several categories including celebrations (*Tribute to Our Ancestors*, 1994; *World Celebration of Indigenous Art and Culture*, 1993); identification of artists (*Artists Who Are Indian*, 1994); multiculturalism and ethnicity (*Multiplicity: A New Cultural Strategy*, 1994; *Half Indian, Half Artist*, 1992); new directions (*New Expressions in Native Art*, 1989; *Contemporary North American Indian Art*, 1983); continuity and tradition (*100 Years of Native American Art*, 1989; *The Pathway of Tradition: Indian Insights in Indian Worlds*, 1992; *Native American Artists Today: Preserving a Heritage*, 1993); activism (*Art and Environment*, 1993; *Columbus Drowning*, 1992; *Decolonizing the Mind*, 1992); spiritualism (*The Spiritual World of American Indians*, 1993; *Myth and Memory*, 1993); aestheticism and style (*The Human Figure in American Indian Art: Cultural Reality or Sexual Fantasy*, 1991; *Visions of the People*, 1992); media types (*Masks: Cultural and Contemporary*, 1989; *Pictorial Beadwork*, 1986; *Life of Clay: Contemporary Pueblo Clay Potters*, 1992), and gender (*Sisters of the Earth, Contemporary Native American Ceramics*, 1994; *As in Her Vision*, 1989).

The Arena of Definitions: Art versus Material Culture, "Tourist Art" versus "Fine Art"

Is Native American art "really" art? The question has more salience for scholars than for Native Americans, who often produce items for internal use in their home communities. Art is not generally a distinct or separate category for Native societies, which "do not separate art and life or draw comparisons between what is beautiful and what is functional. Art, beauty, and spirituality are intertwined in the routine of living" (Farris-Dufrene, 1997: 15). Most of the visual arts produced by Native American cultures are considered utilitarian in the sense that they are not used exclusively for visual pleasure. An artist spends time creating beauty on clothing, a spoon, a folded pouch, a pipe, a clay drinking cup, a house front, or gifts for the gods. A Native American artist does not worry whether he/she has created art; he/she has created beauty and that is what is important. The distinction between utility and "art-for-art's sake" more often reflects a reifying "museum" mentality than it does the intent of the maker.

Each Native culture has concepts that are the equivalent of the English "art-beauty"/"craftsmanship-artifact" categories, but they are embedded in culturally distinct worldviews and philosophies that do not recognize the same hierarchical dichotomy. Because of this variability and the long-term and in-depth research and linguistic knowledge required to access and translate Native philosophical paradigms, it is difficult to make any generalizations about how all Native artists conceptualize and critique their creations, although many writers, especially those writing for popular outlets, have made it appear that they have been able to do so.

Much of the debate about whether Native groups created art before they began producing for Euro-American markets, or whether historic art forms have degenerated from pre-contact art styles, is similarly centered in an unproductive Western oppositional system based on the two polarities of art and craft. The medium and format of the object and the utilitarian/non-utilitarian dichotomization valued in Western markets creates new value frameworks for Native American objects. This specious differentiation of "arts" and "crafts/artifacts" has served to institutionalize a segregation of Native American artists, who by definition produce crafts or "craft-arts," "low" as opposed to "high" art. It has also valorized certain media at the expense of others. Thus painting is high or fine art while baskets and rugs are crafts. A historic Haida mask is primitive art while a Navajo pictorial rug is folk art; neither are simply "art" in an unmarked form.

This hierarchical scheme of artistic value and intent will simply not go away, no matter how often scholars such as Ruth Phillips and Christopher Steiner note its shortcomings:

> The visual aesthetic traditions of the majority of [Native American] peoples are a particularly bad "fit" with the Western classification system, for Western hierarchies of media, genre, and conditions of production rarely match those that have historically operated within Native American communities. In order to identify a corpus of objects that could be identified as fine art – that is, sculpture (monumental if possible) and graphic depiction (painting, if possible) – scholars have often privileged objects of lesser status within their producing communities, arbitrarily promoting some regions of the continent over others and ignoring the indigenous systems of value and meaning attached to objects. (Phillips and Steiner, 1999: 7)

(See also Ames, 1992; Rushing, 1993; Stocking, 1985; Wade, 1986.) Scholars have all but analyzed and deconstructed the phenomenon to death, from the standpoint of primitivism, representation, colonialism and postcolonialism, scientific conceptualizations, commodification, and the reception of commercialization and extended trade by Western audiences. But popular categories are extremely difficult to challenge and change. We should recognize that part of the problem stems, first, from inadequate cross-cultural translations. Concepts in one language generally are not easily translated into another language and in the process lose much of their subtlety. Second, part of the problem stems from different worldviews, a problem compounded by difficult or superficial translations. Third, art works as a form of visual communication, relying on a type of visual language. We do not have very good rules for translating this visual form into words, in any language. Further, pieces contain so much cultural information that reducing an artwork meant to be viewed instantaneously by the eye as a whole unit to a string of sequential words and to a single concept, "art," is inadequate, simplifying, and distorting.

In addition, Native artists today work as part of an international art market in which the assessments of powerful art brokers create value. Even given their acceptance that Native Americans in fact create "art," many critical discussions ironically seek to highlight difference from mainstream art. This in turn again creates value in the marketplace, and is reflected in advertising and popular culture notions of American Indians. As Theresa Harlan has noted, "Contemporary art is often characterized as angry, created from the voices of the defeated, and confined to the realm of the emotions" (Harlan, 1995: 20). It is also, as a quick review of the advertising in a recent issue of *American Indian Art Magazine* reveals, antique, romantic, primitive, naturalistic (i.e., close to nature), tribal, dedicated to tradition, legendary, and spiritual. Indian art is "marked" art; it is ethnic and it is assessed as such. The critical knowledge that forms a large part of the literature on Native American art must be seen as situated knowledge, partially positional (trying to create value while it assesses worth), and political.

One productive way to circumvent the issue is to respect and use Native aesthetic categories and frameworks as basic conceptual tools, that is, to understand, value, and appreciate art using the cultural paradigms of the makers. This is slowly occurring in art scholarship, but the corpus is still small since the research presents a daunting task: it is extremely difficult, requiring the researcher to intimately know all aspects of a culture, and to be linguistically competent. Ethnoaesthetic scholarship concentrates on many specific issues; for example, Zuni "perceptions of Zuniness in pottery decorations" (Hardin, 1983: 108).

Understanding Arts of Culture, Time, and Place

While the debates of the intellectual and popular art worlds have helped to define Native American art and how it is valued and understood, there is always something distinctively "Navajo," "Hopi," or "Seminole" about any piece. Researchers and collectors can generally recognize an Inuit harpoon or distinguish a Mescalero Apache from a Jicarilla Apache basket, just as artists and community members can recognize the art produced by group members as opposed to non-members. While there has been much borrowing of aesthetic ideas among Native societies, there are still recognizable cultural styles of which artists are justly proud. A great deal of the contemporary literature exists to help readers recognize these cultural styles. An important segment also concentrates on a special aspect of this cultural placement – the interaction of artists with their homelands.

One of the most distinguishing features of Native American cultures is their sense of place and their intimate relationship with the land. The sense of place is an important factor in defining a sense of identity. Southwest Indian identity systems, for example, rely on symbols of supernaturally sanctioned, ancient roots regarded as timeless and unchangeable. They are based on strong mythological statements that authorize each group's residence and right to care for the sacred homeland, identified by physical and spiritual features such as bodies of water, mountains, plants, and animals. Each society has an intimate knowledge of these local features. People maintain close spiritual relationships with their environments and these are recorded in oral tradition, song, story, prayer, and art, which are passed on from generation to generation. This is one way that American Indians feel they differ from the general society. Zunis, for example, say that Euro-Americans and Mexicans have no respect for the land and abuse it rather than work with it. The land is not something that can be controlled and changed; it is something of which all humans are a part. Such a perspective provides Native artists not only with strong mythological imperatives for their residence, their fight to live in their homelands, and their views of the land, but also for their rights to make specific forms of art.

This sense of place has been discussed in the literature in several ways, not all of which match the emphasis on distinctive landscapes mentioned by artists themselves. Art historians and anthropologists have for years relied on object types and culture areas to bring order to the diversity of Native media and styles. Probably the most important concept for American Indian Studies is that of the "culture area," which is based largely upon the presence or absence of art – especially key object types – and how they can be classified stylistically (the Plains as a culture area is recognized, for example, by geometric beadwork on clothing). This conceptual device, developed by Otis T. Mason and refined by Clark Wissler at the turn of the twentieth century, was designed to facilitate comparison of different cultures in comparative museum exhibits. Culture areas, defined by economic and material traits, reflect environmental opportunities, limitations, and adaptation (rather than the land itself or the landscape). The concept is still the primary classificatory device for the study of Indian cultures and art, even though anthropologists since the 1930s have discussed the concept's limitations. Culture areas are never perfect and exceptions to any generalization abound. If the Greater Southwest is defined and characterized by the presence of pottery, for example, what does one do with the Seri who do not produce pottery as part of their artistic inventory? Culture areas have some validity but they describe central tendencies, not absolutes. Nevertheless, today the culture area concept is still used as the unquestioned framing device for anthropology, art history, and American Indian Studies courses as well as for all published regional surveys of Native art. The concept's reification has also affected how the general public has viewed issues of authenticity: a Choctaw artist who uses "Plains" beadwork styles is "inauthentic." Unfortunately, the art forms on which these criticisms are based have become canonical objects for scholars as well. Objects that derive from historical moments and places have become the standard by which "modern" is judged in comparison to "traditional." One of the most glaring needs in the study of Indian art is a reanalysis of this pervasive concept and its effect on how Native art is interpreted.

A new general summary of area specializations is penned every few years. Sometimes these surveys simply reiterate existing typologies and parrot accepted knowledge, including preconceptions about tradition and authenticity. In these cases, what authors provide are "classic" traditions with rigid boundaries, little evidence of internal cultural variation, and even less understanding of intertribal contact and cultural influence. It is as if each art tradition were frozen in time and place. Thus readers find reviews of established major traditions: wood carving and masks in the Northwest Coast region, basketry on the Plateau, pottery, textiles, baskets, and jewelry in the Southwest, tanned hide and beadwork on the Northern Plains. But one also finds that the authors ignore creativity and value only changelessness. A very few surveys, however, have presented original information and problematized how Native American art can be better understood using both culturally specific paradigms and universalist criteria. Especially noteworthy since 1980 have been those produced by Christian Feest (1980/1992), Peter Furst and Jill Furst (1982), and Janet Berlo and Ruth Phillips (1998).

Many regional and thematic surveys are published as exhibition catalogues designed for a general audience. The most well known are based on influential exhibitions at the Denver Art Museum, American Museum of Natural History, Walker Art Center, Heard Museum, Philbrook Museum, Gilcrease Institute, and the National Museum of the American Indian. Also common are general surveys of artistic development based primarily on the permanent collections of an institution (for example, Mahey and Strickland, 1980; Penney, 1989; Whiteford, 1989). As such, the publications tell as much about the institutional collecting histories, gift-giving activities of patrons, and curatorial aesthetic preferences as they do about the development of Native art styles. These catalogues also reflect the disciplinary scope of the institution and training of the curators. Quests to associate Native American art with primitivism, for example, led to placing descriptive adjectives such as "primal," "irrational," or "imaginative" on decontextualized pieces in art museums without reference to Native aesthetic goals. Some curators have tried to break through these barriers and past perspectives in their catalogues. Two of the most influential works in this regard are *The Arts of the North American Indian*, edited by anthropologist Edwin Wade (1986), and *Magic Images*, edited with Native lawyer Rennard Strickland (1981).

A new series of survey catalogues is being penned by Native scholars. Although most of these scholars come from intellectual traditions that have not focused on art, all have been influenced by Native artists who are also political activists and by their dealings, particularly in the realm of law. Prominent in this genre are the catalogues produced by Native curators and scholars associated with the National Museum of the American Indian (Hill and Hill, 1994) as well as numerous works from Canada. In addition to opening the exhibition and publishing arena to Native scholars, these successful publications broaden rhetorical and interpretive frameworks as well as politicizing dissemination issues.

Market Economy and Collecting

One of the most extensive topics in the art literature concerns changes in cultural inventories due to contact, trade, and assimilation. Since the first contacts

Europeans have been interested in and desired Native American art just as Native Americans have desired European-produced goods. Items have moved extensively in both directions, spreading technological and aesthetic ideas. Art has been purchased and traded cross-culturally, given as gifts to cement diplomatic relationships, and stolen during raids and military expeditions. Native Americans have valued new materials – broadcloth, ribbon, and beadwork changed the way clothing and the body have been adorned. Guns, steel-headed harpoons, cars, and horse bridles transformed economies and many behavioral activities, such as warfare.

The historic concern with assimilation has affected art studies in that more is known about the transformation of Native industries than is known about the transformations of Euro-American art as a result of contact and borrowing. There are hundreds of works that document how Native communities stopped making pottery when they obtained metal pots and pans. In Wabanaki, Penobscot, and Passamaquoddy communities, for example, snowshoes, wampum, and birchbark baskets were exchanged for canoes, guns, glass beads, and metal tools in the seventeenth and eighteenth centuries. There is also a good deal of information on how creative Native artists changed their manufacturing techniques, styles, and marketing practices in response to changing consumer preferences. In the nineteenth century Native basketmakers created woven pack and utility baskets to meet market demands, while buying metal milk pails for themselves. In the twentieth century, their marketing emphasis has been on decorative items that will grace a living room rather than a kitchen.

While Native American artistic transformations as a result of cultural diffusion or borrowing are well documented in the anthropological literature, a special form of cross-cultural exchange, collecting, has only more recently become the focus of systematic study. From the beginning, Europeans have both haphazardly and systematically collected the art produced by Native North American peoples. One cannot understand contemporary art without understanding past and present collecting behavior and the nature of Euro-American–Native American relations (Lee, 1991). Nor can many forms be understood if they are not recognized as commodities that are sold in an international art market specializing in ethnic art; historic and contemporary Native American art must be contextualized in a framework that includes the political economy of collecting.

Interaction and its effects on the arts were not always consistently steady, but punctuated. Some of the most drastic changes in Southwest Indian art, for example, occurred in the 1880s. Anglo-American pressures to assimilate, coupled with the destruction of the old economic systems, pulled Southwest Indians into a cash, credit, and market economy. Creation of craft objects shifted from home use, with minor trading of surplus goods by barter, to market production. Art became an important cog in the subsistence strategies of many families. Often women made art for sale while men performed outside wage work. The Navajo, for example, greatly expanded their expertise in silversmithing and jewelry production as a result of the railroad and the influence of the Fred Harvey Company. In 1923, it was estimated that 5,500 Navajo women produced rugs for sale as a cottage industry that complemented pastoralism. Art production has given Indian men and women an edge against poverty – a way to obtain cash and to maintain economic flexibility, while living on the margins of expanding industrial, post-industrial, and now service economies.

A great deal of Native American art is made for outside consumption and intended to be sold on the open market. Recent scholarship has been slowly extending our knowledge about the cycles of this production and the economic impact this has had on Native communities and individual families. Much of this information comes from biographies and community studies. Other studies focus on specific art forms and discuss marketing, production, and consumption as facets of economic development (MacDougall, 1997; Parezo, 1983).

For the past 500 years Native American artists have been exposed to Euro-American aesthetic concepts and have assimilated or incorporated them to varying degrees; they have also rejected them when they have not served their cultural and individual purposes. Historic and contemporary Native American artists explore both their own cultural aesthetics and those of American society. This exploration includes styles and art forms developed not only as contemporary experimentation, but also during the reservation era. The beaded vests worn so proudly by Northern Plains men, for example, have become "traditional" in their own right. Much of the contemporary literature deals with documenting the historic development and results of such cultural processes.

These double heritages and aesthetic preferences are crucially bound up in market value, reflecting consumers' stylistic preferences and the requirements of artistic media. The market presents problems: artists must sometimes compromise with the Euro-American art-buying public or compartmentalize the art produced for internal and external use. "Art buyers," notes Price,

> want something distinctively Indian from an Indian artist and that has usually emphasized the primitive, simple, and child-like in technique and the use of traditional Indian symbols and forms. An Indian artist who works with Western techniques and symbols is just another Western artist who must be judged by Western criteria and few people – Indians or Whites – can be financially independent in the competitive field of Western art. Indians usually adjust to this and produce that which sells well to Whites, distinctively "Indian" art. The problem with this is that it tends to reduce the amount of aesthetic play and honest creativity in Indian Art. (Price, 1989: 125)

Collecting and patronage are especially potent topics in this regard. While people in all societies collect, the collection of Native American art is especially extensive and complex, reflecting as it does issues of race, gender, ethnicity, culture, and elitism. Collecting has been structured by the desires of colonial powers to understand and control the goods of colonialized peoples, by the gifts given in diplomatic exchanges, by symmetrical and asymmetrical power relationships, and by the desire of newly established disciplines such as anthropology to save, salvage, and preserve the "vanishing natives." Museums now house millions of pieces of Native American art acquired through colonial collection.

Researchers are focusing on the collecting activities of institutions (Parezo, 1987), individual collectors (Fane, Jacknis, and Breen, 1991; Batkin and Amiotte, 1995; Cohodas, 1999), and the politics of scholarship and collecting itself (Berlo, 1992). The best works are also good ethnographies that contextualize art in relation to collecting activities. The conceptual focus, however, centers on American collecting activity as a noteworthy process of modern society. Other works scrutinize different time periods and the effects of European exploration on Native art (Feest, 1995) and the development of an educated and appreciative audience for Indian art in the twentieth century (Rushing, 1993).

There is now an extensive literature on the development of the decorative and tourist market, especially that which developed during the 1920s and the 1960s and 1970s. Led by Nelson Graburn (1976) and his work with Inuit ivory carvers and print makers, scholars have looked at the development of the range of art forms – inexpensive to expensive – intended solely for sale to Euro-Americans. This work has focused on issues of innovation, continuity and adaptation, historical development, cultural brokerage, cross-cultural aesthetic translations, gender or sexual divisions of labor, miniaturization, stylistic simplification and formalization, stylistic development, and marketing, including the role of Euro-American middlemen/women and patrons.

Institutional Effects on Native American Art Styles and Media

The development of Indian art in the nineteenth and twentieth centuries has been inextricably interwoven with government initiatives, educational institutions and museums, patronage, and business projects. The development of secular and commercial easel art in the Southwest in the mid-twentieth century, for example, was influenced by the patronage of several Santa Fe museum curators and teachers in the Indian schools. So successful was the tutelage of these individuals, especially Dorothy Dunn, and their educational and marketing efforts on behalf of extremely talented Pueblo and Athabascan artists, that the artists' highly stylized, decorative watercolors of traditional activities, especially dances, came to be accepted and almost fossilized as "traditional" Indian painting.

Government patronage of and policies about Indian art production have only begun to attract scholarly attention. Historian Robert Schrader (1983) has documented the Indian Arts and Crafts Board in the 1930s and 1940s as a New Deal program designed to encourage economic development and prevent the fraudulent sales of arts as "Indian-made" when they were not. More recently, cultural anthropologist and attorney Gail Sheffield (1997) has analyzed the controversial Indian Arts and Crafts Act of 1990 with regard to issues of sovereignty, Indian self-identification, authenticity, suppression of free expression, and personal versus cultural rights. Art is never created in a vacuum and it both reflects and comes face to face with contemporary social, economic, and political issues.

Scholars have been exceptionally active in looking at the effects of scholarship itself, particularly in terms of the institutional settings in which Indian art has been presented to the general society. The contested politics of institutional representation have been visible in the many permanent and temporary exhibits that have been recently assembled by anthropology and history museums. Native peoples have increasingly requested and demanded a say in how their cultures, their pasts, presents, and futures are being displayed to multiple audiences. One of the most controversial in recent years has been the 1987 exhibit *The Spirit Sings* at the Glenbow Museum in Calgary. A large reflexive literature has developed, especially in Canada, on the controversy and how institutions dealing with First Nations should conceptualize and mount exhibits (Ames, 1992).

Native artists and critics have also questioned the ways that art galleries and museums have categorized Native artistic production. Native scholar Theresa Harlan has elegantly summarized the problem: "Mainstream museums and publications often set apart 'artists of color,' 'multicultural artists,' and 'ethnic artists,' thereby designating us as the 'other' or 'different.' The art and writings of these 'other' artists are locked into discussion of 'their' art, 'their' people, and 'their' issues. While there are still few opportunities to exhibit works by Native artists, there are even fewer exhibitions that treat these works in terms of their intellectual and critical contribution" (Harlan, 1995: 20). Native women artists have had an especially difficult time gaining access to museum exhibition space, the institutional setting critical for an artist's career. As Powhatan feminist critic Phoebe Farris-Dufrene has argued (1997), the art power brokers assume that the norm for the art world is male, upper-class, and Western. Much of the feminist literature dealing with Native American art describes this ongoing fight against internalized sexism.

NAGPRA and Cultural Patrimony

In historic and contemporary Western society, it is taken for granted that art – transcendent as it may claim to be – nonetheless resides in the world of commodities. Things, and the right to own, represent, and use them as individual property, are considered a moral imperative of exchange and ownership. In the process of exchange, however, new social and cultural values are embedded in the art. A Taos micaceous pot used to cook beans, for example, can be pedestaled in an art museum as an "expressive object" to be admired but not used for food preparation, or even touched. The cooking vessel has been endowed with new cultural meanings and reclassified into the culturally constituted category of "museum quality" object as it moved from Taos to American society. This cultural redefinition and reuse may be acceptable to both the original producers and consumers and add a new dimension to an art form as symbolic capital. But a new meaning and use may also be in conflict with or considered inappropriate by makers who have different conceptions of property, ownership, and the decontextualization and proper use of art, art styles, motifs, and symbols, especially those considered sacred. American and European museums are filled with both uncontested and contested Native American art.

Every society has a symbolic inventory of objects that are precluded from being commodified and alienated in any way from their original purpose. Some of these prohibitions are cultural and upheld collectively, the objects labeled as sacred or cultural patrimony. Power or sovereignty for a society (or nation, social class, race, profession, or ethnic group) is often manifest in its insistence on its rights to exclusively produce specific art forms, styles, and symbols, to define and regulate their appropriate use, and to exclude outsiders (or those without the proper rights or controlling knowledge) from using, collecting, exhibiting, studying, or representing the art. Native Americans have successfully sought to assert these rights over art that they feel has been inappropriately alienated by past collecting activities and sales. They have gained recognition of this quest through federal mandate: Public Law 101-601, the Native American Graves Protection and Repatriation Act (NAGPRA), passed in 1990, and Public Law 101-185, the National Museum of the American Indian Act, passed in 1989, as well as a number of state and federal laws aimed at protecting archaeological sites and encouraging historic preservation.

NAGPRA insists on the return of human remains, funerary objects, and certain kinds of historic art to Native communities. To date, repatriated material cultural items have included wampum belts, masks, rattles, ritual shields and weapons, religious figurines, medicine bundles, items used in ceremonies, and politically important objects such as the Omaha's sacred pole. In a sense this is a reinstitution of culturally specific Native classifications of objects that are considered to be sacred or of extreme cultural importance, not simply those things that were used at one time within a society, are beautiful, or have economic value as a commodity. Because in complex societies, different, publicly recognized commoditization processes operate simultaneously and often in conflict with subgroups' different schemes of valuation and concepts of sacredness, there will always be unresolved conflicts and differing definitions used in the NAGPRA negotiation process.

There is a rapidly expanding literature on NAGPRA, much of which is legalistic or focused on human rights, the correction of past grievances, intellectual property rights, and tribal sovereignty (Thornton, 1998; Echo-Hawk, 1992). Other studies deal with issues of representations and collections management, particularly the proper way to handle sacred objects. A few are now relating the history of the political and social movement to get NAGPRA passed, or documenting and analyzing the repatriation efforts of specific groups (Bray and Killion, 1994; Merrill, Ladd, and Ferguson, 1993). The National Park Service Internet site (www.cr.nps.gov.aad/nagpra.htm) posts a current bibliography as well as a copy of the law, regulations, procedural guidelines, and a summary of the museum inventories demanded by the law.

NAGPRA has the potential to produce an extensive corpus of new scholarship on art, property concepts, ethnographic information on use, concepts of sacredness, and Native worldviews and philosophies, although little has yet been published. Since community scholars from each Native culture must be consulted after the museum produces an inventory, many Native scholars are seeing and discussing their art for the first time. As a result of these consultations, old cultural identifications are being questioned and in many cases corrected and improved. Native scholars have reidentified mislabeled objects and narrowed broad culture area designations to more specific cultural affiliations. In other cases, provenance information has been gathered through oral histories. Some of this information has been shared with museum curators; some has not. For the first time, cultural descendants of the original artists are having a say in deciding what is appropriate knowledge about art to be shared with external communities.

NAGPRA has also forced non-Native scholars to consider Native American conceptions of property and ownership. It has, in many cases, revitalized Native communities, and there is evidence of artistic revivals and the construction of community-initiated and community-run museums and cultural centers. New studies of these institutions, as well as of the art housed within them, is developing in the form of oral histories, interviews with elders on construction techniques, and storytelling programs. As a result, Native histories are being rewritten and presented to the museum-going public in new ways.

Native Voice: Interviews with Famous Artists and Social Commentary

The most rapidly expanding corpus of works is that of biographies of historic artists, interviews, social criticism, and family histories of contemporary artists. There are now popular books on famous artists such as Nampeyo (Kramer, 1996) and works that demonstrate how talent runs in families through several generations (Dillingham, 1994). These studies tend to focus on individual artistic development. They are supplemented by numerous brief biographical sketches in directories (Lester, 1995) and databases on Native artists being compiled by museums. These tend to list basic information considered appropriate by art historians when detailing the provenance of an art work: name of artists, birth and death dates, cultural affiliation, education, awards, scholarships, exhibitions, juried shows. Designed to document authenticity, they generally do not list information considered critical by Native artists: band, community, clan or other kinship affiliation, data that show the viewer that the individual has the right to paint certain motifs.

Better at articulating the worldview and concerns of Native artists are numerous substantive interviews and life history sketches, particularly when combined with critical scholarly writing and assessments. Lawrence Abbott (1994) presents seventeen such interviews in the pathbreaking *I Stand in the Center of the Good*. Rushing and WalkingStick (1992) provide a forum in which artists discuss issues of authenticity, the art market, and the problems of art criticism. These and similar works allow Native artists to talk about their lives and about being successful (for, of course, none of these works documents the lives of artists who have not been recognized as superior by the external art market). There is sometimes a tension in the more sophisticated and sensitive of these works, a tension that mirrors the themes and issues found in the writings of contemporary Native authors/poets and their fiction. This tension is often summarized as the problem of "walking in two worlds." Contemporary artists sometimes tread a fine line between external fame and community-centeredness. This line can be especially evident in those cultures where calling attention to oneself and one's deeds is considered arrogant or constitutes inappropriate behavior.

It is also readily apparent from even a superficial review of artist interviews that there is a multiplicity of artistic intent and practice in the contemporary Native American art worlds. Theories of irony, thematic statements about historic and contemporary life, expressions of alienation from Western culture or reservation life, reactions to modernity and postmodernity, the refutation of stereotypes, metaphors about the place of individuals in the universe – all these are introduced as the intents of Native artists. In many cases, Native art is explicitly aimed at social commentary. The interview literature is particularly good at demonstrating the political symbolisms and the critiques of modern, urban society that are often the basis of modern art. Jaune Quick-To-See Smith, for example, relates how she is concerned with environmental issues affecting Indian country (Lippard, 1990: 28). Following in the footsteps of Fritz Scholder's satirical and biting look at Euro-American stereotyping of Indians, *Indian Kitsch* (Scholder, 1979), many painters and sculptors are also writing about the issues they paint and becoming their own art historians and art critics.

"Resistance to (neo)colonial hegemony" is clearly one of the most salient characteristics of Indian art since the 1960s (Rushing, 1999: 14). Photographer and curator Richard Hill, Jr., a member of the Tuscarora nation, has suggested that his camera is a weapon for "art confrontation." "Indians themselves now have taken the power of the image and begun to use it for their own enjoyment as well as for its potential power as a political weapon" (Hill, quoted in Dixon, 1987: 25). Artists have also used art as an effective tool to rewrite their histories, understanding that images are often more powerful and memorable than high school history texts that marginalize or ignore the place of American Indians in historical rhetoric.

While there is a growing literature on Native American spirituality by Native writers, few artists reveal information about the sacred or symbolic meanings of their art. This is especially true of those art pieces that are meant to be used internally and are not intended for sale to individuals outside the maker's home community. In many Native cultures, religious rituals involve the precise use of knowledge. Words have power, and religious symbolism is taken seriously. Knowledge carries responsibilities, particularly for those who would create representations.

Issues Facing Contemporary Artists

Contemporary Native American art is thriving and dynamic, but often plagued by conceptual dilemmas that stem in part from past research, in part from definitions of "tradition," "traditional," "contemporary," and "modern," and in part from the nature and processes of the fine art market. Only recently have scholars begun to dissect and analyze the wealth of critical issues to which artists have drawn attention as they have struggled to carve out a niche for themselves as practitioners in the fine art world while, at the same time, refusing to be pigeon-holed or marginalized. Is it possible for Native people to be respected as modern artists as well as Native American artists? Janet Berlo and Ruth Phillips have developed a definition of modern Native artists that overcomes some of these persistent problems. "Modern," they insist, "is defined not by a particular set of stylistic or conceptual categories, but by the adoption of Western representational styles, genres, and media in order to produce works that function as autonomous entities and that are intended to be experienced independently of community or ceremonial contexts" (1998: 210). Modern Native American art, then, has been shaped – and ironically so – by the socio-economic contexts of marketing and capitalism. In the midst of a wealth of "modern" Native art, patrons have been especially concerned with traditionalism and ensuring that artists adhere to pre-contact forms and aesthetic principles; that is, that Indian art does not become contaminated by Western modernity.

Some of these issues are definitional and reflect familiar identity dilemmas (see Harmon, this volume). Who has the right to produce and sell "Indian" art? Who is an "Indian" artist? Is it only someone who has full ancestry and who has grown up on a reservation? Consumer protection laws have been enacted in the United States and Canada which demand that only artists who are legally recognized by the federal governments – that is, enrolled in a recognized tribe – can call them-selves Native artists and market their work as "Indian" art. The most recent law, the 1990 Indian Arts and Crafts act, legislates ethnicity for artists. It requires that tribal enrollment numbers, state census roll numbers, or a special "Indian art" status be provided by an artist's tribal council in order for an artist to sell his/her work as "Indian" art. Excluded are artists who are Indian according to ancestry, but not political status or sociocultural traits. The law has arbitrarily disenfran-chised several recognized artists and given rise to conflict and lawsuits.

To be recognized as artists rather than strictly Indian artists, Native people confront the difficulty of breaking into the fine art market. Berlo and Phillips (1998: 209) note that Native artists are often considered provincial, historicist, and quaint – in a word, premodern – by the art community and critics. They sug-gest that this is due in part to a time lag: Native artists became concerned with modernist issues of abstraction and expressionism, a rejection of strict illusionist pictorialism, and a reflexive search for individual expression only in the later twentieth century. Will indigenous artists – whether they work in Western art media or in more "traditional" forms and styles, whether they deal with post-modern avant-garde issues or aesthetic concerns rooted in ancestral heritages, whether they are formally trained in professional art schools or self-taught – be accepted by the fine art market on an equal footing with non-ethnic artists?

Non-professionally trained artists, those who learn in their home communities using established and time-honored methods, also face additional problems when their art is made for external consumption. To sell products as art in the market-place, artists must clear a space in which the maker is distinguished from other producers and their products. One does this by the construction and marking of difference – in style, vision, or quality. To create a market for her pottery, a new Pueblo potter must establish that subtle differences in construction or design are essential modes of distinction, yet simultaneously she must adhere to the accepted parameters of what is thought to be, recognized as, and valued as the pottery of her native community.

Conclusion

Every piece of art contains Native voices and Native perspectives which scholars have striven for years to hear, appreciate, translate, understand, and interpret. While scholars have discovered much over the last century, they still have much to learn. A great deal of research remains to be done on both traditional and contemporary art. While thousands of works have been written on the Greater Southwest, for example (see Parezo, Allen, and Perry, 1991 for an extensive bibliography of over 10,000 references on the Greater Southwest alone), the coverage remains patchy. While there is good information about technology and production processes, traditional functions, and the sexual division of labor in many cultures, more work needs to be undertaken on stylistic innovation, both within traditional frameworks and in new arenas. Much of the existing research on style is still overly concerned with simply documenting sequences of formal and successful stylistic innovations, not with the processes of meaning formation and aesthetic experimentation.

The "to do" list is long: still lacking is a revaluation of previously marginalized and underestimated work. We need, as well, more historiographical work on how scholarship, museums, collecting, and similar activities have affected individual artists and their work, and on groups of artists in general. Likewise, we need better to understand, on the one hand, the criteria of legitimation and the politics of artistic critique and, on the other, the points of view of Native artists and cultures. There are opportunities for Native art critics who will analyze art produced for external consumption in culturally specific as well as generalized art historical terms. Luckily, there are some good scholars who are finding mainstream outlets for their assessments – Theresa Harlan's 1995 work on photography is an excellent model. In some senses, this need parallels the calls for "Indian-centered" histories and will have the same strengths and encounter the same weaknesses being addressed by Native historians and ethnohistorians (see White, 1998). While there are now a number of biographies, biographical sketches, autobiographies, interviews, and "conversations" with Native artists, there is yet no comprehensive and comparative work that discusses the commonalities of experiences of being a Native artist in contemporary American society.

Above all, there is a critical need to pull all the various threads together into a unified theoretical framework. This will be a Herculean effort, interdisciplinary in nature. The envisioned theory would connect, among other things, the continuing colonization and commodification of all parts of Native cultures with the ways Euro-American fictions about American Indians have influenced the art market and the arts themselves, especially those intentionally produced for external sale. It would connect as well Native meanings, understandings, and criticisms, past, present, and future. Perhaps such a unified field theory of Native art and material culture lies beyond our grasp. It seems, however, a worthy goal at which to aim.

BIBLIOGRAPHY

Abbott, Lawrence (ed.) 1994: *I Stand in the Center of the Good. Interviews with Contemporary Native American Artists* (Lincoln: University of Nebraska Press).

Ames, Michael M. 1992: *Cannibal Tours and Glass Boxes: The Anthropology of Museums* (Vancouver: University of British Columbia Press).

Archuleta, Margaret and Rennard Strickland 1991: *Shared Visions: Native American Painters and Sculptors in the Twentieth Century* (Phoenix: Heard Museum).

Bates, Sara 1995: *Indian Humor* (San Francisco: American Indian Contemporary Arts).

Batkin, Jonathan 1987: *Pottery of the Pueblos of New Mexico, 1700–1940* (Colorado Springs: Colorado Springs Fine Art Center).

Batkin, Jonathan and Arthur Amiotte 1995: *Splendid Heritage: Masterpieces of Native American Art from the Masco Collection* (Santa Fe: Wheelwright Museum of the American Indian).

Berlo, Janet C. (ed.) 1992: *The Early Years of Native American Art History: The Politics of Scholarship and Collecting* (Seattle: University of Washington Press and UBC Press).

Berlo, Janet C. and Ruth B. Phillips 1998: *Native North American Art. Oxford History of Art* (Oxford and New York: Oxford University Press).

Bray, Tamara L. and Thomas W. Killion (eds.) 1994: *Reckoning with the Dead: The Larsen Bay Repatriation and the Smithsonian Institution* (Washington, D.C.: Smithsonian Institution Press).

Cohodas, Marvin 1999: *High on the Rivers: The Hickoxes of Somes Bar and Constructions of the California Basket Curio* (Tucson: University of Arizona Press).

Cole, Douglas 1985: *Captured Heritage: The Scramble for Northwest Coast Artifacts* (Seattle: University of Washington Press)

Dillingham, Rick 1994: *Fourteen Families in Pueblo Pottery* (Albuquerque: University of New Mexico Press).

Dixon, Susan R. 1987: "Images of Indians: Controlling the Camera," *North East Indian Quarterly* (Spring/Summer): 25.

Dobkins, Rebecca J. 1997: *Memory and Imagination: The Legacy of Maidu Indian Artist Frank Day* (Oakland: Oakland Museum of California).

Doxtator, Deborah 1996: "Basket, Bead and Quill, and the Making of 'Traditional' Art," *Basket, Bead and Quill* (Ontario) 2: 10–18.

Duncan, Kate C. 1988: *A Special Gift: The Kutchin Beadwork Tradition* (Seattle: University of Washington Press).

Echo-Hawk, Walter 1992: "The Native American Grave Protection and Repatriation Act: Background and Legislative History," *Arizona State Law Journal* 24: 35–77.

Fane, Diana, Ira Jacknis, and Lise M. Breen 1991: *Objects of Myth and Memory: American Indian Art at the Brooklyn Museum* (New York and Seattle: University of Washington Press).

Farris-Dufrene, Phoebe 1997: "Reaching In and Taking Out: Native American Women Artists in a Different Feminism," in *Voices of Color. Art and Society in the Americas,* ed. Phoebe Farris-Dufrene (New Jersey: Humanities Press), pp. 11–19.

Feest, Christian F. 1980: *Native Arts of North America* (London and New York: Thames and Hudson, 1980, revised edition, 1992).

Feest, Christian F. 1995: "The Collecting of American Indian Artifacts in Europe, 1473–1750," in *America in European Consciousness, 1493–1750,* ed. Karen O. Kupperman (Chapel Hill: University of North Carolina Press).

Furst, Peter T. and Jill L. Furst 1982: *North American Indian Art* (New York: Rizzoli).

Glenbow Museum 1987: *The Spirit Sings: Artistic Traditions of Canada's First Peoples* (Toronto: McClelland and Stewart for the Glenbow Museum).

Graburn, Nelson H. H. (ed.) 1976: *Tourist and Ethnic Arts: Cultural Expressions from the Fourth World* (Berkeley: University of California Press).

Graburn, Nelson H. H. 1987: "Inuit Art and the Expression of Ethnic Identity," *American Review of Canadian Studies* 17(1): 47–66.

Hardin, Margaret A. 1983: *Gifts of Mother Earth: Ceramics in the Zuni Tradition* (Phoenix: Heard Museum).

Harlan, Theresa 1995: "Creating a Visual History: A Question of Ownership," *Aperture* 139: 20–33.

Hill, Tom and Richard W. Hill, Sr. (eds.) 1994: *Creation's Journey: Native American Identity and Belief* (Washington, D.C.: Smithsonian Institution Press).

Jackna, Jerry and Lois E. Jackna 1998: *Art of the Hopi. Contemporary Journeys in Ancient Pathways* (Flagstaff, AZ: Northland Press).

Jonaitis, Aldona 1988: *From the Land of the Totem Poles: The Northwest Coast Indian Art Collection at the American Museum of Natural History* (Seattle: University of Washington Press).

Jonaitis, Aldona 1991: *Chiefly Feasts: The Enduring Kwakiutl Potlatch* (Seattle: University of Washington Press).

Kramer, Barbara 1996: *Nampeyo and Her Pottery* (Albuquerque: University of New Mexico Press).

Krinsky, Carol 1996: *Contemporary Native American Architecture* (Oxford and New York: Oxford University Press).

Lee, Molly 1991: "Appropriating the Primitive: Turn-of-the-Century Collection and Display of Native Alaskan Art," *Arctic Anthropology* 28(1): 6–15.

Leroux, Odette, Marion E. Jackson, and Minnie A. Freeman 1994: *Inuit Women Artists: Voices from Cape Dorset* (Hull, Quebec: Canadian Museum of Civilization).

Lester, Patrick D. 1995: *The Biographical Directory of Native American Painters* (Tulsa: SIR Publications, distributed by University of Oklahoma Press, Norman).

Lippard, Lucy 1990: *Mixed Blessings: New Art in a Multicultural America* (New York: Pantheon Books).

MacDougall, Pauleena 1997: "Native American Industry: Basket Weaving among the Wabanaki," in *American Indian Studies: An Interdisciplinary Approach to Contemporary Issues,* ed. Dane A. Morrison (New York: Peter Lang), pp. 167–92.

Mahey, John A. and Rennard Strickland 1980: *Native American Art at Philbrook* (Tulsa, OK: Philbrook Art Museum).

Mathews, Zena Pearlsone and Aldona Jonaitis 1982: *North American Art History: Selected Readings* (Palo Alto, CA: Stanford University Press).

McMaster, Gerald 1999: *Reservation X. The Power of Place in Aboriginal Contemporary Art* (Seattle and Ottawa: University of Washington Press and Canadian Museum of Civilization).

Merrill, William L., Edmund J. Ladd, and T. J. Ferguson 1993: "The Return of the Ahayu:da: Lessons for Repatriation from Zuni Pueblo and the Smithsonian Institution," *Current Anthropology* 34(5): 523–67.

Nabokov, Peter and Robert Easton 1989: *Native American Architecture* (Oxford and New York: Oxford University Press).

Parezo, Nancy J. 1983: *Navajo Sandpaintings: From Religious Act to Commercial Art* (Tucson: University of Arizona Press).

Parezo, Nancy J. 1987: "The Formation of Ethnographic Collections: The Smithsonian Institution in the American Southwest," in *Advances in Archaeological Method and Theory*, vol. 10, ed. Michael Schiffer (Orlando, FL: Academic Press), pp. 1–47.

Parezo, Nancy J. 1991: "A Multitude of Markets," *Journal of the Southwest* 32(4): 563–75.

Parezo, Nancy J. 1996: "Southwestern Art Worlds," *Journal of the Southwest* 38(4): 499–511.

Parezo, Nancy J., Rebecca Allen, and Ruth Perry 1991: *Southwest Native American Arts and Material Culture: A Guide to Research*, 2 vols. (New York: Garland Publications).

Parezo, Nancy J., Kelley A. Hays, and Barbara Slivac 1987: "The Mind's Road. Southwest Indian Women's Art," in *The Desert Is No Lady: Southwestern Landscapes in Women's Writing and Art*, eds. Vera H. Norwood and Janice Monk (New Haven: Yale University Press), pp. 146–73.

Penney, David W. (ed.) 1989: *Great Lakes Indian Art* (Detroit: Wayne State University Press and Detroit Institute of Arts).

Pheps, Elisa 1995: *Dialogues with Zuni Potters* (Zuni, New Mexico: privately printed).

Phillips, Ruth B. 1990: "Moccasins into Slippers: Woodland Indian Hats, Bags and Shoes in Tradition and Transformation," *Northeast Indian Quarterly* 7(4): 26–36.

Phillips, Ruth B. 1994a: "Why Not Tourist Art? Significant Silences in Native American Museum Collections," in *After Colonialism: Imperial Histories and Post-Colonial Displacements*, ed. G. Prakash (Princeton, NJ: Princeton University Press).

Phillips, Ruth B. 1994b: "Fielding Culture: Dialogues between Art History and Anthropology," *Museum Anthropology* 18(1): 39–64.

Phillips, Ruth B. 1998: *Trading Identities: The Souvenir in Native North American Art from the Northeast, 1700–1900* (Seattle: University of Washington Press).

Phillips, Ruth B. and Christopher B. Steiner (eds.) 1999: *Unpacking Culture: Art and Commodity in Colonial and Postcolonial Worlds* (Berkeley: University of California Press).

Price, Sally 1989: *Primitive Art in Civilized Places* (Chicago: University of Chicago Press).

Rushing, W. Jackson 1993: *Native American Art and Culture and the New York Avant-Garde, 1910–1950* (Austin: University of Texas Press).

Rushing, W. Jackson 1999: *Native American Art in the Twentieth Century: Makers, Meanings and Histories* (London and New York: Routledge).

Rushing, W. Jackson and Kay WalkingStick (guest eds.) 1992: "Recent Native American Art," *Art*, 51(3).

Scholder, Fritz 1979: *Indian Kitsch: The Use and Misuse of Indian Images* (Flagstaff, AZ: Northland Press).

Schrader, Robert F. 1983: *The Indian Arts and Crafts Board: An Aspect of New Deal Indian Policy* (Albuquerque: University of New Mexico Press).

Sheffield, Gail K. 1997: *The Arbitrary Indian: The Indian Arts and Crafts Act of 1990* (Norman: University of Oklahoma Press).

Stocking, George W. (ed.) 1985: *Objects and Others: Essays on Museums and Material Culture* (Madison: University of Wisconsin Press).

Szabo, Joyce M. 1994: *Howling Wolf and the History of Ledger Art* (Albuquerque: University of New Mexico Press).

Tanner, Clara Lee 1983: *American Indian Baskets of the Southwest* (Tucson: University of Arizona Press).

Thompson, Raymond H. and Nancy J. Parezo 1989: "Historical Survey of Material Culture Studies in American Anthropology," in *Perspectives on Anthropological Collections from the American Southwest. Proceedings of a Symposium*, ed. Ann Hedlund (Tempe: Arizona State University Anthropological Research Papers No. 40), pp. 33–66.

Thornton, Russell 1998: "Who Owns the Past? The Repatriation of Native American Human Remains and Cultural Objects," in *Studying Native America. Problems and Prospects*, ed. Russell Thornton (Madison: University of Wisconsin Press), pp. 385–415.

Vastokas, Joan 1986–7: "Native Art as Art History: Meaning and Time from Unwritten Sources," *Journal of Canadian Studies* 21(4).

Wade, Edwin L. 1985: "The Ethnic Art Market in the American Southwest, 1880–1890," in *Objects and Others: Essays on Museums and Material Culture*, ed. George W. Stocking, Jr. (Madison: University of Wisconsin Press), pp. 167–91.

Wade, Edwin L. (ed.) 1986: *The Arts of the North American Indian: Native Traditions in Evolution* (New York and Tulsa: Hudson Hills and Philbrook Art Center).

Wade, Edwin L. and Rennard Strickland 1981: *Magic Images: Contemporary Native American Art* (Norman: University of Oklahoma Press).

West, W. Richard 1993: "Research and Scholarship at the National Museum of the American Indian: The New Inclusiveness," *Museum Anthropology* 12(1): 5–8.

West, W. Richard et al. 1999: *The Changing Presentation of the American Indian. Museums and Native Cultures* (Seattle: University of Washington Press and Smithsonian Institution).

White, Richard 1998: "Using the Past: History and American Indian Studies," in *Studying Native America: Problems and Prospects*, ed. Russell Thornton (Madison: University of Wisconsin Press), pp. 217–46.

Whiteford, Andrew H. 1988: *Southwestern Indian Baskets: Their History and Their Makers* (Santa Fe: School of American Research).

Whiteford, Andrew H. 1989: *I Am Here: Two Thousand Years of Southwest Indian Art and Culture* (Santa Fe: School of American Research).

Whitten, Dorothea and Norman Whitten (eds.) 1993: *Imagery and Creativity: Ethnoaesthetic and Art Worlds in the Americas* (Tucson: University of Arizona Press).

13

Native American Literatures

P. JANE HAFEN

Indian written expression rests at the center of a series of seeming contradictions. The literary traditions of indigenous peoples are, in a certain sense, timeless. Fundamental characteristics, such as the ritual of storytelling, trickster humor, sacredness of place, and mythic time have remained largely unchanged. Yet Indian writings have also been subject to historical transformations that have come with European contact: orthography, translation, and English-language expression. Likewise, Indian literary traditions have been concerned with the particularity of individual tribal experience. At the same time, however, they have also used "tribal" to signify more generalized pan-Indian expressions that evoke the common experiences of Native peoples. Indian writers exist in complex relation to multiple traditions: the Western literary canon, the particular oral traditions of their peoples, the political discourses of the time in which they live, the experience of universities and other educational institutions, and, as Robert Warrior has pointed out, an indigenous intellectual tradition that has taken shape around both the spoken and the written word (Warrior, 1995). These traditions occupy familiar literary forms: the oral narrative, the treaty oration, the autobiography, the ethnographic "as-told-to" story, the novel, and the critique. Indian writers have of course blurred the boundaries between these forms. Autobiographies incorporate oratory and sermon. Novels work with oral tradition and play-off of other writings. Despite their blurred nature, such forms nonetheless offer a useful way to begin a discussion of Native literatures.

In most American literature anthologies published in the latter half of the twentieth century, a reader will find writings arranged in a linear chronology. The early sections will often be devoted to various collections of indigenous oral traditions, meant to represent a pre-contact past. More often than not, these stories and songs are presented without cultural or tribal contexts, geographic locations, or temporal identification. Incorporation into such a canon claims Indian expression as a Europeanized literary "art." And as art, it floats free of historical or cultural contexts. Who contributed or collected the text? Who translated it? Is it a fragment of ethnography?

Or the "re-expression" of a sympathetic non-Indian writer? Is the piece "traditional" but not necessarily pre-Columbian? And does that distinction really matter when the text is viewed as art?

Such issues confront both informed readers and Native authors, but the missing context that matters most to Indian people is that of performance. Passed from generation to generation, songs, stories, rituals, histories, and genealogies can never truly be recreated in print. All are dependent upon gesture, language, tone, setting, and audience interaction. In short, oral literatures require a theatricality absent from the printed page. Still, nearly all contemporary American Indian writers incorporate orality in their works. Orality may flow through the narrative strategies of a writer such as Louise Erdrich (Turtle Mountain Chippewa, 1954–), through N. Scott Momaday's use of storytelling as trope (Kiowa, 1934–), or through the visual presentations of Leslie Marmon Silko (Laguna, 1948–) found, for example, in *Storyteller* (1981). In addition to content and literary strategy that contextualize oral expressions, such texts often include "spoken" rhetoric, continually reminding the reader that these literatures are heard as well as read.

Oral literatures that have been translated and/or transcribed should therefore be surrounded by information. The reader should also remember that most tribes continue to maintain private oral literatures – sacred stories that may be related only in particular circumstances of time, place, and audience. Among the helpful contemporary retellings of traditional stories are Alfonso Ortiz (San Juan Pueblo, 1939–95) and Richard Erdoes' *American Indian Myths and Legends* and Brian Swann's *Coming to Light: Contemporary Translations of the Native Literatures of North America*. Both texts try to give readers at least a basic sense of tribal and historical context.

Placed in a more political context, oral storytelling can quickly blur into oratory. Ceremonial oratory, in Indian traditions, pre-dated European contact and included "speeches... at council meetings, coups counts, formal petitions, addresses of welcome, battle speeches to warriors, and statements of personal feelings or experiences" (Ruoff, 1990: 50). Too, Europeans often commented on Native oratorical skill – and on the inadequacy of their own translations. Cadwallader Colden, for example, in *The History of the Five Indian Nations of Canada*, noted that "Indians use many metaphors in their discourse, which interpreted by an unskilful tongue, may appear mean and strike our imagination faintly, but under the pen of a skilful representor might strongly move our passions by their lively images" (1747). Oratory, then, marks one of the earliest instances in which Indian oral expression became part of a written record, one subject, in this case, to literary criticism of a favorable sort.

Europeans responded to indigenous oratory, in part, because of their own rhetorical traditions (Wiget, 1996: 108). Oratory has offered an imaginative meeting place in contact situations ever since. Many prominent Indian speeches have been translated and recorded, including speeches by Powhatan (Powhatan) in 1609, Tecumseh (Shawnee) in 1811, and Chief Joseph (Nez Perce) in 1879. The supposed speech of Logan ("Who is there to mourn for Logan? Not one"), presented by Thomas Jefferson, became a staple for the classrooms and tutors of the early republic.

In the eighteenth and nineteenth centuries, Indian oratory sometimes took on a Christian cast. The Protestant preacher Samson Occam (Mohegan, 1723–92), in

Sermon Preached at the Execution of Moses Paul, an Indian (1772), produced the first publication by an American Indian. Occam's oratorical writing complied with the tenets of his faith while protesting against alcohol abuse among Natives. Writing in the same evangelical genre, William Apess (Pequot, 1798–1839?) published his *Eulogy on King Philip* (1837), which elevated the seventeenth-century Native leader to the heroic status of George Washington. Both works were produced by Christianized Indians for a mostly non-Indian audience. Nonetheless, they illustrate the links between mainstream "literature" and continuing tribal literary traditions, literacy and orality, and English and tribal languages.

Gertrude Simmons Bonnin, also known as Zitkala Sä (Yankton, 1876–1938), carried on oratorical conventions with her award-winning student speech, "Side by Side" (1896), couched in Christian rhetoric. Although known primarily for her autobiographical writings, Bonnin's life-work was based in oratory, with speeches for women's groups in the 1920s and public testimony on political issues. Her political compatriots in the Society of American Indians were said to be excellent speakers. Some, like Sherman Coolidge, served as ministers, following in the oratorical footsteps of Occam and Apess. Oratory continues today as a living tradition among indigenous peoples, taking form in political discourse, sermons, and the written and spoken poetry and fiction of Indian authors.

In addition to his oratorical writings, William Apess also entered the literary realms of autobiography and history. He outlined his difficult childhood and experiences in *Son of the Forest* (1829) and *The Experiences of Five Christian Indians of the Pequot Tribe* (1833). Apess condemns racism against Indians, and his was among the first indigenous voices to transform a personal story told through an oral tradition into a literary and historical document. Such tribal voices could not be bound by mainstream definitions of literary genres. Indeed, most American Indian writing almost inevitably challenges literary and cultural boundaries. George Copway's (Ojibwa, 1818–69) *Life, History, and Travels of Kah-ge-ga-gah-bowh* (1847), for example, melds personal history, tribal storytelling, and an ethnohistory of the Ojibwa with his own Christian conversion narrative. Copway's account also attempts to dispel the image of Indians as savages, with a benign portrayal of his childhood and family. Likewise, Sarah Winnemucca Hopkins' (Pyramid Lake Piute, 1844?–91) *Life among the Piutes: Their Wrongs and Claims* (1883) mixes tribal history, self-writing, and oratory in blurring literary boundaries. Authenticated by a prominent white woman, it is structurally similar to African-American slave narratives. Mrs. Horace Mann frames the book, telling of Sarah's conversion from "savage" child to civilized Christian, promoting "true" Christianity while critiquing exploiters and hypocrites, and advocating justice for her causes. Like slave narratives, Sarah's autobiography contains a rhetoric that unmasks her own anger within the language of her oppressors.

Autobiographies from the nineteenth and twentieth centuries are often studied for their ethnographic information. The writers frequently find themselves in the rhetorical position of making the unfamiliar familiar to the reader, of explaining the tribal to the mainstream through the medium of foreign language and literacy. While satisfying public curiosities about exotic Indians, these autobiographies also served political ends. Apess published his work during the debate over Cherokee Removal.

Copway's publication coincided with protests against Ojibwa removal from Minnesota. Winnemucca's book appeared in the East just prior to the Dawes Severalty Act of 1887. Later, Bonnin would reissue her autobiographical essays in the campaign for Indian Citizenship, while Luther Standing Bear's autobiography would appear as John Collier was pushing the reforms of the 1934 Wheeler-Howard Act.

Many autobiographies have been filtered through an editor and shaped for a mainstream audience. As assisted self-narratives, they set a pattern that continues today and includes such notable works as John Neihardt's *Black Elk Speaks* (1932/2000), Walter Dyk's *Son of Old Man Hat* (1938), and Richard Erdoes' collaborations with Mary Crow Dog (*Lakota Woman*, 1990) and Leonard Crow Dog (*Crow Dog: Four Generations of Sioux Medicine Men*, 1995). Such "as-told-to" texts appear, at first glance, to preserve a sense of orality, as the speaker tells his/her life to the recorder/editor. And yet, readers should consider the same suite of questions: who is really telling the story? Whose voice is really being heard? What are the motives of the translators/editors? And perhaps most interestingly, how is an indigenous worldview based in orality and community shaped by more individualistic literary forms such as the biography?

Perhaps *Black Elk Speaks* is the prime example of how complicated an as-told-to autobiography can be. As Raymond DeMallie has shown, much of Black Elk's story was transformed by John Neihardt (DeMallie, 1984). Yet Black Elk's voice continues to sound throughout the text, in part through the specificity of the Lakota context and in part through the universalism of his Christian belief. The inclusion of additional narrators reminds the reader again of the tribal community. And although Neihardt imposes a tragic ending, adding a heart-rending final paragraph concerning Wounded Knee, it is clear that Lakota culture and society hardly died in the bloody snow. Moreover, the current University of Nebraska Press edition includes an introduction by Vine Deloria that suggests the book is a sacred text, a pan-Indian Bible. Indeed, the wider significance of the book to Indian peoples demonstrates the ways that a single, particular tribal work can both transcend and embrace tribal distinction. H. David Brumble's *American Indian Autobiography* has treated these and other issues surrounding the autobiographical form.

"As-told-to" autobiographies continue to this day, but by the early twentieth century, an increasing number of Indian people had started to tell their own stories in their own voices. Those voices, however, were ironically shaped through the imposition of a foreign language and educational system (Lomawaima, this volume). Yet as Native peoples developed the genre of autobiography and connected it to tribal literatures, they began to define their own space in relation to mainstream literature, utilizing colonial education to create a critical and oppositional voice.

Zitkala Sä's articles, "Impressions of an Indian Childhood," "The School Days of an Indian Girl," and "Why I am a Pagan," for example, found a broad audience at the turn of the twentieth century in popular periodicals such as *Atlantic Monthly* and *Harper's Magazine* (they were collected and published in 1921 as *American Indian Stories*). Her short story "The Soft-Hearted Sioux" drew the wrath of reviewers for its criticism of Christianity. Narrating her childhood and her educational experiences, she criticized the institutional powers of the government and of Christianity. Zitkala Sä's early fiction writings also combined personal experience and the sentimental stylistics of her time with social protest. Likewise, Charles Eastman (Sioux, 1858–1939) sought, in *Indian Boyhood* (1902), *Soul of the Indian* (1911), and *The Indian To-day* (1915), to offer a cultural explanation of Sioux history and values. Luther Standing Bear (Sioux, 1868–1939) in *My Indian Boyhood* (1931), and Francis La Flesche (Omaha, 1857–1932) in *The Middle Five* (1900) recreate their own life stories. In each case the authors occupy a position that poet Joy Harjo (Harjo and Bird, 1997) refers to as "Reinventing the Enemy's Language" with subjectivity created in an oppressive educational context that is then turned back upon that context, yet never fully free of it.

These three prominent Sioux authors – Bonnin, Eastman, and Standing Bear – turn back to tribal stories in separate volumes. Their immensely popular books recount the stories the authors heard in their childhood, and they were marketed toward a mainstream audience of children. Contemporary literary criticisms, particularly tribal studies and dialogic approaches, show these stories to be sophisticated retellings of traditional literatures.

Along with these authors, other Indians have been cited with increasing frequency by historians, literary analysts, and Native Studies scholars. Taken together, these writers and their works make up a canon – still forming, to be sure – of Indian literary expression. These are the texts and authors that have been labeled "significant." It is worth noting a few things about this canon. First, its writers may usefully be seen in generational terms, each building on the writers who came before. Second, each tends to blur genres and forms, linking, for example, Western "art" literature with oral tradition or the particularistic tribal with the universal pan-Indian. Third, they often mediate between Indian and non-Indian worlds, both describing boundaries of difference while at the same time questioning those boundaries. And finally, the very Western notion of a canon itself suggests that there are issues of inclusion and exclusion that require further study.

Among transitional American Indian writers of the first half of the twentieth century were a number of university-trained educators and scientists who ventured beyond the boundaries of their disciplines. Ella C. Deloria (Dakota, 1889–1971) studied anthropology with Franz Boas. Like African-American writer and fellow Boas student Zora Neale Hurston, Deloria turned her trained observations on her own culture. Deloria's *Dakota Texts* (1932), for example, offers an anthropological retelling and linguistic examination of Dakota oral traditions. Yet, fearing that her novel, *Waterlily*, would be considered more for its ethnographic information than its narrative of a Sioux woman's life, publishers shied away and the 1944 manuscript was not published until 1988. In its engagement with contemporary questions concerning ethnographic authority and the politics of representation, many critics now consider it surprisingly prescient.

Oxford-trained D'Arcy McNickle (Cree/Flathead, 1904–77) established his reputation as an educator and historian. Yet McNickle, too, turned to fiction. His first novel, *The Surrounded* (1936), portrays the internal conflicts within a mixed-blood family and suggests that alienation can be followed by reconciliation through oral traditions. That same year McNickle began a distinguished career in Indian policy positions. His later non-fiction works, *Indians and Other Americans* (with Harold

Fey, 1959) and *Native American Tribalism* (1973), were college classroom staples in many infant Native American Studies programs. McNickle's last novel, *Wind from an Enemy Sky* (1982), was published posthumously. Reflecting issues central to his historical moment, both of McNickle's novels address cultural conflicts and characters in transition from traditional lifestyles to more contemporary and political conflicts.

Educated as a natural scientist, John Joseph Mathews (Osage, 1894–1979) traveled the globe. Upon returning to Pawhuska, Oklahoma, he wrote *Talking to the Moon* (1945), a literary biography influenced by John Muir and Henry David Thoreau (Ruoff, 1990: 58), and a novel, *Sundown* (1934). As in so many of the autobiographical accounts, the mixed-blood protagonist of *Sundown* also relates events in Osage history: allotment, oil boom and bust. Robert Allen Warrior (Osage) offers a detailed reading of *Sundown* from tribal contexts, placing Mathews in the context of an Indian intellectual tradition. In *Tribal Secrets*, Warrior argues that *Sundown*'s significance is that it relocates the primary conflict from Indians versus whites to "internal political and social strategies in the midst of an oppressive situation" (1995: 54).

Like Gertrude Simmons Bonnin, Mourning Dove (Christine Quintasket: Okanogan, 1882–1936) claimed her Native name to fit a complicated Indian persona. As she lacked literary training, her works were collaborative. Both her novel, *Cogewea, the Half-Blood* (1927), and a collection of tales, *Coyote Stories* (1933), were filtered through the writing assistance of L. V. McWhorter. Nevertheless, both books emphasized the familiar themes surrounding orality. *Cogewea*, in particular, introduces other issues that would emerge as primary twentieth-century concerns: mixed-bloods and American Indian identity.

The literature created by writers such as Bonnin, Eastman, Standing Bear, Deloria, McNickle, Mathews, and Mourning Dove fell into relative obscurity in the mid-twentieth century. With a renewed interest in American Indian literature and scholarship, however, these early writers – as well as those of the nineteenth century – have been re-examined and recontextualized in the light of recent theories of language and postcolonial studies. The University of Nebraska Press has reprinted many out-of-print works, making them widely accessible for readership and classroom study. In addition to their literary contributions, many of these writers were significant players in American Indian politics and history. Their writings should be considered in these terms as well. Likewise, each produced works in various literary genres, obfuscating traditional Western literary distinctions and categories.

In the last three decades of the twentieth century, Indian literature blossomed, with generational cohorts of successful writers publishing in the mixed and multiple genres of fiction, prose non-fiction, self-writing, and poetry. And often, no matter the literary category, tribal stories, orality, and memoir infuse these writings.

The 1968 publication of N. Scott Momaday's Pulitzer Prize-winning first novel, *House Made of Dawn*, and the appearance the following year of Vine Deloria Jr.'s *Custer Died for Your Sins* mark a watershed in mainstream acceptance of contemporary Indian writing. Momaday was among the first contemporary Native authors to combine a tribal consciousness with academic training in literature, mixing his studies at Stanford under narrative theorist Yvor Winters with his Kiowa heritage and upbringing among the Navajos and the people of Jemez Pueblo. A pathbreaking book, *House Made of Dawn* has been the object of intense literary analysis. Combining the tribally specific with more general Indian experiences of alienation in post-World War II America, Momaday uses a circular structure that suggests the possibilities for regeneration and wholeness when tribal pasts (in this case, Jemez, Kiowa, and Navajo) speak to Indian presents. If *House Made of Dawn* cycles, Momaday's second novel, *Ancient Child* (1989), appears more explicitly postmodern in its non-linearity. In many ways, *Ancient Child* is the same story as *House Made of Dawn*, with different signifiers that lead back to Momaday's own Kiowa origins. In the years between the novels, Momaday published poetry, essays, and memoirs, often illustrating his work.

Originally a chapter in *House Made of Dawn*, Momaday's memoir, *The Way to Rainy Mountain* (1969), plays on orality through visual imagery and an intense focus on storytelling. Unlike Apess, Eastman, Standing Bear, or Bonnin, Momaday has not necessarily sought to inform the mainstream world about his culture, but rather to recreate the Kiowa world through language, the English language: "A word has power in and of itself. It comes from nothing into sound and meaning; it gives origin to all things. By means of words can a man deal with the world on equal terms" (*The Way to Rainy Mountain*, 33). Momaday tells his origin story more conventionally in *The Names: A Memoir* (1976), imaginatively extending his family tree and recounting incidents from his youth.

In the late 1960s and early 1970s, some audiences saw American Indian literatures as metaphors for the imperialist policies of the United States in Vietnam. The Indian Civil Rights movement also helped create larger and more sympathetic audiences for Indian writing. Although some critics have suggested that this period marks a renaissance or a revitalization of American Indian literatures, it is perhaps more accurate to think of the creation of a mainstream audience. Momaday did not give new birth to these literatures so much as he established an institutional space for a continuing literary tradition. Among the American Indian writers who entered that space were Leslie Marmon Silko (Laguna, 1948–), James Welch (Blackfeet-Gros Ventre, 1940–), and Vine Deloria, Jr. (Sioux, 1933–), all university trained and inclined to mingle Western, tribal, and pan-Indian sensibilities.

As with Momaday, ritual storytelling is a central theme for Leslie Marmon Silko. Her first novel, *Ceremony* (1977), is nearly a retelling of Momaday's novel. Its main character, Tayo, like Momaday's Abel, is an alienated war veteran who finds reconciliation through ritual, storytelling, and tribal sensibilities, this time Laguna rather than Jemez. Circularity and storytelling are also major tropes in Silko's *Storyteller* (1981). The volume contains short fictions, poetry and memoir, and is illustrated with family photographs taken by her father, Lee Marmon. Silko structures the text to create the experience of hearing stories from her Great Aunt Susie and her grandmother. From the publication of *Storyteller* in 1981 until 1991, Silko was consumed with producing *Almanac of the Dead* (1991), a complex tome that addresses hemispheric indigenous political issues, portraying unremitting evil while continuing to recognize the redemptive power of tribal diversity and ritual. Through storytelling, in a collection of political essays in *Yellow Woman and a Beauty of the Spirit* (1996), Silko recapitulates familiar narratives from her other works while advocating her agenda of resistance literature.

The alienated and unnamed protagonist in James Welch's *Winter in the Blood* (1974) echoes Momaday's Abel and Silko's Tayo, finding harmony through tribal stories and history and a subtle, dry humor. One might suggest that this particular narrative structure – a move from alienation to tribal centeredness – has characterized the early works of this generation of writers, and that it speaks to the historical experiences of Indian people in the postwar period. Their later writings tend to focus more on questions surrounding memoir and collective history and memory.

More focused on a specifically Blackfeet world, for example, is Welch's amazing novel *Fools Crow* (1986), the story of youthful White Man's Dog's transformation to the tribally responsible Fools Crow. For the majority of the novel, Welch maintains an insulated, Blackfeet point of view in which signifiers are transliterated into English. Unlike Momaday, who tells Kiowa history as reminiscence, Welch rewrites Blackfeet history with an insider's voice and the point of view of the late nineteenth century. Like other contemporary American Indian writers, Welch also writes in a variety of genres. His early work is poetry, including *Riding the Earthboy 40* (1976). He also offers a non-fiction account of his tribal background and filmmaking experiences in *Killing Custer: The Battle of the Little Bighorn and the Fate of the Plains Indians* (1994).

Vine Deloria, Jr.'s work has not been generally identified as literary *per se*, but was part of the late 1960s groundswell of interest in American Indians. *Custer Died for Your Sins* (1969) was decisively political, with pointed humor that challenged mainstream America. It is so delightfully written that it should remind scholars, once again, that tribal issues and means of expressing them are not limited to constructs of genre and academic discipline.

Just as 1968 changed the landscape for American Indian writers, one might point to 1984 as another landmark year for a new generation of Indian literature. Louise Erdrich's *Love Medicine* (1984) won the National Critics Circle Book Award and became a bestseller. In a cycle of five novels set in North Dakota, Erdrich spans the twentieth century with a large cast of characters, multiple storytellers, a devotion to the land, and a wickedly funny survival humor. These novels are not published in the chronological order of the stories they tell, but should be read in this order: *Tracks* (1988), *The Beet Queen* (1986), *Love Medicine* (1984; revised and expanded, 1993), *The Bingo Palace* (1994), and *Tales of Burning Love* (1996). While Erdrich's characters are clearly tribal, they also reflect the realities of the modern world in which they live. By juxtaposing traditional tribal signifiers, such as the trickster Nanapush, with contemporary imagery, Erdrich refigures tribal life at the end of the twentieth century with its powwows, cars, casino gambling, marketing of curios, land development, and religious conflict and overlap. Erdrich's recent novel *The Antelope Wife* (1998) abandons her familiar North Dakota characters and introduces urban Indians in Minneapolis.

Erdrich has been the most successful member of the generation of Indian writers, including Linda Hogan, Sherman Alexie, and Susan Powers, who appeared in the 1980s and 1990s. She is, in some ways, emblematic of this new writing. Where the early twentieth-century authors sought to describe Indian life in order to win white sympathy, and writers such as Momaday, Silko, and Welch recapture tribal memory as restoratives to the alienations of modernity, this latter generation has self-consciously asked Indian and white audiences to consider new understandings of what it means to be an Indian person in postmodern America.

Erdrich credited much of her success to the co-authorship of her husband, Michael Dorris (Modoc, 1945–97). Dorris and Erdrich consciously deconstructed the idea of individual artistic production. They collaborated deeply; the resulting novels themselves do not contain a singular hero, but a tribal community of protagonists. Dorris also succeeded in his own literary pursuits. His early work in Native studies carved out standards for Indian intellectual criticism. His study of fetal alcohol syndrome, *The Broken Cord* (1989), won the National Critics Circle Book Award for nonfiction. He wrote two novels, *A Yellow Raft in Blue Water* (1987) and *Cloud Chamber* (1997), as well as collections of short stories and essays. Determined to educate the public, he also wrote a series of young adult novels that depicted events from an Indian point of view.

Linda Hogan (Chickasaw, 1947–) has also enjoyed popular success, publishing with major presses to critical acclaim. Her historical novel *Mean Spirit* (1990) tells the story of the Osage "reign of terror," and her subsequent novels, *Solar Storms* (1995) and *Power* (1998), promote environmental awareness. Both novels have strong Chickasaw female characters, but like Hogan herself, they are displaced within a foreign tribe.

One of the most visible Indian writers at century's end, Sherman Alexie (Spokane/Coeur D'Alene, 1966–) uses popular culture and current reservation life to disrupt and refigure contemporary ideas surrounding Indians. In poetry, short story collections such as *The Lone Ranger and Tonto Fistfight in Heaven* (1993), and novels such as *Reservation Blues* (1995) and *Indian Killer* (1996), he plays with the reader through imaginative titles and subversive imagery. Alexie has also ventured into filmmaking, expanding the short story "This is What it Means to Say Phoenix Arizona" into the critically acclaimed movie *Smoke Signals* (1997).

Even as Alexie uses familiar literary categories, he destroys them. In *Indian Killer*, for example, Alexie rethinks the genre of the mystery novel, using it to excoriate Indian "wannabees" and academics who exploit Native peoples. He mixes graphic violence with Indian insider humor. The result is a mystery that is about the deeper mysteries of race, culture, and identity.

With *Smoke Signals*, Alexie became one of the first Indians to break into the institutional structure of Hollywood. One should note, however, that Indian filmmakers have long been working through other production and distribution outlets. And if Alexie's filmic success echoes that of Indian writers who have placed their work with major trade publishers, so too does the presence of Indian alternative film production (often in the documentary genre) point to alternative venues for Native authors. Such venues have primarily existed at university presses.

In addition to its republication of works by Ella Deloria, Charles Eastman, and other early twentieth-century writers, the University of Nebraska Press has published a number of contemporary Indian writers, including Diane Glancy (Cherokee, 1941–) and William S. Penn (Nez Perce, 1949–), among others. Many of the works in the Nebraska catalogue are autobiography, memoir, or "as-told-to" stories. On the other hand, the University of Arizona Press series, Sun Tracks, emphasizes poetry. Founded in 1971, its offerings range from first-time publications to the works of major authors such as Momaday, Wendy Rose (Hopi/Miwok, 1948–), Simon Ortiz (Acoma, 1941–), Luci Tapahonso (Navajo, 1953–), Carter Revard (Osage, 1931–), Ofelia Zepeda (Tohono O'Odham), Janice Gould (Maidu/Konkow, 1949–), Nora Naranjo-Morse (Santa Clara Tewa Pueblo, 1953–), and Joy Harjo (Muscogee, 1951–).

Also influential has been the University of Oklahoma's American Indian Literature and Critical Studies series. Oklahoma has published Native authors such as Glancy, Penn, Betty Louise Bell (Cherokee, 1949–), A. A. Carr (Navajo/Laguna Pueblo, 1963–), and Maurice Kenny (Seneca-Mohawk, 1929–). But its most significant role has been in fostering a literary criticism that emphasizes tribal and pan-Indian issues and perspectives. Such critics work in various genres, but together they have worked to establish what Robert Allen Warrior (Osage) calls an "intellectual sovereignty."

General editor Gerald Vizenor (White Earth Chippewa, 1934–) has been among the most prolific and complex of Indian critics, using postmodern theoretical discourse to create both challenging tribal fictions and Native literary critique. Perhaps his greatest critical contribution is his theoretical discussion of trickster narratives in *Narrative Chance* (1989). Vizenor models trickster narratives himself in his own fictions, the Bearheart chronicles and Almost Browne stories. In an example of Warrior's "intellectual sovereignty," Kimberly Blaeser (White Earth Chippewa, 1955–), a noted poet in her own right, has written Vizenor's literary biography (1996). Likewise, Louis Owens (Choctaw/Cherokee, 1948–), who served with Vizenor as editor of the series, has been a major interpreter as well. Owens is a complex writer; his mystery novels complement his literary critiques *Other Destinies* (1992) and *Mixed Blood Messages* (1998), which is also a memoir.

If this critical tradition relies on university presses, other Native literary critics have challenged the academy to assess Native literature from the inside out. Elizabeth Cook-Lynn (Dakota, 1930–), who with anthropologist Beatrice Medicine (Lakota, 1924–) and William Willard, founded the journal, *Wicazo Ša Review*, stands as a prime example. The journal has a specific political agenda devoted to tribal sovereignties and tribal voices, and Cook-Lynn's *Why I Can't Read Wallace Stegner and Other Essays* sets a standard for evaluating works by both non-Indians and Indians. Still other Indian critics have adopted other perspectives. Paula Gunn Allen's (Laguna-Sioux, 1939–) definitive feminist interpretations in *The Sacred Hoop* (1992) and *Off the Reservation* (1998) seem to have had more impact than her many creative writings. Additionally, her anthologies have promoted lesser-known Indian authors. Joy Harjo and Gloria Bird's (Spokane, 1951–) *Reinventing the Enemy's Language* (1997) offers an extensive collection of writings by women and a significant discussion of literary issues.

Although American Indian literatures have primarily relied upon English, some tribes have developed their own literacy and orthographies. Critic Julian Rice asserts that Ella Deloria's ethnographic work laid the foundation for a Dakota-language literature. As tribal peoples reclaimed languages and cultures in the latter part of the twentieth century, many tribes initiated language preservation projects (see Darnell, this volume). Perhaps more pertinent to this discussion, however, is the inclusion of orthographies in prominent English-language publications. Louise Erdrich uses a spattering of Ojibwa words, first in the chapter titles of *Tracks* (1988) and then more significantly in *The Antelope Wife*. Some authors, such as Navajo poets Luci Tapahonso and Laura Tohe (Navajo, 1953–), have deliberately included their Native language in their writings. Most striking is Ray Young Bear's (Mesquakie, 1950–) *Black Eagle Child: The Facepaint Narratives*. Besides being pointedly funny in its portrayal of contemporary Indian issues, particularly blood quantum, the novel boldly includes major sections of Mesquakie orthographies, some translated, some not. The Mesquakie are a small tribe of several thousand people in central Iowa and it is questionable whether or if many tribal peoples would read and understand the text. Nevertheless, Young Bear asserts tribal discourse and sovereignty, regardless of who may or may not understand the indigenous language.

As American Indian peoples continue to write and publish in the modern market, many also continue oral traditions in practice and they manifest those traditions through the writing itself. It should come as no surprise that autobiography, memoir, oratory, and "as-told-to" stories permeate Native writing, for these are quintessentially oral forms. While many American Indian authors are telling their tribal stories for the first time, or retelling traditional stories, they are also creating a Native American canon that has its own peculiar relationship with the mainstream Western literary canon. American Indian writing has been used to demonstrate postcolonial theories and relationships, yet when critics fail to assess tribal and pan-Indian contexts, many of the mainstream critiques can simply reflect a continued colonialism. Native American literatures reflect any number of paradoxes – between, for example, orality and literacy; the individualized genres of poetry and the collective, tribal voice; tribal particularity and shared pan-Indian experience; intellectual sovereignty and mainstream success. In each of these paradoxes, however, one can see the ways in which these literary traditions represent and seek to shape the ongoing transformations and survivals of indigenous voices and peoples.

BIBLIOGRAPHY

Alexie, Sherman 1993: *The Lone Ranger and Tonto Fistfight in Heaven* (New York: Atlantic Monthly Press).

Alexie, Sherman 1995: *Reservation Blues* (New York: Atlantic Monthly Press).

Alexie, Sherman 1996: *Indian Killer* (New York: Atlantic Monthly Press).

Alexie, Sherman 1998: *Smoke Signals: A Screenplay* (New York: Hyperion Press).

Allen, Paula Gunn (ed.) 1990: *Spider Woman's Granddaughters: Traditional Tales and Contemporary Writing by Native American Women* (New York: Fawcett Columbine).

Allen, Paula Gunn 1992: *The Sacred Hoop: Recovering the Feminine in American Indian Traditions* (Boston: Beacon Press).

Allen, Paula Gunn (ed.) 1994: *Voice of the Turtle: American Indian Literature, 900–1970* (New York: Ballantine Books).

Allen, Paula Gunn (ed.) 1996: *Song of the Turtle: American Indian Literature, 1974–1994* New York: Ballantine Books).

Allen, Paula Gunn 1998: *Off the Reservation: Reflections on Boundary-busting Border-Crossing Loose Canons* (Boston: Beacon Press).

Apess, William 1992: *On Our Own Ground: The Complete Writings of William Apess, a Pequot*, Barry O'Connell (ed.) (Amherst: University of Massachusetts Press).

Blaeser, Kimberly 1994: *Trailing You* (Greenfield Center, NY: Greenfield Review Press).

Blaeser, Kimberly 1996: *Gerald Vizenor: Writing in Oral Tradition* (Norman: University of Oklahoma Press).

Brumble, H. David III 1988: *American Indian Autobiography* (Berkeley: University of California Press).

Cook-Lynn, Elizabeth 1996: *Why I Can't Read Wallace Stegner and Other Essays* (Madison: University of Wisconsin Press).

Crow Dog, Leonard and Richard Erdoes 1995: *Crow Dog: Four Generations of Sioux Medicine Men* (New York: HarperCollins).

Crow Dog, Mary, with Richard Erdoes 1990: *Lakota Woman* (New York: G. Weidenfeld).

Deloria, Ella Cara 1932/1974: *Dakota Texts* (G. E. Stechert & Co., 1932; New York: AMS Press, 1974).

Deloria, Ella Cara 1988: *Waterlily* (Lincoln: University of Nebraska Press).

Deloria, Vine, Jr. 1969: *Custer Died for Your Sins: An Indian Manifesto* (New York: Macmillan).

DeMallie, Raymond (ed.) 1984: *The Sixth Grandfather: Black Elk's Teachings Given to John G. Neihardt* (Lincoln: University of Nebraska Press).

Dorris, Michael 1987: *A Yellow Raft in Blue Water* (New York: Holt).

Dorris, Michael 1989: *The Broken Cord* (New York: Harper & Row).

Dorris, Michael 1994: *Paper Trail* (New York: HarperCollins).

Dorris, Michael 1997: *Cloud Chamber* (New York: Scribner).

Dyk, Walter, with Left Handed 1938/1967: *Son of Old Man Hat: A Navaho Autobiography* (Lincoln: University of Nebraska Press).

Eastman, Charles 1902/1971: *Indian Boyhood* (New York: Dover).

Erdoes, Richard and Alfonso Ortiz 1984: *American Indian Myths and Legends* (New York: Pantheon).

Erdrich, Louise 1984/1993: *Love Medicine* (New York: Holt, Rinehart, and Winston, 1984; revised and expanded, New York: HarperCollins, 1993).

Erdrich, Louise 1986: *The Beet Queen* (New York: Holt).

Erdrich, Louise 1988: *Tracks* (New York: Harper & Row).

Erdrich, Louise 1994: *The Bingo Palace* (New York: HarperCollins).

Erdrich, Louise 1996: *Tales of Burning Love* (New York: HarperCollins).

Erdrich, Louise 1998: *The Antelope Wife* (New York: HarperFlamingo).

Harjo, Joy and Gloria Bird 1997: *Reinventing the Enemy's Language* (New York: W. W. Norton).

Hogan, Linda 1990: *Mean Spirit* (New York: Atheneum).

Hogan, Linda 1995: *Solar Storms* (New York: Scribner).

Hogan, Linda 1998: *Power* (New York: W. W. Norton).

Hopkins, Sarah Winnemucca 1883/1994: *Life among the Piutes: Their Wrongs and Claims*, Mrs. Horace Mann (ed.) (New York: G. P. Putnam, 1883; Reno: University of Nevada Press, 1994).

Krupat, Arnold 1989: *The Voice in the Margin: Native American Literature and the Canon* (Berkeley: University of California Press).

Mathews, John Joseph 1934/1988: *Sundown* (Norman: University of Oklahoma Press).

Mathews, John Joseph 1945: *Talking to the Moon* (Chicago: University of Chicago Press).

Mathews, John Joseph 1961: *The Osages, Children of the Middle Waters* (Norman: University of Oklahoma Press).

McNickle, D'Arcy 1936/1992: *The Surrounded* (New York: Dodd, Mead, 1936; Albuquerque: University of New Mexico Press, 1992).

McNickle, D'Arcy 1973: *Native American Tribalism: Indian Survivals and Renewals* New York: published for the Institute of Race Relations by Oxford University Press).

McNickle, D'Arcy 1982: *Wind from an Enemy Sky* (San Francisco: Harper & Row).

McNickle, D'Arcy and Harold Edward Fey 1959: *Indians and Other Americans* (New York: Harper Brothers).

Momaday, N. Scott 1968: *House Made of Dawn* (New York: Harper & Row).

Momaday, N. Scott 1969: *The Way to Rainy Mountain* (Albuquerque: University of New Mexico Press).

Momaday, N. Scott 1976: *The Names: A Memoir.* Sun Track Series No. 16 (Tucson: University of Arizona Press).

Momaday, N. Scott 1989: *Ancient Child* (New York: Doubleday).

Mourning Dove 1927/1991: *Cogewea, the Half Blood* (Boston: Four Seas Co., 1927; Lincoln: University of Nebraska Press, 1991).

Mourning Dove 1933/1990: *Coyote Stories* (Caldwell, ID: Caxton Printers, 1933; Lincoln: University of Nebraska Press, 1990).

Neihardt, John (1932) 2000: *Black Elk Speaks: Being the Life Story of a Holy Man of the Oglala Sioux*, Twenty-First Century Edition. As told through John G. Neihardt by Nicholas Black Elk. Foreword by Vine Deloria, Jr. Illustrations by Standing Bear (Lincoln: University of Nebraska Press).

Owens, Louis 1992: *Other Destinies: Understanding the American Indian Novel.* American Indian Literature and Critical Studies Series, vol. 3 (Norman: University of Oklahoma Press).

Owens, Louis 1998: *Mixedblood Messages: Literature, Film, Family, Place.* American Indian Literature and Critical Studies Series, vol. 26 (Norman: University of Oklahoma Press).

Penn, William S. 1995: *All My Sins are Relatives* (Lincoln: University of Nebraska Press).

Penn, William S. (ed.) 1997: *As We Are Now: Mixblood Essays on Race and Identity* (Berkeley: University of California Press).

Ruoff, A. LaVonne Brown 1990: *American Indian Literatures: An Introduction, Bibliographic Review, and Selected Bibliography* (New York: Modern Language Association).

Silko, Leslie Marmon 1977: *Ceremony* (New York: Viking).

Silko, Leslie Marmon 1981: *Storyteller* (New York: Little, Brown & Co.).

Silko, Leslie Marmon 1991: *Almanac of the Dead* (New York: Simon & Schuster).

Silko, Leslie Marmon 1996: *Yellow Woman and a Beauty of the Spirit: Essays on Native American Life Today* (New York: Simon & Schuster).

Standing Bear, Luther 1931/1972: *My Indian Boyhood* (Lincoln: University of Nebraska Press).

Standing Bear, Luther 1934/1988: *Stories of the Sioux* (Lincoln: University of Nebraska Press).

Swann, Brian (ed.) 1994: *Coming to Light: Contemporary Translations of the Native Literatures of North America* (New York: Random House).

Vizenor, Gerald (ed.) 1989: *Narrative Chance: Postmodern Discourse on Native American Indian Literatures* (Albuquerque: University of New Mexico Press).

Warrior, Robert Allen 1995: *Tribal Secrets: Recovering American Indian Intellectual Traditions* (Minneapolis: University of Minnesota Press).

Welch, James 1974: *Winter in the Blood* (New York: Harper & Row).

Welch, James 1976: *Riding the Earthboy 40* (New York: Harper & Row).

Welch, James 1986: *Fools Crow* (New York: Viking).

Welch, James 1990: *The Indian Lawyer* (New York: W. W. Norton).

Welch, James 1994: *Killing Custer: The Battle of the Little Bighorn and the Fate of the Plains Indians* (New York: W. W. Norton).

Wiget, Andrew (ed.) 1996: *Handbook of Native American Literature* (New York: Garland Publishing, Inc.).

Young Bear, Ray 1992: *Black Eagle Child: The Facepaint Narratives* (Iowa City: University of Iowa Press).

Zitkala Sä (Gertrude Simmons Bonnin) 1901/1985: *Old Indian Legends* (Boston: Ginn, Co., 1901; Lincoln: University of Nebraska Press, 1985).

Zitkala Sä 1921/1986: *American Indian Stories* (Boston: Ginn, Co., 1921; Lincoln: University of Nebraska Press, 1986).

14

Wanted: More Histories of Indian Identity

ALEXANDRA HARMON

Before 1492 none of North America's inhabitants called themselves Indians. Yet today several million residents of the United States and Canada call themselves Indians in part because of their descent from pre-Columbian inhabitants. For this reason if for no other, virtually every history of American Indians is an implicit study of Indian identity. It asserts, in effect, that its subjects are a distinctive people who merit the name "Indians" even if their indigenous ancestors did not.

Indian identity deserves more than tacit attention from historians, however. Because people were identified as Indians only in the context of relations with other kinds of people, and because those relations have changed over time, Indian identity is a legitimate subject – indeed, an essential subject – for historical investigation.

By Indian identity I mean a manifest affiliation with people known to themselves and others as Indians. Individuals consider themselves Indians when they believe they have values, symbols, interests, and a history in common with Indians. If they demonstrate that belief in ways that most other people acknowledge as Indian, they are Indian, at least for some purposes. "Indianness," by one anthropologist's definition, is "self-conscious symbolic representation of…distinctiveness" commonly attributed to Indian people (Paredes, 1995: 341).

The need for historical investigations of Indian identity is clear from contemporary controversies about the subject. People claiming to be Indians or groups claiming to be Indian tribes have touched off academic as well as political and legal debates. Evaluating their claims requires reference to the past. And even when their Indianness is not disputed, Indian people debate and reformulate their past, as all humans do, and thus reformulate their identity. Since the basis and meaning of Indian identity are unavoidable issues for anyone professing to be Indian, they should be central issues for historians. In fact, scholars in all disciplines should consciously and consistently historicize Indian and tribal identities.

Scholars who have undertaken to do this are on a promising path. They have turned away from stereotypes – Indians who are either surviving or endangered relics of a timeless aboriginal past – in search of Indians who have the full range of human attributes, including the capacity to modify their own societies. By asking how Indian people have defined and redefined themselves, historians can explain Indians' power to change without forfeiting a collective existence. And by investigating Indians' part in the establishment and maintenance of ethnic boundaries, historians can invigorate not only Indian studies but also the broader field of North American studies.

So far, relatively few scholars have taken this path. Explicit histories of Indianness north of Mexico are still scarce because scholars were slow to acknowledge the diachronic, contingent nature of Indian identities. Until the late twentieth century, North American historians did not produce narratives about evolving racial and tribal categories or about change over time in the meanings of names such as "Indian" or "Cherokee." Indeed, most did not even ask when, why, and how some people identified themselves as Indians or as Cherokees. Although historians were interested in whites' ideas about Indians, few made it their business to chronicle the changing bases, parameters, manifestations, and uses of Indianness, especially from Indian points of view.

This void in the historical literature has its own history. Resistance to thinking historically about North American Indian identity stems from the interaction of several factors: Indians' early and enduring role as a negative reference group for other Americans, nineteenth-century theories of human development, the conceptual price of ethnic and racial labeling, and laws that privilege simplistic measures of Indianness.

In the process of struggling to forge their own collective identities, European-Americans of the eighteenth and nineteenth centuries came to associate Indians with the past. Histories such as *Savagism and Civilization*, *The White Man's Indian*, and *The Vanishing American* document whites' perceptions of themselves, in contrast to indigenous people, as agents of progress (Pearce, 1988; Berkhofer, 1978; Dippie, 1982). Indians became symbols of what whites had to overcome in order to colonize America. As such, they were defined by their supposed aboriginal state. It followed that "real" Indians could not continue to exist in a "tamed" America (McCulloch and Wilkins, 1995: 366). They would either become something else – civilized people – or they would die out.

The ideology of race perpetuated ahistorical thinking about Indianness. By the middle of the nineteenth century, most European-Americans not only sorted humans into races but also thought of race as an immutable, inheritable, biological essence (Gates, 1985: 3; Stein, 1989: 80; Winant, 1994: xi). This ideology allowed non-Indians and eventually some Native people to define away the Indianness of individuals with substantial non-Indian ancestry, whatever their social and cultural orientation. Contrarily, it prompted many people to discount the significance of culture change among known descendants of aborigines (Plane and Button: 1993, 595, 598).

The modern academic disciplines most concerned with Indians – history and anthropology – came of age in this cultural and ideological context. History in nineteenth-century European-America was the art of writing epic narratives, and the standard metanarrative was a Eurocentric story of human advancement. To historians of the United States and Canada, the events worth recounting were those that had transformed a "wilderness" into the tractable possession of enlightened Europeans and their descendants. The history of North America became a heroic saga of civilization superseding primitivism.

The conviction that Indians would not survive this historical sequence motivated proto-anthropologists. Nineteenth-century intellectuals paired a belief in universal, unilear social evolution with a perception that American Indians had not yet surpassed a barbaric stage of development. By their logic, attaining a higher stage and remaining Indian were mutually contradictory. In the late 1800s and early 1900s, therefore, ethnographers hurried to salvage information about Indian societies because they believed that those societies were on the verge of evolving rapidly and thus losing their Indian identities (Finger, 1991: 16).

The analytical paradigm of twentieth-century anthropology – culture – also discouraged the historicization of Indian identity. In order to catalogue and analyze cultures, anthropologists assembled models of societies in an "ethnographic present." Their subject was tradition, understood as the opposite of modernity and change (Frye, 1996; Paredes, 1995: 343–4). This orientation fostered a tendency to interpret social change among Indians as loss of culture and loss of culture as loss of group identity (Rosenthal, 1970: 83; Collins, 1998: 113).

Ethnic and racial labels have inhibited historical analysis of Indian identity as well. Names such as "Indian" or "Cherokee" have supplied scholars with ready-made subjects for historical narratives. They carry misleading connotations of naturalness, clarity, homogeneity, and permanence. The creators of historical records and historians, too, have used racial and tribal names without noticing or acknowledging that their usage and meanings change over time (Forbes, 1993: 3). But even if scholars acknowledge such changes, they must do so using the very terms that should be historicized. It is hard to portray an ethnic group as provisional and mutable when the only available vocabulary presupposes the group's existence and continuity (Harmon, 1995: 432; Clifton, 1989: 22).

Along with the meanings of labels, the consequences of being labeled Indian have changed; and some twentieth-century consequences have promoted conceptions of Indian identity that are ahistorical, even though they incorporate elements of the past. By the 1900s "Indian" had become a category of U.S. and Canadian law that entailed a unique mix of benefits and liabilities. For most legal purposes the indispensable criterion of Indian identity was biological descent from someone acknowledged as Indian by the federal government, rather than meaningful participation in a dynamic, self-defining cultural group. Since the 1970s the United States has conditioned its coveted acknowledgment of Indian groups on prescribed continuities of lineage, location, external relations, and political life (Campisi, 1991: 56). Such legal criteria require people to identify themselves by reference to a category that presumably resists historical changes in its defining characteristics.

Reified notions of Indianness have endured because many people have had reasons to promote them. For rewards ranging from material gain to a sense of their own superiority, some non-Indians have campaigned to dismantle Indian societies by depicting those societies as static and anachronistic. Other non-Indians – some seeking alternatives to their own society's values – have defended or glorified "traditional" Indianness (Hatt, 1997: 100; Moses, 1996). Such glorification and other strong incentives have influenced people who claim an Indian heritage to oversimplify that heritage. Sociologist C. Matthew Snipp (1989: 34) notes the current material incentive to embrace Indian identity and equate it with biological lineage. "American Indians," he says, "are the only group in American society for whom pedigreed bloodlines have the same economic importance as they do for show animals and race horses." Indians also have had non-material and negative motivations to characterize their Indianness in simplistic ways. Medical anthropologist Theresa O'Nell (1994) found, for example, that their psychological health may be at stake. Indians on the Flathead Reservation, she writes, have responded to racism and U.S. duplicity by visualizing their history as a conflict with morally defective whites, even though most of them have white ancestors, relatives, and neighbors (see also McIlwraith, 1996: 53).

The factors that have deterred historical studies of Indianness are at last losing force. Several developments have converged to give scholars the motivation and the tools they need to historicize Indian and tribal identity. These include new ways of thinking about race and ethnicity, new methods of unearthing and recounting Indians' histories, and new or louder professions of Indianness from a variety of people.

One intellectual development inspiring scholars to think historically about Indianness is a radical shift in our understanding of race. Since the 1960s scientists and social scientists have assembled convincing evidence that racial categories are not biologically defined. Although some human populations – America's first inhabitants among them – developed distinctive genetic patterns by interbreeding in isolation for long periods, humans are a single species with a common set of ancestors and a species-wide pool of potential sexual partners. Sexual crossing of social boundaries followed Europeans' discovery of the Americas and destroyed any genetic pattern that might reliably have identified all descendants of pre-Columbian Americans. Instead of biology, social relations and history must explain a classification such as "Indian" (Winant, 1994: 2, 4; McCulloch and Wilkins, 1995: 367; Snipp, 1989: 31).

Meanwhile, ideas about ethnicity have undergone comparable, complementary changes. Rather than thinking of ethnicity as an essence or an expression of "primordial" sentiments, most social scientists now see it as contingent and variable. Persuaded by Fredrik Barth (1969: 9–11, 15) to shift focus from the content of ethnic identity to the process of ethnic "boundary maintenance," they have produced studies validating Barth's hypotheses: ethnic groups can persist despite changes in membership and culture, culture is as much the result as the defining characteristic of ethnic group organization, and the salience of ethnicity changes with the context of intergroup relations. Few scholars now would disagree with William Simeone's assertion that contemporary Indian identity is a "product of the dynamic relationship between Natives and non-Natives" (1995: xxi).

The realization that ethnicity is a fluid product of particular human relations has intensified social scientists' interest in history. To understand individual Flathead Indians' self-images, O'Nell needed to learn their shared history and views of history. Other anthropologists, sociologists, and political scientists have relied on historical data to explain why people claim identity with ancient Indians despite dissimilarities in customs, beliefs, and appearance; and they have turned to historical data to explain the undisputed Indian identity of groups that post-date Columbus (Albers, 1996: 90; Alfred, 1995; Blu, 1980: ix; Collins, 1998: 6–7; Roosens, 1989: 21–100). Because Indian cultures are no less dynamic than other cultures, sociologist Joane Nagel (1996: 72) urges scholars to document Indian identity by asking not what was and what has survived but what is and how it became.

Ethnohistory – a term coined in the 1950s for a new scholarly methodology – has also fostered willingness to historicize Indian identity. Ethnohistorians meld the methodologies of history and anthropology in an effort to understand culture change. They track peoples whose stories would not otherwise emerge from academic historians' typical sources, and they aspire to see past events from those peoples' points of view. Some of the techniques developed to achieve these ends – life histories, genealogies, analyses of oral tradition, ethnological interpretations of historical texts – have revealed that Indians continually redefine themselves and their societies (Edmunds, 1995: 725; Bahr, 1993; Rafert, 1996; Snow, 1997; Williams, 1979).

Scholars' new willingness to historicize Indian identity is tied to trends outside academia. It cannot be separated from political and legal developments or from concurrent changes in Indians' public image. Since the 1960s the United States and Canada have witnessed a remarkable surge in Indian pride and assertiveness. As growing numbers of individuals and groups have proclaimed themselves Indians, many scholars have sought to explain why.

Historians now credit the black Civil Rights movement, which drew inspiration from African-American spiritual traditions, the anti-fascist rhetoric of World War II, and postwar anti-colonialism, with initiating a general abatement of racial and ethnic repression. By the 1960s Americans were showing unprecedented tolerance of and interest in ethnic differences. Indian organizations and cultural displays proliferated in the new milieu, bolstering Indians' respectability and political clout. Politicians instituted programs that sustained the trend by adding to the material and other benefits of Indian identity (Edmunds, 1995: 724–5; Nagel, 1996: 122, 125, 130, 158; Paredes, 1974: 63).

One outgrowth of these developments – the heightened desire of many people for official Indian status – has drawn some scholars into the business of writing histories focused explicitly on ethnic identity. For example, groups intent on winning government recognition as the historic Mashpee, Lumbee, and Miami Indian tribes retained ethnohistorians to document their continuity, and those scholars subsequently published the groups' stories (Campisi, 1991; Sider, 1993; Rafert, 1996).

Those historians and ethnohistorians who focus on Indian identity have proved the value of that focus many times over. They have documented numerous instances of Indian and tribal ethnogenesis, revealed the myriad varieties and levels of Indian identity, elucidated the relationships that generate and reshape Indian identities, and analyzed some strategic functions of Indian identity.

In 1971 William Sturtevant published an account of the process by which the Seminoles differentiated themselves from Creeks. The term "ethnogenesis" has been in American anthropologists' vocabulary at least since then. Nevertheless, Patricia Albers laments (1996: 90–1), few anthropologists have exploited North America's rich opportunities to study past ethnogenesis. Yet Albers's observation appears alongside essays by a few colleagues who have done just that; and although they may be rare birds, those essayists are not the only members of the species. Anthropologists as well as historians have mustered evidence of tribal and other Indian group formation in all eras, from the protohistoric to the late twentieth century.

Each aboriginal North American group emerged from a process we can call ethnogenesis. To appreciate this, we need only consider ancient humans' dispersal across the continent and their eventual founding of hundreds of linguistically and culturally distinctive societies. Moreover, many of the societies that awaited European colonists were newborns, even younger than Europeans' romance with the New World. Patricia Galloway's *Choctaw Genesis* (1995) is a model effort to determine the birthdate of one such society. Combining archaeological data with painstaking, ethnologically informed analysis of early European observations, she concludes that the Choctaw tribe did not exist before the 1530s but did exist by the 1670s, when it was a confederation of diverse groups occupying a previously uninhabited Mississippi district. Bruce Bourque believes that there were many such "changes in the nature, distribution, and naming of ethnic groups" just before and after Europeans' arrival (1989: 257). On the basis of archaeological evidence and cross-checked European records, Bourque infers that indigenous peoples of Canada's Maritime Peninsula not only relocated but also reorganized and merged in the seventeenth century.

The principal impetus for the reorganizations and mergers that Galloway and Bourque describe was population loss due to diseases imported from Europe and disseminated in advance of colonists. But deadly pandemics were just the first of many twists of the kaleidoscope that fragmented and recombined indigenous peoples after 1500. Magisterial studies by James Merrell (1989) and J. Leitch Wright (1986) show that new, multi-ethnic nations such as Catawbas and Creeks formed not only because of population changes (which followed from warfare and subsistence needs as well as epidemics) but also because of political, economic, and ideological pressures and opportunities associated with European activity. For example, the unique Quebec community of Kahnawake owed its birth in the 1600s to such factors as European-induced changes in Mohawk economics, the conversion of some Mohawks to Christianity, fur trade wars, and Mohawks' practice of replenishing their numbers with foreign captives (Alfred, 1995: chapter 2).

Although many of today's Indian groups took root in ground broken by the earliest European intruders, some grew from newer seeds. The Navajo nation, for example, coalesced in the nineteenth and twentieth centuries as a result of events that gave its scattered and loosely affiliated constituent groups a common history and a common relationship to the U.S. government (Iverson, 1983). In the Navajo case and in many others, U.S. law and the Indian reservation system created conditions favoring ethnogenesis, but they could not guarantee or invariably expedite it. Previously separate groups shared some reservations for many decades, even well into the twentieth century, before becoming a single tribal entity. The present Colville

Confederated Tribes are such a recent amalgam (Gooding, 1994; Harmon, 1998). Segregation on reservations probably delayed but did not prevent the development of a continent-wide Indian identity that extends across tribal boundaries. Today's broad, generic American Indian ethnicity is indisputably younger than the term "Indian" and did not reach maturity until the late twentieth century (Cornell, 1988; Nagel, 1996; Edmunds, 1995: 733; Hertzberg, 1971).

Taken together, the historical scholarship on Indian identity argues for conceiving of Indianness as a multitude of identities. "Indian" refers to a sense of self that has had hundreds of formulations at a tribal or community level and millions of formulations at an individual level. It also refers to an identity that transcends tribal and individual differences – an overarching social category variously defined by such factors as racial traits, descent, and political status. In other words, there have been many, many ways to be Indian.

Tribal histories, including those that treat tribal identity as unproblematic, show that the numerous aggregations labeled "Indian" have been diverse, multifaceted, and elastic. Not only have Indian societies extant at a particular time differed in structure and culture, but each society has changed over time, sometimes quite rapidly. This is evident in microcosm from Michael McConnell's study (1992) of refugee groups that shared the upper Ohio Valley in the middle decades of the eighteenth century. While a few groups merged with their new neighbors, most strengthened their tribal identities, but they did so in varied ways.

A shift of focus from tribes to individuals suggests that Indian groups owe their elasticity to the multivalent and contingent nature of their members' social affiliations. Like other humans, individual Indians have had multiple loyalties and multiple ways of situating themselves or conceiving of themselves in relation to other people (Moses and Wilson, 1985: 4). Susan Gooding (1994) finds this true of the people now included in the Colville tribal confederation. From historical and ethnographic literature she draws evidence that those people have conceived of their group memberships in several overlapping ways, each of them allowing for ethnic realignment. In different contexts people have identified themselves by area of residence, language, lineage and kin ties, or strategic associations. Gooding calls this multiplicity "layered identity" (pp. 1206–13).

Furthermore, individuals' sense of Indianness has not depended on their participation in historic tribal groups. In cities far from their indigenous forebears' various homelands, Indians have found each other and created new Indian communities, partly by sharing stories from their respective tribal pasts and partly by making their own urban experiences into a shared Indian story (Blackhawk, 1995: 16; Danziger, 1991). For the youngest woman in a Los Angeles family that Diana Bahr interviewed (1993), having a mother and grandmother who insisted they were Indian was sufficient to instill a sense of Indian identity, notwithstanding her blonde hair and limited knowledge of her indigenous heritage.

Can people as different as the women Bahr studied and black-haired members of cohesive, landed tribes all be Indians? Would they recognize each other as ethnic kin? Intrigued by the fact that these questions appear to have affirmative answers in many cases, sociologists Nagel (1996) and Stephen Cornell (1990) looked to history for an explanation. Their important books trace the recent evolution of Indianness at the supratribal level. This general Indian ethnicity has not replaced tribal identities or individual identities rooted in descent but encompasses and supplements them.

In addition to exposing the varieties and levels of Indian identity, recent studies elucidate the processes shaping those identities. Indians' self-definitions are the outgrowth of complicated dialectics. Indianness has been defined and redefined in continual give-and-take between outsiders' ascriptions and insiders' self-representations, between government policy and actual practice, between national or international forces and local conditions, between the adverse and the beneficial consequences of being Indian, and between Indians with differing self-conceptions.

"Indian" is not an imported name for a category that pre-dated Columbus; it is a name that brought a new ethnic or racial category into being by precipitating extended, multilateral discourse about the name's meaning. Europeans triggered the discourse when they applied Columbus's misnomer to everyone they found in the Western Hemisphere. Because their heirs gained the upper hand in the discussion, it is tempting to emphasize non-Indian initiatives when explaining Indians. Howard Winant, for example, says that whites' attitudes and actions forced non-whites to suppress their differences and unite (1994: 44; see also Jaimes, 1992). And it is true that by labeling, excluding, and wielding political and economic power, European-Americans eventually set the important parameters of Indianness. But it would be a mistake to downplay the power of Indian people in the definition process, and it would be foolish to assume that Indians' and non-Indians' definitions have coincided (Plane and Button, 1993: 598). As ethnohistorian James Collins says (1998: 195–9), "Indian" and "Tolowa" may be classifications forced by non-Indians; but they are classifications that Indians and Tolowas have given content to, sometimes in defiance of non-Indian expectations (see also Harmon, 1998; Sider, 1993: xvi).

That outsiders' conceptions of Indians have strongly influenced Indians' self-definitions is undeniable. In countless instances this influence began with a name. Like the word "Indian," many a modern tribal name or its applications – Navajo, Creek, and Nez Perce, for example – originated with Europeans. Even if the name meant nothing at first to the people tagged with it, some soon used it for themselves when dealing with Europeans; and in the course of ensuing relations, the name acquired new uses and meanings for both sets of people (Bourque, 1989: 271; Harmon, 1998). The Europeans often thought – erroneously, in many cases – that they had named a category familiar to the Indians; but sometimes they consciously misused a name to encourage the creation of a new group. For instance, by addressing all culturally similar people on the southern Plains as "Comanches," non-Indian leaders hoped to make them act as a political unit. After non-Indians, by conquest and law, created other conditions that impelled the so-called Comanches to act in unison, the name took on more consonant meanings for the two sets of people (Foster, 1991: 36).

Outsiders' ascriptions and concepts of Indian identity have influenced both collective and individual self-conceptions. To make the argument that a comprehensive racial consciousness developed much later among Indians than among African-Americans, Cornell (1990: 375, 381) emphasizes white colonists' inclination to view Indians not as potential laborers but as numerous separate groups, each controlling particular lands and resources. To explain the simultaneous development of Indian political identities based in tribes and in a supratribal ethnic group, Carole Goldberg-Ambrose turns to U.S. law (1994: 1123). And to make the point that some people feel a loss of Indian identity if they leave Robeson County, North Carolina, Karen Blu (1980: 82) cites a Lumbee man's reason for going home after World War II: in North Carolina, he said, he knew what he was because others there knew what he was.

How could Indians help but define themselves in contradistinction to the people around them? "It is otherness," Greg Dening writes (1997: 5), "that prompts self-description." As surely as indigenous Americans' differences inspired Europeans to say what they valued about themselves, encounters with Europeans made indigenous Americans conscious of their own distinguishing characteristics. Whites' oppression of African-Americans gave indigenous people reason to focus on what distinguished them from that group, too. There are poignant accounts of Indian groups' efforts to define themselves as "not black" in New England as well as the South (Blu, 1980: 127; Williams, 1979; Finger, 1991; Plane and Button, 1993; Herndon and Sekatau, 1997).

The interplay of external and internal determinants of Indianness has had some ironic results. To show that they are neither white nor black, tribes and individuals have borrowed emblems from outsiders as well as from their aboriginal forebears. Witness the ubiquity of eagle feather bonnets. After Wild West shows encouraged Americans to associate Indians with these and other appealing features of Plains nomad culture, Indians in all corners of the continent incorporated the bonnets in their pageantry (Moses, 1996: 275; Campisi, 1991: 136; Finger, 1991: xiv; Harmon, 1998: plates). Practices introduced by European-Americans, often in a deliberate effort to eradicate Indianness, have also demarcated Indian groups. Thus, for many Indian communities, a particular Christian church became a unifying and identifying institution (Baird, 1990: 8; Boissevain, 1959; Paredes, 1995: 348).

Government policies and the laws that embody them have been especially important external determinants of Indian identity. When the U.S. government allotted tribal lands to individuals under treaties or statutes such as the Dawes Act of 1887, it took action that marked thousands of landholders and their descendants as Indians and tribe members (Harmon, 1998: chapter 6). As Goldberg-Ambrose says (1994: 1124), law has created "an official vocabulary for the discussion of group life that reinforces certain conceptions of political identity and excludes others." The Canadian Indian Act of 1885 and the U.S. Indian Reorganization Act of 1934 guided the expression of Indian political identity into government-prescribed levels and forms (Alfred, 1995: chapter 3; Edmunds, 1995: 733–4). Some local laws had similar effects. After Massachusetts entrusted Mashpee town government to landowners of Indian descent in 1723, "[t]ribal membership assured the individual the right to land, and, conversely, having a right to land identified an individual as a member of the group. Descent from a proprietor thus became a defining characteristic of tribal membership" (Campisi, 1991: 82).

On the other hand, governments cannot define Indians unilaterally. For one thing, laws and government programs have unintended effects. They have affected Indians' sense of themselves by provoking resistance as often as compliance. Thus during the 1950s and 1960s, alarm about federal plans to terminate Indians' special legal-political status spurred U.S. tribes not only to insist on that status but also to articulate more clearly their conceptions of it. For another thing, government officials have needed information from Indians in order to identify Indians. When allotting Colville Reservation lands, for example, officials convened councils of male residents, told them that land could only go to persons of Native descent who belonged to one of their bands, and asked them to say which applicants belonged. By construing the term "belong" in hundreds of individual cases, the councils helped to give Colville tribal identity its operative meaning (Harmon, 1997). Similar processes have played a part in identifying Indians and defining tribes nationwide.

Furthermore, policies and laws enacted by a national legislature, often with stereotypical Indians in mind, have played out in diverse ways at the local level. The U.S. policy of sorting Indians into reservation-based tribes was more efficacious on the militarized Plains than in western Washington, where the descendants of Native villagers – peaceable, interrelated, and eager for economic relations with whites – moved frequently from reservations to cities to fishing grounds to other reservations (Harmon, 1998).

The reservation policy's peculiar fate in western Washington is but one of many possible reminders that Indian identity also bespeaks the mixed influence of local and national or international conditions. Local history and local laws of the eighteenth and nineteenth century (which in turn reflected national economic and political developments) established the framework for a parochial Mashpee Indian identity. But Mashpees' view of their identity broadened in the twentieth century when individuals left the community and encountered national Indian movements. On their return, the emigrants added pan-Indian symbols and rituals to Mashpee emblems of identity. Campisi (1991: 149, 152) insists that this use of borrowed symbols did not signal Mashpee insecurity about their Indianness, which still rested on a local foundation of land use patterns, family relations, autonomy, and insularity (see also Danziger, 1991: 62; McIlwraith, 1996). Everywhere tribes have engaged in the same process, adapting their distinctive traditions to changes in the world around them while also selecting features of other societies for use in the tribal world.

The national and international factors affecting Indians' self-definitions are economic as well as political and cultural. Indian people have been entangled in global economic networks since their earliest trade relations with Europeans, and the consequences of that entanglement have included changes not only in Indians' material well-being but also in the very foundations of group life (Merrell, 1989). Once people of Native descent had reserved lands and other valuable entitlements under federal law, they tended to define themselves by those assets. Many subsequently adopted tribal membership criteria designed to protect their assets, even though the criteria contravened older ideas about the defining features of their community (Trosper, 1976: 257). The loss of reserved land, on the other hand, has in some instances demoted land from its pre-eminent place among the symbols of Indian identity. Melissa Meyer (1994: 225) implies that such was the case when legislators and businessmen dispossessed certain Anishinaabeg of the White Earth Reservation, forcing them to disperse to cities. Expanding market capitalism, Meyer concludes, was a more powerful agent of Indian assimilation than U.S. policy.

Another dualism that shapes Indian identity is the counterpoise of its shifting advantages and disadvantages. Since people of European descent attained hegemony in the U.S. and Canada, Indians have suffered for their distinctiveness in numerous ways, from genocidal attacks to economic discrimination, legal disabilities, and forced resocialization. Some people have tried to avoid such misery (and perhaps share in whites' privileges) by downplaying, hiding, or changing characteristics that identify them as Indians. For example, Paredes (1974: 68–9) says that well-founded fears of discrimination explain the near-invisibility of Alabama Creek Indians between World Wars I and II. Not surprisingly, those unable to avoid discrimination, like most Creeks, have developed a sharper sense of group identity as a result.

On the other hand, being Indian has not consistently hurt. Assorted laws and policies have attached material and political benefits to Indian status: employment, rights to land, opportunities for education, self-government. Such laws and policies have had a direct bearing on whether people define themselves as Indians at all. When the U.S. government allotted reservation lands to individuals, it received applications from thousands of people who had not previously associated with an Indian community, and hundreds of people who had earlier severed their ties to such communities. Many had a preponderance of non-Indian ancestors (Clifton, 1989: 18). Laws giving preference in employment to individuals "of Indian blood" or fostering tribal government and businesses have arguably been as important as discrimination in determining the self-definition and self-representation of many groups and individuals (Edmunds, 1995: 732; Goldberg-Ambrose, 1994).

Indian identity has also had its non-material rewards. Recent U.S. censuses seem to show the encouraging influence of such intangibles as a right of self-government, media attention to Indians, the vogue for Indian art and spirituality, and public celebrations of multiculturalism. Statisticians cannot entirely account for the rapid increase in enumerated Indians without assuming that people who have a choice are more inclined to identify themselves as Indians (Snipp, 1989: 57). But even in the worst of times for Indians, the non-material rewards of being Indian have not been insignificant. Many people have found greater solace in a sense of belonging among Indians, however disadvantaged in the larger society, than they could imagine finding as detribalized individuals.

Thus, in hundreds of times and places, people with various ancestries and experiences have weighed the benefits and penalties of being Indian, have considered the choices and constraints that their physiognomy and history and immediate circumstances present, and have decided how to present themselves in a racialized world. Some have insisted on their Indian identity; some have renounced or downplayed their claim to an Indian identity; and some have done one and then the other, according to their situations (Merrell, 1997).

From the histories and biographies that show people making varied choices about whether and how to display Indianness, we can glean another important lesson: we can see that Indians or tribes are not monolithic blocs, constituting themselves in unison vis-à-vis outsiders. The several kinds of give-and-take that mold Indians include give-and-take – even conflict – among people who consider themselves Indians. Indians have defined themselves in opposition to presumed members of their own communities or race as much as they have defined themselves in opposition to outsiders.

A theme of Eastern Cherokees' history, according to John Finger (1991: xiii–xiv), is factionalism. In particular, "a division between so-called white Indians who have minimal Cherokee ancestry and those who have more … is perhaps the most fundamental fact of life for today's Eastern Cherokees and raises the perplexing question of who is a 'real' Cherokee." Historians could say the same in the past tense about Eastern Cherokees and about other tribes. During the nineteenth century, when Miami chiefs strayed too far from a consensus worked out in tribal councils, the councils disowned them, declaring to U.S. agents that the chiefs were not really Miamis (Rafert, 1996: 72). During the 1940s competing factions of the group now known as the Lumbee Tribe wanted to claim different identities – Cherokee and Siouan (Sider, 1993).

Is there an Indian group whose history has not included internal disputes about the defining traits of group members or the nature of the group? Only in fiction. Even in tribes with longstanding, institutionalized boundary markers such as reservations, community members have differed about the characteristics and traditions that define them. A historical perspective enables us to see that such differences are as integral to the evolution of identity as commonalities are (Fowler, 1987; Hoxie, 1997: 610; McIlwraith, 1996: 46). In fact, Blu (1980: 66) and Rafert (1996: 24) argue from Lumbee and Miami history, respectively, that heterogeneity and the contentiousness it engenders can be a basis of group durability. The more diverse are the people responding to change, they say, the more likely it is that some of them will have the experience or perspective needed to propose an effective survival strategy.

By now it should come as no surprise to see the word "strategy" in an essay about Indian identity. People known as Indians, no less than other ethnic groups, have consciously strategized to perpetuate themselves in a state that comports with their understanding of who they are or want to be. They have plotted to achieve or retain economic resources, power and autonomy, safety, supportive companionship, and the other necessities of human existence. The decisions they have reached – multitudes of individual decisions as well as collective ones – are apparent in the ways they express their identity.

Potential examples of Indian groups strategizing to salvage their identity are as numerous as the groups themselves. Was it not a defense of identity for Mashpee Indians, shortly after they lost control of their town's government, to organize a tribal corporation? (Campisi, 1991: 147.) Was it not a strategy of self-preservation for the government of the Flathead Reservation, where Indians and non-Indians have intermarried at a high rate, to limit tribal membership by "blood quantum"? (Trosper, 1976.) When Blu says (1980: 134) that the Lumbees have tended "to interpret threats to their social and economic well-being as threats to their identity," she could be referring to any Indian group.

Indians do not just work to preserve identity; they use their identity as a strategic weapon and shield. This is one function of the often-romanticized cultural displays that Indians have directed primarily at non-Indians – powwows and craft sales, for example. Paredes (1995: 352) describes them as "the means by which Indian communities purchase good will" and win non-Indians' acceptance of the less palatable "instruments" that secure their political and economic viability, such as tribal sovereignty and "socialistic" enterprises. Thus in the 1920s, when anti-Indian sentiment was rampant, Indiana Miamis initiated an annual pageant, hoping to give the public a positive impression of their history and culture. This strategy had an important rebound effect. by pulling old and young into a collaborative effort to define Miamis to the world, it helped to create a modern Miami tribe (Rafert, 1996: 212).

The literature reviewed here has the power to undermine assumptions that are deeply ingrained in the popular culture, laws, and political dynamics of the U.S. and Canada. First, history contradicts the still-prevalent notion that culture change destroys Indianness; it shows that Indianness cannot be calibrated to degrees of cultural continuity. Group after group has maintained a strong sense of Indian identity despite wholesale changes in structure, customs, beliefs, and personnel. While the characteristics that identified Indians in the past have altered radically, Indians have refused to disappear.

Consider the people known collectively as the Five Civilized Tribes of Oklahoma: Cherokees, Chickasaws, Choctaws, Creeks, and Seminoles. They have a history of embracing change. In the nineteenth century many of them exchanged centuries-old customs and beliefs for such European-American culture features as market economics, private landownership, Christianity, and centralized government based on written laws. The tribes even incorporated European-Americans themselves; some of their citizens had far more non-Indian than indigenous ancestors. Yet thousands of people today, many of whom live and look like non-Indians, call themselves Indians of the Five Tribes. Why? According to W. David Baird (1990), because of this very history. It is a history of people who have insisted on their peoplehood even at the cost of practices that once seemed proof of that peoplehood. Everyone who is, in some meaningful way, a product of this history has reason to feel like an Indian.

Baird precedes this argument with the statement that the Five Tribes of Oklahoma "have behaved differently" from other Indians by changing so radically; but he is wrong. The Five Tribes are no more unique in this respect than the Lumbees who embraced European-American education, the Mashpees who adopted Christianity and town government, the Stó:ló community that organized under a new government, the Flathead Reservation residents who adopted a new measure of tribal affiliation, or the Comanches who began speaking English in community gatherings (Blu, 1980: 62; Campisi, 1991: 158; Trosper, 1976; Collins, 1998: 167; Foster, 1991: 21). Even resistance to change has required Indians to revise their self-characterizations, often by elevating taken-for-granted activities to sacred emblems of identity (Collins, 1998: 10; Harmon, 1998: chapter 8). Thus, the identifying characteristics of virtually all contemporary Indians and tribes are different from the characteristics that identified their forebears.

Second, historical studies should disabuse people of the notion that Indianness, no matter how altered, has an irreducible essence – a primal core that authenticates its possessors. In truth, there has never been an essential identifying characteristic of

Indians or Indian groups except perhaps their belief in their descent from pre-Columbian Americans. The evidence is overwhelming that a population need not preserve any specific cultural or genetic profile in order to perpetuate its Indian identity. Virtually every characteristic or practice that has marked Indians in the past – name, physical appearance, language, location, method of governance, religion, kinship system, and even group life itself – can lapse without necessarily dimming people's determination to be counted as Indians.

If there is a universal reason for that determination to be counted as Indian, it is history. More precisely, it is a sense of having an Indian history or a historical link to undisputed Indians of the past. People have derived this sense from sources as diverse as family lore, a knowledge of genealogy, a multi-generational attachment to place, similar stories about their forebears' treatment by non-Indians, or a common pattern of experiences while trying to live by shared norms (Bahr, 1993: 23; Rafert, 1996: 239; Snow, 1997; Collins, 1998: 10; Finger, 1991: 181; Iverson, 1994: 7; Moses and Wilson, 1985: 9).

Blu (1980: 1–2) asks what holds the Lumbees together despite their lack of formal organization; and she answers: their shared ideas about themselves as a people. Such ideas usually go by the name "tradition." But tradition need not be venerable or indigenous to make a group cohesive or Indian. In the case of the Five Civilized Tribes, the very adaptations that have cast doubt on their credentials as Indians have become tribal traditions (Baird, 1990). Just as imported horses became integral to the identity of nineteenth-century Plains Indians, imported institutions have become integral to the identities of Indian groups whose survival they helped to ensure.

"Tradition," says Jocelyn Linnekin (1983: 241), "is a conscious model of past lifeways that people use in the construction of their identity." Because "the selection of what constitutes tradition is always made in the present," people create a culture as they rediscover a heritage. Indians, too, have created their cultures by remembering or recovering and reinterpreting their past; but their Indianness does not depend on preserving a requisite portion of that past. Indian identity is not quantifiable or residual; it does not "progress in one direction toward disappearance" (Rafert, 1996: 295). It flowers and wilts and perhaps flowers again, depending on how zealously people cultivate it (Sider, 1993: xvii).

Thus, the studies that illustrate this essay should dispel any inclination to define Indianness solely as something that the descendants of aboriginal people have managed to preserve through centuries of assault on their identities. Instead, the lesson of history – when written as much as possible to give voice to all the participants – is that Indianness is an ongoing creation, and Indians are chief among its creators. They have taken active roles in shaping the identities we know as Indian. They have asserted their identities in strategic ways. And again and again, they have sought change as a means of maintaining their societies and their distinctiveness.

The historicization of North American Indian identities is such a new scholarly enterprise that all the issues mentioned here, and more, beg for further investigation. If this survey cites too few long-term studies of the contingencies that have shaped and reshaped Indian identities, it is because the literature is still deficient. Scholars could profitably answer Albers's plea for additional studies of Indian ethnogenesis. And because many people assume that government-mandated culture change undermined the foundations of Indian tribal life, it behooves historians to document the numerous ways and reasons that Indians have proved them wrong. On the other hand, some Indian societies have in fact disappeared, and there is much more to know about the circumstances of these ethnocides and ethnosuicides.

Future historical inquiries will tell us more about the relative importance of the factors that determine Indian identity and its expressions. In particular, focusing on the relationship of economics to Indian identity should yield a wealth of information. We have barely begun to explore the effects of Indians' urbanization on their identities. And literature on the origins and effects of identifying Indians by "blood quantum" is still scanty and speculative. Numerous revelations surely await scholars who analyze the interplay of local and national developments, especially the influence of local formulations on national formulations of Indianness. We also need comparative studies – comparisons of Indians in the U.S. and Canada and comparisons that tap the rich historical literature on ethnicity in Latin America.

As historians broaden and deepen their analyses of Indian identity, new questions will occur to them. We can expect questions about the relationship of family and gender constructions to ideas about race, ethnicity, and tribe. We should hope, too, for efforts to link insights about Indianness to studies of other ethnic groups: what can the historicization of Indian identity contribute to our understanding of other American ethnicities? Can it inform the growing body of scholarship on the constructed and contingent nature of "whiteness"? And what can the histories of other American ethnicities, especially "whiteness," contribute to our understanding of Indianness? There is ample reason to ask these questions and to expect answers of considerable significance to all North Americans; for Indian and non-Indian identities became inseparable subjects in 1492 and have remained so ever since.

BIBLIOGRAPHY

Albers, Patricia C. 1996: "Changing Patterns of Ethnicity in the Northeastern Plains, 1780–1870," in *History, Power, and Identity: Ethnogenesis in the Americas, 1492–1992*, ed. Jonathan D. Hill (Iowa City: University of Iowa Press), pp. 90–118.

Alfred, Gerald R. 1995: *Heeding the Voices of Our Ancestors: Kahnawake Mohawk Politics and the Rise of Native Nationalism* (Don Mills, Ontario and New York: Oxford University Press).

Bahr, Diana Meyers 1993: *From Mission to Metropolis: Cupeño Indian Women in Los Angeles* (Norman: University of Oklahoma Press).

Baird, W. David 1990: "Are the Five Tribes of Oklahoma 'Real' Indians?," *Western Historical Quarterly* 21 (February): 5–18.

Barth, Fredrik 1969: *Ethnic Groups and Boundaries: The Social Organization of Culture Difference* (Boston: Little, Brown).

Berkhofer, Robert F., Jr. 1978: *The White Man's Indian: Images of the American Indian from Columbus to the Present* (New York: Vintage Books).

Blackhawk, Ned 1995: "I Can Carry on from Here: The Relocation of American Indians to Los Angeles," *Wicazo-Sa Review* 11 (Fall): 16–30.

Blu, Karen I. 1980: *The Lumbee Problem: The Making of an American Indian People* (New York: Cambridge University Press).

Boissevain, Ethel 1959: "Narragansett Survival: A Study of Group Persistence through Adopted Traits," *Ethnohistory* 6 (Fall): 347–62.

Bourque, Bruce J. 1989: "Ethnicity on the Maritime Peninsula, 1600–1759," *Ethnohistory* 36 (Summer): 257–84.

Campisi, Jack 1991: *The Mashpee Indians: Tribe on Trial* (Syracuse: Syracuse University Press).

Clifton, James A. 1989: *Being and Becoming Indian: Biographical Studies of North American Frontiers* (Chicago: Dorsey Press).

Collins, James 1998: *Understanding Tolowa Histories: Western Hegemonies and Native American Responses* (New York: Routledge).

Cornell, Stephen 1988: *The Return of the Native: American Indian Political Resurgence* (New York: Oxford University Press).

Cornell, Stephen 1990: "Land, Labour, and Group Formation: Blacks and Indians in the United States," *Ethnic and Racial Studies* 13 (July): 368–88.

Danziger, Edmund Jefferson, Jr. 1991: *Survival and Regeneration: Detroit's American Indian Community* (Detroit: Wayne State University Press).

Dening, Greg 1997: "Introduction: In Search of a Metaphor," in *Through a Glass Darkly: Reflections on Personal Identity in Early America*, eds. Ronald Hoffman, Mechal Sobel, and Fredrika Teute (Chapel Hill: University of North Carolina Press), pp. 2–5.

Dippie, Brian W. 1982: *The Vanishing American: White Attitudes and U.S. Indian Policy* (Middletown, CT: Wesleyan University Press).

Edmunds, R. David 1995: "Native Americans, New Voices: American Indian History, 1895–1995," *American Historical Review* 100 (June): 717–40.

Finger, John R. 1991: *Cherokee Americans: The Eastern Band of Cherokees in the Twentieth Century* (Lincoln: University of Nebraska Press).

Forbes, Jack D. 1993: *Africans and Native Americans: The Language of Race and the Evolution of Red–Black Peoples*, 2nd edn. (Urbana and Chicago: University of Illinois Press).

Foster, Morris W. 1991: *Being Comanche: A Social History of an American Indian Community* (Tucson: University of Arizona Press).

Fowler, Loretta 1987: *Shared Symbols, Contested Meanings: Gros Ventre Culture and History, 1778–1984* (Ithaca: Cornell University Press).

Frye, David 1996: *Indians into Mexicans: History and Identity in a Mexican Town* (Austin: University of Texas Press).

Galloway, Patricia 1995: *Choctaw Genesis: 1500–1700* (Lincoln: University of Nebraska Press).

Gates, Henry Louis, Jr. 1985: "Writing 'Race' and the Difference It Makes," *Critical Inquiry* 12 (Autumn): 1–6.

Goldberg-Ambrose, Carole 1994: "Of Native Americans and Tribal Members: The Impact of Law on Indian Group Life," *Law and Society Review* 28 (December): 1123–48.

Gooding, Susan Staiger 1994: "Place, Race, and Names: Layered Identities in *United States v. Oregon*, Confederated Tribes of the Colville Reservation, Plaintiff-Intervenor," *Law and Society Review* 28 (December): 1181–229.

Harmon, Alexandra 1995: "Lines in Sand: Shifting Boundaries between Indians and Non-Indians in the Puget Sound Region," *Western Historical Quarterly* 26 (December): 429–53.

Harmon, Alexandra 1997: "The Colville Tribe: Defining What Should Survive," unpublished paper presented at the 1997 conference of the American Society for Legal History.

Harmon, Alexandra 1998: *Indians in the Making: Ethnic Relations and Indian Identities around Puget Sound* (Berkeley and Los Angeles: University of California Press).

Hatt, Michael 1997: "Ghost Dancing in the Salon: The Red Indian as a Sign of White Identity," *Diogenes* 177 (Spring): 93–111.

Herndon, Ruth Wallis and Ella Wilcox Sekatau 1997: "The Right to a Name: The Narragansett People and Rhode Island Officials in the Revolutionary Era," *Ethnohistory* 44 (Summer): 433–62.

Hertzberg, Hazel W. 1971: *The Search for an American Indian Identity: Modern Pan-Indian Movements* (Syracuse: Syracuse University Press).

Hoxie, Frederick E. 1997: "Ethnohistory for a Tribal World," *Ethnohistory* 44 (Fall): 595–615.

Iverson, Peter 1983: *The Navajo Nation* (Albuquerque: University of New Mexico Press).

Iverson, Peter 1994: *When Indians Became Cowboys: Native Peoples and Cattle Ranching in the American West* (Norman: University of Oklahoma Press).

Jaimes, M. Annette 1992: "Federal Indian Identification Policy: A Usurpation of Indigenous Sovereignty in North America," in *The State of Native America*, ed. M. Annette Jaimes (Boston: South End Press), pp. 123–38.

Linnekin, Jocelyn S. 1983: "Defining Tradition: Variations on the Hawaiian Identity," *American Ethnologist* 10: 241–52.

McConnell, Michael N. 1992: *A Country Between: The Upper Ohio Valley and Its Peoples, 1724–1774* (Lincoln: University of Nebraska Press).

McCulloch, Ann Merline and David E. Wilkins 1995: "Constructing Nations within States: The Quest for Federal Recognition by the Catawba and Lumbee Tribes," *American Indian Quarterly* 19 (Summer): 361–89.

McIlwraith, Thomas 1996: "The Problem of Imported Culture: The Construction of Contemporary Stó:ló Identity," *American Indian Culture and Research Journal* 20: 41–70.

Merrell, James H. 1989: *The Indians' New World: Catawbas and Their Neighbors from European Contact through the Era of Removal* (Chapel Hill: University of North Carolina Press).

Merrell, James H. 1997: "'The Cast of His Countenance': Reading Andrew Montour," in *Through a Glass Darkly: Reflections on Personal Identity in Early America*, eds. Ronald Hoffman, Mechal Sobel, and Fredrika Teute (Chapel Hill: University of North Carolina Press), pp. 13–39.

Meyer, Melissa L. 1994: *The White Earth Tragedy: Ethnicity and Dispossession at a Minnesota Anishinaabe Reservation, 1889–1920* (Lincoln: University of Nebraska Press).

Moses, L. G. 1996: *Wild West Shows and the Images of American Indians, 1883–1933* (Albuquerque: University of New Mexico Press).

Moses, L. G. and Raymond Wilson (eds.) 1985: *Indian Lives: Essays on Nineteenth- and Twentieth-Century Native American Leaders* (Albuquerque: University of New Mexico Press).

Nagel, Joane 1996: *American Indian Ethnic Renewal: Red Power and the Resurgence of Identity and Culture* (New York: Oxford University Press).

O'Nell, Theresa D. 1994: "Telling about Whites, Talking about Indians: Oppression, Resistance, and Contemporary American Indian Identity," *Cultural Anthropology*, 9 (February): 94–126.

Paredes, J. Anthony 1974: "The Emergence of Contemporary Eastern Creek Indian Identity," in *Social and Cultural Identity: Problems of Persistence and Change*, ed. Thomas K. Fitzgerald (Athens: University of Georgia Press), pp. 63–80.

Paredes, J. Anthony 1995: "Paradoxes of Modernism and Indianness in the Southeast," *American Indian Quarterly* 19 (Summer): 341–88.

Pearce, Roy Harvey 1988: *Savagism and Civilization: A Study of the Indian and the American Mind* (Berkeley and Los Angeles: University of California Press).

Plane, Ann Marie and Gregory Button 1993: "The Massachusetts Indian Enfranchisement Act: Ethnic Contest in Historical Context, 1849–1869," *Ethnohistory* 40 (Fall): 587–618.

Rafert, Stewart 1996: *The Miami Indians of Indiana: A Persistent People, 1654–1994* (Indianapolis: Indiana Historical Society).

Roosens, Eugeen E. 1989: *Creating Ethnicity: The Process of Ethnogenesis* (Newbury Park, CA: Sage Publications).

Rosenthal, Elizabeth Clark 1970: " 'Culture' and the American Indian Community," in *The American Indian Today*, eds. Stuart Levine and Nancy Oestreich Lurie (Deland, FL: Everett Edwards), pp. 82–9.

Sider, Gerald 1993: *Lumbee Indian Histories: Race, Ethnicity, and Indian Identity in the Southern United States* (New York and Cambridge: Cambridge University Press).

Simeone, William E. 1995: *Rifles, Blankets, and Beads: Identity, History, and the Northern Athapaskan Potlatch* (Norman: University of Oklahoma Press).

Snipp, C. Matthew 1989: *American Indians: The First of This Land* (New York: Russell Sage Foundation).

Snow, Dean R. 1997: "The Same but Different: Penobscot Indian Ethnic Survival," unpublished paper presented to conference of the American Society for Ethnohistory in Mexico City, November.

Stein, Judith 1989: "Defining the Race 1890–1930," in *The Invention of Ethnicity*, ed. Werner Sollors (New York: Oxford University Press), pp. 77–104.

Sturtevant, William 1971: "Creek into Seminole," in *North American Indians in Historical Perspective*, eds. Eleanor Leacock and Nancy Lurie (New York: Random House), pp. 92–128.

Trosper, Ronald 1976: "Native American Boundary Maintenance: The Flathead Indian Reservation, Montana, 1860–1970," *Ethnicity* 3: 256–74.

Williams, Walter L. (ed.) 1979: *Southeastern Indians since the Removal Era* (Athens: University of Georgia Press).

Winant, Howard 1994: *Racial Conditions: Politics, Theory, Comparisons* (Minneapolis: University of Minnesota Press).

Wright, J. Leitch, Jr. 1986: *Creeks and Seminoles: The Destruction and Regeneration of the Muscogulge People* (Lincoln: University of Nebraska Press).

Part Four

Exchange and Social Relations

15

Labor and Exchange in American Indian History

PATRICIA ALBERS

Labor and exchange carry fairly straightforward meanings in their historical use and application. Labor consists of actions both mental and manual by which humans, acting socially, transform nature into products for their own use and exchange. Exchange is an act by which the products of one person's labor are alienated and consumed by another. Labor and exchange are universal processes, fundamental features of human life; how they are carried out is highly variable.

Over time, scholars of different backgrounds and locations have endeavored to understand both the experience and the expression of these economic acts not only in their own historical contexts but in foreign ones as well. Over the past century, writings on labor and exchange in American Indian history have been especially prolific. It is a daunting task to reflect on this massive body of scholarship. The literature now extends across many different fields including, among others, anthropology, history, geography, economics, sociology, and political science. As a consequence, only a few of its major trends are highlighted here.

This chapter reflects my own training and experience as an anthropologist; yet, its focus is also justified on the grounds that until the 1960s the discourse on American Indian economic thought and activity was largely framed around prevailing paradigms within the field of anthropology. Historians and geographers entered discussions on this topic at an early date but it was only after the 1950s that their contributions became significant. The growing presence of scholars outside anthropology helped to broaden perspectives not only by widening the temporal and spatial boundaries within which the scholarship on labor and exchange was conventionally defined, but also by expanding the sources of evidence typically associated with studies of American Indian economies. In the late 1960s, sociologists, economists, and political scientists started to join the discussion as well, and with their arrival, the field of study was stretched even further by the inclusion of perspectives that reached beyond the local to dimensions of national and global scale. It is against such a background that this essay on labor and exchange in American Indian history unfolds.

Technique, Tools, and Trade

From the earliest writings of traders, explorers, and missionaries to the more recent publications of ethnographers, scores of first-hand accounts contain information on every possible facet of work performed in American Indian communities. Until the third decade of the twentieth century, much of the treatment of American Indian labor focused on the products of work and the techniques and tools of production. Scholars offered detailed descriptions of how particular tasks were performed, the technologies associated with them, and the material products made from these efforts. Much of the early writing was concerned with subsistence production and material manufacture for domestic use. Without question, such compendiums of material culture and its associated work effort left us with an unparalleled legacy of information on everything from salmon fishing and buffalo hunting to basket making and totem carving. Notwithstanding the volume and weight of this literature, however, it left untouched much about the theory and practice of labor and exchange in historic and modern American Indian communities.

The early writings often stripped the rich layers of meaning that defined labor and gave it expression. With few exceptions, these writings provided little material on the cultural knowledges and agencies behind certain forms of work. This is not to say that meaning was entirely absent or that it cannot be imputed from early texts. But much of the early writing lacked semantic referents, an understanding of the native languages within which people thought and talked about the labor they performed for their own use or exchange.

Much of the writing was also divorced from the needs and desires that drew individuals toward certain labors and pulled them away from others. Gilbert Wilson's writings (1917, 1971) on Hidatsa agriculture are exceptional in this regard, but they constitute only a small fraction of the massive literatures which emerged on American Indian work in the early twentieth century. Generally speaking, we find little about how the laborer thought about her role in procural, processing, and manufacture.

Early scholarship also avoided the social relations in which labor was embedded, treating it mechanistically and with scant attention to its social bearings. It is not uncommon to find in these writings lengthy descriptions of plant cultivation without any consideration of who performed the work or how it was divided by gender, age, kinship affiliation, or rank. By and large, descriptions of work are sequestered from narratives of social life, kinship, and politics, much less descriptions of religion, spirituality, and worldview. And they are even further removed from the relations which brought American Indian labor into articulations of trade with neighboring groups and into a world-system of mercantile commerce.

Early ethnographic accounts generally decontextualized and divorced work from the forces of production, including the environmental conditions under which nature was appropriated and transformed into products for local use and exchange. They sometimes provided general information about local environments, but only rarely did they offer specific details on the location and timing of procurement, processing, or manufacturing activity. Today, such data must be gleaned from the notebooks and diaries of explorers, traders, and missionaries. Yet, even these writers are often frustratingly vague, recording information when their own experience depended on knowing geographic and temporal markers but otherwise ignoring details. For example, early documents on the Shoshone-Bannock offer many solid details on local fishing and hunting sites along with the seasons of their use, but much less on the plant resources on which this population also relied heavily.

As with labor, early scholars tended to reduce exchange to descriptions of the goods pooled, shared, gifted, bartered, or stolen and the mechanical basics of reciprocity. In the area of intertribal trade, for instance, little consideration was given to how this activity was linguistically constructed in local or regional settings or what constituted the overall social context of the commerce. In northern California, where this sort of trade was vitally linked to family standing and property ownership, much of the literature is strangely silent about it. Again, today's scholars must turn to the records of earlier observers. For the Assiniboine, Cree, and Ojibwa populations that occupied the parklands bordering North Dakota and Manitoba, scholars (Ray, 1974; Milloy, 1988; Peers, 1994) are able to rely on the accounts of several different early observers in reconstructing local trade relations, but comparably detailed historic documents are largely lacking for many other regions.

Ethnographers' preoccupation with the products and techniques of labor was, in part, an extension of the nostalgia motivating the early twentieth-century crafts movement, in which scholars devoted considerable effort to documenting the manufacture of American Indian material culture. This interest in labor as embodied in its products also bespoke the wider set of interests embraced by Victorian imperialism and capitalism. Ethnographic fieldwork was largely financed with the intent to collect material objects for display in museums and at exhibitions. Much has been written about this and does not need to be elaborated upon here. It is enough to say that the priorities of early ethnography contributed to representations that objectified and commodified work activity in American Indian communities and robbed it of its richest meanings. Indeed, it can be argued that an understanding of labor in its most complete conceptual sense was irrelevant, even troublesome, in contexts where objects were appropriated and consumed as "trophies" of colonial control and domination. By removing objects from their makers and distorting their origins, which often included their made-for-museum status or outright theft, ethnographers mystified the objects in popular and serious scholarship. Such dehistoricizing continues even today, as evidenced in the creation of myths that surround the making of American Indian art and crafts for tourists, interior designers, and art collectors (e.g., Parezo, this volume).

Subsistence, Reciprocity, and Redistribution

As the twentieth century progressed, studies of American Indian labor and exchange continued to focus on singular, ethnically marked "tribes," envisioning them as closed systems with only limited connections to the worlds around them. Notwithstanding this myopia, many of the ethnographic writings that appeared after 1930 started to link American Indian economies and economic activity to some sort of cultural, environmental, and/or social context. Largely in reaction to the disjointed and encyclopedic nature of earlier approaches, ethnographers began to think about production, distribution, and consumption in relation to patterns, usually designed around a particular theory of integration or causation. Labor and exchange became interlocking parts of larger systems constructed through the force of dominant cultural values, prevailing techno-environmental conditions, or primary social structures.

In the leading scholarly trend of this period, some authors attempted to identify cultural constructs that informed the conduct of economic activity and motivated people to work and reciprocate in particular ways. *Cooperation and Competition among Primitive Peoples*, edited by Margaret Mead (1937), exemplifies this approach. Its various articles focus on the ways in which tribal economies in North America and other parts of the world were integrated through prevailing cultural sensibilities. For example, Jeanette Mirsky describes how the values of generosity, sharing, and egalitarianism influenced the reciprocal character of economic integration in Teton societies. While writings such as Mirsky's started to give meaningful texture to tribal economic activity, much was still missing. Generally, they provided little if any linguistic analysis, and what they did provide did not grasp the idiomatic intricacies of expression behind any given labor or exchange transaction. What does it really mean to say that generosity is a value, sharing an imperative, and cooperation a necessity – all guiding principles in the historic production and distribution of the Teton – unless we know how these economic acts were expressed and applied in Lakota terms? Similarly, from Irving Goldman's contribution and other writings of the time (e.g., Barnett, 1938), we learn how ideas of prestige and privilege were related to the gifting of property on the Northwest Coast. But again, the authors attach little of this interpretation to the semantic markers of rank and redistribution within which the Kwakiutl and others so ardently labored to "make their names good" (Drucker and Heizer, 1967). These remarks are not intended to devalue this work, only to say that it does not go far enough in exploring the cultural constructions behind labor and exchange. Also, much of this literature focuses on normative discourse without attending to the actual practice of labor, to the concrete transactions within which goods circulate, or to the wider political economic contexts of reciprocity and redistribution.

Techno-environmental approaches occupied the opposite end of the "causal" spectrum. Although techno-environmentalism had been anticipated in earlier scholarship, it became definitive and influential only with the appearance of Julian Steward's work (1938, 1955). Steward and his followers saw American Indian economies as adaptations to the constraints of local environments and the technologies a people used to exploit those environments. In their argument that environment and technology were the "prime movers" of labor and exchange, they ignored many of the cultural and even social dimensions that surrounded work and trade. In his work in the Great Basin, Steward largely reduced Shoshone and Paiute life to a mechanistic search for food and the fulfillment of basic "alimentary" needs (Steward, 1938: 238; 1955: 112). The aesthetics of taste, much less the symbolic importance of local flora and fauna, carried little weight in Steward's understandings of patterns of subsistence and reciprocity. Furthermore, his work was largely silent about how the forced removal of Shoshone and Paiute from their primary procurement sites may have altered their productive strategies and the social formations within which they performed their work in post-contact times (Blackhawk, 1997).

Another explanatory tradition, known as structural-functionalism, focuses on the integrating features of social relationships in kinship, residence, rank, and politics. Labor and exchange are included insofar as they are an outcome of a particular structural-functional contingency. Labor is largely a function of necessity, the result of an elemental need such as food procural, or of a derived need created from within the structure of a social system and its associated cultural logic. Labor is organized and understood in terms of its capacity to keep the system integrated and running. E. Adamson Hoebel's monograph (1960) on the Cheyenne is a classic work in this mode. In his treatment of the labor behind horse acquisition, Hoebel linked raiding to a prestige structure supporting the internal cohesiveness of the tribe in the face of warfare. While this sort of argument helps us understand what motivated Cheyenne to raid, it fails to account for the complex uses to which horses were put and the fact that they were not simply a means of production for warfare and hunting but a central commodity in trade (Albers and James, 1991). Moreover, works like Hoebel's tend to overdetermine the cohesiveness of tribes and the internal workings of their politics and economies (Moore, 1974). Nevertheless, structural-functional studies offer some of the best methods for understanding how the conduct of labor and exchange was nested historically in kinship relations. Such works implicate kinship in the organizational formations that sustained production and distribution in American Indian communities, and suggest how certain economic transactions were constituted by and for these formations.

The treatment of labor and exchange within generalized schemes bound together by the forces of culture, society, or the environment represented a step beyond the piecemeal approaches found in early ethnographic writings. Yet, much was still lacking. As noted above, these accounts failed to interpret economic activity in relation to the language categories and concepts that framed it. Also, the continuing use of the ethnographic present as a rhetorical device to frame ethnographic texts deflected attention away from the wider historical worlds within which American Indian labor and exchange were situated and transformed. Although many of the writings from this period offered historical information, much of it was confined to an introductory chapter and removed from the body of the text in ways that make it appear that tribal economic life unfolded in the absence of history.

Change, Commerce, and Cultural Convention

The scholarship that prevailed in the years after World War II departed from earlier work in that it was explicitly historical as well as better attuned to the impacts of the Euro-American presence in American Indian economies. There were three major trajectories in this work: one associated with acculturation theory, a second linked to historical materialism, and a third combining ecological with structural-functional analysis. In the first trajectory, the discussion of labor and exchange took place in models that implicitly separated the cultural worlds of American Indians and Euro-Americans. For the most part, these works were guided by theories that explained economic activity in institutional economic terms. The authors largely equated American Indian labor with subsistence work and defined it as such, even when much of the product of this labor entered into one form of trade or another. And they largely confined descriptions of exchange to the internal circulation of goods, even when these were closely linked to external lines of distribution. Still conceptualizing American Indian economies as self-contained systems, these writers understood them to be driven by cultural logics radically different from those of European colonizers, and situated in spaces largely outside the worlds of colonialist commerce and manufacture. Indeed, some scholars maintained that much of the change taking place in native economies prior to the reservation period only involved a replacement in technology that did not fundamentally alter the conduct of native labor or exchange. Out of this tradition came some very important, pathbreaking works including John Ewers' classic study (1955) of the horse in Blackfoot culture. Ewers offered detailed evidence of how the adoption of horses was accompanied by changes in the technologies and techniques of warfare and hunting; yet, he did not move on toward analyzing the horse's impact on transformations in wider relations of production and distribution.

Other post-World War II ethnographers turned to the experiences of tribal nations in the twentieth century and the post-reservation era more generally. Much of the scholarship in what was then called "acculturation" theory chronicled transformations in cultural values and their material and social expressions in order to understand the degree to which tribes and their cultures had changed and to explain the mechanisms by which change had come about. Some writers (Thompson and Joseph, 1944) pointed to continuity in native values to explain the persistence of subsistence production and indigenous forms of reciprocity. By contrast, the assimilation of values from the "dominant" society ostensibly led to the abandonment of native economic activity, greater participation in wage labor, and the adoption of "progressive" entrepreneurial practice. Most of these scholars assumed that the persistence of native cultural values led either to an avoidance of work in capitalist markets or to the inevitable failure of their work effort once they participated (Moore, 1989). Indeed, in some of the popular acculturation and modernization schemes of the time one is hard pressed to know what work people actually carried out, much less how they survived at all in post-reservation times. With the treatment of labor so truncated, it was easy for some authors to assert that once the proverbial buffalo were gone, American Indians fell into desperation and total despair. Relying on their understanding of cultural values rather than on solid information on American Indian economic life, these scholars mystified the ways in which American Indians actually labored, exchanged, and survived.

By contrast, historical materialist writings argued that indigenous modes of production were fundamentally altered not only by the adoption of European technologies but also through the commerce that made access to these commodities possible.

Labor and exchange were not isolated or enclosed within self-contained systems, and the transformations of native societies were best understood in terms of the articulations between indigenous and capitalist modes of production (Klein, 1980). Influenced by the writings of Karl Marx and Friedrich Engels, this tradition found expression in the work of a number of ethnographers and ethnohistorians whose publications first appeared in the 1940s and 1950s. Examining very different histories, Oscar Lewis (1942), Joseph Jablow (1951), Eleanor Leacock (1954), and Harold Hickerson (1960, 1971) demonstrated how the fur and hide trades transformed not only the conditions of indigenous labor and exchange but also the cultural constructs and social formations in which these were nested. Their work gave new life to lively debates over the degree to which capitalism had actually penetrated native economic activity, including a well-known dispute about the origins of private property among Subarctic hunting populations. From the perspective of today's literature, it may well be argued that historical materialist writing overplays the hand of capitalism as a force in American Indian economic history, denying local agency and the persistence of important cultural forms. But such writing has the merit of generally avoiding the cumbersome dualisms of more culturally oriented theories.

After the 1940s, many scholars started to push the structural-functional envelope to include an analysis of demographic change and ecological adaptation. Without question, the limits and opportunities for prestige giving that supported, for example, the Northwest Coast potlatch in historic times were influenced by ecological and demographic factors. It is problematic, however, to argue that these conditions necessitated, much less created, the complex cultural constructions that occasioned potlatching in the first place (Drucker and Heizer, 1967; Kan, 1993), or the intricate and stratified structures of alliance in which potlatch goods circulated (Rosman and Rubel, 1971).

During the same period, another tendency in American ethnography moved toward an in-depth understanding of how culture molded individual life experience. Life history studies (e.g., Underhill, 1936; Simmons, 1942; Lurie, 1961) from this and earlier eras offer one of the few sources from which we can gain a glimpse of how cultural agency motivated individuals to action and inaction in particular areas of labor and exchange. Notwithstanding recent critiques about their "authenticity," works such as James Sewid's *Guests Never Leave Hungry* (Spradley, 1969) tell us a great deal about how choices were made over where and when to labor, at what kinds of work, and to what ends. They also reveal a lot about the sharing and pooling that sustained everyday life, and the means by which ceremonial goods were assembled and given to sustain rank and prestige. In a way not typically found in the ethnographic monographs of the time, life histories often cut through the conceptual dichotomies that falsely separated work that was "native" from labor in the larger economies of Canada and the United States. And again, James Sewid's story is instructive, insofar as it tells us that much of his labor, while squarely situated in a capitalist sector of production, was motivated toward, ends and carried out in relation to ideals that were Kwakiutl, not European, in origin.

Sewid's account corresponds with other historical writings (e.g., Chute, 1998; Hosmer, 1999) that show how an adherence to tribal values was not necessarily inconsistent with, nor did it necessarily militate against, active participation in the wider economies of Canada and the United States. Moreover, most scholars now recognize that values alone do not account for the conditions and histories of American Indian economic activity. As the abundance of recent writing on Indian involvement in the capitalist economy (e.g., Boxberger, 1989; Carter, 1990; Littlefield and Knack, 1996; Iverson, 1997; Lewis, 1997) documents, many people succeeded at wage work and small business before and during the reservation era. When these efforts failed, the failures derived from factors that were both more complex and inclusive than the press of traditional cultural values alone.

Imperialism, Injustice, and Inequality

Studies devoted to labor and exchange in American Indian economies reached a peak in the 1970s. At the same time, the profile of scholars doing research on economic subjects became more diversified. The result was an era of vibrant interdisciplinary exchange, in which new bodies of scholarship were separated by the "colors" of prevailing theoretical paradigms rather than the disciplinary backgrounds of their authors. Also, whether researchers followed a formalist (neoclassical), substantivist (institutional), or materialist (Marxist) paradigm, the general lines of inquiry were much the same. In the 1970s, the central questions being addressed related to how American Indian economies became dependent on mercantile or industrial capital, and how this dependency contributed to their growing impoverishment and marginalization. The scholarship from this era gave rise to a rich literature that found its greatest expression in research on the fur and hide trades and in the area of policy and development.

The history of the fur trade was a central point of synergy in the 1970s. For discussions of the fur trade literature, see the stunning critical review by Jacqueline Peterson and Gary Anfinson in Swagerty (1984) and the regional surveys by Eccles, Gibson, Ray, and Swagerty in Washburn (1988). It is hardly necessary to retravel roads that have been mapped so well, except to highlight a few of the more important issues. Among other contributions, the new fur trade studies provided evidence of the complex impacts that mercantile capitalism had on divisions of labor in native communities. Some writings (Ray, 1974; Sprenger, 1988) documented how mercantile commerce contributed to the emergence of complex productive specializations among native populations who provisioned the trade with food versus those who supplied it with furs. Other studies (e.g., Bishop, 1974; Knight, 1978; Krech, 1984; Cox and Klein in Moore, 1993) revealed some of the economic differences separating a proletarianized native labor force from one engaged in petty commodity production. In general, the modern fur trade literature not only provided a fuller appreciation of the complexities of American Indian divisions of labor within the context of mercantile commerce, but also offered a deeper assessment of its impact on the capital accumulation of the fur trade companies (Ray and Freeman, 1978; Ray, 1990; Moore in Littlefield and Knack, 1996).

Beyond the fur trade, scholars also began to look more seriously at American Indian work in other contexts, including the labor systems of the Spanish in the

Southwest and California (Hurtado, 1988; Heizer, Schroeder, and Stewart in Washburn, 1988). The new scholarship is dispelling the notion that tribes were embedded exclusively in subsistence economies, presenting compelling evidence of the complex ways in which American Indians engaged in labor that both sustained their own communities and provisioned foreigners in their midst. This evidence is especially obvious for the eastern United States where local Indian populations entered into a variety of working relations with settlers in colonial times (Kawashima, Wood, Usner in Washburn, 1988; O'Brien, 1997). Although much of their labor represented a form of petty commodity production, some of it can be classified with slavery and with various types of bonded and wage labor.

While scholars of the fur trade were providing more detailed readings of economic activity in localized settings, a countervailing movement sought to understand tribal economies in the context of wider regional, continental, and even global arenas of commerce. Even studies of specific groups endeavored to demonstrate how local actions were a product of articulations within wider and more encompassing economic formations, especially those operating under mercantile and industrial capital. Arthur Ray's geographic study (1974) of the Canadian fur trade was pathbreaking in this regard, as was Bruce Trigger's (1976) monumental study of the Huron. A decade later, Richard White's historical case studies (1983) of Choctaw, Pawnee, and Navajo represented a significant effort to understand the transformative impact of such articulations and the dependencies these created for specific tribal nations. Last but not least, Eric Wolf's (1982) important comparative study examined historic articulations between capitalism and indigenous modes of production not only in North America but throughout the non-European world.

These and many other works (e.g., Peterson and Brown, 1985; White, 1991) demonstrate that American Indian labor was interwoven into social, political, and economic networks that extended well beyond local tribal boundaries. They show how the threads of one group's making radiated out and became tied to others in regional, even global, tapestries. In the process, the designs of these wider tapestries returned and altered both the position and the course of more localized efforts. As various writings (e.g., Wishart, 1979; Milloy, 1988; Swagerty in Washburn, 1988) have demonstrated, the vast transcontinental trade that linked tribes throughout the historic Plains and Intermountain regions of the West exerted a critical force on production and distribution at the local level.

The growing recognition that tribes throughout North America were engaged in widespread trade also raises the possibility that there were regional, transethnic cultural practices that encompassed yet transcended local tribal constructs. In other words, different groups shared rules of conduct and institutions of commerce. Such shared rules have been documented in studies of the fur trade that show how native terms of kinship and their associated reciprocities helped fashion the conduct of their trade with Europeans (Van Kirk, 1980; B. White, 1982; Peterson and Brown, 1985; R. White, 1991; Albers in Moore, 1993; Dean, 1995). Although embellished by local practices, European and intertribal trade often operated at a level of discourse that enabled communication and action among culturally diverse communities. Indeed, it is difficult to comprehend how native peoples and their goods moved across the North American landscape with such fluidity and resiliency in historic times without understanding the interethnically constituted terms of such communication.

The fur trade literature of the 1970s and 1980s also sparked contentious debates (Ray and Freeman, 1978; Peterson and Anfinson in Swagerty, 1984) around questions regarding the motivations that led American Indians to become involved in and dependent on the trade. Central to this discord, as well as to theoretical polarizations in environmental history (White in Swagerty, 1984; White and Cronon in Washburn, 1988), was the question of whether American Indian economic conduct was governed by any notion of maximization. Although some neoclassical economists and evolutionary ecologists continue to explain American Indian labor and exchange through an essentialist discourse, most historians and ethnographers of the fur trade have weighed in against this mode of interpretation. The debates over the economic "rationality" of American Indian conduct in indigenous and fur trade contexts are not likely to be resolved until there are more refined analyses of the linguistic and cultural constructs within which the fur trade and native economic activity more generally were situated. What is needed are more studies like Adrian Tanner's (1979) masterful work on the Mistassini Cree that give concrete evidence of the cultural understandings that motivated and framed hunting, trapping, and economic activity in general.

As the study of American Indian labor and exchange in pre-reservation histories was being placed in the context of regional and world systems of appropriation and commerce, so understandings of treaty-making and government policy were being cast in the light of larger political economic forces and formations. Many studies in the 1970s were concerned with the widespread poverty and economic marginalization of reservation communities and the conditions that created these. But as David Wilkins' fine review essay (1993) points out, Joseph Jorgenson (1971) was the first to introduce dependency theory as an explanatory framework for understanding this "underdevelopment." Jorgenson's (1972, 1978) and other studies (e.g., Clemmer, 1977; Anders, 1980; Cornell, 1988; Biolsi, 1992) established how capitalist formations absorbed American Indian economies into relations of unequal exchange. The focus of this research was the macro-conditions by which native lands and resources were expropriated and exploited, leaving native populations without a means of production to support themselves independently, either inside or outside capitalism's avaricious grasp. Some studies pushed their analyses even further by showing how the appropriation of native resources placed American Indian communities in the position of "internal colonies" (Anders, 1979; Jacobson, 1984; Snipp, 1986; Hall, 1988).

Much of the early dependency literature, however, largely avoided the question of American Indian labor, except to address its marginalization and the high levels of unemployment in Indian country. A few writers (Jacobson, 1984; Snipp, 1986) even assert that the primary source of exploitation for American Indians is land rather than labor. Given recent histories of American Indian participation in the labor force (Knight, 1978; Moore, 1989; Littlefield and Knack, 1996), it is hard to justify this claim. Indeed, land and labor are inextricably connected to one another, for land comes into human consciousness through the labor applied to it. And the uses of land and the conditions of its "ownership" frame the limits and possibilities within which a community's labor power gets realized, exploited, and often marginalized in local, regional, and global markets.

Generally speaking, dependency literature operates at levels of abstraction where individual actors are hidden by the workings of larger systems. As a result, American Indians appear as pawns to forces and formations outside their control, and indeed a serious criticism leveled at this type of theorization is that it denies American Indian people agency. But while it may be true that some of the dependency literature of the 1970s and 1980s paid insufficient heed to pre-existing native cultural constructs and social formations, it introduced perspectives that required scholars to come to grips with the impact of global forces on native communities (Dirlik, 1999).

Indeed, it is hard to make sense of the constraints and opportunities under which American Indian tribes exert cultural agency in modern-day economic enterprises unless we understand how tribes are also shaped by wider national and global conditions. Studies of American Indian gaming and manufacturing must confront the complex and ever-shifting political and economic grounds on which tribes wage their rights to build sovereign enterprises (Cornell and Kalt, 1998; Jorgenson, 1998). The motivations of tribal agencies alone do not offer sufficient explanation, but they cannot be ignored either. Much of the more recent research (e.g., Huff, 1986; Hall, 1988; Anders, 1990; Cornell and Kalt, 1992; Champagne, 1992; Cornell et al., 1998) suggests that while American Indian industries are squarely situated in a capitalist marketplace, operate within a capitalist mode of production, and are governed by the forces of capital accumulation, local tribal values and agencies create unique economic accommodations and outcomes. The recent success of tribally and individually owned American Indian businesses raises a number of questions about the interplay between local agencies and wider conditions of production. However the questions get defined, their answers will require approaches radically different from the so-called "primitive" economic models of the past, approaches that draw instead on macro- and micro-economic theories that render intelligible the historical embeddedness of tribal economies in the capitalist markets of the United States and Canada.

Paralleling and often intersecting the studies on the fur trade and on post-reservation economic development was a growing body of research on gender. Initially, this literature was preoccupied with understanding how economic conditions, including the division of labor and the ownership of property, served as measures of female status in indigenous settings (Brown, 1970; Leacock, 1981). One of the most significant results of this research was the recognition that American Indian women played a much more significant role in the productive and distributive activities of their communities than previously reported (Albers and Medicine, 1983; Klein and Ackerman, 1995). Another important outcome was the realization that colonization had varied consequences for women and their economic activity, consequences that differed not only from one group to another but even within the same group at different points in its history (Rothenberg, 1980; Albers, 1985). More recent studies of gender in American Indian communities have shifted their emphasis away from

the material conditions under which women secure a livelihood and achieve standing in their communities, and toward the cultural constructs and agencies that shape
women's economic, social, and political conduct (Shoemaker, 1995; O'Brien, 1997;
Perdue, 1998). This shift follows the more general theoretical and interpretive
trends in the disciplines that study labor and exchange in American Indian history.

Agency, Resistance, and Assimilation

Toward the end of the twentieth century, many researchers turned away from studies that focus primarily on global sites of economic appropriation. Starting in the
1980s, they paid more attention to the ways in which tribes and their individual
members resist and/or accommodate themselves to the economic forces of imperialism and colonialism. Some of the recent work on federal boarding schools, for
instance, shows how these institutions operated as contractors for local labor markets, and how they socialized American Indian children for particular kinds of
menial employment (e.g., Littlefield in Moore, 1993; Child, 1998). Yet, these same
studies also show how the students and their families resisted this employment and
its associated messages. Generally speaking, more press is now given to the cultural
agencies by which the mercantile, industrial, and computer-age markets of capitalism
are engaged to meet American Indian interests (Huff, 1986; Biolsi in Moore, 1993;
Hosmer, 1999).

Some of the newer literature on American Indian economies and economic activity
follows variants of modernization theory which place greater emphasis on values as a
way of explaining the character of American Indian economic participation and performance. But unlike earlier works, these studies do not assume that assimilation is
an inevitable outcome. However, some of this writing (Trosper, 1999) needs to go
beyond the oft-stated litanies of American Indian value-orientation, frequently
described in such abstract and vague terms that they have little connection to any
concrete act. For cultural constructs to be something more than vacuous abstractions, they need to be grounded in solid research and interpreted through the voices
of those who actually work and trade. Although some may consider this assertion
excessively relativistic, it is safe to say that we cannot discuss historic or modern
American Indian economic activity in English or any other language unless we can
be sure we are talking about the same thing from an Ojibwa, Hupa, or Muscogee
perspective. Without specific linguistic and cultural referents to guide our interpretation, it is easy to get trapped by the kinds of misplaced categories and assumptions
that dominate mainstream economic thinking, especially its neoclassical varieties.

Scholarship that examines labor, exchange, and economic activity in general has
recently fallen out of favor. It is probably fair to say, however, that economic issues
are not being abandoned entirely but simply turned on their head. The thrust of
current economic interest lies in the arena of consumption, rather than distribution
and production, where emphasis is placed on understanding how cultural desire,
agency, and taste fashion the ways people come to make their material worlds
(Brightman, 1993; DeMallie, 1993; Kan, 1993; B. White, 1994). Scholars have paid

particular attention to the commerce in ideology and information, especially as these have become manifested in the making of leisure and play, resulting in a spate of studies on art, tourism, media representation, and identity formation.

As one example, food is no longer examined simply as a feature of subsistence production but as a symbolic metaphor (Brightman, 1993). Food is loaded with meanings beyond nutrition that account for labor investments that neoclassicists would deem "irrational." The cultural conventions surrounding consumptive acts clearly define, engage, and direct people's labor in specific ways. "I'd walk a mile for a fry bread," a popular bumper sticker in the 1980s, becomes part of a discourse that locates modern American Indian food production in worlds of identity formation. However, to say that certain foods are procured for their ritual and symbolic weight rather than their nutritional value is not to dismiss the fact that their origins and the conditions of their existence and production may reside outside the cultural forces which drive people to consume them. Thomas Vennum's exhaustive study (1988) of Ojibwa wild rice production amply attests to this fact, as does recent research (Hayden, 1992) on traditional Stl'átl'imix resource use. The two are related, and as Sidney Mintz (1996) has argued so eloquently in his various writings on food, it is the relationships between agency and condition that give clarity and power to our interpretations and explanations.

Today, it may appear we are shifting from a world where value is no longer analyzed in terms of labor effort and productivity and where material forces and conditions are irrelevant to our interpretations and explanations. But the fact remains that behind the information commerce of the modern era are people who labor and people who control labor and exchange through differential access to the means of production, whether the latter is constituted in acres of land, genetically modified seeds, or megabytes of information. We are entering a new era where the forces of production have been radically transformed by computers, the internet, and new information technologies, and with this will come different relations of production. The manufacturing of, and commerce in, information remains to this day dependent on human labor. To deny this simple fact only obfuscates our understanding of the workings of systems under which large segments of humanity, including those of American Indian ancestry, still remain economically marginalized, impoverished, and without access to any means of participating in today's global systems of production and distribution. And it also limits our ability to fully understand the situations where tribes have been able to successfully enter and compete in modern markets and the grounds on which they have built some semblance of economic sovereignty.

Conclusion

In this chapter, I have endeavored to trace the directions of scholarship on labor and exchange in American Indian history over the past century. Admittedly, this review has been painted with very broad strokes that do not give adequate coverage to the rich and varied texture of existing literatures on the subject. It has focused on a few of the issues which not only have defined this area of inquiry over the past century but which will likely influence it in the future as well. Whether they frame their historical studies of labor and exchange in terms of constructs and agencies or conditions and causes, scholars in coming years will need to find a middle ground – a space where they can interpret the cultural agencies behind peoples' economic activity while explaining the conditions in which these agencies become engaged.

BIBLIOGRAPHY

Albers, Patricia 1985: "Autonomy and Dependency in the Lives of Dakota Women: A Study in Historical Change," *Review of Radical Political Economics* 17(3): 109–34.

Albers, Patricia and William James 1991: "Horses Without People: A Critique of Neoclassical Ecology," in R. K. Kanth and E. K. Hunt (eds.), *Explorations in Political Economy: Essays in Criticism* (Savage, MD: Rowman and Littlefield Publishers), pp. 5–31.

Albers, Patricia and Beatrice Medicine (eds.) 1983: *The Hidden Half: Studies of Plains Indian Women* (Lanham, MD: University Press of America).

Anders, Gary 1979: "The Internal Colonization of Cherokee Native Americans," *Development and Change* 10(1): 41–55.

Anders, Gary 1980: "Theories of Underdevelopment and the American Indian," *Journal of Economic Issues* 14(3): 681–701.

Anders, Gary 1990: "Indians, Energy and Economic Development." *Journal of Contemporary Business* 9: 57–74.

Barnett, Homer 1938: "The Nature of the Potlatch," *American Anthropologist* 40(3): 349–58.

Biolsi, Thomas 1992: *Organizing the Lakota: The Political Economy of the New Deal on the Pine Ridge and Rosebud Reservations* (Tucson: University of Arizona Press).

Bishop, Charles A. 1974: *The Northern Ojibwa and the Fur Trade: A Historical and Ecological Analysis* (Toronto: Holt, Rinehart and Winston of Canada).

Blackhawk, Ned 1997: "Julian Steward and the Politics of Representation: A Critique of Anthropologist Julian Steward's Ethnographic Portrayals of the American Indians of the Great Basin," *American Indian Culture and Research Journal* 21(2): 61–82.

Boxberger, Daniel 1989: *To Fish in Common: The Ethnohistory of Lummi Indian Salmon Fishing* (Lincoln: University of Nebraska Press).

Brightman, Robert 1993: *Grateful Prey: Rock Cree Human–Animal Relationships* (Berkeley: University of California Press).

Brown, Judith K. 1970: "Economic Organization and the Position of Women among the Iroquois," *Ethnohistory* 17: 151–67.

Carter, Sarah 1990: *Lost Harvest: Prairie Indians and Reserve Farming* (Montreal: McGill-Queen's University Press).

Champagne, Duane 1992: "Economic Culture, Institutional Order, and Sustained Market Enterprise: Comparisons of Historical and Contemporary American Indian Cases," in T. Anderson (ed.), *Property Rights and Indian Economies* (Lanham, MD: Rowman and Littlefield), pp. 195–213.

Child, Brenda 1998: *Boarding School Seasons. American Indian Families, 1900–1940* (Lincoln: University of Nebraska Press).

Chute, Janet E. 1998: "Shingwaukonse: A Nineteenth-Century Innovative Ojibwa Leader," *Ethnohistory* 45(1): 65–101.

Clemmer, Richard 1977: "Hopi Political Economy: Industrialization and Alienation," *Southwest Economy and Society* 2(2): 4–33.

Cornell, Stephen 1988: *The Return of the Native: American Indian Political Resurgence* (New York: Oxford University Press).

Cornell, Stephen et al. 1998: *American Indian Gaming Policy and Its Socio-Economic Effects: A Report to the National Gambling Impact Study Commission* (Cambridge, MA: The Economics Resource Group).

Cornell, Stephen and Joseph Kalt (eds.) 1992: *What Can Tribes Do? Strategies and Institutions in American Indian Economic Development* (Los Angeles: University of California American Indian Studies Center).

Cornell, Stephen and Joseph Kalt 1998: "Sovereignty and Nation-Building: The Development Challenge in Indian Country Today," *American Indian Culture and Research Journal* 22(3): 187–214.

Dean, Jonathan 1995: "'Uses of the Past' on the Northwest Coast: The Russian American Company and Tlingit Nobility, 1825–1867," *Ethnohistory* 42(2): 265–302.

DeMallie, Raymond 1993: "'These Have No Ears': Narrative and the Ethnohistorical Method," *Ethnohistory* 40(4): 515–38.

Dirlik, Arif 1999: "The Past as Legacy and Project: Postcolonial Criticism in the Perspective of Indigenous Historicism," in T. R. Johnson (ed.), *Contemporary Native American Political Issues* (Walnut Creek, CA: AltaMira Press), pp. 73–98.

Drucker, Philip and Robert F. Heizer 1967: *To Make My Name Good: A Reexamination of the Southern Kwakiutl Potlatch* (Berkeley: University of California Press).

Eggan, Fred 1966: *The American Indian: Perspectives for the Study of Social Change* (Chicago: Aldine).

Ewers, John 1955: *The Horse in Blackfoot Indian Culture: With Comparative Material from Other Western Tribes*. Bureau of American Ethnology, Bulletin 159 (Washington, D.C.: Smithsonian Institution Press).

Gilbreath, Kent 1973: *Red Capitalism: An Analysis of the Navajo Economy* (Norman: University of Oklahoma Press).

Hall, Thomas D. 1988: "The Patterns of Native American Incorporation," in C. M. Snipp (ed.), *Public Policy Impacts on American Indian Economic Development* (Albuquerque: Native American Studies, Institute for Native American Development), University of New Mexico Development Series, 4: 23–38.

Hayden, Brian (ed.) 1992: *A Complex Culture of the British Columbia Plateau: Traditional Stl'átl'imix Resource Use* (Vancouver: University of British Columbia Press).

Hickerson, Harold 1960: "The Feast of the Dead among Seventeenth Century Algonkian of the Upper Great Lakes," *American Anthropologist* 62: 81–107.

Hickerson, Harold 1971: *The Chippewa and Their Neighbors: A Study in Ethnohistory* (New York: Holt, Rinehart and Winston).

Hoebel, E. Adamson 1960: *The Cheyennes: Indians of the Great Plains* (New York: Holt, Rinehart and Winston).

Hosmer, Brian 1999: *American Indians in the Marketplace: Persistence and Innovation among the Menominees and Metlakatlans, 1870–1920* (Lawrence: University Press of Kansas).

Huff, Delores 1986: "The Tribal Ethic: The Protestant Ethic and American Indian Economic Development," in Jennie R. Joe (ed.), *American Indian Policy and Cultural Values: Conflict and Accommodation* (Los Angeles: American Indian Studies Center), pp. 75–89.

Hurtado, Albert 1988: *Indian Survival on the California Frontier* (New Haven: Yale University Press).

Iverson, Peter 1997: *When Indians Became Cowboys: Native Peoples and Cattle Ranching in the American West* (Norman: University of Oklahoma Press).

Jablow, Joseph 1951: *The Cheyenne in Plains Indian Trade Relations, 1795–1840*. Monographs of the American Ethnological Society, 19 (Seattle: University of Washington Press).

Jacobson, Cardell K. 1984: "Internal Colonialism and Native Americans: Indian Labor in the United States from 1871 to World War II," *Social Science Quarterly* 65(1): 158–71.

Jorgenson, Joseph 1971: "Indians and the Metropolis," in J. O. Waddell and O. M. Watson (eds.), *The American Indian in Urban Society* (Boston: Little, Brown and Co.), pp. 67–113.

Jorgenson, Joseph 1972: *The Sun Dance Religion: Power for the Powerless* (Chicago: University of Chicago Press).

Jorgenson, Joseph 1978: "A Century of Political Economic Effects on American Indian Economy, 1880–1980," *Journal of Ethnic Studies* 6(3): 1–82.

Jorgenson, Joseph 1998: "Gaming and Recent American Indian Economic Development," *American Indian Culture and Research Journal* 22(3): 157–72.

Kan, Sergei 1993: *Symbolic Immortality: The Tlingit Potlatch of the Nineteenth Century* (Washington, D.C.: Smithsonian Institution Press).

Klein, Alan 1980: "Plains Economic Analysis: The Marxist Complement," in W. R. Wood and M. Liberty (eds.), *Anthropology on the Great Plains* (Lincoln: University of Nebraska Press), pp. 129–40.

Klein, Laura and Lillian Ackerman (eds.) 1995: *Women and Power in Native North America* (Norman: University of Oklahoma Press).

Knight, Rolf 1978: *Indians at Work: An Informal History of Native American Labour in British Columbia, 1858–1930* (Vancouver: New Star Books).

Krech, Shepard III 1984: *The Subarctic Fur Trade: Native and Social Adaptations* (Vancouver: University of British Columbia Press).

Leacock, Eleanor 1954: *The Montagnais "Hunting Territory" and the Fur Trade*. Memoirs of the American Anthropological Association, 78 Mensaha, WI: American Anthropological Association).

Leacock, Eleanor 1981: *Myths of Male Dominance* (New York: Monthly Review Press).

Lewis, David Rich 1997: *Neither Wolf Nor Dog: American Indians, Environment, and Agrarian Change* (New York: Oxford University Press).

Lewis, Oscar 1942: *The Effects of White Contact upon Blackfoot Culture*. Monographs of the American Ethnological Society, 6 (Seattle: University of Washington Press).

Littlefield, Alice and Martha C. Knack (eds.) 1996: *Native Americans and Wage Labor: Ethnohistorical Perspectives* (Norman: University of Oklahoma Press).

Lurie, Nancy 1961: *Mountain Wolf Woman: The Autobiography of a Winnebago Indian* (Ann Arbor: University of Michigan Press).

Mead, Margaret (ed.) 1937: *Cooperation and Competition among Primitive Peoples* (New York: McGraw-Hill; rev. edn., Boston: Beacon Press, 1961).

Milloy, John S. 1988: *The Plains Cree: Trade Diplomacy and War, 1790 to 1870* (Winnipeg: University of Manitoba Press).

Mintz, Sidney 1996: *Tasting Food, Tasting Freedom: Excursions into Eating, Culture and the Past* (New York: Beacon Press).

Moore, John H. 1974: "Cheyenne Political History, 1829–1894," *Ethnohistory* 2: 329–59.

Moore, John H. 1989: "The Myth of the Lazy Indian: Native American Contributions to the U.S. Economy," *Nature, Society, and Thought* 2(2): 195–215.

Moore, John H. (ed.) 1993: *The Political Economy of North American Indians* (Norman: University of Oklahoma Press).

O'Brien, Jean M. 1997: "Divorced from the Land: Accommodation Strategies of Indian Women in 18th Century New England," in M. J. Maynes et al. (eds.), *Gender, Kinship, and Power* (New York: Routledge).

Peers, Laura 1994: *The Ojibwa of Western Canada: 1780–1870* (St. Paul: Minnesota Historical Society Press).

Perdue, Theda 1998: *Cherokee Women: Gender and Culture Change, 1700–1835* (Lincoln: University of Nebraska Press).

Peterson, Jacqueline and Jennifer S. H. Brown (eds.) 1985: *The New Peoples: Being and Becoming Métis in North America* (Lincoln: University of Nebraska Press).

Ray, Arthur J. 1974: *Indians in the Fur Trade: Their Role as Trappers, Hunters, and Middlemen in the Lands Southwest of Hudson's Bay, 1660–1780* (Toronto: University of Toronto Press).

Ray, Arthur J. 1990: *The Canadian Fur Trade in the Industrial Age* (Toronto: University of Toronto Press).

Ray, Arthur J. and Donald Freeman 1978: *Give Us Good Measure: An Economic Analysis of Relations Between Indians and the Hudson's Bay Company before 1763* (Toronto: University of Toronto Press).

Rosman, Abraham and Paula Rubel 1971: *Feasting with Mine Enemy: Rank and Exchange among Northwest Coast Societies* (New York: Columbia University Press).

Rothenberg, Diane 1980: "The Mothers of the Nation: Seneca Resistance to Quaker Intervention," in M. Etienne and E. Leacock (eds.), *Women and Colonization: Anthropological Perspectives* (New York: Praeger), pp. 63–87.

Shoemaker, Nancy (ed.) 1995: *Negotiators of Change: Historical Perspectives on Native American Women* (New York: Routledge).

Simmons, Leo (ed.) 1942: *Sun Chief: The Autobiography of a Hopi Indian* (New Haven: Yale University Press).

Snipp, C. Matthew 1986: "The Changing Political and Economic Status of American Indians: From Captive Nations to Internal Colonies," *American Journal of Economics and Sociology* 45: 457–74.

Spradley, James P. (ed.) 1969: *Guests Never Leave Hungry: The Autobiography of James Sewid, A Kwakiutl Indian* (New Haven: Yale University Press).

Sprenger, Herman 1988: "The Métis Nation: Buffalo Hunting versus Agriculture in the Red River Settlement, 1810–1870," in B. Cox (ed.), *Native Peoples, Native Lands* (Ottawa: Carlton University Press), pp. 120–35.

Steward, Julian 1938: *Basin-Plateau Aboriginal Sociopolitical Groups.* Bureau of American Ethnology, Bulletin 120 (Washington, D.C.: Smithsonian Institution Press).

Steward, Julian 1955: *Theory of Culture Change* (Urbana: University of Illinois Press).

Swagerty, William R. (ed.) 1984: *Scholars and the Indian Experience: Critical Reviews of Recent Writings in the Social Sciences* (Bloomington: Indiana University Press).

Tanner, Adrian 1979: *Bringing Home the Animals: Religious Ideology and Mode of Production of the Mistassini Cree Hunters* (New York: St. Martin's Press).

Thompson, Laura and Alice Joseph 1944: *The Hopi Way* (Chicago: University of Chicago Press).

Trigger, Bruce 1976: *The Children of Aataentsic: A History of the Huron People to 1660*, 2 vols. (Montreal: McGill-Queen's University Press).

Trosper, Ronald 1999: "Traditional American Indian Economic Policy," in T. R. Johnson (ed.), *Contemporary Native American Political Issues* (Walnut Creek, CA: AltaMira Press), pp. 139–62.

Underhill, Ruth 1936: *The Autobiography of a Papago Woman*. Memoirs of the American Anthropological Association, 46 (Menasha, WI: American Anthropological Association).

Van Kirk, Sylvia 1980: *Many Tender Ties: Women in Fur Trade Society, 1670–1870* (Winnipeg: Watson and Dwyer).

Vennum, Thomas, Jr. 1988: *Wild Rice and the Ojibway People* (St. Paul: Minnesota Historical Society Press).

Washburn, Wilcomb E. (ed.) 1988: *Handbook of North American Indians*, vol. 4: *History of Indian–White Relations* (Washington, D.C.: Smithsonian Institution Press).

White, Bruce 1982: "'Give Us a Little Milk': The Social and Cultural Meanings of Gift Giving in the Lake Superior Fur Trade," *Minnesota History* 48: 2–12.

White, Bruce 1994: "Encounters with Spirits: Ojibwa and Dakota Theories about the French and Their Merchandise," *Ethnohistory* 41(3): 369–406.

White, Richard 1983: *The Roots of Dependency: Subsistence, Environment, and Social Change among the Choctaws, Pawnees, and Navajos* (Lincoln: University of Nebraska Press).

White, Richard 1991: *The Middle Ground: Indians, Empires, and Republics in the Great Lakes Region, 1650–1815* (New York: Cambridge University Press).

Wilkins, David E. 1993: "Modernization, Colonialism, Dependency: How Appropriate Are These Models for Providing an Explanation of North American Indian 'Underdevelopment'?" *Ethnic and Racial Studies* 16(3): 390–419.

Wilson, Gilbert L. 1917: *Agriculture of the Hidatsa Indians: An Indian Interpretation* (Minneapolis: Bulletin of the University of Minnesota, Studies in the Social Sciences 9).

Wilson, Gilbert L. 1971: "Waheenee: An Indian Girl's Story Told by Herself to Gilbert L. Wilson," *North Dakota History* 38(1–2): 2–187.

Wishart, David J. 1979: *The Fur Trade of the American West: 1807–1840: A Geographical Synthesis* (Lincoln: University of Nebraska Press).

Wolf, Eric. R. 1982: *Europe and the People without History* (Berkeley: University of California Press).

16

The Nature of Conquest: Indians, Americans, and Environmental History

Louis S. Warren

To judge from popular culture, the connection between Indians and nature needs no explaining. The notion that Indians were "in harmony with nature," that they were "the first conservationists," or "the first environmentalists," endures, indeed flourishes. Among the more recent examples of this treatment is the Disney film *Pocahontas.* Ensuring that we in the audience do not overlook the close bond between Indians and nature, one scene features Pocahontas cuddling bear cubs and pet racoons as she croons to John Smith, "Can you sing with all the voices of the mountains? Can you paint with all the colors of the wind?" The grasping, materialist Smith cannot do these things, of course, although he is big-hearted enough to give it a try. As the film ends, Smith makes peace between Indians and colonists before sailing away. But, those of us in the audience who are older than about six know that eventually Smith's compatriots will take the land Pocahontas is so attached to. A happy Disney film, to be sure, but a fable not without its darkness for anyone who knows what happened after the credits.

In reinforcing popular notions that Indians were "more environmental" than their conquerors, the film – like much of popular culture – suggests that dispossessing the Indians was the first step colonists made on their quick and dirty journey to despoiling the American earth. This notion hinges on a much older one – older in fact than the United States – that Indians were once "people of nature," that they did not work but lived off nature's bounty, as noble, natural savages. In the myth perpetuated in "Pocahontas" and a thousand other places, conquering Indians becomes equivalent to reducing nature itself.

Environmental historians might appear to be following this old tradition, but in fact the principal contribution of the field has been to challenge many of the more romantic ideas that swirl around stories of Indians, nature, and conquest. Indeed, there is little of historical value in the perception that Indians were primitive environmentalists who lived without changing nature. It can be a deceptively malevolent ideology, for it carries on another tradition of seeing Indians as people without history, which is to say their status as people becomes highly questionable. It renders Indian history before the time of Europeans a static, edenic story, in which there is no change, no drama, and no human experience. It implies that Indians had no history before their encounter with white people.

By exploring how Indian people have perceived the earth, how they shaped and changed its natural systems, and how those changes in nature required changes in economy and culture, environmental history undermines the simpler myths of Indians as "nature's children." While demonstrating Indian power, innovation, and ingenuity, it also sheds new light on Indian conquest and its ambiguities. At the same time, as we shall see, exploring the nature of conquest and its aftermath in this way is not without problematic implications for Indian politics today.

Indian Environments

Perhaps no conclusion of environmental scholarship so challenges the myth of Indians as "first environmentalists" living in a pristine Eden as this one: from their earliest days in the Americas, long before Europeans arrived, Indians inscribed into the land markers of their respective cultures and history, profoundly shaping the natural environment.

Indian lifeways were never determined by the environment so much as selected from a range of options within it. From the combined farming, hunting, and gathering regimes of the Naragansetts and Wampanoags in the eastern forests, to the less diversified hunting and gathering economies of the Abenaki and Cree further north, from the adobe villages of agrarian Hopis and Zunis in the Southwest to the huge wooden dwellings of the Kwakiutl, Haida, and Tlingit along the salmon streams and whaling grounds of the Pacific Northwest, Indian activities changed American natural systems. Some had more obvious impacts than others, but collectively, Indians created extensive networks of trails, roads, and causeways, huge ceremonial mounds, terraced fields, irrigation systems, and settlements with populations in the thousands, sometimes tens of thousands.

As is the case everywhere in the world, nature and people in pre-contact America shaped each other. Patterns of use altered animal and plant distribution. Ancestral Indians may have played a role in the extinctions of mastodons, camels, and other animals in the late pleistocene. Later, hunting pressure suppressed game species in core hunting areas, with the animals being most numerous in "buffer zones" between enemy tribes because hunters avoided these regions for fear of bringing on war. Many prized species of plants grew near village sites and along trails because Indians planted, transplanted, and protected them there (Hickerson, 1965; Denevan, 1992: 374; West, 1995; Martin and Szuter, 1999; Martin and Klein, 1984).

Even more pervasively, from one end of the Americas to the other, Indians shaped the land through intentional burning of forests and grasslands. Burning replenished the soil with essential nutrients and speeded up the rate at which they were recycled. It allowed sunlight to fall on the soil, thereby encouraging vigorous new growth. This practice was ideal for a new planting of maize, beans, and squash – crops which

Indians developed from wild stock in the millennia before Columbus landed – but burning could facilitate Indian prosperity in other ways, even for those who did not farm. Grasses, shrubs, and non-woody plants would grow thick and fast on a burned-over area, providing food for elk, deer, beaver, and other animals. The Midwestern prairies probably reflected this kind of "fire management," which prevented re-forestation on their eastern perimeter. In many parts of the Americas, long years of Indian firing of the land resulted in a patchwork of plant and forest stands in varying stages of ecological development. Clearly, Indian America was no "virgin land." Many forests in the pre-contact Americas, from the Amazon to the Northern Rockies, developed through a fertile mixing of natural and cultural systems (Pyne, 1982: 71–83; Cronon, 1983: 19–33, 51; Denevan, 1992: 375).

If the New World was in fact an old world shaped by generations of Indian residents, then clearly it was not a wilderness. But what was it? The answers remain problematic. Some have recently described the landscapes of Indian America as gardens. Even non-horticultural peoples, in the words of one scholar, were "domesticators," living in "a garden of human artifice," for "in a number of important respects all had domesticated portions of their habitat in order to induce greater subsistence" (Preston, 1998: 264–5; see also Blackburn and Anderson, 1993: 18; Anderson, Barbour, and Whitworth, 1998: 14).

The idea of Indian settlement as a series of domestications is potentially helpful. It suggests how much Indians saw American landscapes as intimate homelands, even when they looked like stark wilderness to Europeans. But to what extent can European terms describe Indian ideas of nature? Does replacing "wilderness" with "garden" in our texts merely trade older assumptions for new ones (White, 1997)? Indian homelands were internally diverse, often comprising planted fields, hunting grounds, distinctive gathering areas like camas fields or mussel beds, and border areas with neighboring rivals. Can "garden" be a blanket term for all of these places? Was there no place that was more "wild" in the sense that its forests were thicker or its water more scarce, its human or non-human creatures more dangerous? Was the ocean a "garden" for the whaling tribes of the Pacific Northwest?

Definitional shortcomings are compounded by rhetorical problems. In America, a garden is usually a small place, and describing an Indian homeland of a million acres or more as a garden seems forced. More than this, in American popular culture, gardens are strongly gendered spaces, and many of their associations are feminine. To suggest that Indians were pre-eminently gardeners or domesticators may be historically more accurate than the older stereotypes of wilderness hunters, but one wonders how Indians will be "engendered" in the narratives that flow from this careful shift in terms. Will expansionist, white hunters, miners, ranchers, and farmers be seen as more masculine, and therefore destined to overpower the domesticating, taming Indians? In Western culture, the idea of the garden is at least as freighted with meaning – and baggage – as wilderness ever has been.

The inadequacy of modern terms for describing Indian landscapes and regimes of collecting, gathering, and cultivating makes it all the more essential to find ways of describing environmental relations from Indian perspectives. Sources for such a project are hard to come by, and they are complicated by the diversity of Indian peoples in space and time. To assume that any one Indian culture will have the same views about nature as the next, or that later Indian peoples necessarily express the same ideas as their ancestors, can lead to egregious errors. As Richard White has observed, the challenge of such questions will hopefully motivate more scholars to devote more time to Indian languages, and especially to Indian word-lists (White, 1997).

For many, the most obvious place to discover Indian perceptions of nature is in Indian spirituality. But here the seemingly obvious facts are most perilous. Chief Seattle's environmental elegy – now so renowned as to appear on T-shirts, greeting cards, and posters as a call to environmentalism – is almost certainly an invention of later writers. According to Sam Gill, the ostensibly ancient, pan-Indian belief in "Mother Earth" is a twentieth-century invention, created by scholars searching for supposedly "universal" religious ideas and by savvy Indians who for their own reasons cultivated the notion (White, 1997; Kaiser, 1987: 497–537; Gill, 1987).

At a more basic level, even the pervasive, popular connection between Indian beliefs and modern environmental ideas is questionable. Undeniably, many Indian religions in ages past centered – as many do today – on beliefs in powerful spirits residing in the creatures, plants, and geographic features around them. For hunting peoples – and much of the best ethnography on this subject has focused on hunting peoples – animals offered up their bodies after the spirit of the animal received gifts and prayers from the hunter. If the hunter or his family violated sacred rites or taboos associated with the spirit, the creatures would withhold themselves from the hunter and his family could suffer starvation, injury, or death (Nelson, 1983; Tanner, 1979).

As much as these beliefs appear to discourage wastefulness and facilitate a kind of proto-environmentalism, some skepticism is advisable. Robert Brightman argues that Rock Cree belief systems encouraged what outsiders might consider profligacy. According to Brightman, Rock Cree hunters are obligated to take all the bounty offered by the spirits, to kill every animal they can after making the proper offerings. Leaving one fat caribou alive because one has taken "enough" is to refuse a gift from the spirits, sending a message that the hunter no longer needs or wants them. Starvation is the inevitable consequence. Brightman concludes that these beliefs, combined with pervasive faith in the regenerative capacities of animals – once killed, they are re-born instantly somewhere else – militate *against* Western notions of con-servation, at least among the Rock Cree (Brightman, 1993: 281–90; see also Krech, 1994).

Whether Brightman is correct or not, his arguments caution us against seeing Indian spirituality as a kind of environmental functionalism or as tools of "environ-mental management" in the modern sense of the term. To many Indians, animal spir-its retain their powers of independent thought and supernatural action down to the present day. The idea that people could control animal populations through restraint of hunting is hubris, a cardinal sin before the animal spirits, and itself almost certain to bring on their wrath.

Issues of spirituality are enormously complicated, and even traditional aversions to wastefulness need to be contextualized in their respective cultures. Obviously, to explore issues of resource management among Indians in the more remote past is even more difficult, given the problems of sources. In any case, even where sources exist, historians of Indian attitudes toward the environment do well to question all of their own, most basic assumptions about nature and environmentalism before applying them to historical Indian peoples.

Environmental Change in Indian Conquest

If Indians created and maintained an astonishing array and diversity of connections to the natural world, it is safe to say that the coming of the Europeans would touch all of them, and transform most. From 1492 until 1900, biotic changes were so momentous that they can easily dominate environmental narratives of the period. The decline of post-contact Indian populations through pathogens after contact and the subsequent collapse of Indian political economy over large sections of the continent meant radical shifts in Indian lifeways and in many cases limited options for resisting the European incursions that followed. European plants and animals remade the landscape in profound ways. Pigs demolished clam banks, cattle ate deer meadows, and domestic livestock deposited European seeds in their droppings. In the end, older Indian lifeways often became impossible amidst the imported plantains, dandelions, mustard grass, and Russian thistle.

But the nature of conquest was not strictly biological; biology had to be shaped by social action. The dangers of "biological determinism" in history become apparent in the very influential arguments made by Alfred Crosby. In two witty and erudite books, *The Columbian Exchange* (1975) and *Ecological Imperialism* (1986), Crosby argues that Europeans with their plants and animals constituted a kind of environmental package, a "portmanteau biota" (1986: 270). Once opened, the "portmanteau" became a Pandora's Box for Indians. The long-term result was the transforming of America into a "neo-Europe," a region with an environment so similar to Europe that European economies – and therefore peoples – could flourish in it.

This is an argument with many strengths, and with good reason it has become central to the field. There is no denying the enormous environmental transformation that accompanied the conquest and, in many places, preceded it. Isolated for millennia from the pathogens of the Old World, Indians fell in vast multitudes to smallpox, chickenpox, measles, and other European illnesses. Estimates of the devastation vary, and are a subject of some dispute. Most students of the problem suggest that Indians in North America (excluding Mexico) declined between 1492 and 1800 from between 4 and 7 million to somewhere around 1 million (Denevan, 1992: 371; Crosby, 1986: 195–216; Henige, 1998; see also Thornton, this volume). In some places Europeans benefitted directly from this calamity. Exhausted from their trans-Atlantic journey, English Pilgrims in the 1620s moved onto the site of an Indian village destroyed in an epidemic just four years before, and the abandoned fields soon greened with colonists' corn (Cronon, 1983: 90).

But usually it would take many years for Europeans and Africans to fill the ecological niche left by this catastrophe. There were only 16 million people in the Americas as late as 1750, and most of these lived along rivers or on the coast. In the interior, without the constraints of Indian hoes, fires, or trampling feet, resurgent undergrowth overwhelmed old Indian fields, hunting areas, and settlements. Small wonder that when many Americans first encountered this "widowed land," in the nineteenth century, they thought they were seeing "virgin wilderness" (Jennings, 1976; Denevan, 1992: 375).

As profound as these developments were, terms like "neo-Europes" and "portmanteau biota" are of limited use for understanding them. The very idea of "neo-Europes" supports a misconception that the European conquest progressively made the Americas more like Europe, a contention that would often have struck witnesses of the period as bizarre. Examples abound, but a West Coast case study makes the point. Prior to contact, California Indian hunters and gatherers were so numerous as to suppress big game populations, to the point that the animals' relative scarcity made hunting them a marginal activity, superseded in most places by gathering of wild seeds, roots, and fruit (Anderson, Barbour, and Whitworth, 1998: 18; Preston, 1998: 266, 269).

European diseases ravaged California before the Spanish ever settled north of present-day Mexico, with a decline in Indian settlements and a resurgence of large animal populations an almost certain result. When the Spanish arrived to settle in California in 1769, they found a land less "settled" with Indians and more "wild" with big game than the one that had existed only fifty years before. As Indian numbers continued to decline, their fire maintenance of the California landscape receded, and coastal oak forests and chaparral communities thickened and in many places advanced (Preston, 1998: 274). Had any Spanish colonists been aware of these changes, it seems unlikely they would have concluded that their impact at this point had made the region "more like Europe." If anything, the higher animal numbers, the lower human population, and the thick undergrowth made California seem *less* like the cleared and cultivated Old World, and more like a primeval wilderness. The idea that Spanish colonists were somehow "Europeanizing" this landscape makes sense in retrospect from the twentieth century, but it might have inspired a lively debate in 1769.

Where the landscape was transformed by European arrival, concepts of "portmanteau biota" can obscure how that happened. Envisioning organisms loosed on the land like so many demons (or, as some colonists might have thought, angels) risks discounting people's intentions and choices in misleading ways. To be sure, Crosby emphasizes that Europeans and their biota acted as a "team," supporting one another. But uncomfortable questions arise after one reads the litany of environmental eruptions that Europeans could not control, such as epidemics that advanced far ahead of European conquerors, herds of feral mustangs that stretched to the Texas horizon, weeds that choked out Australia's native grasses days or even weeks away from the nearest colonial outpost. We ponder intentions in any historical event – the intent of the perpetrator determines whether the killing was homicide or accident, after all. But do the intentions of historical actors matter in this story? If the ecological shifts that created "neo-Europes" were the result of largely autonomous portmanteau biota like smallpox, weeds, and feral livestock "out-competing" indigenous biota, then the conquest of the Americas begins to look like a result of natural selection. What does it matter if Euro-Americans were aggressive or not? If Europeans had left the Americas after unloading their pathogens, plants, and animals, could Indians have put the biotic genie back in the European bottle? Or would European biota have "conquered" America without the Europeans?

Crosby's is only the most compelling articulation of a biological thesis that necessarily informs much of environmental history, but which can also obscure important aspects of Indian history. Partly, the problem stems from the way environmental historians have borrowed concepts and terminology from evolutionary theory. The tropes of "competition" and "succession," so useful in studying natural systems and their histories, are easily transferred, explicitly or implicitly, to historical narratives about cultures and peoples, with decidedly mixed results.

Specifically, such facile connections between nature and conquest can easily subvert narratives of Euro-American aggression. We cannot accuse Old World germs, plants, or animals of being aggressive. They had staying power, but they did not have malice, or anything else we can construe as intent. And the conquerors themselves are easily folded into their biological context, as when Alfred Crosby writes that the European human was "the dominant member" of the portmanteau biota (Crosby, 1986: 293). In such treatments, the conquest becomes a Darwinian process, in which settler biology, not settler ambition, is the decisive factor.

Crosby himself is almost always more careful than this, and he has in other contexts argued that political and cultural dynamics among Indians shaped the progress of epidemics among them (Crosby, 1976). But there can be little doubt that biotic themes of environmental history can be used to trivialize the very important issue of settler goals and desires. Increasingly, the field seems to be moving toward agreement with scholars such as Noble D. Cook, who writes that military force was a "key factor" in the conquest, but epidemic disease, for the most part accidental, was "even more important" (Cook, 1998: 202). The conquest was coincidental with settler will, but not a product of it. In such narratives, Euro-Americans become the beneficiaries of biology; they are naturally selected to rule, and, in some sense, conquest becomes a natural process.

A closer look at Indian environmental history can reveal the misleading assumptions in such narratives. The reshaping of Indian environments was not just biological, or natural. Horses, pigs, and weeds were not just proliferating organisms. Often, they were tools, even weapons, cultivated, propagated, and reconfigured by colonists and Indians alike.

In many places, Indians used European biota to reshape their economies in their own interests, and in doing so changed both the European organisms and local landscapes. Perhaps the best case study of this pattern is the rise to power of the horse-mounted peoples of the Great Plains. Indian traders and raiders facilitated the spread of horses onto the Great Plains beginning in the late seventeenth century, transmitting the knowledge of horsecraft to allies and observant enemies. The constituents of horse domestication – not only capture of wild animals, but limited selective breeding, healing, training for the race, the hunt, or combat – became valued and pervasive elements of Plains cultures. In a relatively brief time, Indians distinguished themselves as horse catchers, healers, trainers, and gelders (Roe, 1955: 74–7, 258; Dobie, 1954: 43; Ewers, 1955: 57–62; Wyman, 1963: 84).

One product of these cultural developments was a remarkable shift in the nature of horses, insofar as Indian mounts often behaved in ways strikingly different from their European forebears. To charge alongside buffalo and carry a hunter from one animal to the next in the midst of a stampede, changing direction with a nudge from the rider's knees or a shift in his weight to leave his arms free for the bow, all the while evading the defensive thrusts of wounded bison, was something relatively few horses did well. Many, quite sensibly, refused to do it at all. Indian trainers selected horses by their strength and temperament, and taught them the necessary skills with numerous forays into bison herds and ample use of the whip. Their abilities honed, the animals took to the chase with the alacrity of racehorses to the track. When Lewis and Clark were returning from their expedition to the West Coast, the horses they bought from the Shoshones so persistently dashed after buffalo herds that the party sent advance scouts to frighten any bison away from the oncoming pack horses (Ewers, 1955: 153; Dobie, 1954: 38).

Although there is little scholarship on horse breeds in this period, by most accounts Indian domestication and limited selective breeding changed the horses at an even more fundamental level. Indian horses over time became smaller, renowned for their ability to travel vast distances on limited food, and – unlike the horses of the U.S. cavalry, for example – able to secure sustenance even in two feet of snow by pawing down to the grass (Ewers, 1955: 33–4, 42–3; Dobie, 1954: 39, 47–8; Roe, 1955: 135; Sherow, 1992). Hardy "Indian ponies" were much sought after by white traders in the inter-mountain region of the American West by the early nineteenth century, and Nez Perce horse keepers maintained the larger, spotted Appaloosa (Dobie, 1954: 44–5; Roe, 1955: 153; Josephy, 1997: 29). Horses like these would not have existed were it not for Indian handlers. To think of these animals merely as transplanted European biota is to miss the profound mixing of nature and culture they embodied.

Environmental history is most promising when it reveals not just the biotic processes of the past, but how intertwined natural dynamics and people's actions, intentional and unintentional, became. The nexus of horse and people was a complicated mixture of natural conditions and human choice. Great Plains environments were not always suitable for horses. Often, Indians helped make them so, and Indian actions were even essential to the biological success of the horse in some places. Harvesting cottonwood for them during the winter, and burning grasses in the late winter to bring on new growth for horse forage weeks early, Indians reshaped local ecosystems to support horses (Dobie, 1954: 38; Roe, 1955: 248; White, 1983: 185–6; Sherow, 1992). Mandans and Hidatsas provided both bark and hay for their horses, and in the fierce winter kept the most prized animals in special stables inside their earthen lodges (Roe, 1955: 252; Hanson, 1986: 97). In fact, across much of the Plains, especially in the colder north, horse herds would have vanished without Indian caretakers and breeders to maintain them (Ewers, 1955: 53; Dobie, 1954: 58).

In addition to hiding this historical "nature" of the Great Plains, to consider the Great Plains as a "neo-Europe" in the making masks the very un-European cultural changes and politics at work there. Specifically, it encourages a false notion that all environmental changes after contact were bad for all Indians. The post-contact epidemics were most virulent among larger, sedentary gatherings of people. As waves of disease wracked the villages of the Missouri, the once powerful horticulturalists – the Arikaras, Mandans, and Hidatsas – lost populations and power to the growing tribes of horse nomads, especially the Sioux and Cheyenne. Partly because buffalo hunters lived in more dispersed bands and moved regularly, fewer of them fell victim to small-pox, measles, or other deadly pathogens (White, 1978: 328–30).

The new disease environment therefore placed a higher premium on mobility and dispersion than ever before in the lives of the Plains peoples. Nomadic practices were further encouraged by the availability of horses and by the U.S. Cavalry's Indian Wars in the latter nineteenth century, which targeted Indian villages, making them espe-cially vulnerable. American missionaries and government officials would have liked to see the Plains become more like Europe, to see Indians settle in fixed towns and till the soil like Euro-Americans. How ironic, then, that the impact of European organ-isms could do so much to drive Indians away from fixity and farming. If the spread of the horse was supposed to be creating a "neo-Europe," the gathering hegemony of mounted warriors over farmers in this arid grassland during the first three-quarters of the nineteenth century might better have been described as a "neo-Mongolia."

Within tribes, horses created new bonds and drove new wedges between people. Among the Pawnees and Hidatsas, and also among the Cherokees of the Southeast, horses (owned by men) ate the crops women were responsible for tending and there-by contributed mightily to gender conflict (White, 1983: 181; Hanson, 1986: 103; Hatley, 1991: 45). Horse ownership distinguished wealthy from poor Indians in new ways, and among some peoples horse-poor men as a group acquired a reputation for being desperate fighters, anxious for combat and the opportunities it offered to acquire enemy horses (Hanson, 1986: 99; Ewers, 1955: 69, 138, 244).

To describe this complicated history as but an episode in the creation of a "neo-Europe" is to miss its remarkable potential for reminding us how much cultural choice shapes biotic events, and how "biota" like the horse can have radically differ-ent historical meanings and impacts in distinctive cultures. Recent scholarship moves further away from narratives of biological determinism, suggesting the interdepen-dence of environmental, cultural, and political factors in shaping North American ecosystems in the nineteenth century. By the 1800s, Indian and wild horse herds were serious competitors with approximately 30 million bison for range and fresh water. This competition helped force bison numbers downward, particularly when it was combined with Indian hunters' harvest of buffalo cow hides for the robe trade, the expansion of white settlement onto the eastern edge of the Plains, and the probable spread of cattle diseases such as anthrax, bovine tuberculosis, and brucellosis to bison herds. It would take a resurgent drought cycle, a new tanning process converting buf-falo hides to leather, and droves of white hide hunters to deliver the *coup de grâce* to the great bison herds after the American Civil War. But already by 1850, many white observers were noting a decrease in northern and southern Plains buffalo herds, and Indians from the Assiniboines of southern Canada to the Comanches of Texas were eating large numbers of horses to avert starvation (Flores, 1991: 481–3; Flores, 1996; Isenberg, 1999; West, 1995).

The many causes of these environmental changes suggests how persistent we must be in our search for multiple causalities in environmental history. In the story of the bison decline, as with the spread of horses, we must look beyond biological process to explain events. Political forces were paramount. Indians participated in the bison robe trade in no small part to gain guns, both for hunting and to defend old hunting territories from whites and Indians or acquire new ones from Indian enemies (White, 1978). As American conquest lurched nearer, hostilities between whites and Indians and among Indian rivals intensified, thereby increasing demand for guns and driving more Indian men to pursue the robe trade with ever more desperation. To some degree, the near-extinction of the buffalo (a biological event) was underwritten by the willingness of peoples to trade with one another (a cultural practice) which in turn was stimulated by the eagerness of people to kill one another (a profoundly cultural phenomenon).

The new scholarship on bison suggests strong parallels with earlier developments in other parts of Indian America. The fur trade in the first three centuries of contact decimated populations of beaver and other fur bearers over much of North America, and European demand for deer skins helped drive deer sharply downward over much of the Southeast by 1800. In both cases, Indians were the principal hunters and providers of hides to Euro-American agents. Mounted buffalo hunting may have followed a similar pattern, with Indian hunters harming their livelihood as they pursued the market goods of Europeans.

Such developments have long troubled historians. In an argument as intriguing as it was dubious, one scholar maintained that Indians blamed animal spirits for the great plagues of the contact period, and waged vengeful war on the animals as a result (Martin, 1978). More convincing theses focus on the role of the market in creating new demands and new ecological relationships among Indian communities (Cronon, 1983: 82–107; White, 1983: 69–96). In the ground-level view these histories offer of cultures and ecosystems transformed and sometimes destroyed, environmental history of Indian peoples suggests how promising and how devastating – socially and ecologically – the expansion of the European market economy could be. The dispossession of Indians was not just the result of biological dynamics. Indians came to want and need European and American trade goods, and guns became vital for defence of trading territories and hunting grounds. Beaver, marten, and weasel did not approach extinction because of European biota, but more because of choices Indians made in response to European markets.

If the needs of war drove much of the fur and hide trade, settler military power was integral to other environmental changes of the conquest period, too. We must tread carefully here. Tales of smallpox-infected blankets bulk large in popular American renderings of conquest, but while colonists occasionally resorted to germ warfare (during Pontiac's Rebellion, in one of the best documented cases), their understandings of pathogenic transmission were usually too limited and their technology too primitive for these campaigns to be effective (Cook, 1998: 213–15).

In fact, war and settler biota were connected in other, powerful ways, often overlooked. Perhaps no episodes in American history so clearly demonstrate the limitations of a reductive, biotic approach to environmental history as the weaving of settler hostility and settler pastoralism. Colonists often exploited the ability of horses, cattle, sheep, and pigs to transform Indian lands. Already by the seventeenth century, settlers in Pennsylvania and New England were aware that depasturing sheep would obliterate native grasses and spread English seeds, allowing colonists' livestock to advance into the interior, so that their owners could follow not long after (Crosby, 1986: 289; Cronon, 1983: 142–6). Two centuries later, in California, American farmers were still erecting fences to shut out Indian hunters and gatherers, who watched as cattle and sheep ate the wild grass seeds – and hogs the acorns – that Indians needed to survive. As one emigrant commented in 1856, Indians' "spring and summer food … [has] been this season, and will hereafter be, consumed by cattle, horses, and hogs. …" The pervasiveness of such observations suggests that for colonists, depasturing livestock and dispossessing Indians often went hand in hand (Cooke, 1943: 35).

Indian responses to this threat were not uniform, and on more than a few occasions – in colonial New England, among the Cherokee of the South and the Navajo of the Southwest – Indians became pastoralists (Virginia Anderson, 1994: 615–17; Hatley, 1991: 44). But in general Indian adoption of livestock was the exception. Domestic animals too frequently ate plants and seeds needed by Indians, and too often, keeping animals would require radical changes in labor patterns. Hay gathering and lambing, for example, clashed with other tasks most Indian communities performed in the summer and spring, and tending animals in the winter conflicted with itinerant winter hunting practices in many places (Virginia Anderson, 1994: 606; White, 1983).

If the depasturing of livestock could so damage Indian resources, and if Indians could not become pastoralists themselves, then it should hardly be surprising that a prominent Indian tactic in war was to kill livestock in large numbers. In New England, Indians in King Philip's War "began their hostilities with plundering and destroying cattle," according to one witness. Large-scale killings of domestic animals continued throughout the war, and Indian hostility to the animals – and their owners – extended to mutilation and torture of cows in particular (Virginia Anderson, 1994: 622–3).

Such events were not confined to the East. California Indians complained often to Franciscan missionaries in the eighteenth century about the way settler livestock demolished their acorn and chia reserves, and it was not long before Indian raiders began slaughtering the animals (Milliken, 1995: 72–3). Now, had this struggle been one between Indians and imported "biota," as some scholars would put it, Indians would have vanquished the cows, pigs, and sheep, and lived off their meat, even after virgin soil epidemics diminished Indian numbers. The full assemblage of organisms imported from Europe – all the weeds, diseases, and animals Europeans could muster – could not dispossess Indians alone.

The deciding factor, of course, was the will and intent of the colonizers, and their superior numbers and arms. Whites defended their animals with severe military campaigns. Again and again in California, whites sallied to war over pork, milk, and horse-flesh. So many of these bloodthirsty campaigns erupted over livestock it staggers the imagination, and although some of the subsequent stock killings no doubt stemmed from Indian displacement and hunger, there is ample evidence that Indian retribution came to focus on domestic animals as much as it did on the settlers themselves.

In 1858, a California newspaper reported that white men's "outrages" against Indian women occasionally provoked retribution by Indians "shooting the aggressors or killing their stock." In 1860, in Mendocino County, Indians were killing from ten to fifteen head of livestock every night during otherwise one-sided skirmishes with white settlers. Indians often killed hundreds of animals in a single raid, and after whites massacred a large party of Indians at Eureka, one white observer wrote that where Indian men only occasionally had "killed a 'beef' ... before the late grand massacre ... they now kill ten." One white man, renowned among whites and Indians as a brutal slayer of Indian children, faced such enormous losses to his herds that he was "compelled to leave for some other range for his stock" (Heizer, 1974: 35, 42, 44–8).

The displacement of deer by cattle is a biological process, arguably without moral implications. But peoples, white and Indian, are part of the same species, and one when one kills another, that is an event of moral, not merely biological, significance. To see biology as the key to conquest obscures the fact that large-scale homicide often cleared the ground for the environmental revolution the settlers brought with them. There was no way to install livestock on the land alongside Indians who resisted, and so, went the remorseless logic of Indian wars, better remove the Indians (Cooke, 1943: 35–7). The environmental tool kit that Europeans brought with them could not have transformed the Americas the way it did without a conventional war chest, bristling with guns and clubs and knives, and a good many Europeans and Euro-Americans hell-bent on killing Indians.

To reduce environmental history to strictly biological arguments is to beggar its most telling moral and historical insights. Environmental change was bound up with both cultural tolerance and mutual hostility in profound ways. The braiding of biotic shift with race hatred and war, comity and exchange was a subtle weave, and it is the job of environmental historians to separate out the strands and show their relation to one another. War, trade, and environmental change share a relationship as intimate as the passing of a smallpox virus in a mother's embrace, or the germination of a dandelion seed on an overgrazed patch of broomgrass.

Environmental History of Modern Indian America

The paucity of environmental scholarship on twentieth-century Indians reinforces a common assumption that the closure of the frontier – the conquest of nature – spelled the end of Indian history. And yet, it may be that relations between Indians and nature in the twentieth century reveal even more about the ambiguities of conquest than those of the nineteenth century. In defying a multitude of predictions regarding their inevitable demise, in turning consignment to reservations into the defense of reservation homelands, in asserting distinctive cultural, economic, and political ties to vast sections of the American outback and their resources, Indian history since 1900 is in many ways a remarkable display of changing connections between people and nature.

Alongside these material changes, pervasive American beliefs regarding Indian connections to nature have shaped genuine environmental relationships. As Indians have sought to reform or maintain connections to the environment, the mythology of Indian environmentalism has become a tool of Indians and non-Indians alike. Indians may resist it or appropriate it; non-Indians may adopt it in support of Indian political agendas or to critique them. However they are used, myths about Indians and the environment are rarely avoided by anyone who deals with Indian environmental issues.

The interplay of real-world environmental changes and popular ideas about Indian environments is especially stark in the twentieth-century history of Indians, wildlife, and wilderness. The end of the Indian wars in the late 1800s often obscures the ways Indians challenged the authority of the conquerors by carrying on subsistence traditions such as hunting, fishing, and gathering, often on remote, customary lands outside of reservation boundaries. Not only were such activities an economic necessity, but they also reinforced traditions and could serve as a continuing claim to alienated lands.

They also conflicted with game and fish laws, passed in increasing numbers at the turn of the century as American social elites began a sustained effort to reserve wildlife as a recreational resource. In turn-of-the-century New Mexico, local ranchers and urban sportsmen formed posses to arrest parties of Pueblo, Navajo, and Apache hunters for game law violations in the national forests, which Indians had used as hunting grounds for many years, but which ranchers now coveted for grazing and sportsmen for recreational hunting (Warren, 1997).

As much as they involved hunting rights, these struggles featured profound differences in perceptions of nature. For Indians, animals came from the spirit world, and there were no taboos against killing does or fawns once the proper prayers had been offered. Conservationists, defending their own, gendered notions of "proper" hunting, assailed such practices as unmanly and wasteful. Despite severe penalties for their transgressions, including days in jail and heavy fines, Indians continued to claim hunting grounds in various national forests in New Mexico, and have done so up to the present day. Similar disputes in Wyoming, Montana, and elsewhere have occasionally led to violence and murder of Indians. Obviously, these confrontations – which combine animals, perceptions about animals, and issues of land tenure and use rights – have deep resonance with hunting and fishing rights clashes in the present (Warren, 1997). The resumption of whaling by the Makah people of Washington state offers a case in point, with environmentalists criticizing Indian hunting not only for its substance but for its *style* – and its quarry. Whales have been the poster children for wildlife conservation for several decades. Despite a recent resurgence in whale numbers, the thought of Indians hunting them – using only a few pieces of modern technology – further strained the typically tense relationship between environmentalists and Indians.

Indian collisions with conservationists perhaps have been most visible in the national parks. These vast scenic landscapes are ostensibly vestiges of America's primeval "uninhabited wilderness." But as Mark Spence has shown, the uninhabited wilderness had to be created, often by expelling Indians who continued to utilize these ancestral lands for hunting, gathering, religious observances, and living space, well into the twentieth century. Authorities banished Indians from Yellowstone,

Glacier, and Grand Canyon national parks, but Yosemite National Park has seen perhaps the most unusual story of Indian persistence and Indian removal. Yosemite
Indians lived in the park, gathering acorns, fishing, and earning wages as domestic
and manual laborers until the 1930s. They played on tourist affections for Indians as
part of the "wilderness experience," and eventually cultivated a bountiful trade in baskets, souvenir photographs (of themselves), and tourism, sometimes even hosting
meals for tourists in their small lodges. But administrators became concerned that
these modern Indians failed to evoke the "natural" setting of the park, and removed
them by the 1950s. Today, Yosemite Indians live mostly in villages west of the park,
returning for acorn harvests and traditional celebrations, and for spiritual observances
(Spence, 1999; Warren, 1997; Jacoby, 2001).

Conflicts over Indian use rights to national parks highlight how romantic ideas of
Indians as primal environmentalists have simultaneously empowered and dispossessed
real Indians. At Glacier, the Great Northern Railway employed Blackfeet Indians to
greet tourists, and establish in their minds a connection between Indians and the
park's scenic wonderland; at Yosemite, Indians took the initiative and satisfied tourist
market demand for "wilderness people" to complement the scenery. In both cases,
Indians made wages from tourist assumptions about primitive Indians being "part of
nature," but in doing so, they demonstrated to authorities and the public that present-
day Indians were "too modern" to deserve ancestral connections to the land. So it was
that Indians could be hired at the front gates while being expelled from hunting
grounds or gathering areas in the backcountry (Spence, 1999; Jacoby, 2001).

An additional irony flows from a common Indian response to this predicament.
Even as conservation has pushed Indians toward the modern wage economy, separating them from customary uses of the natural world, the trope of "first conserva-
tionist" has in many cases become all the more attractive for Indians. By claiming an
ancient, enduring status as original conservationists, Indians may challenge "official"
conservationists' exclusive rights to manage resources and their use. In this way,
appeals to American cultural myths about Indians can underwrite tribal sovereignty
and Indian claims to wildlife as tribal common property (Johansen and Maestas,
1979: 146, 169–79; Warren, 1997; Spence, 1999; Jacoby, 2001).

It seems very likely that Indians will employ and defend this practice by challenging some conclusions of environmental history, since the idea that Indians shaped the
land in a multitude of ways before and after European contact, even abetting the
decline of the buffalo, is incompatible with the mythology of indigenous environmentalism. In yet another paradox, then, environmental historians' attempts to
ascribe agency and power to historical Indians in nature has undermined some of the
most potent rhetorical tools at the disposal of Indians today.

The effort to retain use rights to ancestral lands and stave off encroachment on
reservations preoccupied Indians throughout the twentieth century, and the history
of allotment is one case study that suggests the distinctive ways Indians perceived,
bounded, defended, and utilized reservations. Federal attempts to end Indian communal ownership of land through the process of allotment began in the 1880s, and
accelerated through the opening decades of the twentieth century. As Indians took
up individual holdings, often under duress, "surplus" lands were sold to whites.

Collectively, between 1880 and 1900, Indians lost almost 80 million acres (Parman, 1994).

The environmental implications of this process were profound. As Emily Greenwald has observed, allotment was a means for authorities to manipulate inhabited space – one of the most fundamental expressions of human relationships with nature – in an effort to contain and control Indian peoples. By putting nuclear families on separate, demarcated parcels, reformers intended to break up customary extended family and communal living patterns, and turn Indians into modern agriculturalists.

As Greenwald reveals, Indian choices in allotment reflected distinctive cultural perceptions of land and resources. Among the Nez Perce, allottees defied the wishes of white reformers, passing over arable prairie in favor of seemingly barren canyon parcels, containing Nez Perce burial sites. In preserving ties to deceased loved ones and the spirit world in the sheltered ravines, some Nez Perce saw to it that the connection between inhabited space in this world and the power of spirits in the next survived the allotment process. Among both Nez Perce and Jicarilla Apaches, inadequacy of land and water often helped turn allottees away from farming their allotments and toward leasing them – as range land to white ranchers. Allotment advocates watched as the dream of Indian free-hold farmers on "rational" grid holdings living in nuclear families gave way to a new reality, of Indian landlords, often on odd-shaped (to whites) adjoining parcels, alongside extended families (Greenwald, 2001).

The histories of conservation and allotment both suggest powerful Indian attachments to particular places and forms of lived space. Environmental historians would do well to pay more attention to these issues. According to Keith Basso, among the Western Apache, places on the land are the most important ties to historical events and tribal identity. "What matters most to Apaches is *where* events occurred, not when, and what they serve to reveal about the development and character of Apache social life" (Basso, 1996: 31). Apache place-names, derived from the historical experience of those places, in many cases refer to historical events that illuminate the causes and consequences of immoral conduct. In this way, place-names inscribe layers of history and social identity into the land, and locales become invested with historical, social, and ritual meaning (Basso, 1996).

Relations with land surely differed among distinctive Indian peoples over time, but parallels to the Western Apache case probably abound. N. Scott Momaday has written that there is a close connection, a "reciprocal appropriation," between Indians and particular landscapes. Vine Deloria, Jr. long ago argued that "American Indians hold their lands – places – as having the highest possible meaning..." (Momaday, 1974: 80; Deloria, 1975). How Indians were connected to particular places, how allotment and other developments challenged those connections, and how Indians resisted or accommodated themselves to the new order might all be explored through deeper scholarship of Indian place-names, a subject for the most part ignored in recent decades.

Place is a particularly salient issue insofar as Indians have been vulnerable to government relocation and environmental management programs throughout the twentieth century. Some of these have stripped Indians of hard-won gains. Among the

Navajo, successful adjustments to the post-conquest period fell victim to federal stock reduction to reduce erosion and silting at Hoover Dam in the 1930s, with devastating consequences (White, 1983). In North Dakota, the Hidatsa community survived allotment and remained vibrant through the mid-twentieth century, relying on agriculture, gathering, domestic manufactures, and wage labor to support homes in the bottomlands of the Missouri River. But Garrison Dam inundated Hidatsa homes in the late 1940s, forcing upon them a struggle to reinvent a lost community life in the new homes to which they had been relocated (Hanson, 1987).

Even more pervasive than the problem of being "managed" in this way have been struggles concerning mineral development on reservations. After decades of seeing tribal resources treated like federal property, Indians anxious to negotiate more lucrative deals with energy companies founded the Council of Energy Resource Tribes (CERT), in 1975. CERT became an adviser for Indians on energy resource matters, often providing technical expertise, accounting, and negotiating help to member tribes. Partly as a result of CERT's influence, Indian control over energy resources has grown substantially in recent decades (Ambler, 1990).

For all its successes, CERT has also found itself caught in some of the paradoxes of modern Indian environmental politics. On many occasions, Indian supporters of energy development have collided with Indian critics. The most famous intra-Indian dispute over energy resource development is perhaps the Big Mountain controversy in Arizona, where the Hopi Tribal Council has asserted claims to coal seams under land occupied by poor Navajos, many of whom are descended from shepherds who moved onto the land in the late nineteenth century when it was still legally a "joint-use area" for Hopis and Navajos. In the 1960s and 1970s, the Hopis – whom courts have named the legal owners of the land – sought to develop the coal resources in partnership with Peabody Coal Company. Navajo residents often see the landscape as a series of places imbued with intense religious and social significance, and a landscape where sheep pastoralism is still viable. Offers of settlement benefits have done little to persuade them to find new homes.

The dispute has divided Indians in complicated ways. Some Hopis, seeing the coal development as a potential environmental disaster and as a means to aggrandize an illegitimate tribal council, have joined Navajos in petitions to stop it. Other Hopis seek to consolidate their hold over the land and develop the mine. Among Indians and non-Indians alike, this complex struggle is often described as a fight between "traditional" and "progressive" tribal factions (Matthiessen, 1979; Kammer, 1980). In this paradigm, "traditional" is almost always synonymous with "environmental," an implication that should make scholars leery. Are "traditional" goals of cultural revival necessarily more in keeping with custom and more environmentally responsible than "progressive" goals of economic security and tribal autonomy? If Indian lifeways in centuries past had some environmental impact, are there reservation developments that might be in keeping with some traditions?

Parallels to the Big Mountain controversy abound, but resolutions are scarce. The Goshutes of Utah and the White Mountain Apache peoples have both petitioned the federal government to locate nuclear waste dumps on their reservations. Such requests usually divide Indians and almost always drive wedges between Indians and neighboring non-Indians, as arguments flare over the right of Indian people to self-determination and economic security and the rights of Indians and others to customary uses of the land and a voice in determining the future of waste disposal plans that could have long-term effects – both environmental and economic – outside reservation boundaries.

However we interpret these conflicts, the continuing cash value of Indian minerals, wildlife, and open space seems to make their proliferation likely. How Indians will defend those interests from non-Indians, and manage resources to secure the competing goals of distinctive Indian groups, remains an open question. Such disputes are not entirely new. Indians argued over who would be most benefitted by adopting horses, and who would suffer from the fur trade. In this context, modern controversies assume traditional proportions.

To contemplate the connections between Indians and the earth will remain a vital historical enterprise for American historians. In the twenty-first century, issues of land tenure and allotment, energy development and the "proper" use of tribal homelands and places, are only a few of the ways historians can see the continuing interaction between Indians and the natural world. Rather than showing us how far Indians have moved "away" from nature, such modern case studies remind us all the more of the many ways that Indian history and the history of contact with Europeans and Euro-Americans is inscribed in the land itself. Indeed, of all the things that connect other Americans to the past, and to Indians, the land is perhaps the most tangible and enduring artifact of our mutual histories. Indians have bounded and shaped the land in a multitude of ways, some of which resonate right down to the new millennium. Whether it be oil wells pumping scarce cash into tribal coffers, a fence separating Indian property from public land along the highway, or a faint trail, the remnant etchings of a footpath two thousand years old, curving along the shoulder of a foothill in the Mojave Desert, a close look at enduring Indian connections to the land reveals the surprising legacies that have grown from the nature of conquest.

BIBLIOGRAPHY

Ambler, Marjane 1990: *Breaking the Iron Bonds: Indian Control of Energy Development* (Lawrence: University Press of Kansas).

Anderson, M. Kat, Michael G. Barbour, and Valerie Whitworth 1998: "A World of Balance and Plenty: Land, Plants, Animals, and Humans in pre-European California," in *Contested Eden: California Before the Gold Rush*, eds. Ramón Gutiérrez and Richard Orsi (Berkeley: University of California Press), pp. 12–47.

Anderson, Virginia DeJohn 1994: "King Philip's Herds: Indians, Colonists, and the Problem of Livestock in Early New England," *William and Mary Quarterly* 3rd series, 51(4) (October): 601–24.

Basso, Keith H. 1996: *Wisdom Sits in Places: Landscape and Language Among the Western Apache* (Albuquerque: University of New Mexico Press).

Blackburn, Thomas C. and Kat Anderson 1993: "Managing the Domesticated Environment," in *Before the Wilderness: Environmental Management by Native*

Californians, eds. Thomas C. Blackburn and M. Kat Anderson (Menlo Park: Ballena Press).

Brightman, Robert 1993: *Grateful Prey: Rock Cree Human–Animal Relationships* (Berkeley: University of California Press).

Burton, Lloyd 1991: *American Indian Water Rights and the Limits of the Law* (Lawrence: University Press of Kansas).

Carson, James Taylor 1995: "Horses and the Economy and Culture of the Choctaw Indians, 1690–1840," *Ethnohistory* 42(3) (Summer): 495–513.

Cook, Noble David 1998: *Born to Die: Disease and New World Conquest 1492–1650* (New York: Cambridge University Press).

Cooke, Sherburne F. 1943: *The Conflict Between the California Indian and White Civilization*, Vol. III: *The American Invasion, 1848–1870* (Berkeley: University of California Press).

Cronon, William 1983: *Changes in the Land: Indians, Colonists, and the Ecology of New England* (New York: Hill and Wang).

Crosby, Alfred 1975: *The Columbian Exchange: The Biological and Cultural Consequences of 1492* (Westport, CT: Greenwood).

Crosby, Alfred 1976: "Virgin Soil Epidemics as a Factor in the Aboriginal Depopulation in America," *William and Mary Quarterly* 3rd series, 33: 289–99.

Crosby, Alfred 1986: *Ecological Imperialism: The Biological Expansion of Europe, 900–1900* (New York: Cambridge University Press).

Deloria, Vine, Jr. 1975: *God Is Red* (New York: Dell).

Denevan, William 1992: "The Pristine Myth: The Landscape of the Americas in 1492," *Annals of the Association of American Geographers* 82.

Denhardt, Robert 1947: *The Horse of the Americas* (Norman: University of Oklahoma Press).

Dobie, J. Frank 1954: *The Mustangs* (New York: Bantam Books [1934]).

Ewers, John C. 1955: *The Horse in Blackfoot Indian Culture: With Material from Other Western Tribes*. Bureau of American Ethnology, Bulletin 159 (Washington, D.C.: Smithsonian Institution Press).

Flores, Dan 1991: "Bison Ecology and Bison Diplomacy: The Southern Plains from 1800 to 1850," *Journal of American History* 78 (September): 465–85.

Flores, Dan 1996: "The Great Contraction," in *Legacy: New Perspectives on the Battle of Little Big Horn*, ed. Charles E. Rankin (Helena: Montana Historical Society Press).

Gill, Sam D. 1987: *Mother Earth: An American Story* (Chicago: University of Chicago Press).

Greenwald, Emily 2001: "Allotment in Severalty: Power, Geography, and the Dawes Act" (Albuquerque: University of New Mexico Press).

Hanson, Jeffrey R. 1986: "Adjustment and Adaptation on the Northern Plains," *Plains Anthropologist* 31(112): 93–107.

Hanson, Jeffrey R. 1987: "The Hidatsa Natural Environment," in *The Way to Independence: Memories of a Hidatsa Indian Family, 1840–1920*, eds. Carolyn Gilman and Mary Jane Schneider (St. Paul: Minnesota Historical Society Press), pp. 333–9.

Hatley, Thomas 1991: "Cherokee Women Farmers Hold Their Ground," in *Appalachian Frontiers: Society and Development in the Preindustrial Era*, ed. Robert D. Mitchell (Lexington: University Press of Kentucky).

Heizer, Robert F. (ed.) 1974: *They Were Only Diggers: A Collection of Articles from California Newspapers, 1851–1866, on Indian–White Relations* (Ramona, CA: Ballena Press).

Henige, David P. 1998: *Numbers from Nowhere: The American Indian Contact Population Debate* (Norman: University of Oklahoma Press).

Hickerson, Harold 1965: "The Virginia Deer and Intertribal Buffer Zones in the Upper Mississippi Valley," in *Man, Culture, and Animals: The Role of Animals in Human Ecological Adjustments*, eds. Anthony Leeds and Andrew P. Vayda (Washington, D.C.: American Association for the Advancement of Science), pp. 43–65.

Isenberg, Andrew 1999: *The Destruction of the Bison: Social and Environmental Changes in the Great Plains, 1750–1820* (New York: Cambridge University Press).

Jacoby, Karl 2001: *Crimes Against Nature: Squatters, Poachers, Thieves, and the Hidden History of American Conservation* (Berkeley: University of California Press).

Jennings, Francis 1976: *The Invasion of America: Indians, Colonialism, and the Cant of Conquest* (New York: Norton).

Johansen, Bruce and Roberto Maestas 1979: *Wasi'chu: The Continuing Indian Wars* (New York: Monthly Review Press).

Josephy, Alvin M., Jr. 1997: *The Nez Perce Indians and the Opening of the Northwest*, 2nd edn. (New Haven, 1965; New York: Houghton Mifflin, 1997).

Kaiser, Rudolf 1987: "Chief Seattle's Speech(es): American Origins and European Reception," in *Recovering the Word: Essays on Native American Literature*, eds. Brian Swann and Arnold Krupat (Berkeley: University of California Press), pp. 497–537.

Kammer, Jerry 1980: *The Second Long Walk: The Navajo–Hopi Land Dispute* (Albuquerque: University of New Mexico Press).

Krech, Shepard III 1994: "Ecology and the American Indian," *Ideas from the National Humanities Center* 3 (Summer): 4–22.

Martin, Calvin 1978: *Keepers of the Game: Indian–Animal Relations and the Fur Trade* (Berkeley: University of California Press).

Martin, Paul S. and R. G. Klein (eds.) 1984: *Quarternary Extinctions: A Prehistoric Revolution* (Tucson: University of Arizona Press).

Martin, Paul S. and Christine R. Szuter 1999: "War Zones and Game Sinks in Lewis and Clark's West," *Conservation Biology* 13(1) (February): 36–45.

Matthiessen, Peter 1979: *Indian Country* (New York: Penguin).

Milliken, Randall 1995: *A Time of Little Choice: The Disintegration of Tribal Culture in the San Francisco Bay Area 1769–1810* (Modesto, CA: Ballena Press).

Momaday, N. Scott 1974: "Native American Attitudes to the Environment," in *Seeing With a Native Eye: Essays on Native American Religion*, ed. Walter Holden Capps (New York: Harper & Row), pp. 79–85.

Nelson, Richard 1983: *Make Prayers to the Raven: A Koyukon View of the Northern Forest* (Chicago: University of Chicago Press).

Parman, Donald 1994: *Indians and the American West in the Twentieth Century* (Bloomington: Indiana University Press).

Preston, William 1998: "Serpent in the Garden: Environmental Change in Colonial California," in *Contested Eden: California Before the Gold Rush*, eds. Ramón Gutiérrez and Richard Orsi (Berkeley: University of California Press).

Pyne, Stephen 1982: *Fire in America: A Cultural History of Wildland and Rural Fire* (Princeton: Princeton University Press).

Roe, Frank Gilbert 1955: *The Indian and the Horse* (Norman: University of Oklahoma Press).

Sherow, James E. 1992: "Workings of the Geodialectic: High Plains Indians and Their Horses in the Region of the Arkansas River Valley, 1800–1870," *Environmental History Review* (Summer): 61–84.

Spence, Mark 1999: *Dispossessing the Wilderness: Indian Removal and the Creation of the National Parks* (New York: Oxford University Press).

Tanner, Adrian 1979: *Bringing Home Animals: Religious Ideology and Mode of Production of the Mistassini Cree Hunters* (New York: St. Martin's Press).

Warren, Louis S. 1997: *The Hunter's Game: Poachers and Conservationists in Twentieth-Century America* (New Haven: Yale University Press).

West, Elliott 1995: *The Way to the West: Essays on the Central Plains* (Albuquerque: University of New Mexico Press).

White, Richard 1978: "The Winning of the West: The Expansion of the Western Sioux in the Eighteenth and Nineteenth Centuries," *Journal of American History* 45 (September): 319–43.

White, Richard 1983: *The Roots of Dependency: Subsistence, Environment, and Social Change among the Choctaws, Pawnees, and Navajos* (Lincoln: University of Nebraska Press).

White, Richard 1997: "Indian Peoples and the Natural World: Asking the Right Questions," in *Rethinking American Indian History*, ed. Donald Fixico (Albuquerque: University of New Mexico Press), pp. 87–100.

Wyman, Walker D. 1963: *The Wild Horse of the West* (Lincoln: University of Nebraska Press [1945]).

17

Gender in Native America

BETTY BELL

"I am only an Indian woman ... I know what an Indian woman can do."
Sarah Winnemucca, 1888

In a 1990 interview, Akwesasne Mohawk activist Shirley Hill Witt described the social organization of her nation. "It's matrilocal," Witt said. "Where we go, the men follow." A moment before, Witt had located her understanding of Iroquois gender – broadly speaking – within personal and historical memory: "The women in [my] family carried with them, and carry with them to this very day, the very strong matrilineal and matrilocal tradition of our people" (Ford, 1997: 43). As depicted by Witt, Iroquois women are culturally defined by continuous and uninterrupted histories of power and authority within their tribal societies.

Consider another 1990 interview conducted by gender historian Ramona Ford, in which Verna Williamson spoke of the opposition she encountered when she ran for governor of the matrilineal Isleta Pueblo: "I knew [the tribal leaders] were going to say, 'You can't run because it is against tribal tradition.'" Williamson, who was later elected governor, sees this opposition as a conflict between tribal and colonial "traditions": "We didn't have a constitution. We're matrilineal ... So where did the story change here?" (Ford, 1997: 43).

As the experiences of Witt and Williamson demonstrate, "the story" of Native women and their relation to power and authority is often told, or lived, between conflicting "traditions": on the one hand, the precolonial or "traditional" status of women; on the other, the postcolonial advance of patriarchy into tribal nations. At the turn of the twenty-first century, it is not difficult to see the lives of Native American women defined by multiple and co-creative tribal and Western "traditions." Even prior to contact, however, tribal gender roles were often just as "plural," composed, in Ramona Ford's words, "of a number of statuses" (Ford, p. 43).

Within matrilineal societies, which represent the strongest convergences of women and power, the positions of women were variously determined within the specific economic, political, and ceremonial practices of individual nations. And in some patrilineal societies, women owned domestic goods, were honored for their ceremonial craft work, and gained prestige from their identification with men or male roles. Bilateral societies, in which descent can come from the mother or the father, allowed women greater latitude in their ownership of property, recognition in council, and roles as traders and shamans. Thus, the degree of a Native woman's status or power was determined by the particularities of her cultural, historical, and situational positions.

The difficulties and inconsistencies that mark discussions of Native American gender arise from the fact that even though gender is central to the organization of Native nations as distinct social and cultural systems, it is often not closely related to power or biology. Kinship, or the individual's relation to the community, is realized through matrilineal, patrilineal, or bilateral descent (see Miller, this volume). There is, however, no universal or necessary correlation between male or female descent and gendered positions of power and authority. Nor are gender and sex defined, necessarily, as culturally equivalent categories. Contested, as well, are the methods or approaches used to secure an understanding or representation of "traditional" women's roles and gender practices. All of these points, of course – gender as a social construction, as an analytical category, as a relational object, and as a key factor in the contemporary production of knowledge – were effectively drawn together by Joan Wallach Scott in her touchstone essay on gender (Scott, 1988).

If feminist scholarship and, more recently, gender studies have transformed the larger practice of history, they have also influenced and given prominence to more specific debates on Native American gender. Current interest in Native women has been shaped by many of the issues first raised in *Women, Culture and Society*, edited by Michelle Z. Rosaldo and Louise Lamphere (1974). Considered by many scholars as the first introduction to an anthropology of women, it inspired further investigations into the cultural, historical, and class differences among women. The major assumption of the book is that the subordination of women is a cultural and historical universal. In it, scholars adopted a theory of "separate spheres" in order to address the construction and maintenance of male dominance in all cultures.

In particular, two essays in that volume informed future work on Native American women. In "Women, Culture and Society: A Theoretical Overview," Rosaldo (1974) argues that the distinctions between private/female and public/male spheres exist in all cultures and that men's work and activities are given greater prestige. Sherry Ortner's "Is Female to Male as Nature is to Culture?" (1974) proposes that women's subordination is a consequence of a universal privileging of culture over nature. Feminist anthropologists and historians countered these arguments with evidence of societies in which the "separate spheres" distinctions were blurred, the work of women was valued, and the authority of the natural world respected.

Many scholars found in Ruth Landes' earlier and seminal ethnographic study, *The Ojibwa Woman* (1997), grounds to challenge the ethnocentric assumptions of the Rosaldo and Ortner essays. Based on her work with the Ojibwa in the 1930s, Landes' text details the rigorous and conventional gender training of boys and girls. The "separate spheres" of men and women, however, are often experienced as situations and as complementary distributions of power that allow, as well, for gender variance:

> Even the most conservative women usually find it necessary to take up some prescriptively masculine work at one time or another ... Those women whose behavior is exceptional [shamans, "manly women"] are not judged with reference to the

conventional standard but with reference to their individual fortunes only. The conduct of the ideal woman, therefore, and the behavior of any individual woman may be quite at variance. (Landes, 1997: 135)

In recent years, scholars of Native American gender have emphasized the value attached to women's work and the possibilities of a third gender recorded in *The Ojibwa Woman*. Ironically, previous scholarship had criticized the text as male-oriented and its portrayal of Native gender as asymmetrical. This criticism addresses the "natural" privilege and superiority accorded to men in the study. "The Ojibwa make the generalization," Landes reported, "that any man is intrinsically and vastly superior to any woman" (Landes, p. 148). Like Louise Spindler's classic study *Menomini Women and Culture Change* (1962), however, Landes' significant contribution to the contemporary debate is her representation of Native gender as contested and contradictory.

Anthropologist Eleanor Leacock argued that Rosaldo's, Ortner's, and, in her view, Landes' theories of universal male dominance reflect, in fact, the consequences of specific historical events such as colonization and the development of private property. In her articles "Women in Egalitarian Societies" (1977) and "Montagnais Women and the Jesuit Program for Colonization" (1980), Leacock correlates the rise of the state with the diminishment of women's power. In her work, the greater power and prestige of precolonial Native women is seen as evidence of women's empowerment in communal economies. Her studies of Native women have provided many of the commonplace examples in contemporary discussions of gender: the precolonial power of Iroquois women; for example; the effect of trade – particularly the fur trade – on the status of women, and the subordination of women through the valued sites of "civilization" (nuclear families, male authority, Western sexual mores, and female dependence).

The explicit purpose of the feminist contributions to *Women, Culture and Society* was to address and correct the problem of male bias and male privilege in the cultural representation and interpretation of women. Through the 1980s and 1990s, the interest in Native American gender roles was inspired by an even larger corrective measure. "Native American women's history," Ramona Ford explains, "forces us to rethink what is 'normative' or possible in women's roles" (Ford, 1997: 43). The assumption is that Native women represent the gender histories of all women, suppressed by patriarchy. If gender has been a useful way of considering Native histories, so too have Native histories been appropriated to make more general arguments about gender.

In the first studies by Native women on gender identities, this assumption was modified by region or race, but Native women remained a (unified) category of woman primarily defined by suppressed histories of power. In Beatrice Medicine's "'Warrior Women': Sex Role Alternatives for Plains Indian Women" (1983) and Paula Gunn Allen's *The Sacred Hoop: Recovering the Feminine in American Indian Traditions* (1986), the emphasis is on a covert female power and alternative socially authorized expressions of gender. As these and other earlier works demonstrate, Native women are perceived as having been produced by but, ultimately, remaining outside of the hegemonic discourses of patriarchy and colonization.

To be sure, the effects of colonization on gender are best measured by the increase in patriarchal and heterosexual privilege in tribal nations. Yet such readings assume that the discourses of Western feminism are less hegemonic, and more responsive to an "authentic" Native gender, than the discourses of patriarchy or the more traditional disciplines of history and anthropology. These readings ignore the roles women played in the colonization of Native nations and the ways in which feminism has codified and replicated Native women as the Other. Whether Native women are read as universal sites of female subordination or universal sites of female power, the "true 'subjects'" of these counter-histories, as Chandra Mohanty argues in her critical essay on third-world women, are "western feminists" (1994: 213).

Three Stories of Gender

The problem in Native gender studies, as it was in pre-feminist anthropology, is how to represent Native women and Native gender practices as the real and material subjects of their own collective histories. Given the paucity of historical evidence, most of it refracted through colonial eyes, it is difficult to determine or document precolonial or preindustrial Native gender roles. In recent scholarship, there has been a considerable recovery and re-examination of old documentary evidence in an attempt to place and historicize those roles and practices. Scholars have also undertaken the equally important task of reviewing and debating the approaches used to read existing materials and the effects of methodology on representation. The gender studies of Beatrice Medicine (1983), Theda Perdue (1998), Ramona Ford (1997), and Devon Mihesuah (1998) caution against unified or ahistorical readings of Native women and stress the importance of representing Native American gender in terms of plural and diverse cultural/historical locations.

In her essay "Native American Women: Changing Statuses, Changing Interpretations," Ford identifies three scholarly approaches to the study of Native gender: (1) historical materialism, which traces the effects of European contact on Native social systems; (2) social/cultural constructionism, which emphasizes the recovery and representation of Native cultural values and social construction; and (3) processual analysis/community interaction, which stresses the contemporary dynamics of gender in local/national political arenas (1997, 43–5). These approaches are primarily distinguished by the knowledge and location being contested and/or privileged: how strongly should studies of Native gender rely on the oral tradition? On written documentation? How can traditional value systems be recuperated through colonial and postcolonial literature? What did power and authority mean in tribal cultures? Were they equally available to women? What are their present expressions in tribal communities? The first approach relies on historical or situational data to trace diverse and interactive post-contact social/cultural constructions of Native gender. By emphasizing particularities of time and place, these studies problematize any unitary concept of history of Native women or Native cultures. The oft-cited case of Iroquois women, for example, has been used both to support and to refute evidence of female power. In her study of the effects of Indian women on the

nineteenth-century suffrage movement, Gail Landsman (1996) argues that suffrag-
ists utilized Iroquois women's rights to property and children, as well as their political influence, as a model of " 'the Matriarchate' in recent history." Diane Rothenberg
(1980), on the other hand, has argued that colonization, in particular the Quakers'
introduction of the nuclear family and private property into the Seneca, diminished
the status of Iroquois women.

Less situational and more universal in practice, social/cultural constructionism is
also more firmly situated in presentist knowledges. In methodology and conclusion,
for example, Paula Gunn Allen's landmark study *The Sacred Hoop* (1986) provides a
counter-mythology to that available in historical and anthropological scholarship.
Allen circumvents colonial and postcolonial written literature by reading traditional
practices, such as kinship and gender roles, through tribal female creation mythologies. Her book continues the work of earlier feminist recoveries of matriarchy – in particular Peggy Reeves Sanday's *Female Power and Male Dominance* (1981) – to argue
that the importance of female deities, such as Corn Woman or Grandmother Spider,
express either explicitly or symbolically the values and cultural construction of tribal
societies. This mythological/cultural constructionist approach reads female power and
gender flexibility as the primary characteristic of all tribal peoples, who were "always
already" positioned in opposition to patriarchy and free from imperialistic ambitions.

The third and less common approach to the study of Native women and the
dynamics of gender calls for an attention to "microlevel social interaction" in tribal
communities. Founded on the scholarship of JoAnne Fiske and Robert Lynch, this
approach considers "how individual women and their voluntary groups and kinship
networks operate in face-to-face encounters today within both local and dominant
society power structures and cultural formations" (Ford, 1997: 46). This method
focuses on local and national tribal political coalition, and the ways in which activism
redefined women's roles and gender in the late twentieth century.

These three approaches attempt to account for traditional, historical, and, to a
much lesser extent, contemporary tribal gender practices. The most common and,
thus far, compelling questions within this continuing and increasingly popular debate
address the status and fluidity of gender: (1) did women have power and status equal
to men? (2) If so, how was female authority expressed in traditional cultures?
(3) How did European colonization impact Native gender and sexuality? And
(4) what do "third genders" or otherwise more complex shapings of gender tell us
about the practice of gender-making in general? In the end, these questions cannot
be pursued as distinct and separate, but rather as mutually dependent counter-
colonization histories of Native gender. Likewise, the rough temporal categories
"traditional," "historical," and "contemporary" blur together in similar ways around
the historical development and the politics of gender studies.

There are, for example, few pre-contact answers to the questions we have posed.
Even if a scholar, such as Allen, relies almost entirely on the oral tradition to discover
those answers, the sources have, over time, undergone translation, cultural evolution,
transcription, and pan-tribal circulation. Studies of historical and pre-contact pasts,
such as Allen's *The Sacred Hoop*, have assisted in the contemporary organization of an
anti-colonial and pan-tribal Native gender identity. In the nineteenth century and for

much of the twentieth century, there was no history or public space for the representation of female Indians that was not constructed by popular American culture. The significance of female deities such as Corn Woman (Selu), Grandmother Spider, or Changing Woman was understood and embraced only within specific tribal communities. As contemporary pan-tribal mythologies, however, they have facilitated the recovery of a (gendered) spiritual core in Native America and aided the self-representation of Native women. In many ways, contemporary indigenous feminism and the popularity of the present debate on Native gender has been fashioned from a cultural circulation and affirmation that was previously unavailable to communities of Native women: a Native reading audience and a popular pan-tribal culture. The contents of these practices, however, are firmly located in the past.

Gender Representations

The Native woman figures prominently in the first pictorial representations of the New World. In Philipp Galle's portrait (1592) of America, for example, the nude muscular body of an Indian woman strides, with spear and beheaded enemy, across a landscape of war and carnage. She is seductive and threatening, representing the national enterprise and the Other within it: she is victimizer and victim, colonizer and colonized. The body of the Indian woman in these early representations symbolizes, as well, the gendered body of the landscape. In Jan Van der Staet's "Vespucci Discovering America" (1580) she is supported by a hammock, caught between action and rest and between recognition and confrontation with a new European, who holds in his hands the symbols of Christianity and civilization. Later she will become the Indian Queen, who beckons, with a warning, all to the New World, and in the nineteenth century, she will serve as the model for the statue of Lady Liberty, situated, ironically, on the dome of the United States capitol (Fleming, 1965, 1967; Higham, 1990). In early representations, the Native woman inhabits, simultaneously, indigenous and foreign locations, and her power comes from her ability to hold conflicting allegories of nation and gender.

From John Smith's *The Generall Historie of Virginia* (1986) and other records of the Jamestown settlement, eighteenth-century historians fashioned their own image of the Native woman as the symbol for America in the form of the "Indian princess." In that century, the few "facts" of Pocahontas' life were augmented to emphasize her conversion to Christianity, her 1614 marriage to John Rolfe, and the birth of their child Thomas. Nineteenth-century romancers drew on the themes of white/Indian intermarriage and white indigenous inheritance but were more interested in her relationship with John Smith, and the political uses of her nobility and conversion. As narrated through this relationship, the stories of European conquest or "discovery" of America were transformed into a romance of mutual, but unconsummated, seduction in which the noble Indian woman is willing to sacrifice her life and her people for the love of an English settler. In the hundreds of plays, poems, and paintings produced in that century on the subject of Pocahontas, her royal birth and identification with colonial interests are the most prominent themes.

From Simon Van de Passe's *Matoaks als Rebecka* (1793) to Robert Matthew Sully's *Pocahontas* (1855), the pictorial representations of Pocahontas are informed by highly gendered European and classical maternal allegories for nation. During this time, the images trace her evolution from a stern white/Indian matriarch to an increasingly classical and whiter, more malleable image of feminine fecundity. As the daughter of a "King," her romance with Smith, baptism as Rebecca, marriage to Rolfe, and birth of the "first" indigenous (mixed-blood) American carry the authority of cultural and legal transfers of allegiance, identity, inheritance, and land. Pocahontas, as Philip Young tells us, represents an original and common American mother: "the mother of us all" (1967: 175).

For Native peoples and particularly for Native women, popular stereotypes of the Indian princess or squaw drudge are non-recuperable sites of early Native woman-hood. Within America's "Pocahontas Perplex," as defined by Rayna Green (1975: 701), the primitive illiterate squaw is the "darker, more negatively viewed" sister to the princess. As Hortense Spillers has written concerning negative images of black women, the princess and the squaw are so "loaded with mythic prepossession that there is no way for the agents buried beneath them to come clean" (1987: 65). Like "Sapphire" or "Brown Sugar," these Indian female images are ciphers and cultural inventions that cannot be reappropriated by Native women without complicity in or service to their enterprise. The first Native women writers, in the nineteenth century, did borrow Pocahontas' nobility, authority, and visibility to make their self-representations coherent and acceptable to white audiences. For them, however, the Indian princess remained performative, a piece of Indian vaudeville, and was denied a presence or a voice in their written work.

While the genesis of America and the "crossing of the cultural rift" is gendered and represented around the image of the Native woman, the violent and oppositional histories of that encounter have been just as powerfully gendered masculine (Hulme, 1986: 142). This is not to suggest that Native men have been depicted as independent and active agents in history or that they have not been subsumed by colonial history. Yet, in a history conceived and presented as a universal story exemplified by the lives of men, Native men did have a historical status greater than Native women did. By virtue of gender, they were granted the positions of male agency, particularly when the subject was resistance. Yet their representation as savages or noble savages helped undercut those positions and delegitimized their ability to act, to defend, to govern, or to represent national enterprises. Indeed, often Indian men were represented in terms of femininity. The narrative of the contest for America is nonetheless a story of male confrontation, in which Indian men are simultaneously represented as powerful masculine warriors and as weak, effeminate pushovers. Not surprisingly, representations of Indian women sometimes followed the same pattern. When womanhood was the thing at stake, Indian women were easily seen in the masculine terms first laid out by Philipp Galle.

The first Native male writers in the late eighteenth century avoid discussions of gender in the Christian confessional writings. With the advent of ethnography and the Indian "autobiography," however, gender played a significant role in the selection of subjects and the ways in which Native cultures would be "preserved." Just as the stories of the Republic and manifest destiny were told through the lives of extra-ordinary men, the stories of savagery and surrender were told through the lives of great and defeated chiefs. *Black Hawk: An Autobiography* (1833), for instance, one of the most popular Indian "autobiographies" of the nineteenth century, is a model of how the spectacle of Indian war and defeat was used to tell the story of American victory culture. Its editor/writer, J. B. Patterson, privileged the Sauk war chief's memories of constant intertribal warfare and the Indian slaughter of Indian women and children over his subject's cultural formation or the wrongs of the United States to the Sauk and Fox.

Black Hawk: An Autobiography provides a good example of the difficulty of recu-perating gender roles and practices from previous sources on Native subjects. In Patterson's text, the status of Sauk and Fox women is as unreliable, finally, as the por-trait of Black Hawk as a worthy but culturally and morally inferior opponent of the United States. As argued by many scholars of Native American literature, these ethnographic "autobiographies" are collective creations (editor/translator/subject) of a plural (white/Native) Indian self. The consequence for gender studies is that it is difficult to distinguish between the views of white patriarchy and the traditions of the Native subject or to determine whether these are conflicting views or evidence of the plural and complex statuses of Indian women.

In Black Hawk's narrative, for instance, the division of labor is seen as comple-mentary – women provided agricultural subsistence; men acted as warriors and hunters – but the distribution of male/female authority is disputed. The Sauk chief often dismisses the significance or influence of women in his nation: "It is not cus-tomary for us to say much about our women, as they generally perform their part cheerfully, and *never interfere with business belonging to the men*!" (1833/1990: 73, emphasis in original). When he is opposed by rival Keokuk, however, Black Hawk does not locate his power to resist in male warriors or leaders but in the agricultural empowerment of Sauk and Fox women:

> Ke-o-kuck, who has a smooth tongue, and is a great speaker, was busy in persuad-ing my band that I was wrong – and thereby making many of them dissatisfied with me. I had one consolation – for all the women were on my side, on account of their corn-fields. (1833/1990: 107–8)

In this instance, women are depicted as having a significant voice in tribal decision-making and agency in historical events. Even though the Sauk and Fox are repre-sented, in the text, as equally dependent on agricultural production and hunting for subsistence, male/female authority is expressed within forms of subsistence associated with matrilineal and patrilineal societies.

Contemporary scholarship has demonstrated the interrelations between early tribal social organization, the position of women, and the dominant means of subsistence. Wherever horticulture was the dominant means of subsistence, for example, it was likely that the tribe was matrilineal or matrilocal. Not all agricultural-dependent tribes – the patrilineal Shawnee and Pima, for example – were matrilineal. Nor were all hunter societies – the matrilineal Crow, for example – patrilineal (see Miller, this volume). In matrilocal societies, where the emphasis on farming was greatest, the high status of women was expressed in female property rights, governance of women's clans, and a privileging of the bond between mother and daughter over husband or son. It is clear, however, that increasing tribal dependence on the horse, the plow, irrigation, and available or authorized forms of subsistence altered tribal relations with the land and the positions of women in relation to it. In Anthony Wallace's interpretation of the Code of Handsome Lake, for example, the sedentary nuclear family replaces broader matrilineal kinship patterns, functioning as a key site of social changes influencing marriage, residence, intergenerational relations, and, perhaps most of all, gender (Wallace, 1970: 285; but see also Rothenberg, 1980).

Civilization and Gender

The idea of "civilization," argues Gail Bederman (1995: 56), "simultaneously denoted attributes of race and gender." Human races, it was assumed, evolved to a precise stage of civilization. Racially, this stage was marked as white, and its advancement was identified by the degree of sexual differentiation. The savagery or barbarism of Native peoples has, since contact, been supported by representations of tribal gender as insufficiently differentiated or perversely blurred. Lewis Henry Morgan's *Ancient Society* (1877/1985) traces seven evolutionary steps from simple savagery to barbarism to civilization. From an examination of the institutions of family, government, property, and technology, Morgan argued that the most advanced "Village Indians" had reached the middle stage of barbarism (Shoemaker, 1995a: 4). In Morgan's earlier study of kinship and family among the Iroquois, which he saw as representative of all Natives, matrilineality does not grant women greater prestige, but rather denies women the protection and status of civilized societies. Iroquois women, he claimed, were "the inferior, the dependent, and the servant of man" (Morgan, 1962: 324).

Despite (and because of) such negative theorizing, the discourses of civilization – Christianity, literacy, republican government – have been adopted and manipulated for centuries by Native American people who wished to retain or to gain recognition of their humanity and their rights. For instance, the moral authority and persuasive skills of early Native writers depended entirely on their ability to present themselves as converted, detribalized, and educated subjects. In their studies of Cherokee women in the eighteenth and nineteenth centuries, Theda Perdue (1989, 1998) and Devon Mihesuah (1998) argue that the present construction of Native women is informed, for the most part, by the personal narratives selected for preservation by Euro-American culture. What, Perdue and Mihesuah ask us to consider, would Native women's history look like if Native Americans had been able to circulate and safeguard their written histories? This historical selection and survival of documentation has affected the representation of all America's most marginalized groups. In the instance of Native women, however, the historical privileging of assimilationist narratives has distorted not only the histories of Native women, but the very organizational systems – kinship, social practices, and gender – in which those histories could be fully interpreted.

In her recent historical study of Cherokee women, Perdue (1998) traces the conversion of a matrilocal society into a patriarchal and constitutional tribal government. She argues that in anticipation of their removal from ancestral lands, the Cherokee adopted a centralized government that was responsive to the gender and racial conventions of "civilized" nations. At their constitutional convention of 1827, the tribe voted to limit the privileges of citizenship to "free" male citizens. This disenfranchisement of women and blacks from tribal representation and property was an effort to effect a public cultural and racial reconstruction of the Cherokee nation as Christian, literate, and "civilized."

Within the ideologies that shifted and restaged the debate on "savagism and civilization" to accommodate federal removal or reservation strategies, gender – and particularly as it has been constructed around women – has been a constant and critical site in the detribalization of Native peoples. By the nineteenth century, the power of Native women had been steadily diminished by trade and negotiation with Europeans and Americans, who preferred and recognized male representation in such transactions. There were earlier and notable exceptions, however, in the experiences of Native women in the fur trade and on the frontier. Consider Richard White's (1991) metaphorical "middle ground," in which liminality and hybridity were privileged and where Native women became principal agents in the negotiation of mutually interdependent Native/white and male/female economies of trade, family, and social custom (see also Van Kirk, 1980). This negotiation, as Nancy Shoemaker (1995b) reminds us in her essay on Kateri Tekakwitha's uses of Christian conversion, was not simply committed to assimilation nor was it confined to Native/white interaction but was used, as well, by Native women to secure further empowerment within their tribal communities.

With the installation of the reservations, work and education were identified as two interrelated locations from which Natives could learn "appropriate" gender roles and practices. On the reservation, the separate spheres of male and female were organized through a redefinition of "work." Labor (or "work") was introduced as a sign of masculine superiority over women who, confined to domestic and gardening chores, did not "work." In Sarah Winnemucca's autobiography, *Life among the Piutes* (Hopkins, 1883/1994), the men learnt to laugh, from their training by reservation agents, at the idea that women, may work. By regulating the sexual distribution of work, federal agencies determined how Native peoples and communities would perceive their own labor in terms of gender conventions.

The aim of Indian education, at the end of the nineteenth century, was to inculcate Native children with the beliefs and values of the ideal United States citizen (see Lomawaima, this volume). Academic instruction was supplemented with lessons in self-reliance, Christian morality, and vocational training. But gender determined the content and direction of students' instruction. Richard Pratt, founder of the Carlisle Indian Industrial School, defined his mission as teaching "the Indian boy to till the soil, shove the plane, strike the anvil, and drive the peg, and the Indian girl to do the work of the good and skillful housewife" (Pratt, 1908: 21). Female vocation, in off-reservation boarding schools, was clearly domestic. "Home economics," or domestic science, raised the status of the home at the turn of the century, and home management took on an important role in the education of Indian girls. The educated female elite, such as Dakota writer Zitkala Sä, were enlisted into the field matron service in order to bring domestic science to the reservation and to educate the reservation women on hygiene, diet, the care and maintenance of children and home, and the necessity of keeping a household budget. In addition to instruction in academics, Christianity, and housewifery, the Indian girl was provided with introductions to, and possible coalitions with, white women's Christian reform organizations, such as the Young Women's Christian Association and the Women's Christian Temperance Union. These groups, appropriately enough, concerned themselves with the maintenance of popular gender roles among the non-Indian population.

The Third Gender

With the advent of gender studies, scholars since the 1980s have attempted to recover and recuperate the histories of third or intermediate genders, once commonly referred to under the generic term "berdache." As with questions concerning the historical status of Native women, there are few unmediated documents on these particular gender issues. The berdache – or, in its more contemporary term, "two-spirited people" – represents, like indigenous matriarchy, sexual histories that have been repressed under patriarchal colonization. Drawn from the oral tradition and historical and anthropological documentation, the works of Beatrice Medicine (1983), Walter Williams (1986), Will Roscoe (1991, 1998), and Sue-Ellen Jacobs, Wesley Thomas, and Sabine Lang (1997) argue that fixed gender roles and heterosexuality are neither natural, essential, nor universal. Gender diversity – including but not necessarily paired with sexual variance – is described by these scholars as a desirable and honored social construction in many North American tribal nations. As seen in Medicine's depiction of the Manly Woman, or the Plains warrior woman, an individual – male or female – with extraordinary skills or courage had both social and sexual latitude in some tribal communities (Medicine, 1983: 267–80).

There is some evidence that early European/American anxieties about undifferentiated or blurred gender roles and practices were, in fact, informed by encounters with the berdache, a figure more explicitly linked with homosexuality in white perceptions of tribal communities. Studies on the figure of the two-spirit are burdened by the need to provide counter-histories, recuperate preindustrial traditions, and negotiate the historical and cultural particularities of those often conflicting traditions. Roscoe's work, for example, documents – some might say celebrates – the spiritual and ceremonial roles of the Lakota berdache (1998). In her ethnographic novel *Waterlily*, however, Dakota writer Ella Deloria represents the male berdache as a "peculiarly delicate matter," since it was the tribe's concern "that its girls should become women and its boys men through normal and progressive steps without complications" (Deloria, 1988: 136). Was Deloria's interpretation informed by her deep knowledge of Dakota culture or by her Christian missionary upbringing? It is difficult to find clarity on such questions, which often underpin the studies of two-spirit individuals and their larger cultural meanings.

Writings on the berdache or third gender are powerfully informed by tribal and pan-tribal traditions, and by the current debate on the social and political construction of the sexed and gendered body. Contemporary constructionist readings of gender emphasize the material concept of sex as a thoroughly political and regulatory, unified fiction (Butler, 1999). Like the homosexual, the lesbian, and the transvestite, the two-spirit is defined by his/her opposition to the seeming materiality of the sexed and gendered body. As presented in much scholarship, however, two-spirit people are not defined, as well, by social and political marginalization but, instead, are authorized by cultural and spiritual tribal traditions.

Contemporary Gender Traditions

At the beginning of the twenty-first century, it is difficult to use a word like "tradition" in reference to Native cultures and histories without self-consciousness as to what, exactly, is being claimed. On the one hand, the word represents the continuity and survival of tribal cultures; on the other, it authorized ahistorical and holistic narratives concerning tribal peoples. Popular discussions, including those surrounding indigenous feminism, rely on both claims for their authority. Counter-histories or counter-mythologies built on tribal gender provide interesting examples of pan-tribal and postmodern traditions, whose true subject is often located in a desire for real and material indigenous difference in the West. It is significant, and not coincidental, that this desire to speak of tribal peoples and histories as "traditional" is shared, equally, by Native and non-Native America.

The contemporary status of women and the existence of the third gender in native communities have been influenced by the highly divers and hybridized experiences of native peoples. As modern subjects, native lives have been affected by "traditional" tribal social organization and cultural values, by shared histories of colonization and adaptation, and by Western feminism and gay pride. As historical subjects that have undergone and are undergoing complex cultural processes, tribal gender roles and practices are and will continue to be contradictory and contested. If the recovery of native gender roles is to be serviceable to native peoples, then it has to address not only the loss of power and status to women and third genders in Euro-American culture, but also how the loss of such power and status is evident within Native America itself.

BIBLIOGRAPHY

Allen, Paula Gunn 1986: *The Sacred Hoop: Recovering the Feminine in American Indian Traditions* (Boston: Beacon Press).

Bederman, Gail 1995: *Manliness and Civilization* (Cambridge: Cambridge University Press).

Black Hawk 1833 (1990): *Black Hawk: An Autobiography* (Urbana: University of Illinois Press).

Butler, Judith 1999: *Gender Trouble: Feminism and the Subversion of Identity*, 2nd edn. (New York: Routledge).

Deloria, Ella 1988: *Waterlily* (Lincoln: University of Nebraska Press).

Fleming, E. McClung 1965: "The American Image as Indian Princess, 1765–1783," *Winterthur Portfolio* 2: 65–81.

Fleming, E. McClung 1967: "From Indian Princess to Greek Goddess: The American Image 1783–1815," *Winterthur Portfolio* 3: 37–66.

Ford, Ramona 1997: "Native American Women: Changing Statuses, Changing Interpretations," in Elizabeth Jameson and Susan Armitage (eds.), *Writing the Range: Race, Class, and Culture in the Women's West* (Norman: University of Oklahoma Press).

Green, Rayna 1975: "The Pocahontas Perplex: The Image of Indian Women in American Culture," *Massachusetts Review* 16: 4.

Higham, John 1990: "Indian Princess and Roman Goddess: The First Female Symbols of America," *Proceedings of the American Antiquarian Society* 100(1): 45–79.

Hopkins, Sarah Winnemucca 1883 (1994): *Life among the Piutes: Their Wrongs and Claims* (Reno: University of Nevada Press).

Hulme, Peter 1986: *Colonial Encounters: Europe and the Native Caribbean, 1492–1797* (London: Routledge).

Jacobs, Sue-Ellen, Wesley Thomas, and Sabine Lang (eds.) 1997: *Two-Spirit People: Native American Gender Identity, Sexuality, and Spirituality* (Urbana: University of Illinois Press).

Landes, Ruth 1938 (1997): *The Ojibwa Woman* (Lincoln: University of Nebraska Press).

Landsman, Gail 1996: "Studies of Native Women and the Development of the Anthropology of Gender," in Harvey Markowitz (ed.), *Papers in Curriculum* Series (Chicago: Newberry Library).

Leacock, Eleanor 1977: "Women in Egalitarian Societies," in Renate Bridenthal and C. Koonz (eds.), *Becoming Visible: Women in European History* (Boston: Houghton Mifflin).

Leacock, Eleanor 1980: "Montagnais Women and the Jesuit Program for Colonization," in Mona Etienne and Eleanor Leacock (eds.), *Women and Colonization: Anthropological Perspectives* (New York: Praeger).

Medicine, Beatrice 1983: "'Warrior Women' – Sex Role Alternatives for Plains Indian Women," in Patricia Albers and Beatrice Medicine (eds.), *The Hidden Half: Studies of Plains Indian Women* (Lanham, MD: University Press of America).

Mihesuah, Devon 1998: *Cultivating the Rosebuds: The Education of Women at the Cherokee Female Seminary 1851–1909* (Urbana: University of Illinois Press).

Mohanty, Chandra Talpade 1994: "Under Western Eyes: Feminist Scholarship and Colonial Discourse," in Patrick Williams and Laura Chrisman (eds.), *Colonial Discourse and Post-Colonial Theory: A Reader* (New York: Columbia University Press).

Morgan, Lewis Henry 1962 (1851): *League of the Ho-de-no-sau-nee, or Iroquois* (Seacaucus, NJ: Citadel).

Morgan, Lewis Henry 1877 (1985): *Ancient Society, or Researches in the Line of Human Progress from Savagery through Barbarism to Civilization* (Tucson: University of Arizona Press).

Ortner, Sherry 1974: "Is Female to Male as Nature Is to Culture?" in Michelle Z. Rosaldo and Louise Lamphere (eds.), *Women, Culture and Society* (Stanford: Stanford University Press).

Perdue, Theda 1989: "Cherokee Women and the Trail of Tears," *Journal of Women's History* 1(1) (Spring).

Perdue, Theda 1998: *Cherokee Women: Gender and Culture Change, 1700–1835* (Lincoln: University of Nebraska Press).

Pratt, Richard H. 1908: *The Indian Industrial School: Its Origins, Purposes, Progress, and the Difficulties Surmounted* (Carlisle, PA: Hamilton Library Association).

Rosaldo, Michelle Z. 1974: "Women, Culture and Society: A Theoretical Overview," in Michelle Z. Rosaldo and Louise Lamphere (eds.), *Women, Culture and Society* (Stanford: Stanford University Press).

Roscoe, Will 1991: *The Zuni Man-Woman* (Albuquerque: University of New Mexico Press).

Roscoe, Will 1998: *Changing Ones: Third and Fourth Genders in Native North America* (New York: St. Martins Press).

Rothenberg, Diane 1980: "The Mothers of the Nation: Seneca Resistance to Quaker Intervention," in Mona Etienne and Eleanor Leacock (eds.), *Women and Colonization: Anthropological Perspectives* (New York: Praeger).

Sanday, Peggy Reeves 1981: *Female Power and Male Dominance: On the Origins of Sexual Inequality* (Cambridge: Cambridge University Press).

Scott, Joan Wallach 1988: "Gender: A Useful Category of Historical Analysis," in *Gender and the Politics of History* (New York: Columbia University Press). (Originally published in *American Historical Review* 91: 5 (1986).)

Shoemaker, Nancy 1995a: "Introduction," in Nancy Shoemaker (ed.), *Negotiators of Change: Historical Perspectives on Native American Women* (New York: Routledge).

Shoemaker, Nancy 1995b: "Kateri Tekakwitha's Tortuous Path to Sainthood," in Nancy Shoemaker (ed.), *Negotiators of Change: Historical Perspectives on Native American Women* (New York: Routledge).

Smith, John 1986: *The Generall Historie of Virginia*, ed. Philip L. Barbour (Chapel Hill: University of North Carolina Press).

Spillers, Hortense 1987: "Mama's Baby, Papa's Maybe: An American Grammar Book," *Diacritics* 17(2): 65–81.

Spindler, Louise S. 1962: *Menomini Women and Culture Change*. American Anthropological Association, Memoir 91 (February).

Van Kirk, Sylvia 1980: *Many Tender Ties: Women in Fur Trade Society, 1670–1870* (Norman: University of Oklahoma Press).

Wallace, Anthony F. C. 1970: *Death and Rebirth of the Seneca* (New York: Knopf).

White, Richard 1991: *The Middle Ground: Indians, Empires, and Republics in the Great Lakes Region, 1650–1815* (Cambridge: Cambridge University Press).

Williams, Walter 1986: *The Spirit and the Flesh: Sexual Diversity in American Indian Culture* (Boston: Beacon).

Young, Philip 1967: "The Mother of Us All: Pocahontas," in *Three Bags Full: Essays in American Fiction* (New York: New York University Press).

18

Métis, Mestizo, and Mixed-Blood

JENNIFER BROWN AND THERESA SCHENCK

The mixing of ethnic groups is an integral part of human history, and varying degrees of mixed ancestry are characteristic of most or all of the world's peoples. This sharing of genetic heritage contributes to great variability within the human species. At the same time it assures a biological unity that defies efforts to compartmentalize *homo sapiens* into separate races. Ample evidence has demonstrated the fallacy of race as a scientific construct; as the American Anthropological Association recently declared, "any attempt to establish [racial] lines of division among biological populations [is] both arbitrary and subjective," and DNA and other studies have shown that "there is greater variation within racial groups than between them" (1998). Seen from this perspective, "racial" mixing is commonplace, not abnormal, and it may or may not give rise to a new ethnic group. In the Americas, as elsewhere, persons of mixed European and indigenous ancestry are not necessarily destined to form a distinct people; biology predetermines only the possibility that they might, never the certainty that they will. In sum, it is time to acknowledge the racial – and racist – ideology that underlies spurious classifications based on biological differences.

Terms and Their Problems

"Race," in older usage, referred simply to a group or class of persons or animals having some features in common or connected by descent or origin. Early nineteenth-century European ethnologists and linguists, however, gave the term new meanings. In Britain, for example, ideas about the Teutonic origins of the English and their distinctness from the Celts came together in the construct of an Anglo-Saxon "race" whose members, "enterprising, liberty-loving, … self-reliant and self-controlled," were "juxtaposed against the impulsive, imaginative, violent, and somewhat childish Celt, … [and] on a broader stage contrasted with the savages of the non-Western world" (Stocking, 1987: 62–3). Racial thinking reinforced European feelings of superiority; it also helped to provide rationales for conquest, colonization, and slavery. By extension, it furnished the folk biology that underlies the notion of mixed-blood, which has become a widely used term denoting racial mixture. In reality, of course, it is not blood that mixes, but people and their cultures.

It is a complex historical fact that racial and ethnic terms have shifted and varied considerably across time and space; words accepted in some periods and places become offensive in others. Their meanings also evolve and take on new connotations. Anyone employing terms for groups of mixed ancestry needs to take into account the particular communities being referred to, and to assess whether a given word is historically appropriate or anachronistic; how would the groups so labeled respond to a given descriptor, past or present? Today, the term "half breed" is offensive to most, although it was evidently not pejorative when it came into wide use in the early 1800s. Yet here and there it has persisted locally as a term of choice, for example, among the older Scots-Cree at Moose Factory on James Bay. The spreading Canadian usage of the term "Métis" strikes these offspring of old Hudson's Bay Company-connected families as irrelevant (Long, 1985); they have had community histories and political concerns very different from those of the descendants of the largely Francophone, Roman Catholic Métis who supported Louis Riel on the western Canadian plains.

The sensitivities of past communities deserve equal concern since the dead have no protection against our projections of current categories into past settings. This essay seeks to point out and respect varying historical usages as they appear. Its title resorts, however, for the sake of brevity, to the three general terms most frequent in current usage: "Métis," referring to the largely Western-Canadian-based population of mixed native–European ancestry; "Mestizo," pertaining to mixed groups of Spanish affiliation, and "Mixed-blood," a category in wide use in the United States in reference to people of mixed descent who may live on or off Indian reservations, but who do not necessarily coalesce into distinct ethnic communities.

Ethnogenesis and Historical Diversity

Although people of mixed native–European ancestry have existed in North America for five centuries, their relatively late and regionally focused emergences as distinctive groups and communities long delayed scholars' recognition of their numbers and importance. Space does not allow review of all relevant North American writings on peoples of mixed descent, but a look at their historiographical discovery through the lens of Métis history illustrates how work on the topic has intensified in recent decades. The growth trajectory of Métis history and the reasons for it parallel the rising attention lately given to mixed-blood populations elsewhere in the Americas.

Twentieth-century Métis historiography began with the works of French ethnologist Marcel Giraud in the 1930s, and of American journalist Joseph Kinsey Howard, whose finely romantic biography of Métis hero Louis Riel, *Strange Empire*, appeared in 1952 (reprinted 1994). Giraud's monumental doctoral thesis, *Le Métis Canadien: son role dans l'histoire des provinces de l'Ouest* (available since 1986 in English translation), appeared in 1945. The book was both ahead of its times and behind them. Giraud later recalled the difficulty he had getting his thesis subject approved; many professors at the University of Paris found it "too remote, of too limited a scope, to arouse any interest" (Peterson and Brown, 1985: xiii). The work, of over 1,300 pages on yellowing acidic paper, lay largely unused in university libraries until the 1970s, when several doctoral students, John Foster, Jacqueline Peterson, Sylvia Van Kirk, and Jennifer Brown, independently came across it during their researches on fur trade and Métis history, and were amazed at its rich content and documentation, notably from the Hudson's Bay Company Archives (then housed in London, and now in Winnipeg). Giraud was the first scholar to write comprehensively on the Métis and to demonstrate, in particular, the remarkable productivity of the HBC Archives for both fur trade history and the history of all the native and European communities, old and new, involved in the trade. Yet viewed in the context of Boasian anthropology, his analytic framework was flawed and old-fashioned, even in the 1940s. Situating the Métis along a social-evolutionary continuum between primitive and civilized, he described them as indolent, volatile, weak-willed, in danger of regressing to their primitive Indian side – perpetuating old evolutionist and racialist conflations of culture, ethnicity, character, and mentality that long characterized much other writing about peoples of mixed descent, and about native people generally.

The early 1980s saw a blossoming of Métis studies, in tandem with new social histories that began to highlight other previously neglected groups. Fur trade scholars in the 1970s turned from company histories and explorers to women, Indians, and fur trade families, bringing new angles of vision that, as a matter of course, led them toward Métis history. As well, Métis writers, most notably Maria Campbell, whose autobiographical book, *Halfbreed*, appeared in 1973, began publishing stories drawn from their own lives, families, and communities. Then, thirty-six years after Giraud's book appeared, Jacqueline Peterson took the initiative of organizing a historic Conference on the Métis in North America at the Newberry Library in Chicago (1981). That seminal gathering, which Giraud attended, brought together for the first time a wide range of scholars, Métis and others, who held in common their interest in Métis studies. It and the resulting book, *The New Peoples: Being and Becoming Métis in North America* (Peterson and Brown, 1985) were among the numerous catalysts for the attention that "new peoples" generally have received in recent years.

We can mention here only a few other important works appearing since 1985. In 1994, eight years after Giraud's work reappeared in English translation, Howard's *Strange Empire* was reprinted with a new introduction by Nicholas C. P. Vrooman, director of the Institute for Métis Studies at the College of Great Falls, Montana (one of several academic institutions where Métis studies are now established). Besides works cited elsewhere in this essay, the studies of Van Kirk (1980) on women in the fur trade, and of Tanis Thorne (1996) on French–Indian fur trade relations and the roles of people of mixed ancestry in tribal politics on the lower Missouri, require mention, as do the writings of John E. Foster (1986). Since Maria Campbell's book appeared, Métis lives, both as told by Métis themselves (Welsh, 1991) and as constructed from the more distant past by others, have been an increasing focus of publication. In 1989, James A. Clifton edited *Being and Becoming Indian: Biographical*

Studies of North American Frontiers, a collection of essays about individuals who played various roles between Indian and outsider communities; several are thoughtful studies of persons of mixed descent whose identities developed in a variety of directions. Margaret Connell Szasz's edited book, *Between Indian and White Worlds: The Cultural Broker* (1994), is similarly useful for its essays on Andrew Montour, D'Arcy McNickle, and others. The best new literature tends toward analyses that are both fine-grained and intensively researched from all available written, oral, pictorial, and other sources, and interdisciplinary in scope, bringing together the best possible analytical tools for the understanding of Métis and other mixed-blood people and their multiple origins and histories.

Early Meetings and Minglings: French Colonial Contexts

Upon the European discovery of North America its native people were seen as distinct yet inferior, and the nature and extent of their humanity were much debated (Dickason, 1984: 32–4). The ways these peoples were treated varied according to the motives and ideology of the conquerors or other visitors. The new arrivals generally saw themselves as superior, but that was no barrier to miscegenation, a common feature of all except the most transitory contacts.

Soon after the beginnings of colonization by the French in the Northeast, Champlain told the Huron: "Our young men will marry your daughters, and we shall be one people" (Thwaites, 1896–1901, vol. 5: 211). His promise was never fulfilled in the manner he intended. To Champlain, marriage was a European, Christian institution in which wives took their husbands' (French) name, identity, and faith; his "one people" was French. The numerous French traders who married Native women, however, usually followed Native rather than European Christian marriage conventions, and most of their progeny took aboriginal identities. In Acadia, in the Great Lakes region, and in the Mississippi Valley, fur traders allied themselves to Native women for both companionship and improved trading possibilities, often living in Native villages and participating fully in their activities. So attached did these young men become to their unaccustomed freedom from clergy and colonial authorities that by 1685 the governor was lamenting the loss of so many to the savage life (Archives des Colonies: NAC, C11A, F7, 88v–90v). By the early 1700s, French officials as well as the leaders of the Catholic Church no longer approved of marriages with Native women (Dickason, 1985: 28). It was, however, too late: such unions had already proven useful and even essential concomitants to successful trading relationships with Native peoples whose social relations centered upon familial and kin ties.

Although the children of these French/Native unions were generally raised among their maternal relatives, a few were brought to Quebec by their fathers and raised as French. Those who remained in their aboriginal communities were considered to have their mothers' tribal identity. In the tradition of most North American aboriginal people, children belonged wholly to the culture in which they were born and raised, even if one parent was of another group. There was as yet no distinct category for children who had one European parent.

French thinking did allow, however, for the idea that children of European–Native parentage might be culturally as well as biologically mixed. The French had long had a word for mixed in the biological sense: *métis* (with the *s* pronounced), derived from the past participle, *mixtus*, of the Latin verb *miscere*. (The Latin etymology of the Spanish *mestizo* is identical.) The word was applied to the mixing of two species or breeds, of farm animals, for example, usually for the purpose of improving the one viewed as inferior. In New France of the 1600s, *métis* was occasionally used to refer to people or animals of mixed ancestry, but since the concept was not of great importance, the word is seldom found in early Canadian French texts.

In Acadia, intermarriage can be traced back to the first residency of the French in the Port Royal area in the early 1600s. The French and Mi'kmaq families associated in these interactions were considerably intertwined by 1750; the descendants of the Sieur de la Tour and of Richard Denys and their Mi'kmaq wives were among the best known. Some who took up farming were said to "live like Europeans"; one such community, at La Have on the east coast of Nova Scotia, was said to number more than seventy-five by the late 1600s. Most others, however, remained with their Mi'kmaq families and did not assimilate into French culture (Prins, 1996: 68–9). Many of the leading families could move easily between the two worlds, and had relatives in each (Upton, 1979: 26–7).

Wherever the French went in the seventeenth and eighteenth centuries, they made alliances with aboriginal people through their women. Some Frenchmen lived for extended periods in Native villages. Most begot children whom they left behind on their return to New France. A few brought a son or two east for education. But the greatest number of their progeny settled in trading communities along the waterways of the Great Lakes and the Mississippi River where Native and French worlds intersected. These settlements were truly mixed. The Jesuit priest Louis Vivier noted on his visit to the Illinois in 1750: "Les habitants sont de trois espèces: des Français, des Nègres et des Sauvages, sans parler des Métis, qui naissent des uns et des autres pour l'ordinaire, contre la Loi de Dieu" (Thwaites, 1896–1901, vol. 69: 169). Vivier was perhaps the first writer to recognize that *métis* offspring of such mingling might be tri-ethnic: French, Indian, and African. He also asserted that they were illegitimates, born out of Christian wedlock contrary to the law of God; what is not clear, however, is whether he also disapproved of all intermarriage across ethnic lines. Although these trading communities were mixed, their mixed-descent members were not a separate people from the other inhabitants; they formed vital connections among a variety of related ethnic groups.

British and Canadian Fur Trade Families in the Northwest

Meanwhile, another kind of mixing was quietly underway to the north and west, in what the French called *le pays d'en haut*, the upper country around and beyond the upper Great Lakes. Employees of the Hudson's Bay Company in Rupert's Land (the Hudson Bay watershed chartered to the Company by King Charles II in 1670) had formed many unions with Native women, largely Cree, by the late 1700s, despite their employer's rules against such ties. Men of the Montreal-based North West Company, which was the most active competitor of the Hudson's Bay Company from the 1780s to 1821, also formed relationships with Ojibwa, Cree, and other Native women, as had the French voyageurs who preceded them. By 1790 all posts of both companies had at least some residents of mixed ancestry (Brown, 1980). Before the early 1800s, however, they were not identified as a distinct group, except that in HBC usage, a Native employee's parish of birth might be listed as "Hudson's Bay" or an HBC officer's half-Cree son such as Charles Isham might be described as an Indian son of Mr. James Isham (Brown, 1994: 203; 1980: 56). The only incipient group differentiation by 1800 was found in the Montreal-based fur trade. Former employees no longer under contract to the company, a group that included both Canadians and their numerous Native families, became known as "freemen" or *gens libres*. Some of these were described by Donald McKay in 1793 as "those vagabonds of Canadians who has [*sic*] abandoned themselves to live as the Indians" (HBCA B. 22/a/1, 26 Sept.). In 1809, when HBC man John McKay found St. Louis trader Pierre Chouteau and some of his men living among the Mandans and Gros Ventres, he described them as "Mullatoes, Negroes, Creoles and Canadians" (HBCA B. 22/a/17, 6 Dec.). No English term was then in regular use for people of mixed parentage; *mulatto* is a borrowing from Spanish (meaning "young mule" and by extension, someone of mixed race), while "creole" refers to native-born (e.g., colonials or sons of traders) but does not denote racial ancestry.

The Métis of Red River

The year 1812 saw the founding of a colony that became the nucleus of Métis identity formation and power in Rupert's Land over the next six decades. Thomas Douglas, Earl of Selkirk, a large stockholder in the Hudson's Bay Company, was granted in 1811 a territory known as Assiniboia, surrounding the lower reaches and the confluence of the Red and Assiniboine rivers in present-day Manitoba. His aim was to establish a new home for Scottish and Irish emigrants displaced by economic developments in Britain. Simultaneously, the Hudson's Bay Company saw the colony as providing homes and a land-base for the many fur traders with Native families who, having left their service, could not readily resettle in England or Scotland (Brown, 1980: 168).

The settlement that took root became Red River, situated at the forks of the two rivers on the site of present-day Winnipeg. There the Métis attained unquestioned visibility as a separate people, although at first they were indistinguishable from freemen or *gens libres* in fur trade records. The term "halfbreed" first entered Hudson's Bay Company records at Carlton House in 1814, as Englishman John Peter Pruden began to differentiate "half-breeds" from freemen among his North West Company rivals (HBCA B. 27/a/5, 1 Nov.). In the winter of 1815, the Métis freemen encamped on the Turtle River (near the North Dakota–Manitoba border) were noted as considering themselves to have a separate group identity (Selkirk Papers, vol. 5: 1586–9). "At this period, for the first time," wrote former

Nor'Wester John Pritchard, "the Half-breed Servants of the North West Company, assumed a new Character, called themselves the 'Bois-brulés' ['burnt-wood people,' a seeming reference to complexion] and the 'New Nation'" (HBCA E. 8/5, fo. 137d). The designation "Métis" did not appear in the earliest Métis document, dated June 25, 1815; its authors, in claiming that they and not the Red River settlers were the owners of the soil, identified themselves as "The four chiefs of the half Indians by the mutual consent of their Fellows" (HBCA B. 235/a/3, Brown, 1980: 173). Variants of the term must have been in oral use by then, however. On July 20, 1815, when HBC clerk Peter Fidler at Brandon House (Manitoba) mentioned that HBC property at Red River had been burned or stolen, he attributed these acts to "Canadians and half-Breeds, Brulees or Mitifs" (HBCA B. 22/a/19). One of the earliest Métis leaders, Cuthbert Grant, Jr., used "halfbreed" when he wrote in English and *brulé* or *bois brulé* in French (Selkirk Papers, vol. 6: 1876–7).

English-language usage did not stabilize until well after the Battle of Seven Oaks (June 1816), considered by many to be the defining moment in Métis origins. On that occasion, twenty-one Red River residents were killed in a conflict with Métis linked with the North West Company. Subsequent events and conflicts in Rupert's Land (which did not become western Canada until Louis Riel's provisional government of 1869–70 negotiated the founding of the province of Manitoba) served to meld this growing regional population of Scots, French, Cree, Ojibwa, and to a lesser extent Athapascan and Siouan ancestry into a new people. Its Francophone members were most commonly known in English as Métis, but the most usual English rubric for the whole category remained "halfbreed" well into the twentieth century.

From the 1820s on, Métis people increasingly saw themselves, and were seen by the surrounding Indians and European colonists, as different from though connected to all those entities. As their population base in and around Red River grew to several thousand, their political consciousness and activity increased, manifest notably in the successful challenge of Guillaume Sayer to the HBC trade monopoly in 1849, and the rise of Red River Métis opposition to Canada's effort, without consultation, to claim the region for its new confederation. The Métis linked with Riel stand out as the only mixed-blood group in North America to take both political and military action to form a new or separate nation, a goal that foundered, however, with Riel's exile from the new province of Manitoba in 1870, and with his return, military defeat, and execution by Canada in the Northwest Rebellion of 1885 in Saskatchewan (for overviews of these developments, see Friesen, 1984; Ens, 1996).

Métis Diasporas

From the early 1800s on, Red River Métis buffalo hunters traveled seasonally to hunt in North Dakota and Montana as well as to the north. Many also became known for their extensive Red River cart trade (Gilman et al., 1979). Their distinctive wooden cart trains became a hallmark of Métis entrepreneurship reaching south to St. Paul, Minnesota, with connections down to Prairie du Chien (Wisconsin) on the Mississippi

River, and westward to the Dakotas and Montana as well as across the plains of Rupert's Land. Some were to establish communities as far west as Idaho, Washington, and Oregon.

Growing populations of mixed descent, less visible to outsiders than their Red River congeners, were also spreading across the subarctic regions to the north. Connected largely with Cree and Dene people, they worked for the Hudson's Bay Company or increasingly trapped and traded on their own. Their labor and skills were key to water transport, whether by canoe, York boat, or barge, and later, steamships on the major lakes and the Mackenzie River. Some worked for the incoming missionaries; some helped negotiate the Indian treaties of the 1870s and after. The Métis Heritage Association of the Northwest Territories (1998) has recently published a work offering a broad view of their roles and activities and bringing new recognition to their history and their many descendants in the north.

Canadian federal and provincial policies toward the Métis have varied. Prime Minister John A. Macdonald was obliged to recognize the Métis of the Red River region as a political force when negotiating the entry of the province of Manitoba into Canadian confederation in 1870, but dismissed their distinctiveness by 1885. During the late 1800s and early 1900s, when Canada was negotiating its major western Indian treaties, the government recognized and then sought to extinguish Métis claims by issuing "Halfbreed" scrip certificates which individuals could turn in for land or an equivalent monetary sum convertible to land; however, speculators seeking cheap land offered cash at discount to a great many Métis for their money scrip. Needful of the money and in no position to develop the sometimes distant lands they might have claimed or to become farmers, the sellers thereby lost rights to further claims. The province of Alberta, through its Métis Betterment Act in 1938, became the only province explicitly to set aside a land-base for Métis use. The act created twelve Métis settlements in the province; the eight that still exist gained title to their lands in the 1980s.

In 1982, when Canada's Constitution Act was passed, section 35 recognized three aboriginal peoples in Canada: Indians, Inuit, and Métis (for an overview of governmental responses to Métis issues, see Brown, 1988). The implications of constitutional recognition are still being explored. In December 1998, a provincial court ruling in Ontario, echoing decisions already handed down in Saskatchewan and Manitoba, affirmed that Métis people have the same rights to hunt and fish for food as do status Indians. Land claims, the issue of federal tax exemption entitlement similar to that of status Indians, and other issues also loom on the legal horizon. As Gerald Morin, Métis National Council president, commented after the hunting and fishing case, "We have always asserted we have [aboriginal] rights and they have never been extinguished or altered by any treaties" (Owens, 1998). He speaks from a growing demographic base. After Canada's census forms reinstituted in 1981 a category for mixed descent ("Métis" instead of the "Halfbreed" category used through 1941 and then deleted), Métis population estimates in Canada have soared. They now range from 500,000 to 800,000 (Owens, 1998), as growing numbers of people affirm and (re)discover their Native ancestry. Political and legal debates about definitions, rights, and criteria for recognition and community membership will continue.

Miscegenation Issues in the English Atlantic Colonies
and the United States

Unlike the French and Hudson's Bay traders of the 1600s and 1700s, English colonists to the south generally avoided intermarriage on either Indian or European terms. The early presence of white women made it unnecessary, while prejudice against "Savages" and a history of Indian wars made it unlikely (Axtell, 1985: 304). Nevertheless, throughout the colonial period, sexual contacts between English colonists and Native women were frequent enough to be seen as a recurring problem. In 1642 Connecticut passed a law forbidding its citizens to "take up theire aboade with the Indians, in a prophane course of life." Similarly, in 1679 the Boston Synod complained of men who left the colony "to forsake Churches and Ordinances and to live like Heathen." Fines and punishments were instituted to no avail (Axtell, 1981: 156, 275–6). The racial fears of numerous colonial and later state governments found expression in the anti-miscegenation laws that were on the books from the 1600s to the mid-twentieth century. Virginia in 1691, for example, outlawed unions of whites with "Negroes, mulattoes, and Indians" to prevent "that abominable mixture and spurious issue which hereafter may increase in this dominion." Sexual encounters between Indians and African-Americans, however, did increase in the 1700s, and their children might be defined as either Negro or Indian (Mandell, 1998: 466–501). As of 1930, twenty-nine of forty-eight states had anti-miscegenation laws directed mainly against "Negroes" but also in a number of instances against "Indians" and "Mongolians" (Reuter, 1969 [1931]: 80–4).

The offspring of Indian–white sexual contacts in the American colonies were generally known as "half breeds," a term found as early as 1760 (*Newport Mercury*, April 22, 2/1). They do not, however, seem to have formed a separate people, and most generally lived with their Indian maternal relatives. In the southeastern United States by the mid-1700s, numerous Scottish-American traders began to forge alliances for trade in a manner comparable to their trading counterparts in Rupert's Land, and they became connected with important families among the Cherokee and other "Civilized Tribes." The offspring of these families often prospered as they followed their fathers into entrepreneurial activities such as the operation of mills, stores, inns, and ferries. Their presence contributed to internal divisions between conservatives and adopters of the newcomers' culture and way of life, though tribal identities of the mixed-bloods endured (Champagne, 1994: 98).

Anglo-American colonization was marked largely by displacement or removal rather than intermingling (Prucha, 1962: 6). The pushing aside of Indians to replace them with whites began early in Virginia and New England, aided by tremendous Native mortality from European diseases in the 1600s. The end of the Seven Years War in 1763 saw the end of French power in North America and the intended establishment of an Indian Territory under British sovereignty west of the Appalachian Mountains; but within forty years after American independence was won, Indian removals beyond the Mississippi River and their replacement by American settlers were increasingly both standard practice and policy.

Not every American writer, however, recommended racial isolation; some saw benefits in mixing. In 1803, President Thomas Jefferson expressed his personal views on the Indian problem in a letter to Colonel Benjamin Hawkins. Acknowledging that Indians would have to "learn to do better on less land," he suggested agriculture and household manufacturing as suitable occupations to replace hunting. The object was "to let our settlements and theirs meet and blend together, to intermix, and become one people" (Bergh, 1903, vol. 10: 363). While this statement did not specifically mention intermarriage, Jefferson did raise that subject with a group of Delaware and Mohicans in 1808. In order to learn to cultivate the land and live like whites, he told them, "you will unite yourselves with us, join in our Great Councils and form one people with us, and we shall all be Americans; you will mix with us by marriage, your blood will run in our veins, and will spread with us over this great island" (Bergh, 1903, vol. 16: 452). Several decades later, the ethnologist Lewis Henry Morgan concluded that racial mixing could speed the Indians' mental and physical progress without detriment to the whites (Bieder, 1986: 231–3). Such outlooks were in the minority, however; Jefferson's assertion about one people would not have been accepted by most of his contemporaries, who viewed such unions as unnatural and their children as likely to inherit the worst traits of both parents.

American Mixed-Bloods, Land, and Assimilationist Goals

Jefferson's larger objective was the peaceful acquisition of Native lands. In a letter to William Henry Harrison, governor of the Indiana Territory, he proposed that the newly established trading houses allow the "good and influential Indians" to run into debt, because "when these debts get beyond what the individuals can pay, they become willing to lop them off by a cession of lands" (Prucha, 1975: 22). The mixed-bloods were to become useful in achieving this end.

As land cessions were secured, the United States aimed to assimilate Native peoples into mainstream society by promoting Christianity and agriculture and allotting land to individuals. In the forefront of this effort would be the mixed-bloods, those people seen as already genetically predisposed to receive civilization, such as the American authorities imagined it to be.

At first, most treaties between the United States and Native peoples were either acknowledgments of boundaries or affirmations of friendship. A strong emphasis on land cession began in 1816, however. In particular, tribes containing notable mixed-blood contingents received numerous individual land grants in hopes that the mixed-bloods would lead the way to assimilation. In an 1817 treaty with all the tribes then in Ohio, the government granted the Indians' request that numerous individuals connected to them by blood or adoption receive grants, typically of 140 acres (Kappler, 1904, vol. 2: 146). This policy continued for more than a quarter of a century.

In 1825 the powerful mixed-blood factions of the Osage and Kansa tribes, descendants of eighteenth-century French traders, were each able to acquire by treaty a reservation for the use of the half-breeds (Kappler, 1904, vol. 2: 218, 223). Other tribes that had mixed-bloods were persuaded to grant them individual tracts for farming, usually on ceded land. Some grants were made to chiefs and heads of families, although most of those who received land grants were connected through marriage to traders or interpreters.

A notable addendum to the 1826 treaty with the Chippewa at Fond du Lac on the south shore of Lake Superior reflected the fact that trader-connected mixed-bloods were likely to receive more advantages than others; almost all the intended recipients of land were children of prominent traders or of Native women married into trading families. By no means were all mixed-bloods included. And since none of the area was suitable for farming, this addendum was evidently a ploy of the traders to acquire power through their relatives' land holdings. The United States Senate did not ratify this article of the treaty.

The traders of Lake Superior were still determined to get some of the money being distributed to the Ojibwa in treaties. At first they tried to call in their debts to be paid out of treaty money. Then they continued to try to acquire land for their mixed-blood children, emphasizing the capacity of these children to aid their Indian relatives. To achieve this end, they persuaded some of the tribal leaders that the mixed-bloods should be provided for. The treaty of 1837 set aside $100,000 to be distributed among the mixed-bloods. A commissioner was appointed to take testimony from all those who believed themselves entitled to shares of the payment, and 879 mixed-bloods presented themselves, some from as far away as Red River (Manitoba) and Mackinac. The chiefs in council determined who should be accepted, based on ancestry and residence. Only 392 were recognized as belonging to the nations in the area ceded in the treaty, and the $100,000 was divided among them. Three traders succeeded in getting debt payments put into the treaty. The rest were able to call in their payments out of the money paid to the mixed-bloods (Kappler, 1904, vol. 2: 492; State Historical Society of Wisconsin, "A List of the Mixed-Blood Chippewa of Lake Superior, 1839").

It is evident that both the traders and the United States government at this time wanted to separate the mixed-bloods from the rest of the Native people. The Indians were not always in agreement, and considered those who remained on their reservations as equals. They won their point in the treaty of 1847 which stipulated: "the half or mixed bloods of the Chippewa residing with them shall be considered Chippewa Indians, and shall, as such, be allowed to participate in all annuities which shall hereafter be paid to the Chippewa of the Mississippi and Lake Superior" (Kappler, 1904, vol. 2: 568).

Nevertheless the government still tried to separate those mixed-bloods who were "sufficiently advanced in civilization" and encouraged them to become educated and settle on lands which they would possess in fee simple (Kappler, 1904, vol. 2: 746, 889). The general response from the Indians was to withhold membership and annuities from those who thus separated themselves. "Halfbreeds" were to be considered Indians unless they elected to leave the community. The government, meanwhile, continued to try to entice mixed-bloods to leave the reservations and become citizens (Kappler, 1904, vol. 2: 813, 975, 940, 972). By the mid-nineteenth century, many had sold their lands and either moved back among their Native relatives or, disavowing their Native ancestry if they could, moved into the American mainstream.

Métis Status Issues in the United States in the Later 1800s

The Métis who left Rupert's Land (or Canada after 1870) for the American West moved into a land with a long and quite distinct history of outlooks toward people of mixed descent, and faced a quite different future. Some, through marriage into American Indian communities, were accepted onto tribal rolls. The U.S. government never recognized the Métis as a distinct group, however, and many of their descendants, lacking a community base and under pressure to deny Indian ancestry, were assimilated into the dominant society.

In those areas where Red River (Canadian) Métis were living, some special problems arose. The U.S. government would negotiate only with individual Indian tribes who were long-time tenants/possessors of the land. These Métis were neither Indian nor white; and their Indian ancestry was often, in any case, Canadian Cree rather than from American groups. The Plains Ojibwa who had gradually moved west from the headwaters of the Mississippi and the Red Lake area considered the Métis to be intruding on their increasingly limited food supply. In 1852 the Ojibwa leader Way-shaw-wush-ko-quen-abe complained of these interlopers to Isaac Stevens from the Office of Indian Affairs, asking that the "half-breeds" remain in Pembina (North Dakota), and go hunting on the plains only once a summer (U.S. Department of the Interior, 1854: *Report of the Commissioner of Indian Affairs*, p. 398). As it had done with other tribes, the U.S. government would treat with mixed-bloods only as part of a full-blood group, and even attempted to get the Pembina Métis to join the Red Lake or the White Earth (Minnesota) bands. Some did. In the treaty of 1863, those who were related by blood to the Chippewa of the Red Lake and Pembina bands were granted homesteads in the ceded territory, but that still left many Métis living around Turtle Mountain as outsiders. The following year the treaty was amended to grant individual scrip certificates instead of land to the mixed-bloods, who thereby lost their claim to future annuities (Kappler, 1904, vol. 2: 853, 861).

It was evident that the other Métis would not be recognized unless they were attached to an Indian band. Many of those who had fled from Manitoba after Louis Riel's exile in 1870 moved between 1876 and 1880 to Montana, where they later became known as Landless Indians (Dusenberry, 1985: 120). Those who remained at Turtle Mountain were finally joined to the Plains Ojibwa when a reserve was established for them in 1882, and are now recognized as part of the Turtle Mountain Chippewa (Camp, 1987: 110–22).

U.S. Mixed-Blood Policies into the Twentieth Century

When individual allotments were finally made under the Dawes Act of 1887, there was no distinction based on "degree of blood." Mixed-bloods, if recognized by the individual tribe from which they were descended or where they lived, were considered Indian. Nevertheless, government officials still had hopes of assimilating all

Natives and making them full citizens. In his first report as Commissioner of Indian Affairs in 1889, Thomas J. Morgan described what this process would require:

> The tribal relations should be broken up, socialism destroyed, and the family and the autonomy of the individual substituted. The allotment of lands in severalty, the establishment of local courts and police, the development of a personal sense of independence, and the universal adoption of the English language are means to this end. (Prucha, 1975: 177)

In 1892, in a document providing rules for Indian courts, Commissioner Morgan determined that "all mixed bloods and white persons who are actually and lawfully members, whether by birth or adoption, of any tribe residing on the reservation shall be counted as Indians" (Prucha, 1975: 186). The goal of assimilation continued, however. In 1901, Commissioner William A. Jones stated that, as soon as "an Indian of either mixed or full blood" proved that he could take care of himself, Jones considered it his duty to "sever forever the ties which bind him either to his tribe, in the Communal sense, or to the Government" (Prucha, 1975: 186).

Thereafter, eager to reduce the number of Indians considered wards of the government, the Department of Indian Affairs decided that those of less than one-half Indian blood would be given "complete control of all their property," while those of more than one-half might also be released if they were found competent to manage their own affairs. In language reflecting the racial thinking of the day, Commissioner Cato Sells explained, "it is almost an axiom that an Indian who has a larger proportion of white blood than Indian partakes more of the characteristics of the former than of the latter" (Prucha, 1975: 211–13).

In the Wheeler-Howard Act of 1934, the government still preferred to consider as Indian only those of "one-half or more Indian blood" (Prucha, 1975: 225). However, the criteria for tribal membership were to be determined by each individual Native group. In general today, mixed-bloods are no longer separated from full-bloods, and it is acceptance by a recognized tribal group or band which determines one's status.

Mestizos in Early Spanish Contexts

Just as *métis* developed wherever the French had contact with native people, and the mixed-blood or half-breed arose wherever the English penetrated, so also did the *mestizo* come into being wherever the Spanish conquered. In contrast with the English, however, the Spanish colonial system needed native people for its population base and as a major source of its labor. Spanish authorities therefore encouraged, or tolerated, miscegenation (Cook, 1976: 258; Axtell, 1992: 206). What distinguished this *mestizaje* from the mixing that occurred farther north was that it resulted in a single society in which class distinctions with racial undertones played an important role (Esteva-Fabregat, 1995: 57). Not only was social stratification rooted in Spanish culture, but it likewise mirrored the structure of some of the native societies that contributed to the mixing.

By the close of the seventeenth century, the population of Ibero-America was already to a great extent mixed, due to the large influx of Spanish men in proportion to Spanish women (Axtell, 1992: 226). Thus, as New Spain pushed its boundaries northward into what is now the United States, its mestizo population played a large role in its conquests; likewise mixed-blood women were brought in from Mexico for purposes of settlement. In colonial New Mexico people were ranked hierarchically according to the degree of racial mixing and Christianization; unconverted Indians, being *gente sin razon*, were ranked as children, "lacking reason" (Gutiérrez, 1991: 195–8). Various distinctions were made among both men and women of mixed descent; Hernandez lists for the latter in the late 1600s *mestizas* (women who were European/Indian), *muletas* (European/African), *lobas* (Indian/African), and *coyotas* (*mestiza*/Indian) (Hernandez, 1986: 92).

When North American colonists arrived in the Southwest in the early decades of the nineteenth century they found a society already "steeped in a tradition of racial and cultural assimilation" (Craver, 1982: 16–17). In fact, male newcomers found that only through marriage with women from the upper ranks of this mestizo population could they achieve economic success, a testimony to the importance of these women in the social hierarchy.

Another kind of *mestizaje* occurred throughout New Spain. As the Spanish, and later the American, newcomers came into direct conflict with the Native population, rape and prostitution became common. The large number of mixed-blood children born soon after initial contact in California were "almost without exception absorbed into the Indian, rather than the white, community" (Cook, 1976: 336–7). Looked upon as inferior by their white progenitors, excluded from white society, these children, like the mixed-bloods of so many other American tribes, were culturally native. In the Pueblo Southwest, however, mixed-blood children were either expelled or abandoned (Gutiérrez, 1991: 174).

The Spanish mestizos of the Southwest, so long the objects of North Americans' discrimination, both religious and racial, have begun to rediscover and emphasize their indigenous roots (Vento, 1998: 276–86). Descendants of African slaves and Indians are also reaffirming and researching their native heritage (Walton-Raji, 1993; Katz, 1986). In most of these cases, as with so many other Americans who discover some Native ancestry, official recognition is not at issue and will probably never be achieved. Nevertheless, origins that were a source of shame to many even a few decades ago have become a source of pride to their descendants.

Conclusions

Mixed ancestry, as noted at the outset, is a commonplace among human beings. This essay has explored the ramifications of the mixings of indigenous peoples and newcomers in North America over the last five centuries. The overall picture is of a diversity that has emerged in a wide range of historical, socioeconomic, cultural, and political settings. Blood and "race" mixture in themselves are no predictors of ethnic identity; they only open possibilities. The question is always, how do human beings screen or filter the results of such mixture through their perceptions, values, interests, cultures, and even the linguistic categories that they apply to unions that cross ethnic lines, and to the progeny of those unions? Why and when do such things come to matter historically, and to whom – and why do they often not matter, in the many instances of mixing that have not resulted in constructions of new ethnic categories?

This comparative overview provides no simple answers, but may offer a few guidelines for study. Demography is key; no mixed population will be objectified as a new social entity if it does not reach a critical mass, observable by others as somehow distinct. In turn, observations by others play critical roles in pointing to a newly available identity, as in Red River in 1814–16; and outsiders' observations upon and interactions with a group, whether favorable or ill-disposed, often heighten its sense of boundaries and difference. Factors of political and economic interest also enter the equation. What, for example, may some interest groups have gained by stereotyping a category of people of mixed ancestry as distinct? The North West Company in 1815 did not create the Métis out of thin air, but some of its leaders made powerful use of a recognition of their presence in a time of violent fur trade competition.

Later, after Louis Riel's death in 1885, racial stereotyping in western Canada served to marginalize and dismiss the Métis as half-savage troublemakers with no prospects, fostering their invisibility such that their continued existence and problems could be ignored. It also placed tremendous pressures on those Métis who could assimilate into mainstream society to do so – until changing interests and balances of power in the 1980s and 1990s fostered, for many, a return to identities left in abeyance for three generations or more (for a powerful cinematic statement of this experience, see Welsh, 1991).

Canadian governmental policies, which both frame and are shaped by evolving constructions of the meanings of Métis, Indian status, treaties, and aboriginality itself, have developed within parameters that essentialize "Métis" in ways very different from the meanings given to "mixed-blood" or "mestizo" in the United States. The descendants of native–European unions in the United States were typically not isolated as a group and did not see themselves as a new or distinct people. Rather, most eventually were assimilated into one of several categories – most often, Indian, Hispanic, or American – and so they remain today.

The term "mixed-blood" and its variants have lately been appropriated as powerful metaphors, however. Numerous writers of mixed heritage now invoke blood as a metaphorical symbol of vitality and strength, and of the ability to function in two cultures. Gerald Vizenor, for example, describes "crossbloods" as "agonistic survivors ... a postmodern tribal bloodline" (1990: vii), and William S. Penn writes of "mixbloods" who "express the unified and inseparable strands of their heritage and experience" (1997: 9). Mixed descent in itself becomes a source of personal identity and pride, a marker of particular historical experiences and consciousness. The extent to which the new awareness will bring about efforts to draw new boundaries and definitions, for example, in the creating of new categories in the U.S. Census, remains to be seen. In the meantime, human history itself continues to see the merging of ethnic peoples at their borders and to demonstrate mixing as normal rather than exceptional. The fascination of the topic lies in the many and complex ways that

human beings construct ethnic mixture, or its supposed lack, in the process of negotiating the boundaries and the differences that they superpose upon their shared
genetic heritage as a species.

BIBLIOGRAPHY

American Anthropological Association Executive Board 1998: "AAA statement on
'race'," *Anthropology Newsletter* 39(6): 3.

Axtell, James 1981: *The European and the Indian: Essays in the Ethnohistory of Colonial
North America* (New York: Oxford University Press).

Axtell, James 1985: *The Invasion Within: The Contest of Cultures in Colonial North
America* (New York: Oxford University Press).

Axtell, James 1992: *Beyond 1492: Encounters in Colonial North America* (New York:
Oxford University Press).

Bergh, Albert Ellery 1903: *The Writings of Thomas Jefferson*, vols. 10, 16 (Washington,
D.C.).

Bieder, Robert E. 1986: *Science Encounters the Indian, 1820–1880: The Early Years of
American Ethnology* (Norman: University of Oklahoma Press).

Brown, Jennifer S. H. 1980: *Strangers in Blood: Fur Trade Company Families in Indian
Country* (Vancouver: University of British Columbia Press).

Brown, Jennifer S. H. 1988: "Métis," in *The Canadian Encyclopedia* (2nd edn.)
(Edmonton: Hurtig), vol. 2, pp. 1343–6.

Brown, Jennifer S. H. 1994: "Fur Trade as Centrifuge: Familial Dispersal and Offspring
Identity in Two Company Contexts," in *North American Indian Anthropology: Essays
on Society and Culture*, eds. Raymond J. DeMallie and Alfonso Ortiz (Norman:
University of Oklahoma Press), pp. 197–219.

Camp, Gregory Scott 1987: "The Turtle Mountain Plains-Chippewas and Métis,
1797–1935." Unpublished dissertation, University of New Mexico.

Campbell, Maria 1973: *Halfbreed* (Toronto: McClelland and Stewart).

Champagne, Duane (ed.) 1994: *Native America: Portraits of the Peoples* (Detroit: Visible
Ink Press).

Clifton, James A. (ed.) 1989: *Being and Becoming Indian: Biographical Studies of North
American Frontiers* (Chicago: Dorsey Press).

Cook, Sherburne F. 1976: *The Conflict Between the California Indian and White
Civilization* (Berkeley: University of California Press).

Craver, Rebecca McDowell 1982: *The Impact of Intimacy: Mexican-Anglo Intermarriage
in New Mexico, 1821–1846* (El Paso: Texas Western Press).

Dickason, Olive Patricia 1984: *The Myth of the Savage and the Beginnings of French
Colonialism in the Americas* (Edmonton: University of Alberta Press).

Dickason, Olive Patricia 1985: "A Look at the Emergence of the Métis," in *The New
Peoples: Being and Becoming Métis in North America*, eds. Jacqueline Peterson and
Jennifer S. H. Brown (Winnipeg: University of Manitoba Press), pp. 19–36.

Dusenberry, Verne 1985: "Waiting For a Day That Never Comes: The Dispossessed Métis
of Montana," in *The New Peoples: Being and Becoming Métis in North America*, eds.
Jacqueline Peterson and Jennifer S. H. Brown (Winnipeg: University of Manitoba
Press), pp. 119–36.

Ens, Gerhard J. 1996: *Homeland to Hinterland: The Changing Worlds of the Red River Métis in the Nineteenth Century* (Toronto: University of Toronto Press).

Esteva-Fabregat, Claudio 1995: *Mestizaje in Ibero-America*, trans. John Wheat (Tucson: University of Arizona Press).

Fogelson, Raymond 1998: "Perspectives on Native American Identity," in *Studying Native America: Problems and Prospects*, ed. Russell Thornton (Madison: University of Wisconsin Press), pp. 40–59.

Foster, John E. 1986: "The Plains Métis," in *Native Peoples: The Canadian Experience*, eds. R. Bruce Morrison and C. Roderick Wilson (Toronto: McClelland and Stewart), pp. 375–403.

Friesen, Gerald 1984: *The Canadian Prairies: A History* (Toronto: University of Toronto Press).

Gilman, Rhoda H., Carolyn Gilman, and Deborah M. Stultz 1979: *The Red River Cart Trails: Oxcart Routes between St. Paul and the Selkirk Settlement 1820–1870* (St. Paul: Minnesota Historical Society Press).

Giraud, Marcel 1986: *The Métis in the Canadian West*, 2 vols., trans. George Woodcock (Edmonton: University of Alberta Press [1945]).

Gutiérrez, Ramón A. 1991: *When Jesus Came, the Corn Mothers Went Away: Marriage, Sexuality, and Power in New Mexico, 1500–1846* (Stanford: Stanford University Press).

Hernandez, Salome 1986: "Nuevas Mexicanas as Refugees and Reconquest Settlers 1680–1696," in *New Mexico Women: Intercultural Perspectives*, eds. Joan M. Jensen and Darlis A. Miller (Albuquerque: University of New Mexico Press), pp. 41–69.

Howard, Joseph Kinsey 1994: *Strange Empire: A Narrative of the Northwest* (St. Paul: Minnesota Historical Press [1952]).

Hudson's Bay Company Archives: B. 22/a/1, 17, 19; B. 27/a/5; B. 235/a/3; E. 8/5 (Winnipeg: Provincial Archives of Manitoba).

Kappler, Charles J. 1904: *Indian Affairs: Laws and Treaties*, 5 vols., vol. 2 (Washington, D.C.: Government Printing Office).

Katz, William Loren 1986: *Black Indians: A Hidden Heritage* (New York: Atheneum).

Lomawaima, K. Tsianina 1994: *They Called It Prairie Light: The Story of Chilocco Indian School* (Lincoln: University of Nebraska Press).

Long, John S. 1985: "Treaty No. 9 and Fur Trade Company Families: Northeastern Ontario's Halfbreeds, Indians, Petitioners and Métis," in *The New Peoples: Being and Becoming Métis in North America*, eds. Jacqueline Peterson and Jennifer S. H. Brown (Winnipeg: University of Manitoba Press), pp. 137–62.

Mandell, Daniel R. 1998: "Shifting Boundaries of Race and Ethnicity: Indian–Black Intermarriage in Southern New England, 1760–1880," *Journal of American History* 75: 466–501.

Métis Heritage Association of the Northwest Territories 1998: *Picking up the Threads: Métis History in the Mackenzie Basin* (MHANT).

National Archives of Canada, Archives des Colonies: C11A, F7 (Ottawa).

Newport Mercury 1760: Newport, RI, April 22.

Owens, Anne Marie 1998: "Landmark Ruling Gives Métis Aboriginal Rights – Stage Set for New Fights" (Toronto: *National Post*, December 22).

Penn, William S. 1997: *As We Are Now: Mixblood Essays on Race and Identity* (Berkeley: University of California Press).

Peterson, Jacqueline and Jennifer S. H. Brown (eds.) 1985: *The New Peoples: Being and Becoming Métis in North America* (Winnipeg: University of Manitoba Press).

Prins, Harald 1996: *The Mi'kmaq: Resistance, Accommodation, and Cultural Survival* (Fort Worth: Harcourt Brace College Publishers).

Prucha, Francis Paul 1962: *American Indian Policy in the Formative Years: The Indian Trade and Intercourse Act, 1790–1834* (Cambridge, MA: Harvard University Press).

Prucha, Francis Paul (ed.) 1975: *Documents of United States Indian Policy* (Lincoln: University of Nebraska Press).

Reuter, Edward Byron 1969: *Race Mixture: Studies in Intermarriage and Miscegenation* (New York: Negro Universities Press [1931]).

Selkirk Papers (Thomas Douglas, Earl of Selkirk): transcripts. Winnipeg: Provincial Archives of Manitoba.

State Historical Society of Wisconsin: "A List of the Mixed-Blood Chippewa of Lake Superior, 1839" (unpublished).

Stocking, George W., Jr. 1987: *Victorian Anthropology* (New York: Free Press).

Szasz, Margaret Connell (ed.) 1994: *Between Indian and White Worlds: The Cultural Broker* (Norman: University of Oklahoma Press).

Thorne, Tanis C. 1996: *The Many Hands of My Relations: French and Indians on the Lower Missouri* (Columbia: University of Missouri Press).

Thornton, Russell 1998: "The Demography of Colonialism," in *Studying Native America: Problems and Prospects*, ed. Russell Thornton (Madison: University of Wisconsin Press), pp. 17–39.

Thwaites, Reuben Gold (ed.) 1896–1901: *Jesuit Relations and Allied Documents*, 73 vols., vols. 5, 69 (Cleveland: Burrows Brothers).

Upton, Leslie F. S. 1979: *Micmacs and Colonists: Indian–White Relations in the Maritimes, 1713–1867* (Vancouver: University of British Columbia Press).

U.S. Department of the Interior, 1854: Report of the Commissioner of Indian Affairs. In *Message from the President of the United States to the Two Houses of Congress*, Part I (Washington: Beverley Tucker), pp. 211–544.

Van Kirk, Sylvia 1980: *Many Tender Ties: Women in Fur Trade Society, 1670–1870* (Norman: University of Oklahoma Press).

Vento, Arnoldo Carlos 1998: *Mestizo: The History, Culture and Politics of the Mexican and the Chicano* (Lanham, MD: University Press of America).

Vigil, James Diego 1998: *From Indians to Chicanos: The Dynamics of Mexican-American Culture* (Prospect Heights, IL: Waveland Press).

Vizenor, Gerald 1990: *Crossbloods: Bone Courts, Bingo and Other Reports* (Minneapolis: University of Minnesota Press).

Walton-Raji, Angela Y. 1993: *Black Indian Genealogy Research: African American Ancestors among the Five Civilized Tribes* (Bowie, MD: Heritage Books).

Welsh, Christine 1991: *Women in the Shadows* (Direction Films).

19

Transforming Outsiders: Captivity, Adoption, and Slavery Reconsidered

PAULINE TURNER STRONG

The capture and social transformation of outsiders was a widespread but varied practice in indigenous North America. Depending upon the society and time period in question, captivity was followed by incorporative practices such as adoption and resocialization as well as a variety of subordinating practices ranging from confinement and involuntary labor to torture and death. Although underrepresented in popular imagery and in scholarly accounts, Native American captives of Europeans and Euro-Americans were also subjected to a variety of incorporative and subordinating practices.

This essay explores the assumptions embedded in conceptualizing indigenous practices under such rubrics as "captivity," "adoption," and "slavery," arguing that the use of these translation devices (Cheyfitz, 1997) has led to blind spots, misconceptions, and poorly framed controversies. "Incorporation" and "subordination" are offered as more satisfactory analytical terms for the range of transformative processes that follow in the wake of "captivity," itself understood as the assertion of power over a person or group resulting in dislocation, physical confinement, and social transformation. These more abstract terms and definitions have the advantage of grouping together phenomena that might otherwise be viewed separately (e.g., kidnapping, incarceration, forced relocation and schooling, and various forms of servitude), while calling our attention to the complex ways in which incorporative and subordinating practices are combined in particular instances.

There are significant regional and historical variations in captivity practices, and the scholarly literature has developed rather independently from one region to another. Therefore, after a discussion of literary and ethnohistorical scholarship on colonial and frontier captivity narratives – the most compelling, if problematical, documents concerning captivity – this essay reviews the central themes, debates, and lacunae in the historical and ethnohistorical scholarship on (1) the Northeast, (2) the Southeast, (3) the Plains and Southwest, and (4) the Northwest. As the literature on captivity is immense and interdisciplinary, this review privileges analytical scholarship over descriptive accounts, anthologies, and primary sources; comparative research over case studies; histories and ethnohistories over literary criticism; and recent scholarship over classics. Many excellent works have been omitted in which captivity, adoption, and slavery are incidental rather than central, and several important and prolific authors are represented by a single title. With the exception of two works of enduring theoretical importance, none of the works considered here were published prior to the 1970s, when new interpretations of captivity, adoption, and slavery began to appear in the interdisciplinary fields of ethnohistory, American Studies, and Women's Studies.

For these reasons this essay should be supplemented with other recent bibliographies. For captivity, see Derounian-Stodola and Levernier (1993), Magnaghi (1998), Sayre (2000), Strong (1999), and Vaughan (in Washburn, 1977–83, vol. 112); for adoption, see Kan (2001) and Strong (2001); for slavery and other forms of servitude, see Donald (1997), Magnaghi (1998), and Sturtevant (1988: 404–16).

Captivity Narratives

Since the late seventeenth century the published narratives of colonial and frontier captives have been compelling to Euro-American scholars and popular audiences alike. Annotations upon the most popular narratives, anthologies of captivities and "Indian atrocities," popular histories, and literary critiques have often replicated the stereotypes found within the narratives, reinscribing the selective tradition of captivity (Strong, 1999) within new genres directed to new audiences. Scholars achieve independence from the selective tradition of captivity to varying degrees, and even contemporary works of scholarship may perpetuate stereotypes, generally through insufficient attention to the cultural and historical contexts within which captivity occurred.

Contemporary interpretations of captivity narratives fall under two main rubrics: (1) literary history, and (2) ethnohistory or social history. In the first category are two landmark works in American Studies: Richard Slotkin's *Regeneration through Violence* (1973) and Annette Kolodny's feminist response, *The Land Before Her* (1984). These works follow in the path of Roy Harvey Pearce's inquiries into how Anglo-American "civilization" has been defined in relation to the American "wilderness" and Indian "savagery." Pearce (1947) outlines the development of successive genres in which captivity serves as a vehicle for particular cultural "functions" or "significances": (1) religious confession (during the late seventeenth and early eighteenth centuries); (2) political propaganda (in the early through the mid-eighteenth century); (3) the expression of sensationalism and sensibility (from the mid-eighteenth century into the nineteenth century); and (4) historical and ethnological knowledge (in the nineteenth and twentieth centuries). While there is actually more overlap and longevity in the various ideological functions of the narratives, Pearce's schematic model has basically stood the test of time. James Levernier and others have elaborated the model in studies emphasizing the role of captivity narratives as propaganda for Western expansion (e.g., in Derounian-Stodola and Levernier, 1993). Recent studies by Faery (1999), Scheckel (1998), and Strong (1999) have situated the publication and performance of popular captivity tales, both historical and fictional, in relation to the development of Anglo-American ideologies of nation, race, and gender. The religious significance of captivity narratives has also received considerable attention, most recently by Ebersole (1995) and Strong (1999), while the theme of sensationalism and sensibility has been developed in a variety of feminist studies inspired by Kolodny (e.g., Burnham, 1997; Faery, 1999; Namias, 1993; Strong, 1999).

While most literary historians have followed Pearce's lead in tracing the development of captivity narratives as a historically variable set of genres, Slotkin (1973) analyzes the content of captivity narratives at an archetypal level. As one of the earliest forms of a distinctly American mythology of "regeneration through violence," captivity narratives constitute, for Slotkin, a variation of the universal archetypal pattern of the heroic quest: at first a heroine (Mary Rowlandson) who resists and exorcizes the threat of the wilderness and its inhabitants, the exemplary captive is transformed by the late eighteenth century into a heroic hunter (Daniel Boone) who allows himself to be initiated into the mysteries of the wild. Scholars need not share Slotkin's Jungian orientation to benefit from his analysis, for the structuring metaphor of "regeneration through violence" can also be understood in more culturally and historically specific terms.

Slotkin, like Pearce, stresses the progressive secularization of captivity narratives, but he finds in the narratives of the eighteenth and nineteenth centuries a marked increase in both the realism with which the captivity experience is portrayed and the degree of intimacy that may obtain between captive and captor. The contrast with Pearce's emphasis on the propagandistic and sensationalistic qualities of the narratives of the eighteenth and nineteenth centuries can be explained by Slotkin's attention to adopted "White Indians" such as Mary Jemison and partly transculturated captives such as Boone (see also Axtell, 1981: 168–206; Kolodny, 1984; Namias, 1993; Scheckel, 1998). Like James Fenimore Cooper's Natty Bumppo (for whom he served as a model), Boone prized the wilderness skills and "natural" virtues he learned from (and then utilized against) his captors.

Inspired by Slotkin's study of the mythologizing of Daniel Boone, Robert Tilton (1994) has recently offered a detailed exploration of the "evolution" of the figure of Pocahontas in the literature and art of the eighteenth and nineteenth centuries. Tilton's attention to visual representations of captivity is a significant departure from a text-based scholarly tradition (but see Kasson, 1990; Scheckel, 1998). His focus on the permutations of a particular captivity narrative is also significant, for it is more typical for literary studies to cast themselves quite broadly, as indicated, for example, by the subtitle of a recent literary study: *Puritan to Postmodern Images of Indian Captivity* (Ebersole, 1995). While broadly defined studies reveal the persistence of the selective tradition of captivity, they tend not to offer the detailed sociocultural and historical contextualization essential to understanding relationships between captivity narratives as a literary tradition and captivity as a culturally and historically variable practice.

The indigenous context of captivity has been neglected or distorted in many literary histories. As Pearce (1974) acknowledged, studies of captivity narratives and other images of Indians carried out under the rubric of the "history of ideas" disregard Indians as a cultural and historical (as opposed to an ideological) reality. This applies not only to Tilton and Slotkin, but also to the valuable feminist studies of Kolodny (1984) and Laurel Thatcher Ulrich (1982), which are more concerned with the perspectives and experiences of Euro-American captive women than with those of their Native American captors. Several recent literary interpretations, however, consider Native American perspectives and experiences alongside those of Euro-American captives (e.g., Burnham, 1997; Faery, 1999; Sayre, 2000; Scheckel, 1998).

In contrast to literary historians, up until the 1990s ethnologists and ethnohistorians generally considered captivity narratives less as coherent literary texts than as documents from which to abstract details regarding the nature of indigenous beliefs and practices, processes of accommodation and conflict between indigenous and immigrant peoples, and the transformative process Hallowell (1963) called "transculturation." While ethnohistorical interest in captivity narratives dates to Lewis Henry Morgan, Henry Rowe Schoolcraft, and John R. Swanton, a new generation of researchers were inspired by James Axtell's 1975 article, "The White Indians of Colonial America" (reprinted in Axtell, 1981: 168–206; see also pp. 39–128, 245–71). In "White Indians" and other works Axtell culls ethnographic details from a variety of colonial narratives in order to analyze the attraction that indigenous societies held for those transculturated captives who resisted repatriation – an attraction that Axtell contrasts effectively with the generally unsuccessful assimilation of Native Americans into British colonial society. Axtell's rather impressionistic conclusions regarding the extent to which non-Indian captives were successfully adopted into Indian societies have been challenged by Vaughan and Richter (1980), who utilize the statistical techniques and concern for local detail characteristic of social history. A recent study of captivity in colonial New Mexico (Brooks, 1996) considers the partial transculturation of Native American and colonial captives alike.

Recent research on captivity narratives has been facilitated by the publication of a comprehensive set of facsimiles, unfortunately without annotation (Washburn, 1977–83). The most satisfying of the recent studies follow Pearce's (1974) forward-looking program in melding literary and ethnohistorical approaches. In the introduction to an excellent anthology, Vaughan and Clark (1981) demonstrate the value of an interdisciplinary approach, analyzing Puritan and Quaker narratives in the context of other contemporary literary genres, Puritan social structure, and the course of British/Indian relations. In the 1990s a number of social historians and ethnohistorians have demonstrated how fully certain individual narratives can be contextualized culturally and historically. Particularly notable are Neal Salisbury's (1997) edition of Mary Rowlandson's captivity narrative; John Demos's (1994) multivocal history of the life of the adopted Puritan captive, Eunice Williams; Haefeli and Sweeney's (1995) delineation of the indigenous context of the same captivity; and June Namias's (1993) rendering of the relationship between Sarah Wakefield and her Dakota captor. The results of John Fierst's extensive research on the narrative of the transculturated Ottawa captive, John Tanner, are eagerly awaited (but see Fierst's preview in Brown and Vibert, 1996: 220–41).

A serious limitation to the narrative-based approach is its privileging of literate captives and those with access to an amanuensis or editor and a publisher (but see Calloway, 1992). This approach also downplays the existence of Native American captives, whether held by indigenous people or by Europeans or Euro-Americans. Several recent works (Brooks, 1996; Faery, 1999; Namias, 1993; Salisbury, 1997; Sayre, 2000; Strong, 1999) demonstrate the value of expanding the definition of "captivity narrative" to include European and Euro-American accounts of kidnapping, incarcerating, enslaving, adopting, and resocializing Indians. The following survey of regional scholarship illustrates the value of approaches that make use of a wide variety of unpublished sources in order to illuminate the experiences of a broader array of captives than are represented in the selective tradition of captivity.

The Northeast

Scholarship on captivity in the Northeast is dominated by the highly ritualized and well-documented practices of the Iroquoians. Although interpretations vary, there is a fair amount of agreement as to a general Iroquoian captivity pattern. (The central source for the following summary is Richter, 1983; see also, in addition to references cited below, Fenton's and Tooker's contributions to Kan, 2001; Fenton's, Tooker's, and Trigger's articles in Sturtevant, vol. 15, 1978: 296–321, 418–41, 798–804; and Strong, 1999.)

As in many parts of North America, captivity among Iroquoians was generally initiated in a "mourning war." Typically, a bereaved clan matron whose grief (or that of a clan member) remained unassuaged after a series of condolence rituals would persuade her brothers' sons (or other young male members of the matrilineage) to obtain one or more captives. The fate of captives was contingent upon a variety of circumstances, including their own deportment, and their status was ambiguous until clarified by ritual action, if not permanently ambiguous. Upon the war party's return a captive would be submitted to a sequence of ritual actions designed to transform his or her social status and revitalize the matrilineage and clan. First the mourners would vent their rage as captives were forced to "run the gauntlet," i.e., to run between two parallel lines of villagers who administered physical and verbal abuse. Next the captives would be divided among bereaved lineages, if necessary, and incorporated through adoption. Women and children would often be welcomed as valuable additions to a bereaved lineage, their social identity transformed through an astute mixture of inducements and punishments. An adolescent or adult male, expected to be less malleable and compliant, was more likely to be tortured and sacrificed – if not already killed and scalped during battle or on the homeward journey.

A victim of torture was expected to face his pain courageously, mocking or cursing his tormentors, who would try to goad him on to ever more impressive displays of bravery. The victim's status as an adopted member of the matrilineage would be underscored through repeatedly addressing him as "sister's son." Women took an active part in the proceedings, which served as an arena for avenging the death of clan members. Following torture a captive would be sacrificed at dawn. Portions of the captive's flesh were offered to the spiritual powers considered responsible for success in warfare, followed by collective consumption, particularly of the soul-infused heart and blood.

The adoption of a captive filled the vacant social position left by the deceased and was thought to replenish the spiritual power of the lineage. Similarly, ritually ingesting the heart and blood of a captive was a way of revitalizing a lineage, especially when the captive had exhibited uncommon strength and bravery under torture. In the absence of a captive, a bereaved lineage might be revitalized through a presentation of wampum or through performing an adoption ceremony over a dead enemy's scalplock or a sacrificed bear. The performance of a scalp ceremony, the ingestion of a heart or blood, the adoption of a captive or bear, and the presentations of wampum were all rituals of incorporation that restored life and power to a bereaved lineage.

The symbolic equivalence among captives, bears, scalplocks, hearts, blood, and wampum lent considerable flexibility to this set of transformative practices. Such flexibility facilitated the adaptation of these practices to a wide variety of circumstances. Historical adaptations are well documented for Iroquoians, whose warfare and captivity practices changed significantly after the European invasion. The major colonial source on Iroquoian captivity, the *Jesuit Relations*, documents events in the mid-seventeenth century, when warfare and captivity reached an unprecedented intensity, largely in response to the European presence. In contrast to colonial warfare, indigenous conflicts were limited in scale, in large part due to the goal of taking captives without sustaining casualties (since any additional casualties among the raiding party would require the mounting of still another raid). Following the onset of sustained contact with Europeans in the early seventeenth century, however, warfare and disease led to a demographic crisis of unparalleled proportions. This dramatically intensified the Iroquoian search for captives to revitalize their lineages.

During the seventeenth century Iroquoians adopted many non-Iroquoian captives, mainly Algonquian-speakers, probably contributing to a convergence of Iroquoian and Algonquian captivity practices. By the 1660s, according to French missionary estimates, the foreign-born outnumbered natives in many Iroquoian villages. Even so, massive adoptions could not offset losses to disease, Christian missions, and warfare – losses augmented by serious conflicts with the French after 1674. In the early eighteenth century the Five Nations of Iroquois turned increasingly to the peaceful incorporation of weak or remnant Indian groups, notably, the Tuscaroras (after which the league became known as the Six Nations).

Debates concerning Iroquoian captivity practices fall into three general areas: (1) the extent and nature of European or Euro-American interpretive biases; (2) the extent to which former captives retained a marginal or subordinate status within Iroquoian society; and (3) continuities and variations in captivity practices across Northeastern Indian societies. The question of observer bias arises in any interpretation based primarily upon European and Euro-American accounts; in this case, critiques focus upon the treatment of captives who were not adopted. Scalping, torture, human sacrifice, and ritual cannibalism are central components of Western representations of the savage Other (Sayre, 1997; Strong, 1999). Furthermore, Christian doctrine offers distinct interpretations of torture and sacrifice (in the forms of mortification, penance, and martyrdom) and ritual cannibalism (in the form of the Eucharist). For these reasons, European accounts of scalping, torture, human sacrifice, and ritual cannibalism must be treated with care, as in a 1980 article by Axtell and Sturtevant demonstrating that scalping was indigenous to North America (in Axtell, 1981: 16–35; see also pp. 207–41). Similarly convincing is Thomas Abler's defense of the existence of Iroquois ritual cannibalism (e.g., in Abler and Logan, 1988; see also Axtell, 1981: 168–206). Another important contribution is Nancy Shoemaker's (1995) discussion of the beatified Iroquois convert, Kateri Tekakwitha, which suggests how converts and missionaries alike may have perceived parallels between Iroquois torture and sacrifice rituals and Catholic penitential practices.

Tekakwitha, whose mother was Algonquian, may also be taken as an illustration of the marginality of adopted captives within Iroquois society, which Starna and Watkins (1991) have emphasized in claiming that adopted Iroquois captives held a "quasi-kin" status consistent with sociologist Orlando Patterson's (1982) influential definition of slavery as "social death." Emphasizing the vulnerability of Iroquois adoptees, Starna and Watkins have offered a forceful challenge to the dominant interpretation of Iroquois captivity. In their view, adoption did not terminate the ambiguous status of captives, nor incorporate them fully into Iroquois society. Rather, Iroquois rituals placed captives in a state of social death, offering them only a subordinate status.

Starna and Watkins rely on the same evidence as previous ethnohistorians, viewing the practices that others have interpreted as a mourning complex or incorporative rituals, instead, as ways of transforming captives from the status of persons to the status of powerless and dishonored slaves. This view takes into account the practices of adopting and then sacrificing captives, linguistically equating captives to dogs, mutilating captives' fingers (interpreted as a visible mark of enslavement), compelling them to perform labor inconsistent in kind or quantity with the status of a family member, and transferring captives from one family to another (which European captives often conceptualized as being "sold" from one "master" to another). It is also consistent with an authoritative account of indigenous slavery among the Cherokees, a southern Iroquoian group (Perdue, 1979).

Whether we consider Iroquois captives as incorporated kin or subordinated slaves depends not only upon whether we emphasize incorporation or subordination but also upon how we conceptualize "adoption" and "slavery." Adoption, like kinship itself, varies widely across societies, and depends upon the cultural construction of personhood, social identity, power relations, and rights over property (Kan, 2001; Strong, 2001). Practices grouped under the rubric of "slavery" vary in similar ways. Patterson's definition, upon which Starna and Watkins rely, is construed broadly and contested by those who emphasize a master's property rights in a slave or who associate slavery with a capitalist or proto-capitalist economy (see Donald, 1997, which compares the status of captives in the Northeast and Northwest). Whether or not Starna and Watkins's interpretation becomes widely accepted, they have performed a valuable service in forcing ethnohistorians to define more clearly such terms as "adoption" and "slavery," and insisting that the extensive Iroquois use of the idiom of kinship be considered with the question of power relations in the foreground.

Another area open to interpretation concerns the range of variation across indigenous societies in the Northeast. Bruce Trigger (1976) has pointed to differences between the Hurons and the Five Nations – particularly involving the greater likelihood that captured women and children would be killed by the Hurons; the enhanced role of Huron headmen in decision-making and torture rituals; and the farewell feast that Hurons gave to fulfill captives' desires before their death. Continuities and divergences between Iroquoian practices and those of their Algonquian-speaking neighbors are less clear. Captives of Algonquians served as informants, interpreters, and mediators; they also served as hostages who could be exchanged for wampum or other valuables, pledges of peace, political subordination, or other captives (Haefeli and Sweeney, 1995; Salisbury, 1997; Vaughan and Richter, 1980). While this is true of Iroquoian captives as well, it may have been more common among Algonquians to treat captives within what Sayre calls an "economy of exchange" rather than within an "economy of vengeance" (Sayre, 1997; Strong, 1999).

The famous captivities of Rowlandson, Tanner, and John Smith are the most well-known accounts of captivity among eastern Algonquians, and each captive was treated differently – Rowlandson as a valuable hostage; Tanner as an adopted, but transferable, relative; and Smith as an adopted, hence subordinate, political leader (Salisbury, 1997; Fierst's and Gleach's articles in Brown and Vibert, 1996: 220–41, 21–42). There are other examples of Algonquian captives treated more as subordinated outsiders than as kin or quasi-kin (Haefeli and Sweeney, 1995), but this is clearly an area in which further research is needed.

Always diverse and flexible, Northeastern captivity practices were transformed in significant ways by the colonial invasion. Algonquians seem to have adopted certain incorporative rituals from their Iroquoian neighbors, while Iroquoians may have adopted from Algonquians and Europeans a more exchange-oriented approach to captivity. Notably, both Iroquoian and Algonquian war parties in the late seventeenth and eighteenth centuries took captives, heads, and scalps in order to fulfill conditions of alliance imposed by French and English colonial officials as well as to obtain ransom or bounty payments. When they chose to keep European captives among themselves, their treatment of those captives may have been influenced by European patterns of servitude and slavery, with which Native Americans became familiar through personal experience (Salisbury, 1997; Kawashima in Sturtevant, 1988: 404–6). At the same time, Indian allies of the English and French insisted on utilizing captives, refugees, and scalps in indigenous (if syncretic) ways, adopting captives or refugees to replenish their numbers and offering captives and scalps as sacrifices to spiritual forces.

In its intercultural scope, expanded scale, and responsiveness to demographic, political, and economic changes, captivity in the colonial era was part of the complex conjuncture of practices and meanings that ethnohistorian Richard White has called the "middle ground." Viewing captivity as a middle ground (Haefeli and Sweeney, 1995; Salisbury, 1997; Strong, 1999) is a fruitful new perspective that promises to expand our understanding not only of Euro-American captives but also of the many Native Americans who were captured by Europeans or Euro-Americans and imprisoned, enslaved, transculturated, employed as intermediaries, or executed.

The Southeast

In contrast to scholarship on captivity in the Northeast, research focused on the Southeast has largely been carried out under the rubric of slavery rather than that of captivity and adoption. (Scholarship on John Smith and Pocahontas, as discussed above, is a significant exception.) The literature on the Southeast also features a more developed discussion of the captivity and enslavement of Native Americans by Europeans and Euro-Americans. The emphasis on slavery is due both to the existence of a distinct category of subordinated captives in the ranked societies of the Southeast (Hudson, 1976) and to the articulation of plantation slavery with indigenous practices. Nevertheless, both indigenous slavery and Indian involvement in plantation slavery remain surprising and controversial to many non-specialists (see "Indian Slavery," H-Net, 1998).

Our understanding of the history of captivity, adoption, and slavery in the Southeast is most complete for the Cherokees due to Theda Perdue's *Slavery and the Evolution of Cherokee Society* (1979; see also Shoemaker, 1995: 90–114). Perdue's analysis of the Cherokee treatment of war captives has important implications for the debate regarding the nature of northern Iroquoian practices, for she views full adoption into a clan as only one possible treatment for those war captives (primarily women and children) who were preserved from torture and sacrifice (a subject discussed more generally in Hudson, 1976). The other alternatives are (1) ransom and (2) a precarious existence as an *atsi nahsi'i* ("one who is owned" or "dependent"). Unlike adopted captives, *atsi nahsi'i* remained outside the kinship system until they were adopted or died, their fate depending entirely upon their masters' protection and good will. Perdue views the function of *atsi nahsi'i* as more symbolic than economic prior to the participation of Cherokees in the colonial slave trade; in other words, *atsi nahsi'i* conferred prestige upon their masters and served as an anomalous or deviant "other" against which the social order of kinship was defined. (See Kan, 1989, for a similar structuralist argument about Tlingit slavery.) Although *atsi nahsi'i* would be viewed as slaves within Patterson's model (because they suffered "social death" and were both powerless and dishonored), in Perdue's analysis *atsi nahsi'i* did not become true slaves until the establishment of the South Carolina Indian trade in the seventeenth and eighteenth centuries, when slaves were commodified and the taking of captives replaced vengeance as the primary motivation for warfare.

If we remain skeptical about the usefulness of translation devices, the crucial issues are not whether Cherokee *atsi nahsi'i* were slaves, but (1) that the Cherokee had a category of subordinated captives distinct from adoptees, and (2) that Cherokee processes of incorporating and transforming captives were transformed by the colonial trade in captives (and, later, by the adoption of plantation slavery by the Cherokee elite). Although Perdue discusses the impact of the slave trade upon the Cherokees in some depth, scholarship on the trade in Indian captives in the Southeast remains fragmentary (but see Hudson, 1976; Duncan, 1982; Usner, 1992; and Wood in Sturtevant, 1988: 407–9). The legal and illegal Indian slave trade centered in South Carolina and Louisiana was a major cause of hostilities among Native American groups as well as colonial hostilities against them. At its peak, in the early eighteenth century, there were significant numbers of Native American slaves in both regions, and many others had been sold into slavery in the West Indies and New England. But the Indian slave trade declined for a variety of reasons: the susceptibility of Native American slaves to European diseases; the ease with which Native American slaves could successfully run away; fear that runaways and their relatives would join Africans in revolt; and a desire on the part of colonial officials to secure good relations with neighboring tribes and to use Native Americans to catch runaway African slaves.

While certain Native American groups, including the Catawbas, served Europeans as slave catchers (Merrell, 1984), others assisted runaways, while still others adopted plantation slavery themselves. For elite Cherokees and others emulating Southern patterns of "civilization," chattel slavery replaced indigenous patterns of captivity, adoption, and servitude. But many Cherokees opposed plantation slavery and the repression of African freedmen that was enshrined in the 1827 Cherokee constitution and subsequent legislation, and the status of African slaves and freedmen was a source of major political conflict before, during, and after the Civil War. Perdue (1979) describes the legacy of chattel slavery among the Cherokees as a racially mixed population with persistent economic and social inequalities; this observation is developed by Circe Sturm (1998) in an article on racial formation in the Cherokee Nation. Some four thousand black slaves were emancipated by an 1863 proclamation of the Cherokee chiefs in Oklahoma, and freed slaves were admitted to full Cherokee citizenship and provided an allotment of land in a treaty signed in 1866 with the United States. Over the next century, however, Cherokee Freedmen were marginalized by Cherokee laws that define identity through "blood" (descent from an enrolled Cherokee ancestor) rather than through the naturalization (sometimes referred to as "adoption") of Cherokee Freedmen, most of whom have no Cherokee ancestry. These laws have been upheld in U.S. courts due to the sovereign right of the Cherokee Nation to define its membership.

Quite a different relationship to plantation slavery developed among the Florida Seminoles, who offered refuge to runaway African slaves. Living under Seminole protection in exchange for providing food, fighting as warriors, and serving as intermediaries with whites, Black Seminoles lived in separate towns and combined African cultural, religious, and linguistic practices with new practices adopted from the Seminoles. Rebecca Bateman (1990) has interpreted Black Seminole history through the model of ethnogenesis, which emphasizes the social, cultural, linguistic, and political processes that lead to the emergence of new ethnic groups, often through amalgamation. Having fought with Seminoles during the Seminole Wars, the Freedmen were among those removed to Indian Territory when the wars ended in 1842. Settled in an area that included slave-holding Creeks, Black Seminoles were vulnerable to Creek raids, and many emigrated southward, where their descendants still live in Nacimiento and Múzquiz, Coahuila, and Brackettville, Texas. Some of the Black Seminoles who stayed in Indian Territory into the Civil War period were enslaved by Confederate Seminoles, while others took refuge among non-slaveholding Indians. Like their counterparts among the Cherokees, Seminole Freedmen were granted citizenship in an 1866 treaty with the U.S. government. Subsequently many Black Seminoles lost their allotments of land when restrictions against alienating land from Freedmen and mixed-bloods were lifted. Like the Black Seminoles in Texas, Seminole Freedmen in Oklahoma were racialized as black, subordinated under Jim Crow laws enacted after statehood, and affected by Civil Rights legislation in the twentieth century. The complex identities and historical experiences of Seminole and Cherokee Freedmen reflect a variety of incorporative and subordinating processes on the part of their respective Indian nations, the states of Texas and Oklahoma, and the U.S. and Mexico.

The theoretical models of comparative slavery, racial formation, and ethnogenesis have been fruitful in conceptualizing the transformative processes associated with captivity, adoption, and slavery in the Southeast. Current ethnohistorical scholarship is centrally concerned with the complex and shifting identities, alliances, and divisions generated through these processes. Contemporary theoretical approaches allow for a nuanced treatment of the changing ways of incorporating and subordinating outsiders in Southeastern Indian societies, and could be usefully employed in scholarship on other regions.

The Plains and Southwest

Recent ethnohistorical scholarship on captivity, adoption, and slavery on the Plains and in the Spanish borderlands (including Florida) coalesces around two themes: (1) forced labor within the Spanish mission system and in other colonial and postcolonial institutions, and (2) the commerce in captives through which Native American, Spanish, Mexican, and Anglo-American women and children crossed cultural borders in a variety of modes ranging from full incorporation to extreme subordination. The scholarship of the 1990s, influenced by feminist theories and the work of Native American scholars such as Edward Castillo (Jackson and Castillo, 1995; Sturtevant, vol. 8, 1978: 99–127, 713–18), offers a much more critical view of the exploitation of Native American labor in the Spanish and Mexican colonies than is characteristic of much of the previous scholarship (but see Cook in Sturtevant, vol. 8, 1978: 91–8; 1988: 472–80). A body of sophisticated scholarship on indigenous captivity practices and their historical transformation is beginning to emerge, although much work remains to be done.

Although slavery was formally outlawed by the Spanish Crown, colonists relied on forced Indian labor in several contexts: (1) through enslaving Native Americans who refused to submit to Spanish rule (*indios sirviendos*) as well as captives ransomed or purchased from Plains Indians (*indios genízaros*); (2) through the *repartimiento* system of conscripted labor, which was employed in missions and elsewhere; and (3) more indirectly, through the compulsory tribute payments known as the *encomienda* system. Scholars have debated whether the servitude of mission Indians is properly characterized as slavery or "near slavery" (Weber, 1990; Jackson and Castillo, 1995; Heizer in Sturtevant, 1988: 414–16; and "Indian Slavery," 1998). Regardless of terminology, there is no doubt that mission Indians were a highly subordinated labor force subject to forced relocation, confinement, devastating epidemics, and physical punishment, abuse, and deprivation. It is also certain that the exploitation of Pueblo Indian labor and resources were among the grievances that led to the successful Pueblo Revolt of 1680. After the reconquest of 1696, New Mexican colonists relied more upon non-Pueblo captives for labor, engendering an Indian slave trade that thrived until outlawed by the U.S. in 1867. In California, Indians labored in Franciscan missions between 1769 and 1834, and the capture, sale, indenture, and conscription of Native Americans continued under Mexican and U.S. rule until the end of the Civil War and, in some cases, beyond (Jackson and Castillo, 1995).

A notable account of captivity, adoption, and slavery in New Mexico is Ramón Gutiérrez's *When Jesus Came, the Corn Mothers Went Away* (1991). While Gutiérrez's interpretation of indigenous Pueblo culture has been roundly criticized, his interpretation of status differences in eighteenth-century New Mexican colonial society is an important contribution to our understanding of the relations among Spanish gentry, mestizo peasantry, Pueblo Indians, and the hispanicized Indians known as *genízaros*. The latter, or their ancestors, were generally ransomed from Plains Indian traders for payments of manufactured goods, metal tools, and horses. If retained rather than resold, they were baptized, given Christian names, and often incorporated into Spanish society through adoption and *compadrazgo* (godparent-hood). But Gutiérrez argues (against Chávez, in Sturtevant, 1979: 198–200) that even adopted *genízaros* remained subordinated outsiders rather than true kinfolk. *Genízaros* were used for menial tasks, exchanged as moveable wealth, and settled in outlying villages to offer protection from nomadic Indians. They eventually amalgamated into the colonial and Pueblo Indian populations, although even today some villages are known as originally *genízaro* settlements.

The trade in Indian captives – which took place at Pueblo trade fairs as well as in more informal exchanges – is much better documented for the Southwest than for the Northeast or Southeast. In a recent article on the commerce in captives in colonial New Mexico, James Brooks (1996) argues that both Indian and colonial captives became central to the creation of "borderlands communities of interest" that bound New Mexican colonists more closely to neighboring Indians than to Spanish and Mexican elites. Some three thousand Indians, mainly children, ransomed between 1700 and 1850 entered colonial society under conditions ranging from full adoption and intermarriage to "near slavery." At the same time, Spanish and Mexican captives were incorporated into Navajo, Apache, Ute, Comanche, and other Native American groups. Brooks is particularly interested in those captives, whether situated in colonial or indigenous society, who were able to attain some degree of power and autonomy, primarily through intermarriage and maternity (in the case of women) or through warfare and diplomacy (in the case of men).

Brooks's interest in the agency of Native American and European captives and their role in establishing a middle ground between indigenous and colonial societies articulates with current work on captivity outside the Southwest. Other scholars studying captivity, adoption, and slavery in the Southwest and Plains are beginning to examine critically the claims made in captivity narratives and frontier literature about the brutal treatment of captives, particularly among the Comanches, who played a central role in the trade in captives. Michael Tate (1994) surveys the narratives of Texan captives among the Comanches published over the century between 1836 and 1930, taking care to situate these captivities within the New Mexican slave economy as well as within the Comanche practice of adopting captive children in order to replenish a population depleted by frontier warfare and smallpox and cholera epidemics (also see Foster, 1990 for an account of historical changes in the Comanche trade in captives). Tate also discusses Comanche attitudes toward adult male captives (likely to be tortured and/or killed) versus adult women and their children, who were generally treated with respect and adopted or returned unless their existence endangered the war party. Unlike much literature on the region, in Tate's account resocialization joins vengeance as a motivation for the harsh treatment of captives. Also notable is Tate's differentiation of individual Comanche actions from a general cultural pattern in which some actions were sanctioned while others (especially rape) were condemned. He attributes the incorporation of the famous Cynthia Ann Parker to the protection and mentorship of an elderly Comanche woman, and, in contrast, the hardships of captives who remained in the role of subordinated outsiders to the lack of such protection.

Another recent work on captivity in the Southwest is Marc Simmons's (1997) account of the capture, in 1883, of six-year-old Charley McComas by Chiricahua Apaches. Simmons's book offers a valuable description of the dissemination of alternate narratives of the captivity of a judge's son in the late nineteenth century, but despite Simmons's incorporation of the accounts of descendants of McComas's captors, Chiricahua motivations remain obscure. This is largely because Simmons focuses nearly exclusively on one notorious captivity rather than on a historically variable set of captivity practices. While there is value in focusing in depth on particular instances of captivity, the contrast between Simmons's book and the more balanced accounts of Brooks, Tate, and Foster indicates the value of bringing the techniques of social history and ethnohistory to the study of particular captivities. At the same time, Simmons has demonstrated well that family records and oral history can still illuminate the experiences of certain captives.

The northern Plains has not inspired much recent work on captivity, but Namias (1993) has pointed the way toward what might be done in her nuanced analysis of the Wakefield captivity. Blackfoot adoption practices in the mid-twentieth century are discussed by Marjorie Lismer (1974), who observed fluid families with frequent adoptions and fosterage of infants and young children by grandparents, other relatives, and bereaved persons replacing a dead relative. Accounts by Black-Rogers, Powers and Powers, and Straus (in Kan, 2001) are valuable additions to the literature on adoption in the Plains. Also enhancing our understanding of the various means of adopting and treating kinfolk in Plains societies are the works of the Dakota ethnographer Ella Deloria. Notably, the fictional *Waterlily* (1988) illustrates how various ways of treating a captive fit into a larger Dakota pattern of extending what Deloria elsewhere calls "social kinship." The emerging scholarship on indigenous patterns of adoption and historical changes in captivity practices provide a context within which the many captivity narratives located in this region can be read with increasing sophistication.

The Northwest

Like the scholarship on the Southeast, Southwest, and Plains, that on the indigenous societies of northern California, the Northwest Coast, and the Plateau frequently refers to slavery. Until recently, however, there has been little sustained attention to the stigmatized and subordinated status of "debt slaves" (who assumed the status on a temporary or permanent basis in order to fulfill an obligation), illegitimate children, war captives, and their descendants. This is partly the consequence of a rather sterile debate as to whether these societies were organized by rank or class, one in which those favoring "rank" argued that (1) although slaves were forms of wealth and markers of status for the aristocracy, they were economically unimportant, and (2) because they were defined and treated as non-persons, slaves were situated entirely outside of the social structure, and thus outside the realm of social analysis (see Donald, 1997 for references to the long-lived debate). The relative neglect of slavery in the Northwest also stems from the reluctance of Native American consultants to discuss this now stigmatized practice, which was criticized by missionaries and outlawed under U.S. and Canadian law. Former slaves were adopted into the lineages of their owners, but like the black Freedmen of the Southeast, they often retained the stigma of their former status.

Recently, however, two monographs have been devoted entirely to slavery in the Northwest. Ruby and Brown (1993) focus especially upon the Chinookan and Klamath trade in Indian slaves and other valuables that was centered at the Dalles on the Columbia River. Especially after the adoption of the horse, an expansive trade network bound together the Plateau, the Northwest Coast, northern California, the Great Basin, the Rocky Mountains, and even the Plains (see also Sturtevant, 1988: 414–16; 1990: 533–46; 1998: 641–52). A more theoretically ambitious account, by Leland Donald (1997), compares Northwest Coast slavery with that found in other regions of North America, arguing against what he has described elsewhere as an egalitarian bias in scholarship on Native Americans. Both monographs offer important documentation concerning the capture, trade, treatment, and ritual sacrifice of captives in the Northwest, but should be read in concert with accounts that offer a symbolic and experiential perspective on kinship, personhood, and social inequality in the Northwest (e.g., Kan, 1989; and Harkin, Kan, Miller, and Buckley in Kan, 2001).

The incorporative practice of adoption into a clan existed side by side with the subordinating and dehumanizing practice of slavery in the ranked societies of the Northwest. Aristocratic women were sometimes taken as wives by their captors, and aristocrats of both genders might be ransomed by their people and ritually cleansed of their slave status. Captive commoners, however, could expect to remain slaves, and were distinguished through naming practices, lack of material and symbolic property, linguistic differences, and physical features that revealed their foreign origin. Slaves' labor contributed to the wealth of their owners, and although they might improve their status through exhibiting conspicuous bravery, displaying unusual artistic, shamanic, or linguistic talents, or playing certain ceremonial roles, slaves had little control over their lives. As in the Northeast, a set of symbolic correspondences equated subordinated captives with other valuables used in ritual transformations and exchanges: if captives were associated with wampum, bears, and scalplocks in the Northeast, they were associated with coppers and salmon in the Northwest. At a potlatch slaves might be given away or freed; they might also be sacrificed and buried under house posts, subjected to ritual cannibalism, or burned with their owners' bodies in order to accompany them to the next world. Lacking a clan affiliation, slaves were outside the moral universe; if they died naturally, their bodies were simply discarded in the sea or forest.

Contemporary traditionalists practice both formal and informal adoption. In an edited volume concerning the adoption of anthropologists by Native Americans (Kan, 2001), Thomas Buckley recounts his adoption by Yuroks, while Sergei Kan discusses the increasing number of adoptions of non-Tlingits as well as his own adoption into two traditionalist families. Another contemporary perspective is offered by Lillian Petershoare (1985), who considers the diminishing role of the matrilineage and clan in contemporary Tlingit life, while maintaining that the ethic of caring for one's (bilateral) extended family is still observed in many informal adoptions. This article also considers the implications of traditional adoption practices for the implementation of the Indian Child Welfare Act of 1978, which returned jurisdiction over the adoption of Native American children in the U.S. to their tribes and nations. Although the legal literature is extensive, ICWA is only beginning to receive the scrutiny of anthropologists and historians (but see Strong, 2001).

Conclusion

In popular representations and, until recently, most scholarship, captives, adoptees, and slaveholders are racialized as White, captors as Red, slaves as Black. An interdisciplinary body of scholarship published over the last quarter-century has blurred this picture, revealing that a multiracial cast has played each of these roles, albeit in distinctive ways. Many productive approaches to the study of captivity, adoption, and slavery have emerged, including the ethnohistorical contextualization of captivity narratives (particularly those emerging from the colonial Northeast); feminist and postcolonial approaches to power relations (especially in scholarship on captivity narratives and on the Southwest); a focus on "middle ground" or "borderland" phenomena (particularly in research on the Northeast and Southwest); theories of racial formation and ethnogenesis (particularly regarding the Southeast and Southwest); and the perspective of comparative slavery (particularly regarding the Southeast and Northwest). The author hopes that this essay contributes to a cross-fertilization of studies across regional and disciplinary divides as well as to a broader and more complex understanding of the incorporation and subordination of outsiders in Indian and non-Indian societies alike.

BIBLIOGRAPHY

Abler, T. S. and M. H. Logan 1988: "The Florescence and Demise of Iroquoian Cannibalism: Human Sacrifice and Malinowski's Hypothesis," *Man in the Northeast* 35: 1–26.

Axtell, J. 1981: *The European and the Indian: Essays in the Ethnohistory of Colonial North America* (New York: Oxford University Press).

Bateman, R. B. 1990: "Africans and Indians: A Comparative Study of the Black Carib and Black Seminole," *Ethnohistory* 37: 1–24.

Brooks, J. F. 1996: " 'This Evil Extends Especially ... to the Feminine Sex': Negotiating Captivity in the New Mexico Borderlands," *Feminist Studies* 22(2): 279–309.

Brown, J. S. H. and E. Vibert (eds.) 1996: *Reading Beyond Words: Contexts for Native History* (Petersborough, Ont.: Broadview Press).

Burnham, M. 1997: *Captivity and Sentiment: Cultural Exchange in American Literature, 1682–1861* (Hanover, NH and London: University Press of New England).

Calloway, C. 1992: *North Country Captives: Selected Narratives of Indian Captivity from Vermont and New Hampshire* (Hanover, NH: University Press of New England).

Cheyfitz, E. 1997: *The Poetics of Imperialism: Translation and Colonization from "The Tempest" to Tarzan*, 2nd edn. (Philadelphia: University of Pennsylvania Press).

Deloria, E. C. 1988: *Waterlily* (Lincoln and London: University of Nebraska Press).

Demos, J. 1994: *The Unredeemed Captive: A Family Story from Early America* (New York: Alfred A. Knopf).

Derounian-Stodola, K. Z. and J. A. Levernier 1993: *The Indian Captivity Narrative, 1550–1900* (New York: Twayne and Maxwell Macmillan International).

Donald, L. 1997: *Aboriginal Slavery on the Northwest Coast of North America* (Berkeley: University of California Press).

Duncan, J. D. 1982: "Indian Slavery," in B. A. Glasrud and A. M. Smith (eds.), *Race Relations in British North America, 1607–1783* (Chicago: Nelson-Hall), pp. 85–106.

Ebersole, G. L. 1995: *Captured by Texts: Puritan to Postmodern Images of Indian Captivity* (Charlottesville and London: University Press of Virginia).

Faery, R. B. 1999: *Cartographies of Desire: Captivity, Race, and Sex in the Shaping of an American Nation* (Norman: University of Oklahoma Press).

Foster, M. W. 1990: *Being Comanche: A Social History of an American Indian Community* (Tucson: University of Arizona Press).

Gutiérrez, R. 1991: *When Jesus Came, the Corn Mothers Went Away: Marriage, Sexuality, and Power in New Mexico, 1500–1846* (Stanford: Stanford University Press).

Haefeli, E. and K. Sweeney 1995: "Revisiting *The Redeemed Captive*: New Perspectives on the 1704 Attack on Deerfield," *William and Mary Quarterly* 3rd series, 52, 3–46.

Hallowell, A. I. 1963: "American Indians, White and Black: The Phenomenon of Transculturalization," *Current Anthropology* 4, 519–31.

Hudson, C. 1976: *The Southeastern Indians* (Knoxville: University of Tennessee Press).

"Indian Slavery" 1998: "H-Net List for American Indian Studies" <gopher.h-net.msu.edu>, June–October.

Jackson, R. H. and E. Castillo 1995: *Indians, Franciscans, and Spanish Colonization: The Impact of the Mission System on California Indians* (Albuquerque: University of New Mexico Press).

Kan, S. 1989: "Why the Aristocrats Were 'Heavy', or How Ethnopsychology Legitimated Inequality among the Tlingit," *Dialectical Anthropology* 14: 81–94.

Kan, S. (ed.) 2001: *Relatives to Strangers: Native American Adoption and Naming of Anthropologists* (Lincoln and London: University of Nebraska Press).

Kasson, J. S. 1990: *Marble Queens and Captives: Women in Nineteenth-Century American Sculpture* (New Haven: Yale University Press).

Kolodny, A. 1984: *The Land Before Her: Fantasy and Experience of the American Frontiers, 1630–1860* (Chapel Hill: University of North Carolina Press).

Lismer, M. 1974: "Adoption Practices of the Blood Indians of Alberta, Canada," *Plains Anthropologist* 19(63), 25–33.

Magnaghi, R. M. 1998: *Indian Slavery, Labor, Evangelization, and Captivity in the Americas: An Annotated Bibliography* (Lanham, MD: Scarecrow Press).

Merrell, J. H. 1984: "The Racial Education of the Catawba Indians," *Journal of Southern History* 50, 363–84.

Namias, J. 1993: *White Captives: Gender and Ethnicity on the American Frontier* (Chapel Hill: University of North Carolina Press).

Patterson, O. 1982: *Slavery and Social Death: A Comparative Study* (Cambridge, MA: Harvard University Press).

Pearce, R. H. 1947: "The Significances of the Captivity Narrative," *American Literature* 19, 1–20.

Pearce, R. H. 1974: "From the History of Ideas to Ethnohistory," *Journal of Ethnic Studies* 2: 86–92.

Perdue, T. 1979: *Slavery and the Evolution of Cherokee Society, 1540–1866* (Knoxville: University of Tennessee Press).

Petershoare, L. 1985: "Tlingit Adoption Practices, Past and Present," *American Indian Culture and Research Journal* 9(2): 1–32.

Richter, D. K. 1983: "War and Culture: The Iroquois Experience," *William and Mary Quarterly* 3rd series, 40: 528–59.

Ruby, R. H. and J. A. Brown 1993: *Indian Slavery in the Pacific Northwest* (Spokane, WA: Arthur H. Clarke).

Salisbury, N. (ed.) 1997: *The Sovereignty and Goodness of God by Mary Rowlandson, with Related Documents* (Boston: Bedford Books).

Sayre, G. M. 1997: *"Les Sauvages Américains": Representations of Native Americans in French and English Colonial Literature* (Chapel Hill and London: University of North Carolina Press).

Sayre, G. M. (ed.) 2000: *American Captivity Narratives: Selected Narratives with Introduction.* New Riverside Editions (Boston and New York: Houghton Mifflin).

Scheckel, S. 1998: *The Insistence of the Indian: Race and Nationalism in Nineteenth-Century American Culture* (Princeton, NJ: Princeton University Press).

Shoemaker, N. (ed.) 1995: *Negotiators of Change: Historical Perspectives on Native American Women* (New York: Routledge).

Simmons, M. 1997: *Massacre on the Lordsburg Road: A Tragedy of the Apache Wars* (College Station: Texas A & M University Press).

Slotkin, R. 1973: *Regeneration through Violence: The Mythology of the American Frontier, 1600–1860* (Middletown, CT: Wesleyan University Press).

Starna, W. A. and R. Watkins 1991: "Northern Iroquoian Slavery," *Ethnohistory* 38: 34–57.

Strong, P .T. 1999: *Captive Selves, Captivating Others: The Politics and Poetics of Colonial American Captivity Narratives* (Boulder and Oxford: Westview Press/Perseus Books Group).

Strong, P. T. 2001: "To Forget Their Tongue, Their Name, and Their Whole Relation: Extra-tribal Adoption, the Indian Child Welfare Act, and the Trope of Captivity," in S. Franklin and S. McKinnon (eds.), *Relative Values: Reconfiguring Kinship Studies* (Durham, NC and London: Duke University Press).

Sturm, C. D. 1998: "Blood Politics, Racial Classification, and Cherokee National Identity: The Trials and Tribulations of the Cherokee Freedmen," *American Indian Quarterly* 22: 230–58.

Sturtevant, W. C. (gen. ed.) *Handbook of North American Indians*, 20 vols. Vol. 4, *History of Indian–White Relations*, ed. W. E. Washburn (Washington, D.C.: Smithsonian Institution Press, 1988); vol. 7, *Northwest Coast*, ed. W. Suttles (1990); vol. 8, *California*, ed. R. Heizer (1978); vol. 9, *Southwest*, ed. A. Ortiz (1979); vol. 12, *Plateau*, ed. D. E. Walker, Jr. (1998); vol. 15, *Northeast*, ed. B. Trigger (1978).

Tate, M. L. 1994: "Comanche Captives: People between Two Worlds," *The Chronicles of Oklahoma* 72: 228–63.

Tilton, R. S. 1994: *Pocahontas: The Evolution of an American Narrative* (Cambridge: Cambridge University Press).

Trigger, B. G. 1976: *The Children of Aataentsic: A History of the Huron People to 1660*, 2 vols. (Montreal: McGill-Queen's University Press).

Ulrich, L. T. 1982: *Good Wives: Image and Reality in the Lives of Women in Northern New England, 1650–1750* (New York: Alfred A. Knopf).

Usner, D. 1992: *Indians, Settlers, and Slaves in a Frontier Exchange Economy: The Lower Mississippi Valley before 1783* (Chapel Hill: University of North Carolina Press).

Vaughan, A. T. and E. W. Clark (eds.) 1981: *Puritans among the Indians: Accounts of Captivity and Redemption* (Cambridge, MA: Harvard University Press).

Vaughan, A. T. and D. K. Richter 1980: "Crossing the Cultural Divide: Indians and New Englanders, 1605–1763," *Proceedings of the American Antiquarian Society* 90(1), 23–99.

Washburn, W. E. (comp.) 1977–83: *The Garland Library of Narratives of North American Indian Captivities*, 112 vols. New York: Garland.

Weber, D. J. 1990: "Blood of Martyrs, Blood of Indians: Toward a More Balanced View of Spanish Missions in Seventeenth-Century North America," in D. H. Thomas (ed.), *Columbian Consequences*, vol. 2: *Archaeological and Historical Perspectives on the Spanish Borderlands East* (Washington, D.C. and London: Smithsonian Institution Press), pp. 429–48.

20

Translation and Cultural Brokerage

ERIC HINDERAKER

Culture has generally been treated by historians and anthropologists as "an historically transmitted pattern of meanings embodied in symbols" (Geertz, 1973: 89),
especially the symbol systems associated with language, religion, production and
exchange, and political ritual. Together these symbol systems define the unique,
organic character of a coherent social group. Johann Herder employed the term as
an antidote to the universalism of the Enlightenment. "Unlike 'civilization,' which
was transferable between peoples (as by a beneficent imperialism), culture was what
truly identified and differentiated a people" (Sahlins, 1995: 11–12). While these
characterizations might be debated or refined, they establish a useful starting point
for this essay. Above all, the concept of culture raises the question of commensurability: if culture is the uniquely defining symbolic universe of a human society,
how is meaningful communication across the boundaries of culture possible? This
question carries us into the realm of translation and cultural brokerage.

Translators and cultural brokers have long attracted interest from both scholarly
and popular audiences. In part this is because they often lived fascinating, paradoxi-
cal lives. In part, too, brokers have claimed a disproportionate share of attention
because, central as they were to contact situations, they are often overrepresented in
the surviving records. We simply know more about the activities of cultural brokers
and translators than we do about the great majority of their contemporaries. Brokers
also serve as focal points for important interpretive and theoretical issues. Daniel
Richter (1988) has argued that cultural brokers can help scholars link the broad patterns of imperial histories with the complex dynamics of local settings. Brokerage
and translation also challenge anyone who seeks to conceptualize culture *per se*; for
this reason, they have long been of interest to anthropologists, particularly given
that discipline's widespread reliance on native informants to interpret cultural phenomena. It might even be argued that the study of cultural brokers has played a
kind of brokerage role between the disciplines of history and anthropology: one of
the most enduring threads in the ethnohistorical literature of North America traces

the activities of cultural brokers in the post-Columbian era. This essay will consider various ways in which cultural brokerage might be defined, explore the ways in which brokers and translators have been treated biographically, identify key theoretical challenges implied by the study of cultural brokerage, and touch on current approaches that have been formulated in response to those challenges.

Definitions

In the 500 years of interaction between Europeans and Native Americans, many discrete activities might be identified as examples of translation and cultural brokerage. At the most basic level, and from the very earliest period of contact, brokers translated words from one language to another. This is the most obvious and ubiquitous form of brokerage, but by no means the only one. Brokers were also responsible for interpreting diplomatic and political concepts between cultures, for facilitating commercial relationships, and for informing outsiders about the religious or symbolic content of their own people's traditions. Nor does this list exhaust the possibilities: brokers sometimes crossed from their own cultural realm to another and became symbols in their own right, laden with meanings ascribed to them by members of another culture (Hinderaker, 1996; Deloria, 1998).

A list of brokerage acts can be useful, but it misses crucial elements of any effective definition of brokerage and translation. Its emphasis on single, discrete acts fails to communicate the ways in which many prominent brokers combined a variety of roles and gained their identities through long service in multiple contexts. One important characteristic of brokers was their ability to move easily from language translation to more complex forms of intermediation (Hagedorn, 1988). If we seek to understand brokers, as distinct from brokerage acts, we must consider their relationships to the communities they served as well as the particular acts they performed. Many of the most effective brokers in the Americas were exposed to hybrid cultural influences for long periods of time, and gained through their experiences a unique ability to perform a variety of cross-cultural tasks. From this point of view, it might be argued that brokers were defined less by what they did than by who they were.

Another shortcoming of any list of brokerage acts is its inability to account for power relations between cultures. All brokerage and translation was shaped by the relationship between a cultural intermediary and the communities or individuals for whom he or she was working. The efforts of cultural brokers could always be compromised by their interests, loyalties, and dependencies; to be effective, brokers had to establish relationships of trust with everyone who relied on their honesty and judgment. Brokers were repeatedly scrutinized for evidence of their integrity, and any perceived inconsistencies could jeopardize their credibility. This left many brokers and translators in an oddly uncomfortable position, at the center of important activities yet isolated and vulnerable as a result of their unique roles (Merrell, 1997). Brokers and translators were often caught between two powerful, contrary streams. As long as members of both cultures considered them useful they could stay afloat, but when the currents shifted, their reputations and livelihoods were easily dashed

(Gillespie, 1997). Any effective definition of brokerage must address the issue of power and capture the liminal character of many brokers' experiences.

Nor can brokerage acts be understood apart from the settings in which they occurred. Where Spaniards encountered fully sedentary cultures in central Mexico and the Andean highlands, they negotiated with indigenous nobles for tribute and labor (Gibson, 1964); as Spain extended its power into northern New Spain, where the non-sedentary natives were generally hostile to Spanish intrusions, it resettled Christianized Indians from central Mexico to act as cultural brokers with the local populations (Hobgood and Riley, 1978). English and French colonists, by contrast, generally encountered semi-sedentary peoples in the Eastern Woodlands and required brokers who could mediate between the very different assumptions that animated tribal chiefdoms and kin-based communities, on the one hand, and nascent European nation-states on the other, a context that Richard White (1991) has illuminated especially well. Differences among European cultures could influence the forms of brokerage as strongly as differences among Indian cultures could. Patricia Seed (1995) has demonstrated how widely the values and motives of European colonizers could vary, and those variations shaped the forms of negotiation each colonizing power pursued with native peoples. Where possible, Spain exploited pre-existing structures of authority to extract labor, and later land, from local communities (Horn, 1997). English colonists sought brokers who could temper conflicts over land and facilitate transfers of property, while brokers in New France mediated spiritual, commercial, and military alliances but rarely dealt with transfers of labor or property (Hinderaker, 1997). The nature of mediation in any setting depended on a complicated interplay of local and extralocal influences, and can only be understood in context.

Finally, all of these abstract descriptions of brokerage and translation assume two entirely distinct cultural realms. That assumption makes most sense for the very earliest period of contact between Europeans and Native Americans. Over time, however, contact settings produced a great variety of social and cultural hybrids which did not eliminate the need for brokerage and translation but which substantially altered their dynamics. The fur trading region of the Great Lakes, for example, gave rise to a large Métis, or mixed-race, population that grew up at the interstices of French and Indian cultures and contributed in its own way to the processes of brokerage and translation (Peterson and Brown, 1985; see Brown and Schenck, this volume). *Métissage* highlights the difficulty of offering a wholly satisfactory definition of brokerage and translation, at the same time that it anticipates theoretical challenges to the ways we employ the idea of culture itself.

Persons

The essential fascination of brokers is biographical. Cultural brokers are often uniquely interesting figures who give a human focus to complex stories of intercultural contact. Several early brokers and translators have risen to mythic status. Malinche, the Nahua woman who became a translator, ally, and partner to Hernando Cortés, played a crucial role in the conquest of Mexico and remains central to popular and scholarly reconstructions of the early contact era (Cypess, 1991). Her mystique is based in part on her extraordinary facility with languages, but it was her gift for shrewd and sometimes duplicitous negotiation and her unwavering loyalty to Cortés that has marked her as an especially powerful and controversial figure. In some contexts her name "has become synonymous with selling out to foreigners" (Kartunnen, 1997), while in others she has been credited with originating the "cosmic race" of modern Mexico (Vasconcelos, 1997). In the United States, too, the most cherished founding myths are linked to brokers who lived extraordinary, contradictory lives. Squanto, the Patuxet Indian whose aid to the Plymouth colony continues to be celebrated in grade schools throughout the United States, is popularly understood as a local Indian who came out of the woods to offer advice on planting corn. His real story is much more complex. Kidnapped from his New England home in 1614 by an English captain, he crossed the ocean four times and lived in both Spain and England before he returned to his home village in 1619, only to discover that an epidemic had wiped out his people. By the time the Pilgrims arrived at Plymouth in 1621, Squanto was a more experienced traveler than many of the colonists, which helps explain why he was such an effective broker between the settlers and the local Indians (Salisbury, 1981). The founding of Virginia is also connected to a mythic broker whose life is often misunderstood. Pocahontas, daughter of the great werowance Powhatan, is linked to John Smith in popular memory but married another Englishman, John Rolfe, converted to Christianity, and traveled to London, where she attended a Ben Jonson masque with King James I (Tilton, 1994). All these figures remain controversial because they allied themselves with imperial powers at a time when the success of the colonizing ventures remained in doubt; each has been celebrated as a national hero and reviled as a traitor to his or her race.

Scholarly interest in cultural brokers and translators has extended far beyond such familiar figures as Malinche, Squanto, and Pocahontas to include dozens of people who played comparable roles in a variety of settings. There is now such a rich biographical literature on cultural brokers that it is impossible to do it justice in a brief essay, but a survey of key texts can illuminate its animating concerns. Despite their differences, biographies of cultural brokers tend to share in common, explicitly or implicitly, a central question: how is the psychological experience of the broker shaped by his or her attempts to inhabit two cultural worlds at the same time, or to cross from one culture to another? The work of Anthony F. C. Wallace provides a rich point of departure for an exploration of the biographical literature. Son of an accomplished historian of colonial Pennsylvania, Wallace studied under the distinguished anthropologists Frank Speck and A. Irving Hallowell. Hallowell was deeply interested in the relationship between personality and culture and wrote an influential essay on the phenomenon he called "transculturalization," the process by which outsiders were adopted into American Indian cultures (Hallowell, 1963). Wallace became a leading proponent in American ethnohistory of the "culture-and-personality school" that is identified especially with Margaret Mead and Ruth Benedict. He wrote influential biographies of two important Indian brokers, and taken together they illustrate especially well the strengths and limitations of this approach.

The first of Wallace's Indian biographies, *King of the Delawares: Teedyuscung, 1700–1763* (1949), is both a pathbreaking study of intercultural relations between Pennsylvania and its Indian population, and a psychological profile of the Delawares' most important mediator during the crisis that culminated in the Seven Years War. Though Teedyuscung succeeded for a time in a very difficult situation, Wallace emphasizes his instability and self-doubt. Wallace implies, for example, that Teedyuscung's insecure family background may have created uncertainty about core values. His Delaware culture was "shattered" by mid-century, and Teedyuscung could not help but be attracted to "the successes and luxuries of the aggressive, self-confident Europeans" (Wallace, 1990 [1949]: 43). He converted to Christianity, dressed in European clothes, and, as his situation became increasingly untenable, displayed an alarmingly "sharpened appetite for liquor" (Wallace, 1990 [1949]: 223). (Like many commentators before and since, Wallace treats alcohol consumption as a barometer of psychic well-being.) Teedyuscung's role as broker generated immense psychic strains and, as his influence waned, his behavior became more erratic. In the end he was murdered as he slept, a tragic victim of the conflict between cultures. For Wallace, Teedyuscung illustrated the psychological dangers of an insecure cultural foundation. He suggests that, for someone with a confused sense of identity, a brokerage role only exacerbated the problem; as pressures mounted Teedyuscung, in Wallace's account, became steadily less honorable and trustworthy.

Wallace's second and more famous book, *The Death and Rebirth of the Seneca* (1970), presents the obverse case. Its subject, the famous Seneca prophet Handsome Lake, observed the decline of the Senecas from a once powerful and respected nation to a people decimated by disease and plagued by "alcohol, violence, witch fear, [and] disunity" (Wallace, 1970: 199). Community leaders were divided between traditionalists, who clung to the old ways, and assimilationists who argued that the Senecas must adopt European practices, including Christianity, to survive. In 1799 Handsome Lake fell ill and, near death, experienced a vision that gave him new life and purpose. The first vision was followed by several more; together they laid the foundation for a new religion, which was still practiced in 1970 by about 5,000 Iroquois Indians in the United States and Canada. Wallace presents Handsome Lake's gospel as a creative adaptation of Christian tenets to traditional Seneca religious forms. Faced with a psychic crisis that was similar to Teedyuscung's, Wallace implies that Handsome Lake succeeded where Teedyuscung failed: he invented a new, hybrid religion that established a durable bridge between Indian and European cultures. Rather than choosing between a Seneca past or a white future, Handsome Lake's revelations made it possible to envision a third alternative, a syncretic cultural form that honored tradition at the same time that it addressed the most pressing social problems of the day. Rooted in religious practice, it established a code of values that allowed Indians to maintain a distinctive sense of identity in a rapidly changing world.

In his creative integration of history, anthropology, and psychology, Wallace consistently implies that a stable cultural context is essential to psychological well-being. Teedyuscung, who tried to shuttle between cultures without being rooted securely in either, became steadily more erratic. Handsome Lake escaped the plight of most brokers through prophecy, which established an adaptive, syncretic cultural foundation for his Seneca followers. Wallace's approach suggests that the cultural crossings of a broker are dangerous because they threaten to unmoor him from the traditions that impart moral values to behavior. Other scholars have resisted this view. In the wake of Hallowell's pioneering work on transculturalization, American anthropologists became increasingly interested in cross-cultural influence. In a brief but suggestive essay, Malcolm McFee (1968) challenged the assumption that acculturation entailed "cultural loss and replacement," and argued instead that "biculturism" could enrich its subject to create a "150% man." Most scholarship on cultural brokers in North America since Wallace and McFee has tended toward one of these two positions: brokerage is represented either as a creative act that enhances identity, or as a marginalizing process that alienates the broker from his or her cultural roots.

Two recent collections of biographical essays illustrate the tendency to gravitate toward one of these positions. In *Being and Becoming Indian* (1989), James Clifton presented thirteen essays that share a common focus on culturally marginal figures. Like McFee, Clifton looks favorably upon brokers. Though the book's subjects are widely scattered in time and space, Clifton's preface stresses the common features of their experience. "We use biography not as an end in itself but as a method....We aim at revealing more texture and intricacy than what emerges from other types of anthropological and historical studies, and at generating some new insights" (Clifton, 1989: ix). Clifton decried the tendency in both popular and scholarly contexts to essentialize Indian identity. Most Indians, he argued, had a mixed cultural heritage and experienced "mobility ... between ethnic and racial categories" (Clifton, 1989: 17). Yet scholars commonly treat bicultural people as "suspended between two cultures," a condition often regarded as "inherently disabling." Clifton argued instead that "such people become more complicated psychologically.... In such settings, people master knowledge of both cultures, which is used to organize their behavior as called for and appropriate in different social contexts. Such people become, not diminished, but culturally enlarged" (Clifton, 1989: 29).

Colin Calloway's essay "Simon Girty: Interpreter and Intermediary," like many in the volume, amplifies Clifton's point but also complicates it. Girty, the son of an Irish immigrant, was raised in western Pennsylvania, captured by a Delaware war party during the Seven Years War, and adopted into a Seneca community. At the war's end he became a trader and gradually earned a reputation as a skilled interpreter and intermediary. He also commanded respect among the Ohio Indians as a man of uncommon courage, integrity, and generosity, and he became increasingly prominent in intercultural relations. When the American Revolution began, Girty chose to serve the British Indian Department, and so has been vilified by American writers as a vicious traitor, lacking both culture and conscience. Calloway demonstrates instead that Girty was an important "bridge between cultures." As Clifton suggested, Girty's cultural resources were enhanced, not diminished, by his extraordinary range of influences. But his world was transitory. By the end of his life, the cultural context of his youth had passed. Like Andrew Montour, who played a similar role on the Pennsylvania frontier a couple of decades earlier, Girty came of age when the Ohio frontier was – in James Merrell's memorable phrase – a "debatable land" (Merrell, 1997: 20). Both men's talent was to facilitate the debate between cultures; when the debate was over, the cultural space in which they had operated quickly closed.

The impossibility of finding a balance between two competing cultures is a recurring theme in *Between Indian and White Worlds: The Cultural Broker* (Szasz, 1994) – a theme that echoes Wallace's work. In a broadly framed historiographical introduction (which serves as a valuable supplement to this essay), the volume's editor, Margaret Connell Szasz, is particularly critical of Clifton. "The mid- to late 1980s," she writes, "saw a backlash against native people," especially in Clifton's Wisconsin, and "Clifton reflected the milieu of his time" (Szasz, 1994: 18). This context helps to explain, in Szasz's view, why Clifton looked so favorably on people with hybrid identities and decried those who saw themselves in racial terms – especially if they were using their Indian identities "to 'manipulate ... guilt feelings' ... in order to secure 'a larger share of the resources available'" (Szasz, 1994: 19). Szasz, like Clifton, is sympathetic to cultural brokers. "Over the centuries," she contends, "their successes and failures have served as a barometer of the health of cultural pluralism in American and Canadian societies" (Szasz, 1994: 20). But she and her contributors emphasize the stress, confusion, and indecision that often accompanied brokerage roles. In an essay on several brokers in Spanish–Pueblo relations in New Mexico at the end of the seventeenth century, John Kessell notes that brokers faced bewildering and complicated choices. Their circumstances were always unstable. Neutrality, he concludes, was "almost impossible. Brokers went too far and became part of the other, drew back disillusioned into their own culture, or found themselves ostracized by both" (Szasz, 1994: 26). In her essay on Andrew Montour, Nancy Hagedorn argues that an "identity crisis" underlay his brokerage activities. "[H]e probably identified himself primarily as Indian in his values and beliefs, but found it necessary to adopt many English ways to maintain his position as interpreter" (Szasz, 1994: 57, 59). Similarly, Szasz argues in her essay on the Mohegan Samson Occam, who became a renowned Christian missionary, that Occam's brokerage activities were both stressful and compromising. Only when he "alter[ed] the direction of his brokerage ... [and] centered his energies on his own people" (Szasz, 1994: 72) did Occam become a valuable resource to his own community. In the end, he helped the Mohegans "merge nonconformist Protestantism into their native world view without losing their sense of community" (Szasz, 1994: 78). In turning from an English Christian constituency to a Mohegan one, Szasz argues that Occam rediscovered himself and helped to reinvigorate his community.

Both of these volumes focus primarily on men, and gender remains a background issue. In *Between Worlds: Interpreters, Guides, and Survivors* (1994), Frances Kartunnen notes that women have often been especially effective – and controversial – brokers. Ten of her sixteen subjects are women, and the book's most effective sections include meditations on gender as a variable in brokerage. The essays range from the sixteenth to the twentieth centuries, and from central Mexico, the Yucatan, the rain forest of Ecuador, and the American West, to Australia, the Cape of Good Hope, and the borderlands of Russia and Finland. Kartunnen suggests that all the people she profiles were in some way "set apart" from their communities "before they began to speak to outsiders" (Kartunnen, 1994: 286). Several had become human property before they emerged as brokers; most had attenuated ties with families and loved ones. All were apparently marked by unusual intellectual abilities, a characteristic that often singled them out for malicious treatment. Most came from structured and intolerant cultures. The collision with colonialism brought her subjects forward from their own communities, but Kartunnen emphasizes that the special opportunities and challenges of brokerage could paradoxically liberate unusual individuals from the narrow constraints of their native societies.

If all of this can be said of brokers generally, it applies especially to women. Writing of Cortés's translator Malinche, Kartunnen emphasizes that "her own world was generally characterized by stringently defined social roles that were taught in childhood and enforced throughout life. Deviation from the ideal brought dreadful punishments" (Kartunnen, 1994: 77). As women entered into brokerage roles, they were often profoundly alienated from the expectations and roles of their own communities. For women, roles as translators and brokers could also lead to roles as wives or concubines of foreign men. Kartunnen is careful not to idealize these unions; several women she profiles had deeply unsatisfactory, if not disastrous, relationships with non-native men. But coming from marginal positions in their own society, women brokers sometimes won a measure of protection, and even companionship, through such unions.

Finally, Kartunnen emphasizes that "informants were open to intense criticism, slander, and shunning" (Kartunnen, 1994: 298), and this, too, was doubly true of women. Through their roles as intermediaries, Kartunnen's subjects risked criticism and ostracism from both sides. Lacking a secure place in their native cultures, brokers often had no one who would come strongly to their defense. Because they traveled widely and moved through shifting contexts that forced them to form and re-form personal alliances, brokers could appear inconstant or untrustworthy to others. Some women brokers endured constant sexual threats as they moved in unfamiliar contexts without male protectors. If they did try to live as "women alone," as Sarah Winnemucca discovered, they could be subjected to humiliating criticism and slander that centered on unorthodox or promiscuous sexual behavior. Despite all the risks they took, brokers nearly always struggled to make a living. False promises; underpayment, late payment, or non-payment for services; prolonged dependency: these were the common experiences of translators and brokers.

Brokers have often been subjected to questions about the authenticity of their public selves. Native autobiographies and "told-to" biographies offer one illustration of this problem. The earliest Indian autobiographers – Samson Occam, Hendrik Aupaumut, and William Apess – were Christians. Though these writers might "exploit the ambiguities" of their identities to defend the interests of their people, their texts were produced for white audiences by individuals who were substantially acculturated to European values (Murray, 1991: 57). In "told-to" biographies the distance between the purported narrator and the final text has raised a similar concern. The autobiography of Black Hawk, for example, was produced collaboratively under circumstances that may have substantially altered its content. Black Hawk narrated his experiences to Antoine LeClair, a government interpreter of mixed descent, who translated and transcribed the account in English. LeClair then turned over his notes to a journalist named J. B. Patterson, who produced the final version of the autobiography (Krupat, 1994: 5–6).

As the discipline of anthropology emerged in the latter half of the nineteenth century, a new kind of cultural broker began to define Indian cultures for non-native audiences. Lewis Henry Morgan relied for his landmark ethnographic account of the Iroquois League on information supplied by Ely Parker (Seneca) and his siblings (Deloria, 1998). As anthropologists such as James Mooney, James Dorsey, and Paul Radin entered the field, they interpreted Indian cultures with the help of Native informants. George Sword (Oglala Sioux) wrote an important account of the Ghost Dance that helped to establish its validity as a prophetic movement (Mooney, 1965 [1896]). The Smithsonian's Bureau of American Ethnology relied heavily on the work of this first generation of anthropologists, among them the Tuscarora-descended J. N. B. Hewitt, who pioneered the formal study of the Tuscarora language and played a central role in the Bureau's development for half a century (Rudes and Crouse, 1987; Fenton, 1998: 36–8). A generation of autobiographer-informants, including Sam Blowsnake (Winnebago), Francis La Flesche (Omaha), Charles Eastman (Santee Sioux), and Zitkala Sä (Yankton), sought to document and legitimize their Indian backgrounds for readers and scholars who were increasingly receptive to an anti-modernist celebration of Indian practices and beliefs (Hoxie, 1992).

Yet the problems of authenticity and authorship have continued to shape critical responses to Indian texts. Like their predecessors, many autobiographer-informants of the late nineteenth and early twentieth centuries came from mixed backgrounds and traveled extensively. Their unusual life experiences prepared them to communicate with a non-Indian audience but also opened them to charges of inauthenticity. Such is the case with one of the most influential Indian biographies of the twentieth century, *Black Elk Speaks* (1932; Neihardt, 1972). Though Black Elk has been widely regarded as a prophet of Native American spirituality (my own copy, a 1972 paperback, claims to be "a book of personal vision that makes the LSD trip seem pale by comparison"), his famous autobiography is a complex and ambiguous text. Black Elk narrated the story of his life through his son, who acted as translator, to John Neihardt, the book's author, and Neihardt's two daughters, one of whom, Enid, transcribed the tale using the Gregg shorthand method (Neihardt, 1995: 20). Neihardt employed considerable license in retelling Black Elk's story. Black Elk is himself a paradox: converted by Episcopalian missionaries in his youth, he spent three years touring Europe with Buffalo Bill's Wild West Show. Upon his return to South Dakota he joined the Ghost Dance before eventually being baptized as a Catholic (Holler, 1995). Though his account has often been read as a "pure" rendering of Lakota spirituality, William Powers argues that Black Elk tailored his account to a white audience and obscured much of Lakota religion in the process (Powers, 1990).

In a sense this problem is inherent to all Indian autobiographies, since the autobiographical form is itself a Western conceit that has no direct parallel in Native American cultures. In recent years a generation of Indian writers, including N. Scott

Momaday, Gerald Vizenor, Leslie Marmon Silko, James Welch, and Louise Erdrich, have sought to invest written forms that are derived from a European tradition with content that reflects Indian subjects and sensibilities (see Hafen, this volume). Together they have created a rich, varied, and powerful body of literature. Yet, as David Murray has commented, "to write about Indian experience and be published in English is inevitably to be involved in an ambiguous area of cultural identity" (Murray, 1991: 92). Modern novelists stand far removed from the translators and negotiators of the sixteenth and seventeenth centuries, but in both cases individuals who can be called cultural brokers moved into arenas of ambiguous identity and experience to construct a bridge between cultures. In most cases the language barriers of the early contact period are more easily overcome today, but larger issues of identity and authenticity – and, by extension, of the commensurability of alien cultures – continue to be debated.

Structures

While the meaning of brokerage appears self-evident in many biographical treatments, any systematic attempt to understand the phenomenon introduces difficult theoretical challenges. The discipline of anthropology has been shaped in part by ongoing debates about how to define culture and conceptualize relationships among cultures; those debates, in turn, help to illuminate the phenomena of translation and cultural brokerage.

For a time in the first half of the twentieth century, the evolution of anthropology was driven by a debate between the two "schools" of functionalism and structuralism. In Britain, functionalism was associated with the work of Bronislav Malinowski, whose *Argonauts of the Western Pacific* (1922) pioneered the practice of intensive fieldwork in native communities and placed a new emphasis on understanding the interrelated functions of cultural phenomena. For Malinowski, the essential work of an anthropologist was to uncover the coherence of a cultural *system*, to recognize its integrity and internal unity. But while Malinowski revolutionized the practice of fieldwork in his discipline, critics regarded his investigations to be unsystematic and his monographs to be sprawling and anecdotal. E. E. Evans-Pritchard advocated a structuralist alternative. In place of the functionalists' extended descriptions of single cultures, he argued that anthropologists should compare societies "to discover general tendencies...that are common to human societies as a whole" (Kuper, 1996: 82). To this end, Evans-Pritchard and others sought to develop cross-cultural perspectives on such basic human institutions as marriage, kinship systems, and political structures. They advocated rigor in terminology and method to allow for such comparisons and searched for the universal structures that underlay particular cultural forms.

But if functionalism and structuralism seemed antagonistic at the time, they were eventually recognized to be complementary and mutually reinforcing. They are the twin epistemological pillars of modernist anthropology; together they have sustained the coherence of the discipline for more than half a century. Functionalism allows anthropologists to assume that individual cultures are coherent, self-contained systems of meaning, in which all the parts work together to contribute to a larger whole that is susceptible to description and interpretation, while structuralism posits the existence of universal patterns of meaning in human languages and societies, without which cultural systems might be mutually unintelligible. The anthropological enterprise has always been premised on such underlying structures: they explain anthropologists' capacity to understand, and brokers' capacity to mediate between, cultures.

Island societies are especially well suited to functionalist-structuralist analysis. The essays of Clifford Geertz on Bali (1973) and Marshall Sahlins on the South Seas islands (1985) have been influential both in their brilliant ethnographic analysis and in their reconsideration of the nature and meaning of culture. Sahlins, in particular, has challenged anthropologists working in the structuralist tradition to adopt a more dynamic approach to culture. In *Islands and Beaches* (1988), Greg Dening explored the significance of beaches as zones of cultural contact in the Marquesas Islands and argued that the phenomena of intercultural contact, even in these relatively remote and isolated contexts, were surprisingly varied and complicated. When the object of study is a larger, more complex society, or a region occupied by diverse peoples subject to repeated contact, invasion, reformation, and rapid adjustment to change, as the Americas have been, it becomes still more difficult to employ a traditional notion of culture. American ethnohistorians have tried to represent historic Indian cultures as coherent and integrated systems, but the evidence for such systems is often fragmentary and the historical experience of Indian peoples too tangled to allow descriptions of culture systems to be fully integrated into historical accounts. Many ethnohistories begin with a set-piece ethnographic chapter that discusses important myths, rituals, and community structures, then turn to the historical record and largely abandon those topics. Where analyses of Indian culture are more fully integrated into a historical account it may still be necessary to acknowledge, as Richard White does in *The Middle Ground*, that "the world that had existed before they [Frenchmen] arrived was no more. It had been shattered. Only fragments remained" (White, 1991: 1).

While functionalist methods have proven to be of limited usefulness to American ethnohistorians, the structuralist assumptions that undergird the anthropological enterprise have come under increasing scrutiny in recent years. The confident assertion that Western ways of knowing can serve as a master key to human cultures has been attacked as an imperialist conceit (Asad, 1991), and the "fables of rapport" upon which ethnographers have always relied to establish their authoritative knowledge of other cultures have been called into question (Clifford, 1988). In a similar way, recent studies of language translation emphasize the impossibility of "mere" translation, the pure transposition of ideas from one language to another (Murray, 1991). All such transfers occur in specific contexts that charge them with particular meanings and relations of power, which in turn shape the process of translation itself. Lydia Liu argues that any study of language in cross-cultural settings must ask, "In whose terms, for which linguistic constituency, and in the name of what kinds of knowledge or intellectual authority does one perform acts of translation between cultures?" (Liu, 1995: 1).

These questions challenge the notion of cultures themselves as self-contained systems of meaning. Such systems are first and foremost the intellectual constructs of Western observers and academics; as Talal Asad has noted, "anthropological assumptions about cultural continuity, autonomy and authenticity must be questioned" (Asad, 1991: 316). Here we have a radical critique of both the practices and the underlying assumptions that ground our understanding of translation and cultural brokerage. If cultures cannot be conceptualized as self-contained, self-perpetuating systems, and translation and brokerage cannot be treated as transparent acts, the task of explaining those acts becomes much more complicated. The old metaphors – crossing a cultural divide, living in two worlds – no longer ring true. But these challenges are liberating as well as threatening. While they complicate any attempt to theorize cultural brokerage, they also make translation and brokerage look different, both less aberrant and more complex than they have often been represented to be.

Performances

One important alternative to structuralist-functionalism has been offered by James Clifford, in what might be termed a *relationalist* view of culture. Clifford has argued that, while anthropologists and historians have generally assumed that individuals establish identities within their own social groups and then carry those identities with them when they encounter others, it might make more sense to suggest that identity is shaped in the experience of encounter itself. He criticizes both disciplines for assuming that cultural contact can produce only two outcomes: absorption or resistance. "A fear of lost identity, a Puritan taboo on mixing beliefs and bodies, hangs over the process. Yet what," he asks, "if identity is conceived not as a boundary to be maintained but as a nexus of relations and transactions actively engaging a subject?" (Clifford, 1988: 344). This metaphor of identity reshapes the relationship between culture and broker. It suggests that brokers, rather than being marginalized or endangered by forays across boundaries, were especially active in *inventing* the cultural identities that they were empowered to represent. Ella Deloria offers one example of this pattern. A Dakota linguist who worked for Franz Boas at Columbia University, she also taught Indian songs, dances, and ideas to Camp Fire Girls (an organization created to transmit Indian traditions and lore to young American girls). In each context, Deloria – herself from a bicultural background – was engaged in a fundamentally inventive activity. As a linguist, she adapted her local knowledge to academic needs; as a resource for the Camp Fire movement, she tailored her presentation of Indian culture to the sensibilities of a young, female, middle-class audience (Deloria, 1998). Clifford's most recent book, *Routes* (1997) (its title a play on the idea of cultural "roots") extends this view by exploring the significance of travel in shaping cultures, and especially in shaping informants, those individuals who translate or broker between cultures. "Practices of displacement," he suggests, "might emerge as *constitutive* of cultural meanings rather than as their simple transfer or extension" (Clifford, 1997: 3).

A second, and related, approach to cultural mediation might be termed *performativism*. If brokers help to constitute their cultures through the processes of mediation, the nature of those processes demands careful reconsideration. A performative explanation of brokerage assumes that shared meanings in contact settings do not derive from individuals who have mastered two distinct symbol systems and can therefore mediate between them by translating, explaining, or enacting operative concepts; they emerge instead from acts of invention and improvisation, some of which are more effective than others. Performativism implies that cultures can be reinvented through acts of mediation. Thus Richard White has argued that the "middle ground" of French–Algonquian relations in the Great Lakes region originated in "congruences" that "often seemed – and, indeed, were – results of misunderstandings or accidents" (White, 1991: 52). White's notion of creative misunderstandings resonates with the phenomenon James Lockhart has called "Double Mistaken Identity" in Spanish–Nahua relations (Lockhart, 1992: 445).

These formulations are both appealing and problematic. Their appeal lies in their powerful resonance with post-structuralist developments throughout the humanities and social sciences, which seem to demand corresponding innovations in the ways we conceptualize such basic notions as "culture" and "cultural broker." But they are problematic because they fundamentally change the status of brokerage acts and threaten to rob brokerage of its distinct character and meaning. From within a structuralist-functionalist framework, brokers appear to perform unique tasks that demand unique skills. The post-structuralist sensibility, on the other hand, regards liminality and the need to enact identity through performance to be a universal condition. Greg Dening's introduction to *Through a Glass Darkly: Reflections on Personal Identity in Early America* (1997) captures the ease with which scholars can move from a discussion of cultural brokerage to a discussion of the human condition. "Early America was a place of thresholds, margins, boundaries," he writes. "It was a place of ambivalence and unset definition. The search for identity in that place was multivalent and unending.... Maybe edginess is the paramount feeling of the human condition itself. Perhaps it is not necessarily specific to such situations as early America.... The self is always on edge, always contingent, dependent on all the exchanges with otherness around" (Dening, 1997: 2–3). He invokes the metaphor of theater and, following Erving Goffman's *The Presentation of Self in Everyday Life* (1959), suggests that identity is shaped, not in some larger cultural inheritance, but in the everyday performance of the self.

For the scholar of European–Indian contacts, the challenge of post-structuralism is to return the discussion to Indian communities and the problems of intercultural relations. Brian Hosmer has recently argued that we need "a rigorous definition" of cultural brokerage if it is to remain a useful concept. "If most twentieth-century Indians are forced to come to terms with the mainstream world, in some way or other, then it may be argued that most are involved in some sort of cultural brokerage every day," he writes. "But are we then in danger of expanding this concept until it describes a condition common to most Indians rather than a feature that distinguishes the few from the many?" (Hosmer, 1997: 494). Hosmer's essay on two recent Menominee leaders, Reginald Oshkosh and Mitchell Oshkenaniew, emphasizes that a simple analysis of their personal identities or cultural loyalties does little to clarify their relative abilities as cultural brokers. Both sought a middle way between the opportunities of commercial logging and the need to maintain broad-based, communal well-being for the Menominees, and in that sense both can be called cultural brokers. Hosmer argues, though, that Oshkosh was a more able broker both because of his lineage, "which provided him with a certain prestige and a platform from which to influence tribal members," and because he was able to encourage "economic modernization" at the same time that "he refused to accept social fragmentation or stratification as its inevitable consequence" (Hosmer, 1997: 503). Hosmer consistently tests each man's brokerage strategies against the standard of community cohesion, and argues that an effective broker, in the late twentieth century as in the early seventeenth, is capable of extracting some benefits of inter-cultural contact without allowing his community to be destroyed by it.

While Hosmer presents a case in which a strict definition of brokerage seems to work well, there are other contexts in which terminological rigor is elusive and recent theoretical innovations in the study of culture appear to be indispensable guides to the politics of modern Indian communities. James Clifford's essay "Identity in Mashpee," in *The Predicament of Culture* (1988), offers a case in point. Clifford analyzes a lawsuit in which the Mashpee Wampanoag Tribal Council asserted its claim to about 16,000 acres of land on Cape Cod. The trial turned on the question of whether the Mashpees were a tribe, and if so whether the tribe had existed continuously throughout the historic period. In the courtroom, most Mashpee Indians seemed to identify strongly with their "Indianness," but the components of their identities, and the nature of the community and culture to which they belonged, were hard to pin down. In part, Clifford suggests, this is because the court wanted evidence of tribal political structures, while much of the Mashpees' testimony described something more subtle and variable. In part, too, the Mashpees were handicapped by the prominence of written records as evidence. "Until recently," Clifford notes, "nearly everything most characteristically Indian in Mashpee would have gone unrecorded. The surviving facts are largely the records of missionaries, government agents, outsiders. In the rare instances when Indians wrote – petitions, deeds, letters of complaint – it was to address white authorities and legal structures" (Clifford, 1988: 340).

The few Indians who emerge clearly from the historical record of Mashpee, and some of the Europeans as well, are cultural brokers. One of the community's original brokers was Richard Bourne, an English tenant farmer on Indian lands in the mid-seventeenth century who "studied the language of his landlords and soon became an effective mediator between the societies" (Clifford, 1988: 294). In partnership with a Cotachesset Indian named Paupmunnuck, Bourne propagated Christianity among Indians from several Cape Cod communities and created the "South Sea Indian Plantation" to protect their land claims. But if these two men were brokers, what was being brokered? Under Bourne's leadership the Indians of Mashpee became "praying Indians" and laid aside many outward trappings of their native cultures. But as a result of their affiliation with Bourne's church and their newfound plantation status, they could protect their land-base, kinship networks, and elements of their native cultures and identities. Did the creation of the "South Sea Indian Plantation," which evolved into the town of Mashpee, mark the end of several Indian communities on the Cape, or were the terms of their existence simply renegotiated?

Three hundred years later two brothers described their ties to the Mashpees in court. John Peters identified himself as a medicine man for the Mashpee Wampanoag tribe, but his descriptions of that status sounded strikingly informal and vague. Though he called many Mashpee residents Indian "traditionalists," he admitted that he could not say with confidence exactly which residents merited that label. Most of the ritual events that Peters discussed were shaped by a confusing combination of Christian and generic "Indian" elements, many of which had been only recently appropriated by the community. John's brother Russell Peters was also a paradox. "Dressed in a blue three-piece business suit," he was "indistinguishable from a half-dozen lawyers in the courtroom" (Clifford, 1988: 310). Russell was president of the Mashpee Wampanoag Tribal Council, the "business arm" of the tribe; at the time of the trial he was also directing a television documentary series on eastern Indians. Though both John and Russell Peters appeared, on the stand, to be contradictory figures with questionable claims to any real "Indian" identity, both took their roles as Indian leaders seriously. Each could be described as a cultural broker who joined in an old and still unfinished conversation about the nature and validity of their Indianness. In the end, Clifford suggests, "the trial was less a search for the facts of Mashpee Indian culture and history than it was an experiment in translation, part of a long historical conflict and negotiation of 'Indian' and 'American' identities" (Clifford, 1988: 289). The Mashpee story is not unique; the Lumbee Indians offer another example of a people whose identity was forged by the processes of contact and colonization and who have struggled to gain official recognition in the face of prevailing definitions of tribal legitimacy and cultural authenticity (Sider, 1993). The Mashpees lost their case, but paradoxically the struggle to define themselves in court may have done more to strengthen their bonds of community than anything they had experienced in a very long time.

Recent scholarship suggests a series of questions that can clarify the study of cultural brokers. Where do brokers come from? Brokers who emerge from marginal positions in their own societies might already possess brokerage skills as a result of "counter-discursive" practices within their own cultures (Terdiman, 1985). Kartunnen's brokers, for example, were mostly marginal to their communities, and that fact fundamentally shaped their experiences as brokers. Many of the individuals considered in this essay, however, were brokers of a different type, drawn from the leadership ranks of their own communities. This essential distinction between types of brokers raises additional questions: how are brokers selected, and to what ends? To answer these questions is to clarify the power relations that give shape to a particular brokerage context. Finally, scholars should be attentive to the contexts in which brokerage takes place. Effective brokerage at a council fire in the seventeenth-century backcountry is something quite different from effective brokerage in a twentieth-century courtroom, or for that matter in modern literature. Each situation has its own poetic, the terms of which are shaped by the culture in which it originated. Council fires originated in Native American settings, and the role of brokers was to facilitate the process by which Europeans could adapt to their form. Courtrooms derive from English precedents; there, brokers must adapt the needs of Indian communities to Anglo-American norms. In either case, the rules and expectations of a particular context must be clearly understood from the perspective of the dominant culture, and problematized from the perspective of the subordinate one, to elucidate the challenges of brokerage.

When we complicate our ideas of culture, community, and identity, the processes of brokerage become richer and more interesting than ever, if also more varied in their forms. But an uncritical understanding of culture is no longer tenable. Essentialist definitions of Indian and European cultures must be challenged by a recognition of the wrenching changes that have accompanied intercultural contact and the dynamic processes through which cultures and identities take shape. From this point of view the experience of dissonance and instability that has long been associated with brokers no longer appears unique. What makes brokers stand out in the historical record is instead their performances: the moments in which they stepped forward to offer their own creative and often unstable contributions to the ongoing dialogue between peoples.

BIBLIOGRAPHY

Apess, William 1829: *A Son of the Forest: The Experience of William Apess a Native of the Forest, Written by Himself* (n.p.).

Asad, Talal 1991: "Afterword: From the History of Colonial Anthropology to the Anthropology of Western Hegemony," in *Colonial Situations: Essays on the Contextualization of Ethnographic Knowledge*, History of Anthropology vol. 7, ed. George Stocking (Madison: University of Wisconsin Press), pp. 314–24.

Barbour, Philip 1970: *Pocahontas and Her World: A Chronicle of America's First Settlement* (Boston: Houghton Mifflin).

Blu, Karen 1980: *The Lumbee Problem: The Making of an American Indian People* (New York: Cambridge University Press).

Clifford, James 1988: *The Predicament of Culture: Twentieth-Century Ethnography, Literature, and Art* (Cambridge, MA: Harvard University Press).

Clifford, James 1997: *Routes: Travel and Translation in the Late Twentieth Century* (Cambridge, MA: Harvard University Press).

Clifton, James (ed.) 1989: *Being and Becoming Indian: Biographical Studies of North American Frontiers* (Chicago: Dorsey Press).

Cypess, Sandra Messinger 1991: *La Malinche in Mexican Literature From History to Myth* (Austin: University of Texas Press).

Deloria, Philip 1998: *Playing Indian* (New Haven: Yale University Press).

Dening, Greg 1988: *Islands and Beaches. Discourse on a Silent Land: Marquesas 1774–1880* (Chicago: Dorsey Press).

Dening, Greg 1997: "Introduction: In Search of a Metaphor," in *Through a Glass Darkly: Reflections on Personal Identity in Early America*, eds. Ronald Hoffman, Mechal Sobel, and Fredrika J. Teute (Chapel Hill: University of North Carolina Press), pp. 1–6.

Fenton, William 1998: *The Great Law and the Longhouse: A Political History of the Iroquois Confederacy* (Norman: University of Oklahoma Press).

Geertz, Clifford 1973: *The Interpretation of Cultures* (New York: Basic Books).

Gibson, Charles 1964: *The Aztecs under Spanish Rule: A History of the Indians of the Valley of Mexico, 1519–1810* (Stanford: Stanford University Press).

Gillespie, Michele 1997: "The Sexual Politics of Race and Gender: Mary Musgrove and the Georgia Trustees," in *The Devil's Lane: Sex and Race in the Early South*, eds. Catherine Clinton and Michele Gillespie (New York: Oxford University Press), pp. 187–201.

Goffman, Erving 1959: *The Presentation of Self in Everyday Life* (Garden City, NY: Doubleday).

Grumet, Robert S. (ed.) 1996: *Northeastern Indian Lives, 1632–1816* (Amherst: University of Massachusetts Press).

Hagedorn, Nancy 1988: "'A Friend to Go between Them': The Interpreter as Cultural Broker during Anglo-Iroquois Councils, 1740–1770," *Ethnohistory* 35: 60–80.

Hallowell, A. Irving 1963/1976: "American Indians, White and Black: The Phenomenon of Transculturalization," *Current Anthropology*, 4: 519–31; reprinted in A. Irving Hallowell, *Contributions to Anthropology: Selected Papers of A. Irving Hallowell* (Chicago: University of Chicago Press), pp. 498–529.

Hinderaker, Eric 1996: "The 'Four Indian Kings' and the Imaginative Construction of the First British Empire," *William and Mary Quarterly* 3rd series, 53: 487–526.

Hinderaker, Eric 1997: *Elusive Empires: Constructing Colonialism in the Ohio Valley, 1673–1800* (New York: Cambridge University Press).

Hobgood, John and Carroll L. Riley 1978: "Mesoamericans as Cultural Brokers in Northern New Spain," in *Cultural Continuity in Mesoamerica*, ed. David L. Browman (The Hague: Mouton Publishers).

Holler, Clyde 1995: *Black Elk's Religion: The Sun Dance and Lakota Catholicism* (Syracuse: Syracuse University Press).

Horn, Rebecca 1997: *Postconquest Coyoacan: Nahua–Spanish Relations in Central Mexico, 1519–1650* (Stanford: Stanford University Press).

Hosmer, Brian C. 1997: "Reflections on Indian Cultural 'Brokers': Reginald Oshkosh, Mitchell Oshkenaniew, and the Politics of Menominee Lumbering," *Ethnohistory* 44: 493–509.

Hoxie, Frederick E. 1992: "Exploring a Cultural Borderland: Native American Journeys of Discovery in the Early Twentieth Century," *Journal of American History* 79: 969–95.

Kartunnen, Frances 1994: *Between Worlds: Interpreters, Guides, and Survivors* (New Brunswick, NJ: Rutgers University Press).

Kartunnen, Frances 1997: "Rethinking Malinche," in *Indian Women of Early Mexico*, eds. Susan Schroeder, Stephanie Wood, and Robert Haskett (Norman: University of Oklahoma Press), pp. 290–312.

Krupat, Arnold (ed.) 1994: *Native American Autobiography: An Anthology* (Madison: University of Wisconsin Press).

Kuper, Adam 1996: *Anthropology and Anthropologists: The Modern British School*, 3rd edn. (London: Routledge).

Liu, Lydia 1995: *Translingual Practice: Literature, National Culture, and Translated Modernity – China, 1900–1937* (Stanford: Stanford University Press).

Lockhart, James 1992: *The Nahuas after the Conquest: A Social and Cultural History of the Indians of Central Mexico, Sixteenth through Eighteenth Centuries* (Stanford: Stanford University Press).

Malinowski, Bronislav 1922: *Argonauts of the Western Pacific* (London: G. Routledge; New York: E. P. Dutton).

McFee, Malcolm 1968: "The 150% Man, a Product of Blackfeet Acculturation," *American Anthropologist* 70: 1096–103.

Merrell, James 1997: "'The Cast of His Countenance': Reading Andrew Montour," in *Through a Glass Darkly: Reflections on Personal Identity in Early America*, eds. Ronald Hoffman, Mechal Sobel, and Fredrika J. Teute (Chapel Hill: University of North Carolina Press), pp. 13–39.

Mooney, James 1965: *The Ghost-Dance Religion and the Sioux Outbreak of 1890*, ed. and abr. Anthony F. C. Wallace (Chicago: University of Chicago Press [unabr. edn. orig. pub. 1896]).

Murray, David 1991: *Forked Tongues: Speech, Writing and Representation in North American Indian Texts* (Bloomington: Indiana University Press).

Neihardt, Hilda 1995: *Black Elk and Flaming Rainbow: Personal Memories of the Lakota Holy Man and John Neihardt* (Lincoln: University of Nebraska Press).

Neihardt, John 1972: *Black Elk Speaks: Being the Life Story of a Holy Man of the Oglala Sioux* (New York: Simon & Schuster [orig. pub. 1932]).

Peterson, Jacqueline and Jennifer S. H. Brown (eds.) 1985: *The New Peoples: Being and Becoming Métis in North America* (Lincoln: University of Nebraska Press).

Powers, William 1990: "When Black Elk Speaks, Everybody Listens," in *Religion in Native North America*, ed. Christopher Vecsey (Moscow, ID: University of Idaho Press), pp. 136–51.

Richter, Daniel 1988: "Cultural Brokers and Intercultural Politics: New York–Iroquois Relations, 1664–1701," *Journal of American History* 75: 40–67.

Rudes, Blair and Dorothy Crouse 1987: *The Tuscarora Legacy of J. N. B. Hewitt: Materials for the Study of the Tuscarora Language and Culture*, 2 vols. (Ottawa: National Museums of Canada).

Sahlins, Marshall 1985: *Islands of History* (Chicago: University of Chicago Press).

Sahlins, Marshall 1995: *How "Natives" Think: About Captain Cook, for Example* (Chicago: University of Chicago Press).

Salisbury, Neal 1981: "Squanto: Last of the Patuxets," in *Struggle and Survival*, eds. David Sweet and Gary Nash (Berkeley: University of California Press), pp. 228–46.

Seed, Patricia 1995: *Ceremonies of Possession in Europe's Conquest of the New World, 1492–1640* (New York: Cambridge University Press).

Sider, Gerald 1993: *Lumbee Indian Histories: Race, Ethnicity, and Indian Identity in the Southern United States* (New York: Cambridge University Press).

Szasz, Margaret Connell (ed.) 1994: *Between Indian and White Worlds: The Cultural Broker* (Norman: University of Oklahoma Press).

Terdiman, Richard 1985: *Discourse/Counter-Discourse: The Theory and Practice of Symbolic Resistance in Nineteenth-Century France* (Ithaca: Cornell University Press).

Tilton, Robert 1994: *Pocahontas: The Evolution of an American Narrative* (New York: Cambridge University Press).

Vasconcelos, Jose 1997: *The Cosmic Race: A Bilingual Edition*, trans. and ann. Didier T. Jaen (Baltimore: Johns Hopkins University Press).

Vizenor, Gerald 1991: *Landfill Meditation: Crossblood Stories* (Hanover, NH: Wesleyan University Press, published by University Press of New England).

Wallace, Anthony F. C. 1970: *The Death and Rebirth of the Seneca: The History and Culture of the Great Iroquois Nation, Their Destruction and Demoralization, and Their*

Cultural Revival at the Hands of the Indian Visionary, Handsome Lake (New York: Alfred A. Knopf).

Wallace, Anthony F. C. 1949/1990: *King of the Delawares: Teedyuscung, 1700–1763* (Philadelphia: University of Pennsylvania Press, 1949; reprint edn., Syracuse: Syracuse University Press, 1990).

White, Richard 1991: *The Middle Ground: Indians, Empires, and Republics in the Great Lakes Region, 1650–1815* (New York: Cambridge University Press).

Part Five

Governmental Relations

21

Federal and State Policies and American Indians

Donald Fixico

Federal and state policies involving American Indians date back more than 250 years, to the earliest colonial manifestations of what would become the United States. Given this long history, the question surrounding tribal–governmental relations has offered one of the most familiar structures for organizing the larger narrative of Indian history. Tribal experiences have been diverse, but they can usually be viewed in common through the lens of the federal government. Similarly, one should note that state relations have also been less frequently the subject of study. This structure – primarily political rather than social or cultural – has often focused on federal policies. Scholars have frequently conceptualized an oscillating pendulum, with policy swinging between opposing poles: accommodation and dispossession, assimilation and segregation, acculturation and cultural pluralism, quasi-foreign and quasi-domestic status. While this structure has indeed offered a useful way of organizing and periodizing Indian history, we should also note that the "pendulum's" wide sweep obscures as much as it reveals. Federal policies have originated in and been administered from a wide array of ideological, economic, and political positions. Likewise, taking stock of the role of states, other colonial nations, corporations, and other private entities throws the entire question of policy into a more complicated relief. In the context of treaties, for example, Vine Deloria, Jr. and Raymond DeMallie have revealed the surprising multitude of parties entering into a broad range of treaty agreements with tribes (Deloria and DeMallie, 1999).

It is useful to consider together with the oscillating pendulum some of the central goals of federal policies, which have consistently focused on Indian land, religion, economy, and education. It is also important to consider at least two of the central notions driving policy formation. As federal Indian policy moved during the nineteenth century from the foreign to the domestic realm, it was consistently articulated as a "problem" to be solved. Sometimes the problem was articulated as one of "administration"; at other times as a problem of social and cultural advancement on the part of Indian people themselves. White Americans devised various means of dealing with their "Indian problems," and they struggled as their solutions became worn out, demonstrable failures. And thus, the second notion – that of reform. New policy – even when it looks back to earlier policies – has been consistently articulated in terms of reform, suggesting that policy studies need concern themselves not simply with policy, but with ideology as well. The ideologies surrounding reform have been powerful in American culture, and Indian reform has drawn extensively on that power.

Moving chronologically, this essay will note certain key moments in American Indian policy. It will suggest some of the ideological currents flowing beneath policy formation and it will note the existence of complex and interlocking cycles of problem, solution, implementation, and reform. The essay will conclude with a brief consideration of the role of Indian scholars and critics in policy history and a few thoughts on its possible futures.

Initial political relations with European colonies centered on what might be called "foreign relations," primarily around questions of war and peace, land (for colonial settlement), economy (trade, particularly that surrounding fur), and religion (present in all colonial situations, but marked in New Spain and New France). As the British won intra-European imperial contests against the Spanish, French, and Dutch, the thirteen British colonies set the tone for later American policy practices with native nations (see Edmunds, this volume, for a national comparative approach). These early "government to government" practices involved treaty-making with Indian leaders, trade relations policies, and the willingness to wage war against the tribes. Each colony developed its own distinct Indian policy in order to address its particular situation. In New York, for example, the Dutch and English colonists tended to see Indians in two distinct categories – the "local" coastal and Hudson River Algonquians and the more distant Iroquois. The former were "expendable," as they failed to bring in enough fur from their trapped-out lands; the latter were "valuable" for exactly these economic reasons. The Dutch, and later the English developed a variety of policies that juggled the omnipresent elements of war, trade, and treaty (Trelease, 1960). Virginia, Connecticut, Massachusetts, and the other colonies – each had their own interests and policies for maneuvering through the thicket of native and colonial allies and rivals. In general, however, the British colonies and the Crown viewed Indian people as nations, thus validating a certain kind of national status for each tribe or group of native communities. In most cases, of course, "nations" came to exist out of village worlds, formed, many scholars have suggested, in the cauldron of an intercultural middle ground (see Dowd, this volume).

Since both "sides" – Indian tribes and European colonizers – acknowledged the sovereign rights of each other, they essentially established the earliest history of Indian–white relations within the context of international law. With the colonial practice of treaty-making, a contractual model often came to structure relations and policy – at least in the European perspective from which most of these negotiations have been studied, interpreted, and enforced. With the success of the American Revolution, the new United States inherited these broader colonial legacies, as well as the inclinations of individual colonies (now states) to negotiate their own interests with local Native people.

The first treaty between Indian people and the United States occurred in 1778 with the Delaware Indians (Kappler, 1903). As John Wunder points out, power in the new republic was so diffuse that many states concluded their own treaties with nearby tribes (Wunder, 1994: 19). In order to consolidate the new nation's federal power and insure a relatively coherent and consistent structure for treaty negotiations, Congress passed the Trade and Intercourse Act of 1790 (Prucha, 1962). In addition to regulating trade, this legislation forbid states, corporations, or individual citizens from entering into land cession agreements with Indian people. From 1790 on, the federal government claimed a nearly exclusive right to oversee political and economic relations with Indians. As a result, while the relations between Indians and individual colonies had proved critical, those between Indians and states were relatively less so, and they have, not surprisingly, attracted relatively less attention from scholars.

In theory, the two "sides" were equal partners in treaty agreements. In practice, Indian people, initially the more powerful, found themselves negotiating from increasingly weaker positions, from the fall of France through the defeat of the Old Northwest tribes in the early 1790s (Jones, 1982). Many scholars have examined the policies of the new republic, formed in this particular context. Francis Paul Prucha offered notable starting points, examining trade and diplomacy (Prucha, 1962), while Reginald Horsman considered larger questions surrounding race and American expansion (1981). A recent collection of original essays (Hoxie et al., 1999) provides some new perspectives and insights into this little understood era.

While one might track federal policy changes in each administration, a natural periodizing line – the Removal Act of 1830 – suggests a broader categorization, defined by the policies of Thomas Jefferson and Andrew Jackson. As Anthony Wallace (1999) and Bernard Sheehan (1973) have argued, Jefferson appeared to embrace an enlightened notion of assimilation and agrarian acculturation while in fact ruthlessly pursuing a policy marked by war and concomitant treaties of land cession. Trade remained a part of treaty provisions – indeed, trade regulation, religious instruction, and educational provisions were critical to Jefferson's policy vision. The standard treatment of this policy in the wake of Jefferson's administration has been biographical – Herman Viola's *Thomas L. McKenney: Architect of America's Early Indian Policy, 1816–1830* (1974). The frequent warfare that accompanied this policy produced a popular body of writing and imagery, often focused on violence, noble savagery, and imperial nostalgia, which has received treatment from Robert F. Berkhofer Jr. (1978) and Brian Dippie (1982), among others. Both Berkhofer and Dippie take notable pains to connect their discussions of ideology and imagery back to concrete policy formations.

The federal government's war policy has been a long one, involving 1,642 official military engagements with Indian tribes. Naturally most written accounts came from the perspective of Anglo-American journalists and mainstream writers who chronicled the victories of the United States and who vilified Native Americans. Such military history has captured the imagination of general readers of American history, although these typically imbalanced accounts have described American Indians as "wild savages" on the frontier who had to be defeated in order for manifest destiny to overspread the continent. Military history remains today an important part of the wider world of federal–Indian policy.

The fall of Indian nations on Jeffersonian battlefields – the War of 1812, when Tecumseh's confederation faltered, the Black Hawk War of 1832, and the Seminole wars of 1817–18, 1835–42, and 1855–8 – also point to a new theme, that of Indian removal. Defeated Indian tribes faced removal treaties, which were part of Jefferson's program for exchanging eastern lands for western. Indeed, the program was wide-reaching, and many Indian groups were removed without first suffering military defeat. If the impetus for removal was Jeffersonian, however, the key figure in its policy development and implementation was undoubtedly Andrew Jackson. Jackson's role in the removal of the Southwest tribes to Indian Territory – most famously the Cherokee "Trail of Tears" – marks with a certain clarity the passing of the imbalance of power from Indian advantage to that of white Americans. Indian policy began to make an ambiguous, still-unfinished shift from foreign to domestic, perhaps nowhere so clearly articulated as in John Marshall's 1831 Supreme Court decision in *Cherokee Nation v. State of Georgia*, which marked tribes as "domestic dependent nations" (Wunder, 1994: 26). Numerous scholars have considered the shifts in Indian status that took place under the Jacksonian policies. Perhaps the baseline study is Ronald Satz's *American Indian Policy in the Jacksonian Era* (1975). Michael Paul Rogin (1975) has offered an intriguing psychological reading of policy and person, while Grant Foreman (1953), Angie Debo (1940), Anthony Wallace (1993), and many others have treated the actual dimensions of removal. The "Cherokee Cases" have been examined in a range of contexts by scholars too numerous to mention (see Harring, this volume).

By the middle of the nineteenth century, many Americans had started to rethink these older policies, which centered around conflict, cession, and removal. Indeed, even in the midst of Removal, reformers had called for a more humanitarian, "Christian" policy toward Indians. During the administration of Ulysses S. Grant following the Civil War, they got their wish, with the implementation of what came to be known as the "Peace Policy." Humanitarians allied themselves with practical-minded individuals who believed that fighting Indians was simply too expensive. They argued that, in order to solve the Indian problem, the United States should settle peacefully with Indian people, feed them, teach them agriculture, and establish them in organized Christian churches. The new policy centered on an administrative unit – the reservation – and a figure of authority – the agent. Neither idea was new. Indeed, if historian Bernard Sheehan had seen in Jeffersonian policy the "seeds of [Indian] extinction," only a few years later Robert Trennert argued that the reservation system was conceived as early as the 1850s as an "alternative to extinction" (1975). Reservation and agent, however, both took on new importance under the Peace Policy. In one of the most extraordinary breakdowns of the separation of church and state in American history, agents were appointed from the ranks of Christian missionaries. The treaties of the 1860s reflect the new dimensions of the Peace Policy, with almost inevitable provisions for agents, charged with civilizing and Christianizing Indian people within the confines of the reservation.

The standard treatment of the period is Loring B. Priest, *Uncle Sam's Stepchildren: The Reformation of United States Indian Policy, 1865–1887* (1969). Francis Paul Prucha's *American Indian Policy in Crisis: Christian Reformers and the*

Indian, 1865–1900 (1976) and Robert Keller Jr.'s *American Protestantism and United States Indian Policy, 1869–1882* (1983) are notable treatments of the relation between Christian mission and federal policy. Norman Bender's *New Hope for the Indians: The Grant Peace Policy and the Navajos in the 1870s* (1989) provides a focused tribal case study. Also useful are biographies and memoirs of individual missionaries and agents who helped establish the reservation order.

During the last half of the nineteenth century, writers and scholars began to realize that there were many stories to be told about Anglo-Americans winning the continent and Native Americans losing their homelands. Initially seen as the red villains of the frontier, American affection for the now-defeated underdogs led to a new collection of nostalgic Indian heroes – Geronimo, Chief Joseph, Sitting Bull, Black Hawk, Crazy Horse, and other famed leaders. Biographers guessed at the early life histories of Indian chiefs, thereby adding to the standard imagery found in the popular press. Indian leaders in other sectors of Indian history – policy matters, for example – were ignored. Take, for instance, Ely S. Parker (Seneca), the first significant Indian in a policy-making position. Commissioner of Indian Affairs between 1869 and 1871, he led the early implementation of the Peace Policy itself (Armstrong, 1978: 137–51).

The failures of that policy have been well documented – allegations of fraud and graft, the appointments of incompetent agents from the clergy, jurisdictional fights between the Indian Office and the Board of Indian Commissioners, which had been created in 1869 to provide oversight. Although one could hardly call it a culmination of these problems, the 1871 abandonment by Congress of the treaty system marks a critical turning point in policy history. Parker was forced to resign in that same year, and the Indian Office held completely accountable to the Board. Created in 1832 and housed in the War Department, the Office of Indian Affairs had moved to Interior in 1849. In the mid- and late 1860s, policymakers engaged in a substantial debate as to its appropriate location. The resolution of this debate, considered in tandem with the shift from treaty to agreement, suggests another sea change in the relation between foreign and domestic approaches to Indian policy.

If the Peace Policy originated in reform movements, so too did it generate its own set of opponents, bent on yet another round of reform. Appalled by military escapades such as the Sand Creek massacre and roused by the abuses that characterized the reservations of the mid- and late nineteenth century, a new group of sympathetic reformers rallied around the name "the Friends of the Indian." They aimed to help the government solve the "Indian problem" and, in 1883, inaugurated a series of annual meetings at Lake Mohonk, New York, designed to develop solutions. Out of this and other "Friends" meetings came many of the personalities and the policies of the late nineteenth and early twentieth centuries.

Perhaps the earliest nationally recognized Indian reformer was Helen Hunt Jackson. Her descriptive exposé, *A Century of Dishonor: A Sketch of the United States Government's Dealings with Some of the Indian Tribes*, appeared in print in 1881. It aimed to create an effect similar to Harriet Beecher Stowe's *Uncle Tom's Cabin*, describing the atrocities of poverty on reservations and blaming the United States government for violating its treaties with the tribes. Other reformers wrote similar accounts, decrying the conditions that led to a decline in Indian population from an initial 5 million to 250,000 by the late nineteenth century (see Thornton, this volume, for a discussion of population estimates). Disease, poverty, and despair spread throughout Indian reservations which, for many, resembled prisoner of war camps. These accounts enlightened readers who had little knowledge of Native Americans outside of stereotypes, and they usually pointed fingers at government policies. In *The Indian Dispossessed* (1905), for example, Seth K. Humphrey describes various reservations, paying particular attention to the government's role as trustee (see also Wissler, 1971).

This particular understanding of the "Indian problem" offered a focus for some of the earliest scholarly literature dealing with federal Indian policy. Among the earliest is George Manypenny's *Our Indian Wards* (1880), a survey of Indian history published the year before Jackson's book. Lawrie Tatum's *Our Red Brothers and the Peace Policy of President Ulysses S. Grant* (1899) was also aimed at reform. Frances E. Leupp, Commissioner of Indian Affairs between 1904 and 1909, described Indians in terms of social welfare issues in his *The Indian and His Problem* (1910). Later scholars have identified certain reformist bureaucrats and organizations that tried to help Indians and improve reservation conditions. Francis Paul Prucha's edited collection, *Americanizing the American Indians: Writings by the "Friends of the Indian" 1880–1900* (1973) is a notable example, as is Robert Mardock's *The Reformers and the American Indian* (1971).

One of the key policy reforms of the late nineteenth century – indeed, the policy that basically superceded the Peace Policy – was allotment in severalty, the division of collectively held Indian lands into individually owned parcels. It took coherent form in 1887, with the passage of the General Allotment Act – also known as the Dawes Act after its sponsor, Lake Mohonk regular Senator Henry Dawes (Washburn, 1975; Otis, 1973). Allotment, some have argued, pointed to the destruction of Indian societies. Forced to become part of the larger colonized cultures of the mainstream, Indians were victimized in numerous ways as, with land to sell and lease, they were forced into a capitalist economic system. Allotment was modified several times, as reformers and bureaucrats scrambled to force Indian landholders out of their native cultures and into American culture and society. The 25-year period during which the government could hold an individual's land in trust was often waived by "competency commissions," which would designate "competent" Indians who would be issued a patent and proclaimed ready to sell or manage their lands. The pattern of abuse and the resulting land loss is ably recounted in Janet McDonnell's *The Dispossession of the American Indian, 1887–1934* (1991). Yet, as Emily Greenwald has argued (2001), the selection of allotments was in itself a critical moment in which Native people acted to reassert their own social and cultural values. Likewise, tribes like the Mescalero Apaches actually requested allotment in order to gain clear and unambiguous title to land they feared could be alienated. Although allotment was clearly a disaster for many Native people, the picture is surely more complicated than we have assumed. Classic works on allotment include those by D. S. Otis (1973), J. P. Kinney (1937), and Leonard Carlson (1981).

If land has been critical to policy and scholarship, so too has the question of legal status. Usurped of much of their sovereignty when placed, by the end of the nineteenth century, upon an estimated 200 reservations, Indians were governed by agents of the federal government – yet they were not citizens of the United States. What were their legal rights? In response to this question, individuals and organizations began speaking on behalf of Indians, offering legal advice and assistance in the strange world of federal–Indian law. Perhaps the most notable of these groups was the Indian Rights Association. The definitive scholarly work on the Association remains William T. Hagan's *The Indian Rights Association: The Herbert Welsh Years, 1882–1904* (1985). Five years earlier, lawyers Russel Barsh and James Youngblood Henderson collaborated on the first "legal history" of federal–Indian policy, *The Road: Indian Tribes and Political Liberty* (1980). Among the many works on Indian legal status are those by Charles Wilkinson (1987), Oren Lyons (1992), David Wilkins (1997), and John Wunder (1994) (see also Harring, this volume).

United States policy aimed at the cultural transformations characterized by the word "assimilation." The ultimate solution to the Indian problem, reformers argued, rested upon bringing Indian people into the mainstream of white American life, economy, and culture. Land allotment, for example, was only a means to this end (Fritz, 1963; Hoxie, 1984). Likewise, citizenship, legislated in 1924, was only a formal naming of the wish for Indian assimilation.

Like the Peace Policy, however, allotment only produced more challenges for Native Americans and bureaucrats. The administration of allotment required more bureaucrats, not fewer. Non-farming Indians did not become agrarians – indeed in many places, they watched their new white neighbors fail on lands not suited to agriculture. Instead of assimilation and prosperity, a new generation of reformers began to see in allotment continued segregation and poverty. And, undeniably, Indian people were in the process of losing millions of acres of their lands to unscrupulous Americans. Later scholars, struck as well by the losses produced by allotment, began to look closely at other kinds of fraud and dispossession, including land loss among the Oklahoma tribes (Debo, 1940) and the scams surrounding Indian oil (Wilson, 1985).

By the 1920s, the failure of the allotment policy had become painfully apparent, leading to yet another public round of reform. One of the critical documents of the period is the Meriam Report, published in 1928 as *The Problem of Indian Administration*. Compiled by Lewis Meriam, the Task Force report surveyed Indian conditions and considered policy failures and reforms, revealing the devastations of allotment on Indian reservations. In 1933, one of the key reformers of the 1920s, John Collier, was appointed Commissioner of Indian Affairs by Franklin D. Roosevelt (Philp, 1977; Kelly, 1983). Collier was a cultural pluralist who believed that Indian cultures had much to teach Americans and that they needed to be protected, preserved, and reinvigorated. He worked diligently to integrate Indian legislation into Roosevelt's New Deal programs, succeeding in 1934 with the passage of the Wheeler-Howard bill, also known as the Indian Reorganization Act or IRA (Deloria and Lytle, 1984).

The Indian New Deal (Collier also pushed through Congress provisions for revolving credit funds and the promotion of Indian arts and crafts) has undoubtedly been a watershed moment in policy history. Radical in nature, it swung the pendulum of

federal Indian policy back in a direction that favored tribes – at least in the understanding of John Collier. It formally ended the allotment policy. Many contemporary
tribal governments were organized under the IRA and, indeed, one could argue that
Indian policy and politics for the remainder of the twentieth century were the products of the changes introduced by the Indian New Deal. Yet many Indian people
experienced the IRA as simply a new form of federal paternalism, one that reshaped
Indian social and political organization into constitutional forms resembling the
United States far more than they resembled anything native. Among the most impor-
tant works dealing with the period are Donald Parman's *The Navajos and the New
Deal* (1976), Laurence Hauptman's *The Iroquois and the New Deal* (1981), Graham
Taylor's *The New Deal and American Indian Tribalism* (1980), and Thomas Biolsi's
Organizing the Lakota (1992). Robert Fay Schrader examines the Indian Arts and
Crafts Board, an important subsidiary part of the Indian New Deal (1983), while
Kenneth Philp has edited the proceedings of a major conference on tribal govern-
ment and sovereignty, *Indian Self-Rule: First-Hand Accounts of Indian–White
Relations from Roosevelt to Reagan* (1986).

The Indian New Deal did little to stop the suffering caused by the Great
Depression. Nonetheless, in its rejection of allotment, creation of political structures
recognizable to white Americans, loan programs, and efforts to consolidate fragmented lands, it utterly transformed many native lives. Perhaps just as critical, however, was a different New Deal agency, the Civilian Conservation Corps, which
included an Indian division. Designed to provide jobs to the unemployed, the CCC
brought Indian men from reservations to work on bridges, schools, libraries, shel-
ters, and other public works. The fact that native men left their families and communities, returning later with much-needed wages, seemed to many to recapture the
movements of warriors and hunters and brought a new measure of self-respect to
some native men. Yet the CCC also marked a significant moment in the integration
of Indian people into the wage labor economy (see Albers, this volume).

That integration was hastened by the onset of World War II. Many Indian people
left reservations to work in the war industries producing jeeps, boots, and other
items needed on the battlefields of Europe and the Pacific. Equally important,
25,000 Indian men and 500 Indian women served in the armed forces, which gave
them the opportunity to travel around the nation and the world (Bernstein, 1991).
During World War I, Indian people had served in numbers disproportionate to their
population. Indeed, their wartime service contributed to the passage of the Indian
Citizenship Act in 1924 (Britten, 1997). Now, in the wake of a similar display of
service and patriotism in World War II, white Americans sought to repudiate the
cultural pluralist tenets of the New Deal and pushed once again for Indian assimilation. Kenneth Philp's *Termination Revisited: American Indians on the Trail to Self
Determination* (1999) offers a fine overview of the period.

Postwar policy took shape first around a program of "relocation" to urban areas. In
1947–8, confronting blizzards and poor conditions on the Navajo reservation, the
government removed starving Navajos (Dene) to Salt Lake City, Denver, and Los
Angeles. The relocation policy assumed certain things: that Indians were in fact wage
workers ripe for the postwar economy and that the reservations, which once served as

sites of social control and assimilation, actually enabled Indians to preserve cultural traditions and social fabrics. Reservation poverty was the problem; urban prosperity was the answer. In 1951, the federal government began offering "relocation" to all Native people, and the program became official with the 1952 arrival of Indian people in Chicago (Fixico, 1986). Throughout the 1950s and 1960s, and into the 1970s, Indians relocated to Chicago, Seattle, Denver, Los Angeles, Detroit, San Francisco, and Minneapolis-St. Paul, among other cities. Los Angeles became the largest urban Indian area in America, with 60,000 Indian people living there. In order to assist Indians in finding jobs, Congress passed a vocational education law in 1957, which aimed to help train Native people in skilled professions. By the 1990s, more than two-thirds of the total Indian population in the United States lived in urban areas.

Urbanization created a new set of policy problems and procedures, centered around familiar issues – education, economics, spatial autonomy, freedom of religion and other legal rights – reshaped into different problems in urban contexts. In addition to the federal government, states, counties, and cities found that they needed to pay attention to Indian people. Rather than assimilate into the urban setting, Native people have instead tended to retain substantial ties to home reservations and, at powwows and community centers, to "re-tribalize" their communities (Weibel-Orlando, 1991). Scholars too have, over the last decades, become interested in the question of urban Indians. Alan Sorkin's *The Urban American Indian* (1978) offers an early overview, while Edmund Danziger Jr.'s *Survival and Regeneration: Detroit's American Indian Community* (1991) examines a specific case study of an urban community and its social and political contexts. Donald Fixico's *The Urban Indian Experience in America* (2000) offers a thorough survey of urban Indian life.

Postwar urbanization brought Indian people together into political alliances, which were increasingly capable of affecting the course of federal and state policy. Similarly, other policy changes helped mobilize Indian political involvement in critical ways. Congress passed two bills with particularly profound repercussions. The Indian Claims Commission Act (1946) created an Indian Claims Commission, chartered for ten years to hear and decide Indian land claims against the United States once and for all. Native appeals to the commission proved voluminous and complex, however, and the commission continued to function until 1978. Although the federal government was clearly attempting to get out of the Indian business, in fact the Claims Commission mobilized and solidified Native people while making them keenly aware of the government's long history of unfulfilled obligations.

The second major legislation occurred in 1953, when the Congress passed House Concurrent Resolution 108. This resolution laid the foundation for a new federal policy based on the "withdrawal" of federal trust responsibilities to Indian people (Burt, 1982). As many scholars have observed, the relocation policy went hand in hand with this new "termination" policy. A small but influential bloc of terminationist Congressmen in the House and the Senate passed bills to terminate trust status for a total of 109 tribes between 1954 and the early 1970s. The pendulum had swung again and, although many legislators argued that they were advocating a simple egalitarianism – no special privileges for minority groups – Indian people tended to see the policy as more clearly anti-Indian. Termination also took Indian policy deliberations more directly to the state level, as terminated tribes were often slated to become counties. With federal status "withdrawn" and reservation sovereignty not yet viable, they would look to state government as the superior governmental agency (Fixico, 1986). Such, for example, was the case with the Menominee tribe of Wisconsin, the first tribe scheduled for termination. As a tribe receiving some federal services, the Menominee had done well. As a county, overseen by a board of local white businessmen and responsible for providing county services, Menominee fared poorly. Nicholas Peroff's *Menominee Drums: Tribal Termination and Restoration, 1954–1974* (1982) describes not only the termination, but also the political battle waged by the Menominees in order to reclaim federal trust status.

Nor were the Menominee the only Indian people trying to alter the course of federal and state Indian policies. The National Congress of American Indians, organized in 1944, found a new focus, as tribal leaders vehemently opposed the termination policy (Cowger, 1999). The first major national conference of Indian political organizers occurred in 1961 on the University of Chicago campus. The Chicago Indian Conference's "Declaration of Indian Purpose" called for Indian input into the formation of federal policy and, indeed, throughout the 1960s, increasingly savvy tribal leaders journeyed to Washington to put in their bids for programs and other funding.

At the same time, however, Indian activists were also taking their concerns to the streets, and those concerns were often aimed at state and local entities as much as they were the federal government. Indian protests aimed at reclaiming fishing rights in the state of Washington in the mid-1960s, for example, brought Native people into national consciousness. The issue, however, originated in the state's repressive efforts to control Indian fishing in order to further its own economic objectives. The 1969 seizure of Alcatraz Island in San Francisco Bay mushroomed from a local event – the loss of San Francisco's Indian Center catalysed larger issues surrounding relocation and racism – into a national one (Johnson, 1996: 50). Likewise, the 1968 founding of the American Indian Movement (AIM) in Minneapolis came as an effort to combat local police violence. All these movements took on national dimensions as Red Power began to emerge as part of the larger pattern of civil rights activism across the country. Over the next few years, for example, as many as forty AIM chapters were organized in the United States and Canada and AIM began shifting its focus to what might be called "federal" issues. The 1972 "Trail of Broken Treaties" caravan to Washington resulted in the takeover of the Bureau of Indian Affairs. Lost in the media coverage, however, was a comprehensive intellectual and political platform concerning federal policy and its basis in treaty relations (Deloria, 1974). Likewise, AIM's 1973 takeover of the small town of Wounded Knee, South Dakota fused local, regional, and federal grievances together, most of which the media ignored.

The Red Power movement generated a wave of contemporary writing and it has become the focus of increased scholarly attention today. Vine Deloria, Jr.'s *Custer Died for Your Sins* (1969) and N. Scott Momaday's Pulitzer Prize-winning *House Made of Dawn* (1968) put Americans on notice that Indians were no longer a silent minority. Dee Brown's *Bury My Heart at Wounded Knee* (1971) was a bestseller among a sympathetic white reading public. Amidst such public writings, however, a growing cadre of Native scholars also sought to provide intellectual bedrock for Indian political argument. Deloria's *Of Utmost Good Faith* (1971), *We Talk, You Listen* (1970), and later, *God Is Red* (1973) did exactly that, offering a range that spanned polemic to collections of useful documents. Another important contemporary collection is Alvin Josephy's *Red Power: The American Indian's Fight for Freedom* (1971). Robert Warrior and Paul Chaat Smith (1996), Troy Johnson (1996), Joane Nagle, Troy Johnson, and Duane Champagne (1997), among others, have looked back at the history of the Red Power movement.

The changes in policy that came in the wake of the 1960s bear a certain resemblance to the changes encapsulated in the Indian New Deal. Once again, federal policy reversed course, rejecting termination in favor of tribal "self-determination." Yet again, policies overlapped and stood in complex relation to one another, marked by borrowing of ideas, common ideological underpinnings, and a shared sense of righteous origin in "reform." Termination, functionally dislodged as policy by the early 1960s, remained on the books, a threat to tribal people until the early 1970s. However, as George Pierre Castile notes, Indian self-determination took root as policy with *both* Indian and federal support (Castile, 1998). Jack Forbes's *Native Americans and Nixon* (1981) details the policy shift that led to Nixon's announcement of Self-Determination as government doctrine. Self-Determination meant, in many cases, Indian administration of federal funds and programs in ways consistent with tribal customs and understandings and it was given formal policy standing with the Indian Self-Determination and Education Act of 1975.

The 1970s proved to be a productive decade for Native people. In addition to the policy innovations that came with Self-Determination, several legal decisions suggested that Indians would be able to set precedents in court. Perhaps the most significant of these was the Penobscot-Passamaquoddy case (1975), which pitted tribes and the federal government against the state of Maine. Massachusetts (Maine did not exist at the time) had violated the Trade and Intercourse Act of 1790 in acquiring Indian land in 1794; Maine continued to do so in the following years. In theory, no claims to Maine land were valid. In practice, the tribes accepted a 1980 settlement that included a 24 million dollar trust fund and a 54 million dollar land acquisition fund (Brodeur, 1985). The 1970s were also marked by the passage of several other important pieces of legislation. The American Indian Policy Review Commission Act mandated the first comprehensive look at Indian affairs since the Meriam Commission of the 1920s. The Alaska Native Claims Settlement Act (1971), the Menominee Restoration Act (1973), the American Indian Religious Freedom Act (1978), the Indian Child Welfare Act (1978) – these pieces of legislation, along with struggles to regain hunting and fishing rights, innovations in the right to tax, and many other Native initiatives suggest that the 1970s saw more victories than losses for Indian people. Yet in almost every case, Indian people found themselves constrained even in the midst of what looked like positive changes. The Menominees received no restitution for all that they had lost under termination. The Religious Freedom Act mandated no penalties for infringements upon Native religious practice; indeed, it was effectively gutted by an increasingly conservative Supreme Court before it was a decade old.

Self-Determination took on new meanings during the Reagan years, as the federal dollars flowing to reservations – never more than a tiny stream – slowed to a scant trickle. In response, tribal governments often went aggressively in search of resources, in the process putting real teeth into contemporary claims for tribal sovereignty (although see Alfred, this volume). Perhaps the most noticeable of the tribal innovations of the 1980s was gaming. Tribes took advantage of their position between state and federal statuses in order to argue that state rules allowing charitable gaming allowed Indians to use their (federal) lands to run gaming operations outside the regulation of the states. Congress addressed this situation in 1988, with the Indian Gaming Regulatory Act, which mandated a series of compacts between individual tribes and the states in which they reside (Wunder, 1994: 204–7). Gaming has opened up new arenas for conflict between tribes and states. Arizona, New Mexico, Kansas, and many other states have tried to restrict or counter the effect of Indian gaming. At the same time, however, gaming has also forced some states and tribes to sit down in a productive political relationship. The Mashentucket Pequot gaming operation, for example, did much to salvage the economy of Connecticut in the early 1990s. Able to bring substantial economic power to the table, some tribes have found common ground with state governments, which have often tended to be hostile to tribal governments and initiatives.

The question of state–tribal relations has been seriously understudied, particularly when considered in relation to the vast literature on federal policy. Yet states and localities have typically been active players in Indian policy history. Consider issues surrounding water rights, voting rights, local taxation, regional development – all these are as often state-level questions as they are federal. One of the most intriguing works to look at state policy is George Harwood Phillips's *Indians and Indian Agents: The Origins of the Reservation System in California, 1849–1852* (1997), which argues that the modern reservation system stemmed, in part, from the efforts of agents to spare one-seventh of California for Indian occupancy. George Pierre Castile and Robert L. Bee's edited volume, *State and Reservation: New Perspectives on Federal Indian Policy* (1992) examines the responses of a number of tribal communities and their governments to state and federal policies. Sharon O'Brien's *American Indian Tribal Governments* (1990) is the only comprehensive volume on the subject of tribal governments.

Indian tribes' relations with state governments have been most complicated and longstanding in the thirteen original states which, under the federal Constitution, retained some of the power and jurisdiction over subject Indians they had exercised as colonies. Although there are no comprehensive studies of the relations for any of the states, a number of studies offer useful insights in the course of examining particular tribes, time periods, or developments, especially land claims cases. For Massachusetts, see Brodeur (1985), Clifford (1988), Campisi (1991), and Plane and Button (1993); on New York, consult Hauptman (1986, 1988); also Rountree (1990) on Virginia, and Merrell (1989) on South Carolina. It is apparent that state relations with Indians, which have gained in importance over the last decades, offer a critically important site for new scholarship.

The work on federal and state policy has changed course with each new generation of scholars, moving from exercises in description and periodization to analytical treatments of certain periods. By the mid-1980s, scholars were investigating case studies within policy periods, while some senior scholars ventured to provide comprehensive coverage of the history of federal–Indian relations (Prucha, 1984). Each generation, however, has faced similar questions about federal and state relations with Indian people. And while these have tended to center on issues of law, education, economy, religion, and land, new work has also broadened the field to include topics such as tribal government, health care, repatriation, and perhaps most importantly, Indian response to policy initiatives (see especially Cornell, 1988). As a result, the scholarship has evolved to transcend older, one-sided views of policy as something formed and implemented in a cultural vacuum. Over the last few decades, scholars have used policy to get at even larger questions. In a sociological study, for example, Joane Nagel addresses "identity" as a key to understanding Indian activism and federal policies during the 1960s and 1970s (Nagel, 1996). Troy Johnson's *The Occupation of Alcatraz Island: Indian Self-Determination and the Rise of Indian Activism* (1996) functions in a similar way. The Native American Graves Protection and Repatriation Act (1990) has required new kinds of research on the part of both Native and non-Native scholars. It too suggests new ways of considering the relation between identity, history, and policy, most especially from an Indian perspective.

Federal and state policy has undoubtedly changed Indian lives and histories. Rarely, however, have those changes reflected the desires of policymakers. Removal did not lead to assimilation. Nor did the reservation system or allotment. The Indian New Deal did not restore Indian land-bases and traditional forms of government. Termination was unsuccessful in eliminating tribes' unique legal status and their accompanying claims on the federal government. If many Indian people relocated, they also maintained ties to home reservations. With the massive budget cuts of the 1980s, Self-Determination was revealed to include economic dependency, and the Reagan-Bush policy of retrenchment in fact led to gaming, other forms of economic development, and a larger and louder assertion of Native sovereignty.

The challenge of writing about policy and its relation to Indian people lies in understanding the roots of these surprises. In almost every case, those roots need to be traced back to the responses of Indian people, whether it be the choosing of an allotment, a vigorous lobbying session, a street demonstration, or a casino deal. In many cases, particularly when discussing the eighteenth and nineteenth centuries, historians will find themselves at a disadvantage. In the past, the lack of Indian sources has allowed historians to focus on the relative abundance of government documents and to produce histories that speak almost exclusively to the non-Indian side of the policy equation. Federal policy, as well, has offered the only single opportunity for discussing Indian history from a broad perspective. The problem, of course, is that such histories tell us more about governments, policies, and bureaucrats than they do about Indian people. In the future, those familiar sources will need to be re-evaluated and made, as much as possible, to speak more fairly to the perspectives and responses of Native people. In conjunction with the development of new sources and new techniques of analysis, such a re-evaluation may well produce yet another burst of scholarship concerning federal and state policy with regard to Indian people.

BIBLIOGRAPHY

Armstrong, William 1978: *Warrior in Two Camps: Ely S. Parker, Union General and Seneca Chief* (Syracuse: Syracuse University Press).

Barsh, Russel and James Youngblood Henderson 1980: *The Road: Indian Tribes and Political Liberty* (Berkeley: University of California Press).

Bender, Norman 1989: *New Hope for the Indians: The Grant Peace Policy and the Navajos in the 1870s* (Albuquerque: University of New Mexico Press).

Berkhofer, Robert F., Jr. 1978: *The White Man's Indian: Images of the American Indian from Columbus to the Present* (New York: Vintage).

Bernstein, Alison R. 1991: *American Indians and World War II: Toward a New Era in Indian Affairs* (Norman: University of Oklahoma Press).

Biolsi, Thomas 1992: *Organizing the Lakota: The Political Economy of the New Deal on the Pine Ridge and Rosebud Reservations* (Tucson: University of Arizona Press).

Britten, Thomas A. 1997: *American Indians in World War I: At War and at Home* (Albuquerque: University of New Mexico Press).

Brodeur, Paul 1985: *Restitution: The Land Claims of the Mashpee, Passamaquoddy, and Penobscot Indians of New England* (Boston: Northeastern University Press).

Brown, Dee 1971: *Bury My Heart at Wounded Knee: An Indian History of the American West* (New York: Holt, Rinehart and Winston).

Burt, Larry 1982: *Tribalism in Crisis: Federal Indian Policy, 1953–1961* (Albuquerque: University of New Mexico Press).

Campisi, Jack 1991: *The Mashpee Indians: Tribe on Trial* (Syracuse: Syracuse University Press).

Carlson, Leonard 1981: *Indians, Bureaucrats, and Land: The Dawes Act and the Decline of Indian Farming* (Westport, CT: Greenwood Press).

Castile, George Pierre 1998: *To Show Heart: Native American Self Determination and Federal Indian Policy, 1960–1975* (Tucson: University of Arizona Press).

Castile, George Pierre and Robert L. Bee (eds.) 1992: *State and Reservation: New Perspectives on Federal Indian Policy* (Tucson: University of Arizona Press).

Clifford, James 1988: "Identity in Mashpee," in Clifford, *The Predicament of Culture: Twentieth-Century Ethnography, Literature, and Art* (Cambridge, MA: Harvard University Press).

Cornell, Stephen 1988: *The Return of the Native: American Indian Political Resurgence* (New York: Oxford University Press).

Cowger, Thomas 1999: *The National Congress of American Indians: The Founding Years* (Lincoln: University of Nebraska Press).

Danziger, Edmund, Jr. 1991: *Survival and Regeneration: Detroit's American Indian Community* (Detroit: Wayne State University Press).

Debo, Angie 1940: *And Still the Waters Run: The Betrayal of the Five Civilized Tribes* (Princeton: Princeton University Press).

Deloria, Vine, Jr. 1969: *Custer Died for Your Sins: An Indian Manifesto* (New York: Macmillan).

Deloria, Vine, Jr. 1970: *We Talk, You Listen: New Tribes, New Turf* (New York: Macmillan).

Deloria, Vine, Jr. 1971: *Of Utmost Good Faith* (San Francisco: Straight Arrow Books).

Deloria, Vine, Jr. 1973: *God Is Red: A Native View of Religion* (New York: Dell).

Deloria, Vine, Jr. 1974: *Behind the Trail of Broken Treaties: An Indian Declaration of Independence* (New York: Delacorte Press).

Deloria, Vine, Jr., 1985: *American Indian Policy in the Twentieth Century* (Norman: University of Oklahoma Press).

Deloria, Vine, Jr. and Raymond J. DeMallie (eds. and compilers) 1999: *Documents of American Indian Diplomacy: Treaties, Agreements, and Conventions, 1775–1979* (Norman: University of Oklahoma Press).

Deloria, Vine, Jr. and Clifford Lytle 1984: *The Nations Within: The Past and Future of American Indian Sovereignty* (Austin: University of Texas Press).

Dippie, Brian 1982: *The Vanishing American: White Attitudes and U.S. Indian Policy* (Middletown: Wesleyan University Press).

Fixico, Donald L. 1986: *Termination and Relocation: Federal Indian Policy, 1945–1960* (Albuquerque: University of New Mexico Press).

Fixico, Donald L. 2000: *The Urban Indian Experience in America* (Albuquerque: University of New Mexico Press).

Forbes, Jack 1981: *Native Americans and Nixon: Presidential Politics and Minority Self-Determination, 1969–1970* (Los Angeles: American Indian Studies Center, UCLA).

Foreman, Grant 1953: *Indian Removal: The Emigration of the Five Civilized Tribes of Indians* (Norman: University of Oklahoma Press).

Fritz, Henry 1963: *The Movement for Indian Assimilation, 1860–1890* (Philadelphia: University of Pennsylvania Press).

Greenwald, Emily 2001: *Allotment in Severalty* (Albuquerque: University of New Mexico Press).

Hagan, William T. 1985: *The Indian Rights Association: The Herbert Welsh Years, 1882–1904* (Tucson: University of Arizona Press).

Hagan, William T. 1997: *Theodore Roosevelt and Six Friends of the Indian* (Norman: University of Oklahoma Press).

Hauptman, Laurence M. 1981: *The Iroquois and the New Deal* (Syracuse: Syracuse University Press).

Hauptman, Laurence M. 1986: *The Iroquois Struggle for Survival: World War II to Red Power* (Syracuse: Syracuse University Press).

Hauptman, Laurence M. 1988: *Formulating American Indian Policy in New York State, 1970–1986* (Syracuse: Syracuse University Press).

Hertzberg, Hazel W. 1971: *The Search for an American Indian Identity: Modern Pan Indian Movements* (Syracuse: Syracuse University Press).

Horsman, Reginald 1981: *Race and Manifest Destiny: The Origins of American Racial Anglo-Saxonism* (Cambridge, MA: Harvard University Press).

Hoxie, Frederick 1984: *A Final Promise: The Campaign to Assimilate the Indians, 1880–1920* (Lincoln: University of Nebraska Press).

Hoxie, Frederick et al. (eds.) 1999: *Native Americans and the Early Republic* (Charlottesville: University Press of Virginia).

Humphrey, Seth K. 1905: *The Indian Dispossessed* (Boston: Little, Brown and Company).

Jackson, Helen Hunt 1881: *A Century of Dishonor: A Sketch of the United States Government's Dealings with Some of the Indian Tribes* (New York: Harper and Brothers).

Johnson, Troy 1996: *The Occupation of Alcatraz Island: Indian Self-Determination and the Rise of Indian Activism* (Urbana: University of Illinois Press).

Johnson, Troy, Joane Nagel, and Duane Champagne (eds.) 1997: *American Indian Activism: Alcatraz to the Longest Walk* (Urbana: University of Illinois Press).

Jones, Dorothy 1982: *License for Empire: Colonialism by Treaty in Early America* (Chicago: University of Chicago Press).

Josephy, Alvin, Jr. (ed.) 1971: *Red Power: The American Indian's Fight for Freedom.* (New York: McGraw-Hill) (2nd edition 1999).

Kahn, Edgar 1969: *Our Brother's Keeper: The Indian in White America* (New York: New Community Press).

Kappler, Charles (ed. and compiler) 1903: *Indian Affairs. Laws and Treaties* (Washington, D.C.: Government Printing Office).

Keller, Robert H., Jr. 1983: *American Protestantism and United States Indian Policy, 1869–82* (Lincoln: University of Nebraska Press).

Kelly, Lawrence C. 1983: *The Assault on Assimilation: John Collier and the Origins of Indian Policy Reform* (Albuquerque: University of New Mexico Press).

Kinney, J. P. 1937: *A Continent Lost – A Civilization Won: Indian Land Tenure in America* (Baltimore: Johns Hopkins University Press).

Leupp, Frances E. 1910: *The Indian and His Problem* (New York: Charles Scribner's Sons).

Lyons, Oren et al. 1992: *Exiled in the Land of the Free: Democracy, Indian Nations, and the U.S. Constitution* (Santa Fe: Clear Light Publishers).

McDonnell, Janet A. 1991: *The Dispossession of the American Indian, 1887–1934* (Bloomington: Indiana University Press).

Manypenny, George 1880: *Our Indian Wards* (Cincinnati: Robert Clarke and Company).

Mardock, Robert Winston 1971: *The Reformers and the American Indian* (Columbia: University of Missouri Press).

Meriam, Lewis et al. (comps.) 1928: *The Problem of Indian Administration* (Baltimore: Johns Hopkins University Press).

Merrell, James 1989: *The Indians' New World: Catawbas and Their Neighbors from European Contact through the Era of Removal* (Chapel Hill: University of North Carolina Press).

Momaday, N. Scott 1968: *House Made of Dawn* (New York: Harper & Row).

Nagel, Joane 1996: *American Indian Ethnic Renewal: Red Power and the Resurgence of Identity and Culture* (New York: Oxford University Press).

O'Brien, Sharon 1990: *American Indian Tribal Governments* (Norman: University of Oklahoma Press).

Otis, D. S. 1973: *The Dawes Act and the Allotment of Indian Lands* (Norman: University of Oklahoma Press).

Parman, Donald L. 1976: *The Navajos and the New Deal* (New Haven: Yale University Press).

Peroff, Nicholas 1982: *Menominee Drums: Tribal Termination and Restoration, 1954–1974* (Norman: University of Oklahoma Press).

Phillips, George Harwood 1997: *Indians and Indian Agents: The Origins of the Reservation System in California, 1849–1852* (Norman: University of Oklahoma Press).

Philp, Kenneth R. 1977: *John Collier's Crusade for Indian Reform, 1920–1954* (Tucson: University of Arizona Press).

Philp, Kenneth R. (ed.) 1986: *Indian Self-Rule: First-Hand Accounts of Indian–White Relations from Roosevelt to Reagan* (Salt Lake City: Howe Brothers).

Philp, Kenneth R. 1999: *Termination Revisited: American Indians on the Trail to Self Determination, 1933–1953* (Lincoln: University of Nebraska Press).

Plane, A. M. and G. Button 1993: "The Massachusetts Indian Enfranchisement Act: Ethnic Contest in Historical Context, 1849–1869," *Ethnohistory* 40: 587–618.

Priest, Loring B. 1969: *Uncle Sam's Stepchildren: The Reformation of United States Indian Policy, 1865–1887* (New York: Octagon Books).

Prucha, Francis Paul 1962: *American Indian Policy in the Formative Years: The Indian Trade and Intercourse Act 1790–1834* (Cambridge, MA: Harvard University Press).

Prucha, Francis Paul (ed.) 1973: *Americanizing the American Indians: Writings by the "Friends of the Indian" 1880–1900* (Cambridge, MA: Harvard University Press).

Prucha, Francis Paul 1976: *American Indian Policy in Crisis: Christian Reformers and the Indian, 1865–1900* (Norman: University of Oklahoma Press).

Prucha, Francis Paul 1984: *The Great Father: The United States Government and the American Indians*, 2 vols. (Lincoln: University of Nebraska Press).

Rogin, Michael Paul 1975: *Fathers and Children: Andrew Jackson and the Subjugation of the American Indian* (New York: Knopf).

Rountree, Helen 1990: *Pocahontas's People: The Powhatan Indians of Virginia through Four Centuries* (Norman: University of Oklahoma Press).

Satz, Ronald N. 1975: *American Indian Policy in the Jacksonian Era* (Lincoln: University of Nebraska Press).

Schrader, Robert Fay 1983: *The Indian Arts and Crafts Board: An Aspect of New Deal Indian Policy* (Albuquerque: University of New Mexico Press).

Sheehan, Bernard W. 1973: *Seeds of Extinction: Jeffersonian Philanthropy and the American Indian* (Chapel Hill: University of North Carolina Press).

Sorkin, Alan L. 1978: *The Urban American Indian* (Lexington, MA: Lexington Books).

Tatum, Lawrie 1899: *Our Red Brothers and the Peace Policy of President Ulysses S. Grant* (John C. Winston and Co.).

Taylor, Graham D. 1980: *The New Deal and American Indian Tribalism: The Administration of the Indian Reorganization Act, 1934–45* (Lincoln: University of Nebraska Press).

Trelease, Allen W. 1960: *Indian Affairs in Colonial New York: The Seventeenth Century* (Ithaca: Cornell University Press).

Trennert, Robert A. 1975: *Alternative to Extinction: Federal Indian Policy and the Beginnings of the Reservation System, 1846–1851* (Philadelphia: Temple University Press).

Viola, Herman 1974: *Thomas L. McKenney: Architect of America's Early Indian Policy, 1816–1830* (Chicago: The Swallow Press).

Wallace, Anthony F. C. 1993: *The Long, Bitter Trail: Andrew Jackson and the Indians* (New York: Hill and Wang).

Wallace, Anthony F. C. 1999: *Jefferson and the Indians: The Tragic Fate of the First Americans* (Cambridge, MA: Harvard University Press).

Warrior, Robert and Paul Chaat Smith 1996: *Like a Hurricane: The Indian Movement from Alcatraz to Wounded Knee* (New York: New Press).

Washburn, Wilcomb 1975: *The Assault on Indian Tribalism: The General Allotment Law (Dawes Act) of 1887* (Philadelphia: J. B. Lippincott Company).

Weibel-Orlando, Joan 1991: *Indian Country, L.A.: Maintaining Ethnic Community in Complex Society* (Urbana: University of Illinois Press).

Wilkins, David E. 1997: *American Indian Sovereignty and the U.S. Supreme Court: The Masking of Justice* (Austin: University of Texas Press).

Wilkinson, Charles F. 1987: *American Indians, Time, and the Law: Native Modern Constitutional Democracy* (New Haven: Yale University Press).

Wilson, Terry P. 1985: *The Underground Reservation: Osage Oil* (Lincoln: University of Nebraska Press).

Wissler, Clark 1971: *Red Man's Reservations* (New York: Collier Books).

Wunder, John 1994: *"Retained by the People": A History of American Indians and the Bill of Rights* (New York: Oxford University Press).

_____

22

Native Americans and the United States, Canada, and Mexico

R. DAVID EDMUNDS

The Indian policies that have emerged in the United States, Canada, and Mexico are products of their colonial past and reflect the aspirations of European colonial powers and their colonists, moderated by the impact of geography and transformed by historical events since the end of each country's colonial period. This essay will first survey the history of Indian policies developed in the United States, using them as a springboard for comparisons with Canada and Mexico, the other two nations involved in colonial relations with indigenous people. By looking for similarities and discontinuities, unique developments and those that echo or parallel policies in different nations, we can place both national and tribal histories in broader context.

In the decade immediately following the American Revolution, relations between Native Americans and the new American government were marked by uncertainty. Most of the tribes had supported the British during the conflict, and although American military forces had defeated the Iroquois and the Cherokees, other tribes had successfully defended their homeland against the Americans. Many envisioned themselves as victors in the conflict. Colin Calloway (1987) shows that although the Crown had been forced to relinquish its claims to the region east of the Mississippi, British agents continued to exercise considerable influence, particularly among the Great Lakes and Ohio tribes. Both Reginald Horsman (1964) and Larry Nelson (1999) trace the personal careers of British Indian agents and indicate that they encouraged Indian people to resist American demands for land cessions.

In contrast, the Americans believed they had won the revolutionary war and that the Indians, who were allies of the British, were a conquered people. Consequently the Articles of Confederation government attempted to gain Native American acquiescence to the American occupation of Ohio through a series of questionable treaties, which the Shawnees, Delawares, and other Midwestern tribes resisted, leading to warfare (Horsman, 1967; Dowd, 1992; Sword, 1985).

Attempting to centralize and consolidate Indian affairs, during the 1790s the Congress passed the Indian Intercourse Acts, which established federal hegemony over Indian policy and forbade state or local governments from negotiating with the tribes. The acts also provided for the punishment of whites who committed crimes against Indians, established federal trading posts or Indian "factories," and generally encouraged Native Americans to become small yeoman farmers and acculturate toward the Anglo-American way of life. Bernard Sheehan (1973) explores the rationale behind the government's well intentioned, yet disastrous efforts to promote agriculture among the tribes. Francis Paul Prucha's masterful *The Great Father: The United States Government and the American Indians* (1984) remains the standard volume on the formulation and administration of federal Indian policy during these years, despite criticisms that it depicts its subject from the government's perspective.

The Indian Intercourse Acts met with only limited success. Although members of some tribes (e.g., Moravian Delawares, Cherokees) attempted "to walk the white man's road," other tribespeople rejected the federal acculturation programs. Yet with the fur trade declining and Americans expanding westward onto the remaining Indian land-base east of the Mississippi, the tribes were hard-pressed to provide for their families and maintain political autonomy. As Native American frustration increased, new leaders emerged, offering religious deliverance from the problems besetting the tribes. Anthony F. C. Wallace (1970) shows how Handsome Lake, a holy man who had experienced visions, championed a new syncretic faith which promised to revitalize peacefully the Seneca communities. R. David Edmunds (1983) offers a comparable treatment of Tenskwatawa, the Shawnee Prophet. Tenskwatawa professed a nativistic doctrine that urged tribespeople throughout the Old Northwest to sever their ties with the Americans, whom he blamed for most of the Indians' troubles. The relation between politics and religion is a central theme in this literature. Dowd (1992), for example, argues that Tecumseh's and Tenskwatawa's attempts to unite the tribes prior to the War of 1812 were a logical outgrowth of previous Native American attempts at political confederation. Edmunds (1983, 1984), on the other hand, asserts that this pan-Indian movement coalesced initially around Tenskwatawa's religious teachings, and only later was politicized by his brother, Tecumseh. Joel Martin (1991) provides an interesting analysis of the religious foundations of intra-tribal conflict among the Creeks during this period, and subsequent Creek resistance to American expansion.

The two decades following the war witnessed the rapid expansion of whites westward to the Mississippi River, and the subsequent purchase of Indian lands in the Midwest and South by the federal government. Prucha (1984) provides detailed information on the establishment of an Office of Indian Affairs in 1824, and the government's decision to "save" the eastern tribes by removing them to lands west of the Mississippi. Herman Viola (1974) examines the career of Thomas McKenney, the first commissioner of Indian Affairs. Viola suggests that McKenney's support of Indian removal was motivated by the genuine, if misguided, belief that eastern Indians removed to lands beyond the white frontier could pursue their traditional way of life until missionaries and other reformers prepared them for assimilation into white society.

Although some reformers were motivated by such altruism, most American frontiersmen wanted the Indians removed west of the Mississippi so that their lands would be opened to white settlement. In 1830, after Andrew Jackson was elected president, Congress passed the Indian Removal Bill and the removal process was accelerated. Many historians and Native Americans have been justly critical of Jackson's policies, although Ronald Satz (1975) provides a balanced account.

Native American people were almost unanimous in their opposition to the government's removal policies. Since the removal era itself, most historians have emphasized the acculturation of the southern tribes, particularly the Cherokees. However, the most recent studies argue that although the Cherokees were led by a cadre of relatively well-educated, acculturated mixed-bloods, much of the tribe remained tied to traditional ways. Perdue (1979, 1998), for example, suggests that the Cherokees incorporated Anglo-American values and institutions, yet molded them to particular Cherokee parameters. McLoughlin (1984, 1986a, 1986b), on the other hand, focuses upon missionaries, Christianity, and the Cherokees' changing concepts of religion as key to cultural evolution during this period. Historians have generally been sympathetic to those Cherokees who endeavored to remain in their homelands, but Thurman Wilkins (1970) argues that those Cherokees who accepted removal and negotiated with the government were more perceptive than their opponents and wisely attempted to make the best of a bad situation. Richard White (1983) suggests that among the Choctaws an acculturated elite fought removal primarily to protect their privileged economic status, including their plantations, while more traditional Choctaws wished to remain in Mississippi through their emotional attachment to their homeland. Such dichotomies also may have been prevalent among the Cherokees, Creeks, and other southern tribes.

The American impetus for removal, while contested among whites, nonetheless operated at all levels of government. Mary Young (1961) discusses the chicanery and fraud perpetrated by state and local officials in Alabama, for example, while Michael Green (1982) demonstrates that the Creeks failed to develop a unified tribal response to federal attempts to purchase their lands in Georgia and Alabama. Encouraged by the Jackson administration, state and local officials in the South harassed the tribespeople and passed legislation designed to weaken their tribal governments. Meanwhile, federal officials coerced tribal leaders to sell their lands and remove to the west. On the Cherokee "Trail of Tears," approximately 4,000 Cherokees – about 25 percent of the tribe's population – died. The physical removal of the tribes, including the suffering encountered by the emigrants, has been chronicled by many historians, but a pioneering work still relevant today is Grant Foreman's *Indian Removal* (1932).

Considerable acculturation also took place north of the Ohio River but, as Richard White (1991) points out, Indians in this region intermarried with Creole French, adopting the cultural patterns of these traders and entrepreneurs. Edmunds (1985) argues that American settlers disliked the Creole French almost as much as they detested Indians, and since Native Americans in the Midwest refused to become small yeoman farmers, they were removed to western Iowa or Kansas. Eventually, most of these Midwestern tribes were consolidated with the southern tribes in the Indian Territory (eastern Oklahoma), although some tribal communities (Ojibwas, Ottawas, Menominees, etc.) in northern Michigan and Wisconsin continued to occupy reservations within their former homelands. The federal government's removal policies lumped diverse tribes together on a limited, partially segregated land-base. They also ignored Native American people such as the Osages, Pawnees, and Dakotas who lived on the eastern edge of the Great Plains, and who resented the new Indian emigrants.

Meanwhile, the Great Plains also was invaded by growing numbers of white Americans who passed through the region en route to New Mexico, California, and Oregon. To minimize contact between the plains tribes and white emigrants, in 1851, at the Treaty of Fort Laramie, federal officials attempted to extend earlier policies by concentrating the plains people north of the Platte River and south of the Arkansas. Yet the concentration policy failed. Both Donald Berthrong (1963) and Elliott West (1998) illustrate how the gold trails bisected Cheyenne lands in Colorado and touched off a wave of violence that swept the central plains in the late 1850s and 1860s. West's study, which examines the environmental impact of human habitation on the central plains, suggests that Indian horse herds overgrazed the region, leading to the demise of the bison. West's work has been praised by academic historians, but has been sharply criticized by many Native Americans.

Robert Utley (1967, 1973) indicates that after almost a decade of warfare federal policymakers attempted to further concentrate the southern plains tribes in western Oklahoma and the Texas panhandle, while the northern plains tribes were assigned lands in western South Dakota, eastern Wyoming, and southeastern Montana. The resulting treaties of Medicine Lodge Creek (1867) and Fort Laramie (1868) were broken by white buffalo hunters in the south and by gold-seekers in the Black Hills region. The resulting warfare ended with the plains tribes' defeat in the 1870s and further concentration on reservations. Meanwhile, President Ulysses S. Grant's Peace Policy, which provided missionaries as Indian agents to the western tribes, generally failed. As Clyde Milner (1982) argues, missionaries acting as Indian agents reduced corruption in the Bureau of Indian Affairs (BIA), but their lack of experience prevented them from dealing effectively with the western tribes. The Peace Policy illustrates the continual blurring of missionary church and imperial state that has characterized so much of United States policy.

In the following decade, the Apaches in Arizona and New Mexico maintained a sporadic armed resistance. Although, as Dan Thrapp (1984) and Eve Ball (1980) point out, the Apaches initially utilized the border to elude and minimize control by either the United States or Mexico, they had neither the numbers nor the logistical support to prevail against a combination of American and Mexican arms. After 1886 the Apaches also were defeated and either imprisoned or confined to their reservation.

With Native Americans finally concentrated on reservations, federal policymakers renewed their attempts to transform tribespeople into small yeoman farmers. In 1871 Congress forbade any further treaties with Indian tribes, and although the federal government was legally obligated to honor past treaties, in actuality Native Americans were arbitrarily governed by acts of Congress and executive orders of the president. Historians such as Prucha (1976) and William T. Hagan (1985) argue that well-meaning philanthropists still championed acculturation, but these policies often were ethnocentric and fraudulently administered.

The acculturation programs had several facets. To limit the influence of "degrading tribalism," federal agents removed Indian children from their families and enrolled them in boarding schools, sometimes located hundreds of miles from their homes. Robert Trennert (1988) points out that these institutions attempted to "whitewash" Indians students and sever their ties to tribal cultures. Other scholars, including Michael Coleman (1993), Tsianina Lomawaima (1993), and Brenda Child (1998), amply illustrate that although the boarding school experience created a sense of camaraderie among the students, it was also horribly disruptive to Indian families.

Champions of acculturation also assaulted the remaining Indian land-base. In 1887 Congress passed the General Allotment Act (the "Dawes Act"), which decreed that upon the discretion of the president, most reservations would be divided. Heads of families would receive 160-acre "allotments," the title to be held in trust by the federal government for twenty-five years, after which the Native American would be given the land "in fee simple" (complete, unrestricted ownership), and the owner would be accorded the full rights of American citizenship. In theory, tribal members would then be integrated into the larger fabric of American society.

As many historians, from Angie Debo (1940, 1941) to Melissa Meyer (1994), have illustrated, most Native Americans opposed the Dawes Act; moreover, it often was fraudulently administered. In 1906 the Burke Act allowed the president to waive the twenty-five-year trust period for "competent" Indians, opening the allotments of non-literate tribespeople and even children for exploitation. Moreover, the Supreme Court ruled, in *Lone Wolf v. Hitchcock* (1902), that Congress could arbitrarily abrogate Indian treaties. This decision, discussed by Blue Clark (1994), established congressional plenary power over all Indian reservations. Tragically, of the 138,000,000 acres of land held by Native Americans in 1888, following passage of the Dawes Act, only 48,000,000 acres were in Native American hands in 1934, when the policy of allotment was officially terminated.

Although Native American people reached their demographic and spiritual nadir during the first two decades of the twentieth century, they persisted. Indeed, according to Frederick E. Hoxie (1984), by 1920 most federal officials had abandoned plans to assimilate Indians into the American mainstream in favor of policies that would integrate Indian economic resources while keeping Native American communities marginalized from American society. Nevertheless, in 1919 Congress decreed that any of the 15,000 Native Americans who had served in the armed forces during World War I would be eligible for United States citizenship. And five years later, Congress extended citizenship to all Indians. The Indian Citizenship Act of 1924 completed a sequence of processes: consolidation, acculturation, and the incorporation of Indian people into the civil framework of the United States.

The act also heralded a decade of reform. Following a series of investigations, in 1928 the federal government published reports that exposed the poor economic and social conditions within the reservation communities. Lawrence Kelly (1983) discusses reservation conditions in the 1920s and indicates that some reforms were initiated during the Hoover administration, whereas Kenneth Philp (1978) focuses on John Collier's administration of the BIA during the New Deal period. While Collier was a romantic whose attitudes toward Indians were shaped by his familiarity with

Pueblo communities in the Southwest, Philp argues that his policies, encapsulated in the Indian Reorganization (Wheeler-Howard) Act of 1934, did much to protect Indian land rights and spur a Native American cultural renaissance.

The Wheeler-Howard Act terminated the allotment of Indian lands and provided federal funds for tribes to purchase new lands to be held in common. The act also championed new tribal constitutions, with elected tribal officials who would control reservation governments, and it provided funds for bilingual education and renewed cultural activities.

Historians still debate the merits of the act. Harry Kersey (1989), for example, argues that Collier's policies reversed a pattern of division and displacement among the Seminoles and laid the base for subsequent innovations in self-government and economic activities. Donald Parman (1976) points out that while the Navajos opposed Collier's attempts to prevent overgrazing by forcing them to reduce their flocks and herds, New Deal programs eventually fostered better health care, a growing pride in Navajo identity, and an interest in self-government. Thomas Biolsi (1992) is more critical in his appraisal of Collier's policies among the Lakota. If the Wheeler-Howard Act "awakened" the Lakota to the recognition that their opinions could influence government agents, it also established a Native American bureaucracy that perpetuated the economic dependency of the Lakotas upon the federal government and exacerbated divisions between "traditionals" and "progressives" within the tribe.

Obviously, the Indian New Deal was not a panacea for all tribes, but by 1947 tribal communities had used federal loans to purchase nearly 4 million acres, which were returned to the tribal land-base. The value of Indian agricultural production during this period climbed from $1,850,000 to $50,000,000 per annum. More important, for the first time in the twentieth century the Native American birth rate climbed. Native American people could again look forward to the future.

During the 1940s, Native American men and women enlisted in the armed forces in unprecedented numbers and many others left their reservations to work in defense industries in major urban areas. Alison Bernstein (1991) argues that their wartime experiences provided Indian military personnel and defense workers with a new sense of independence and confidence that they could both manage their own affairs, and function outside of the reservation communities. That sense was challenged after the war when the federal government reversed the progressive policies epitomized by the Wheeler-Howard Act and adopted the goal of "termination," designed to abolish reservation communities, "liberate" Native Americans from their "coddling" by the BIA, and speed their assimilation into American society. To facilitate this process, federal agents encouraged Indian people to leave the reservations and move to the cities, where they supposedly would lose much of their traditional Indian identity.

Although some reformers advocated termination in an honest effort to free Native Americans of BIA restraints, Burt (1982) points out that the policy also was championed by western economic interests and politicians who wished to open the remaining reservation lands to economic development. Donald Fixico (1982) discusses the termination programs in relation to BIA attempts to "relocate" rural or reservation Indians into major metropolitan centers. He points out that many of the 12,000 relocated Native Americans were unprepared for urban life and returned to their reservation communities. Burt and Fixico agree that the termination policies did augment the number of Native Americans residing in urban regions, but note that many remained unhappy and resentful toward the federal government.

In 1961 the federal government abandoned its policies of termination and relocation and, during the ensuing decade, Native Americans benefited from the Johnson administration's War on Poverty, which channeled federal funds into both reservation and urban communities. Stephen Cornell (1988) shows how agencies arising from these programs, such as the Office of Economic Opportunity (OEO) and the Comprehensive Employee Training Act (CETA), allowed tribal and community leaders to bypass the BIA and secure federal funds for local social and economic programs. Participation in these programs also provided valuable administrative experience for a cadre of new Native American leaders who emerged in the late 1960s and 1970s. Vine Deloria, Jr. and Clifford Lytle (1984) argue, however, that Native American reliance upon these programs continued a dependency upon federal funding that had existed for decades. Indians administered the programs, but most of the guidelines were still made by bureaucrats in Washington. Meanwhile, in 1968 Congress passed the American Indian Civil Rights Act, guaranteeing reservation residents the same rights and liberties in relation to reservation governments that other U.S. citizens enjoy in their interactions with state and local officials. The act measurably increased the influence of tribal courts but, as Deloria and Lytle point out, such gains sometimes came at the expense of more traditional methods of solving problems and reconciling differences.

By 1970 the American Indian Movement (AIM) and other Native American activists were demanding further reforms, and in July President Richard Nixon presented Congress with an agenda that urged a broadening of Native American self-determination and ushered in a decade of reform. In November 1971 the Alaska Native Claims Settlement Act extinguished native claims to much of Alaska, but set aside 44 million acres for Native Americans in the state and paid these communities almost one billion dollars. The Boldt decision in *United States vs. Washington* (1974) markedly strengthened Indian fishing rights, but the philosophical cornerstones of federal policy in the 1970s were the Indian Self-Determination and Education Act, and the American Indian Policy Review Commission Act, both passed in 1975.

The Self-Determination and Education Act pledged that the federal government would support Native American self-determination while maintaining the tribes' trust relationship with the United States. In particular, the act increased Native American control over Indian education and encouraged the tribes to subcontract for schools and other educational programs. The Policy Review Commission Act created a commission to assess historical and legal relations between the United States and Indian people. It instructed the commission to suggest means of strengthening tribal governments and guaranteeing the rights of individual Indians, and to recommend legislation that would enable tribes to "realize their political and legal self-determination." In 1977 the commission recommended giving tribal governments full sovereignty over reservations, with the status of state or local governments, criminal and civil jurisdiction over both Indians and non-Indians on reservation lands, and control of reservation watersheds.

Deloria and Lytle (1984) argue that both the Self-Determination Act and the Policy Review Commission promised more than they delivered. Many of the educational programs established under the Self-Determination and Education Act floundered through lack of funding and accreditation problems, while the Policy Review Commission was plagued by insufficient funds, politics, and major philosophical differences among its members. Other scholars have been more sanguine. While admitting that the legislation initially fell short of many Indians' expectations, Stephen Cornell (1988) argues that Native Americans gained a greater influence over federal actions, and markedly increased their control over "the financial and organizational resources of tribal government." Donald Parman (1994) agrees that the commission fell short of its aspirations, but argues that the educational provisions of the Self-Determination Act were successful. Among its other results was the Tribally Controlled Community College Assistance Act (1976) which led to the foundation and subsequent growth of tribal community colleges. Parman also points to passage of the Indian Health Care Improvement Act (1976), the Indian Child Welfare Act (1978), and the Joint Resolution on American Indian Religious Freedom (1978) during these years.

During the 1980s, neither the Reagan nor the Bush administration sponsored legislation focusing upon Native American civil rights or education, and the Supreme Court, following the Reagan appointments, limited some of the gains made during the previous decade. Native American hunting and fishing rights were challenged and, while the Supreme Court upheld some treaty rights, it redefined and limited others (Wunder, 1994). For example, the Winters Doctrine of Indian water rights, established in 1908, was limited considerably by the Court in *Cappert vs. United States* (1976). And the Court seriously weakened the American Indian Religious Freedom Act by refusing to review an Oregon decision restricting use of peyote, a drug central to the ceremonies of the Native American Church (*Employment Division, Department of Human Resources et al. vs. Alfred L. Smith et al.* [1990]).

Yet some gains were registered during these years. As Parman (1994) points out, in 1983 the Reagan administration issued a policy statement advocating increased self-government and economic self-sufficiency for the tribes, and promised to negotiate with the tribes on a "government to government" basis. It cut funding for many Indian programs, but offered block grants to the tribes so they could administer many of their own programs. Encouraged by this "new federalism," tribal governments began to exercise increased sovereignty and extended their authority (revenue and otherwise) over non-Indians living on reservation lands. They also utilized the unique tax status of reservation or tribally owned land to lure industrial development and to market commodities (tobacco, gasoline, etc.) free from state or local taxes. Fergus Bordewich's controversial *Killing the White Man's Indian* (1996) discusses the rise of Indian entrepreneurship, particularly among the Mississippi Choctaws, although he also questions the validity of many Native American claims to sovereignty.

The most controversial of these entrepreneurial initiatives during the 1990s was the tribal embrace of gaming as an important economic activity. As Native American bingo halls emerged and prospered in California, Oklahoma, and other states in the 1980s, Congress approved the Indian Gaming Regulatory Act (1988), which delineated separate types of gaming and established a National Indian Gaming Commission to regulate Indian-owned gambling operations. The act also regulates the relationship between tribal casinos and the states, but generally guarantees the rights of tribes to establish casinos on tribally held trust lands in all states that allow similar gaming, even when such gaming is only for charities (Wunder, 1994).

Since the 1990s, casinos have proliferated amidst much fanfare and controversy. Their proponents, including the National Indian Gaming Commission, point out that gaming has provided an economic windfall for many tribes, transforming some formerly impoverished tribal communities into economic powerhouses. Tribes whose lands are located near population centers have attracted large numbers of gaming patrons and now provide their members with generous per capita payments. They have established trust funds for the education of their children and even have erected museums and cultural centers celebrating their traditions and history. But the economic prosperity has not been universal. Tribes whose lands are isolated from population centers have fared more poorly, and some casinos have closed. Moreover, some critics of the gaming phenomenon argue that the casinos may spur compulsive gambling in Indian communities, and that the infusion of material wealth has been disruptive to traditional tribal life.

Although Native Americans disagree among themselves over gaming, there is a general consensus about recent gains in religious rights. In 1990 Congress passed the Native American Graves Protection and Repatriation Act which provided for the protection of burial sites and initiated procedures for the return of skeletal remains and sacred objects. More recently, in 1994, with the support of the National Congress of American Indians, the Native American Rights Fund, and other Native American organizations, Congress passed the American Indian Religious Freedom Act that legalized peyote for the religious use of Native American people.

In the United States, Indian policies have evolved from a colonial past, the linchpin of which included white land acquisition, Indian consolidation, and forced cultural transformation. In the later nineteenth and throughout the twentieth century, Indians and non-Indians struggled to define their relations legally, politically, and economically, leading to a range of evolving initiatives – the New Deal, termination and relocation, self-determination, new federalism, and economic entrepreneurship. Undoubtedly, tribal communities will continue in their struggle for sovereignty and self-determination, and just as predictably, the federal government will continue to exercise some control over tribal governments. Although many Native Americans are critical of various facets of federal Indian policy, they are aware that tribal governments are bound to the federal government through an evolving historical process that has created obligations for both sides. That relationship will change, but it also will continue.

Like that of the United States, Canadian Indian policy developed from British colonial roots, but it has been influenced by different factors. Since the population of Canada has remained much smaller, and since most non-Indians live in the southern portions of the country, pressure for the acquisition of Native American lands, particularly in northern Canada, has been generally less than in the United States.

Moreover, Canada's continued association with the British Empire initially ameliorated the relationship between Native Americans and the Canadian government.

Robert Allen (1992) argues that unlike the United States, which treated Indian people as defeated enemies in the post-revolutionary period, Canada envisioned Native Americans as allies and encouraged their settlement in Upper Canada, particularly in the area encompassed by Lakes Ontario, Erie, and Huron. British officials hoped to use settlements of Mississauguas and loyal Iroquois, particularly the followers of Joseph Brant, as buffers against any American invasion of this region. British Indian agents periodically purchased lands from Indians along the northern shores of Lakes Erie and Ontario during the 1790s, but with few whites moving into the region, Indian–white conflict remained minimal. Indeed, as George Stanley (1963) points out, during the War of 1812 the Mohawks from Brantford assisted the British in repulsing American incursions in the Niagara region.

Following the Treaty of Ghent (1815), however, the strategic value of these Indian settlements as buffers against an American invasion declined, and Canadian policies began to resemble those that had emerged earlier in the United States. Robert Surtees (1983) observes that both the British government and the government of Upper Canada reduced expenditures for support of the eastern tribes, and officials auctioned off lands already ceded by the tribes to white settlers, utilizing the funds as annual payments to the tribes. And J. R. Miller (1989) argues that officials in Canada unofficially adopted a policy of "amalgamation" which urged the tribes to adopt a sedentary, agricultural life, similar to that of the white settlers in the region. By 1828, Native Americans in Ontario were no longer envisioned as valued allies, but as "wards" of the government who needed education, Christianity, and agriculture as tools to facilitate their acculturation and to lessen their dependence on the government.

Like their American counterparts, most Indians in Ontario had little interest in the government's programs. They resented the Indian Department's attempts to turn them into sedentary farmers, and although their lands were almost depleted of game, they refused to cede additional acreages to the government. In response, L. S. F. Upton (1973) notes, Canadian officials took a clue from their neighbors to the south and, during the 1830s, removed many of the tribespeople remaining in Upper Canada to Manitowaning, a new multi-tribal settlement established on Manitoulin Island, off the northern shore of Lake Huron. Yet as both the Indians and many white reformers pointed out, Manitoulin Island was composed of a rocky, infertile soil hostile to agriculture. In that respect, Canadian removals differed from those of the United States, where much of Indian Territory was at least capable of providing subsistence. During the 1840s Canadian Potawatomis, Ottawas, and Ojibwas, assisted by the Indian Department and missionaries, barely eked out an existence and, as Douglas Leighton (1977) points out, in the following decade many Indians abandoned the island. By 1856 the population had dwindled, and five years later the settlement was almost deserted.

Upton (1979) maintains that Indian policies in the Maritime Provinces also proved unsuccessful. In 1819 Nova Scotia attempted to set aside a plot of land for Indians in each county, but the land was held in trust by local officials, and was not deeded directly to the tribes. Moreover, when these maritime people periodically left their assigned lands on seasonal hunting or fishing trips, white squatters occupied their homes and refused to allow the tribespeople to return to their property. As in the United States, local magistrates failed to support the Indians' claims, and many Native Americans wandered homeless among the growing white settlements. In addition, the seasonal migration of Native Americans in the region led most Indian parents to withdraw periodically their children from schools, and during the 1820s British philanthropists condemned the institutions as failures and withdrew much of their funding (Chalmers, 1972).

Dissatisfied with provincial Indian policies, the government of Canada attempted to standardize Indians' status. While both Canada and the United States asserted a centralist uniformity toward Indians, the results differed distinctly. As Duncan Scott (1913) points out, unlike the United States, where Indians were declared "wards" of the federal government and denied citizenship, Canada officially declared Native people "amenable to the laws of the land," capable of making civil contracts and pursuing legal action within the country's judicial system. Moreover, policies of land allotment and forced acculturation that culminated in the Dawes Act in the United States, emerged thirty years earlier in Canada. "An Act for the Gradual Civilization of the Tribes in the Canadas" (1857) encouraged Indians to withdraw from the tribe and enabled them to secure the private ownership of a plot of land formerly included in the tribal reserve. One year later the Pennefeather Commission recommended the allotment of remaining reservation lands and an increased effort to educate Indian children in preparation for their assimilation into Canadian society.

In 1860 the British government relinquished all control over Indian affairs in Canada and the pressure for assimilation increased. Eighteen years before the Dawes Act, Canada enacted the Enfranchisement Act of 1869, which discarded earlier attempts at "gradual civilization" in favor of more stringent policies. Enfranchisement policy was buttressed by a series of "Indian Acts," designed to break up the reserves, assign plots of land to individual Indians, and force Native American children into a government-sponsored educational system. Milloy (1983) indicates that initially these acts were applied only to Indians in eastern Canada, but by the mid-1880s the Indian Department supported acts that outlawed traditional ceremonies and potlatches in the Canadian west. Meanwhile, as Chalmers (1972) argues, the Canadian government provided financial support to a proliferation of parochial boarding and day schools whose curriculums championed English and vocational training, but discouraged tribal traditions and languages. Jacqueline Gresko (1986) also points out that when Indian parents resisted the enrollment of their children in these institutions, Parliament amended the Indian Act (1890). This legislation enabled Manitoba and the Northwest Territories to extend their hunting and fishing laws over Indian people in an effort to make hunting and fishing tribes more sedentary so that their children could be kept in school for longer periods.

The Canadian government sought to assimilate the Native American population within its borders, but viewed Indians differently from its counterpart to the south. Unlike the United States, which "lumped" all Native American people, regardless of their biological descent, into a general category of "Indian," Canadian Indian policy in the late nineteenth century established four distinct categories of tribal people that have persisted ever since. As Roger Nichols' (1988) study of Indian policy in both countries clearly delineates, Canadian "status Indians" are either tribal people of Indian blood who live with their tribe, persons who are married to tribal people living with the tribe, persons living with the tribe with a parent who is an Indian, or persons adopted into the tribe as children who live with the tribe. Non-status Indians are either persons of Indian descent or persons who subscribe to an Indian culture but do not qualify as status Indians. Inuit are people of the far north, previously referred to as "Eskimos." The final group consists of "Métis," people of Indian-French, or Indian-Scots-English descent who are considered indigenous, but whose primary identification is with other mixed-blood persons. Métis have generally formed separate communities and have an identity and legal status distinct from those of both "Indians" and "whites." Nichols points out that in the United States such individuals traditionally have not been envisioned as "Indians" unless they are members of a specific tribe.

As the essays in Peterson and Brown (1985) indicate, Métis people posed a particular challenge for Canadian Indian policy. Prior to the Act of Dominion (1867), many Métis resided in Rupert's Land, which comprised the modern prairie provinces and Northwest Territories and was then administered by the Hudson's Bay Company. A large number of these Méti settlers lived on small farms near the forks of the Red and Assiniboine rivers in modern Manitoba, but hunted bison on the plains during summers. Wary that the Canadian government would attempt to alter their land claims, in December 1869 the Red River Métis established their own provisional government under Louis Riel, and declared their independence from Canada. The Canadian government suppressed the rebellion and Riel and some of his followers fled to Montana, while many other Métis moved to Saskatchewan. Yet as Canadian settlement expanded, the bison herds again were decimated and the Métis who had fled to Saskatchewan again found their land claims threatened. Sprague (1980) argues that the Métis were remarkably patient in response to Ottawa's "dishonesty and manipulation," but in 1885 Riel returned from Montana and again led Métis and their Cree and Blackfeet allies against the government. The Métis were defeated; Riel was captured, tried, and hanged for treason. Many Métis again fled south to North Dakota and Montana, but Blackfoot and Cree leaders who supported the Riel rebellion were sentenced to prison. In addition, Native American people in the prairie provinces retreated onto reserves while Canadian officials purchased the productive agricultural lands in southern Saskatchewan and Alberta from bewildered tribal leaders.

Further west, in British Columbia, conditions also deteriorated. Since Canada had no central government prior to 1867, local and provincial governments traditionally had exercised more control over regional Indian policy than in the United States. Following the Treaty of 1846, British or Canadian Indian policy in the region was managed by the Hudson's Bay Company, which exercised a virtual trade monopoly in the territory. The company promoted Canadian settlement on Vancouver Island, but chief factor and colonial governor James Douglas attempted to protect the coastal tribes by locating reserves around traditional fishing and gathering areas. To safeguard the tribes from unscrupulous land brokers, he retained titles to the reserves for the Crown. Douglas did not regard tribal people as sovereign, but as British subjects entitled to the rights and protection of British law. His policies protected valuable tribal lands and fishing grounds but, as Robin Fisher (1977) points out, they also made the tribes singularly dependent upon the good will of the governor's office.

Douglas left office in 1864, just as Indian–white relations began to change dramatically. The discovery of gold in the province's interior spurred an influx of gold-diggers that threatened the Chilcotin people who lived near the gold fields. Violence erupted and in 1864 the Chilcotins killed eighteen whites. In response, British Columbia's provincial government executed seven Indians. Five years later the provincial government rejected all tribal claims to any lands not included within reserves. And when British Columbia joined the Dominion of Canada in 1871, provincial officials secured an agreement with Ottawa that limited future reserves in the province to no more than ten acres per family. As Paul Tennant (1990) demonstrates, provincial claims to lands formerly occupied or utilized by tribal communities created a morass of ill will and legal entanglements that plagued Indian affairs in British Columbia well into the twentieth century.

The advance of white settlement into the Canadian west, and the resulting pressure on Native American people, created the need for organized law enforcement in the region. Unlike the United States, which relied upon its military to enforce Indian policy but required that individuals accused of breaking the law be relinquished to civilian courts for trial and punishment, Canada created a unique force with both police and judicial powers. Canada maintained no standing army, but in 1873 the Canadian government created the North West Mounted Police to maintain law and order on the Canadian frontier. Given considerable authority over both Native Americans and non-Indians, Mounties could investigate crimes, collect evidence, arrest those accused of crimes, try the accused, pass sentences, and escort the guilty to prison. Since their formation, as Desmond Morton (1977) indicates, the Mounties have served as the most important arm of law enforcement between Native Americans and the broader spectrum of Canadian society.

By the beginning of the twentieth century the Indian policies of Canada and the United States converged around similar goals. Both countries either encouraged Native Americans to relinquish tribal traditions and assimilate into the mainstream culture, or assigned them to isolated reservations where they could cling to those cultures but remain condemned to a marginal economic existence. Brian Titley (1986) demonstrates that although many young Native American men enlisted in Canadian regiments during World War I, their homelands remained subject to government expropriation. The Oliver Act of 1911 made reserve lands adjacent to white communities vulnerable to seizure, while the government's "Greater Production Effort" program, launched during World War I, provided for the sale or lease of "surplus" reserve lands to white farmers and ranchers. James Dempsey (1983) argues that wartime programs bypassed tribal control over these lands and consigned their administration entirely to government bureaucrats.

Not surprisingly, such policies engendered resentment among Indian people. In 1918 Frederick Loft, a World War I veteran from the Six Nations reserve in Ontario, founded the League of Indians of Canada, and he spent the early 1920s visiting

Native American reserves and soliciting members. The League declined in the late 1920s but the banner of protest was picked up by the Six Nations of Ontario, who claimed that Ontario held no authority over them because the British government had granted them lands as equal allies for their service in the American Revolution (Montgomery, 1963). Officials in Ontario denounced the claim and harassed tribal leaders, but the Six Nations, led by Chief Deskeheh (Levi General), took their case to the League of Nations in the Netherlands. Britain intervened and the Six Nations' petition failed, but the affair caused considerable embarrassment to the Canadian government.

As in the United States, Native people made substantial contributions to the Canadian armed forces during World War II (Gaffen, 1985). After the war the government appointed a special commission to investigate Canadian Indian policy. Yet after six years of hearings and debates, the resulting Indian Act of 1951 brought few basic changes. Leslie and Maguire (1978) argue that the act did limit the power of Indian Department officials to intervene in the affairs of recognized tribes, but the government remained committed to assimilating Native Americans into Canadian society.

This commitment was reflected in the government's attempt to relocate Indian people from rural reserves to the cities during the late 1950s and 1960s. Arthur Davis (1968) notes that while Canada's relocation program was considerably smaller than its counterpart in the United States, its goals were similar. Tribespeople relocated to cities such as Toronto, Calgary, Winnipeg, and Saskatoon enjoyed a higher income than their relatives on the reserves, but they also experienced the isolation and social problems faced by Indians relocated to cities in the United States during these years (Price and McCaskill, 1974; Nagler, 1970).

Although the American government's attempts to terminate tribes peaked during the 1950s, Canadian interest in termination emerged only during the following decade. In 1969 the government issued its notorious "White Paper," which urged that Canadian Indians be given title to their lands, and that provincial governments administer all tribal education and health programs. Moreover, the White Paper recommended the repeal of all the Indian acts and the eventual dissolution of the Indian Department. Weaver (1981) argues that Native Americans in Canada were almost unanimous in their negative response and, supported by academics and other Canadians interested in Native American affairs, denounced the White Paper so strongly that officials abandoned the program.

Meanwhile, progress was occurring on other fronts. Chalmers (1972) shows that during the 1960s many boarding schools (both private and government-operated) closed, and Indian children began to attend neighboring public schools. Yet as Buckley (1992) illustrates, many of these provincial schools made few attempts to meet the cultural needs of Native American students. Accordingly, the Canadian government in 1973 directed that funds appropriated for Native American education be paid directly to reserves that wished to establish their own primary and secondary education programs. In the following year, the government established an Office of Native Claims, similar to the Indian Claims Commission in the United States, to hear tribal land claims.

Like their AIM counterparts in the United States, Indians in Canada also strove for greater sovereignty during these years. As Miller (1989) points out, the National Indian Brotherhood emerged as the representative of status Indians during the 1970s and asserted that its members were separate nations with sovereignty over their homelands. During the 1980s they changed their name to the Assembly of First Nations and were joined by the Inuit Tapirisat of Canada, a national Inuit organization, and the Native Council of Canada, who represented Métis and non-status Indians. The three groups convinced the government to recognize their "existing aboriginal and treaty rights" in the 1983 Constitutional Act. One year later the government's "Penner Report" also supported Indian land claims and urged that the "Indian First Nations" be given "a distinct order of government" in Canada.

During the final two decades of the twentieth century relations between the government and Indian people in Canada followed an uncertain course. Weaver (1986) argues that the Conservatives were alarmed by separatists in Quebec and reassessed any political movements that they believed might contribute to the atomization of Canada. In 1985 the Nielsen Task Force suggested that the government cut expenses by assigning most Indian services to provincial governments, and tried to convince the tribes to reorganize as municipal governmental units under provincial supervision. Most tribes resisted the pressure, and the task force only furthered a growing suspicion among Indian people of the government's intent. Hornung (1991) and York and Pindera (1991) indicate that Indian–government relations also were strained when intra-tribal disputes on the Mohawk reservation astride the New York–Quebec border spilled over into other Canadian Six Nations communities. Local attempts to expand a golf course at Oka, near Montreal, encountered stiff Mohawk resistance. One law officer was killed, and although the confrontation eventually was defused, suspicion and bitterness on both sides continued.

In contrast, the government was more receptive to the aspirations of tribal people in the Far North and in British Columbia. The James Bay Agreement (1975) provided substantial funds, over 13,000 square kilometers of land, and exclusive hunting rights for Cree and Inuit people in eastern Quebec. Similarly, during the 1980s, Dené and Métis people in the Northwest Territories were awarded a large cash settlement, title to 180,000 square kilometers, and a portion of royalties from oil and other minerals in the McKenzie Valley (Morrison, 1983). In 1974, following a favorable ruling in the Calder Case, the Nisgha people initiated legal action to have former lands returned to them in British Columbia. The litigation continued for twenty-five years until the province agreed, in 1999, that the tribe was entitled to a reserve of about 2,000 square kilometers, over which it should exercise limited sovereignty. In 1990, after almost two decades of negotiations, Canadian officials also agreed to the creation of a new territory, Nunavut ("Our Land"), to be populated primarily by Inuit people and formed from the eastern portions of the Northwest Territories. Nunavut's territorial government was to be guided by its own legislature, and the territory was deemed a potential province. Nunavut became a reality on April 1, 1999.

In 1996 the Royal Commission on Aboriginal Peoples issued a 4,000-page report urging the Canadian government to provide better housing, education, and job training to the Native population. As this came during a period of budget restraints, the government was slow to address these recommendations. As the twenty-first century began, Indian policies in Canada remained less centralized and more varied than in the United States. While the Inuit people of Nunavut have moved toward virtual self-rule, First Nations people in more populous provinces and territories face a far less friendly political environment. Throughout Canada Native peoples still strive for sovereignty, economic self-sufficiency, and acceptance of their way of life. As in the United States, their struggle continues.

Unlike the United States and Canada, Mexico attempted to break from the Indian policy of its colonial past. Having achieved independence from Spain in 1820, Mexico formulated provisions designed to accelerate the integration of Indian people into the mainstream of Mexican society. Spicer (1960) points out that the new Mexican constitution of 1821 rejected the transitional communities fostered by the Spanish mission system, granted full citizenship to all Indians in the new republic, and theoretically guaranteed to them political rights equal to those of other Mexican citizens. But the government also demanded that Indian communities restructure their political systems so that all adult males would vote for a prescribed set of local officials whose duties and obligations would be established by Mexican law. And in policies similar to those that would emerge half a century later in the United States, Mexican officials decreed that most tribal lands were to be divided among individuals, with sufficient acreage to support their families. Surplus lands (particularly those previously held by missions) were to become the property of the state. Officials argued that such policies would eliminate Mexico's "Indian problem," and that Indians would cease to exist as a separate ethnic group. Federal statutes and policies were forbidden to include the term "Indian," and state constitutions (Sonora, Chihuahua) which were forced to deal specifically with remaining Indian communities were instructed to use the term "indígene" rather than "Indian."

David Weber (1982) indicates that such policies were easier to formulate than to enforce. Mexican control over Native American people in its northern provinces was limited by shortages of manpower and other resources, and nomadic tribes such as the Comanches and Apaches ignored the new mandates. While state and local officials attempted to stop the raids in northern states, even offering bounties on Apache scalps, their efforts proved ineffective.

The kind of central policymaking and implementation found in the United States, and to a lesser degree in Canada, was even more attenuated in Mexico. When officials in Sonora or Chihuahua petitioned the federal government for assistance, bureaucrats in Mexico City generally ignored their pleas; consequently Indian policies formulated in the capital were poorly implemented. Bowen (1983) and Pennington (1983) show how Seri and Tarahumara tribespeople refused to accept state attempts to restructure their societies and withdrew into isolated desert or mountainous regions where state officials exercised little authority. The Yaquis, also a sedentary people, resisted the government reforms so staunchly that first the state of Sonora, and finally the federal government conducted a series of military campaigns which reduced their population but failed to break their spirit. Finally, as Evelyn Hu-DeHart (1984) points out, between 1900 and 1910 Mexican officials resettled many Yaquis to Oaxaca and the Yucatan, but most of these exiles returned to Sonora after the fall of the Díaz regime in 1911.

The various regimes that governed Mexico between 1820 and the end of the French Intervention (1867) exercised more control over the administration of Indian affairs in central and southern Mexico, but in these regions they also encountered difficulty implementing policies that reinforced liberal democracy, individual land ownership, and assimilation. As Charles Hale (1968) indicates, much of the difficulty emerged because policymakers in Mexico City were far removed from rural Indian communities. In theory, federal and state policies were designed to redistribute communally held land and assign small farms to former members of the Indian community, but in actuality much of the redistributed land was purchased by large haciendas which then employed the individual Indians (indígenes) as rural laborers. Indian communities managed to retain some communal pasture and woodland as "ejidos," but such ownership was more tolerated than encouraged.

The Ley Lerdo, passed in 1856 and incorporated into the new Constitution of 1857, effectively terminated the ejido landholdings. Designed primarily to limit the power of the Catholic Church, the law forced the church to sell most of its vast landholdings at auction, but it also stipulated that lands held by other corporate bodies, including ejidos, were eligible to be purchased. Jan Bazant S. (1971) argues that policymakers in Mexico City naively assumed that individual Indians would purchase many of these lands, and that the number of small individual landholders would increase. Instead, foreigners and wealthy landowners purchased nearly all the lands and Indians became, as Richard Sinkin (1979) points out, economically and politically dependent upon the haciendas. Unlike in the United States and Canada, where Native American populations were isolated on relatively undesirable lands with little opportunity to participate in the economic life of the nation, many of Mexico's Indians lost control of their lands and were forced to labor for large landowners at subsistence wages.

The administration of Porfirio Díaz (the Porfiriato, 1876–1911) paid little attention to Indian people except as laborers on ranches and haciendas. Intent upon modernizing Mexico, Díaz was heavily influenced by "Científicos," young Mexican intellectuals who in turn had been swayed by their admiration of the emergent industrial economies in Britain and Germany. Eager to attract foreign capital and present an image of a "modernizing Mexico," the Científicos denigrated Indian people as obstacles to modernization, either denouncing them in racist terms or arguing that they would have to abandon their cultures and embrace Western civilization before becoming a viable part of the new Mexico (Stabb, 1959; Powell, 1968). Ironically, although the Díaz administration provided funds for the construction of schools and the development of education, most of the funds were spent in urban areas, far from significant Indian populations. Meanwhile, as Nash (1970) illustrates, most Indians resided in small rural villages, continued to speak their native languages, labored for *hacendados,* and subsisted on a scant diet of tortillas, beans, chilies and pulque. As with reservation conditions in the United States, infant mortality rates were high, life expectancy was low (less than thirty years), and modern medical care was non-existent.

Indians participated in the upheavals of the revolutionary period (1910–17), but generally focused their efforts on land reforms rather than ethnic aspirations. Whereas many Native Americans in the United States opposed the Dawes Act and wished to retain their communal land-base, Indians from southern Mexico fought with the Zapatistas (the followers of Emilio Zapata), whose primary goal was the seizure of land from large haciendas and its redistribution to the landless (Womack, 1968). Others, influenced by local caciques, supported Díaz or Huerta but their primary purpose also was to regain lost lands, not protect reservation lands from development.

Ironically, as Alan Knight (1986, 1990) argues, many of the reforms later adopted under the Constitution of 1917 were initiated during the brief Huerta dictatorship (1913–14). Rejecting the policies of the Científicos, in 1914 the Huerta regime began the construction of rural schools in Indian villages, sent government agents into the pueblos to assist in organizing community projects, and restored seventy-eight ejidos to the Yaqui and Mayo Indians of Sonora.

Cumberland (1972) and Hall (1981) note that the Constitution of 1917 institutionalized these reforms and added to them. Drawing on policies championed by reformist or revolutionary groups during the preceding decade, Article 27 required that lands taken from Indian communities during the Porfiriato be returned, and authorized legal assistance for communities who charged that their lands had been seized illegally. Private ownership of real estate was no longer promoted as the ultimate form of land tenure, and large landholders who did not use such land or natural resources "in the public interest" could have their lands seized by the government. In theory, some of these confiscated lands would be returned to the remaining Indian communities. Thus during the early twentieth century, while the United States continued to implement the allotment process, Mexico officially returned to a policy of promoting communal lands for indígenes or Indian citizens. Indeed Mexico anticipated the intent, if not the actual practice, of the land consolidation provisions of the Indian New Deal in the United States.

During the 1920s, the federal government's new commitment to its Indian population increased. Knight (1990) argues that the Científicos' disdain for anything Indian was replaced by "indigenismo," the acknowledgement that although Indians' role in the political and social development of Mexico had been minimized since independence, Indians and their cultures were critical to the development of Mexico in the twentieth century. Indigenismo also asserted that the racial and cultural qualities of Indian people were basic hues in the broader spectrum of Mexican identity, and the government would assist the Indian communities in their integration into the formal structure of Mexican society. Unlike the earlier attempts at such integration, which had attempted to eradicate all things Indian, the federal government optimistically planned to proceed "without de-Indianization." Educated, bilingual, and politically mobilized Indian communities would take their place in a modern Mexico, but they would retain their own distinct cultures.

Championed by Manuel Gamio, who served as an Undersecretary of Education, between 1920 and 1940 the Mexican government trained bilingual teachers (many of them Indian) and established schools in many rural Indian villages. Although Spanish did not completely replace Indian languages, most Indians were bilingual by

1940. Ejidos were both encouraged and romanticized as part of the Aztec past. Following the election of Lázaro Cárdenas to the presidency in 1934, the number of ejidos increased. As Knight (1990) shows, Indian traditions in dance, music, and art were co-opted as part of a greater Mexican culture. Similarly, the vivid murals of Diego Rivera and other artists, celebrating Indian valor and suffering in opposition to the "Black Legend" of Spanish colonialism, proliferated in the capital and in other cities. In 1935 Gregorio López y Fuentes was awarded Mexico's first National Prize for Literature for the publication of *El Indio*, which examined the position of Indians in Mexican society. Four years later the Mexican government established the prestigious Instituto Nacional de Antropología e Historia which has devoted much of its focus to the Indian cultures of Mexico. Although federal policies in the United States during the halcyon days of the Indian New Deal also attempted to assist tribal people reassert their identity and cultures during the 1930s, they obviously were far overshadowed by the "indigenismo" in Mexico.

Following World War II the federal government established the Instituto Nacional Indigenista which, as Martin C. Needler (1971) indicates, attempted to promote reform through local Indian communities. Prometores, or "agents of change," were dispatched to the villages where they championed new bilingual programs, health clinics, and cooperative retail stores. Although land reform had languished in the 1940s, during the administration of Adolfo López Mateos (1958–64) almost 30 million acres, much of it in the southern states, was redistributed. Yet Neil Harvey (1990) argues that many Indians believed they did not receive a fair share of this acreage in comparison to the Ladino population. During the late 1960s and 1970s, while the government focused on problems of urbanization and Mexico's international balance of payments deficit, resentment smoldered in some of Mexico's Indian communities. Like reservation residents in the United States, many indígenes remained impoverished and they focused their hostility toward local or state officials whom they accused of corruption.

Nowhere in Mexico were Indians more suspicious of the federal government than in Chiapas. The poorest and most isolated of Mexico's states, Chiapas included regions in which large landowners and local officials had consistently thwarted land and election reforms, and where educational and medical services were minimal. In 1988, following the election of Carlos Salinas de Gortari to the presidency, the federal government again emphasized the role of privatized, individual agriculture. Moreover, as Morris (1992) points out, the Salinas administration charted an economic and political course designed to develop closer ties with the United States, especially through the North American Free Trade Association (NAFTA). Abandoning the agrarian reform of its predecessors, the Salinas regime criticized the communal ejido system as "unproductive" and fostered legislation turning the ejido lands over to individuals, while selling many government-owned public services back to large corporations. George Collier (1994) argues that in Chiapas these activities were interpreted as a further betrayal by the dominant Partido Revolucionario Institucional (PRI) of the Indian communities, and Salinas' policies sparked an armed uprising among the Maya population.

Led by an officer known only as "Sub-Comandante Marcos," in January 1994 an armed contingent of Mayas from Chiapas' eastern lowlands blocked the Pan-American highway and temporarily seized control of municipal buildings in San Cristóbal, the state capital, and in several other cities in Chiapas. Heavily armed Mexican troops eventually recaptured the buildings, but the Ejército Zapatista Liberación Nacional (the "Zapatistas"), the rebel army, has continued to conduct a sporadic guerrilla campaign against the federal government since that time.

Although the federal government conducted military campaigns against the Zapatistas, and subsequently concluded an uneasy truce, the Zapatistas remain adamant in their demands. Envisioning a Mexico in which Indian people retain their political and cultural autonomy, the Zapatistas have demanded that the government honor its commitments to Indian people and permit Indian communities to continue in their communal economic activities. The Zapatista rebellion reminds us that although the Mexican government first attempted to legislate Indians out of existence, then celebrated their historic past without providing a place for them within the political power structure of the ruling party, Indian communities with a strong sense of ethnic identity still persist (Nash, 1995). Like their counterparts in the United States and Canada, Indian people from Sonora to Chiapas envision themselves as citizens of Mexico, but also as Indians. While recognizing the discrete histories that place them in varying relations to national, state, provincial, and local governments, indigenous people in the Northern Hemisphere share the common desire to (re)establish control over their lands and cultures. Indeed, the rise of transnational ties among North, Central, and South American Indians may constitute the foundation of the histories to be written during the coming generation, histories that will be both comparative and synthetic.

BIBLIOGRAPHY

Allen, Robert S. 1992: *His Majesty's Indian Allies: British Indian Policy in the Defense of Canada* (Toronto: Dundurn Press).

Ball, Eve 1980: *Indeh, an Apache Odyssey* (Provo: Brigham Young University Press).

Bazant S., Jan 1971: *Alienation of Church Wealth in Mexico: Social and Economic Aspects of the Liberal Revolution, 1856–1857* (ed. and trans. Michael P. Costeloe) (Cambridge: Cambridge University Press).

Bernstein, Alison R. 1991: *American Indians and World War II* (Norman: University of Oklahoma Press).

Berthrong, Donald J. 1963: *The Southern Cheyennes* (Norman: University of Oklahoma Press).

Biolsi, Thomas 1992: *Organizing the Lakota: The Political Economy of the New Deal on the Pine Ridge and Rosebud Reservations* (Tucson: University of Arizona Press).

Bordewich, Fergus 1996: *Killing the White Man's Indian: Reinventing Native Americans at the End of the Twentieth Century* (New York: Anchor Books).

Bowen, Thomas 1983: "Seri," in Alfonso Ortiz (ed.), *Handbook of North American Indians*, vol. 10: *Southwest* (Washington, D.C.: Smithsonian Institution), pp. 220–49.

Buckley, Helen 1992: *From Wooden Plows to Welfare: Why Indian Policy Failed in the Prairie Provinces* (Montreal: McGill-Queens University Press).

Burt, Larry W. 1982: *Tribalism in Crisis: Federal Indian Policy: 1953–1961* (Albuquerque: University of New Mexico Press).

Calloway, Colin G. 1987: *Crown and Calumet: British–Indian Relations, 1783–1815* (Norman: University of Oklahoma Press).

Chalmers, John W. 1972: *Education Behind the Buckskin Curtain: A History of Native Education in Canada* (Edmonton: University of Alberta Press).

Child, Brenda J. 1998: *Boarding School Seasons: American Indian Families, 1900–1940* (Lincoln: University of Nebraska Press).

Clark, Blue 1994: *Lone Wolf vs. Hitchcock: Treaty Rights and Indian Law at the End of the Nineteenth Century* (Lincoln: University of Nebraska Press).

Coleman, Michael C. 1993: *American Indian Children at School, 1850–1930* (Jackson: University Press of Mississippi).

Collier, George A. 1994: "The New Politics of Exclusion: Antecedents to the Rebellion in Mexico," *Dialectical Anthropology* 19: 1–44.

Cornell, Stephen 1988: *The Return of the Native: American Indian Political Resurgence* (New York: Oxford University Press).

Cumberland, Charles C. 1972: *The Mexican Revolution: The Constitutionalist Years* (Austin: University of Texas Press).

Davis, Arthur K. 1968: "Urban Indians in Western Canada: Implications of Social Theory and Social Policy," *Transactions of the Royal Society of Canada* 6th series, 4: 217–28.

Debo, Angie 1940: *And Still the Waters Run* (Princeton: Princeton University Press).

Debo, Angie 1941: *The Road to Disappearance: A History of the Creek Indians* (Norman: University of Oklahoma Press).

Deloria, Vine, Jr. and Clifford Lytle 1984: *The Nations Within: The Past and Future of American Indian Sovereignty* (New York: Pantheon Books).

Dempsey, James 1983: "The Indians and World War I," *Alberta History* 31: 1–8.

Dowd, Gregory Evans 1992: *A Spirited Resistance: The North American Indian Struggle for Unity, 1745–1815* (Baltimore: Johns Hopkins University Press).

Edmunds, R. David 1983: *The Shawnee Prophet* (Lincoln: University of Nebraska Press).

Edmunds, R. David 1984: *Tecumseh and the Quest for Indian Leadership* (Boston: Little, Brown, and Co.).

Edmunds, R. David 1985: "'Unacquainted with the Laws of the Civilized World': American Attitudes Toward the Métis Communities in the Old Northwest," in Jacqueline Peterson and Jennifer S. H. Brown (eds.), *The New Peoples: Being and Becoming Métis in North America* (Winnipeg: University of Manitoba Press).

Fisher, Robin 1977: *Contact and Conflict: Indian–European Relations in British Columbia, 1774–1890* (Vancouver: University of British Columbia Press).

Fixico, Donald L. 1982: *Termination and Relocation: Federal Indian Policy, 1945–1960* (Albuquerque: University of New Mexico Press).

Foreman, Grant 1932: *Indian Removal: The Emigration of the Five Civilized Tribes* (Norman: University of Oklahoma Press).

Gaffen, Fred 1985: *Forgotten Soldiers* (Penticon, B.C.: Theytus Publishers).

Green, Michael D. 1982: *The Politics of Indian Removal: Creek Government and Society in Crisis* (Lincoln: University of Nebraska Press).

Gresko, Jacqueline 1986: "Creating Little Dominions Within the Dominion: Early Catholic Indian Schools in Saskatchewan and British Columbia," in Jean Barman, Yvonne Hebert, and Donald McCaskill (eds.), *Indian Education in Canada* (Vancouver: University of British Columbia Press), vol. 1, pp. 88–109.

Hagan, William T. 1985: *The Indian Rights Association: The Herbert Welsh Years* (Tucson: University of Arizona Press).

Hale, Charles A. 1968: *Mexican Liberalism in the Age of Mora* (New Haven: Yale University Press).

Hall, Linda B. 1981: *Alvaro Obregón: Power and Revolution in Mexico, 1911–1920* (College Station: Texas A & M University Press).

Harvey, Neil 1990: "Peasant Strategies and Corporatism in Chiapas," in Joe Foweraker and Anne L. Craig (eds.), *Popular Movements and Political Change in Mexico* (Boulder: Lynne Rienner Publishers), pp. 183–98.

Hornung, Rick 1991: *One Nation under the Gun* (New York: Pantheon Books).

Horsman, Reginald 1964: *Matthew Elliott, British Indian Agent* (Detroit: Wayne State University Press).

Horsman, Reginald 1967: *Expansion and American Indian Policy, 1783–1812* (East Lansing: Michigan State University Press).

Hoxie, Frederick E. 1984: *A Final Promise: The Campaign to Assimilate the Indians, 1880–1920* (Lincoln: University of Nebraska Press).

Hu-DeHart, Evelyn 1984: *Yaqui Resistance and Survival: The Struggle for Land and Autonomy, 1821–1910* (Madison: University of Wisconsin Press).

Kelly, Lawrence C. 1983: *The Assault on Assimilation: John Collier and the Origins of Indian Policy Reform* (Albuquerque: University of New Mexico Press).

Kersey, Harry A. 1989: *The Florida Seminoles and the New Deal, 1933–1942* (Boca Raton: Florida Atlantic University Press).

Knight, Alan 1986: *The Mexican Revolution: Counter Revolution and Reconstruction* (New York: Cambridge University Press).

Knight, Alan 1990: "Racism, Revolution, and Indigenismo: Mexico, 1910–1940," in Richard Graham (ed.), *The Idea of Race in Latin America, 1870–1940* (Austin: University of Texas Press), pp. 71–113.

Leighton, Douglas 1977: "The Manitoulin Incident of 1863: An Indian–White Confrontation," *Ontario History* 69: 113–24.

Leslie, John and Ronald Maguire (eds.) 1978: *The Historical Development of the Indian Act* (Ottawa: Indian and Northern Affairs).

Lomawaima, K. Tsianina 1993: *They Called It Prairie Light: The Story of Chilocco Indian School* (Lincoln: University of Nebraska Press).

Martin, Joel W. 1991: *Sacred Revolt: The Muskogees' Struggle for a New World* (Boston: Beacon Press).

McLoughlin, William G. 1984: *Cherokees and Missionaries, 1789–1832* (New Haven: Yale University Press).

McLoughlin, William G. 1986a: *The Cherokee Ghost Dance: Essays on the Southeastern Indians, 1789–1861* (New Haven: Yale University Press).

McLoughlin, William G. 1986b: *Cherokee Renascence in the New Republic* (New Haven: Yale University Press).

Meyer, Melissa L. 1994: *The White Earth Tragedy: Ethnicity and Dispossession at a Minnesota Anishinaabe Reservation, 1889–1920* (Lincoln: University of Nebraska Press).

Miller, J. R. 1989: *Skyscrapers Hide the Heavens: A History of Indian–White Relations in Canada* (Toronto: University of Toronto Press).

Milloy, John S. 1983: "The Early Indian Acts: Development Strategy and Constitutional Change," in Ian Getty and Antoine Lussier (eds.), *As Long as the Sun Shines and Water Flows: A Reader in Canadian Native Studies* (Toronto: University of Toronto Press), pp. 39–64.

Milner, Clyde A. 1982: *With Good Intentions: Quaker Work among the Pawnees, Otoes, and Omahas in the 1870s* (Lincoln: University of Nebraska Press).

Montgomery, Malcolm 1963: "The Legal Status of the Six Nations in Canada," *Ontario History* 55: 93–105.

Morris, Stephen 1992: "Political Reformism in Mexico: Salinas at the Brink," *Journal of Inter-American Studies and World Affairs* 34: 27–58.

Morrison, William R. 1983: *A Survey of the History and Claims of the Native People of Northern Canada* (Ottawa: Treaties and Historical Research Centre).

Morton, Desmond 1977: "Cavalry or Police: Keeping the Peace on Two Adjacent Frontiers, 1870–1900," *Journal of Canadian Studies* 12: 27–37.

Nagler, Mark 1970: *Indians in the City: A Study of the Indians in Toronto* (Ottawa: St. Paul University Press).

Nash, June C. 1995: "The Reassertion of Indigenous Identity: Mayan Responses to State Intervention in Chiapas," *Latin American Research Review* 30: 7–42.

Nash, Manning 1970: "The Impact of Mid-Nineteenth Century Economic Change upon the Indians of Middle America," in Magnus Morner (ed.), *Race and Class in Latin America* (New York: Columbia University Press), pp. 170–83.

Needler, Martin C. 1971: *Politics and Society in Mexico* (Albuquerque: University of New Mexico Press).

Nelson, Larry L. 1999: *A Man of Distinction amongst Them: Alexander McKee and British–Indian Affairs along the Ohio Country Frontier, 1754–1799* (Kent, OH: Kent State University Press).

Nichols, Roger L. 1988: *Indians in the United States and Canada: A Comparative Study* (Lincoln: University of Nebraska Press).

Parman, Donald L. 1976: *The Navajos and the New Deal* (New Haven: Yale University Press).

Parman, Donald L. 1994: *Indians and the American West in the Twentieth Century* (Bloomington: Indiana University Press).

Pennington, Campbell W. 1983: "Tarahumara," in Alfonso Ortiz (ed.), *Handbook of North American Indians*, vol. 10: *Southwest* (Washington, D.C.: Smithsonian Institution), pp. 641–89.

Perdue, Theda 1979: *Slavery and the Evolution of Cherokee Society 1540–1866* (Lincoln: University of Nebraska Press).

Perdue, Theda 1998: *Cherokee Women: Gender and Culture Change, 1700–1835* (Lincoln: University of Nebraska Press).

Peterson, Jacqueline and Jennifer S. H. Brown (eds.) 1985: *The New Peoples: Being and Becoming Métis in North America* (Winnipeg: University of Manitoba Press).

Philp, Kenneth R. 1978: *John Collier's Crusade for Indian Reform, 1920–1954* (Tucson: University of Arizona Press).

Powell, T. G. 1968: "Mexican Intellectuals and the Indian Question, 1876–1911," *Hispanic American Historical Review* 48: 19–36.

Price, John and Donald McCaskill 1974: "The Urban Integration of Canadian Native People," *Western Canadian Journal of Anthropology* 4: 29–74.

Prucha, Francis Paul 1976: *American Indian Policy in Crisis: Christian Reformers and the Indian, 1865–1900* (Norman: University of Oklahoma Press).

Prucha, Francis Paul 1984: *The Great Father: The United States Government and the American Indians* (Lincoln: University of Nebraska Press).

Satz, Ronald N. 1975: *American Indian Policy in the Jacksonian Era* (Lincoln: University of Nebraska Press).

Scott, Duncan 1913–17: "Indian Affairs, 1840–1867," in Adam Short and Arthur G. Doughty (eds.), *Canada and Its Provinces* (Toronto: Publishers Assoc. of Canada), vol. 5, pp. 331–62.

Sheehan, Bernard W. 1973: *Seeds of Extinction: Jeffersonian Philanthropy and the American Indian* (New York: W. W. Norton and Co.).

Sinkin, Richard N. 1979: *The Mexican Reform, 1855–1876: A Study in Liberal Nation Building* (Austin: Institute of Latin American Studies).

Spicer, Edward H. 1960: *Cycles of Conquest: The Impact of Spain, Mexico, and the United States on the Indians of the Southwest, 1533–1960* (Tucson: University of Arizona Press).

Sprague, D. N. 1980: *Canada and the Métis, 1869–1885* (Waterloo: Wilfrid Laurier University Press).

Stabb, Martin 1959: "Indigenism and Racism in Mexican Thought, 1857–1911," *Journal of Inter-American Studies* 1: 405–23.

Stanley, George F. G. 1963: "The Significance of the Six Nations in the War of 1812," *Ontario History* 55: 215–31.

Surtees, Robert J. 1983: "Indian Land Cessions in Upper Canada, 1815–1830," in Ian Getty and Antoine S. Lussier (eds.), *As Long as the Sun Shines and Water Flows: A Reader in Canadian Native Studies* (Vancouver: University of British Columbia Press), pp. 65–84.

Sword, Wiley 1985: *President Washington's Indian War* (Norman: University of Oklahoma Press).

Tennant, Paul 1990: *Aboriginal People and Politics: The Indian Land Question in British Columbia, 1849–1989* (Vancouver: University of British Columbia Press).

Thrapp, Dan L. 1984: *The Conquest of Apacheria* (Norman: University of Oklahoma Press).

Titley, Brian 1986: *A Narrow Vision: Duncan Campbell Scott and the Administration of Indian Affairs in Canada* (Vancouver: University of British Columbia Press).

Trennert, Robert A. 1988: *The Phoenix Indian School: Forced Assimilation in Arizona, 1891–1935* (Norman: University of Oklahoma Press).

Upton, L. S. F. 1973: "The Origins of Canadian Indian Policy," *Journal of Canadian Studies* 8: 51–61.

Upton, L. S. F. 1979: "Indian Policy in Colonial Nova Scotia," *Acadiensis* 5: 11–23.

Utley, Robert M. 1967: *Frontiersmen in Blue: The United States Army and the Indian, 1848–1865* (New York: Macmillan).

Utley, Robert M. 1973: *Frontier Regulars: The United States Army and the Indian, 1866–1890* (New York: Macmillan).

Viola, Herman J. 1974: *Thomas L. McKenney: Architect of America's Early Indian Policy* (Chicago: Sage Books).

Wallace, Anthony F. C. 1970: *The Death and Rebirth of the Seneca* (New York: Alfred A. Knopf).

Weaver, Sally M. 1981: *Making Canadian Indian Policy: The Hidden Agenda* (Toronto: University of Toronto Press).

Weaver, Sally M. 1986: "Indian Policy in the New Conservative Government, Part One: The Nielsen Task Force of 1985," *Native Studies Review* 2: 1–43.

Weber, David J. 1982: *The Mexican Frontier, 1821–1846: The American Southwest Under Mexico* (Albuquerque: University of New Mexico Press).

West, Elliott 1998: *The Contested Plains: Indians, Goldseekers, and the Rush to Colorado* (Lawrence: University Press of Kansas).

White, Richard 1983: *The Roots of Dependency: Subsistence, Environment, and Social Change among the Choctaws, Pawnees, and Navajos* (Lincoln: University of Nebraska Press).

White, Richard 1991: *The Middle Ground: Indians, Empires, and Republics in the Great Lakes Region, 1650–1815* (Cambridge: Cambridge University Press).

Wilkins, Thurman 1970: *Cherokee Tragedy* (New York: Macmillan).

Womack, John, Jr. 1968: *Zapata and the Mexican Revolution* (New York: Alfred A. Knopf).

Wunder, John 1994: *Retained by the People: A History of American Indians and the Bill of Rights* (New York: Oxford University Press).

York, Geoffrey and Loreen Pindera 1991: *People of the Pines: The Warriors and the Legacy of Oka* (Toronto: Little, Brown).

Young, Mary 1961: *Redskins, Ruffleshirts, and Rednecks: Indian Allotment in Alabama and Mississippi* (Norman: University of Oklahoma Press).

23

American Indian Education: *by* Indians versus *for* Indians

K. Tsianina Lomawaima

The term "American Indian education" has referred to the education of Indian people *by* Indian people. The term has also referred to the education designed *for* Indian people by colonizing nations. For the last five centuries, education *by* Indians and education *for* Indians have stood at loggerheads. The former has been dedicated, as in all human societies, to perpetuating family values, language, religion, politics, economies, skills, sciences, and technologies. Colonial education *for* Indians has been dedicated to eradicating Native knowledge and values, and substituting values and knowledge judged to be "civilized."

In the "American" era (from 1776 through the present), "civilized" education has usually meant instruction in English and the suppression of Native languages; conversion to Christianity and the criminalization of Native religions; an emphasis on manual labor, and on "industrial" or "vocational" rather than academic training; strict regimentation of dress, emotional expression, and physical activity through military discipline; and physical disruption of family/community by removing Indian children into boarding schools, tuberculosis sanatoria, orphanages, and non-Indian foster homes (see Qoyawayma, 1964; Giago, 1978; St. Pierre, 1991; Skolnick and Skolnick, 1997). Despite generations of efforts to "civilize" them, Native people have vigorously defended education *by* Indians, and have vigorously resisted colonial education in both overt and covert ways.

One of the most overt student rebellions took place in 1919 at the off-reservation boarding school, Haskell Institute, in Lawrence, Kansas. Students ran "amok" one evening, shouting "'Let's string him up!' as the principal worked to restore order" (Child, 1996: 54). Parents protested by keeping students home, or by writing letters. Filling box after box in the National Archives, parental letters address enrollment policies, severe discipline, poor nutritional and health standards, heavy workloads, academic under-preparation, and other issues (see Child, 1998; Lomawaima, 1994). Sometimes parents and students acted in concert. When Phoenix Indian School began recruiting students from diverse tribes, the local Pimas who had dominated school enrollment protested, and Pima student desertions "jumped dramatically" (Trennert, 1988: 62). Students did more than desert. In April 1899, Pima, Maricopa, and Papago students petitioned the Indian Commissioner, decrying the Phoenix Superintendent's disregard for them in his zeal to enroll "foreign" Indians, and his cultural insensitivity in forcing the girls to dance with "strangers," an "outrage imposed on their maidenly modesty" (cited in Trennert, 1988: 66).

Covert resistance has been a hallmark of colonial education. Native people have devised ingenious ways to escape or ameliorate the very real powers and consequences of federal control. Authorities pressured Indian parents to surrender their children – through military and police powers, prosecution and incarceration, withholding of goods, services, and food rations – but parents hid children, sheltered school runaways, and procrastinated when enrolling or returning students to school. Students, both voluntary and involuntary school-goers, resisted authoritarianism and regimentation. Smuggling bean sandwiches up to their dorm rooms; telling ghost stories after "lights out"; stealing apples, eggs, chickens, and parching corn from school commissaries; passing notes in class; building illicit gang "clubhouses" out of scrap lumber; even constructing disguised stills or conducting secret peyote meetings in secluded dorm rooms – students devised strategies to assert independence, express individuality, develop leadership, use Native languages, and undermine federal goals of homogenization and assimilation (Child, 1998; Lomawaima, 1994).

The confrontation between education *by* Indians and education *for* Indians means that all histories of Indian education have been constructed within a context of powers and sovereignties. Indian education has been adversarial for generations, pitting federal powers against tribal powers, federal sovereignty against tribal sovereignties. Indian education has fit within larger political agendas: whether to create reservations or allot lands, to terminate tribes and relocate families to cities, or to foster tribal self-determination. The history of Indian education is a history of Indian people trying, through whatever means possible, to control the education of their children. Local control over education continues to be a critical factor in successfully implementing tribal sovereignty.

Native people have always valued education. The educational systems designed to transmit tribal knowledge over the centuries are formally organized, consciously constructed systems that value student initiative and intellectual engagement (Johnston, 1988; Eastman, 1991 [1902]; Eggan, 1974). But tribal people also recognized the value of colonial education as a training ground for successful relations with Euro-American governments and citizens. From the earliest European contacts, Native societies have sought out colonial educational opportunities, for at least some Native people (Szasz, 1988). Enrollment in mission and federal boarding schools has been both voluntary and involuntary (LaFlesche, 1978 [1900]; Lomawaima, 1994). In the twentieth century, as opportunities for higher education expanded, the majority of Native graduates earned undergraduate and graduate degrees in Education (see Lomawaima, 1995: 333–4).

As tribal governments have asserted their sovereignty in the decades since the Civil Rights movements, the first strides toward self-empowerment have often been strides in education. The first community-controlled school enabled under the Economic Opportunity Act of 1964 was established at the Diné (Navajo) community of Rough Rock, Arizona, in 1966. The first tribal college, Navajo Community College (renamed Diné College in 1998), was established in 1969. In 1970, Native educators, students, and parents formed the National Indian Education Association (NIEA). The Coalition of Indian-Controlled School Boards (CICSB) was established in 1971. The American Indian Higher Education Consortium (AIHEC), which oversees more than two dozen tribal colleges, was established in 1972.

By and large, contemporary Native educational programs focus on developing effective local control, and locally relevant curriculum, language materials, and pedagogical methods. They are not interested in "multicultural" initiatives that incorporate discrete "traits" of varied cultures into an overarching curricular plan. That trend is understandable if one understands the relations of contested powers that surround American Indian education. Indigenous systems of knowledge, and the educational processes that perpetuate them, are complex systems that are profoundly different from so-called "mainstream" systems of knowledge and pedagogy. Indigenous knowledge can not – *should not* – be easily reduced to lesson plans featuring favorite foods, or "costumes," or Disney-esque moments valorized by Euro-American history: helpful Indians "celebrating" the first Thanksgiving with the noble Pilgrims, or Pocahontas bravely "saving" John Smith.

The distinction between education *by* Indians and education *for* Indians is still salient, but since the 1960s there has been significant progress. American Indian parents and communities now have much more claim (based on political power, economic development, and myriad social changes) to what many Americans have long assumed are basic rights of citizenship: the right to make choices about their children's education, and the right to control schools. Like Americans everywhere, American Indian parents are struggling with educational issues: private versus public schools; control of curriculum versus censorship; responsibilities of teachers versus responsibilities of parents and communities; how best to inculcate "family values"; how to enhance language facility; how to improve – or whether to use – test scores. Prior to World War II, most American Indian parents were denied any influence, let alone any choice, in these matters. Today, the answers may not be easier to find, but Indian parents do have more chances to decide the future of American Indian education.

The Meaning of Education in Native Communities

Basil Johnston, Anishinabe scholar and educator, chronicled his experiences in the Canadian Jesuit mission school known as "Spanish" in the moving memoir, *Indian School Days* (1988). He has also written eloquently about tribal education. Johnston proposes that the best way to understand "Native peoples and their heritage … [is] by examining native ceremonies, rituals, songs, dances, prayers, and stories" (1976: 7). In these sources are found the "fundamental understandings, insights, and attitudes toward life and human conduct, character, and quality" that bind every human society. Johnston stresses the experiential and engaged quality of Native learning. Native education demands commitment:

> [I]t is not enough to listen or to read or to understand the truths contained in stories; according to the elders the truths must be lived out and become part of the being of a person. The search for truth and wisdom ought to lead to fulfillment of man and woman. (1976: 7)

The oral literature and history which transmit Native knowledge are not transparent or literal genres; "listeners are expected to draw their own inferences, conclusions, and meanings according to their intellectual capacities," and "time and deliberation are required for adequate appreciation" (1976: 8).

Johnston's characterizations of Anishinabe education resonate in many Native authors' autobiographies. Although cultural particulars vary widely among Native nations, pedagogical themes recur. A dependence on oral genres requires serious memory training, and an analytical, intellectual engagement with oral texts that are highly condensed, metaphorical masterpieces. The texts are not easily understood: they demand lifetimes of study. As one Native consultant, known as Hand, told the ethnographer George Dorsey after narrating the Arikara origin story: "This will give an idea to all how the Arikara originated under the earth. Yet it seems a mystery to us, and it is for us to solve" (Dorsey, 1904: 25).

As Johnston and other Native autobiographers document, indigenous educators do not imagine that children are passive learners. Native education demands "active learners," willing to experiment, practice, and eventually display mastery of skills or knowledge. Learning is often accomplished through doing. Charles Eastman (Dakota, or Eastern Sioux) relates in his autobiography how he was instructed by his grandmother in the bravery and deep personal sacrifice required to petition the Great Mystery, when at age 8 he sacrificed his beloved pet dog (1991 [1902]: 101–12). Even though Euro-American-style "lecturing" is probably a rarely used method, Native education is a language-rich activity. Eastman also recalled how his uncle would "catechize" him at the end of each day, asking him to recall, describe, and analyze the events, and his observations, of the day (Eastman, 1991 [1902]: 52–3).

Indigenous education has not typically been defined by the walls of "schools," but it does utilize structured and age- or ability-graded curricula developed by social and ceremonial groups such as kivas (Pueblo), houses (Northwest Coast), kin-defined clans (nearly everywhere), social classes (such as the Yurok Talth), women's or men's societies (Plains), or the Midewiwin lodge (Great Lakes Anishinabeg). Native educational systems are conscious systems. They build on knowledge and skills in successive layers; they use specialists as instructors; they differentiate among learners – whether by heritage and/or aptitude, certain students may be singled out for instruction; certain bodies of skills or knowledge are transmitted only within select groups; "higher" education is not necessarily open to, or sought out by, everyone.

The details of indigenous educational systems are embedded within diverse sources – autobiographies, anthropological monographs, Native literature and so-called "myths" – but most published histories of Indian education begin and end with the concerns of colonial education.

Colonial Education

The United States has shared the earlier assumptions of imperial France, Spain, and Great Britain about "appropriate" education for Native peoples. "Savage" Native Americans were to be "civilized"; "civilization" requires Christianity; "civilization" requires total subordination of Native communities, frequently achieved through relocation; and the presumed deficiencies of Native people require "appropriate" pedagogical methods. Appropriate methods have "included a military model of mass regimentation, authoritarian discipline, strict gender segregation, an emphasis on manual labor, avoidance of higher academic or professional training, rote memorization, and drill in desired physical and emotional habits" (Lomawaima, 1999: 19). Colonial education has redesigned Native families, architectures, economies, agronomies, foods, and menus. The goal of Indian education has been total transformation, obedience, and assimilation into colonial culture.

Catholic doctrine dictated that "wild" Indians be "reduced" from chaotic freedom to settled, organized life. Hence the terminology applied to mission communities, *reducciones* in New Spain and *reductions* in New France. *Reductions* were effective foci for French power: residents were closely supervised, travel was restricted, weekdays were regimented into prayer periods, and every Sunday was consumed by pageantry. In 1529 the Franciscans established schools in central Mexico. Students labored, kept a discipline of silence, were constantly supervised, and subject to a uniformity so strict that there was not "a difference among them, even as regards a ribbon" (Barth, 1945: 102).

By the 1600s, manual labor was integral to Jesuit education for Indians in New France, and later Spanish missions in the Southwest were self-supporting, thanks to Indian labor. The Franciscan fathers in the California missions did not classify their converts by intelligence, character, or spirituality, but by their ability to work (Jackson and Castillo, 1995: 13). French and Spanish missions offered important models, but the British most directly influenced American education for Indians.

In New England as in New Spain and New France, education *for* Indians was the responsibility of missionaries (Szasz, 1988: 5). Christian Natives were relocated to new communities under British control, into the "praying towns" such as Natick, Massachusetts, rather than absorbed into English congregations. Cultural assimilation was not a precursor to integration; Natives and non-Natives remained segregated. Anglo-American education for Indians has been excellently documented by Margaret Connell Szasz in *Indian Education in the American Colonies, 1607–1783* (1988). Szasz describes the remarkable diversity of educational efforts throughout the colonies, while recognizing their shared goal to "Christianize and civilize the natives" (1988: 5). In New England, she painstakingly reconstructs how the Puritan John Eliot's mission was enabled by Algonkian translators and assistants Cockenoe, Job Nesuton, and "James" Wowaus (pp. 113–15).

The "separate but civilized" model for Indian communities persisted through the early 1800s. As colonial claims over American Indians passed from British to U.S. hands, the federal government subsidized mission education. In 1819, Congress initiated an annual appropriation known as the "Civilization Fund" to underwrite mission expenses. Some fifty years later, in at least partial recognition of the limited number of Indian students in the missions, the federal government adopted more direct responsibility for Indian education.

New initiatives in education stemmed from the changing circumstances of American expansion. As early as 1802 Thomas Jefferson had articulated a "removal" policy that went far beyond the British practice of segregating English and Native societies. Removal was made law in 1830, and tribes east of the Mississippi were forced west, to so-called "Indian Territory" stretching across what is now Nebraska, Kansas, and Oklahoma. By the 1870s, the idealistic view that the removed (and indigenous western) tribes could assimilate at their own pace in large territories was doomed. Removal policy was replaced by reservation policy, and most Americans imagined reservations to be temporary enclaves where Natives could be effectively schooled, civilized, trained as domestic or manual laborers, and then swallowed into the lower strata of American life.

"Indian affairs" and administration of reservations are federal responsibilities, and so federal schools, on and off reservation, have educated Indian youth. Federal subsidy of mission efforts was gradually curtailed – mostly as a Protestant assault against Catholic schools – and ended by 1917 (Prucha, 1979). Prucha's *The Churches and the Indian Schools, 1888–1912* (1979) describes the political setting for the transition from church to government schools. The mission model of educational goals and practices, however, was carried forward.

From the 1880s through the 1920s, debate raged over how education for Indians should best be designed. Policymakers, professional educators, federal bureaucrats, and interested citizens argued over Indian abilities as they proposed radically different visions of the Indian "place" in America. Indian people were the only interested party excluded from the dialogue. Office of Indian Affairs (OIA) policymakers had a pessimistic, racial, and segregationist view of morally, intellectually, even physically "inferior" Indians who might be educated in the rudiments of American life as individuals; but whose societies would soon vanish. Members of "reform" groups such as the Indian Rights Association had a more egalitarian, positive view of the abilities of individual Indians to learn, assimilate, and succeed, but they shared prevalent beliefs in the inescapable extinction of tribal cultures. Intellectuals such as the white educator Elaine Goodale Eastman, and the Lakota writer Gertrude Bonnin (also known as Zitkala Sä), who praised the virtues of tribal lifestyles and Native knowledge, were unquestionably in the minority.

Eastman particularly detested OIA policymakers' favorite catch-phrase, "the dignity of labor." She flatly repudiated their claim that instilling respect for "the dignity of labor" in their Indian pupils was a nobler calling than academic instruction or professional training:

It is perfectly clear to everybody, including those who flatter the workingman with fair words, that the comforts and refinements of our civilization, the higher pleasures of art, literature, and travel, the society of cultivated men and women – all that the world calls success and honor—are the rewards of the *mind*, not muscle. (Eastman, 1900; emphasis in the original)

Federal Indian policy scholar Frederick Hoxie (1989 [1984]) proposes that the turn of the century heralded a policy change, from reformist notions of unlimited possibilities for Indians who had been "civilized," to much more racist notions of Indians' inherited or conditioned limitations. Francis Paul Prucha (1984) has a more generous view of policy continuity and cultural tolerance during this period. Michael Coleman (1985, 1993) has persuasively argued, on the other hand, that the rhetoric of federal officials during this time was deeply ambiguous, and subject to readings as "either romantic racist sentimentality ... or a genuine growth of sensibility – or, more likely, a confused blending of both" (1993: 47). The ambiguity that Coleman identified can be better understood if we examine the constraints on a "genuine growth of sensibility," if we understand that officials were grappling with differentiating "safe" from "dangerous" kinds of cultural difference.

Federal tolerance of certain Indian "traits" did not go far. Complete intolerance was the norm applied to non-Christian religious expression, or to "dangerously" different economic, political, or social beliefs or practices (such as marriage rules). The tolerance extended only to difference perceived to be "safe" or "innocent." "Safe" difference included the production of arts and crafts, the recording of "tales" classified as mythical or fictional, and the preparation of Native foods (as long as they did not require subversively different, outlawed, or competitive economies, such as buffalo hunting, gill netting of salmon, or harvesting of "wild" foods such as acorns on white-owned lands).

The ambiguities for educators, and later scholars, raised by "safe" toleration are apparent in Superintendent of Indian Schools (1898–1910) Estelle Reel's experiment with Native arts in the standard curriculum, as she laid it out in *Uniform Course of Study* (1901). Native teachers were employed in the federal schools to teach economically viable crafts such as basket and rug weaving. Prucha sees Reel's encouragement of select crafts as examples of "occasional breaks in the absolute ethnocentrism" of the *Uniform Course* (1984: 829). He proposes that it reflected Commissioner Jones's "remarkable sensitivity for his times in recognizing the deep value that Indianness gave to the products" (p. 829). After Jones, Commissioner Leupp also "systematically hoped to save instead of crush what was characteristically Indian. He promoted a revival of Indian music and plastic arts in the schools" (p. 829).

Prucha may be too uncritical. A close examination of Leupp's ideas about music, juxtaposed to Reel's experiment of hiring Native teachers, illustrates the fundamental "Indianness" that schools simply could not tolerate:

> I have, in a few speeches and other public utterances, made special mention of the successful practice of one of our teachers in the Southwest, of inducing her pupils to bring to the classroom the little nursery songs of their homes, and sing them there in concert, in their own tongue ... As everyone who reads this letter probably knows, I have none of the prejudice which exists in many minds against the perpetuation of Indian music and other arts, customs, and traditions, provided *they are innocent in themselves and do not clash needlessly with the new social order.* (emphasis added; cited in Lomawaima, 1996)

Leupp apparently perceived these "little nursery songs" as culturally innocuous. The challenge was to find "innocent" expressions of Indian identity and cultural life that did not clash with the new social order. That challenge was practically impossible to meet, as Reel's short-lived experiment with Native crafts teachers reveals. Since "instruction by native women ... inevitably brought girls into contact with the kind of tribal women whose authority and respectability the schools were trying to undermine, that part of Reel's plan ... did not survive her retirement" (Lomawaima, 1996: 19).

Even after Leupp's pronouncement, the tension between "innocent" and "dangerous" cultural expression continued to haunt the OIA. A 1908 circular issued by the Superintendent of Indian Schools reiterated Leupp's interest in Native music.

> [P]upils should be encouraged to practice singing the native songs of their people and of the Nation, the home, the fireside, the nursery.... The Office is especially anxious that the singing of native tribal songs be given a prominent place in the musical exercises, so that pupils may not drop and forget the music of their ancestors. (Reel, 1908)

However, in real life on reservations the perpetuation of Native music and song – typically through religious life – was not tolerated by federal authorities. A more typical federal stance presents itself in the events described below, drawn from the National Archives records of the Pima reservation (just southeast of Phoenix, Arizona).

In the fall of 1912, Superintendent Frank Thackery of the Pima reservation wrote to Mr. Anton White, who had been charged with organizing "Indian songs and dances of the old style." The Superintendent prohibited White's dances because they "would hinder industrial and social progress." After being entreated by a returned student, fresh from boarding school (and Reel's *Uniform Course*), to allow two or three simple songs, the Superintendent met with White again to remind him "that the holding of his Indian dances and the singing of his foolish, meaningless songs are forbidden." In a subsequent, transcribed hearing on the matter, Anton White himself mustered in his defense an argument reminiscent of the federal "educational" use of songs:

> I have made out this song, not because I want the people to sing it. It is because I want to sing it myself. But other young men have gotten interested in my singing and they have come over to listen to me ... I suppose it is because they have heard American songs in school and they were interested in those songs because it was for their education and for their amusement. (National Archives, 1912–13)

Recent scholars in Indian educational history have applied the theoretical perspectives of Michel Foucault, Pierre Bourdieu, and political economy, in an effort to understand apparent contradictions between federal policies and practices, as well as to better represent the experiences of Indian students. These scholars view Indian education as an exercise of the power of the state, as an institutional structure dedicated to instilling new practices or habits into American Indian subjects. For example, D. W. Adams, in his groundbreaking article about the "deep meaning" of Indian education (1988), probed the agendas behind assimilationist schooling.

He proposed that one of the "fundamental considerations" behind school policy was the transfer of real estate from Indian to white hands (pp. 16–21). School practices fit hand-in-glove with Congressional passage of the 1887 General Allotment Act, and were designed to condition Indians to surrender tribally controlled lands and accept individual land allotments. Littlefield (1989, 1993) has examined Indian colonial education from a political economy perspective, and proposed that "'proletarianization' better characterizes the efforts of the federal Indian schools than assimilation" (1993: 43). Both Littlefield and Lomawaima (1993, 1994, 1996) have emphasized that educational practice was designed to train Indians for subservience, and for entry only into the manual/domestic labor market.

The emphasis on manual labor, and low expectations of Indians, were clearly articulated in an OIA Education Division publication at the turn of the century. The document stressed "thorough industrial training," and so assigned half the school day to the industrial departments, where students worked in the barns, the fields, and the shops (in trades such as blacksmithing, harness-making, painting, and repair). The other half of the day was spent in the "literary" departments which emphasized basic skills in reading, writing, and arithmetic, since "[h]igher education in the sense ordinarily used has no place in the curriculum of Indian schools." "Higher education" was defined as beyond the sixth to the eighth grade. The circular specified that boys' training should not exceed the level of polytechnic institutes and that girls should be trained to serve "good wholesome meals at tables of moderate means" but not to aspire to hotel or restaurant style (National Archives, 1900).

Native students and parents frequently protested the low academic standards of the Indian schools, and limited job opportunities after graduation, but to little avail. One example of alumna dissatisfaction can be found in a letter from Miss Priscilla LaMote, of Neopit, Wisconsin, responding to an inquiry from the OIA:

> It gave me courage to receive such a friendly letter from you. When I left Hampton I intended to return in the fall but conditions have changed my plans. Also, I thought it useless as other pupils who have taken the post graduate course get no higher positions than those who simply graduate from the Senior class. ... The agent here wished me to teach in this government school. The principal said that Indian teachers were forbidden to teach members of their own tribe. Naturally I became discouraged, and have not tried to do anything about getting another place. The Tomah Indian School superintendent asked me if I'd accept the position of assistant laundress if it was offered to me. That, of course isn't a sure place and I would like to work as soon as possible. It seems queer though when I've been to school so long and labored so diligently at my school work that I can['t] get a better place than that of an assistant. (LaMote, 1910)

Some federal workers, such as Charles Buchanan at Tulalip Reservation in western Washington state, recognized that employment opportunities for Native people were limited by more than poor educational preparation:

> I regret to state that there is a very serious, deep and positive prejudice, general throughout the Northwest, against the Indian. This makes it difficult if not

impossible for Indian boys, trained in trades, to secure employment side by side with white men. ... this feeling ... for the present at least, effectually closes many of the doors of present opportunity, in mechanical lines, to our Indian boys and girls. (Buchanan, 1914)

Indian education policy and practice altered somewhat through the 1920s and 1930s, as critics of assimilation exerted greater influence in Washington, D.C. After intensive field research, an interdisciplinary team headed by Lewis Meriam wrote an excoriating critique of the government's Indian Service. *The Problem of Indian Administration* (Meriam, 1928) faulted the government for substandard efforts in Indian health, in management of tribal assets, in social services – in fact, in all areas of federal responsibility. The Meriam Report targeted educational efforts, and the conditions in boarding schools in particular, as among the most severely deficient, indeed, as the most actively harmful to the health and well-being of Indian children:

> The survey staff finds itself obliged to say frankly and unequivocally that the provisions for the care of the Indian children in boarding schools are grossly inadequate. (1928: 11)

The Report's recommendations identified education as the keystone to effective administration of "Indian affairs," and offered an alternative to the long-standing assumption that integration was the only option for Native people:

> Recommendations. The fundamental requirement is that the task of the Indian Service be recognized as primarily educational, in the broadest sense of that word, and that it be made an efficient educational agency, devoting its main energies to the social and economic advancement of the Indians, so that they may be absorbed into the prevailing civilization *or be fitted to live in the presence of that civilization at least in accordance with a minimum standard of health and decency.* (emphasis added; p. 21)

An era of reform began when Charles Rhoads became Commissioner of Indian Affairs in 1929, followed by John Collier (1933–45). Rhoads appointed the progressive educator and Meriam Report researcher, W. Carson Ryan Jr., as Director of Education in 1930. Collier brought a radically new vision to the administration of Indian affairs, as he advocated Native religious freedom, self-government, and cultural survival (Philp, 1977; Szasz, 1977). Collier's administration is not without critics, and some would dispute how much autonomy tribes gained during this era, but educational policy was deeply affected.

Assimilationist practice, perhaps, was more enduring than policy, as "Old Guard" employees of the federal schools were slow to respond to new directives from Washington. Collier, through Ryan, directed the federal schools to allow Native religious expression and language use, to liberalize contact between boys and girls, to loosen up military discipline, to improve nutritional and health care standards, to introduce relevant Native curriculum, and to adopt a more humane approach to Indian children. Day school construction was encouraged, boarding school enrollment was discouraged (especially for young children), and the federal government more effectively subsidized the enrollment of Indian children in public schools through the Johnson O'Malley Act (1934). Some of the changes were visible to, and positively acclaimed by, Indian students in the boarding schools, but others seemed to be old ideas in new guises.

Students at Chilocco Indian Agricultural School in Oklahoma, for example, protested the "new vocational program" instituted in 1936 under Collier's directives. A "big group of students went home in a rush at the opening of school," according to Superintendent Correll, because they "misunderstood" the new course of study. In fact, students were justifiably upset, since the new course of study meant that "they were not going to get a diploma showing that they had graduated from an accredited high school" (Correll, 1936). Chilocco's designation as a "vocational" school meant the loss of state accreditation.

Collier's efforts to reform the BIA were cut short by World War II, but his era's educational programs marked key transitions in the history of Indian education. Innovative programs, such as bilingual education, contained both elements of past assimilation agendas and future efforts to develop relevant cultural curricula. The *Indian Life Readers,* published by the BIA in the 1940s, included a Pueblo Series, Sioux Series, and Navajo Series. Some, like *Young Hunter of Picuris* (Clark, 1965 [1943]), were English-only texts that celebrated Native values and practices:

> Mother brought cornmeal in a bowl. ...
> She gave it to Father
>   for him to bless the deer ...
> Father made a prayer
>   as he sprinkled the cornmeal. ...
> Father saved the deer's blood
>   and the women put
>   their finger tips in it
>   and marked their baby boys' feet
>   to make them swift
>   and marked their hands
>   to make them strong
>   and marked their heads
>   to make them gentle and brave.
> Young Hunter said, "I did not know
>   that deer were so important."
> (Clark, 1965: 24–5)

Bilingual texts in English and Navajo, such as *Coyote Tales* (Thompson, Young, and Morgan, 1968 [1949]), introduced Navajo values and moral lessons into classrooms, as they legitimized, even encouraged, the "development of active bilingualism upon the part of both children and their elders" (Beatty, 1943: 91). Some texts, however, such as the "Just-For-Fun" Lakota story *The Hen of Wahpeton* (Clark, 1943), used the bilingual text to promote federal agendas. In an era when reservation agents were promoting sanctioned forms of stock-raising, gardening, and agriculture, *The Hen of Wahpeton* tells the story of the War-Bonnet family's special incubator chick who learns to read and sing opera. The War-Bonnet family itself was an Agency Superintendent's dream come true:

> The War-Bonnet family
> were very fine people.
> They did as they should do
> and they bought
> what was good for them.
> (Clark, 1943: 7–8)

When Collier's tenure ended in 1945, the assimilation agenda resurfaced. Directors of Indian Education Willard Beatty (1936–52) and Hildegard Thompson (1952–65) struggled to maintain 1930s reforms but their work was hampered by the conservative political mood of the country and lack of support from Congress (Szasz, 1977). Some boarding schools closed, but enrollments at others increased as students from isolated, educationally under-served areas such as the Navajo Reservation and rural Alaska, were transported to schools in Oklahoma and Oregon. Throughout the 1940s and 1950s, the enrollment of Native students in public schools continued to rise, but Native parents were often excluded from the local political processes of school governance.

Changes in the political landscape of tribes in the last decades, however, have roots that can be traced back to Collier's era and earlier. Indian education has never been an isolated phenomenon. The move to replace boarding schools with day schools was, it is true, part of a larger movement in Progressive Education. It was also partly a consequence of a shift in personnel in the Education Division, with the appointments of Ryan, Beatty, and Thompson. The move to local schools, however, was more than a swing of the pendulum in educational theory and practice. It was part of a significant re-ordering of the political life of tribes. We cannot understand the changes in Indian education in the 1930s separate from what Collier hoped to accomplish for tribal governments with the Indian Reorganization Act, and what he hoped to accomplish for the safe, legal practice of Native religions with his administrative directives to BIA personnel.

Since the 1960s, Native parents and tribal communities have made miraculous progress in gaining more control of education for their children – miraculous compared to conditions in the 1920s when my grandmother, because she had been abandoned by her husband, was judged an "unfit mother" whose two sons were removed by Court order to the Chilocco Indian Agricultural School, and whose daughter was placed in the Wichita orphanage. Congress passed landmark enabling legislation in the 1960s and 1970s affecting Indian education in federal schools, public schools, and increasingly in schools run by Native people themselves. Federal action and tribal initiatives have expanded the boundaries of Indian education.

The Economic Opportunity Act (1964) supported Head Start, Upward Bound, VISTA (Volunteers in Service to America), and Indian Community Action Programs (CAP) such as the establishment in 1966 of Rough Rock School on the Navajo reservation. The Elementary and Secondary Education Act (P.L. 89–10) (1965), Title I was amended in 1966 to include BIA schools; in 1969 Navajo Community College opened its doors; in 1970 the National Indian Education Association (NIEA) began in Minneapolis; in 1971 the Coalition of Indian-Controlled School Boards (CICSB) was established in Boulder, Colorado; the 1972 Indian Education Act (Title IV of PL 92-318) was amended in 1975 to include Johnson O'Malley (JOM) and BIA programs, setting a precedent for limited Indian control of programs and recognizing urban Indian populations, state-recognized and terminated tribes as eligible for federal educational funds; in 1972 members of the Boards of Regents of tribal colleges assembled in Boulder to form the American Indian Higher Education Consortium (AIHEC); the Indian Self-Determination and Education Assistance Act (PL 93-638) (1975) increased Indian participation in government programs and established the basis for "638 contracting" by tribes or Indian organizations of schools/programs; the Native American Languages Act, Title I of PL 101-477 (1990) recognized the primacy of Native language preservation; in 1991 the Indian Nations at Risk Task Force issued its Final Report; in 1995 the National American Indian/Alaska Native Education Summit assembled in Washington, D.C.

Historians of American Indian education, however, have not (with few exceptions – see Szasz, 1977) focused their attention on recent decades. Either the Meriam Report, its subsequent reforms, or World War II has culminated the narratives of Indian educational history. These chronological boundaries have influenced how Indian educational histories have been constructed; in methodology, boundaries around ideas of what constitutes appropriate evidence have also shaped historical narratives.

Chronological and Methodological Boundaries in the History of American Indian Education

Historians both chronicle and create history. Scholars focus on certain dates, events, evidence, and players that assume the prominence of landmarks, guiding footsteps along accepted narrative trails. The history of American Indian education has established its own canons designating who, what, when, and where "counts" as important. While categories of "important" evidence and players have been expanded, some landmark dates, players, and events – moments such as the Civilization Act of 1819; players such as Richard Henry Pratt, founder of Carlisle Indian School; and events such as the reform movement of the late nineteenth century – are usually reaffirmed as "important."

The entry of Native scholars onto the scene has resulted in reorientations of methodological boundaries, although chronological boundaries remain entrenched. Native scholars (such as Child, Johnston, and Lomawaima) have helped to reshape Indian educational history by opening up the bounds of appropriate evidence to include oral history, personal narrative, and letters by Native students and parents, and by including Indian people in the history of Indian education, but a review of the literature below shows that scholars' genders and disciplinary training have played salient roles as well.

Many scholars, Native and non-Native, agree on the "important" chronological landmarks in the history of American Indian education. The 1928 publication of the Meriam Report is typically presented as a watershed event. It begins, or more usually ends, historical narratives. Szasz (1977) begins with the Meriam Report. It and the 1969 Kennedy Report are "natural boundaries" for a study of "education directed by the Indian Bureau and … [more recently] on schools controlled by the Indian people themselves" (p. vii). The Meriam Report marks the end, not the beginning, of Adams' study *Education for Extinction: American Indians and the Boarding School Experience, 1875–1928* (1995). Adams' narrative begins as the Indian Rights Association, at the helm of the reform movement, undertakes to "secure the civilization" of the Indians and "to prepare the way for their absorption into the common life of our own people" (p. 9). Prucha's 1979 work, *The Churches and the Indian Schools, 1888–1912*, nearly coincides with Adams' start date, although Prucha concludes his more focused study before the Meriam Report. Hoxie (1984/1989), in *A Final Promise: The Campaign to Assimilate the Indians, 1880–1920*, neatly splits the chronological disparity between Adams' and Prucha's beginning and end-points. Coleman (1993) pushes the starting line back a bit in *American Indian Children at School, 1850–1930*, but his choice of 1930 as a critical post-Meriam Report end date is mirrored by most scholars of the boarding schools (Child, 1998; Littlefield, 1993; Lomawaima, 1993, 1994; McBeth, 1983). Clearly the need that Szasz articulated in 1977 for more study of recent events and players in Indian education is still with us.

Methodological boundaries have been expanded in Indian educational history in the areas of evidence and viewpoint. Interdisciplinary exchanges within American Indian studies, the cross-fertilization of historic and anthropological approaches within ethnohistory, and the introduction or resurrection of Indian voices, perspectives, and interpretations have all enriched the study of Indian education. The evidentiary base of traditionally respectable documents has been expanded to include oral historical accounts (Szasz, 1977), Indian autobiographical accounts (Coleman, 1993), personal narratives of alumni, students (Lomawaima, 1994; McBeth, 1983) and teachers (Horne and McBeth, 1998), and previously untapped documentary records such as the letters of Indian students and parents (Child, 1998).

As evidentiary sources have multiplied, Indian people's experiences and perspectives have moved toward center stage of the historical narrative. In *The Churches and the Indian Schools, 1888–1912*, Prucha wrote about the "tension and conflict between Protestants and Catholics over Indian missions" (1979: ix). "The Indians were only obliquely a part" (p. xi) of the story he had to tell, pawns in the battle but not active participants or policymakers. Szasz (1977), McBeth (1983), Lomawaima (1994), Haig-Brown (1988), and others have assumed that even as pawns in others' educational plans, Native people still thought, acted, and responded. These scholars also see the reality that Indian people were more than pawns; understanding them is necessary to understanding Indian education. Szasz depended on documentary records left by federal policymakers, but she paired them with interviews, "contributions from both Indian students and Indian Bureau administrators" (1977: vii). Surely as those whose lives were being affected, students had meaningful stories to tell. These authors have used the evidence of oral interviews to demonstrate the roles Indian people have played as students, parents, teachers, and administrators in shaping Indian education. In these narratives, Indian people act as well as react. Sally McBeth's scholarship (1983) was among the first to privilege Native experience.

McBeth's Native students in an Oklahoma college taught her that what she assumed would be "normative," i.e., negative, attitudes toward boarding schools were more complex (1983: 4). McBeth listened carefully, and the issues Native people stressed were the clues to the "meaning of the boarding school experience," as institutions that represent "separation from White society and unification with other Indian people" (p. 116), as institutions that symbolize "acceptance of those values or experiences which are interpreted as crucial for survival, and resistance to those values which are deemed as opposed to the 'Indian way'" (pp. 116–17), and as institutions reflective of "*government control* of Indian people" as well as "*government obligations* toward Indian people" (p. 117). McBeth's scholarship set a new standard for Indian educational history, a standard that demands attention to policy, to school practice, and to Indian people.

Adams (1995) used the analytic triad of policy, practice, and student experience (see also Coleman, 1993; Lomawaima, 1993, 1994) to understand more fully how policy rhetoric was institutionalized into practice, and how Native students responded to both rhetoric and reality. Adams strove to give voice to whites responsible for creating the boarding school system, and to Indians, "a group for whom the documentary record is both sparse and unreliable." He found the special challenge of representing Indian children "almost unsurmountable" (p. x).

Recently, Brenda Child (1998) has moved beyond the oral interviews typical of the previous decade's boarding school scholarship. Child searched for documents, hoping to contribute to a "new Indian history" (1998: xiii) with Indian people center stage. In the National Archives she found a rich trove of letters written by students and their families whose "stories were overwhelming" (p. xiii). Red Lake Ojibwa herself, Child pursued letters by and from Ojibwa families so that her resulting work would "have an Ojibwe point of view" (p. xiv). Student letters document "homesickness, disease, rebellion and programs aimed at assimilation" (p. xv) while parents' letters "communicated a determined and passionate commitment to children" (p. xvi). Child found the documentary record not nearly as "sparse and unreliable" as Adams (1995) did, but perhaps being an Ojibwa reading Ojibwa letters made a difference. Adams is not Ojibwa, nor is he Native, but his contributions to Indian educational history are substantial. The many contributions to the history of Indian education considered here require us to think carefully about the roles of Native and non-Native scholars in the construction of history.

The question of how Native and non-Native scholars have changed the ways in which Indian history has been constituted is problematic. How do we sort out factors of Native or non-Native ancestry, of gender, or of disciplinary training in describing the trajectory of scholarship? Non-Native women such as Haig-Brown, Littlefield, McBeth, and Szasz have been instrumental in opening up the boundaries of Indian educational history, in introducing Indian voices, and in validating Indian perspectives. Scholars trained in anthropology (including Lomawaima and McBeth) have injected a willingness to use oral as well as documentary evidence. Native scholars such as Child, Lomawaima, and Molin (Buffalohead and Molin, 1996) have insisted that Indian people are much more than pawns in the history of Indian education.

The historical truth of the matter is that Native people have been for many generations excluded from the realms of academic discourse, from the possibilities of higher educational and professional training, from what Elaine Goodale Eastman called "the rewards of the *mind*." Exclusion from higher training is, after all, the very subject matter of any history of Indian education. My father experienced that exclusion first-hand. As a teenager he had survived childhood at Chilocco Indian Agricultural School, his escape from Chilocco, and hobo life on the rails in the Depression, with its homelessness and poverty. He got a job as a soda jerk, and worked his way through a public high school. When he graduated, with an Honor Society scholarship, to attend a small liberal arts college in Missouri, he was met on his first day on campus by the Dean of Students. "Don't bother to unpack," he told my dad. "We had an Indian boy here once before, and he was no good."

We are all products of our past. Surely historians would be the first to heed the warning that to be ignorant of the past is to repeat its mistakes. Indian people, and women, and anthropologists, and who-knows-else-or-what combinations of the above, have infiltrated American history and history is a better place for it. We are all coming to recognize, perhaps in more insightful ways than in the past, how human lives are enmeshed within written histories. Different people, different perspectives, different histories, different voices, different scholars. Indian people have injected Indian lives into Indian history, and as a result the story of American Indian education is a living, growing story.

BIBLIOGRAPHY

Adams, D. W. 1988: "Fundamental Considerations: The Deep Meaning of Native American Schooling, 1880–1900," *Harvard Educational Review* 58(1): 1–28.

Adams, D. W. 1995: *Education for Extinction: American Indians and the Boarding School Experience, 1875–1928* (Lawrence: University Press of Kansas).

Axtell, J. 1981: *The European and the Indian: Essays in the Ethnohistory of Colonial North America* (New York: Oxford University Press).

Barth, P. J. 1945: "Franciscan Education and the Social Order in Spanish North America, 1502–1821." Ph.D. dissertation, University of Chicago.

Beatty, W. W. 1943: "Bilingual Readers," in *The Hen of Wahpeton*, by A. Clark (Lawrence, KS: Haskell Institute, for Education Division, U.S. Office of Indian Affairs), pp. 90–1.

Buchanan, C. 1914: Letter (National Archives, Record Group 75, Records of the Education Division, Records of Industries Section; Entry 761, Records Concerning Former Students, 1910–25. March, 1914).

Buffalohead, R. W. and P. F. Molin 1996: "'A Nucleus of Civilization': American Indian Families at Hampton Institute in the Late Nineteenth Century," *Journal of American Indian Education* 35(3): 59–94.

Child, B. J. 1996: "Runaway Boys, Resistant Girls: Rebellion at Flandreau and Haskell, 1900–1940," *Journal of American Indian Education* 35(3): 49–57.

Child, B. J. 1998: *Boarding School Seasons: American Indian Families, 1900–1940* (Lincoln: University of Nebraska Press).

Clark, A. 1943: *The Hen of Wahpeton* (Lawrence, KS: Haskell Institute, for Education Division, U.S. Office of Indian Affairs).

Clark, A. 1965: *Young Hunter of Picuris* (Chilocco, 1943) (Chilocco, OK: Chilocco Indian School for Branch of Education, Bureau of Indian Affairs).

Coleman, M. C. 1985: *Presbyterian Missionary Attitudes toward American Indians, 1837–1893* (Jackson: University Press of Mississippi).

Coleman, M. C. 1993: *American Indian Children at School, 1850–1930* (Jackson: University Press of Mississippi).

Correll, L. E. 1936: Letter #2858–1936–800 to CIA, Attn. Mr. A. C. Monahan (National Archives, Record Group 75; Entry 121, Central Consolidated Files, Box 3092: Chilocco 730–1920/101524 to 800–1936/2858. January 13, 1936).

Dejong, D. H. 1993: *Promises of the Past: A History of Indian Education in the United States* (Golden, CO: North American Press).

Dorsey, G. 1904: *Traditions of the Arikara* (Washington, D.C.: Carnegie Institution of Washington).

Eastman, C. A. 1991: *Indian Boyhood* (Boston, 1902) (Lincoln: University of Nebraska Press).

Eastman, E. G. 1900: "The Education of the Indian," *The Arena* (October 1900) (in the Archival collections of the Museum of Native American Cultures/MONAC, transferred to Cheney-Cowles Museum, Spokane, Washington. MONAC filed as: Newspaper Clippings Folder #2: 8-06-1900 through 9-29-00, Item 18).

Eggan, D. 1974: "Instruction and Affect in Hopi Cultural Continuity," in *Education and Cultural Process*, ed. G. Spindler (New York: Holt, Rinehart and Winston), pp. 311–32.

Giago, T. A., Jr. 1978: *The Aboriginal Sin: Reflections on the Holy Rosary Mission School* (San Francisco: The Indian Historian Press).

Haig-Brown, C. 1988: *Resistance and Renewal: Surviving the Indian Residential School* (Vancouver, Tillacum Library).

Horne, E. B. and S. McBeth 1998: *Essie's Story: The Life and Legacy of a Shoshone Teacher* (Lincoln: University of Nebraska Press)

Hoxie, F. E. 1989: *A Final Promise: The Campaign to Assimilate the Indians, 1880–1920* (Lincoln, 1984) (Cambridge: Cambridge University Press).

Jackson, R. and E. Castillo 1995: *Indians, Franciscans, and Spanish Colonization: The Impact of the Mission System on California Indians* (Albuquerque: University of New Mexico Press).

Jennings, F. 1975: *The Invasion of America: Indians, Colonialism, and the Cant of Conquest* (Chapel Hill: University of North Carolina Press).

Johnston, B. H. 1976: *Ojibway Heritage* (New York: Columbia University Press).

Johnston, B. H. 1988: *Indian School Days* (Norman: University of Oklahoma Press).

LaFlesche, F. 1978: *The Middle Five: Indian Schoolboys of the Omaha Tribe* (1900) (Lincoln: University of Nebraska Press).

LaMote P. 1910: Letter (National Archives, Record Group 75, Records of the Education Division, Records of Industries Section; Entry 761, Records Concerning Former Students, 1910–25. Dated April 8, 1910).

Leupp, F. E. 1907: Circular #175 (National Archives, Record Group 75. Entry 718, Circulars Issued by the Education Division, 1897–1909; Box 1. Issued December 5, 1907).

Littlefield, A. 1989: "The B.I.A. Boarding School: Theories of Resistance and Social Reproduction," *Humanity and Society* 13: 428–41.

Littlefield, A. 1993: "Learning to Labor: Native American Education in the United States, 1880–1930," in *The Political Economy of North American Indians*, ed. J. Moore (Norman: University of Oklahoma Press), pp. 43–59.

Lomawaima, K. T. 1993: "Domesticity in the Federal Indian Schools: The Power of Authority over Mind and Body," *American Ethnologist* 20(2): 1–14.

Lomawaima. K. T. 1994: *They Called It Prairie Light: The Story of Chilocco Indian School* (Lincoln: University of Nebraska Press).

Lomawaima, K. T. 1995: "Educating Native Americans," in *Handbook of Research on Multicultural Education*, eds. J. A. Banks and C. M. Banks (New York: Macmillan Publishing), pp. 331–47.

Lomawaima, K. T. 1996: "Estelle Reel, Superintendent of Indian Schools, 1898–1910: Politics, Curriculum, and Land," *Journal of American Indian Education* 35(3) (Spring), 5–31.

Lomawaima, K. T. 1999: "The Unnatural History of American Indian Education," in *Next Steps: Research and Practice to Advance Indian Education*, eds. K. G. Swisher and J. W. Tippeconnic III (Charleston, WV: ERIC Clearinghouse on Rural Education and Small Schools), pp. 3–39.

McBeth, S. 1983: *Ethnic Identity and the Boarding School Experience of West-Central Oklahoma American Indians* (Washington, D.C.: University Press of America).

Meriam, L. 1928: *The Problem of Indian Administration* (Baltimore: Johns Hopkins University Press for the Institute for Government Research).

National Archives 1900: Circular #43 (Record Group 75; Entry 718, Circulars Issued by the Education Division, 1897–1909, Box 1. Issued September 19, 1900).

National Archives 1912–13: Correspondence between Supt. Thackery and Commissioner of Indian Affairs (Record Group 75; Entry 121, Central Consolidated Files Pima, Box 113866-1912-Pima 752, 1912–1913).

Philp, K. R. 1977: *John Collier's Crusade for Indian Reform, 1920–1954* (Tucson: University of Arizona Press).

Prucha, F. P. 1979: *The Churches and the Indian Schools, 1888–1912* (Lincoln: University of Nebraska Press).

Prucha, F. P. 1984: *The Great Father: The United States Government and the American Indians* (Lincoln: University of Nebraska Press).

Qoyawayma, P. 1964: *No Turning Back* (Albuquerque: University of New Mexico Press).

Reel, E. 1901: *Uniform Course of Study for the Indian Schools of the United States* (Washington, D.C: Government Printing Office).

Reel, E. 1908: Circular Issued by the Supt. of Indian Schools (National Archives, Record Group 75; Entry 719, Circulars Issued by the Supt. of Indian Schools, 1899–1908. Issued Feb. 5, 1908).

Skolnick, S. and M. Skolnick 1997: *Where Courage Is Like a Wild Horse: The World of an Indian Orphanage* (Lincoln: University of Nebraska Press).

St. Pierre, M. 1991: *Madonna Swann: A Lakota Woman's Story* (Norman: University of Oklahoma Press).

Szasz, M. C. 1977: *Education and the American Indian: The Road to Self-Determination Since 1928,* 2nd edn. (Albuquerque: University of New Mexico Press).

Szasz, M. C. 1988: *Indian Education in the American Colonies, 1607–1783* (Albuquerque: University of New Mexico Press).

Thompson, H., R. W. Young, and W. Morgan, 1968: *Coyote Tales* (Phoenix, 1949) (Lawrence, KS: Haskell Institute for Branch of Education, Bureau of Indian Affairs).

Trennert, R. A., Jr. 1988: *The Phoenix Indian School: Forced Assimilation in Arizona, 1891–1935* (Norman: University of Oklahoma Press).

24

Indian Law, Sovereignty, and State Law: Native People and the Law

SIDNEY L. HARRING

It is fundamental to the position of American Indians in the United States that they are sovereign people, living under their own law. The recognition that Indian law, the "common law" of Indian communities, operates alongside contemporary United States and Canadian law is the starting point for any discussion of the complexities of "Indian law" in North America. More than a lived reality to Native people, Indian law also has an impact on the nature of American and Canadian law. United States courts have acknowledged Indian law in hundreds of cases. Relationships between the two systems of law are not always easy: there is constant tension as states and tribes repeatedly challenge each other's respective jurisdictions. In the early twenty-first century Indian tribes face renewed attacks on their sovereignty from the states. Conservative federal judges, particularly in the West, have been increasingly unreceptive to broad-based defenses of Indian sovereignty.

Underpinning the abstractions of legal theory have been the countlessly repeated assertions of rights by ordinary Native people, going about their daily lives. In 1996 Hazel Van der Peet went to the Supreme Court of Canada to vindicate her right to sell ten salmon – an "existing aboriginal right" under the Constitution Act of 1982. She lost. In 1998 Harry Catarat and a half dozen fellow Dene were engaging in a traditional moose hunt in Northern Saskatchewan when Canadian Armed Forces helicopters carrying commandos and game wardens descended into their camp. Catarat "volunteered" to be arrested so that he could legally challenge his arrest. In 1994 several semi-trucks filled with gambling equipment "loaned" by American tribes mysteriously made their way across the border to set up a fully operational gambling casino on the White Bear reserve in Saskatchewan. It operated just long enough to get raided by the Royal Canadian Mounted Police – creating another legal test of aboriginal rights. These events are not isolated, but represent a powerful reassertion of aboriginal rights in both the United States and Canada. Contextualizing these legal events requires some understanding of the existing position of Native people in United States and Canadian law (*R. v. Catarat and Sylvestre*, Saskatchewan Provincial Court, September 1998, unreported).

Modern doctrines of Indian law are deeply rooted in history. One important case recognizing both the continued existence of Native American law as well as the right of Native people to be governed by their own laws is *ex parte Crow Dog* (109 U.S. 556 (1883)). In a dispute deeply rooted in tribal politics, Crow Dog, a Brulé Sioux, shot his chief, Spotted Tail, to death on the Rosebud Reservation in 1881. Arrested by the tribal police on the order of an Indian agent, he was turned over to the United States Army, and tried for murder in the Dakota territorial court. Crow Dog admitted the killing. Among other defenses, he challenged the jurisdiction of the United States to try him, arguing that he was a Brulé living under Brulé law and not United States law. His family had met with Spotted Tail's family, and in a traditional legal proceeding designed to restore order and harmony within the community, settled the matter for $600 in cash, eight horses, and one blanket. Crow Dog was nonetheless convicted of murder and sentenced to death. However, the United States Supreme Court (although using racist language that mischaracterized the case as one of "red man's revenge") agreed with Crow Dog: the Brulé were a "domestic dependent nation," retaining inherent sovereignty as a nation, including their own law, the "common law" of the Brulé people. Crow Dog's criminal offense was committed under Brulé law and United States law did not apply. He was freed and lived to be an old man, often reminding his people that his case showed the strength of Brulé traditional law (Harring, 1994).

At the time the case was widely known, coming as an apparent surprise to many whites who, in the era of the end of the Indian wars, were amazed that Indian law not only still existed, but was recognized as law by the United States Supreme Court. The Court, however, had only stated settled law: Native Americans in both the United States and Canada have legal traditions that precede European settlement and that have survived, adapted to changing social and cultural conditions, and are recognized and incorporated, to varying degrees, in the laws of both countries. This "legal dualism," the recognition of two laws, including a distinct body of law for Native people, has been the subject of many legal treatises (Morse, 1985; Wilkinson, 1987; Woodward, 1989), casebooks (Clinton, Newton, and Price, 1990; Getches, Wilkinson, and Williams, 1998), and hundreds of law review articles.

The end of the twentieth century brought renewed assertions of Indian law and Indian sovereignty. The wealth of some Indian nations in the United States from mineral resources, gambling, and tax-free gasoline and tobacco sales, and a wave of litigation in Canada stemming from the argument that sovereignty is a "pre-existing aboriginal right" guaranteed by the Constitution Act of 1982, have promoted renewed assertions by Native people that they have the right to live under their own laws as well as new arguments for a broader scope of Indian common law. The Chippewa of northern Wisconsin, for example, successfully argued not only that they had a right to their own hunting and fishing regulations, but that they had a right to extend these rights beyond their reservations to their traditional treaty lands: the northern third of the state (Whaley and Bresette, 1994). Washington State Indians successfully argued that a treaty right to fish meant a right to a commercial right to half of the fish (Cohen, 1986).

Let us look briefly at the relationship between United States and Canadian laws of Indian rights and the laws maintained by Native nations. Native American law itself – the common law of Native people – is not a single category of law. At the time of European "discovery," over five hundred Native American peoples north of Mexico – now often called "nations" – were as, if not more, diverse than the peoples of Europe. These societies ranged from highly organized nations with clearly defined political hierarchies, laws, and legal institutions; to confederacies of smaller nations, with more decentralized political and legal orders; to both interconnected and isolated family-based bands, governed by basic human agreements, not unlike the norms that might regulate a large family. Native people displayed a wide range of other adaptations including vastly different social organizations, economies, and cultural traditions. Since law, at its basic level, is simply the existence of social norms backed by legitimate coercive mechanisms that insure a level of social order, it follows that the legal traditions of Native North America are many and varied, just as are the legal traditions of European and Asian countries. There is a substantial anthropological literature on these legal traditions that is not studied as carefully as it should be in countries that recognize Native American law (Hoebel, 1940, 1955; Llewellyn and Hoebel, 1941; Cooter and Fikentscher, 1998).

In 1942, Felix Cohen, a lawyer for the Bureau of Indian Affairs, authored his still-influential treatise, *Handbook of Federal Indian Law*, perhaps beginning the modern period of sovereignty-based Indian law jurisprudence in the United States courts. The legal doctrines most often discussed under the rubric "Indian rights" are generally of European origin. They represent efforts by judges and legal scholars formally trained in English, Canadian, or American law to adapt the various European legal traditions to create a structure for the recognition of the laws and legal traditions of Native Americans. The discourse of Native American law, then, has a Eurocentric core, which has distorted the way scholars have approached the discipline. Rather than a discourse of Native sovereignty, we have seen a concern with the "balancing" of Indian rights with the often insensitive needs of the more populous American and Canadian nations (Williams, 1990).

As recently as 1985, Chief Justice William Rehnquist referred to Native American law dismissively (and in complete ignorance of the large literature on Indian law) by saying that "few Indian tribes maintained any semblance of a formal court system ... offenses by one Indian against another were usually handled by social and religious pressure and not by formal judicial processes; emphasis was on restitution rather than punishment" (*Oliphant v. Suquamish* 435 U.S. 191, 197 (1978)). This statement, citing an 1840s Bureau of Indian Affairs Report as its source, puts Native American law in a completely European framework, equating "law" to a formal court system, possessing the attributes of modern European law.

Modern legal anthropologists adopt a much more flexible and functional definition of law. *The Cheyenne Way*, a pathbreaking study of the traditional law of American Indians by legal philosopher Karl Llewellyn and anthropologist E. A. Hoebel, first developed a complex argument about the unique character of Native American law, and dozens of anthropologists and legal scholars have elaborated upon this research. The Cheyenne had an elaborate system of law, which could be carefully adapted to a wide range of social situations. Tribal elders, in deciding legal cases, paid close attention to both precedent, the previous ways that similar problems had been resolved, and to the current needs of both the individuals involved and the band. Far from being "certain" or "neutral," the law was understood to be deeply rooted in the community, flexible, and easily adjusted to the particular needs of a new situation.

The existence of these two distinct lines of "Indian law" requires any student of Indian rights in North America to follow both. On one hand, Native Americans in the United States (the matter is more complex in Canada) live under their own law. On the other hand, the Indian nations live within the United States and Congress has insisted that it has the right to impose United States law over Indian nations if it chooses to do so. Following the *Crow Dog* decision, Congress in 1885 enacted the Major Crimes Act, permitting itself to extend federal criminal law to Indian reservations. The United States Supreme Court, in *United States v. Kagama* (118 U.S. 375 (1886)), upheld this extension of federal plenary power over the Indian tribes. This tenuous balance remains in federal Indian law today. Perhaps the best way to avoid confusion is to refer to the United States or Canadian law of Indian rights as "federal law" or "Indian rights law," leaving the term "Indian law" or "Native law" to refer to the laws of Indian nations. There is no consistent usage of any of these terms in the literature and it is often necessary to resort to contexts to understand exactly what law is being discussed.

After generations of relegation to obscure anthropological texts, there is a renewed interest in the law of Indian nations, both "traditional" as well as evolved "common law," that is rooted in traditional law but transformed after hundreds of years of contact with Europeans and their laws. While the legal history of the extension of United States jurisdiction over Native Americans is important, it is equally critical that we follow the legal history of the right of Native Americans to live under their own law as an attribute of their sovereignty, a right repeatedly affirmed, most importantly in *Williams v. Lee* (358 U.S. 217 (1959)). There is an extensive literature on Native American law that clearly shows its depth and complexity, as well as its continuing strength through the twentieth century and beyond.

Indian Common Law

"Indian law," while deeply rooted in tradition, is not static, but has evolved to meet changing social conditions. Just as scholars of the English common law point out that it changed to incorporate Norse and Norman law, Native American law is also evolving, a lived law, a "common law" of particular Native communities and nations. Native American law at contact was more diverse than that of England, with unique cultures adapting differently to different conditions. Any discussion of a single "Native American law" is as futile as a discussion of "European law": imagine a "common law" of the Irish, Finnish, Lapp, English, Bulgarian, Basque, French, Greek, Lithuanian, Russian, and German peoples!

Similarly, to call Indian law "customary law" sets up a false dichotomy between Indian and English or European law – which is itself rooted in custom. And, to call Indian law "traditional" sets up a similar problem. While Indian law is deeply rooted in tradition, it has evolved over time to meet changing conditions, as any common law does. Moreover, given the rapid pace of social change in North America over the past five hundred years this development has been uneven, affecting even members of the same tribe in different ways. Despite these caveats, however, there are some distinguishing elements of Indian law that can be discussed.

In many cases, Native American law could be immediate and direct, reflecting, for example, the needs of small, close-knit, and homogenous communities. The immediate need was to resolve the legal problem so that the community could move forward – together. For Native economies based on hunting and fishing, any significant disruption of the social order could easily lead to dire consequences for an entire people. This kind of law has been characterized as "a law of blood" because one of the core features was often an immediate right to revenge, held by the close relatives of a victim of violence (Reid, 1970). Most commonly this led to a formal or informal process, not unlike the one that occurred in Crow Dog's case, as the men of the group – and again there were many different units of primary social organization, including small bands, extensive bands, various family and clan structures, and nations of different sizes – met to decide on the appropriate resolution. They would discuss the case, listen to the viewpoints of all of the involved parties, and announce an appropriate resolution. A question of simple revenge might be taken on the spot by the relatives of the victim. But, just as often, the relatives of the victim showed their power and generosity by refusing to take revenge, settling the case with an appropriate gesture from the family or clan of the perpetrator of the misdeed. This generosity raised the prestige of the family. The gifts that Crow Dog's clan gave to Spotted Tail's clan have been characterized as "blood money" but the reality was much more complex. It is not that Spotted Tail's blood was paid for, putting a cheap premium on life, but that Crow Dog's people symbolically recognized their loss and restored a balance within the Brulé nation (Harring, 1994: 1–12).

Most of the accounts of actual cases in Native American law – and there are thousands of surviving accounts, both written and in oral history – involve some physical injury to a person. In addition to intentional murder cases, there are also cases of accidental death or injury, which also required various forms of restitution. Some acts injured an entire nation. Plains nations, for example, had warrior societies to police their lengthy and elaborate hunting and warfare trips. These events required careful coordination, and any departure from the common plan endangered the entire group. Young warriors who aggressively attacked ahead of the plan were disciplined by members of the police societies. They might have their horses shot or confiscated and their weapons broken. But their property was restored as soon as they acknowledged their mistakes and agreed to follow the orders of their leaders. The members of these "police" societies were legal officers, with summary powers of punishment that included the right to inflict violence. The hunt was an immediate concern and its success might mean life or death to a band. There was no time for formal legal process under such conditions. After the hunt or battle ended, the leaders could discuss any problems with an eye toward judgment and conciliation (Provisne, 1934).

There are fewer property cases in Native American law although, as Native people came to recognize new forms of property, these increased in the late nineteenth century. It is clear that many different kinds of property rights existed in Native society, again depending on a group's social organization. Fields, orchards, and other agricultural sites were held as personal or clan property among the Cherokee, Creek, Six Nations, Hopi, Zuni, and the other nations with substantial agricultural economies. Fishing, hunting, and trapping grounds of the Cree and Ojibwa were held by bands and clans with clearly recognized use rights. In the Northwest, individuals or clans owned salmon fishing locations and equipment such as traps and platforms. Early Russian settlers in Alaska were forced to pay the Tlingit for the water they drew from streams owned by Tlingit clans (Harring, 1994). Some of these use rights were exclusive, but some were also shared among different family, clan, or tribal entities, each holding defined rights. Personal property rights were deeply entrenched in many Native American nations, with some large accumulations of personal wealth taking different social forms. Plains warriors personally owned large stocks of horses, with the size and quality of the horse herd representing the prestige of the owner (Llewellyn and Hoebel, 1941). Northwest Coast nations were often led by their richest members, who generated political power through elaborate gift-giving rituals known as potlatches. Obligated rival clans returned these rituals, with further gifts of property binding clans together in a cycle of reciprocal symbolic exchanges (Codere, 1950). Other kinds of property were held communally, meaning that a community or clan owned it. Some property might even be held jointly between different bands, clans, or nations.

As the various Indian nations adapted to the changes that American and Canadian society brought, new forms of property developed, especially incident to Indian farming. Livestock and "improvements" were owned by individuals, while reservation lands were communally owned. Individuals held different kinds of rights to communal lands. Laws of inheritance, unknown in most Native societies as the various clan structures cared for their members, were developed to keep these farms in the hands of the wives and children of Indian farmers. Among the earliest of the Creek laws created to adapt to the needs of the new Creek nation in the Indian Territory was a law that required disinterested parties to "count" each estate and report its contents to the Creek District Courts. The court records reflect a careful "counting" of the small estates of Creek farmers: one pot, two hogs, one saddle, two chairs, one table (Harring, 1994).

Native American legal institutions were generally (but not always) informal. Peacemakers of different types existed in Native communities from the Seneca of New York to the Navajo of the Southwest. Seneca peacemakers were incorporated into the national structure by the mid-nineteenth century, and formally elected as the judicial branch of government. Still, as legal officers, the peacemakers had a very different role than judges in neighboring New York towns. While American judges were (officially at least) "neutral" and "disinterested" parties, Seneca peacemakers were members of the community with knowledge of the dispute and an interest in resolving the problem in a way that insured continuing peace. Indeed, living together in peace was the whole purpose of Seneca social order, the very definition of traditional culture. These peacemaker courts exist today (Porter, 1997). In contrast, Navajo peacemakers serve in an informal capacity and are not part of the tribal government. Rather, two distinct types of legal orders exist on the Navajo Nation: that formal legal order that is a branch of Navajo government, and the peacemakers, who assist at the request of the parties. As with the Seneca, their goal is reconciliation, not assignment of blame and punishment (Zion, 1993).

Even though most petty matters were dealt with informally, many Native nations called formal meetings for explicitly legal purposes. The Dogrib, a Dene people in northern Canada, dealt informally with most problems: a thief of bannock might have a piece of bannock pinned to his shirt for the day; a thief of an animal from a trap would have to replace the stolen property with something of greater value. Serious offenses, however, required the forming of a circle. The offending party sat in the center, while other members of the band, male and female, surrounded him in a circle, discussing the disposition of the case until they reached a consensus. The process emphasized reintegration, and the discussion dealt with the entire context of the deviance. Once the matter was settled, it was over, and never spoken of again. These "circles" are still in use in northern Canada, traditionally, of course, but also as part of the sentencing process of some Canadian judges (Ryan, 1995).

In general, settlers of European origin recognized Native law when used among Native people, and were often impressed by its directness, simplicity, and honesty. But from earliest settlement, colonists also insisted on applying their law to Native people, particularly those living or working among Europeans (Kawashima, 1986; Grabowski, 1996). This insistence reflected a Eurocentric view of Native law, denying it the elevated legitimacy accorded the common or the civil law. But it also reflected the political underpinnings of any legal order: the settlers wanted to control their own communities and European law facilitated this political domination. It followed that two systems of law coexisted literally side by side, one inside of the settlement, the other just outside the walls. Native people who committed crimes within the purview of settler society were punished under American or Canadian law; those outside of the walls were dealt with according to traditional law. While this system regularly produced difficult cases, it fundamentally worked.

Yet, the coexistence of two legal systems inevitably transformed each. New forms of property such as horses, guns, and iron tools gave rise to new forms of law to regulate changing conditions. The fur trade and other changing economic forms also produced changes in Native law. Traditional legal orders that had formerly governed only internal relations had to be expanded to include laws governing relationships between different Native nations, or between Native nations and European peoples. Nor were such adjustments limited to Indian peoples. The Hudson's Bay Company, for example, borrowed many elements of Native law to govern complex trade relationships in the west and north (Reid, 1994). In the Great Lakes area in the seventeenth and early eighteenth centuries, a political and legal order developed that incorporated elements of both Native and European cultures (R. White, 1991).

While these new and changing Native laws varied greatly according to time, region, and nation, that of the Cherokee Nation of the southeastern United States is probably the most thoroughly studied. The Cherokees are both instructive and exceptional. By the 1820s, they had restructured their traditional law, copying many of the forms of United States law and political organization, while retaining core Cherokee values. Laws were formally enacted by a National Council, composed of representatives of various villages. Violations of the law drew penalties, including the death penalty, for selling Cherokee land. Individual property rights were recognized, although lands were still communally held (Strickland, 1975). This new Cherokee legal order was part of an elaborate and carefully thought out plan to protect Cherokee rights against the encroachment of American settlers. It asserted the supremacy of Cherokee law as the political grounds for claiming a national status equal to that of the United States (McLoughlin, 1986). This Cherokee legal order had a great impact on other Native tribes in the southeastern United States. The Choctaws, Chickasaws, Creeks, and Seminoles, who joined the Cherokee in the Indian Territory after removal in the 1840s, built elaborate legal systems, with formal legal codes, two-tiered court systems including both trial and appellate courts, and a pardon system modeled on American law. Most Native nations, however, did not emulate the Cherokee in creating such elaborate formal legal systems. The Six Nations of Canada relied on their Grand Council as a single branch of government, carrying out executive, legislative, and judicial functions, a structure more in keeping with traditional Native councils. The Council discussed complex legal problems, made decisions, kept a record of those decisions that amounts to an evolving common law, and enforced its decisions (Noon, 1949).

Native Law in the Twentieth Century

Events in the twentieth century further changed the evolution of Indian law. Just as a wide variety of tribes created a diversity of Native law, so too are there wide variations in the actual administration of law on Indian reservations in the United States. Beginning in the 1880s, the Bureau of Indian Affairs, the federal agency responsible for administering Indian matters, set up more than one hundred "courts of Indian offenses." Although these courts were often composed of Indian judges, they were directly administered by the Indian agent, and were used as tools of assimilation. The legality of these courts was first challenged in an incident arising on the Umatilla Reservation in 1888. Clapox broke into the jail where his friend, Minnie, was being held as punishment for being "disorderly." When he was arrested for his role in the escape, Clapox challenged the legality of Minnie's original imprisonment. A United States District Court in *U.S. v. Clapox* (34 Fed. Rep. 575 (1888)) held that these courts were not United States courts but more akin to disciplinary codes in schools, punishing children for bad behavior in an effort to socialize them to adult ways, an offensive analogy for socializing Indians to American ways.

A number of BIA courts of Indian offenses still exist. The most common current legal model, however, are tribal courts. Part of the New Deal, the Indian Reorganization Act (IRA) of 1934 permitted Indian tribes to incorporate governments that copied American local governments. A chief and a council were elected by popular vote, with many reservations divided into voting districts. Other officials, such as judges, were also either elected or appointed, according to tribal constitutions. While majoritarian democracy is deeply rooted in Anglo-American culture, it has little meaning in most Indian cultures. In fact, this democratic facade undermines traditional governance mechanisms, often based on a deeply rooted consensus reached over many hours of discussion. Some number of Indian nations either are now or have historically gone through complex factional struggles between adherents of traditional law and adherents of BIA law, as both systems exist side by side on many reservations (Whiteley, 1988; Porter, 1997).

Modern tribal court structures, sometimes including appellate courts, can be as complex as the courts of adjacent states. Tribal judges are often well-trained and while an increasing number are formally trained as lawyers, most are not. A tribal prosecutor may represent the tribe, and a tribal public defender often represents the defendant. Although the full range of procedures of federal or state courts are not required, the proceedings of tribal courts are often quite similar, and most resemble lower court proceedings in neighboring non-Indian communities. Many of these proceedings are held in Indian languages. Most of the tribes have detailed legal codes, often adapted from some American source. Modern court rooms exist on many reservations, often part of a criminal justice complex that includes a police station and a jail. The Bureau of Indian Affairs maintains a police academy, as does the Navajo Nation. Here tribal police officers are trained in a course of study not unlike other police training programs. The criminal justice complexes of populous reservations are sprawling, employing dozens, occasionally even hundreds, of people. Smaller reservations have less elaborate facilities and typically hold court in community halls or schools and often keep their prisoners in "contract jails" – off reservation in local jails with the tribe paying for cell space.

While both the substantive laws applied in these courts and the rules that govern these trials are made by the Indian nations, Congress in 1968 passed the "Indian Civil Rights Act" providing some of the basic features of American due process in tribal courts. The legal proceedings of Native nations do not occur under the United States Constitution, so there is no appeal to United States courts unless some specific federal law or constitutional provision is violated. Federal financial assistance for Indian police forces and jails, however, is dependent on compliance with federally set standards. A good deal of tribal sovereignty is lost in these processes, but most tribes are dependent on the federal government for financial assistance. In this sense Indian sovereignty is often compromised to poverty, much like the sovereignty of third world countries.

With hundreds of different Native legal processes occurring across North America any generalizations about Native American courts of justice are difficult. Many tribes use proceedings that look very much like those of ordinary American small town courts: thousands of petty offenders are tried and sentenced to fines and jail terms, to be served in a tribal jail. Other Indian nations are more concerned with incorporating traditional Native values in their proceedings (Tso, 1989). Some Native scholars have criticized tribal courts for adopting too many of the forms of American law and, in the process, losing their traditional reconciliation function (Porter, 1997). Other scholars have praised these courts, arguing that they provide a structure to protect and defend Native law and tradition (Pommersheim, 1995; Newton, 1998). Nell Jessup Newton has surveyed the reported cases of twenty tribal courts, reporting a subtle and complex jurisprudence in tribal law (Newton, 1998). In any case, it is clear that an Indian common law is being applied in tribal courts, although scholars might disagree about its extent and nature (Cooter and Fikentscher, 1998).

Despite these changes in Native law, one should also recognize that traditional law continues to function in many Native communities in the hands of traditional chiefs and elders. In the United States a number of Indian nations, especially in the Southwest, have never accepted any form of law imposed by the United States and still retain their traditional system of law. Traditional bodies or individual peacemakers apply an unwritten law of the community, a law that has evolved to deal with modern problems. Even Native nations with IRA courts often have different kinds of traditional law operating at the same time, either in competition with the "official" courts, or with their tacit support and consent. In Canada, where Native sovereignty is not recognized by Canadian law, such traditional law has operated without any official sanction, but often quite openly in Native communities.

It is important to remember that, because of economics and geography, most Native people also live under the same state and provincial law as their non-Native neighbors. No more than half of all Native people in the United States live on Indian reservations, and Native people living outside of "Indian country" are under the general law of their state, the same as any other person. Many cities and towns near Indian reservations have developed reputations for racist local law enforcement, filling jails with Indians held on a range of minor changes. In addition, many Indian communities, for various reasons, do not have their own laws or legal institutions. Most of these are in the eastern United States, but Indian communities across the country have been put under state jurisdiction. Different legal actions and historical events led to this result, including the termination of the Indian Territory in Oklahoma in the late nineteenth century, the termination of many tribes during the 1950s, or the abdication of federal protection of Indian rights as in Texas, California, and New York. While traditional peacemaking may go on in these communities, no special regime of Indian law governs. These disparate regimes give rise to many intergovernmental disputes, with states often trying to assert increasing authority over "Indian country."

Although Indian law was as recognized in colonial Canada as it was in the United States, modern Canada does not recognize Indian sovereignty as providing a distinct legal regime on Indian reserves, therefore the ordinary civil and criminal law of Canada generally applies to Indian nations. There has been a good deal of Native resistance to this domination, and it is clear that Native law continues to operate without the formal sanction of Canadian law.

The Cherokee Cases, "Domestic Dependent Nations," and Federal Indian Law

The legal challenge that the Cherokee Nation posed to unfettered settler expansion set the stage for the "Cherokee cases," the foundational United States cases in Indian rights under American law and the common law. In the first of these cases, that of Corn Tassel (an unreported case) in 1830, Chief Justice John Marshall granted a stay of execution, blocking the State of Georgia from executing Corn Tassel, a Cherokee who denied Georgia's legal jurisdiction on Cherokee lands. Georgia hanged Corn Tassel in violation of Marshall's order, a deliberate violation of both Cherokee and federal law (Harring, 1994).

The Cherokees were back in the United States Supreme Court the next year with a lawsuit against the State of Georgia, *Cherokee Nation v. Georgia* (30 U.S. 25 (1831)). The issue this time was jurisdictional: the Cherokees filed their lawsuit directly in the United States Supreme Court as a case between a state and a foreign nation, again asserting their sovereign status as an Indian nation. They lost, with Chief Justice Marshall holding that the Cherokees were not a foreign nation and thus leaving the Supreme Court without jurisdiction over the case.

The next year the Cherokees – with what was now obviously a carefully planned legal strategy – were back in the Supreme Court. This case, *Worcester v. Georgia* (31 U.S. 515 (1832)), is the most critical of the three foundational cases in United States Indian law. The Supreme Court had ruled in *Cherokee Nation v. Georgia* that the Cherokee Nation was a "domestic dependent nation" having a special relationship with the government of the United States, and that no state had jurisdiction over their lands. Chief Justice John Marshall held that this unique legal status had been created through a long history of interaction between the Cherokees and British and United States authorities, including a nation-to-nation treaty process. While the relationship was complex and unique, the Cherokee Nation had many of the attributes of nations. These included a substantial measure of sovereignty, although this did not amount to full sovereignty because of a long history under the protection of the United States (G. White, 1988).

President Andrew Jackson, contemptuous of the Supreme Court's opinion, forced the removal of the Cherokees – and later many other eastern Indian nations – to the west of the Mississippi. The "Indian Territory," most of modern-day Oklahoma, became the home of the Cherokees, Choctaws, Chickasaws, Creeks, and Seminoles. There these nations organized their own political and legal orders, electing chiefs, councils, judges, and other officials. They enacted their own laws, codes that incorporated features from both their traditional cultures as well as American law. These governments were so successful that these nations were dubbed the "five civilized tribes," because they had outwardly taken on so many of the characteristics of the United States. But the reality was far more complex, as Native traditions were protected behind this veneer.

Indian judges regularly held court, with offenders brought in by Indian law enforcement officers. A wide variety of punishments were used, including the death penalty. As late as 1896 in *Talton v. Mayes* (163 U.S. 376), the legality of these proceedings was upheld by the United States Supreme Court. A Cherokee murderer appealed, arguing that his Cherokee Nation death sentence was not legal under United States law. The Supreme Court held that the Cherokee Nation had a sovereign right to its own law, and that United States law did not govern the case, leaving the Court with no jurisdiction over the Cherokee Nation. Talton was promptly executed under Cherokee law but, ironically, by the time of his execution the United States Congress had unilaterally terminated the powers of the courts of the Indian nations in the Indian Territory. After a rebellion by the Creek leader, Crazy Snake, and others, the legal institutions of these nations went underground, not re-emerging until the middle of the twentieth century (Harring, 1994).

Kagama, Lone Wolf, and the Plenary Power Doctrine

Worcester, *Crow Dog*, and *Talton* represent the traditional, "limited sovereignty" position within United States Indian law. This complex position suggests that, unless inconsistent with their dependent position under federal authority, the Indian nations retain their sovereignty. Another line of cases, however, suggests that Congress had a "plenary power" over Indian nations. This doctrine stems from two late nineteenth-century cases, *Kagama* and *Lone Wolf*. *United States v. Kagama* (118 U.S. 375 (1886)) followed directly from *Crow Dog*. Congress reacted to the Supreme Court's holding that the United States lacked jurisdiction over crimes between Indians in "Indian country" by passing the Major Crimes Act, asserting federal jurisdiction over Indians who committed any of seven serious crimes in Indian country. Kagama, a Klamath, killed Pactah Billy in a land dispute on the Hoopa Reservation in northern California. Tried and convicted of murder under this new law, he appealed. The United States Supreme Court upheld federal jurisdiction over Indian crimes, holding that Congress had plenary power over the Indian tribes, a complete power in any area (Harring, 1994: 142–53).

Lone Wolf v. Hitchcock (187 U.S. 553 (1903)) extended this logic to Indian lands. The lands of the Kiowas, Comanches, and Apaches in Oklahoma were taken from them and allocated to white settlers. Lone Wolf, a Kiowa chief, sued, arguing that these Indian lands were protected by treaty rights. The United States Supreme Court held that Congress's power over Indian lands was also plenary, in effect denying the Indians any legal rights (Clark, 1994).

Since *Lone Wolf* there have been thousands of cases decided in American courts, and the tension between the sovereignty line of cases and the plenary power line of cases continues (Wilkinson, 1987). *Lone Wolf*, itself, has never been overruled, but it is now clear that Native people hold definite rights to their land that cannot be unilaterally abrogated by Congress. *United States v. Sioux Nation of Indians* (448 U.S. 371 (1980)) held that Sioux treaty rights to the Black Hills were broken by the United States, and the Nation was awarded money damages – based on the 1876 value of the Black Hills. The Sioux refused the money, arguing that the remedy for unlawfully taking land is the return of the land: the Black Hills are still almost entirely held by the United States government (Lazarus, 1991).

Indian law presumptively governs every matter internal to an Indian nation unless the United States Congress has directly and expressly intervened and asserted federal plenary power. *Williams v. Lee* (358 U.S. 217 (1959)), for example, affirmed the Navajo court's jurisdiction in a civil dispute between a trader and a Navajo citizen, and explicitly declared a United States policy of promoting sovereignty and self-government in Indian communities. The decision enabled Indian nations to establish their own governments and legal systems, make their own laws, provide their own fire and police protection, make their own hunting, fishing, zoning, and environmental regulations, and generally regulate all matters of health, education, and welfare. To finance these functions, Indian nations have the power to levy taxes. In practice the exercise of these powers is complex. Many Indian nations, for example, have such small populations (only a handful have more than 10,000 people; hundreds of Native communities have less than 1,000 people) that the costs of providing government services are prohibitive. Consequently, many small communities have negotiated agreements with other tribes or even with the states to provide such services. Since the relationship between Indian tribes and the United States is a federal matter, the states, following *Worcester*, have no authority over Indians in "Indian country."

Political considerations, including the fact that Congressmen and Senators represent the citizens of individual states, have resulted in even more complex situations. The plenary power doctrine, which puts the Indian tribes under the political control of Congress, has meant that Congress has passed a number of laws subjecting the tribes to various kinds of control by the states. Perhaps typical is the Indian Gaming Regulatory Act of 1988 which requires tribes that operate gambling operations to enter into "compacts" with the state in which they are located. These are agreements that regulate the scope of gambling and often give the states some payment in exchange. *Seminole Nation* holds that it violates the constitutional principle of federalism to force a state into any compact negotiation with an Indian nation, so these compacts can be used to undermine tribal sovereignty. Other agreements between the tribes and the states are founded on a greater degree of mutual respect, and include agreements for mutual police, fire, and emergency services.

Native Law in Canada

Canada and the United States share a common British and French colonial history. The Royal Proclamation of 1763 legally enshrined a broad regime of Native rights throughout British North America, as well as a treaty process required to purchase Indian lands. Hundreds of treaties followed, in both the United States and Canada (Jones, 1982). The core of the relationship between Native people and the Crown derives from this treaty process, and it has been incorporated into the laws of both countries.

The treaty instruments themselves are legal documents, a kind of international contract. There is no question that Native people understood the treaties differently than did Canadians and Americans (Treaty 7 Elders, 1996). The legal concepts "sovereignty," "property," "ownership," and "land sale" cannot have been adequately translated in the treaty process. As a result, a distinct set of rules of treaty interpretation have evolved in both Canada and the United States requiring treaties to be interpreted "largely and liberally" in favor of the Indians. The Washington State fishing treaties, for example, guaranteed the Indians some undefined share of the fish, leading a U.S. District Court to decide that "sharing" meant an even division, 50 percent, the same meaning that it had in a kindergarten class (Cohen, 1986). But most courts have not been so generous and the legal interpretation of treaties continues to be a disputed matter.

Native law in Canada, as in the United States, is a unique area of law with its own interpretive frameworks. But political and cultural differences between the United States and Canada produced a distinct federal law in Canada. Canada, for political reasons, wanted an orderly frontier. As a result the national government kept political control of Native people, and the Canadian courts had much less of a role in defining Native rights during the nineteenth century, deferring instead to the political process. It follows from this that no concept of Native sovereignty emerged from Canadian politics, as it did from the Marshall Court. While Native people clearly had their own laws and legal orders, these primarily functioned beyond the reach of Canadian authorities. Because Canada is a large and sparsely populated country, many northern communities were isolated from Canadian law until well into the twentieth century (Harring, 1988). At the same time, however, Canadian authorities recognized this difficulty and often took extraordinary measures to reach Native communities with Canadian law. A significant part of the history of the Royal Canadian Mounted Police is their long reach, as agents of the Crown, into the most remote parts of Canada (Morrison, 1985; Macleod, 1976). Indeed, Canadian courts still travel to the most remote Native villages, carrying out this tradition of bringing the Queen's law to Native people.

Canadian courts regularly decided Native rights cases conservatively, with little recognition of Native rights. The "Indian Title Case," *St. Catharine's Milling and Lumber Company v. R.*, coursed through three Canadian courts and the Privy Council in the 1880s. Ultimately, it was decided that Native people had a "usufructuary" right to the land, that is, some right to occupy it, but not any kind of land title. Ironically, no Native people were parties in the case: it was between the national government and the Province of Ontario with the question of Native rights underlying each side's claim (Harring, 1998: 125–47). But Native people did make their way to court. As early as the 1880s, the Nisga'a of British Columbia asserted their land rights in a variety of forums, eventually losing in the Supreme Court of Canada in *Calder v. Attorney General of British Columbia* ([1973] S.C.R. 313). Although four justices held that the Nisga'a had clear aboriginal land rights, four held that no such Native land rights existed. With the critical ninth justice holding that the Court lacked jurisdiction, the Nisga'a lost.

Native people, however, did not abandon their land claims and they brought many other cases to Canadian courts. The Gitksan and Wet'suwet'en chiefs of northern British Columbia brought the most elaborate claim, deeply rooted in their traditional law. *Delgamuukw v. Attorney General of British Columbia and Attorney General of Canada* ([1990] 48 B.C. 211; [1993] 5 W.W.R. 97) took two years to try in the Supreme Court of British Columbia. The Gitksan and Wet'suwet'en lost, but the court's 400-page judgment was attacked by many scholars for both its racism and its limited and narrow view of Native land rights. Ultimately, this judgment was reversed in a landmark ruling by the Supreme Court of Canada ([1997] S.C.R. 1010). The ruling held that Native land rights were protected under the Canadian Constitution and that the trial judge had erred in not giving proper weight to Native oral history in deciding whether these rights existed in the context of *Delgamuukw*. The case was sent back to the British Columbia courts for retrial.

Most Native law cases in Canada have concerned land or hunting and fishing rights. Native political sovereignty has not been directly recognized by Canadian courts, a major difference between Canadian and American law. Thus, First Nations in Canada have never had a right, under Canadian law, to their own law as a matter of their sovereignty. Native law, of course, has existed in Canada all of this time, often, as in the Six Nations, in the open, operating in competition with Canadian law. Canada's answer to Native sovereignty had been a comprehensive Indian Act, regulating every aspect of Indian life from "cradle to grave," incorporating a system of legal dualism that treated Indians as children, subject to an entirely different set of legal rights than other Canadians. The most infamous feature of these Indian Acts were laws banning the potlatch, sun dance, and other Native religious ceremonies (Pettipas, 1994; Cole and Chaikin, 1990). While Native people protected their culture by taking many elements of it "underground," incalculable damage was done to Native cultures through these repressive laws.

The Constitution Act of 1982 recognized "existing aboriginal rights," and heralded a new era of Native rights in Canada. The full range of the "existing aboriginal rights" language of the Canadian Constitution is still undefined, and has spurred a rush of litigation. *R. v. Sparrow* ([1990] 1 S.C.R. 1075) sets out a complex test that has been refined in succeeding cases, but it essentially requires each court to make a detailed inquiry into Native history to discover the meaning of each particular right, then to discover whether it has been "extinguished." Finally, if the right still exists it must be balanced against other public policy requirements. *R. v. Van der Peet* ([1996] 25 C.R. 507) showed how limited the *Sparrow* test could be, very narrowly interpreting the meaning of traditional Stó:lõ exchange of fish in such a way as to deny any commercial fishing rights.

The tension inherent in these cases, as in the United States, is that Canadian courts must "balance" Native interests with the interests of the majority population, a process that often does not fully recognize Native interests, nor honor Native history. What is needed is a greater recognition of Native law and Native rights. This, in turn, requires the recognition of a new "common law" in North America that incorporates Native law into the Eurocentric law that United States and Canadian courts now apply, and rejects the inherent ethnocentrism and imperialism that dominates the existing legal relationship between Native people and the Canadian and American states. Accepting Native law and Native legal history as equal to American and Canadian law in deciding cases is an important step in this process. Similarly, a "new sovereignty" that recognizes Native nations with unique and historic relationships with the United States and Canada is also a necessary element of this process.

Conclusion

Since relationships between Native people and the modern Canadian and American states are legally defined, deep conflicts over the content and meaning of Indian law are occurring in both countries. Events at the turn of the twenty-first century sharpened these differences. Native people have taken stock of their situation and put renewed confidence in their own law, increasing its use in order to redefine their position within the United States and Canada and making Indian law an important means for the expression of Indian identity. Canadian historian Tony Hall (1995), for example, describes a conflict between Ojibwa people and Canadian authorities at Long Lake 58 Reserve in northern Ontario. When provincial police attempted to arrest Native protesters for "trespassing," for blocking the main line of the Canadian National Railroad, the Ojibwa challenged the legitimacy of the law itself, demanding to see the title of the Canadian government to their land. Their point is an obvious one: how is it that their Native title is subordinate to a Canadian title based on British feudal land law? Such disputes end up in Canadian and American courts but underlying them are Native conceptions of law and justice that do not depend on the rulings of these courts. Native title exists in Indian common law, whether American and Canadian courts recognize it or not. No Ojibwa at Long Lake 58 particularly cared whether or not they were arrested for "trespassing": their assertion of their legal rights was the only thing that mattered.

At the same time that Native people are putting more stock in their own law and traditions, their recognition that the legal victories won in American and Canadian courts have not resolved claims to land or sovereignty has tempered Native legal activism. This is particularly true in the United States, where two decades of conservative rule has packed the federal courts with judges unsympathetic to Indian matters. The United States Supreme Court itself handed down a long string of losses to the Indian nations in the 1990s. Their interpretation of basic doctrines in Indian law has become increasingly restrictive, often separating doctrine from historical context. The Canadian Supreme Court has refused to define the "existing aboriginal rights" guaranteed in the Constitution Act of 1982, leaving doubtful when, and if, they ever will. This puts much more pressure on Indian nations themselves to assert their own rights, without relying on American or Canadian law. It obviously discourages litigation.

This continued existence of two systems of law and justice, side by side, provides opportunity and challenge, even if there are jurisdictional difficulties. The recognition that Native cultures have unique sets of values that structure "Indian law" implicitly contrasts with both American and Canadian law, forcing both societies to rethink their own cultural values as embodied in their law. It is not clear at all, for example, that the modern criminal justice's punishment-based policy honors the promise of American or Canadian democracy as fully as does a Native insistence on reconciliation and respect. Native communities in Canada have increasingly demanded the right to their own local criminal justice institutions, simply to stop the loss of their young people. United States Indian nations, which have their own courts modeled after nearby state courts, have become increasingly disposed to incorporating more Indian law in their case dispositions in an effort to rebuild their traditions.

The continued recognition of Indian law accords the Indian nations their proper status as nations, holding traditional authority derived not from conquest, nor from the Queen, but from their own continued existence as Native sovereignties. Legal pluralism, the coexistence of different legal systems side by side, has been in effect in North America since the arrival of European settlers. The continued recognition and support of the efforts of Native nations to assert and defend their own laws holds the promise of an enriched law and legal culture for all people.

BIBLIOGRAPHY

Clark, Blue 1994: *Lone Wolf v. Hitchcock: Treaty Rights & Indian Law at the End of the Nineteenth Century* (Lincoln: University of Nebraska Press).

Clark, Bruce 1990: *Native Liberty, Crown Sovereignty: The Existing Aboriginal Right of Self-Government in Canada* (Montreal: McGill-Queens University Press).

Clinton, Robert, Nell Jessup Newton, and Monroe Price 1990: *American Indian Law* (Charlottesville: Michie).

Cohen, Fay G. 1986: *Treaties on Trial: The Continuing Controversy over Northwest Indian Fishing Rights* (Seattle: University of Washington Press).

Cole, Douglas and Ira Chaikin 1990: *An Iron Hand Upon the People: The Law against the Potlatch on the Northwest Coast* (Vancouver: University of British Columbia Press).

Cooter, Robert and Wolfgang Fikentscher 1998: "Indian Common Law: The Role of Custom in American Indian Tribal Courts, Part I," *The American Journal of Comparative Law* 46: 287–337, 509–80.

Codere, Helen 1950: *Fighting with Property: A Study of Kwakiutl Potlatching and Warfare, 1792–1930* (Seattle: University of Washington Press).

Getches, David H., Charles F. Wilkinson, and Robert A. Williams, Jr. 1998: *Federal Indian Law: Cases and Materials* (4th edn.) (St. Paul: West Publishing Company).

Grabowski, Jan 1996: "French Criminal Justice and Indians in Montreal, 1670–1760," *Ethnohistory* 43: 405–29.

Hall, Anthony 1995: "Treaties, Trains, and Troubled National Dreams: Reflections on the Indian Summer in Northern Ontario, 1990," in Louis A. Knafla and Susan W. S. Binnie (eds.), *Law, Society, and the State: Essays in Modern Legal History* (Toronto: University of Toronto Press), pp. 290–320.

Harring, Sidney L. 1989: "The Rich Men of the Country: Canadian Law in the Land of the Copper Inuit, 1914–1930," *Ottawa Law Review* 21(1).

Harring, Sidney L. 1994: *Crow Dog's Case: American Indian Sovereignty, Tribal Law, and United States Law in the Nineteenth Century* (Cambridge: Cambridge University Press).

Harring, Sidney L. 1998: *White Man's Law: Native People in Nineteenth Century Canadian Jurisprudence* (Toronto: Osgoode Society/University of Toronto Press).

Hoebel, E. Adamson 1940: *The Political Organization and Law Ways of the Comanche Indians*. Memoirs of the American Anthropological Association, 54 (Menasha, WI: American Anthropological Association).

Hoebel, E. Adamson 1955: *The Law of Primitive Man* (Cambridge, MA: Harvard University Press).

Johnson, D. Bruce 1986: "The Formation and Protection of Property Rights among the Southern Kwakiutl Indians," *Journal of Legal Studies* 15: 41–67.

Jones, Dorothy V. 1982: *License for Empire: Colonialism by Treaty in Early America* (Chicago: University of Chicago Press).

Kawashima, Yasuhide 1986: *Puritan Justice and the Indian: White Man's Law in Massachusetts, 1630–1763* (Middletown, CT: Wesleyan University Press).

King, Rachel 1998: "Bush Justice: The Intersection of Alaska Natives and the Criminal Justice System in Rural Alaska," *Oregon Law Review* 77: 1–57.

Lazarus, Edward 1991: *Black Hills White Justice: The Sioux Nation Versus the United States, 1775 to the Present* (New York: Harper/Collins).

Llewellyn, Karl and E. A. Hoebel 1941: *The Cheyenne Way: Conflict and Case Law in Primitive Jurisprudence* (Norman: University of Oklahoma Press).

Lowie, Robert 1943: "Property Rights and Coercive Powers of Plains Indian Military Societies," *Journal of Legal and Political Sociology* 1: 59–71.

Lyons, Oren et al. 1992: *Exiled in the Land of the Free: Democracy, Indian Nations, and the U.S. Constitution* (Santa Fe: Clear Light Publishers).

Macleod, Rod C. 1976: *The North-West Mounted Police and Law Enforcement, 1873–1905* (Toronto: University of Toronto Press).

MacLeod, William Christie 1937: "Police and Punishment among Native Americans of the Plains," *Journal of Criminal Law, Criminology, and Police Service* 27: 181–395.

McLoughlin, William G. 1986: *Cherokee Renascence in the New Republic* (Princeton: Princeton University Press).

Mills, Antonia 1994: *Eagle Down is Our Law: Witsuwit'en Law, Feasts, and Land Claims* (Vancouver: University of British Columbia Press).

Morrison, William R. 1985: *Showing the Flag: The Mounted Police and Canadian Sovereignty in the North, 1894–1925* (Vancouver: University of British Columbia Press).

Morse, Bradford 1985: *Aboriginal Peoples and the Law: Indian, Métis and Inuit Rights in Canada* (Ottawa: Carleton University Press).

Newton, Nell Jessup 1998: "Tribal Court Praxis: One Year in the Life of Twenty Tribal Courts," *American Indian Law Review* 22: 285–353.

Niezen, Ronald 1998: *Defending the Land: Sovereignty and Forest Life in James Bay Cree Society* (Needham Heights, MA: Allyn and Bacon).

Noon, John A. 1949: *Law and Government of the Grand River Iroquois* (New York: Viking Fund Publications in Anthropology).

Pettipas, Katherine 1994: *Severing the Ties that Bind: Government Repression of Indigenous Religious Ceremonies on the Prairies* (Winnipeg: University of Manitoba Press).

Pommersheim, Frank 1995: *Braid of Feathers: American Indian Law in Contemporary Tribal Life* (Berkeley: University of California Press).

Porter, Robert B. 1997: "Strengthening Tribal Sovereignty Through Peacemaking: How the Anglo-American Legal Tradition Destroys Indigenous Societies," *Columbia Human Rights Law Review* 28: 235–96.

Provisne, John 1934: "The Underlying Sanctions of Plains Indian Culture." Ph.D. dissertation, University of Chicago.

Reid, John Phillip 1970: *A Law of Blood: The Primitive Law of the Cherokee Nation* (New York: New York University Press).

Reid, John Phillip 1993a: "Principles of Vengeance: Fur Trappers, Indians, and Retaliation for Homicide in the Transboundary North American West," *Western Historical Quarterly* 24: 21–43.

Reid, John Phillip 1993b: "Certainty of Vengeance: The Hudson's Bay Company and Retaliation in Kind against Indian Offenders in New Caledonia," *Montana: The Magazine of Western History* 43: 4–17.

Reid, John Phillip 1994: "Restraints of Vengeance: Retaliation in Kind and the Use of Indian Law in the Old Oregon Country," *Oregon Historical Quarterly* 95: 48–91.

Richardson, Jane 1940: *Law and Status Among the Kiowa Indians* (New York: J. J. Augustin).

Ryan, Joan 1995: *Doing Things the Right Way: Dene Traditional Justice in Lac La Martre* (Calgary: University of Calgary Press).

Smith, Watson and John Roberts 1954: *Zuni Law: A Field of Values* (Cambridge, MA: Peabody Museum, Harvard University).

Strickland, Rennard 1975: *Fire and the Spirits: Cherokee Law From Clan to Court* (Norman: University of Oklahoma Press).

Treaty 7 Elders and Tribal Council 1996: *The True Spirit and Original Intent of Treaty 7* (Montreal: McGill-Queens University Press).

Tso, Tom 1989: "The Process of Decision Making in Tribal Courts," *Arizona Law Review* 31, 225–35.

Whaley, Rick and Walter Bresette 1994: *Walleye Warriors: An Effective Alliance Against Racism and for the Earth* (Philadelphia: New Society Publishers).

White, Bruce M. 1987: "A Skilled Game of Exchange: Ojibwa Fur Trade Protocol," *Minnesota History* (Summer): 229–40.

White, G. Edward 1988: *The Marshall Court and Cultural Change, 1815–35* (New York: Macmillan).

White, Richard 1991: *The Middle Ground: Indians, Empires, and Republics in the Great Lakes Region, 1650–1815* (Cambridge: Cambridge University Press).

Whiteley, Peter M. 1988: *Deliberate Acts: Changing Hopi Culture Through the Oraibi Split* (Tucson: University of Arizona Press).

Wilkins, David 1997: *American Indian Sovereignty and the U.S. Supreme Court* (Austin: University of Texas Press).

Wilkinson, Charles 1987: *American Indians, Time, and the Law* (New Haven: Yale University Press).

Williams, Robert A., Jr. 1990: *The American Indian in Western Legal Thought: The Discourses of Conquest* (New York: Oxford University Press).

Williams, Robert A., Jr. 1997: *Linking Arms Together: American Indian Treaty Visions of Law and Peace, 1600–1800* (New York: Oxford University Press).

Woodward, Jack 1989: *Native Law* (Toronto: Carswell).

Wunder, John 1994: *"Retained by the People": A History of American Indians and the Bill of Rights* (New York: Oxford University Press).

Zion, James 1993: "The Navajo Justice and Harmony Ceremony," *Mediation Quarterly* 10(327).

25

Sovereignty

Taiaiake Alfred

Sovereignty. The word, so commonly used, refers to supreme political authority, independent and unlimited by any other power. Discussion of the term "sovereignty" in relation to indigenous peoples, however, must be framed differently, within an intellectual framework of internal colonization. Internal colonization is the historical process and political reality defined in the structures and techniques of government that consolidate the domination of indigenous peoples by a foreign yet sovereign settler state. While internal colonization describes the political reality of most indigenous peoples, one should also note that the discourse of state sovereignty is and has been contested in real and theoretical ways since its imposition. The inter/counterplay of state sovereignty doctrines – rooted in notions of dominion – with and against indigenous concepts of political relations – rooted in notions of freedom, respect, and autonomy – frames the discourse on indigenous "sovereignty" at its broadest level.

The practice of history cannot help but be implicated in colonization. Indeed, most discussions of indigenous sovereignty are founded on a particular and instrumental reading of history that serves to undergird internal colonization. Fair and just instances of interaction between indigenous and non-indigenous peoples are legion; yet mythic narratives and legal understandings of state sovereignty in North America have consciously obscured justice in the service of the colonial project. From the earliest times, relations between indigenous peoples and European newcomers vacillated within the normal parameters that characterize any relation between autonomous political groups. Familiar relations – war, peace, cooperation, antagonism, and shifting dominance and subservience – are all to be found in our shared history. Yet the actual history of our plural existence has been erased by the narrow fictions of a single sovereignty. Controlling, univerzalizing, and assimilating, these fictions have been imposed in the form of law on weakened but resistant and remembering peoples.

European sovereignties in North America first legitimated themselves through treaty relationships entered into by Europeans and indigenous nations. North

American settler states (Canada and the United States, with their predecessor states Holland, Spain, France, and England) gained legitimacy as legal entities only by the expressed consent through treaty of the original occupiers and governors of North America. The founding documents of state sovereignty recognize this fact: all Dutch and French treaties with indigenous peoples, the Treaty of Utrecht, the Articles of Capitulation and the Royal Proclamation (made in a context of military interdependency between the British and indigenous nations) all contain explicit reference to the independent nationhood of indigenous peoples. As the era of European exploration and discovery gave way to settlement, with its concomitant need for balanced peaceful relations with indigenous nations, the states' charter documents made clear reference to the separate political existence and territorial independence of indigenous peoples.

None of this historical diversity is reflected in the official history and doctrinal bases of settler state sovereignty today. Rather, Canada and the United States have written self-serving histories of discovery, conquest, and settlement that wipe out any reference to the original relations between indigenous peoples and Europeans. This *post facto* claim of European "sovereignty" is limited by two main caveats. The first is factual: the mere documentation of European assertions of hegemonic sovereignty does not necessarily indicate proof of its achievement. European control over actual territory was tenuous at best; and the political existence of European settler states was a *negotiated* reality until well into the nineteenth century (and not completely achieved, even in colonial mythology, until the end of the nineteenth century in the United States and to this day in Canada).

The second limitation is theoretical: the discourse of sovereignty upon which the current *post facto* justification rests is an exclusively European discourse. That is, European assertions in both a legal and a political sense were made strictly vis-à-vis other European powers, and did not impinge upon or necessarily even affect in law or politics the rights and status of indigenous nations. It is only from our distant historical vantage point, and standing upon a counterfactual rock, that we are able to rationalize European usurpations of indigenous sovereignty as justified.

If sovereignty has been neither legitimized nor justified, it has nevertheless limited the ways we are able to think, suggesting always a conceptual and definitional problem centered on the accommodation of indigenous peoples within a "legitimate" framework of settler state governance. When we step outside this discourse, we confront a different problematic, that of the state's "sovereignty" itself, and its actual meaning in contrast to the facts and the potential that exists for a nation-to-nation relationship.

Indigenous scholars have focused on this problematic to profound effect. Russel Barsh and James Henderson, for example, explored the process of intellectual obscurantism in close detail in *The Road: Indian Tribes and Political Liberty*. Barsh and Henderson concentrated on the United States and the creation of a historical narrative that completely ignored basic principles of natural law and the philosophical underpinnings of American notions of liberty and equality. They trace the evolution of the doctrine of tribal sovereignty in United States law through judicial decisions, and demonstrate the ways in which the process misrepresented the true potential of liberal principles – and even the United States Constitution – to accommodate notions of indigenous nationhood.

The Road is a landmark work. It embarked on a critique from within, arguing for recognition of indigenous peoples' rights *within* the historic and legal frame of state sovereignty. Ultimately, Barsh and Henderson subjected the rationale for indigenous or "tribal" liberty to criteria defined by the framers of the United States Constitution. The problem, they argued, was the subjection of principle to politics, and unprincipled decisions by the state judiciaries. Barsh and Henderson designed a "theory of the tribe in the American nation" (p. 205), and in doing so advanced the theoretical notion of a coexistence of indigenous and state sovereignty that was hamstrung as a conceptual tool by the weight of skewed legal precedent and the reality of the political context. In this sense, *The Road* follows the trajectory – native sovereignty within and in relation to state sovereignty – first set forth in the 1830s in the Cherokee decisions, which suggested that tribes were "domestic dependent nations" (see Harring, this volume).

The entanglement of indigenous peoples within the institutional frame of the colonial state of course went beyond legal doctrines. The practice of sovereignty in the structures of government and the building of institutional relationships between indigenous governments and state agencies offered another forum for the subordination of principle. In two volumes, *American Indians, American Justice* and *The Nations Within*, Vine Deloria, Jr. and Clifford Lytle first outlined how the legal denial of indigenous rights in the courts was mirrored in governing structures that embedded the false notion of European superiority in indigenous community life. The example of the United States' usurpation of indigenous nationhood clarified how the state generally uses not only political and economic but also certain intellectual strategies to impose and maintain its dominance. Such linking of the intellectual and structural forms of colonialism have produced some of the deepest analyses of the issue.

In considering the question of the "sovereignty" of indigenous peoples within its territorial borders, the state takes various positions: the classic strategies include outright denial of indigenous rights; a theoretical acceptance of indigenous rights combined with an assertion that these have been extinguished historically; and legal doctrines that transform indigenous rights from their autonomous nature to contingent rights, existing only within the framework of colonial law. Scholars have documented fully the manifestation of these strategies in the various policies implemented by settler states in the modern era: domestication, termination, assimilation (see Edmunds, Fixico, this volume).

With the minor concession that in both Canada and the United States the federal government itself has maintained and defended its powers over indigenous peoples vis-à-vis states and provinces, the potential for recognition of indigenous nationhood has gone unrealized. There has been a total theoretical exclusion and extinguishing of indigenous nationhood, leading to what a recent United Nations Human Rights Commission study (1999) labeled the unjust "domestication" of indigenous nationhood.

Indigenous peoples nonetheless struggled to achieve a degree of freedom and power within the intellectual and political environment created out of the colonial domestication project and settler state sovereignty. For generations, indigenous peoples fought to preserve the integrity of their nations and the independent bases of their existence. They were successful in countering the colonial project to the extent that they survived (a monumental human achievement given the intensive efforts of two modern industrial states to eradicate them). Yet by the late 1980s, the increasing erosions of tribal governing powers in the United States and failed attempts to enshrine a recognition of indigenous nationhood in the Canadian constitution made it clear that the governments of Canada and the United States were incapable of liberalizing their relationships with "the nations within."

As they regained their capacity to govern themselves and began to re-assert the earlier principles of the nation-to-nation relationship between indigenous peoples and states, indigenous people began to question seriously the viability of working within the system, of considering themselves "nations within." The questioning often came out of models – tribal and band councils dependent upon and administering federal funds, for example – that recognized indigenous sovereignty yet always subsumed it to that of the state. A new intellectual approach began to emerge in the critique of the fundamental pillars by which the United States and Canada claimed legal authority over indigenous peoples and lands. Reflecting critical trends in other academic disciplines, legal scholarship began the project of deconstructing the architecture of colonial domination. Perhaps the two most important strategies to re-achieve a political plurality in the face of the dominance of state sovereignty have been woven together: on the one hand, the assertion of a prior and coexisting sovereignty, and, on the other, the assertion of a right of self-determination for indigenous peoples in international law.

The most thorough and illuminating of the critical legal studies of the indigenous–state relationship is Robert Williams' *The American Indian in Western Legal Thought*. Its description of how law – embodying all of the racist assumptions of medieval Europe – has served as the European colonizers' most effective instrument of genocide destroys the arguments of those who would defend the justice of the colonial state. Williams shows how the deep roots of European belief in their own cultural and racial superiority underlie all discussions of the interaction between whites and indigenous peoples on the issue of sovereignty. After Williams' critique, any history of the concept of sovereignty in North America must trace the manipulation of the concept as it evolved to justify the elimination of indigenous peoples. By examining the deep history of European thought on indigenous peoples – what he calls the "discourse of conquest" – Williams showed how the entire discussion of sovereignty in North America represents the calculated triumph of illogic and interest over truth and justice.

After the end of the imperial era and the foundation of the North American states, in no instance did principles of law preclude the perpetration of injustice against indigenous peoples. In Canada, the rights of indigenous peoples were completely denied in the creation of the legal framework for the relationship. And the United States Supreme Court's definition of tribal sovereignty – made by Chief Justice John Marshall in a series of nineteenth-century decisions centered on *Johnson v. McIntosh* – merely gave legal sanction to the unilateral abrogation of treaties by the United States and denial of the natural law rights of indigenous peoples. As Williams argues: "*Johnson*'s acceptance of the Doctrine of Discovery into United States law preserved the legacy of 1000 years of European racism and colonialism directed against non-Western peoples" (p. 317).

Recent assertions of prior and persistent indigenous power have come from two places: first, the intellectual and historical critiques of state legitimacy, and second, the revitalization of indigenous communities. Using "remnant recognitions" in colonial law, Indian critics have sought to deconstruct the skewed legal and institutional frame and to focus directly on the relationship between indigenous peoples and state sovereignty.

Core to this effort is the theoretical attention given to the entire notion of sovereignty as the guiding principle of government in states. What the Canadian philosopher James Tully calls the "empire of uniformity" is a fact-obliterating mythology of European conquest and normality. Tully recognizes the ways in which injustice toward indigenous peoples is deeply rooted in the basic injustice of normalized power relations within the state itself. In his *Strange Multiplicity*, Tully considers the intellectual bases of dominance inherent in state structures, and he challenges us to reconceptualize the state and its relation with indigenous people in order to accommodate what he calls the three post-imperial values: consent, mutual recognition, and cultural continuity.

Taiaiake Alfred, in his *Peace, Power, Righteousness*, has engaged this challenge from within an indigenous intellectual framework. Alfred's "manifesto" calls for a profound reorientation of indigenous politics, and a recovery of indigenous political traditions in contemporary society. Attacking both the foundations of the state's claim to authority over indigenous peoples, and the process of cooptation that has drawn indigenous leaders into a position of dependency on and cooperation with unjust state structures, Alfred's work reflects a basic sentiment within many indigenous communities: "sovereignty" is inappropriate as a political objective for indigenous peoples.

David Wilkins' *American Indian Sovereignty and the U.S. Supreme Court* amply illustrates the futility and frustration of adopting sovereignty as a political objective. Wilkins traces the history of the development of a doctrine of Indian tribal sovereignty in the United States Supreme Court, demonstrating its inherent contradictions for Indian nationhood. From the central Marshall decisions in the mid-nineteenth century through contemporary jurisprudence, Wilkins reveals the fundamental weakness of a tribal sovereignty "protected" within the colonizer's legal system.

Wilkins' exhaustive and convincing work draws on postmodern and critical legal studies approaches to the law. Examining the negative findings of the Court, he deconstructs the facade of judicial objectivity, demonstrating that in defining sovereignty, the "justices of the Supreme Court, both individually and collectively have engaged in the manufacturing, redefining, and burying of 'principles', 'doctrines', and legal 'truths' to excuse and legitimize constitutional, treaty, and civil rights violations of tribal nations" (p. 297). In the United States, the common law provides for recognition of the inherent sovereignty of indigenous peoples, but simultaneously allows for its limitation by the United States Congress. The logic of colonization is clearly evident in the creation of "domestic dependent nation" status, which supposedly accommodates the historical fact of coexisting sovereignties, but does no more than slightly limit the hypocrisy. It accepts the premise of indigenous rights while at the same time legalizing their unjust limitation and potential extinguishment by the state.

Scholars and indigenous leaders, in confronting the ignorance of the original principles in politics today and in the processes that have been established to negotiate a movement away from the colonial past, have usually accepted the framework and goal of "sovereignty" as core to the indigenous political movement. New institutions are constructed in communities to assert indigenous rights within a "tribal sovereignty" framework. And many people have reconciled themselves to the belief that we are making steady progress toward the resolution of injustices stemming from colonization. It may take more energy, or more money than is currently being devoted to the process of decolonization, but the issue is always framed within existing structural and legal parameters.

But few people have questioned how a European term and idea – sovereignty is certainly not Sioux, Salish, or Iroquoian in origin – came to be so embedded in and important to cultures that had their own systems of government since the time before the term "sovereignty" was invented in Europe. Fewer still have questioned the implications of adopting the European notion of power and governance and using it to structure the postcolonial systems that are being negotiated and implemented within indigenous communities today.

These are exactly the questions that have become central to current analyses of power within indigenous communities. Using the sovereignty paradigm, indigenous people have made significant legal and political gains toward reconstructing the autonomous aspects of their individual, collective, and social identities. The positive effect of the sovereignty movement in terms of mental, physical, and emotional health cannot be denied or understated. Yet this does not seem to be enough: the seriousness of the social ills which do continue suggests that an externally focused assertion of sovereign power vis-à-vis the state is neither complete nor in and of itself a solution. Indigenous leaders engaging themselves and their communities in arguments framed within a liberal paradigm have not been able to protect the integrity of their nations. "Aboriginal rights" and "tribal sovereignty" are in fact the benefits accrued by indigenous peoples who have agreed to abandon autonomy to enter the state's legal and political framework.

Yet indigenous people have successfully engaged Western society in the first stages of a movement to restore their autonomous power and cultural integrity in the area of governance. The movement – referred to in terms of "aboriginal self-government," "indigenous self-determination," or "Native sovereignty" – is founded on an ideology of indigenous nationalism and a rejection of the models of government rooted in European cultural values. It is an uneven process of reinstituting systems that promote the goals and reinforce the values of indigenous cultures, against the constant effort of the Canadian and United States governments to maintain the systems of dominance imposed on indigenous communities over the past 100 years. Many communities have almost disentangled themselves from paternalistic state controls in administering institutions within jurisdictions that are important to them. Many more are currently engaged in substantial negotiations over land and governance, hoped and believed to lead to significantly greater control over their own lives and futures.

The intellectuals' rejection of the cooptation of indigenous nationhood, along with the development of assimilative definitions of "sovereignty" in Canada and the United States, followed years of activism among indigenous peoples on the ground. That activism was the direct result of the retraditionalization of segments of the population within indigenous communities – rejection of the legitimacy of the state and recovery of the traditional bases of indigenous political society. In Canada, the movement has taken the form of a struggle for revision of the constitutional status of indigenous nations, focused on forcing the state to break from its imperial position and recognize and accommodate the notion of an inherent authority in indigenous nations. In the United States, where a theoretical, redefined, and arbitrarily limited form of "sovereign" authority still resides with Indian tribes, the movement has focused on defending and expanding the political and economic implications of that theoretical right. In comparison, the struggles can be seen as philosophical vis-à-vis Canada and material vis-à-vis the United States.

There has been a much more substantive and challenging debate in Canada (linked to the struggles of indigenous peoples confronting the Commonwealth legal tradition in Australia and New Zealand) where actual political and legal stature is being contested, as opposed to the United States where indigenous peoples tend to rely implicitly upon the existing legal framework. In Canada, more than any other country, indigenous peoples have sought to transcend the colonial myths and restore the original relationships. It is this effort to transcend the colonial mentality and move the society beyond the structures of dominance forming the contemporary political reality that will drive future activism and scholarship on the question of indigenous peoples' political rights and status in relation to states.

In spite of this progress – or perhaps because of it – people in many Native communities are beginning to look beyond the present, envisioning a postcolonial future negotiated at various levels. There are serious problems with that future in the minds of many people who remain committed to systems of government that complement and sustain indigenous cultures. The core problem for both activists and scholars revolves around the fact that the colonial system itself has become embedded within indigenous societies. Indigenous community life today may be seen as framed by two fundamentally opposed value systems, one forming the undercurrent of social and cultural relations, the other structuring politics. This disunity is the fundamental condition of the alienation and political fatigue that plagues indigenous communities. A perspective that does not see the ongoing crisis fueled by continuing efforts to keep indigenous people focused on a quest for power within a paradigm bounded by the vocabulary, logic, and institutions of "sovereignty" will be blind to the reality of a persistent intent to maintain the colonial oppression of indigenous nations. The next phase of scholarship and activism, then, will need to transcend the mentality that supports the colonization of indigenous nations, beginning with the rejection of the term and notion of indigenous "sovereignty."

A Post-Sovereign Future?

Most of the attention and energy thus far has been directed at the process of decolonization – the mechanics of escaping from direct state control and the legal and political struggle to gain recognition of an indigenous governing authority. There has been a fundamental ignorance of the end values of the struggle. What will an indigenous government be like after self-government is achieved? Few people imagine that it will be an exact replica of the precolonial system that governed communities in the past. Most acknowledge that all indigenous structures will adapt to modern methods in terms of administrative technique and technology. There is a political universe of possibility when it comes to the embodiment of core values in the new systems.

The great hope is that the government systems being set up to replace colonial control in indigenous communities will embody the underlying cultural values of those communities. The great fear is that the postcolonial governments being designed today will be simple replicas of non-indigenous systems for smaller and racially defined constituencies: oppression becoming self-inflicted and more intense for its localization, thereby perpetuating the two value systems at the base of the problem.

One of the main obstacles to achieving peaceful coexistence is, of course, the uncritical acceptance of the classic notion of "sovereignty" as the framework for discussions of political relations between peoples. The discourse of sovereignty has effectively stilled any potential resolution of the issue that respects indigenous values and perspectives. Even "traditional" indigenous nationhood is commonly defined relationally, in contrast to the dominant formulation of the state: there is no absolute authority, no coercive enforcement of decisions, no hierarchy, and no separate ruling entity.

In his work on indigenous sovereignty in the United States, Vine Deloria, Jr. has pointed out the distinction between indigenous concepts of nationhood and those of state-based sovereignty. Deloria sees nationhood as distinct from "self-government" (or the "domestic dependent nation" status accorded indigenous peoples by the United States). The right of "self-determination," unbounded by state law, is a concept appropriate to nations. Delegated forms of authority, like "self-government" within the context of state sovereignty, are concepts appropriate to what we may call "minority peoples" or other ethnically defined groups within the polity as a whole. In response to the question of whether or not the development of "self-government" and other state-delegated forms of authority as institutions in indigenous communities was wrong, Deloria answers that it is not wrong, but simply inadequate. Delegated forms do not address the spiritual basis of indigenous societies:

> Self-government is not an Indian idea. It originates in the minds of non-Indians who have reduced the traditional ways to dust, or believe they have, and now wish to give, as a gift, a limited measure of local control and responsibility. Self-government is an exceedingly useful concept for Indians to use when dealing with the larger government because it provides a context within which negotiations can take

place. Since it will never supplant the intangible, spiritual, and emotional aspirations of American Indians, it cannot be regarded as the final solution to Indian problems. (Deloria and Lytle, 1984: 15)

The challenge for indigenous peoples in building appropriate postcolonial governing systems is to disconnect the notion of sovereignty from its Western, legal roots and to transform it. It is all too often taken for granted that what indigenous peoples are seeking in recognition of their nationhood is at its core the same as that which countries like Canada and the United States possess now. In fact, most of the current generation of indigenous politicians see politics as a zero-sum contest for power in the same way that non-indigenous politicians do. Rather than a value rooted in a traditional indigenous philosophy, indigenous politicians regard the nationhood discourse as a lever to gain bargaining position. For the politician, there is a dichotomy between philosophical principle and politics. The assertion of a sovereign right for indigenous peoples is not really believed, and becomes a transparent bargaining ploy and a lever for concessions within the established constitutional framework. Until "sovereignty" as a concept shifts from the dominant "state sovereignty" construct and comes to reflect more of the sense embodied in Western notions such as personal sovereignty or popular sovereignty, it will remain problematic if integrated within indigenous political struggles.

One of the major problems in the indigenous sovereignty movement is that its leaders must qualify and rationalize their goals by modifying the sovereignty concept. Sovereignty itself implies a set of values and objectives that put it in direct opposition to the values and objectives found in most traditional indigenous philosophies. Non-indigenous politicians recognize the inherent weakness of a position that asserts a sovereign right for peoples who do not have the cultural frame and institutional capacity to defend or sustain it. The problem for the indigenous sovereignty movement is that the initial act of asserting a sovereign right for indigenous peoples has structured the politics of decolonization since, and the state has used the theoretical inconsistencies in the position to its own advantage.

In this context, for example, the resolution of "land claims" (addressing the legal inconsistency of Crown or state title on indigenous lands) are generally seen as marks of progress by progressive non-indigenous people. But it seems that without a fundamental questioning of the assumptions that underlie the state's approach to power, the bad assumptions of colonialism will continue to structure the relationship. Progress toward achieving justice from a indigenous perspective made within this frame will be marginal, and indeed it has become evident that it will be tolerated by the state only to the extent that it serves, or at least does not oppose, the defined interests of the state itself.

In Canada – to note a second example – recognition of the concept of "aboriginal rights" by the high court is seen by many to be such a landmark of progress. Yet those who think more deeply recognize the basic reality that even with a legal recognition of collective rights to certain subsistence activities within certain territories, indigenous people are still subject to the state's controlling mechanisms in the exercise of these inherent freedoms and powers. They must conform to state-derived criteria and represent ascribed or negotiated identities in order to access these legal rights. Not throwing indigenous people in jail for fishing is certainly a mark of progress given Canada's shameful history. But to what extent does that state-regulated "right" to fish represent justice when you consider that indigenous people have been fishing on their rivers and seas since time began?

There are inherent constraints to the exercise of indigenous governmental authority built into the notion of indigenous sovereignty, and these constraints derive from the myth of conquest that is the foundation of mainstream perspectives on indigenous–white relations in North America. The maintenance of state dominance over indigenous peoples rests on the preservation of the myth of conquest, and the "noble but doomed" defeated nation status ascribed to indigenous peoples in the state sovereignty discourse. Framing indigenous people in the past allows the state to maintain its own legitimacy by disallowing the fact of indigenous peoples' nationhood to intrude upon its own mythology. It has become clear that indigenous people imperil themselves by accepting formulations of nationhood that prevent them from transcending the past. One of the fundamental injustices of the colonial state is that it relegates indigenous peoples' rights to the past, and constrains the development of indigenous societies by only allowing that activity which supports its own necessary illusion – that indigenous peoples do not today present a serious challenge to the legitimacy of the state.

Indigenous leaders have begun acting on their responsibility to expose the imperial pretence that supports the doctrine of state sovereignty and white society's dominion over indigenous nations and their lands. State sovereignty can only exist in the fabrication of a truth that excludes the indigenous voice. It is in fact antihistoric to claim that the state's legitimacy is based on the rule of law. From the indigenous perspective, there was no conquest and there is no moral justification for state sovereignty, only the gradual triumph of germs and numbers. The bare truth is that Canada and the United States "conquered" only because indigenous peoples were overwhelmed by imported European diseases, and were unable to prevent the massive immigration of European, African, and Asian populations. Only recently, as indigenous people learned to manipulate state institutions and have gained support from others oppressed by the state, has the state been forced to incorporate any inconsistencies.

Recognizing the power of the indigenous challenge and unable to deny it a voice, the state's response has been to attempt to draw indigenous people closer. It has encouraged indigenous people to reframe and moderate their nationhood demands to accept the *fait accompli* of colonization, to help create a marginal solution that does not challenge the fundamental imperial premise. By allowing indigenous peoples a small measure of self-administration, and by forgoing a small portion of the moneys derived from the exploitation of indigenous nations' lands, the state has created an incentive for integration into its own sovereignty framework. Those indigenous communities that cooperate are the beneficiaries of a patronizing *faux* altruism. They are viewed sympathetically as the anachronistic remnants of nations, the descendants of once independent peoples who by a combination of tenacity and luck have managed to survive and must now be protected as minorities. By agreeing to live as artifacts, such coopted communities guarantee themselves a mythological role, and thereby hope to secure a limited but perpetual set of rights.

Is there a Native philosophical alternative? And what might one achieve by standing against the further entrenchment of institutions modeled on the state? Many traditionalists hope to preserve a set of values that challenge the destructive, homogenizing force of Western liberalism and materialism: they wish to preserve a regime that honours the autonomy of individual conscience, non-coercive forms of authority, and a deep respect and interconnection between human beings and the other elements of creation. The contrast between indigenous conceptions and dominant Western constructions in this regard could not be more severe. In most traditional indigenous conceptions, nature and the natural order are the basic referents for thinking of power, justice, and social relations. Western conceptions, with their own particular philosophical distance from the natural world, have more often reflected different kinds of structures of coercion and social power.

Consider these different concepts of power as they affect one's perspective on the relationship between the people and the land, one of the basic elements of a political philosophy, be it indigenous nationhood, or state sovereignty. Indigenous philosophies are premised on the belief that the human relationship to the earth is primarily one of partnership. The land was created by a power outside of human beings, and a just relationship to that power must respect the fact that human beings did not have a hand in making the earth, therefore they have no right to dispose of it as they see fit. Land is created by another power's order, therefore possession by man is unnatural and unjust. The partnership principle, reflecting a spiritual connection with the land established by the Creator, gives human beings special responsibilities within the areas they occupy, linking them in a natural and sacred way to their territories.

The form of distributive or social justice promoted by the state through the current notion of economic development centers on the development of industry and enterprises to provide jobs for people and revenue for government institutions. Most often (and especially on indigenous lands) the industry and enterprises center on natural resource extraction. Trees, rocks, and fish become resources and commodities with a value calculated solely in monetary terms. Conventional economic development clearly lacks appreciation for the qualitative and spiritual connections that indigenous peoples have to what developers would call "resources."

Traditional frames of mind would seek a balanced perspective on using land in ways that respect the spiritual and cultural connections indigenous peoples have with their territories, combined with a commitment to managing the process respectfully, and to ensure a benefit for the natural and indigenous occupants of the land. The primary goals of an indigenous economy are the sustainability of the earth and ensuring the health and well-being of the people. Any deviation from that principle – whether in qualitative terms or with reference to the intensity of activity on the land – should be seen as upsetting the ideal of balance that is at the heart of so many indigenous societies.

Unlike the earth, social and political institutions were created by men and women. In many indigenous traditions, the fact that social and political institutions were designed and chartered by human beings means that people have the power and responsibility to change them. Where the human–earth relationship is structured by the larger forces in nature outside of human prerogative for change, the human–institution relationship entails an active responsibility for human beings to use their own powers of creation to achieve balance and harmony. Governance structures and social institutions are designed to empower individuals and reinforce tradition to maintain the balance found in nature.

Sovereignty, then, is a social creation. It is not an objective or natural phenomenon, but the result of choices made by men and women, indicative of a mindset located in, rather than a natural force creative of, a social and political order. The reification of sovereignty in politics today is the result of a triumph of a particular set of ideas over others – no more natural to the world than any other man-made object.

Indigenous perspectives offer alternatives, beginning with the restoration of a regime of respect. This ideal contrasts with the statist solution, still rooted in a classical notion of sovereignty that mandates a distributive rearrangement, but with a basic maintenance of the superior posture of the state. True indigenous formulations are non-intrusive and build frameworks of respectful coexistence by acknowledging the integrity and autonomy of the various constituent elements of the relationship. They go far beyond even the most liberal Western conceptions of justice in promoting the achievement of peace, because they explicitly allow for difference while mandating the construction of sound relationships among autonomously powered elements.

For people committed to transcending the imperialism of state sovereignty, the challenge is to de-think the concept of sovereignty and replace it with a notion of power that has at its root a more appropriate premise. And, as James Tully (1995) has pointed out, the imperial demand for conformity to a single language and way of knowing has, in any case, become obsolete and unachievable in the diverse (ethnic, linguistic, racial) social and political communities characteristic of modern states. Maintaining a political community on the premise of singularity is no more than intellectual imperialism. Justice demands a recognition (intellectual, legal, political) of the diversity of languages and knowledge that exists among people – indigenous peoples' ideas about relationships and power holding the same credence as those formerly constituting the singular reality of the state. Creating a legitimate postcolonial relationship involves abandoning notions of European cultural superiority and adopting a mutually respectful posture. It is no longer possible to maintain the legitimacy of the premise that there is only one right way to see and do things.

Indigenous voices have been consistent over centuries in demanding such recognition and respect. The speaker of the Rotinohshonni Grand Council, Deskaheh, for example, led a movement in the 1920s to have indigenous peoples respected by the members of the League of Nations. And more recently, indigenous leaders from around the world have had some success in undermining the intellectual supremacy of state sovereignty as the singular legitimate form of political organization. Scholars of international law are now beginning to see the vast potential for peace represented in indigenous political philosophies. Attention focused on the principles of the Rotinohshonni *Kaienerekowa* (Great Law of Peace) in the international arena, for example, suggests the growing recognition of indigenous thought as a postcolonial

alternative to the state sovereignty model. James Anaya, author of the most comprehensive and authoritative legal text on indigenous peoples in international law, writes:

> The Great Law of Peace promotes unity among individuals, families, clans, and
> nations while upholding the integrity of diverse identities and spheres of auton-
> omy. Similar ideals have been expressed by leaders of other indigenous groups in
> contemporary appeals to international bodies. Such conceptions outside the mold
> of classical Western liberalism would appear to provide a more appropriate founda-
> tion for understanding humanity … (Anaya, 1996: 79)

But the state is not going to release its grip on power so easily. The traditional values
of indigenous peoples constitute knowledge that directly threatens the monopoly on
power currently enjoyed by the state. Struggle lies ahead. Yet there is real hope for
moving beyond the intellectual violence of the state in a concept of legal pluralism
emerging out of the critiques, and reflected in the limited recognition afforded
indigenous conceptions in recent legal argumentation. In a basic sense, these shifts
reflect what many indigenous people have been saying all along: respect for others is
a necessary precondition to peace and justice.

Indigenous conceptions, and the politics that flow from them, maintain in a real
way the distinction between various political communities and contain an imperative
of respect that precludes the need for homogenization. Most indigenous people
respect others to the degree that they demonstrate respect. There is no need, as in
the Western tradition, to create a political or legal hegemony to guarantee respect.
There is no imperial, totalizing, or assimilative impulse. And that is the key difference: both philosophical systems can achieve peace; but for peace the European
demands assimilation to a belief or a country, while the indigenous demands nothing except respect.

Within a nation, one might even rethink the need for formal boundaries and
precedents that protect individuals from each other and from the group. A truly
indigenous political system relies instead on the dominant intellectual motif of balance, with little or no tension in the relationship between individual and the collective. Indigenous thought is often based on the notion that people, communities, and
the other elements of creation coexist as equals – human beings as either individuals
or collectives do not have a special priority in deciding the justice of a situation.

Consider the indigenous philosophical alternative to sovereignty in light of the
effect that sovereignty-based states, structures, and politics have had on North
America since the coming of the Europeans. Within a few generations, "Turtle
Island" has become a land devastated by environmental and social degradation. The
land has been shamefully exploited, indigenous people have borne the worst of
oppression in all its forms, and indigenous ideas have been denigrated. Recently,
however, indigenous peoples have come to realize that the main obstacle to recovery
from this near total dispossession – the restoration of peace and harmony in their
communities and the creation of just relationships between their peoples and the
earth – is the dominance of European-derived ideas such as sovereignty. In the past
two or three generations, there has been movement for the good in terms of

rebuilding social cohesion, gaining economic self-sufficiency, and empowering structures of self-government within indigenous communities. There has also been a
return to seeking guidance in traditional teachings, and a revitalization of the traditions that sustained the great cultural achievement of respectful coexistence. People
have begun to appreciate that wisdom, and much of the discourse on what constitutes justice and proper relationship within indigenous communities today revolves
around the struggle to promote the recovery of these values. Yet there has been very
little movement toward an understanding or even appreciation of the indigenous
tradition among non-indigenous people.

It is in fact one of the strongest themes within indigenous American cultures that
the sickness manifest in the modern colonial state can be transformed into a framework for coexistence by understanding and respecting the traditional teachings.
There is great wisdom coded in the languages and cultures of all indigenous peoples –
this is knowledge that can provide answers to compelling questions if respected and
rescued from its status as cultural artifact. There is also a great potential for resolving
many of our seemingly intractable problems by bringing traditional ideas and values
back to life. Before their near destruction by Europeans, many indigenous societies
achieved sovereignty-free regimes of conscience and justice that allowed for the harmonious coexistence of humans and nature for hundreds of generations. As our
world emerges into a post-imperial age, the philosophical and governmental alternative to sovereignty, and the central values contained within their traditional cultures,
are the North American Indian's contribution to the reconstruction of a just and
harmonious world.

BIBLIOGRAPHY

Alfred, T. 1995: *Heeding the Voices of Our Ancestors: Kahnawake Mohawk Politics and the
Rise of Indigenous Nationalism* (Toronto: Oxford University Press).
Alfred, T. 1999: *Peace, Power, Righteousness: An Indigenous Manifesto* (Toronto: Oxford
University Press).
Anaya, S. J. 1996: *Indigenous Peoples in International Law* (New York: Oxford
University Press).
Asch, M. (ed.) 1997: *Aboriginal Treaty Rights in Canada: Essays on Law, Equality, and
Respect for Difference* (Vancouver: University of British Columbia Press).
Barsh, R. L. and J. Y. Henderson 1980: *The Road: Indian Tribes and Political Liberty*
(Berkeley: University of California Press).
Bartelson, J. 1995: *A Genealogy of Sovereignty* (Cambridge: Cambridge University Press).
Biersteker, J. and C. Weber (eds.) 1996: *State Sovereignty as a Social Construct*
(Cambridge: Cambridge University Press).
Clark, B. 1990: *Indigenous Liberty, Crown Sovereignty: The Existing Aboriginal Right of
Self-Government in Canada* (Montreal: McGill-Queen's University Press).
Cornell, S. 1988: *The Return of the Native: American Indian Political Resurgence* (New
York: Oxford University Press).
Deloria, V., Jr. 1970: *We Talk, You Listen* (New York: Macmillan).
Deloria, V., Jr. 1988: *Custer Died for Your Sins: An Indian Manifesto* (Norman:
University of Oklahoma Press).

Deloria, V., Jr. and C. Lytle 1983: *American Indians, American Justice* (Austin: University of Texas Press).

Deloria, V., Jr. and C. Lytle 1984: *The Nations Within: The Past and Future of American Indian Sovereignty* (Austin: University of Texas Press).

Fleras, A. and J. L. Elliott 1992: *The "Nations Within": Aboriginal–State Relations in Canada, the United States, and New Zealand* (Toronto: Oxford University Press).

Foucault, M. 1980: *Power/Knowledge: Selected Interviews and Other Writings, 1972–1977*, ed. and trans. C. Gordon (New York: Pantheon Books).

Foucault, M. 1997: *The Politics of Truth*, ed. S. Lotringer (New York: Semiotext(e)).

Lyons, O. et al. 1992: *Exiled in the Land of the Free: Democracy, Indian Nations, and the U.S. Constitution* (Santa Fe: Clear Light Publishers).

Patton, P. (ed.) 2000: *Political Theory and Indigenous Rights* (Cambridge: Cambridge University Press).

Rotman, L. I. 1996: *Parallel Paths: Fiduciary Doctrine and the Crown–Indigenous Relationship in Canada* (Toronto: University of Toronto Press).

Royal Commission on Aboriginal Peoples (Canada) 1996: *Report*, 5 vols. (Ottawa: Canada Communication Group).

Spinner, J. 1994: *The Boundaries of Citizenship: Race, Ethnicity, and Nationality in the Liberal State* (Baltimore: Johns Hopkins University Press).

Tully, J. 1995: *Strange Multiplicity: Constitutionalism in an Age of Diversity* (Cambridge: Cambridge University Press).

Wilkins, D. E. 1997: *American Indian Sovereignty and the U.S. Supreme Court: The Masking of Justice* (Austin: University of Texas Press).

Wilkinson, C. F. 1987: *American Indians, Time, and the Law: Indigenous Societies in a Modern Constitutional Democracy* (New Haven: Yale University Press).

Williams, R. A., Jr. 1990: *The American Indian in Western Legal Thought: The Discourse of Conquest* (New York: Oxford University Press).

Bibliography

COMPILED BY TIMOTHY WILLIG

Albers, Patricia and Beatrice Medicine (eds.) 1983: *The Hidden Half: Studies of Plains Indian Women* (Lanham, MD: University Press of America).

Albers, Patricia C. and William R. James 1986: "On the Dialectics of Ethnicity: To Be or Not to Be a Santee (Sioux)," *Journal of Ethnic Studies* 14: 1–27.

Alden, John Richard 1966: *John Stuart and the Southern Colonial Frontier: A Study of Indian Relations, War, Trade, and Land Problems in the Southern Wilderness, 1754–1775* (New York: Gordian Press, Inc.).

Alfred, Gerald R. (Taiaiake) 1995: *Heeding the Voices of Our Ancestors: Kahnawake Mohawk Politics and the Rise of Native Nationalism* (Toronto: Oxford University Press).

Alfred, Gerald R. (Taiaiake) 1999: *Peace, Power, Righteousness: An Indigenous Manifesto* (Don Mills, Ontario: Oxford University Press).

Allen, Paula Gunn 1986: *The Sacred Hoop: Recovering the Feminine in American Indian Traditions* (Boston: Beacon Press).

Allen, Paula Gunn 1998: *Off the Reservation: Reflections on Boundary-Busting Border-Crossing Loose Canons* (Boston: Beacon Press).

Allen, Robert S. 1992: *His Majesty's Indian Allies: British Indian Policy in the Defence of Canada, 1774–1815* (Toronto: Dundurn Press).

Anderson, Gary Clayton 1984: *Kinsmen of Another Kind: Dakota–White Relations in the Upper Mississippi Valley, 1650–1862* (Lincoln: University of Nebraska Press).

Anderson, Gary Clayton 1999: *The Indian Southwest, 1580–1830: Ethnogenesis and Reinvention* (Norman: University of Oklahoma Press).

Anderson, Karen L. 1991: *Chain Her by One Foot: The Subjugation of Women in Seventeenth-Century New France* (London and New York: Routledge).

Anson, Bert 1970: *The Miami Indians* (Norman: University of Oklahoma Press).

Aquila, Richard 1983: *The Iroquois Restoration: Iroquois Diplomacy on the Colonial Frontier, 1701–1754* (Detroit: Wayne State University Press).

Armstrong, William H. 1978: *Warrior in Two Camps: Ely S. Parker, Union General and Seneca Chief* (Syracuse: Syracuse University Press).

Aveni, Anthony F. (ed.) 1975: *Archaeoastronomy in Pre-Columbian America* (Austin: University of Texas Press).

Axtell, James 1981: *The European and the Indian: Essays in the Ethnohistory of Colonial North America* (New York: Oxford University Press).

Axtell, James 1985: *The Invasion Within: The Contest of Cultures in Colonial North America* (New York: Oxford University Press).

Axtell, James 1988: *After Columbus: Essays in the Ethnohistory of Colonial North America* (New York: Oxford University Press).

Axtell, James 1992: *Beyond 1492: Encounters in Colonial North America* (New York: Oxford University Press).

Barsh, Russel Lawrence and James Youngblood Henderson 1980: *The Road: Indian Tribes and Political Liberty* (Berkeley: University of California Press).

Basso, Keith H. 1979: *Portraits of "the Whiteman": Linguistic Play and Cultural Symbols among the Western Apache* (Cambridge: Cambridge University Press).

Basso, Keith H. 1996: *Wisdom Sits in Places: Landscape and Language among the Western Apache* (Albuquerque: University of New Mexico Press).

Battaille, Gretchen and Kathleen Mullen Sands 1984: *American Indian Women: Telling Their Lives* (Lincoln, NE: Bison Books).

Benn, Carl 1998: *The Iroquois in the War of 1812* (Toronto: University of Toronto Press).

Berkhofer, Robert F., Jr. 1965: *Salvation and the Savage: An Analysis of Protestant Missions and American Indian Response, 1787–1862* (Lexington: University of Kentucky Press).

Berkhofer, Robert F., Jr. 1971: "The Political Context of a New Indian History," *Pacific Historical Review* 40: 357–82.

Berkhofer, Robert F., Jr. 1978: *The White Man's Indian: Images of the American Indian from Columbus to the Present* (New York: Alfred A. Knopf).

Bernstein, Alison R. 1991: *American Indians and World War II: Toward a New Era in Indian Affairs* (Norman: University of Oklahoma Press).

Bierhorst, John 1985: *The Mythology of North America* (New York: Morrow).

Biolsi, Thomas 1992: *Organizing the Lakota: The Political Economy of the New Deal on the Pine Ridge and Rosebud Reservations* (Tucson: University of Arizona Press).

Biolsi, Thomas 1997: *Indians and Anthropologists: Vine Deloria Jr. and the Critique of Anthropology* (Tucson: University of Arizona Press).

Bird, S. Elizabeth (ed.) 1996: *Dressing in Feathers: The Construction of the Indian in American Popular Culture* (Boulder, CO: Westview Press).

Blu, Karen I. 1980: *The Lumbee Problem: The Making of an American Indian People* (Cambridge: Cambridge University Press).

Boldt, Menno and J. Anthony Long (eds.) 1985: *The Quest for Justice: Aboriginal Peoples and Aboriginal Rights* (Toronto: University of Toronto Press).

Bowden, Henry Warner 1981: *American Indians and Christian Missions: Studies in Cultural Conflict* (Chicago: University of Chicago Press).

Boxberger, Daniel L. 1989: *To Fish in Common: The Ethnohistory of Lummi Indian Salmon Fishing* (Lincoln: University of Nebraska Press).

Bradley, James W. 1987: *Evolution of the Onondaga Iroquois: Accommodating Change, 1500–1655* (Syracuse: Syracuse University Press).

Bragdon, Kathleen J. 1996: *Native People of Southern New England, 1500–1650* (Norman: University of Oklahoma Press).

Brandão, José António 1997: *"Your fyre shall burn no more": Iroquois Policy toward New France and its Native Allies to 1701* (Lincoln: University of Nebraska Press).

Brightman, Robert A. 1993: *Grateful Prey: Rock Cree Human–Animal Relationships* (Los Angeles: University of California Press).

Britten, Thomas 1997: *American Indians in World War I: At Home and at War* (Albuquerque: University of New Mexico Press).

Brody, Hugh 1982: *Maps and Dreams* (New York: Pantheon Books).

Brown, Jennifer S. H. 1980: *Strangers in Blood: Fur Trade Company Families in Indian Country* (Vancouver: University of British Columbia Press).

Brown, Jennifer S. H., W. J. Eccles, and Donald P. Heldman (eds.) 1994: *The Fur Trade Revisited: Selected Papers of the Sixth North American Fur Trade Conference, Mackinac Island, 1991* (East Lansing: Michigan State University Press; and Mackinac Island, MI: Mackinac Island State Historic Parks).

Brown, Jennifer S. H. and Elizabeth Vibert (eds.) 1996: *Reading Beyond Words: Contexts for Native History* (Peterborough, ON and Orchard Park, NY: Broadview Press).

Brumble, H. David, III 1988: *American Indian Autobiography* (Berkeley: University of California Press).

Buckley, Thomas C. (ed.) 1984: *Rendezvous: Selected Papers of the Fourth North American Fur Trade Conference* (St. Paul: Minnesota Historical Society).

Burt, Larry 1982: *Tribalism in Crisis: Federal Indian Policy, 1953–1961* (Albuquerque: University of New Mexico Press).

Bushnell, Amy Turner 1994: *Situado and Sabana: Spain's Support System for the Presidio and Mission Provinces of Florida* (New York: American Museum of Natural History; and Athens, GA: distributed by the University of Georgia Press).

Calloway, Colin G. 1982: "The Intertribal Balance of Powers on the Great Plains, 1760–1850," *Journal of American Studies* 16 (April): 25–47.

Calloway, Colin G. 1987: *Crown and Calumet: British–Indian Relations, 1783–1815* (Norman: University of Oklahoma Press).

Calloway, Colin G. (ed.) 1988: *New Directions in American Indian History* (Norman: University of Oklahoma Press).

Calloway, Colin G. 1990: *The Western Abenakis of Vermont, 1600–1800: War, Migration, and the Survival of an Indian People* (Norman: University of Oklahoma Press).

Calloway, Colin G. 1995: *The American Revolution in Indian Country: Crisis and Diversity in Native American Communities* (Cambridge: Cambridge University Press).

Calloway, Colin G. 1997: *New Worlds for All: Indians, Europeans and the Remaking of Early America* (Baltimore: Johns Hopkins University Press).

Calloway, Colin G. (ed.) 1997: *After King Philip's War: Presence and Persistence in Indian New England* (Hanover, NH: University Press of New England).

Campisi, Jack 1991: *The Mashpee Indians: Tribe on Trial* (Syracuse: Syracuse University Press).

Campisi, Jack and Laurence M. Hauptman (eds.) 1988: *The Oneida Indian Experience: Two Perspectives* (Syracuse: Syracuse University Press).

Carter, Harvey Lewis 1987: *The Life and Times of Little Turtle: First Sagamore of the Wabash* (Urbana: University of Illinois Press).

Cave, Alfred A. 1996: *The Pequot War* (Amherst: University of Massachusetts Press).

Cayton, Andrew R. L. and Frederika J. Teute (eds.) 1998: *Contact Points: American Frontiers from the Mohawk Valley to the Mississippi, 1750–1830* (Chapel Hill: University of North Carolina Press).

Champagne, Duane 1992: *Social Order and Political Change: Constitutional Governments among the Cherokee, the Choctaw, the Chickasaw, and the Creek* (Stanford: Stanford University Press).

Champagne, Duane (ed.) 1999: *Contemporary Native American Cultural Issues* (Walnut Creek, CA: AltaMira Press).

Champagne, Duane, et al. (eds.) 1997: *American Indian Activism: Alcatraz to the Longest Walk* (Urbana: University of Illinois Press).

Clark, Blue 1994: *Lone Wolf vs. Hitchcock: Treaty Rights and Indian Law at the End of the Nineteenth Century* (Lincoln: University of Nebraska Press).

Clark, Jerry E. 1977: *The Shawnee* (Lexington: University Press of Kentucky).

Clifford, James 1988: "Identity in Mashpee," in James Clifford (ed.), *The Predicament of Culture: Twentieth-Century Ethnography, Literature, and Art* (Cambridge, MA: Harvard University Press), pp. 277–346.

Clifton, James A. 1977: *The Prairie People: Continuity and Change in Potawatomi Indian Culture, 1665–1965* (Lawrence: Regents Press of Kansas).

Clifton, James A. (ed.) 1989: *Being and Becoming Indian: Biographical Studies of North American Frontiers* (Chicago: Dorsey Press).

Cole, D. C. 1988: *The Chiricahua Apache, 1846–1876: From War to Reservation* (Albuquerque: University of New Mexico Press).

Cole, Douglas and Ira Chaikin 1990: *An Iron Hand Upon the People: The Law Against the Potlatch on the Northwest Coast* (Vancouver: Douglas & McIntyre; and Seattle: University of Washington Press).

Coleman, Michael 1993; *American Indian Children at School, 1850–1930* (Jackson: University Press of Mississippi).

Comer, Douglas C. 1996: *Ritual Ground: Bent's Old Fort, World Formation, and the Annexation of the Southwest* (Berkeley: University of California Press).

Cornell, Stephen E. 1988: *The Return of the Native: American Indian Political Resurgence* (New York: Oxford University Press).

Cox, Bruce A. (ed.) 1987: *Native People, Native Lands* (Ottawa: Carleton University Press).

Cronon, William 1983: *Changes in the Land: Indians, Colonists, and the Ecology of New England* (New York: Hill and Wang).

Crosby, Alfred W. 1972: *The Columbian Exchange: Biological and Cultural Consequences of 1492* (Westport, CT: Greenwood Publishing Co.).

Crosby, Alfred W. 1986: *Ecological Imperialism: The Biological Expansion of Europe 900–1900* (Cambridge: Cambridge University Press).

Cruikshank, Julie 1990: *Life Lived like a Story: Life Stories of Three Yukon Native Elders* (Lincoln: University of Nebraska Press).

Cruikshank, Julie 1998: *The Social Life of Stories: Narrative and Knowledge in the Yukon Territory* (Lincoln: University of Nebraska Press).

Cumming, Peter A. and Neil H. Mickenberg (eds.) 1980: *Native Rights in Canada* (Toronto: Indian-Eskimo Association of Canada in association with General Publishing Co.).

Danziger, Edmund J., Jr. 1974: *Indians and Bureaucrats: Administering the Reservation Policy during the Civil War* (Urbana: University of Illinois Press).

Danziger, Edmund J., Jr. 1978: *The Chippewas of Lake Superior* (Norman: University of Oklahoma Press).

Danziger, Edmund J., Jr. 1991: *Survival and Regeneration: Detroit's American Indian Community* (Detroit: Wayne State University Press).

Day, Gordon M. 1998: *In Search of New England's Native Past: Selected Essays*, eds. Michael K. Foster and William Cowan (Amherst: University of Massachusetts Press).

Debo, Angie 1934: *The Rise and Fall of the Choctaw Republic* (Norman: University of Oklahoma Press).

Debo, Angie 1940: *And Still the Waters Run* (Princeton: Princeton University Press).

Debo, Angie 1941: *The Road to Disappearance* (Norman: University of Oklahoma Press).

Debo, Angie 1970: *A History of the Indians of the United States* (Norman: University of Oklahoma Press).

Debo, Angie 1976: *Geronimo: The Man, His Time, His Place* (Norman: University of Oklahoma Press).

Delâge, Denys 1993: *Bitter Feast: Amerindians and Europeans in Northeastern North America, 1600–64*, trans. Jane Brierly (Vancouver: University of British Columbia Press).

Deloria, Philip J. 1996: "'I Am of the Body': Thoughts on My Grandfather, Culture, and Sports," *The South Atlantic Quarterly* 95: 321–38.

Deloria, Philip J. 1998: *Playing Indian* (New Haven: Yale University Press).

Deloria, Vine, Jr. 1969: *Custer Died for Your Sins: An Indian Manifesto* (New York: Macmillan).

Deloria, Vine, Jr. 1972: *God Is Red: A Native View of Religion* (New York: Grossett and Dunlap).

Deloria, Vine, Jr. 1974: *Behind the Trail of Broken Treaties: An Indian Declaration of Independence* (New York: Dell).

Deloria, Vine, Jr. 1981: "Identity and Culture," *Daedalus* 110(2): 13–27.

Deloria, Vine, Jr. (ed.) 1985: *American Indian Policy in the Twentieth Century* (Norman: University of Oklahoma Press).

Deloria, Vine, Jr. 1998: "Intellectual Self-Determination and Sovereignty: Looking at the Windmills in Our Minds," *Wicazo Sa Review* 13(1): 25–31.

Deloria, Vine, Jr. and Clifford M. Lytle 1983: *American Indians, American Justice* (Austin: University of Texas Press).

Deloria, Vine, Jr. and Clifford M. Lytle 1984: *The Nations Within: The Past and Future of American Indian Sovereignty* (New York: Pantheon Books).

Deloria, Vine, Jr. and David E. Wilkins 1999: *Tribes, Treaties and Constitutional Tribulations* (Austin: University of Texas Press).

DeMallie, Raymond J. 1984: "Nicholas Black Elk and John G. Neihardt: An Introduction," in Raymond J. DeMallie (ed.), *The Sixth Grandfather: Black Elk's Teachings Given to John Neihardt* (Lincoln: University of Nebraska Press), pp. 1–99.

DeMallie, Raymond J. and Alfonso Ortiz (eds.) 1994: *North American Indian Anthropology: Essays on Society and Culture* (Norman: University of Oklahoma Press).

DeMallie, Raymond J. and Douglas R. Parks (eds.) 1987: *Sioux Indian Religion: Tradition and Innovation* (Norman: University of Oklahoma Press).

Dennis, Matthew 1993: *Cultivating a Landscape of Peace: Iroquois–European Encounters in Seventeenth-Century America* (Ithaca, NY: Cornell University Press).

Devens, Carol 1992: *Countering Colonization: Native American Women and Great Lakes Missions, 1630–1900* (Berkeley: University of California Press).

Dickason, Olive Patricia 1984: *The Myth of the Savage and the Beginnings of French Colonialism in the Americas* (Edmonton: University of Alberta Press).

Dickason, Olive Patricia 1992: *Canada's First Nations: A History of Founding Peoples from Earliest Times* (Norman: University of Oklahoma Press).

Dippie, Brian 1982: *The Vanishing American: White Attitudes and U.S. Indian Policy* (Middletown: Wesleyan University Press).

Dowd, Gregory E. 1992: *A Spirited Resistance: The North American Indian Struggle for Unity, 1745–1815* (Baltimore: Johns Hopkins University Press).

Downes, Randolph C. 1940: *Council Fires on the Upper Ohio: A Narrative of Indian Affairs in the Upper Ohio Valley until 1795* (Pittsburgh: University of Pittsburgh Press).

Drake, James David 1999: *King Philip's War: Civil War in New England, 1675–1676* (Amherst: University of Massachusetts Press).

Eccles, W. J. 1983: "The Fur Trade and Eighteenth-Century Imperialism," *William and Mary Quarterly*, 3rd series, 40: 341–62.

Edmunds, R. David 1978: *The Potawatomis: Keepers of the Fire* (Norman: University of Oklahoma Press).

Edmunds, R. David (ed.) 1980: *American Indian Leaders: Studies in Diversity* (Lincoln: University of Nebraska Press).

Edmunds, R. David 1983: *The Shawnee Prophet* (Lincoln: University of Nebraska Press).

Edmunds, R. David 1984: *Tecumseh and the Quest for Indian Leadership* (New York: HarperCollins).

Edmunds, R. David 1995: "Native Americans, New Voices: American Indian History, 1895–1995," *American Historical Review* 100: 717–40.

Edmunds, R. David and Joseph L. Peyser 1993: *The Fox Wars: The Mesquakie Challenge to New France* (Norman: University of Oklahoma Press).

Ewers, John Canfield 1958: *The Blackfeet: Raiders on the Northwestern Plains* (Norman: University of Oklahoma Press).

Ewers, John Canfield 1968: *Indian Life on the Upper Missouri* (Norman: University of Oklahoma Press).

Feest, Christian F. 1992: *Native Arts of North America* (New York: Thames & Hudson).

Feest, Christian F. (ed.) 1999: *Indians and Europe: An Interdisciplinary Collection of Essays* (orig. pub. 1987; Lincoln: University of Nebraska Press).

Fenton, William N. 1998: *The Great Law and the Longhouse: A Political History of the Iroquois Confederacy* (Norman: University of Oklahoma Press).

Fey, Harold E. and D'Arcy McNickle 1970: *Indians and Other Americans: Two Ways of Life Meet* (New York: Perennial Library, Harper & Row).

Fisher, Robin 1977: *Contact and Conflict: Indian–European Relations in British Columbia, 1774–1890* (Vancouver: University of British Columbia Press).

Fitzhugh, William W. (ed.) 1985: *Cultures in Contact: The Impact of European Contacts on Native American Cultural Institutions, A.D. 1000–1800* (Washington, D.C.: Smithsonian Institution Press).

Fixico, Donald L. 1986: *Termination and Relocation: Federal Indian Policy, 1945–1960* (Albuquerque: University of New Mexico Press).

Fixico, Donald L. (ed.) 1987: *An Anthology of Western Great Lakes Indian History* (Milwaukee: American Indian Studies, University of Wisconsin-Milwaukee).

Fixico, Donald L. (ed.) 1989: *Native Views of Indian–White Historical Relations.* D'Arcy McNickle Center for the History of the American Indian, Occasional Papers in Curriculum, no. 7 (Chicago: Newberry Library).

Fixico, Donald L. (ed.) 1997: *Rethinking American Indian History* (Albuquerque: University of New Mexico Press).

Fixico, Donald L. 1998: *The Invasion of Indian Country in the Twentieth Century: American Capitalism and Tribal Natural Resources* (Niwot: University Press of Colorado).

Fixico, Donald L. 2000: *The Urban Indian Experience in America* (Albuquerque: University of New Mexico Press).

Flanagan, Thomas 1991: *Métis Lands in Manitoba* (Calgary: University of Calgary Press).

Flanagan, Thomas 2000: *Riel and the Rebellion: 1885 Reconsidered* (Toronto: University of Toronto Press).

Fogelson, Raymond D. 1989: "The Ethnohistory of Events and Nonevents," *Ethnohistory* 36: 133–47.

Forbes, Jack D. 1960: *Apache, Navaho, and Spaniard* (Norman: University of Oklahoma Press).

Forbes, Jack D. 1993: *Africans and Native Americans: The Language of Race and the Evolution of Red-Black Peoples* (Urbana: University of Illinois Press).

Foster, Michael K., Jack Campisi, and Marianne Mithun (eds.) 1984: *Extending the Rafters: Interdisciplinary Approaches to Iroquoian Studies* (Albany: State University of New York Press).

Foster, Morris W. 1991: *Being Comanche: A Social History of an American Indian Community* (Tucson: University of Arizona Press).

Fowler, Loretta 1982: *Arapahoe Politics, 1851–1978* (Lincoln: University of Nebraska Press).

Fowler, Loretta 1987: *Shared Symbols, Contested Meanings: Gros Ventre Culture and History, 1778–1984* (Ithaca, NY: Cornell University Press).

Galloway, Patricia Kay 1995: *Choctaw Genesis, 1500–1700* (Lincoln: University of Nebraska Press).

Geertz, Armin W. 1994: *The Invention of Prophecy: Continuity and Meaning in Hopi Indian Religion* (Berkeley: University of California Press).

Gibson, Arrell Morgan 1963: *The Kickapoos: Lords of the Middle Border* (Norman: University of Oklahoma Press).

Gibson, Arrell Morgan 1971: *The Chickasaws* (Norman: University of Oklahoma Press).

Gidley, Mick 1998: *Edward S. Curtis and the North American Indian, Inc.* (Cambridge: Cambridge University Press).

Gill, Sam D. 1982: *Native American Religions: An Introduction* (Belmont, CA: Wadsworth Publishing Co.).

Gill, Sam 1987: *Mother Earth: An American Story* (Chicago: University of Chicago Press).

Graymont, Barbara 1972: *The Iroquois in the American Revolution* (Syracuse: Syracuse University Press).

Green, Michael D. 1982: *The Politics of Indian Removal: Creek Government and Society in Crisis* (Lincoln: University of Nebraska Press).

Grumet, Robert S. (ed.) 1996: *Northeastern Indian Lives, 1632–1816* (Amherst: University of Massachusetts Press).

Guillemin, Jeanne 1975: *Urban Renegades: The Cultural Strategy of American Indians* (New York: Columbia University Press).

Gutiérrez, Ramón A. 1991: *When Jesus Came, the Corn Mothers Went Away: Marriage, Sexuality, and Power in New Mexico, 1500–1846* (Stanford: Stanford University Press).

Hagan, William T. 1958: *The Sac and Fox Indians* (Norman: University of Oklahoma Press).

Hagan, William T. 1966: *Indian Police and Judges: Experiments in Acculturation and Control* (New Haven: Yale University Press).

Hagan, William T. 1976: *United States–Comanche Relations: The Reservation Years* (New Haven: Yale University Press).

Hagan, William T. 1993: *Quanah Parker: Comanche Chief* (Norman: University of Oklahoma Press).

Hall, Robert L. 1997: *An Archaeology of the Soul: North American Indian Belief and Ritual* (Urbana: University of Illinois Press).

Hall, Thomas D. 1989: *Social Change in the Southwest, 1350–1880* (Lawrence: University of Kansas Press).

Hann, John H. 1988: *Apalachee: The Land Between the Rivers* (Gainesville: University Press of Florida).

Hann, John H. 1996: *A History of the Timucua Indians and Missions* (Gainesville: University Press of Florida).

Harkin, Michael E. 1997: *The Heiltsuks: Dialogues of Culture and History on the Northwest Coast* (Lincoln: University of Nebraska Press).

Harmon, Alexandra 1998: *Indians in the Making: Ethnic Relations and Indian Identities around Puget Sound* (Berkeley: University of California Press).

Harring, Sidney L. 1994: *Crow Dog's Case: American Indian Sovereignty, Tribal Law, and United States Law in the Nineteenth Century* (Cambridge: Cambridge University Press).

Harring, Sidney L. 1998: *White Man's Law: Native People in Nineteenth-Century Canadian Jurisprudence* (Toronto: Osgoode Society for Canadian Legal History by University of Toronto Press).

Harrod, Howard L. 1987: *Renewing the World: Plains Indian Religion and Morality* (Tucson: University of Arizona Press).

Harrod, Howard L. 1995: *Becoming and Remaining a People: Native American Religions on the Northern Plains* (Tucson: University of Arizona Press).

Harrod, Howard L. 2000: *The Animals Came Dancing: Native American Sacred Ecology and Animal Kinship* (Tucson: University of Arizona Press).

Hatley, Tom 1993: *The Dividing Paths: Cherokees and South Carolinians through the Era of Revolution* (New York: Oxford University Press).

Hauptman, Laurence M. 1981: *The Iroquois and the New Deal* (Syracuse: Syracuse University Press).

Hauptman, Laurence M. 1986: *The Iroquois Struggle for Survival: World War II to Red Power* (Syracuse: Syracuse University Press).

Hauptman, Laurence M. 1995: *Between Two Fires: American Indians in the Civil War* (New York: Free Press).

Hauptman, Laurence M. 1999: *Conspiracy of Interests: Iroquois Dispossession and the Rise of New York State* (Syracuse: Syracuse University Press).

Hauptman, Laurence M. and James D. Wherry (eds.) 1990: *The Pequots in Southern New England: The Fall and Rise of an American Indian Nation* (Norman: University of Oklahoma Press).

Hertzog, Hazel W. 1971: *The Search for an American Indian Identity: Modern Pan-Indian Movements* (Syracuse: Syracuse University Press).

Hickerson, Nancy Parrott 1994: *The Jumanos: Hunters and Traders of the South Plains* (Austin: University of Texas Press).

Hill, Sarah H. 1997: *Weaving New Worlds: Southeastern Cherokee Women and Their Basketry* (Chapel Hill: University of North Carolina Press).

Hinderaker, Eric 1997: *Elusive Empires: Constructing Colonialism in the Ohio Valley, 1673–1800* (Cambridge: Cambridge University Press).

Hittman, Michael 1997: *Wovoka and the Ghost Dance,* ed. Don Lynch (Lincoln: University of Nebraska Press).

Holler, Clyde 1995: *Black Elk's Religion: The Sun Dance and Lakota Catholicism* (Syracuse: Syracuse University Press).

Holm, Tom 1996: *Strong Hearts, Wounded Souls: Native American Veterans of the Vietnam War* (Austin: University of Texas Press).

Horsman, Reginald 1967: *Expansion and American Indian Policy, 1783–1812* (East Lansing: Michigan State University Press).

Horsman, Reginald 1981: *Race and Manifest Destiny: The Origins of American Racial Anglo-Saxonism* (Cambridge, MA: Harvard University Press).

Howard, James H. 1981: *Shawnee!: The Ceremonialism of a Native Indian Tribe and its Cultural Background* (Athens: Ohio University Press).

Hoxie, Frederick E. 1984: *The Campaign to Assimilate the Indians, 1880–1920* (Lincoln: University of Nebraska Press).

Hoxie, Frederick E. 1995: *Parading Through History: The Making of the Crow Nation in America, 1805–1935* (Cambridge: Cambridge University Press).

Hoxie, Frederick E., Ronald Hoffman, and Peter J. Albert (eds.) 1999: *Native Americans and the Early Republic* (Charlottesville: University Press of Virginia).

Hoxie, Frederick E. and Peter Iverson (eds.) 1998: *Indians in American History: An Introduction* (Wheeling, IL: Harlan Davidson).

Hudson, Charles M. 1976: *The Southeastern Indians* (Knoxville: University of Tennessee Press).

Hudson, Charles M. and Carmen Chaves Tesser (eds.) 1994: *The Forgotten Centuries: Indians and Europeans in the American South, 1521–1704* (Athens: University of Georgia Press).

Hughes, J. Donald 1983: *American Indian Ecology* (El Paso: Texas Western Press).

Hurt, R. Douglas 1987: *Indian Agriculture in America: Prehistory to the Present* (Lawrence: University Press of Kansas).

Hurt, R. Douglas 1996: *The Ohio Frontier: Crucible of the Old Northwest, 1720–1830* (Bloomington: Indiana University Press).

Hurtado, Albert L. 1988: *Indian Survival on the California Frontier* (New Haven: Yale University Press).

Irwin, Lee 1994: *The Dream Seekers: Native American Visionary Traditions of the Great Plains* (Norman: University of Oklahoma Press).

Irwin, Lee (ed.) 1996–7: *To Hear the Eagles Cry*. Special issues of *American Indian Quarterly,* 20(3–4) (1996): 309–593; and 21(1) (1997): 1–147.

Irwin, Lee (ed.) 2000: *Native American Spirituality: A Critical Reader* (Lincoln: University of Nebraska Press).

Isernhagen, Hartwood 1999: *Momaday, Vizenor, Armstrong: Conversations on American Indian Writing* (Norman: University of Oklahoma Press).

Iverson, Peter 1981: *The Navajo Nation* (Westport, CT: Greenwood Press).

Iverson, Peter 1982: *Carlos Montezuma and the Changing World of American Indians* (Albuquerque: University of New Mexico Press).

Iverson, Peter (ed.) 1985: *The Plains Indians of the Twentieth Century* (Norman: University of Oklahoma Press).

Iverson, Peter 1994: *When Indians Became Cowboys: Native Peoples and Cattle Ranching in the American West* (Norman: University of Oklahoma Press).

Iverson, Peter 1998: *"We Are Still Here": American Indians in the Twentieth Century* (Wheeling, IL: Harlan Davidson).

Jacobs, Wilbur R. 1966: *Wilderness Politics and Indian Gifts: The Northern Colonial Frontier, 1748–1763* (Lincoln: University of Nebraska Press).

Jacobs, Wilbur R. 1972: *Dispossessing the American Indian: Indians and Whites on the Colonial Frontier* (New York: Charles Scribner's Sons).

Jaenen, Cornelius J. 1976: *Friend and Foe: Aspects of French–Amerindian Cultural Contact in the Sixteenth and Seventeenth Centuries* (New York: Columbia University Press).

Jennings, Francis 1975: *The Invasion of America: Indians, Colonialism, and the Cant of Conquest* (Chapel Hill: University of North Carolina Press).

Jennings, Francis 1984: *The Ambiguous Iroquois Empire: The Covenant Chain Confederation of Indian Tribes with English Colonies from its Beginnings to the Lancaster Treaty of 1744* (New York: W. W. Norton & Co.).

Jennings, Francis 1988: *Empire of Fortune: Crowns, Colonies and Tribes in the Seven Years War in America* (New York: Collier Books).

Jennings, Francis et al. (eds.) 1985: *The History and Culture of Iroquois Diplomacy: An Interdisciplinary Guide to the Treaties of the Six Nations and Their League* (Syracuse: Syracuse University Press).

John, Elizabeth A. H. 1975: *Storms Brewed in Other Men's Worlds: The Confrontation of Indians, Spanish, and French in the Southwest, 1540–1795* (Norman: University of Oklahoma Press).

Johnson, Troy R. 1996: *The Occupation of Alcatraz Island: Indian Self-Determination and the Rise of Indian Activism* (Urbana: University of Illinois Press).

Johnson, Troy R. (ed.) 1999: *Contemporary Native American Political Issues* (Walnut Creek, CA: AltaMira Press).

Johnson, Troy R. et al. (eds.) 1997: *American Indian Activism: Alcatraz to the Longest Walk* (Urbana: University of Illinois Press).

Jones, Dorothy V. 1982: *License for Empire: Colonialism by Treaty in Early America* (Chicago: University of Chicago Press).

Jorgensen, Joseph G. 1972: *The Sun Dance Religion: Power for the Powerless* (Chicago: University of Chicago Press).

Josephy, Alvin M., Jr. 1961: *The Patriot Chiefs: A Chronicle of American Indian Leadership* (New York: Viking Press).

Josephy, Alvin M., Jr. 1965: *The Nez Perce Indians and the Opening of the Northwest* (New Haven: Yale University Press).

Josephy, Alvin M., Jr. 1984: *Now that the Buffalo's Gone: A Study of Today's American Indians* (Norman: University of Oklahoma Press).

Josephy, Alvin M., Jr. (ed.) 1992: *America in 1492: The World of the Indian Peoples before the Arrival of Columbus* (New York: Alfred A. Knopf).

Judd, Carol M. and Arthur J. Ray (eds.) 1980: *Old Trails and New Directions* (Toronto: University of Toronto Press).

Kammer, Jerry 1980: *The Second Long Walk: The Navajo–Hopi Land Dispute* (Albuquerque: University of New Mexico Press).

Kan, Sergei 1989: *Symbolic Immortality: The Tlingit Potlatch of the Nineteenth Century* (Washington, D.C.: Smithsonian Institution Press).

Kan, Sergei 1999: *Memory Eternal: Tlingit Culture and Russian Orthodox Christianity through Two Centuries* (Seattle: University of Washington Press).

Kavanagh, Thomas W. 1996: *Comanche Political History: An Ethnohistorical Approach, 1706–1875* (Lincoln: University of Nebraska Press).

Keesing, Felix 1987: *The Menomini Indians of Wisconsin: A Study of Three Centuries of Cultural Contact and Change* (Philadelphia: American Philosophical Society).

Kehoe, Alice 1989: *The Ghost Dance: Ethnohistory and Revitalization* (Fort Worth: Holt, Rinehart and Winston).

Kelly, Lawrence C. 1983: *The Assault on Assimilation: John Collier and the Origins of Indian Policy Reform* (Albuquerque: University of New Mexico Press).

Kelsay, Isabel Thompson 1984: *Joseph Brant, 1743–1807: Man of Two Worlds* (Syracuse: Syracuse University Press).

Kersey, Harry A., Jr. 1989: *The Florida Seminoles and the New Deal, 1933–1942* (Boca Raton: Florida Atlantic University Press).

Kersey, Harry A., Jr. 1996: *An Assumption of Sovereignty: Social and Political Transformation among the Florida Seminoles, 1953–1979* (Lincoln: University of Nebraska Press).

Kessell, John L. 1987: *Kiva, Cross, and Crown: The Pecos Indians and New Mexico, 1540–1840* (Albuquerque: University of New Mexico Press).

Kidwell, Clara Sue 1995: *Choctaws and Missionaries in Mississippi, 1818–1918* (Norman: University of Oklahoma Press).

Kidwell, Clara Sue and Ann Marie Plane (eds.) 1996: "Representing Native American History," *The Public Historian* 18(4): 7–143.

Klein, Kerwin Lee 1997: *Frontiers of Historical Imagination: Narrating the European Conquest of Native America, 1890–1990* (Berkeley: University of California Press).

Klein, Laura F. and Lillian A. Ackerman (eds.) 1995: *Women and Power in Native North America* (Norman: University of Oklahoma Press).

Knaut, Andrew L. 1995: *The Pueblo Revolt of 1680: Conquest and Resistance in Seventeenth-Century New Mexico* (Norman: University of Oklahoma Press).

Krech, Shepard, III (ed.) 1981: *Indians, Animals, and the Fur Trade: A Critique of "Keepers of the Game"* (Athens: University of Georgia Press).

Krech, Shepard, III 1999: *The Ecological Indian: Myth and History* (New York: W. W. Norton).

Kroeber, Karl (ed.) 1994: *American Indian Persistence and Resurgence* (Durham, NC: Duke University Press).

Krupat, Arnold 1985: *For Those Who Come After: A Study of Native American Autobiography* (Berkeley: University of California Press).

Krupat, Arnold 1989: *The Voice in the Margin: Native American Literature and the Canon* (Berkeley: University of California Press).

Kupperman, Karen Ordahl 2000: *Indians and English: Facing Off in Early America* (Ithaca, NY: Cornell University Press).

Lazarus, Edward 1991: *Black Hills Justice: The Sioux Nation Versus the United States, 1775 to the Present* (New York: HarperCollins).

Leacock, Eleanor Burke and Nancy Oestreich Lurie (eds.) 1971: *North American Indians in Historical Perspective* (New York: Random House).

Lepore, Jill 1998: *The Name of War: King Philip's War and the Origins of American Identity* (New York: Alfred A. Knopf).

Lewis, David Rich 1994: *Neither Wolf nor Dog: American Indians, Environment, and Agrarian Change* (New York: Oxford University Press).

Lewis, G. Malcolm (ed.) 1998: *Cartographic Encounters: Perspectives on Native American Mapmaking and Map Use* (Chicago: University of Chicago Press).

Liebersohn, Harry 1998: *Aristocratic Encounters: European Travelers and North American Indians* (New York: Cambridge University Press).

Lincoln, Kenneth 1983: *Native American Renaissance* (Berkeley: University of California Press).

Lincoln, Kenneth 1987: *The Good Red Road: Passages into Native America* (San Francisco: Harper & Row).

Lincoln, Kenneth 1993: *Indi'n Humor: Bicultural Play in Native America* (New York: Oxford University Press).

Lincoln, Kenneth 2000: *Sing With the Heart of a Bear: Fusions of Native and American Poetry, 1890–1999* (Berkeley: University of California Press).

Lippard, Lucy (ed.) 1992: *Partial Recall* (New York: New Press).

Loftin, John D. 1991: *Religion and Hopi Life in the Twentieth Century* (Bloomington: Indiana University Press).

Lomawaima, K. Tsianina 1994: *They Called It Prairie Light: The Story of Chilocco Indian School* (Lincoln: University of Nebraska Press).

McConnell, Michael N. 1992: *A Country Between: The Upper Ohio Valley and its Peoples, 1724–1774* (Lincoln: University of Nebraska Press).

McLoughlin, William G. 1984: *Cherokees and Missionaries, 1789–1839* (New Haven: Yale University Press).

McLoughlin, William G. 1986: *Cherokee Renascence in the New Republic* (Princeton: Princeton University Press).

McLoughlin, William G. 1993: *After the Trail of Tears: The Cherokees' Struggle for Sovereignty, 1839–1880* (Chapel Hill: University of North Carolina Press).

McNickle, D'Arcy 1973: *Native American Tribalism: Indian Survivals and Renewals* (New York: Oxford University Press).

McNickle, D'Arcy 1975: *They Came Here First: The Epic of the American Indian* (New York: Octagon Books).

McReynolds, Edwin C. 1957: *The Seminoles* (Norman: University of Oklahoma Press).

Malone, Patrick M. 1991: *The Skulking Way of War: Technology and Tactics among the New England Indians* (Lanham, MD: Madison Books).

Mancall, Peter C. 1995: *Deadly Medicine: Indians and Alcohol in Early America* (Ithaca, NY: Cornell University Press).

Mandell, Daniel R. 1996: *Behind the Frontier: Indians in Eighteenth-Century Eastern Massachusetts* (Lincoln: University of Nebraska Press).

Martin, Calvin 1978: *Keepers of the Game: Animal–Indian Relationships and the Fur Trade* (Berkeley: University of California Press).

Martin, Calvin (ed.) 1987: *The American Indian and the Problem of History* (New York: Oxford University Press).

Martin, Joel W. 1991: *Sacred Revolt: The Muskogees' Struggle for a New World* (Boston: Beacon Press).

Matthiessen, Peter 1983: *In the Spirit of Crazy Horse* (New York: Viking Press).

Matthiessen, Peter 1984: *Indian Country* (New York: Viking Press).

Merrell, James H. 1987: "Declarations of Independence: Indian–White Relations in the New Nation," in Jack P. Greene (ed.), *The American Revolution: Its Character and Limits* (New York: New York University Press), pp. 197–223.

Merrell, James H. 1989a: *The Indians' New World: The Catawbas and Their Neighbors from European Contact Through the Era of Removal* (New York: W. W. Norton).

Merrell, James H. 1989b: "Some Thoughts on Colonial Historians and American Indians," *William and Mary Quarterly,* 3rd series, 46: 94–119.

Merrell, James H. 1999: *Into the American Woods: Negotiators on the Pennsylvania Frontier* (New York: W. W. Norton).

Meyer, Melissa L. 1994: *The White Earth Tragedy: Ethnicity and Dispossession at a Minnesota Anishinaabe Reservation, 1889–1920* (Lincoln: University of Nebraska Press).

Mihesuah, Devon A. 1993: *Cultivating the Rosebuds: The Education of Women at the Cherokee Female Seminary, 1851–1909* (Urbana: University of Illinois Press).

Mihesuah, Devon A. (ed.) 1998: *Natives and Academics: Researching and Writing about American Indians* (Lincoln: University of Nebraska Press).

Milanich, Jerald T. 1996: *The Timucua* (Oxford, UK, and Cambridge, MA: Blackwell Publishers).

Miller, Christopher L. 1985: *Prophetic Worlds: Indians and Whites on the Columbia Plateau* (New Brunswick, NJ: Rutgers University Press).

Miller, J. R. 2000: *Skyscrapers Hide the Heavens: A History of Indian–White Relations in Canada,* 3rd edn. (Toronto: University of Toronto Press).

Miller, Jay 1997: *Tsimshian Culture: A Light Through the Ages* (Lincoln: University of Nebraska Press).

Miller, Jay 1999: *Lushootseed Culture and the Shamanic Odyssey: An Anchored Radiance* (Lincoln: University of Nebraska Press).

Miller, Jay and Carol M. Eastman (eds.) 1984: *The Tsimshian and Their Neighbors of the North Pacific Coast* (Seattle: University of Washington Press).

Miner, Craig H. 1978: *The End of Indian Kansas: A Study of Cultural Revolution, 1854–1871* (Lawrence: Regents Press of Kansas).

Mooney, James 1896: *The Ghost-Dance Religion and the Sioux Outbreak of 1890*. Annual Report of the Bureau of Ethnology, 1892–1893, part 2 (Washington, D.C.: U.S. Government Printing Office).

Moore, John 1987: *The Cheyenne Nation: A Social and Demographic History* (Lincoln: University of Nebraska Press).

Moore, John (ed.) 1993: *The Political Economy of North American Indians* (Norman: University of Oklahoma Press).

Moore, John 1996: *The Cheyenne* (Cambridge, MA: Blackwell Publishers).

Morrison, R. Bruce and C. Roderick Wilson (eds.) 1986: *Native Peoples: The Canadian Experience* (Toronto: McClelland & Stewart).

Moses, L. G. 1984: *The Indian Man: A Biography of James Mooney* (Urbana: University of Illinois Press).

Moses, L. G. 1996: *Wild West Shows and the Images of American Indians, 1883–1933* (Albuquerque: University of New Mexico Press).

Moses, L. G. and Raymond Wilson (eds.) 1985: *Indian Lives: Essays on Nineteenth- and Twentieth-Century Native American Leaders* (Albuquerque: University of New Mexico Press).

Murray, David 1991: *Forked Tongues: Speech, Writing, and Representation in North American Indian Texts* (Bloomington: Indiana University Press).

Murray, David 2000: *Indian Giving: Economies of Power in Indian–White Exchanges* (Amherst: University of Massachusetts Press).

Nabokov, Peter 1981: *Indian Running: Native American History and Tradition* (Santa Barbara: Capra Press).

Nabokov, Peter and Robert Easton 1989: *Native American Architecture* (New York: Oxford University Press).

Nagel, Joane 1996: *American Indian Ethnic Renewal: Red Power and the Resurgence of Identity and Culture* (New York: Oxford University Press).

Namias, June 1993: *White Captives: Gender and Ethnicity on the American Frontier* (Chapel Hill: University of North Carolina Press).

O'Brien, Jean M. 1997: *Dispossession by Degrees: Indian Land and Identity in Natick, Massachusetts, 1650–1790* (Cambridge: Cambridge University Press).

O'Brien, Sharon 1989: *American Indian Tribal Governments* (Norman: University of Oklahoma Press).

O'Connell, Barry 1992: "Introduction," in Barry O'Connell (ed.), *On Our Own Ground: The Complete Writings of William Apess, A Pequot* (Amherst: University of Massachusetts Press), pp. xiii–lxxvii.

Olson, James C. 1965: *Red Cloud and the Sioux Problem* (Lincoln: University of Nebraska Press).

Ortiz, Alfonso 1969: *The Tewa World: Space, Time, Being, and Becoming in a Pueblo Society* (Chicago: University of Chicago Press).

Ortiz, Roxanne Dunbar (ed.) 1979: *Economic Development in American Indian Reservations* (Albuquerque: Native American Studies, University of New Mexico).

Ourada, Patricia K. 1979: *The Menominee Indians: A History* (Norman: University of Oklahoma Press).

Owens, Louis 1992: *Other Destinies: Understanding the American Indian Novel* (Norman: University of Oklahoma Press).

Owens, Louis 1998: *Mixedblood Messages: Literature, Film, Family, Place* (Norman: University of Oklahoma Press).

Parezo, Nancy J. 1983: *Navajo Sandpainting: From Religious Act to Commercial Art* (Albuquerque: University of New Mexico Press).

Parezo, Nancy J. (ed.) 1993: *Hidden Scholars: Women Anthropologists and the Native American Southwest* (Albuquerque: University of New Mexico Press).

Parman, Donald L. 1976: *The Navajos and the New Deal* (New Haven: Yale University Press).

Parman, Donald L. 1994: *Indians and the American West in the Twentieth Century* (Bloomington: Indiana University Press).

Pearce, Roy Harvey 1988 (1953): *Savagism and Civilization: A Study of the Indian and the American Mind*, revised edn. (Berkeley: University of California Press).

Perdue, Theda 1979: *Slavery and the Evolution of Cherokee Society, 1540–1866* (Knoxville: University of Tennessee Press).

Perdue, Theda 1998: *Cherokee Women: Gender and Culture Change, 1700–1835* (Lincoln: University of Nebraska Press).

Peterson, Jacqueline and Jennifer S. H. Brown (eds.) 1985: *The New Peoples: Being and Becoming Métis in North America* (Lincoln: University of Nebraska Press).

Peyer, Bernd C. 1997: *The Tutor'd Mind: Indian Missionary-Writers in Antebellum America* (Amherst: University of Massachusetts Press).

Philips, George Harwood 1975: *Chiefs and Challengers: Indian Resistance and Cooperation in Southern California* (Berkeley: University of California Press).

Philips, George Harwood 1993: *Indians and Intruders in Central California, 1769–1849* (Norman: University of Oklahoma Press).

Philips, George Harwood 1997: *Indians and Indian Agents: The Origins of the Reservation System in California 1849–1852* (Norman: University of Oklahoma Press).

Philp, Kenneth R. 1977: *John Collier's Crusade for Indian Reform, 1920–1954* (Tucson: University of Arizona Press).

Philp, Kenneth R. 1999: *Termination Revisited: American Indians on the Trail to Self Determination 1933–1953* (Lincoln: University of Nebraska Press).

Plane, Ann Marie 2000: *Colonial Intimacies: Indian Marriage in Early New England* (Ithaca, NY: Cornell University Press).

Powers, Marla N. 1986: *Oglala Women: Myth, Ritual, and Reality* (Chicago: University of Chicago Press).

Powers, William K. 1977: *Oglala Religion* (Lincoln: University of Nebraska Press).

Powers, William K. 1987: *Beyond the Vision: Essays on American Indian Culture* (Norman: University of Oklahoma Press).

Price, Catherine 1996: *The Oglala People, 1841–1879: A Political History* (Lincoln: University of Nebraska Press).

Prins, Harald E. L. 1996: *The Mi'kmaq: Resistance, Accommodation, and Cultural Survival* (Fort Worth: Harcourt Brace).

Prucha, Francis Paul 1962: *American Indian Policy in the Formative Years: The Indian Trade and Intercourse Acts, 1790–1834* (Cambridge, MA: Harvard University Press).

Prucha, Francis Paul 1971: *Indian Peace Medals in American History* (Madison: State Historical Society of Wisconsin).

Prucha, Francis Paul 1976: *American Indian Policy in Crisis: Christian Reformers and the Indian, 1865–1900* (Norman: University of Oklahoma Press).

Prucha, Francis Paul 1979: *The Churches and the Indian Schools, 1888–1912* (Lincoln: University of Nebraska Press).

Prucha, Francis Paul 1984: *The Great Father: The United States Government and the American Indians*, 2 vols. (Lincoln: University of Nebraska Press).

Pryce, Paula 1999: *"Keeping the Lakes' Way": Reburial and the Re-Creation of a Moral World among an Invisible People* (Toronto: University of Toronto Press).

Pyne, Stephen 1982: *Fire in America: A Cultural History of Wildland and Rural Fire* (Princeton: Princeton University Press).

Rafert, Stewart 1996: *The Miami Indians of Indiana: A Persistent People, 1654–1994* (Indianapolis: Indiana Historical Society).

Reff, Daniel T. 1991: *Disease, Depopulation, and Culture Change in Northwestern New Spain, 1518–1764* (Salt Lake City: University of Utah Press).

Reid, John Phillip 1970: *A Law of Blood: The Primitive Law of the Cherokee Nation* (New York: New York University Press).

Reid, John Phillip 1975: *A Better Kind of Hatchet: Law, Trade, and Diplomacy in the Cherokee Nation During the Early Years of European Contact* (University Park: Pennsylvania State University Press).

Richter, Daniel K. 1992: *The Ordeal of the Longhouse: The Peoples of the Iroquois League in the Era of European Colonization* (Chapel Hill: University of North Carolina Press).

Richter, Daniel K. 1993: "Whose Indian History?" *William and Mary Quarterly*, 3rd series, 50: 379–93.

Richter, Daniel K. and James Merrell (eds.) 1987: *Beyond the Covenant Chain: The Iroquois and Their Neighbors in Indian North America, 1600–1800* (Syracuse: Syracuse University Press).

Rice, Julian 1991: *Black Elk's Story: Distinguishing its Lakota Purpose* (Albuquerque: University of New Mexico Press).

Rice, Julian 1992: *Deer Women and Elk Men: The Lakota Narratives of Ella Deloria* (Albuquerque: University of New Mexico Press).

Rice, Julian 1998: *Before the Great Spirit: The Many Faces of Sioux Spirituality* (Albuquerque: University of New Mexico Press).

Riley, Glenda 1984: *Women and Indians on the Frontier, 1825–1915* (Albuquerque: University of New Mexico Press).

Rogin, Michael Paul 1975: *Fathers and Children: Andrew Jackson and the Subjugation of the American Indian* (New York: Random House).

Rollings, Willard H. 1992: *The Osage: An Ethnohistorical Study of Hegemony on the Prairie-Plains* (Columbia: University of Missouri Press).

Ronda, James P. 1984: *Lewis and Clark among the Indians* (Lincoln: University of Nebraska Press).

Roscoe, Will 1991: *The Zuni Man-Woman* (Albuquerque: University of New Mexico Press).

Roscoe, Will 1998: *Changing Ones: Third and Fourth Genders in Native North America* (New York: St. Martins).

Ross, Luana 1998: *Inventing the Savage: The Social Construction of Native American Criminality* (Austin: University of Texas Press).

Ross, Thomas E. and Tyrel G. Moore (eds.) 1987: *A Cultural Geography of North American Indians* (Boulder, CO: Westview Press).

Rountree, Helen C. 1989: *The Powhatan Indians of Virginia: Their Traditional Culture* (Norman: University of Oklahoma Press).

Rountree, Helen C. 1990: *Pocahantas's People: The Powhatan Indians of Virginia through Four Centuries* (Norman: University of Oklahoma Press).

Ruby, Robert H. and John Arthur Brown 1989: *Dreamer-Prophets of the Columbia Plateau* (Norman: University of Oklahoma Press).

Salisbury, Neal 1982: *Manitou and Providence: Indians, Europeans, and the Making of New England, 1500–1643* (New York: Oxford University Press).

Salisbury, Neal 1996: "The Indians' Old World: Native Americans and the Coming of Europeans," *William and Mary Quarterly*, 3rd series, 53: 435–58.

Satz, Ronald N. 1975: *American Indian Policy in the Jacksonian Era* (Lincoln: University of Nebraska Press).

Saunt, Claudio 1999: *A New Order of Things: Property, Power, and the Transformation of the Creek Indians 1733–1816* (Cambridge: Cambridge University Press).

Sayre, Gordon 1997: *Les Sauvages Américains: Representations of Native Americans in French and English Colonial Literature* (Chapel Hill: University of North Carolina Press).

Schenck, Theresa M. 1997: *The Voice of the Crane Echoes Afar: The Sociopolitical Organization of the Lake Superior Ojibwa, 1640–1855* (New York: Garland Publishers).

Schmalz, Peter S. 1991: *The Ojibwa of Southern Ontario* (Toronto: University of Toronto Press).

Schrader, Robert Faye 1983: *The Indian Arts and Crafts Board: An Aspect of New Deal Indian Policy* (Albuquerque: University of New Mexico Press).

Shaffer, Lynda 1992: *Native Americans before 1492: The Moundbuilding Centers of the Eastern Woodlands* (Armonk, NY: M. E. Sharpe).

Shannon, Timothy 2000: *Indians and Colonists at the Crossroads of Empire: The Albany Congress of 1754* (Ithaca, NY: Cornell University Press).

Sheehan, Bernard W. 1973: *Seeds of Extinction: Jeffersonian Philanthropy and the American Indian* (Chapel Hill: University of North Carolina Press).

Sheridan, Thomas E. and Nancy J. Parezo (eds.) 1996: *Paths of Life: American Indians of the Southwest and Northern Mexico* (Tucson: University of Arizona Press).

Shoemaker, Nancy (ed.) 1995: *Negotiators of Change: Historical Perspectives on Native American Women* (New York: Routledge).

Shoemaker, Nancy 1999: *American Indian Population Recovery in the Twentieth Century* (Albuquerque: University of New Mexico Press).

Sider, Gerald M. 1993: *Lumbee Indian Histories: Race, Ethnicity, and Indian Identity in the Southern United States* (Cambridge: Cambridge University Press).

Slotkin, Richard 1973: *Regeneration Through Violence: The Mythology of the American Frontier 1600–1860* (Middletown: Wesleyan University Press).

Slotkin, Richard 1985: *The Fatal Environment: The Myth of the Frontier in the Age of Industrialization, 1800–1890* (New York: Atheneum).

Slotkin, Richard 1992: *Gunfighter Nation: The Myth of the Frontier in Twentieth-Century America* (New York: Atheneum).

Smith, Donald B. 1987: *Sacred Feathers: The Reverend Peter Jones (Kahkewaquonaby) and the Mississauga Indians* (Lincoln: University of Nebraska Press).

Smith, Sherry 2000: *Reimagining Indians: Native Americans through Anglo Eyes 1880–1940* (New York: Oxford University Press).

Snipp, C. Matthew 1989: *American Indians: The First of This Land* (New York: Russell Sage Foundation).

Snow, Dean R. 1994: *The Iroquois* (Oxford, UK and Cambridge, MA: Blackwell).

Spector, Janet 1993: *What This Awl Means: Feminist Archaeology at a Wahpeton Dakota Village* (St Paul: Minnesota Historical Society).

Spicer, Edward H. 1962: *Cycles of Conquest: The Impact of Spain, Mexico, and the United States on the Indians of the Southwest, 1533–1960* (Tucson: University of Arizona Press).

Stanley, Sam (ed.) 1978: *American Indian Economic Development* (The Hague: Mouton Publishers).

Steele, Ian K. 1990: *Betrayals: Fort William Henry and the "Massacre"* (New York: Oxford University Press).

Steele, Ian K. 1994: *Warpaths: Invasions of North America* (New York: Oxford University Press).

Steltenkamp, Michael 1993: *Black Elk: Holy Man of the Oglala* (Norman: University of Oklahoma Press).

Stewart, Omer C. 1987: *Peyote Religion: A History* (Norman: University of Oklahoma Press).

Strickland, Rennard 1975: *Fire and the Spirits: Cherokee Law from Clan to Court* (Norman: University of Oklahoma Press).

Strickland, Rennard 1997: *Tonto's Revenge: Reflections on American Indian Culture and Policy* (Albuquerque: University of New Mexico Press).

Strong, Pauline Turner 1999: *Captive Selves, Captivating Others: The Politics and Poetics of Colonial American Captivity Narratives* (Boulder, CO: Westview Press).

Strong, Pauline Turner and Barrik Van Winkle 1996: " 'Indian Blood': Reflections on the Reckoning and Refiguring of Native North American Identity," *Cultural Anthropology* 11: 547–76.

Sturtevant, William C. and Bruce G. Trigger (eds.) 1978– : *Handbook of North American Indians*, 11 vols. of 20 projected (Washington, D.C.: Smithsonian Institution Press).

Sugden, John 1997: *Tecumseh: A Life* (New York: Henry Holt).

Sugden, John 2000: *Blue Jacket: Warrior of the Shawnees* (Lincoln: University of Nebraska Press).

Sutton, Imre (ed.) 1985: *Irredeemable America: The Indians' Estate and Land Claims* (Albuquerque: University of New Mexico Press).

Svingen, Orlan 1993: *The Northern Cheyenne Indian Reservation, 1877–1900* (Niwot: University Press of Colorado).

Swann, Brian (ed.) 1983: *Smoothing the Ground: Essays on Native American Oral Literature* (Berkeley: University of California Press).

Swann, Brian (ed.) 1992: *On the Translation of Native American Literatures* (Washington, D.C.: Smithsonian Institution Press).

Swann, Brian and Arnold Krupat (eds.) 1987: *Recovering the Word: Essays on Native American Literature* (Berkeley: University of California Press).

Szasz, Margaret Connell (ed.) 1994: *Between Indian and White Worlds: The Cultural Broker* (Norman: University of Oklahoma Press).

Szasz, Margaret Connell 1999a: *Indian Education in the American Colonies, 1607–1783*, 3rd edn. (Albuquerque: University of New Mexico Press).

Szasz, Margaret Connell 1999b: *Education and the American Indian: The Road to Self-Determination since 1928* (Albuquerque: University of New Mexico Press).

Tanner, Helen Hornbeck (ed.) 1987: *Atlas of Great Lakes Indian History* (Norman: University of Oklahoma Press).

Thomas, David Hurst (ed.) 1989–91: *Columbian Consequences*, 3 vols. (Washington, D.C.: Smithsonian Institution Press).

Thomas, David Hurst 2000a: *Exploring Native America* (New York: Oxford University Press).

Thomas, David Hurst 2000b: *Skull Wars: Kennewick Man, Archeology, and the Battle for Native American Identity* (New York: Basic Books).

Thomas, Peter A. 1990: *In the Maelstrom of Change: The Indian Trade and Cultural Process in the Middle Connecticut River Valley, 1635–1665* (New York: Garland Publishers).

Thornton, Russell 1986: *We Shall Live Again: The 1870 and 1890 Ghost Dance Movement as Demographic Revitalization* (Cambridge: Cambridge University Press).

Thornton, Russell 1987: *American Indian Holocaust and Survival: A Population History since 1492* (Norman: University of Oklahoma Press).

Thornton, Russell 1990: *The Cherokees: A Population History* (Lincoln: University of Nebraska Press).

Thornton, Russell (ed.) 1998: *Studying Native America: Problems and Prospects* (Madison: University of Wisconsin Press).

Tinker, George E. 1993: *Missionary Conquest: The Gospel and Native American Cultural Genocide* (Minneapolis: Fortress Press).

Tooker, Elisabeth 1970: *Iroquois Ceremonial of Midwinter* (Syracuse: Syracuse University Press).

Tooker, Elisabeth 1991: *An Ethnography of the Huron Indians 1615–1649* (Syracuse: Syracuse University Press).

Trafzer, Clifford E. (ed.) 1985: *American Indian Identity: Today's Changing Perspectives.* Publications in American Indian Studies, no. 1 (San Diego: San Diego State University).

Trafzer, Clifford E. (ed.) 1986: *American Indian Prophets: Religious Leaders and Revitalization Movements* (Sacramento, CA: Sierra Oaks Publishing Co.).

Trelease, Allen William 1960: *Indian Affairs in Colonial New York: The Seventeenth Century* (Ithaca, NY: Cornell University Press).

Trennert, Robert A., Jr. 1975: *Alternative to Extinction: Federal Indian Policy and the Beginnings of the Reservation System, 1846–51* (Philadelphia: Temple University Press).

Trennert, Robert A., Jr. 1988: *The Phoenix Indian School: Forced Assimilation in Arizona, 1891–1935* (Norman: University of Oklahoma Press).

Trigger, Bruce G. 1976: *The Children of Aataentsic: A History of the Huron People to 1660* (Montreal: McGill-Queen's University Press).

Trigger, Bruce G. 1985: *Natives and Newcomers: Canada's Heroic Age Reconsidered* (Kingston: McGill-Queen's University Press).

Trigger, Bruce G., Toby Morantz, and Louise Dechene (eds.) 1987: *Le Castor Fait Tout: Selected Papers of the Fifth North American Fur Trade Conference, 1985* (Montreal: Lake St. Louis Historical Society).

Trigger, Bruce G. and Wilcomb E. Washburn (eds.) 1996: *The Cambridge History of the Native Peoples of the Americas.* vol. 1: *North America* (2 parts) (Cambridge: Cambridge University Press).

Tyler, Daniel (ed.) 1976: *Red Men and Hat Wearers: Viewpoints in Indian History* (Boulder, CO: Pruett Publishing Co.).

Underhill, Ruth M. 1979: *Papago Woman* (New York: Holt, Rinehart, and Winston).

Usner, Daniel H., Jr. 1992: *Indians, Settlers, and Slaves in a Frontier Exchange Economy: The Lower Mississippi Valley before 1783* (Chapel Hill: University of North Carolina Press).

Usner, Daniel H., Jr. 1998: *American Indians in the Lower Mississippi Valley: Social and Economic Histories* (Lincoln: University of Nebraska Press).

Utley, Robert M. 1963: *The Last Days of the Sioux Nation* (New Haven: Yale University Press).

Utley, Robert M. 1984: *The Indian Frontier of the American West, 1846–1890* (Albuquerque: University of New Mexico Press).

Utley, Robert M. 1993: *The Lance and the Shield: The Life and Times of Sitting Bull* (New York: Henry Holt).

Van Kirk, Sylvia 1981: *"Many Tender Ties": Women in Fur Trade Society, 1670–1870* (Winnipeg: Watson & Dwyer).

Vecsey, Christopher 1980: *American Indian Environments: Ecological Issues in Native American History* (Syracuse: Syracuse University Press).

Vecsey, Christopher 1988: *Imagine Ourselves Richly: Mythic Narratives of North American Indians* (New York: Crossroad).

Vecsey, Christopher 1991: *Handbook of American Indian Religious Freedom* (New York: Crossroad).

Vecsey, Christopher and William A. Starna (eds.) 1988: *Iroquois Land Claims* (Syracuse: Syracuse University Press).

Velie, Alan R. (ed.) 1995: *Native American Perspectives on Literature and History* (Norman: University of Oklahoma Press).

Vibert, Elizabeth 1997: *Traders' Tales: Narratives of Cultural Encounters in the Columbia Plateau, 1807–1846* (Norman: University of Oklahoma Press).

Vizenor, Gerald Robert 1984: *The People Named the Chippewa: Narrative Histories* (Minneapolis: University of Minnesota Press).

Vizenor, Gerald Robert 1994: *Manifest Manners: PostIndian Warriors of Survivance* (Hanover, NH: University Press of New England).

Vizenor, Gerald Robert 1998: *Fugitive Poses: Native American Indian Scenes of Absence and Presence* (Lincoln: University of Nebraska Press).

Wallace, Anthony F. C. 1949: *King of the Delawares: Teedyuscung, 1700–1763* (Philadelphia: University of Pennsylvania Press).

Wallace, Anthony F. C. 1970a: *The Death and Rebirth of the Seneca* (New York: Alfred A. Knopf).

Wallace, Anthony F. C. 1970b: *Prelude to Disaster: The Course of Indian–White Relations which Led to the Black Hawk War of 1832* (Springfield: Illinois State Historical Library).

Wallace, Anthony F. C. 1999: *Jefferson and the Indians: The Tragic Fate of the First Americans* (Cambridge, MA: Belknap Press of Harvard University Press).

Wallace, Ernest and E. Adamson Hoebel 1952: *The Comanches: Lords of the South Plains* (Norman: University of Oklahoma Press).

Warren, Louis S. 1997: *The Hunter's Game: Poachers and Conservationists in Twentieth-Century America* (New Haven: Yale University Press).

Warrior, Robert Allen 1995: *Tribal Secrets: Recovering American Indian Intellectual Traditions* (Minneapolis: University of Minnesota Press).

Warrior, Robert and Paul Chaat Smith 1996: *Like a Hurricane: The Indian Movement from Alcatraz to Wounded Knee* (New York: New Press).

Washburn, Wilcomb E. 1971: *Red Man's Land/White Man's Law: A Study of the Past and Present Status of the American Indian* (New York: Charles Scribner's Sons).

Weaver, Jace 1996: *Defending Mother Earth: Native American Perspectives on Environmental Justice* (Maryknoll, NY: Orbis Books).

Weaver, Jace 1998: *Native American Religious Identity: Unforgotten Gods* (Maryknoll, NY: Orbis Books).

Weeks, Philip (ed.) 1988: *The American Indian Experience: A Profile, 1524 to the Present* (Arlington Heights, IL: Forum Press).

White, Richard 1978: "The Winning of the West: The Expansion of the Western Sioux in the Eighteenth and Nineteenth Centuries," *Journal of American History* 65: 319–43.

White, Richard 1983: *The Roots of Dependency: Subsistence, Environment, and Social Change among the Choctaws, Pawnees, and Navajos* (Lincoln: University of Nebraska Press).

White, Richard 1991: *The Middle Ground: Indians, Empires, and Republics in the Great Lakes Region, 1650–1815* (Cambridge: Cambridge University Press).

Whiteley, Peter M. 1988: *Deliberate Acts: Changing Hopi Culture through the Oraibi Split* (Tucson: University of Arizona Press).

Wilkins, David E. 1997: *American Indian Sovereignty and the U.S. Supreme Court: The Masking of Justice* (Austin: University of Texas Press).

Wilkinson, Charles F. 1987: *American Indians, Time, and the Law: Native Societies in a Modern Constitutional Democracy* (New Haven: Yale University Press).

Williams, Robert A. 1990: *The American Indian in Western Legal Thought: The Discourses of Conquest* (New York: Oxford University Press).

Williams, Robert A. 1997: *Linking Arms Together: American Indian Treaty Visions of Law and Peace, 1600–1800* (New York: Oxford University Press).

Williams, Walter L. (ed.) 1979: *Southeastern Indians since the Removal Era* (Athens: University of Georgia Press).

Williams, Walter L. 1986: *The Spirit and the Flesh: Sexual Diversity in American Indian Culture* (Boston: Beacon Press).

Williamson, Ray A. 1987: *Living the Sky: The Cosmos of the American Indian* (Norman: University of Oklahoma Press).

Wilson, Terry P. 1985: *The Underground Reservation: Osage Oil* (Lincoln: University of Nebraska Press).

Womack, Craig 1999: *Red on Red: Native American Literary Separatism* (Minnesota: University of Minnesota Press).

Wood, Peter H., Gregory A. Waselkov, and M. Thomas Hatley (eds.) 1989: *Powhatan's Mantle: Indians in the Colonial Southeast* (Lincoln: University of Nebraska Press).

Worcester, Donald E. 1979: *The Apaches: Eagles of the Southwest* (Norman: University of Oklahoma Press).

Wunder, John R. 1994: *"Retained by the People": A History of American Indians and the Bill of Rights* (New York: Oxford University Press).

Young, Mary Elizabeth 1961: *Redskins, Ruffleshirts, and Rednecks: Indian Allotments in Alabama and Mississippi, 1830–1860* (Norman: University of Oklahoma Press).

Young, Mary Elizabeth 1981: "The Cherokee Nation: Mirror of the Republic," *American Quarterly* 33: 502–24.

Index